D0559911

P- 0033-17
16 -11- 76
A

# Party Identification
# and Beyond

# Party Identification and Beyond

## Representations of Voting and Party Competition

*Edited by*

**IAN BUDGE**
**IVOR CREWE**
**DENNIS FARLIE**
*University of Essex*

## JOHN WILEY & SONS

London · New York · Sydney · Toronto

JF
2071
B83
1976

3119674
BADADUQ

Copyright © 1976, by John Wiley & Sons, Ltd.

All rights reserved.

No part of this book may be reproduced by any means, nor transmitted, nor translated into a machine language without the written permission of the publisher.

*Library of Congress Cataloging in Publication Data:*
Main entry under title:

Party identification and beyond.

'Originated in the papers and discussions of the Workshop on Participation, Voting, and Party Competition, held at the joint sessions of the European Consortium for Political Research at Strasbourg, Easter, 1974.'
    1. Party affiliation—Congresses. 2. Voting—Congresses. I. Budge, Ian. II. Crewe, Ivor. III. Farlie, Dennis. IV. Workshop on Participation, Voting, and Party Competition, Strasbourg, 1974.
JF2071.P37        324'.2        75-35615
ISBN 0 471 013552

Printed by The Pitman Press Ltd., Bath.

# List of Contributors

OLE BORRE

Institute of Political Science,
University of Aarhus, Denmark

IAN BUDGE

Department of Government,
University of Essex, England

IVOR CREWE

Department of Government,
University of Essex, England

ERIC DAMGAARD

Institute of Political Science,
University of Aarhus, Denmark

DENNIS FARLIE

Department of Mathematics,
University of Essex, England

JACQUELINE FREYSSINET-DOMINJON

Institut d'Études Politiques,
Université des Sciences Sociales de
Grenoble

ANDRE-PAUL FROGNIER

Unité De Science Politique,
Université Catholique de Louvain

RONALD INGLEHART

Center for Political Studies, Institute
for Social Research, University of
Michigan, USA

WILLIAM IRVINE

Department of Political Science,
Queens University, Kingston, Ontario,
Canada

MAX KAASE

Zentrum fur Umfragen, Methoden
und Analysen, University of
Mannheim, West Germany

HANS KLINGEMANN

*Zentrum fur Umfragen, Methoden und Analysen, University of Mannheim, West Germany*

MICHAEL LAVER

*Department of Political Theory and Institutions, University of Liverpool, England*

GARY MAUSER

*Department of Economics and Commerce, Simon Fraser University, Burnaby, British Columbia, Canada*

WARREN MILLER

*Center for Political Studies, Institute for Social Research, University of Michigan, USA*

PETER ORDESHOOK

*Department of Political Science, Carnegie-Mellon University, Pittsburgh, Pennsylvania, USA*

DAVID ROBERTSON

*Department of Government, University of Essex, England*

JERROLD RUSK

*Department of Government, University of Arizona, USA*

DUSAN SIDJANSKI

*Department of Political Science, University of Geneva, Switzerland*

JACQUES THOMASSEN

*Sub-faculteit sociaal-culturele wetenschappen, Katholieke Hogeschool, Tilburg, The Netherlands*

# Preface

This book originated in the papers and discussions of the Workshop on Participation, Voting and Party Competition, held at the Joint Sessions of the European Consortium for Political Research at Strasbourg, Easter 1974. Without Consortium sponsorship it would never have been written, and both editors and contributors therefore owe not only the book but a great deal of stimulation and encouragement to the Consortium (which groups some sixty departments and institutes throughout Western Europe); to its dynamic director, Professor Jean Blondel; and to the Institute of Political Science at the University of Strasbourg, which organized the Joint Sessions. We are also grateful to Professor Henry Valen for being the first to suggest the idea of a book based on the papers, to Professor Hans Daalder for pushing the editors into action, and to John Wiley & Sons, UK, for encouragement and practical help.

A workshop designed to bring together the different research traditions in the study of voting behaviour runs the obvious risk of spreading over a wide range of subjects, with no clear focus or integrating theme. The payoff comes from the ability of discussion to uncover similarities between superficially different approaches. The book has benefited in this respect from the discussions of the workshop; consisting of a series of papers circulated before the meetings and addressed to points the others raised, it develops a dialogue which we trust will lead the reader as it led us to a broader synthesis of the factors affecting voting and party competition. (Verbatim notes on the Workshop discussions are available from the ECPR Central Services, University of Essex, Colchester, England.)

In order to achieve a sharper focus we had regrettably to omit contributions related to participation in general (except ones related to turnout) in spite of the gains that undoubtedly ensue from placing the problem of non-voting in a broader perspective. The contributions related to participation comprised:

Frank Aarebrot and Stein Kuhnle (University of Oslo), 'Nation-building as the Formation of Collective Loyalty';

T.-H. Cao (University of Geneva), 'De l'Apathie Politique en Suisse?';

Andries Hoogerwerf et al. (University of Nijmegen), 'Political Opinion and Class Identification in the Netherlands';

Willy Martinussen (University of Oslo), 'A Resource Perspective on Political Participation';

Pertii Pesonen (University of Helsinki), 'Finland: Party Support in a Fragmented
   System';
Otto Schmidt (University of Amsterdam), 'The Abolition of Compulsory Voting in
   the Netherlands';
R. Serry and Cees van der Eijk (University of Amsterdam), 'Participation in the
   Netherlands: Types and Attitudes: a preliminary investigation'.

For purposes of focus we have explicitly related discussion in the book to the
question of party identification: what it is, how it should be measured, whether the
concept itself or its measures are necessary to any realistic approach to voting. To
widen and strengthen this discussion we invited contributions from Dusan Sidjanski
and Ronald Inglehart on Switzerland, from Ronald Inglehart and Hans Klingemann on
the member nations of the EEC, from Max Kaase on Western Germany and from
David Robertson on theoretical considerations, even though these papers were not
presented at the Workshop itself. The centrality of party identification to our
concerns bears witness to the pervasive influence on election studies of the 'Michigan
School' of Angus Campbell, Warren Miller, Philip Converse, Donald Stokes and their
associates, not only through their original work on American politics but through
their imaginative collaborations with European colleagues. If the extension of their
ideas has now provoked critiques based on European experience (some of which
appear here), this in itself is a tribute to the power of the original. The book tries to
capture some of the intellectual excitement of the current debate on the status of
party identification through a dialectical process of presenting the thesis, then the
antithesis (including newer approaches such as dimensional analyses and rational
choice reasoning), and combining them in a broader synthesis. We are grateful to
Warren Miller for contributing the strong and clear justification of party identification
which sets off the dialectic at a high level.

# Contents

PART I

Party Identification: Its Theoretical and Measurement
Status

# 1

# Introduction: Party Identification and Beyond

In the course of a mere two decades, party identification has become as pervasive a concept as power, authority, legitimacy, stability or any other element in the professional political scientists' vocabulary. Theorists might reply that this is sympotomatic of the narrowing of interests associated with the 'behavioural revolution' to peripheral aspects of politics in a few Western democracies, which can be quantified and investigated through surveys. While voting studies undoubtedly owe some of their appeal to these considerations, party identification has positive conceptual qualities to commend it, even to theorists, one of them being that it offers a new explanation of democratic stability and legitimacy, which in turn confer authority and power. The more electors are attached by enduring psychological links to political parties, the argument runs, the more the polity is insured against 'flash parties' and sudden demagogic incursions. Conversely, the greater the legitimacy, authority and power of established party élites, the greater the time available for the vital bargaining and compromise which allow democracies to solve problems in an orderly and peaceful fashion with the largest possible degree of general consent (Converse and Dupeux, 1962; Converse, 1969). If this is accepted, the growth and development of party identification becomes the central concept not only of voting studies but even more centrally of political socialization (Greenstein, 1965; Easton and Dennis, 1969; Jennings and Niemi, 1968; Langton, 1968). Its importance derives not only—perhaps only slightly—from the direct attachment to a party that it fosters, but even more from its role in simplifying the complex and confusing political world from the viewpoint of the individual elector. Given a basic feeling of trust and confidence in a particular party, the elector can adjust his attitudes to conform to those of chosen leaders on all but exceptional cases—thus avoiding excessive information costs (Goldberg, 1969) and even alienation and anomie (see Miller, Chapter 2 below; for critiques Thomassen, Chapter 4 below and Robertson, Chapter 19 below).

In a manner fairly typical of behavioural developments in political science (which can be parallelled in economics, sociology and the natural and biological sciences), a concept that was at first a narrowly technical summary measure of predispositions to vote for a particular party has by these means been developed over the years to apply to a great variety of contexts. Its explanatory range is moreover accompanied by great simplicity of interpretation at a conceptual level and extreme simplicity of measurement. All these factors make for the widespread popularity of the concept. One important element in the current debate over its status is in fact whether its conceptual and measurement simplicity mask underlying complexities which it does not solve but merely glosses over—again a problem of popular concepts in other disciplines. This question forms the focus of much of the discussion in this book. For a full understanding of its ramifications, and of the background to the various points that will be raised, we must briefly review the history and uses of party identification, and relate these to other developments in the field of voting and party competition.

## PARTY IDENTIFICATION AND VOTING STUDIES

Even in the earliest voting studies electors were classified for some purposes into adherents of the various parties. Originally (Lazarsfeld, *et al.*, 1944; Berelson *et al.*, 1954) this was done on the basis of their vote in the relevant election: thus one could see how the class composition of 'Democrats' differed from that of 'Republicans', or even how it differed between electors who voted for the same party in two successive elections and those who did not. From the association between social background and vote, certain factors emerged as predisposing electors to vote for a particular party. Lazarsfeld and Berelson formalized the associations in a predictive form in the 'Index of Political Predispositions'. This was basically a cross-tabulation of religion (Catholic-Protestant), urban-rural residence and occupation. Urban manual Catholics formed the group with the highest proportion of Democratic voters who were accordingly ranked highest on predispositions to vote Democrat and lowest on predisposition to vote Republican. Rural non-manual Protestants had the extreme set of opposing predispositions and fell at the other end of the rank-ordering. More mixed groups were placed in the middle ranks of the Index.

Studies using social background variables of this kind (which included most of those done in Europe in the fifties and early sixties (Benney *et al.*, 1956; Milne and MacKenzie, 1955 and 1958; Valen and Katz, 1964) tended to discount the independent influence of candidates and issues on electors' votes. This was rather seen as being nullified by the perceptual distortions associated with the electors' sociopolitical allegiances. Much of the Elmira study is focused on the way electors bend candidates' issue-stands to suit their own preconceptions (Berelson *et al.*, 1954, Chapters 5, 6, 10, 11). The basic conception, shaped by the history of the 1948 presidential election, was of electors drifting away from the party as a result of the low salience of politics during the inter-election period, and being drawn back to their original allegiances by the rise in the salience of politics during the campaign itself, bending their original conceptions as they did so.

While such a predispositional approach suited the relatively tranquil American politics of the forties and of Britain in the fifties, it had much reduced explanatory power in the face of the massive vote transfers to Eisenhower in 1952 and 1956, and the obvious contrast between Republican presidential and Democratic congressional majorities (apart from begging the question as to whether correlation should count as causation). Clearly electors could not be voting simply in terms of long-term social predispositions: other influences were deflecting these. The most obvious source of such other influences was to be found in the cues offered by elections themselves, the candidates and issues of the campaign.

Ironically, in view of its later identification with the long-term predisposition tapped by party identification, the real innovation of the Michigan School was its frank recognition of the independent (if short-term) effects of the campaign itself, in the shape of new candidates and new issues. In their first formulation (Campbell *et al.*, 1954) candidates and issue orientations were recognized as independent factors affecting voting choice along with party identification. The influence of each was recognized as varying independently: some elections might be dominated by issues or candidates, others by long-term predispositions measured by party identification. As Miller remarks below, (Chapter 2), it is this recognition that voting in a particular election might in principle be determined almost wholly by reactions to issues that makes nonsense of any critique of party identification based on increases in the amount of issue voting in recent elections (Key, 1966; Pomper *et al.*, 1972). In fact the formulation is so comprehensive as to be tautological, but usefully tautological, in that elections are typed by relative predominance of one of the three main variables. More damaging are criticisms voiced earlier about the lack of theoretical or temporal antecedence between the determinants of voting and the act itself (Rossi, 1959): reactions to issues and candidates might well be formed at the same time as the voting decision itself and can hardly be said to explain it in the sense of preceding and shaping it. And was party identification itself not simply the same thing as consistent voting for the same party? As a surrogate Index of Political Predispositions, did it not suffer in comparison with the original from the absence of clearly antecedent socioeconomic characteristics?

No doubt in response to such criticisms, the status of the various concepts was reformulated in *The American Voter* (Campbell *et al.*, 1960). Candidate and issue orientations were decomposed into six 'components of electoral decision' which immediately preceded voting choice within the 'funnel of causality': these were attitudes (1) to the Democratic and (2) to the Republican candidate; (3) to domestic and (4) to foreign issues; (5) to groups involved in the election and (6) towards the parties as managers of government. Such attitudes were ascertained from the 'open' questions put to electors about the candidates and parties involved in the election. Given a highly pro-Democratic or pro-Republican score on these 'components', electors would vote for the appropriate party with high probability.

This approach is open to all the previous objections about the lack of clear antecedence between determinants and vote. To a considerable extent these are answered by the Michigan authors' concept of a funnel of causality widening back in time from the voting choice itself, incorporating larger and larger numbers of increasingly indeterminate relationships as it does so. At the narrowest point, immediately preceding the vote, choice is almost tautologically determined by the 'components of electoral decision'. Preceding and influencing these, however, are factors whose objective and antecedent status can hardly be in doubt. First come the actual personalities and issues of the election, whose handling by campaign managers crucially affects electors' attitudes on the six components. These are also shaped by the actual record of the incumbent government and the general goodness or badness of the times, as well as by the electors' social class and other group affiliations. Occupying a central place in the 'funnel' however, mediating many of the influences on the components from objective factors further back, and shaping perceptions of candidates and issues, is party identification. A diagram of these interrelationships between various components of the model is given in Figure 1.1. The measure of

6

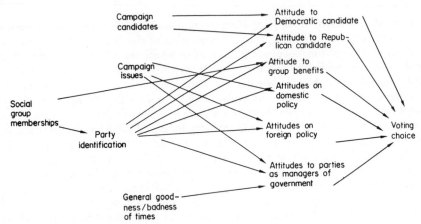

Figure 1.1    Interrelationships between voting choice, party identification and short-term partisan attitudes

long-term predispositions to the parties emerges as the most important single element of the new explanatory scheme, and its relative independence of the other factors becomes a crucial test if not of the validity, at least of the distinctiveness and parsimony, of the Michigan approach. For if the six components of partisan attitudes turn out to be imperfect measures of a Democratic or Republican partisanship they become indistinguishable from party identification itself, and the rationale for separating these two elements in the model is undermined. (See Shaffer, 1972, for findings that seem to show exactly this.) Even worse, if party identification is shown to be no more than current voting intention, all that is left of the explanatory scheme is the 'pull' of candidates and issues and the long-term predispositions fostered by class and other social characteristics, which would leave us where we started with the pure Index of Political Predispositions.

Rightly recognizing that the stability and independence of party identification are crucial to their explanation of voting behaviour, Campbell and his associates went to considerable lengths to show:

(a) that party identification among American electors was independent of voting choice. A man would still view himself as a Democrat while allowing his candidate preferences to sway him towards Eisenhower.

(b) as a corollary, party identification was stable. Normally, people inherited a partisan identity just as they did a religious identity. Here concurrent and later work on the political socialization of children offered much support, showing that party identification was the first piece of political information learned, and that many children were able to identify themselves as Democrat or Republican at as early an age as six (Greenstein, 1965; Easton and Dennis, 1969; Langton, 1968; Zurick, 1974). On the other hand more sophisticated over-time data showed that the recall of parents' partisanship was unreliable and that the correlation between parents and children was of the order of 0.5 (Jennings and Niemi, 1968).

These negative findings however came later (along with the opposing findings on other points which we shall cite below). At the time the full-blown Michigan scheme was elaborated most of the evidence (heavily American) appeared to support very firmly the independent existence and stability of party identification. This led to further developments in the last of the major Michigan volumes, *Elections and the Political Order* (Campbell *et al.*, 1966). Two of these are cited here to illustrate the utility of the concept, once its initial postulates are accepted, as an analytic tool in the study of elections.

(*a*) It was always recognized that party identification could change under the impact of major issues. The two frequently encountered in *The American Voter* are the Depression (which turned many former Republicans into Democrats) and the Civil War, which again favoured the Democrats by giving them the Solid South (at any rate up to the late fifties). The interaction between party identification and issues (once the stability of the former was accepted) could be used to type elections as 'maintaining' (the balance of parties as affected by their underlying proportions of identifiers), 'deviating' (from the balance, but not altering it permanently) and 'realigning' (the underlying proportions of identifiers and thus permanently affecting the party balance). American electoral history could thus be divided into periods of Republican and Democratic dominance marked off by the 'realigning' elections of 1860, perhaps 1896, and 1932. The whole typology depends crucially of course on the assumption that party identification is an independent and stable factor underlying voting.

(*b*) A further analytic tool is provided by Converse's construct of the normal vote. Given that party identification is distinct from actual votes cast and remains stable, and no short-term (issue- or candidate-based) forces operate (or alternatively, that they balance out in their partisan affects), electors will vote in accordance with their partisan attachments. Thus the party with the 'natural majority' of identifiers will win. Less obviously, those short-term forces that are operating may produce proportionately equal defections from the strong and weak identifiers with each party. Here again the party with a 'natural majority' will do best.

Conversely, rates of defection from the various types of identifier with party A that greatly exceed rates from the corresponding types for party B identify the election as one in which short-term issues and candidates strongly favour party B. Precise estimates of the contribution of short-term factors to the vote can then be made by: (1) calculating what *would have been* the parties' share of the vote from the various types of identifier, given actual turnout, had defection rates among them been equal or nil, and (2) subtracting this from what was actually obtained. Observed defection rates can actually be used to set up a figure in which predictions of defection for weak and strong identifiers can be projected for elections categorized as strongly pro-Republican, moderately pro-Republican, moderately pro-Democrat and strongly pro-Democrat. This gives some capability of predicting elections in advance on the basis of simple and easily quantified assumptions, as well as assessing the significance of mid-term congressional, local and byelections—hallmarks of a really powerful and useful concept.

Mention of weak and strong identifiers reminds us that party identification is a measure not only of the direction but also of the strength of partisanship. Differences in involvement exist between weak and strong identifiers—involving higher turnout and greater participation generally—and hold regardless of party. None of the critiques of party identification dispute the assertion that strong identifiers are the more involved, more consistent, more active and more politically committed electors. The question is rather, what are they committed to? Is it undeviating loyalty to a party regardless of new issues and new alternatives? Would strong identifiers under all circumstances be last to leave and first to return? Or is their loyalty strictly conditional on the other alternatives available, so that their very commitment to politics may render them sensitive to the presence of an attractive new alternative and more inclined to defect to it? Goot, in commenting on the expressed support of strong Australian identifiers for a new party alignment, has commented that new parties are commonly founded by former members and leaders of old parties (Goot, 1972). Crewe in Chapter 3 of this book expands this point and raises another disturbing possibility: do strong identifiers share the same kind of attachment to their party? May they not at least fall into two groups: (1) identifiers positively attracted by an existing party, (2) identifiers strongly repelled by existing alternatives to 'their' party. Should the alternatives change, such 'negative' identifiers might well desert their previous parties in large numbers, in spite of displaying the same reactions as 'positive' identifiers under stable conditions. (In this sense Crewe's critique ties in with Robertson's stress on the autonomy of electors' political aims and their independent use of these to evaluate parties rather than having them inculcated by the parties (Robertson, Chapter 19). The 'British Election Studies' of 1974 have devised questions to measure negative as well as positive affect to the parties (Crewe *et al.*, forthcoming), following on a theoretical critique of interpersonal comparisons of intensity which stresses the importance of establishing the other alternatives with which party choice is compared, and of the sense and reference in regard to which it is stated as strong (Rae and Taylor, 1970). The importance of the institutional context is emphasized for example by the fall in the proportion of strong Democratic identifiers from 22 per cent in 1964 to 16 per cent in 1968, presumably under the impact of the Wallace Third Party (Flanagan, 1966), and by the rise in proportions of French self-identifiers after the advent of the Gaullists in 1958 (Cameron, 1972). Damgaard and Rusk's discussion of the dramatic party changes in Denmark in 1973 (Chapter 9 below) also stresses the attraction of the new 'flash' parties to 'strong' identifiers with some of the existing parties.

These points may be met in part by the retort that party identification has worked well for the uses to which it has been put—that strong identifiers under stable political conditions, which are the ones mainly investigated, are homogeneous in terms of the behaviour under investigation (principally turnout and consistency of voting choice) and that under crisis conditions, when the party system changes, proportions of identifiers are also expected to change. But here we are turning from the general conceptual status of party identification to its underlying measurement assumptions, which require separate and more detailed discussion.

## DEFINITION AND MEASUREMENT OF PARTY IDENTIFICATION

Originally—and this point is again emphasized in Miller's restatement (Chapter 2 below)—party identification was conceived as a non-calculative product of early socialization processes—'the individual's affective orientation to an important group-object in his environment' (Campbell *et al.*, 1960). Party identification has been reinterpreted by Goldberg and others, including Stokes, under the influence of rational choice models, as an information-economizing device—having decided at one time that a party supports one's interests, one quite rationally votes for it in the future without further examination of issue-stands (Butler and Stokes, 1969; Golberg, 1969;

Davis *et al.*, 1970). Robertson has argued eloquently that partisan attachments can be viewed *either* as if they were effective group orientations *or* as if they were rational information-economizing devices, but that the two interpretations are inconsistent with each other and cannot be used simultaneously. This is because the first presumes that electors' political aims are inculcated by the parties, and the other that their aims are autonomous and that parties are used as instruments by electors to achieve these aims (Robertson, 1975; see also Chapter 19 below).

To some extent Robertson's criticism rests on moral as well as empirical—descriptive grounds: to assume that electors' goals are inculcated by parties is to reverse the relationship postulated by theories of representative democracy. It does however introduce the broader descriptive consideration that the long-term predispositions of voters to vote for particular parties (their partisanship if you prefer), while it is a factor that must be taken into account in any realistic approach, need not *necessarily* be measured by 'individuals' affective orientations' towards parties. One alternative, the Index of Political Predisposition based on salient background characteristics, has already been mentioned. Since there are alternative methods of measuring long-term predispositions, the debate over party identification should be viewed primarily as a measurement controversy about what constitutes the best method of estimation, rather than assuming from the outset that party identification is in some metaphysical sense the only true method.

The force behind this common if implicit assumption derives from the simplicity and ease of measuring predispositions through electors' own estimates of their proximity to the parties, ascertained from direct survey questions. In keeping with its definition as individuals' affective orientations, the original Party Identification questions ran as follows:

Generally speaking, do you think of yourself as a Republican, a Democrat, an Independent, or what?
(IF REPUBLICAN OR DEMOCRAT) Would you call yourself a strong (Republican, Democrat) or a not very strong (Republican, Democrat)?
(IF INDEPENDENT) Do you think of yourself as closer to the Republican or Democratic Party?

Answers to these questions give rise to a seven-point classification (Strong Democrat, Weak Democrat, Independent Democrat, Independent, Independent Republican, Weak Republican, Strong Republican), which for a two-party system is usually regarded as a rank-ordering, placing individuals in terms of degree of attachment to Republicans. Interpretation of this as a continuum bounded by optimum degrees of partisanship produces interesting contrasts with the spaces produced by dimensional analyses and with those assumed by rational choice models. We develop the interpretation in the next section, but comment first on the complexities that arise when party identification questions are used in a multi-party system, and on the implicit assumptions upon which the use of these questions rest.

Kaase's contribution to this book (Chapter 5) illustrates in particular the influence that the wording of these questions may have on responses. In countries with a long list of parties such as The Netherlands (Thomassen, Chapter 4 below) it is simply not possible to name them all. Kaase's estimates of party adherents in the Federal Republic of Germany fluctuated from 54 per cent in 1967 to 29 per cent in 1969. It is unlikely that actual proportions of partisans fluctuated to this extent within a two-year period: it is much more likely that responses were sensitive to the fact that the question mentioned parties in 1967 and omitted them in 1969, the wording in the latter year being simply: "Do you usually think of yourself as an adherent of a certain party? (IF YES) Which party do you like best?"

Given that exactly the same question cannot be asked everywhere, fluctuations of this kind are extremely damaging to the claims of party identification to measure long-term predispositions on a cross-national basis. This is of course only a special case of the sensitivity and unreliability of survey questions which have been extensively criticized as measures (see for example Webb *et al.*, 1966). Given that comparative survey data provide incomparably the best description of individual voting reactions, it might still be better not to rest the measurement of long-term predispositions on a single set of questions but rather to base it on a multivariate analysis such as that suggested by Farlie and Budge (Chapters 6 and 20 below). Unlike dimensional analyses this would produce a party-bounded space similar to that of party identification but with greater cross-national stability.

Even if the variation due to wording is dismissed as a technical question that will be met by improvements in survey technology, it may be questioned whether the effective orientation tapped by the party identification questions actually exists independently of voting intention (Chapters 3-5 below). This question was first raised in an investigation of British voting behaviour conducted within the Michigan framework itself, and was occasioned by the finding that British electors changed identifications along with voting intentions to a very much greater extent than American electors—indeed, to an extent that cast doubt on party identification as an independent variable at all (Butler and Stokes, 1969). Thomassen and Kaase (Chapters 4 and 5 below) produce findings on German and Dutch panel data that reveal considerable instability in identification over time. Thomassen interprets such instability as demonstrating that, in The Netherlands at least, party identification is no more than an alternative way of measuring current voting intention. Miller points out (Chapter 2 below) that The Netherlands is a party system undergoing considerable social upheaval at present, with a concomitant rise of major new issues. Within the Michigan framework one would therefore expect changes in the proportions of identifiers. This is of course a valid point: but it should be noted that it makes the framework tautologous, for any finding on the relationship between party identification and party choice becomes compatible with it. If electors change votes while maintaining their previous identification this proves the concept valid, but changing both together is simply evidence that an upheaval is taking place with concomitant shifts in the proportions of identifiers.

Miller's argument in Chapter 2 could indeed be seen as a plea that party identification is a tautology, but a useful one. If we assume by definition that most people do identify fundamentally with a party, we can for example type current Dutch elections as 'realigning', and compare their salient features with maintaining elections (identified as such by finding that they occur in countries and at periods with stable proportions of identifiers).

Since tautologies cannot be accepted or rejected through empirical checks, they must be judged on other grounds. Thomassen for example suggests it is simply more illuminating to measure Dutch voters' long-term predispositions through their class and religious affiliations than through questions on direct effect for the parties. This hint that we might in some cases go back to the Index of Political Predisposition (IPP) as a measure makes it relevant to shift discussion from party identification as a unique conception on its own (which we have implicitly taken it to be up to this point), to party identification as one attempt out of many to estimate long-term partisan predispositions. Others are the IPP, the Party-defined Likelihood Ratio Space applied to background characteristics by Budge and Farlie below (Chapters 6, 20); long-term rational choice decisions to support a particular party on grounds that its interests are unlikely to diverge from one's own; and even past voting record and consistency.

When party identification is viewed simply as one out of a set of potential indicators, debate shifts from its unique goodness or badness to its relative merits *vis-à-vis* the other indicators. An empirical examination of these in the Canadian context is contributed by Irvine (Chapters 17 and 18) and across nine democracies by Budge and Farlie (Chapter 6). At a general level the relative merits of party identification surely lie in its simplicity of measurement, location in an internally consistent conceptual scheme (see the next section of this chapter) and ultimate grounding in social psychology. Its weakness (as in our earlier comments), and the thrust of criticisms such as those of Kaase, Thomassen and Crewe, Chapters 3–5 below), lies in its lack of theoretical or even temporal antecedence to the voting decision itself. For short-term predictive success alone, one might for example base one's measure of predisposition on current voting intention, which has a high correlation with actual voting in the next election. But such predictive success has none of the element of surprise, of showing how seemingly unrelated phenomena (like policy distances between elector and party, or membership of a particular class) in fact directly influence the vote. In the context of these extended chains of inference between antecedent predispositions and voting choice, voting intention seems more like the *explicandum* than the *explicans*. The same criticism might be made against using the partisan regularity of past voting.

Even if it is accepted that party identification is not exactly the same as past regularity or present intention, one must still ask how theoretically interesting is the statement that electors vote for the party to which they feel closest? Is it not more interesting to assert that people with specified social characteristics will vote for a particular party—more interesting because these characteristics are more antecedent to the voting decision, both theoretically and temporally, than is party identification?

Miller de-emphasizes the use of party identification as a predictor of voting choice in favour of its more general social-psychological role as a perceptual organizing concept for individual electors. Here again however one could argue with Thomassen that class and other social groupings can fill exactly the same function, and again provide a more interesting explanation: (1) because of their undoubted antecedence to most political phenomena and (2) because they can be used to structure not only the political world but the whole social world, and being more general are on grounds of parsimony to be preferred to a specialized explanatory concept like party identification.

Accepting party identification as a tautology that covers all conceivable findings does not therefore necessarily compel its use, but merely shifts evaluation from empirical judgements to general theoretical criteria. But these do not clearly favour party identification over other estimators of long-term partisan predispositions.

## ASSUMPTIONS INVOLVED IN PARTY IDENTIFICATION

Survey-based analyses of voting behaviour have generally proceeded in an *ad hoc* manner, introducing concepts that serve to explain the data immediately on hand, rather than working out an *a priori*, rigorously formulated and internally consistent body of theory such as that associated with rational choice approaches (for a masterly summary of these see Riker and Ordeshook, 1973, and Ordeshook's contribution to this volume, Chapter 15).

Nevertheless, survey-based interpretations cannot help but rest on some implicit assumptions: those using party identification are no exception. Stating them explicitly aids evaluation and comparison with other approaches. It also enhances appreciation of the concept of party identification itself, for the assumptions, though implicit, hang together well and provide a remarkably consistent picture of influences upon voting. Our statement of these assumptions draws heavily upon a previous evaluation of the application of party identification to Britain (Crewe, 1974). Every assumption may not be involved in every application of party identification but they are all necessary for the range of uses to which it has been put. For reference we number them as follows:

(1) Most electors feel an underlying attachment to a party which can be distinguished from current voting intention (termed party identification).

(2) This underlying attachment is produced by socialization within the family.

(3) Most electors remain attached to their party throughout life, whatever the leadership does.

(4) The minority who change attachments do so from a combination of the following circumstances: absence or weakness of parental attachments; family and own initial attachments different from those of adult reference groups such as class; large-scale economic, social and political change.

(5) Underlying attachments to parties are correctly reflected in electors' direct responses to questions about their self-perceived closeness to parties, and their strength of feeling about this.

(6) The more strongly attached to a party that an elector is, the more likely he is to vote independently for the party to which he is attached:

      (a)      in a particular election,

      (b)      over a series of elections.

(7) The more strongly attached to a party an elector is, the more likely he is to turn out to vote.

(8) The more strongly attached to a party an elector is, the more likely are all his other evaluations and perceptions of politics to be consistent with his party attachment.

(9) Temporary inconsistencies between voting choice and party attachments can be produced by the appeals of issues and candidates, but only over one or two elections, following which the individual generally votes again according to his party attachment.

Readers will recognize in some assumptions points already discussed above. Putting them together enables us to evaluate them as a whole. It will be noted that some assumptions are concerned with much broader questions than pure prediction of the vote: Assumption (8), for example, asserts the uses of party identification in structuring the elector's political world.

Nevertheless, from a combination of certain assumptions, predictions can be drawn which can be evaluated against aggregate voting data. For example, electors are postulated in the absence of strong counteracting forces to vote for the party to which they say they are attached and to inherit their party identification from their parents. Over time, moreover, the short-term cues—issues and candidates—that impinge on electors will cancel each other out: hence in a country where the proportions of party identifiers of different types remained stable or rose slightly, we should expect the aggregate percentage votes to correspond fairly closely to these figures and to show no consistent tendency to decline. Nor should turnout decline or transfers of votes between parties become more volatile. In Britain, however, stable or rising identification with the two main parties has been accompanied by all these trends (Crewe, 1974)—a conjunction that is extremely difficult to interpret within the framework of the assumptions stated above.

This being said, it is not at all clear that we have anything better to take their place, given the weaknesses both of dimensional analysis (Chapter 7) and of rational choice models (Chapters 14 and 15). Perhaps the solution is to be found in some analogue to party identification that can be interpreted along the same lines but which is at once less sensitive to cross-national variations and more sensitive to changes in electors' closeness to parties. Such an analogue is being developed on the basis of Likelihood Ratio Space by Budge and Farlie, forthcoming, and the present volume contains examples of both its empirical and theoretical use (Chapters 6 and 20).

## PARTY IDENTIFICATION, POLICY SPACES AND DIMENSIONAL ANALYSES

The fact that many of the leading ideas associated with long-term partisan predispositions have been developed in an explicitly spatial form draws attention to party identification's own potential as a spatial representation of a two-party system. This can be spelled out by adding to the assumptions stated above the following.

(5a) For a two-party system, underlying attachments to parties can be adequately represented by a line.

(5b) Such a line is bounded by the points of 'very strong attachment' to each of the two parties.

(5c) Electors can be typed in terms of their party attachments by placement at one of the seven positions on the line: very strongly (A), fairly strongly (A), 'independent' (A), independent, 'independent' (B), fairly strongly (B), very strongly (B).

Then assumptions 6—8 can be restated in terms of the influence on voting consistency, turnout and evaluations, of closeness to the 'strongly attached' end-points. An example of a hypothetical distribution of electors over this line is given in Figure 1.2. This interpretation of party identification as a spatial construct is not, as we have already seen, at all essential to its use. The previously stated, non-spatial assumptions already cover the analytic purposes to which it has been put. Nevertheless, viewing the concept spatially is useful for purposes of comparison with rational choice models and dimensional analyses, as follows:

(a) The spatial interpretation strikingly illustrates the way in which the parties are defined within the Michigan framework. Parties are not (as in rational choice models) groups of leaders who manoeuvre in front of the electorate as they compete with policies for their votes. Rather, parties exist among electors quite independently of

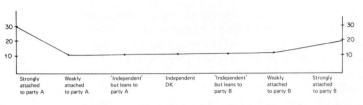

Figure 1.2    A spatial interpretation of party identification for a two-party system

leaders, and are therefore capable of surviving serious errors of judgement on their part (as the Republican party did for example in the Goldwater and Watergate debacles). This is a thoroughly realistic view and conforms much more closely to our intuitive ideas of what a party is than the leadership groups of most rational choice theories.

(b) The purest expression of party is to be found among the strongest electoral partisans; thus the spatial representation of electors is bounded by the most strongly attached positions. Although superficially the party identification line resembles Downs's famous representation of party competition along a left-right continuum (Downs, 1957), the spaces actually contrast sharply. Downs's space is a pure policy space (bounded for example by zero and 100 per cent government intervention in the economy). Thus in principle (although he hedges on this, cf. Barry, 1970) the leadership parties could place themselves anywhere on this space where it was advantageous for them to do so, and electors would react by supporting whichever party was closest to their personal policy-preference. Such a policy space with free movement of parties differs fundamentally from a party-bounded space like that of party identification, where the nature of the space is itself defined by the parties and thus restricts movement. It would be absurd for example to think within this context of a Republican candidate located at the 'fairly strong Democrat' position.

When the contrast between policy and party defined spaces is explicitly stated it appears clear enough. Many rational choice theorists have however suggested that party identification could be viewed as one dimension of a multi-dimensional policy space (for example Davis *et al.*, 1970). If the essential characteristic of a policy space is recognized as free movement, it cannot admit a dimension on which movement is restricted—all the results of mathematical analysis based on rational choice assumptions depend on this (Riker and Ordeshook, 1973; Ordeshook, Chapter 15 below). Less formal rational choice models have introduced the idea that an area of policy space may 'belong' to particular parties (Robertson, 1975; Laver, Chapter 16 below): e.g., Northern Ireland Unionists can never credibly claim to support unification with the South. Such modifications introduce unforeseen complications which have the effect of rendering the policy space with which they began much more analogous to a party-defined space (Budge and Farlie, forthcoming; Chapter 20 below). However that may be, the contrast between pure policy space and party-defined space is fundamental, and viewing party identification as itself a party-defined space helps illuminate it.

(c) We have noted that party identification can be used to represent shifts in attachment to one party or the other (by tracing the movement of individuals from strongly to weakly attached or across the party boundaries in diagrams such as Figure 1.2). Little actual use has been made of such a spatial representation, partly because it is so limited, but survey analysts have relied heavily on the underlying ordinal scale which it generates for a two-party system (at the same time somewhat cavalierly ignoring the problem posed by independents and abstainers). In particular, they have leaned on the assumption that a diminution in support for one party will mean an increase in support for the other. There is therefore no problem estimating which party will benefit by vote transfers from the other—there is only one destination to which they can go.

Such is not the case however with a multi-party system. The prediction of election outcomes obviously depends on knowing whose votes will go to whom if there is a transfer (and beyond that, which party is likely to join with others in a coalition). It is at once more important in a multi-party system to have some kind of spatial representation (and thus to estimate which parties are closer) and more difficult to get one than in a two-party system. Party identification itself cannot form such a representation since it provides no way of ranking many parties in relation to each other (Converse, 1966).

Estimates of distance can however be formed by locating parties in other spaces derived from survey data. Such spaces are generally based on survey responses quite similar in kind to those elicited for party identification; only, instead of self-assessments of proximity to one party alone, as with party identification, these questions obtain rankings of all parties in order of perceived closeness to the respondent (or information on which other parties are closest neighbours). Typically, such rankings are 'averaged' in some way, either by correlating the ranks given to each pair of parties by each individual, or by taking the mid-point between the mean ranks assigned to the other party in the pair by individuals belonging to each party. Some technique is then applied to these averaged rankings which is designed to produce a space in which distances correspond to the proximity measures. The closer the resemblance between two parties (as estimated either by a correlation close to 1.0 or by a high aggregated and averaged rank number), the closer together should be their locations in any ensuing space.

This is usually a highly economical way of representing a party system since the number of dimensions required to represent a highly fragmented party system is low—often no more than two. No direct interpretation of these dimensions is possible—since only party preference rankings have been used to generate the space, dimensions are simply those that characterize the lowest-dimensional space that represents party preferences adequately. Usually however the dimensions can be identified with ideological or other cleavages known independently to exist. Thus, if all parties commonly viewed as left-wing are at opposite ends of a dimension from the parties commonly regarded as right-wing, the dimension will be termed a left–right dimension. Dimensions susceptible to these interpretations which commonly emerge under dimensional analyses are a left–right division, a clerical–anti-clerical division, and a governing–non-governing party division (which often coincides with a pro-system–anti-system split) (Converse and Valen, 1971; Daalder and Rusk, 1972; Chapters 8-13 below).

Some technical weaknesses of these representations are noted below (Chapter 7) such as the suppression of information through averaging and instability of dimensions over time. Here we are particularly concerned with the relationship of such dimensional analyses to policy spaces on the one hand and party identification on the other.

In spite of introductory rhetoric which links them to rational choice models, all dimensional aalyses known to us (with two exceptions, one of them reported in Chapter 9 below) are incapable of operationalizing such models. This is because the models assume a pure policy space while the dimensional analyses use as input perceptions of party closeness. Were issue-preferences and other policy indicators the input, dimensional analyses would operationalize the policy space of rational choice models: only if policy-indicators go in will a police space come out. The only analyses that to our knowledge do produce policy spaces are Robertson's factor analysis of British party manifestos (Robertson, 1975) and Damgaard and Rusk's study of Danish legislative voting (Chapter 9 below). This lends considerable general interest to its discovery of a uni-dimensional left–right space.

Even so, rational choice arguments depend on the representation of individuals as well as parties in the space, which cannot be done with the averaging methods generally employed by dimensional analyses. For its original purposes of estimating where votes for a particular party were likely to go, and what coalitions would form, representation only of parties is of course perfectly adequate.

Going beyond prediction to explanation, however, one may ask as with party identification just how antecedent perceptions of closeness are to the vote transfers and coalitions under study? Which is the independent and which the dependent variable? In Norway, for example, the bourgeois parties moved closer from 1965 to 1970, in a space based on party rankings, *as a result* of having been in coalition during the intervening period (Converse and Valen, 1971). Here the coalition explains perceived closeness, rather than the other way round.

The similarity between this criticism of the dimensional analysis and previous criticisms of party identification is not coincidental, since the spatial modelling of multi-party systems developed from earlier or concurrent uses of party identification. As the latter itself can be interpreted as a (limited) spatial construct, we can ask whether the analogy is complete—whether dimensional analyses based on rankings retain the characteristics, while extending the range, of party identification under a multi-party system.

Surprisingly, the answer is no. The space produced by dimensional analysis of party rankings is a space defined by qualities inferred from the party placements. The parties themselves do not bound or define the space—this is done by the inferred qualities. One might of course maintain that, because party locations form the basis of inference, certain areas of the derived space are reserved to particular parties, and that such a space corresponds to policy spaces with party-reserved areas, which as we noted above are analogous to party-defined spaces. As party identification interpreted spatially is a party-defined space, a link might thus be made with dimensional analyses.

The argument breaks down however because practically any movement of parties in an inferred space—even within a 'reserved' area—changes the basis of inference and hence the nature of the space. For example, if socialist parties and bourgeois parties, which were at the opposite ends of a dimension consequently interpreted as 'left–right', move to the centre, even though they remain apart each in their 'own' direction, the interpretation of the dimension will change. This need not happen in a policy space, and of course a party-defined space will remain stable unless the parties themselves disappear or expand in number.

However useful party-inferred spaces based on dimensional analysis prove to be in interpreting electoral events, they do not take the place of party identification. Nor, as we have seen, do the pure policy spaces that might be derived from dimensional analyses of issue-preferences or other policy indicators. On the other hand policy spaces with areas 'reserved' or 'owned' by the parties do show strong resemblances amounting to practical identity with party-defined spaces such as that based on party identification or on the Likelihood Ratio Space described in Chapter 6. An assessment of these linkages will be made after the presentation of various spatial analyses and models in Parts II and III below.

## PLAN OF DISCUSSION

Consideration of the spatial approaches increasingly applied to voting and party competition does indeed go 'beyond' the party identification in our title, but, as we hope to have shown in the last section, along a perfectly coherent and logical line of development from the original. Because party identification is at once so widely used in survey analysis and capable of spatial interpretation, it forms a criterion against which spatial representations can be evaluated. Since continuity of research is desirable, it can be argued that one spatial representation is preferable to another if it preserves the essential features of party identification while avoiding its weaknesses (Chapters 6 and 20 below). At least we should be clear about the similarities and differences between party identification and the newer concepts, and not fudge the issues, as Robertson argues in relationship to rational choice models (Chapter 19).

The plan of our book, like the sequence of discussion in this chapter, also broadens out from party identification to alternative or related approaches. The rest of Part I is devoted to clarifying the conceptual and empirical standing of party identification at the present time. Miller explicitly takes the concept out of a narrow American setting and views it as a framework for comparative analysis (Chapter 2). In keeping with this it is evaluated in different European contexts: in Britain by Crewe (Chapter 3), in The Netherlands by Thomassen (Chapter 4) and in Germany by Kaase (Chapter 5).

Mindful of the point made earlier, that party identification should not be regarded as unique but as one of several alternative attempts to measure long-term predispositions, Budge and Farlie in Chapter 6 make explicit comparisons between the explanatory power of party identification and of other common social and demographic factors in relation to voting, across nine democracies—introducing in the process the idea of a Likelihood Ratio Space, which they expand as an alternative spatial representation in Chapter 20.

Part II presents the dimensional analyses which as we revealed have developed largely as substitute measures of party closeness in multi-party systems. The first chapter (Chapter 7) is concerned to relate these analyses to what has gone before. Two revealing analyses, by Rusk and Borre in Chapter 8 and Damgaard and Rusk in Chapter 9, link change at legislator and electoral levels in Denmark. The remaining chapters are concerned to map the cleavages existing among various Western party systems. In Chapter 10 Frognier uncovers a complex regional pattern in Belgium, an analysis that also represents a considerable technical achievement in extracting information from limited data. In Chapter 11 Mauser and Freysinnet employ a mixed space to estimate the appeals not only of parties but also of candidates in France. Switzerland turns out to offer less fruitful ground for at least a simple spatial representation in Inglehart and Sidjanski's analysis (Chapter 12). Inglehart and Klingemann in Chapter 13 provide a useful review and synthesis of relationships between party identification and simple spatial modelling in Western countries, fittingly bringing discussion back to party identification on a comparative basis.

Part III contains basically 'rational choice' approaches, which in contrast to party identification place their main emphasis on issue-voting and strategic manoeuvring. As the link Chapter 14 points out, however, the contrast is not complete: attempts can be found inside many rational choice frameworks to introduce party identification either explicitly or by another name. Some of the discussion in Part III focuses on this very point. Ordeshook in Chapter 15 provides a concise overview of mainstream developments of rational choice models, emphasizing their mathematical sophistication but the necessity of relaxing their more stringent assumptions if they are to provide satisfactory empirical models. The papers that follow work within the broad rational choice approach, but are more concerned with realistic representation than mathematical sophistication. Laver's clever reconstruction of voter 'space' in a critical Northern Ireland election involves a discontinuity between Unionist and Nationalist 'spaces' which could be imposed by their basic party identifications (Chapter 16). Irvine explicitly compares the explanatory power of party identification, rational choice and other models within the context of turnout and voting choice in Canada (Chapters 17 and 18). He ends up with a combined model with both party identification and rational choice components. Robertson argues in Chapter 19 however that, although voters must be viewed as having long-term attachments to a party in any realistic rational choice model, this cannot be party identification since its social psychological definition is incompatible with rational choice assumptions. Farlie and Budge seek to resolve this point in Chapter 20 by suggesting the use of a party-defined space that is capable of measuring both long-term predispositions (like party identification) and short-term issue cues (like rational choice models). Hopefully therefore our discussion ends on a synthesis 'beyond', but in line with, the concept of party identification.

## BASIC CONSIDERATIONS

Although our discussion covers much ground and is at points enmeshed in much detail, readers can always clarify the position by referring mentally to three basic considerations.

(1) Few analysts dispute the brilliant simplification involved in the initial Michigan approach, that voting is affected both by long-term predispositions and by short-term cues. Predispositions continue to be much the same from election to election and can be invoked to account for the substantial numbers of electors who always vote for the same party. Short-term cues—issues and candidates—are by their nature peculiar to each election.

There is little disagreement about the measurement of short-term cues (although perhaps there should be). These are nearly always estimated through direct survey questions about preferences on and/or salience of issues and candidates.

On the other hand there is considerable disagreement about the best measure of long-term predispositions: is it party identification, the Index of Political Predisposition, various social background characteristics linked to party support, or what? The papers in Part I can be viewed almost entirely as a measurement controversy based on a fundamental agreement that predispositions are central and need to be estimated: the question is, should they be estimated through party identification or by other means?

(2) In Parts II and III, although the spaces produced by dimensional analysis and postulated by rational choice models come in many shapes and dimensions, they fall

basically into four types, each of which has uses and properties, but some of which are more flexible than others:

> (a) party-defined spaces, like that produced for party identification in a two-party system (Figure 1.1 above);
>
> (b) party-inferred spaces, based on survey rankings of parties, with qualities inferred from party locations;
>
> (c) pure policy spaces, derived from issue-preferences or other policy indicators;
>
> (d) party-reserved policy-spaces, like (c) except that parties 'own' particular areas in the space (e.g. only the British Labour Party and not the Conservative Party can convincingly urge higher welfare benefits in an election).

Once spaces have been reduced to one of these types, they can be related through the discussion above and through our comments in Chapters 8 and 16.

(3) What is the meaning given to party within the approach under consideration? Is party conceived as:

> (a) an ongoing body of adherents with associated loyalties and ideology?
>
> (b) only the package of policies endorsed by current leaders?
>
> (c) purely a leadership group, or something existing among electors independently of leaders?
>
> (d) composed of the most loyal adherents, or as defined in some sense by the position of the average voter?
>
> (e) always united, or composed of internal factions and wings which might act differently under various circumstances?

Endorsement of a subset or any one of these alternative conceptions of party carries consequences for the whole description of the election process.

Although these three basic considerations seem at first sight independent of each other, and are presented separately here, it will become obvious as discussion proceeds that they are closely interrelated. For example, choice of a pure policy space to represent elections implies that the only influence on voting must be short-term cues, since predispositions cannot be represented in a space whose defining characteristic is free movement. Furthermore, parties in such a space can be represented only by a point designating the leaders' or candidates' set of current policy commitments.

Such consequences are drawn out in the introductions to each section. Armed with such distinctions we trust that readers will form their own synthesis of these stimulating discussions and analyses, as a check against ours.

## REFERENCES

Barry, B. M. (1970), *Sociologists, Economists and Democracy*, Collier-Macmillan, London.

Benney, M., R. H. Pear and A. H. Gray (1956), *How People Vote*, Routledge and Kegan Paul, London.

Berelson, B., P. F. Lazarsfeld and W. McPhee (1954), *Voting*, University of Chicago Press, Chicago.

Boyd, R. W. (1972), 'Popular Control of Public Policy: A Normal Vote Analysis of the 1968 Election', *American Political Science Review* 66, 429–49. (See also the 'Comments' in the same issue by R. A. Brody and B. I. Page (pp. 450–8) and by J. H. Kessel (pp. 459–65).)

Budge, I., and D. Farlie (forthcoming), *Voting and Party Competition: A Spatial Synthesis on a Critique of Existing Approaches Applied to Surveys from Ten Democracies*, Wiley, London and New York.

Butler, D. E. and D. E. Stokes (1969), *Political Change in Britain*, Macmillan, London.

Cameron, D. M. (1972), 'Stability and Change in Patterns of French Partisanship', *Public Opinion Quarterly*, 16, 19–30.

Campbell, A., G. Gurin and W. E. Miller (1954), *The Voter Decides*, Row, Peterson & Co., Evanston, Illinois.

Campbell, A., P. E. Converse, W. E. Miller and D. E. Stokes (1960), *The American Voter*, Wiley, New York.

Campbell, A., P. E. Converse, W. E. Miller and D. E. Stokes (1966), *Elections and the Political Order*, Wiley, New York.

Converse, P. E. (1966), 'The Problem of Party Distance in Models of Voting Change', in M. Kent Jennings and L. H. Zeigler (eds.), *The Electoral Process* Prentice Hall, Englewood Cliffs, New Jersey.

Converse, P. E. (1969), 'Of Time and Partisan Stability', *Comparative Political Studies*, 2, 139–71.

Converse, P. E., and G. Dupeux (1962), 'Politicisation of the Electorate in France and the United States', *Public Opinion Quarterly*, 26, 1–26.

Converse, P. E., and H. Valen (1971), 'Dimensions of Cleavage and Perceived Party Distances in Norwegian Voting', *Scandinavian Political Studies*, 6, 107–52.

Crewe, I. M. (1974), 'Do Butler and Stokes Really Explain Political Change in Britain?*European Journal of Political Research*, 2, 47–92.

Crewe, I. M., B. Sarlvik and J. Alt (forthcoming), *The British General Elections of 1974*, Cambridge University Press, Cambridge.

Daalder, H., and J. G. Rusk (1972), 'Perceptions of Party in the Dutch Parliament', in S. C. Patterson and J. C. Wahlke (eds.), *Comparative Legislative Behaviour*, Wiley, New York.

Davis, O. H., M. J. Hinich and P. C. Ordeshook (1970), 'An Expository Development of a Mathematical Model of the Electoral Process', *American Political Science Review*, 64, 426–48.

Downs, A. (1957), *An Economic Theory of Democracy* Harper & Row, New York.

Easton, D., and J. Dennis (1969), *Children in the Political System*, McGraw Hill, New York.

Flanagan, W. (1968), *Political Behaviour of the American Electorate*, Allyn and Bacon, Boston.

Goldberg, A. S. (1969), 'Social Determinism and Rationality as a Basis of Party Identification', *American Political Science Review*, 63, 5–25.

Goot, M. (1972), 'Party Identification and Party Stability', *British Journal of Political Science*, 2, 121–4.

Greenstein, F. (1965), *Children and Politics*, Yale University Press, New Haven, Connecticut.

Jennings, M. Kent, and R. G. Niemi (1968), 'The Transmission of Political Values from Parent to Child', *American Political Science Review*, 62, 169–84.

Key, V. O. (1966), *The Responsible Electorate* Belknap Press, Cambridge, Massachusetts.

Langton, K. P. (1968), *Political Socialisation*, Oxford University Press, New York.

Lazarsfeld, P. F., B. Berelson and H. Gaudet (1944), *The People's Choice*, Duell, Sloane and Pierce, New York.

Milne, R. S., and H. C. Mackenzie (1955), *Straight Fight*, Hansard Society, London.

Milne, R. S., and H. C. Mackenzie (1958), *Marginal Seat*, Hansard Society, London.

Pomper, G. M. (1972), 'From Confusion to Clarity: Issues and American Voters 1956–1968', *American Political Science Review*, 66, 415–28. (See also the 'Comments' in the same issue by R. A. Brody and B. I. Page (pp. 450–8) and by J. H. Kessel (pp. 459–65).)

Rae, C., and M. J. Taylor (1970), *The Analysis of Political Cleavages*, Yale University Press, New Haven, Connecticut.

Riker, W., and P. C. Ordeshook (1973), *Positive Political Theory*, Prentice Hall, Englewood Cliffs, New Jersey.

Robertson, D. (1976), *A Theory of Party Competition*, Wiley, London and New York.

Rossi, P. H. (1959), 'Four Landmarks in Voting Research', in E. Burdick and A. Brodbeck (eds.), *American Voting Behaviour*, Free Press, New York.

Shaffer, W R. (1972), *Computer Simulations of Voting Behaviour*, Oxford University Press, New York.

Valen, H., and D. Katz (1964), *Political Parties in Norway*, Universitatsforlaget, Oslo.

Webb, E. J., D. T. Campbell, R. D. Schwartz and L. Seckart (1966), *Unobtrusive Measures*, Rand McNally, Chicago.

Zurick, E. (1974), 'Political Socialisation of English Schoolchildren', unpublished Ph. D. dissertation, University of Essex.

# 2

# The Cross-National Use of Party Identification as a Stimulus to Political Inquiry

WARREN E. MILLER

Party identification has become one of the ubiquitous concepts in national and cross-national electoral analysis. In one version or another the concept has been used in innumerable studies of mass politics and has now been described or otherwise analysed in investigations in at least fifteen different countries. As the use of the concept has spread, there has also been an increase in scepticism concerning the utility of the concept and the measurements derived from it. This is not to say there have not always been critics. From the first appearance of party identification in the early Michigan studies there have been analysts who have argued that the concept is a figment of the social scientists' imagination, a theoretical construct that is, at best, a weak surrogate for habitual voting behaviour. More recent critics of the Michigan studies have pointed—with a curious kind of emphasis—to the apparent diminution of the importance of party identification as a direct predictor of the vote, almost as though to imply that some earlier postures of theoretically inspired scepticism are now being supported.

The international scene is even more complex as questions are raised about the utility of a concept developed out of the perhaps unique historical background and institutional context of a very non-European American politics. Early excitement shared by a few Europeans working in research partnerships with American scholars (such as Valen and Campbell, Dupeux and Converse, Sarlvik and Miller, Butler and Stokes) was followed by a rather pervasive acceptance of the American export. The current mood, however, threatens to reject the concept as irrelevant to multi-party systems that are apparently undergoing great change. The point of this brief essay is to offer a perspective, and a prospect, that may forestall premature closures that would inhibit the pursuit of intriguing and important problems.

In a brief and very partial reconstruction of the history of party identification, both paradox and irony play a role. One more or less internal paradox lies in the fact that the first major work emphasizing the importance of party identification as an analytic construct (Miller, *et al.*, 1954) was concerned almost exclusively—if implicitly—with party identification as the explanation for various continuities and persistencies in voting behaviour, while the very first Michigan publication on party identification—preceding *The Voter Decides*—was equally single-mindedly focused on party identification as the origin of attitudes toward public policy (Belknap and

Campbell, 1952). The irony may be found in comparing *The American Voter's* subsequent preoccupation with party identification as the moulder of partisan attitudes that precede the vote decision (Miller *et al.*, 1966, pp. 86-96) with more recent assertions that the Michigan obsession with party identification has been challenged with new evidence that attitudes towards questions of public policy are a better direct predictor of the vote than is party identification. Both cases become matters of social commentary rather than instances of intellectual disjuncture when it is recognised that at least two very different functions for party identification are involved in each juxtaposition.

## THE NATURE OF PARTY IDENTIFICATION

It may be that the time has passed when a single 'Michigan view' on the nature of party identification can be specified, and yet it may be useful to restate and summarize one such view. Those most directly associated with the Michigan studies of electoral behaviour have continued to extend and elaborate the basic concept of party identification *without* dramatic changes in the perspective they elaborated throughout *The American Voter*. Assertions of other scholars to the contrary notwithstanding, virtually all of the past as well as the current work of the Michigan Center for Political Studies rests on a number of persistent assumptions concerning the nature of party identification.

Within the psychological life space of the citizen, party identification is held to be one of the dominant relationships that exists between an individual and the political party. The term 'identification' is used quite intentionally to express the assumption that the relationship often involves an extension of ego. This is because an important part of the individual's self-identity as a political actor is assumed to emanate from the sense of belonging to the politcal group.

The basic assumption that people may belong to a party through their sense of personal identification with the party was derived from more generic social-psychological theory which holds that much of our individual sense of *personal identity* is derived from groups to which we belong. Religious identification is thus generically similar to the concept of political party identification: in both instances the institution, that is the group, is concerned with defining the proper relationship between the person and the group-relevant components of social life. Indeed, the existence of the group, with acknowledged leaders who articulate the group's values and interpret the group's interest in the stream of public affairs, is crucial to the group member's ability to relate to the larger world. Neither the communicant nor the party follower often contribute very much as individuals to the structure of attitudes and values that define the belief systems of the group. It is the religious leaders that develop theologies, and the political leaders who develop ideologies.

With the adults as the mediators, the young learn to recongize the good and the bad. Confessional loyalties and political loyalties often begin with the socializing influence of the family and of others, but they come to be incorporated in the self. The maintenance of rituals becomes important to the person's sense of identity. Over time, the definition of self is extended to include belongingness within the group. What happens to the group also happens to the individual; as the group prospers or declines the individual flourishes or suffers, at least in psychological terms.

There are, of course, gradations in the strength of attachment to the group, and therefore in the centrality of the group to the individual's life. At the weakest end of the continuum, the identification may be more akin to that which the casual sports fan has for a preferred team. The consequences of such a limited identification are little more than that of the spectator's interest. However, even with the most limited identification, individuals possessing very limited information may well be able to evaluate, if not comprehend, the relevant events occurring about them. This leads to a second class of assumptions.

A world as complex as the world of politics generates a tremendous amount of information. Given modern industrial society, information is rapidly communicated to all who may be interested. We assume that, without the simplifying function of party identification, the interested citizen is forced to expend considerable energy in order to take constant note of the changes communicated by the flood of information. However, given a sense of belonging to a political party, there are many short cuts immediately available. It becomes a relatively simple matter to discover what one or another political leader, who is understood to be the representative of one's party, thinks about a new event. Just as the leader of a congregation may offer the prescriptions and proscriptions that guide the subsequent thoughts and behaviour of the faithful, so a president or senator or governor or mayor may provide a ready cue to guide the political thought and action of the party identifier. Where inter-group hostilities are widely recognized and accepted by members of the groups, the communications process may be further simplified. To shift the venue, strong labour union identifiers may be able to infer from a pronouncement by corporate management precisely where the union leadership, the membership and they themselves must stand with regard to the pronouncement. In the realm of politics, a statement from a recognized party leader may define the situation for the members of the opposition as well as for his own followers. More generally, party identification permits reliance on many others for cues and guides to one's own beliefs and attitudes.

Finally, if party identification is important to one's understanding of the world of politics, and to one's sense of self in a world of others, it may also perform an even more primitive function in the domain of political action. The group identifier comes to know what to do when placed in a situation that demands the performance of a group-relevant act or behaviour. Church attendance or observance of holy days doubtless becomes a highly ritualistic matter for many religious communicants. In a similar manner, a citizen who identifies with a political party comes to know habitually, if not instinctively, what to do on election day. All other things being equal, and particularly in the absence of ambiguous or contrary information, the party loyalist votes, and votes the party line.

It has also always been assumed that the origins of an individual's identification with a political party may be as varied as the consequences. In general, of course, the acquisition of a sense of party identification is one of the central results of political socialization. Research such as that carried out in Kent Jennings's work at Michigan has modified the early easy assumption that all children of politically committed parents simply inherit parental partisanship (Jennings and Niemi, 1974). Nevertheless, it still seems to be the case that familial transmission of political values and a sense of political identity is a prime source of the party identification of the young citizen. The child's peer group is another early source of political cues and definitions of the politically 'good'. With the more recent recognition that socialization occurs throughout the life of the citizen, the social environment is now seen as a rich and continuing source of guidance to self-identity and, where necessary, socialization in new situations and circumstances.

From the earliest days of the Michigan studies of party identification, it has been apparent that party identification as the source of continuity in individual thought and behaviour is also subject to drastic disruption and change in response to systemic redefinition of the symbols associated with party. The conceptual framework for the development of the concept of a 'realigning' election—in contrast to the ideas of 'deviating', 'maintaining' and 'reinstating' elections—rests on the occurrence of crises associated with the failure of one national policy and its replacement by another with the introduction of a new political regime. (Campbell, 1960). In the contemporary American context, it has been presumed, and with good evidence, that the Democratic majority in the national electorate was created by widespread rejection of Republican economic and social policies at the time of the great depression of the 1930s. This was followed, in turn, by acceptance of the policies of the Democrats which shaped the nation over the ensuing thirty years. Whether the temporal focus lies with the depression of the 1930s or the Civil War of the 1860s, the origin of partisan realignment through change in partisan identifications has clearly been associated with questions of national public policy.

Quite contrary to assumptions about citizens' response to charismatic political leaders, the argument has never been made that the historic origins of party identification are free of policy connotation and reflect only presumed moral or aesthetic qualities inherent in one party or the other. The transmission of a sense of party identification has never been assumed to be antithetical to the coincident transmission of other symbols giving political content to the meaning of party identification. The content is indeed often of a primitive and unsophisticated kind, but it is of the kind that permits an economic recession in 1974 to evoke old feelings that 'our' Democratic party is the party of the common man and will defend those of us in the working class while 'their' Republican party is the party of big business and the upper classes. No matter how limited the content, there has never been any assumption that somehow party identification and party voting must be irrational and at odds with policy-oriented behaviour.

The meaning and function of party identification have been derived from a basic interest in understanding how the ordinary citizen copes with the complexities of political phenomena that are usually so far removed from direct personal experience. Although the evolution of the concept was not prompted by many of the contemporary concerns for understanding the gratifications produced by social behaviour, or for measuring the costs and benefits in some calculus of efficiency of individual behaviour, the concept seems to meet a host of theoretical needs that haunt the quest for an understanding of the individual decisions that aggregate into mass electoral behaviour. If the economizing and satisficing functions we have just described or implied are not met by personal identification with the party, how are they served? There is little evidence that the members of a mass citizenry in any modern country fit any classical model of political man. There is even less satisfaction in employing notions of habit or instinct to describe attributes associated with the party identifier. The synthetic concept of party identification is one vehicle for relating the individual to the collectivity, and if it does not exist its functional equivalent must.

# PARTY IDENTIFICATION AND ACCOUNTING FOR THE VOTE

From *The Voter Decides* on, party identification has often been used by the analyst to account directly for voting behaviour. In that analysis of the 1952 American presidential election, party identification was treated as conceptually coordinate with candidate orientation and issue orientation in explaining the electoral decision (although our definition of its conceptual status changed by the time of *The American Voter*). Since then, a fair share of the credibility of party identification as a useful construct has been based on the presumption—and on growing evidence—that it captures at the individual, or micro, level the foundation for the notable stability of aggregate election returns noted in macro-analysis of American elections. Consequently, the voter's psychological attachment to party has gained prominence as an explanation for continuities in electoral behaviour. The efficiency or usefulness of party identification in such exerises as accounting for the continuous Democratic control of the American Congress, accounting for variation in split-ticket voting or illuminating the turnover in presidential voting (as between 1956 and 1960) does not need further explication. However, the variation, or the change, in the electoral context that makes it possible to exploit party identification as an anlytic construct should be noted. And to the same end, the growing sophistication of political analysis should be brought into the discussion.

It is probably inevitable that some appraisals of the importance of party identification will rest on superficial assessments of how much variance in individual behaviour can be explained or accounted for with the measurement of party identification. By now, however, it should be clear that the questions of 'How much explained variance'? is the wrong question to ask. The change from the 'Issueless' 1950s to the crisis-ridden polarizations of the late 1960s in American politics certainly meant a diminution in the numbers of voters for whom a primitive loyalty to party was the *only* 'operative' political attitude (see Nie and Anderson, 1974). But unless one demonstrates that prior psychological attachments to party were *not* important in the shaping of many of the new concerns with questions of public policy, the sheer decline in the role of party identification as an independent predictor of the vote must be a misleading indicator of the importance of party identification in 'determining' electoral behaviour. This is doubly the case if better measurement of the other predictors accompanies the 'real growth' in their direct contribution to the vote. And it is certainly true that the contributions of partisan attitudes on questions of public policy are assessed with greater subtlety and power in recent electoral research than in years gone by. Both the nature of the political universe under study and the genius of the investigator will determine the residual, direct explanatory power of a measurement of party identification; neither source of variation should be mistaken for a measure of change in the importance of the construct.

More generally, variation in the direct role of party identification in determining electoral behaviour should usually be taken to define new problems for research and not simply as a basis for judging whether party identification is more or less important in some gross quantitative sense. In fact, the increased sensitivity and complexity of political analyses are already providing significant examples of how apparent variations in the importance of party identification as a direct predictor of the vote can stimulate further explorations of great theoretical as well as pragmatic interest. Thanks to the increased sophistication of analysts, neither the bivariate fit of party identifcation and the vote at single points in time nor separate measures of their stability over time can be taken as adequate bases for unadorned conclusions. With the appearance of crucially important panel data, the joint assessment of their stability over time has been demonstrated to be much more revealing. Butler and Stokes used such joint assessments to good effect in their pursuit of comparisons between the American and British contexts (Butler and Stokes, 1971, pp. 13–32). Converse and Pierce, in work still in progress, have generated comparable displays for France; and Thomassen has presented comparable data for The Netherlands in a most provocative paper (Chapter 4 of this volume).

The evolving treatment of the French data perhaps best illustrates the perspective of this essay. The configurations of the French data bear resemblances to both the American and the British, but also match a more general expectation that attributes of French electoral behaviour should reflect highly labile if not chaotically fluid decision-making at the mass level. But since the joint distribution of party identification and vote choice obviously depends on independent factors influencing each attribute, the Converse-Pierce analysis has pursued the institutional factors influencing the stability of the vote as well as those associated with party identification. Preliminary indications are that French voters in situations most like the typical American situation—in constituencies where competition is essentially between two parties and where the competitors include an incumbent and a *new* challenger—show a closer fit to the American configuration involving party identification than do the remainder of the French voters. More generally, the attempt to understand apparent differences in the role and function of party identification in two different national settings has been the stimulus for systematic explorations of yet other institutional differences whose acknowledged existence has not been widely appreciated as relevant to the role of party identification in voting behaviour. It might be noted that the Converse-Pierce analysis appears to be well on its way to specifying populations and situations in France in which party identification enhances sheer ability to predict or account for vote choice with a robustness akin to the American experience.

Thomassen's paper holds out a similar prospect for further inquiry in The Netherlands. The simple joint distribution of vote stability and stability of party identification over three different Dutch elections discloses the kind of anomaly that cries for attention and explication. The fact that the level of instability of party identification *exceeds* the instability of the vote is offered as evidence that party identification is merely an unreliable measurement of current partisan pre-ference—and more unreliable than the vote. It would seem, however, that the hypothesis of measurement error demands no more than *equal* unreliability. Why nineteen per cent of the voters should show unstable party identification in the face of perfect vote stability while only five per cent report stable party identification and unstable vote preference is not intuitively clear. Given the dramatic rate of change in depillarization and deconfessionalization noted by Thomassen at the end of his paper, and given the fluidity of the Dutch party system at the élite level of organizing new parties and joining the electoral contest, it is more than a cliché to suggest that further research should follow. With Jennings' earlier work in mind (Jennings, 1972), it seems reasonable to expect that the Dutch study may do much to elaborate our understanding of the special case of group identification that we know as political party identification. It is equally likely that the elaboration will increase our general understanding of Dutch political institutions, their place in the social and economic structure of Dutch society and their points of similarity and dissimilarity with the political institutions of other Western democracies.

Although there is little in the way of direct tests of the proposition, it may well be that one of the differences between the socializing experiences in the United States and in many Western European countries is to be found in the different location of the political party in the social structure of the national society and, therefore, in the social environment of the average citizen. As has been noted by many scholars, the political party in the European context is often derivative of a prior social or economic grouping. Thus, the labour union or the Church may be the historical locus of a political party and at the same time the immediate primary group attachment for the individual. As a consequence, any sense of preference for the group's party may be *derived* only from the primary sense of belonging to the group. If the primary group thereby mediates between the individual and the group's party, any direct sense of identification with party may indeed be severely limited. The evolution of the political party in the United States has been notoriously different from that of many European parties. This is not to say there have not been many Americans for whom the labour union and the Democratic party or the farmers' association and the Republican party seemed to have a natural affinity. It is simply to argue that inter-continental differences in the chronology of development of political and non-political groups during two hundred years of history have produced different relationships in the individual-group-party triad. These differences may underly some of the empirical irregularities observed in comparing party identification in Europe and the United States.

## PARTY IDENTIFICATION AND POLITICAL BELIEFS AND VALUES

While political analysts have used party identification most heavily to account for voting behaviour, the voters themselves presumably use their attachment to party, albeit without much self-awareness, for closely related but quite different primary purposes. Borre and Katz (1973) summarize the functions of party identification for the voter in a most useful introduction to their excellent analysis of 'Party Identification and Its Motivational Base in a Multiparty System: A Study of the Danish General Election of 1971'. In their summary, '. . . party identification [is] considered as a determinant of participation in political discussions, of stability of political interest and the use of mass media; secondly, it [is] considered [to be] a guide for the voter to opinions on current issues; and thirdly, party identification [is] considered as stimulus for ingroup sympathies and outgroup hostility within the political system'. In short, identification with a party is treated as the psychological mechanism that connects the voter to the world of politics beyond the limited act of voting. It may be argued that the development of that connection and the intermediate consequences of that connection should become the principal foci for the study of party identification.

To illustrate we may note that, because of the general failure to study party identification as 'a guide for the voter to opinions on current issues', at least two lines of inquiry that should be intimately related have been pursued largely as though one or the other did not exist. On the one hand, the study of mass belief systems, ideology and 'issue voting' has been elaborated out of a pressing normative concern to understand the linkage of masses and élites in the process of democratic politics and government. This concern has driven analysts to focus on the quality of electoral response to national crisis and political leadership. Indeed, some to the most interesting work published on American politics in recent years tries to account for an apparently dramatic change in the quality of public response to questions of public policy (Nie and Anderson, 1974). On the other hand, the somewhat earlier tradition of attempting to understand electoral choice in the homely terms of the voters has not prospered. There has been little continuity of effort to extend our knowledge of the role of party attachment in the evolution of partisan attitudes that undergird partisan choice at the polls. And because of the overwhelming concentration on party identifcation as a predictor of the vote, we now have a curious pseudo-debate over whether or not 'issue voting' is replacing 'party voting'. If the debate is to be real it must juxtapose party as one source of 'issue voting' along with the other possible sources of voters' concerns with issues of public policy. The attempt to bring clarity to confusion by arguing over whether 'issues' are in general more important than 'party' must be read in the future as a wilful misunderstanding of the nature of the concept of party identification.

The major exception to this latter line of discussion has been provided by the students of political socialization. Their literature is growing rapidly and promises to redress the balance of emphasis in the study of political values and beliefs. It should be noted, however, that further explication of the role of party identification in shaping political attitudes rests heavily on a simple methodological point. Just as the task of disentangling short-term vote preferences from long-term party attachment rests on the serial collection of evidence across time through the use of the panel design, so the study of the development of party identification and its subsequent impact on the development of political attitudes depends on the same panel design for effective research. And just as two decades of electoral research have extended our appreciation of the need to encompass voting behaviour in entirely different political epochs (as well as under variation in cultural and institutional contexts), so political socialization is now understood to range far beyond childhood and adolescence and to continue—although probably with less dramatic change—throughout adulthood, thus demanding continuous study over very long periods of time indeed. In the face of this realization, even Jennings's truly remarkable eight-year panel study of political socialization is only a beginning on the path that must be followed.

The broadened conception of political socialization deserves emphasis because it gives added point to earlier and largely ignored perspectives on the reciprocal influence relationships uniting party identification and the perceptual and attitudinal components of the citizen's system of political beliefs. It seems likely that in the contemporary experience of many voters, a prior commitment to party creates a perceptual screen or filter through which the events of politics pass and by which new attitudes are shaped or influenced. However, it is also abundantly evident, as noted in *The American Voter*, that changes in party identification can be motivated by prior attitudinal commitment and do occur with some frequency. And consonant with Jennings's most recent data on the malleability of party identification among the young voters, the Michigan report of the 1972 election (Miller *et al.*, 1973) notes that the new voters in that election appear to have *selected* their party loyalties to match their commitments in questions of public policy. Finally, the most dramatically cataclysmic, systemic events, such as depressions and civil wars, have come to be seen as of lasting importance in part just because they reshape the political attitudes *and* the enduring party loyalties of large numbers of citizens.

Party identification is durable but not immutable; party loyalty does much to shape cognitions and evaluations of political events, but political attitudes and, ultimately party loyalties change under the impact of events. The extension of the study of political socialization into the world of the adult citizen extends the study of the origins of party identification and recognizes the dynamic interplay between party identification, the continuing performance of parties and politicians, and the evolution of political attitudes.

At the level of the voter's phenomenology, party identification is an important, often necessary, vehicle for continued involvement in political affairs. The fact that party attachment leads to *continuity* of partisan outlook is probably of little intrinsic value to the voter—apart from the neurotically compulsive few who may place an overt value on consistency in the face of opportunity for change. The explicit role of party as reference group, as a source of cues, as a legitimate source of information as to what should be believed and valued, is much more to the point. But it is this facet of party identification that has been relatively neglected by the social researcher. Recognition of the psychological functions of party attachment should lead to a sustained interest in the phenomenon because the exploration of those functions will necessarily broaden inquiry to include the full range of other institutions that may perform comparable functions for the voter.

Hans Klingemann's current work provides a number of rich illustrations from a comparison of American and German data (Klingemann, 1973). In addition to documenting some remarkable similarities concerning levels of conceptualization expressed by German citizens in 1969 and the American electorate in 1968, Klingemann's analysis suggests that very different roles are played by the trade unions of the respective countries in the inculcation of political values and beliefs. A much greater politicization of German trade union members is sharply reflected in German-American differences in the levels of conceptualization of union members in the two countries.

At the same time, Klingemann's analysis matches that of earlier American data in demonstrating that differences in party attachment are *not* strongly related to the dimensions captured in the measurement of levels of conceptualization. At the most general level, therefore, Klingemann exposes another anomaly demanding explanation. Why, in both Germany and the United States, are there such modest differences in level of conceptualization between those closely attached to political parties and those who deny all party identification? Would similar conclusions be drawn in countries where the role of the party press bulks larger in the total array of media of mass communications—or where political news is less nationalized?

Such a line of inquiry, still prompted by a desire to explicate the role of party attachment in different situations, could lead to research designed to include a host of familiar themes in a single programme of inquiry. Mass communications, interpersonal influence and para-political organizational affiliations are clearly all relevant to an understanding of the origins of political attitudes and beliefs. It seems at least possible that a preoccupation with this role of party attachment would give sharper point to new studies involving these other phenomena and could, perhaps, produce further definitions of intriguing and important problems in need of resolution.

The basic arguments of this essay can be summarized as follows:

(1) Most research involving party identification has been derivative in the sense that it has been concerned with one empirical *consequence* of party attachment—continuity and persistence of partisan loyalty. The most fruitful and provocative research on party identification has, consequently, been concerned with seeking variation and explanation for variation in the institutional and contextual domains thought likely to affect behavioural expressions of that continuity. Much of this work has, however, also expanded our understanding of the conditions predisposing to the development and decay of party identification.

(2) The theoretical basis for an interest in party identification is found in socio-psychological theories about the nature of relationships connecting individuals to secondary groups, and about the need for some of these relationships to exist if individuals are to be active participants in mass society. Where data on such relationships involving voters and national political parties indicate variation across different nations or different sub-groups within one nation, the explication of the variation and its consequences should be taken as a necessary definition of a new research problem.

(3) The quest for evidence of the contribution of party attachment to the values, beliefs and behaviours of the voter is of obvious theoretical importance as long as it either expands or tests our theoretical assumptions. It is not necessary nor important to demonstrate some type of primacy for party identification in the phenomenology of the voter. It *is* important to understand the social psychology of individual political behaviour, and that involves understanding many of the functions attributed to party identification. The search for such knowledge is of central importance, and the awareness that such knowledge may accrue through the study of party identification should be taken as a point of departure in future research.

(4) The continuing study of the interplay between secondary group affiliations and political attitudes promises to enable us to distinguish between the epiphenomena and the essence of electoral stability and change. Attending only to the direct impact of contemporary attitudes on the vote choice is a preoccupation with the unique and the ephemeral and presupposes that a science can be erected on the whimsy of politicians' reactions to unplanned events.

## REFERENCES

Belknap, George, and Angus Campbell (1952), 'Political Party Identification and Attitudes Towards Foreign Policy', *Public Opinion Quarterly*, 15, 601–23.

Borre, Ole, and Daniel Katz (1973), 'Party Identification and its Motivational Base in a Multiparty System: A Study of the Danish General Election of 1971', *Scandinavian Political Studies*, 8, 69–111.

Butler, David, and Donald Stokes (1971), *Political Change in Britain*, St Martin's Press, New York.

Campbell, Angus (1960), 'Surge and Decline: A Study of Electoral Change', *Public Opinion Quarterly*, 24, 397–418.

Jennings, M. Kent (1972), 'Partisan Commitment and Electoral Behaviour in the Netherlands', *Acta Politica*, 7, 455–70.

Jennings, M. Kent, and Richard G. Niemi (1974), *The Political Character of Adolescence: The Influence of Families and School*, Princeton University Press, Princeton, New Jersey.

Klingemann, Hans (1973), 'Dimensions of Political Belief Systems', paper presented to ECPR Workshop on Political Behaviour, Dissatisfaction, and Protest, at Mannheim, Germany, on 12–18 April 1973.

Miller, Warren E., Angus Campbell and Gerald Gurin (1954), *The Voter Decides* Row, Paterson & Co., Evanston, Illinois.

Miller, Warren E., Angus Campbell, Philip E. Converse and Donald E. Stokes (1966), *The American Voter,* Wiley, New York.

Miller, Warren E. Arthur H. Miller, Alden S. Raine and Thad A. Brown (1973), 'A Majority Party in Disarray: Policy Polarisation in the 1972 Election', University of Michigan, *mimeo.*

Nie, Norman H., and Kristi Anderson (1974), 'Mass Belief Systems Revisited: Political Change and Attitude Structure', *Journal of Politics, 36,* 54–91.

# 3

# Party Identification Theory and Political Change in Britain

IVOR CREWE

In the series of election studies conducted over the last two decades by the Survey Research Center (now the Center for Political Studies) at the University of Michigan, the concept of party identification has played a central role in the analysis of electoral change. At the individual level, self-declared strength of party identification has consistently been found to be associated with stability of party choice, turnout and political attitudes over two or more successive elections (Campbell *et al.*, 1960, Chapter 6). Aggregate levels of partisanship have therefore been taken as indicators of the long-term, durable partisan forces operating in the electorate, and thus as a baseline by which to measure the strength and magnitude of transient partisan forces at any single election. This in turn has allowed for a classification of elections (largely confined to the United States so far) according to the size and direction of deviation from the overall distribution of party identification (Campbell *et al.*, 1960, pp.531-8; Campbell *et al.*, 1966, pp. 63-77), and to the existence or absence of accompanying changes in the social alignments of the parties (Pomper, 1967). In particular, it has made it possible to identify 'realigning' elections, in which major and enduring shifts in the overall balance and social composition of partisanship occur.

This mode of analysis is not without its critics. Burnham (1965, 1974), for example, has argued that the Michigan studies have failed to account for a variety of electoral trends in the United States electorate over the twentieth century, in particular the gradual increase in non-voting, ticket-splitting, partisan volatility and 'roll-off' (i.e. failing to complete long ballots for numerous offices). This chapter will not enter into what is developing into a vigorous controversy about American electoral behaviour in the nineteenth and early twentieth centuries and its implications for the Michigan 'paradigm' (Converse, 1972, 1974). Instead it will raise similar types of question about the applicability of the Michigan approach to postwar electoral change in Britain.

---

\* This chapter is an updated and shortened version of 'Do Butler and Stokes Really Explain Political Change in Britain?', *European Journal of Political Research*, **2**, 47–92.

## ELECTORAL CHANGE IN POSTWAR BRITAIN

In order to appreciate the problem that the case of postwar Britain poses, it is first necessary to distinguish between competitive and non-competitive partisan change. The former refers to changes in the distribution of the total *vote between* each major *party* and is the conventional notion of changes in party support. It is called *competitive* partisan change because of its focus on the gains and losses of one party relative to others; and it is the form of partisan change on which the Michigan studies, and in particular *Political Change in Britain* (Butler and Stokes, 1969) almost exclusively concentrate. However, the most distinctive feature of this form of partisan change is its marked absence from Britain since the war. If we follow Rose and Urwin (1970) and measure it by summing the change in the percentage of the poll obtained by each party in each election between 1945 and 1970, and then calculate the mean by dividing by the number of elections, it emerges that Britain has experienced less of

Table 3.1     Trends in British[1] elections 1950–October 1974

| | | | | | | | | | | |
|---|---|---|---|---|---|---|---|---|---|---|
| | Share of the electorate obtained by: | | | | | | | | | |
| Date of general election | Conservative | Labour | Conservatives plus Labour | Liberals | Others | No Party | Turn Out | Constituencies 'won' by non voters[2] | Candidates |
| | % | % | % | % | % | % | % | | |
| 1950 | 37.6 | 39.9 | 77.5 | 7.9 | 1.1 | 13.5 | 86.5 | 3 | 1868 |
| 1951 | 39.6 | 40.3 | 79.9 | 2.1 | 0.6 | 17.5 | 82.5 | 2 | 1376 |
| 1955 | 38.1 | 35.6 | 73.8 | 2.1 | 0.9 | 23.3 | 76.7 | 7 | 1409 |
| 1959 | 38.8 | 34.5 | 73.4 | 4.6 | 0.7 | 21.2 | 78.8 | 8 | 1536 |
| 1964 | 33.4 | 34.0 | 67.5 | 8.6 | 1.0 | 22.9 | 77.1 | 29 | 1753 |
| 1966 | 31.7 | 36.3 | 68.0 | 6.5 | 1.3 | 24.2 | 75.8 | 34 | 1707 |
| 1970 | 33.2 | 31.5 | 64.7 | 5.4 | 2.3 | 28.1 | 72.0 | 89 | 1837 |
| 1974(Feb) | 29.5 | 29.0 | 58.5 | 15.1 | 4.5 | 21.9 | 78.1 | 16 | 2135 |
| 1974(Oct) | 26.1 | 28.6 | 54.7 | 13.3 | 4.7 | 27.2 | 72.8 | 78 | 2252 |

Note:   1.   Figures are for the United Kingdom.

2.   Defined as constituencies in which the number of non-voters exceed the number of votes obtained by the winning candidate.

Sources:   1950;1966: David Butler and Jennie   Freeman, British Political Facts 1900-1968 (3rd ed.), Macmillan, London, 1969) pp.143-4

1970:   David Butler and Michael Pinto-Duchinsky, The British General Election of 1970, Macmillan, London, 1971) p.353

February and October 1974: The Times Guide to the House of Commons 1974 and The Times Guide to the House of Commons October 1974, The Times Newspapers Ltd., London, 1974.

such change than any other of the twenty Western democracies with the exception of Switzerland.

But if our conception of partisan change is expanded to include non-competitive features such as trends in turnout and changes in the share of the *electorate* obtained by the major parties, singly or in combination, then a number of political changes in Britain since the war have been very interesting indeed.

Table 3.1 records some of these trends for the quarter century from the first normal postwar election (1950) to Britain's most recent general election (October 1974). It shows firstly that the support obtained by the Labour and Conservative parties combined, expressed as a proportion of the total electorate, has gradually but persistently fallen since 1951. In the space of twenty-three years the two big parties have lost the support of a quarter of the electorate and now (1975) command the loyalty of barely more than half the electorate: in 1951 four in every five registered electors turned out at the polls to vote Labour or Conservative: by 1970 the figure fell to just over three in five; after a further four years it dropped further to 54.7 per cent. This erosion of two-party support is even more accentuated in certain regions. In Scotland, for example, the Scottish Nationalist Party has replaced the Conservatives as the serious opposition to Labour (in only 14 out of 71 seats in Scotland did Labour and Conservative come first and second); and in the South East and South West, outside London, as well as in rural constituencies in the rest of England, the Liberal Party replaced Labour as the main challenge in over half the Conservative-held seats. Taken individually, the Conservative party obtained its lowest share of both the poll and of the electorate in recorded electoral history by October 1974; but even at its most recent electoral victory, in 1970, it obtained a smaller share of the electorate than in 1950, when it *lost*. Similarly, Labour's share of the electorate in October 1974 was its lowest since 1935, despite the marginal majority of seats it secured, and was considerably lower than in 1959, the year of its worst postwar *defeat*.

These figures may be supplemented by evidence from surveys and the regularly published opinion polls. Reports by the BBC's Audience Research Department show that the public's average 'reaction indices' to the party political broadcasts of the Labour and Conservative parties have steadily declined since 1959.* The proportion of electors claiming to want a form of coalition government was generally between 30 and 40 per cent in the 1960s but had reached 60–65 per cent by February 1974. The proportion who deny that there are any really important differences between the parties steadily grew from 31 per cent in October 1964 to 57 per cent in October 1969, since when the figure has subsided again, but only slightly. Satisfaction with the performance of the leaders of the two major parties sank to a record low level by 1969 (Rose, 1968). There is also considerable evidence that individual membership of the major parties has rapidly declined in recent years (Beer, 1969, pp. 415-16). Thus although there has been no systematic empirical study of British attitudes to the party system and to party politics it seems very likely that such a study would conclude, as Dennis (1970) did of the American public, that there is an ambivalent and far from

---

* Reaction indices are calculated from panel members' use of a rating scale, and range from 0 to 100. Labour and Conservative ratings have steadily declined by very similar proportions among supporters, opponents and the uncommitted alike. The data can be found in the separate post-election reports prepared by the BBC's Audience Research Department. I am grateful to Dr J. Blumler of the Television Research Unit, Leeds University, for bringing these figures to my attention.

overwhelming level of diffuse support for the institution of party, and that indifference is widespread and antipathy substantial. Parties, even in Britain, are simply not as 'loved and trusted' as Graham Wallas once asserted (1910, p. 83).

It could reasonably be argued therefore, that the most important change in support for the two major parties since the war has occurred not in the shifts of support *between* them but in the decline in strength of *both* of them. Moreover, as Table 3.2 shows, this gradual erosion in the two-party share of the British electorate goes against the trend in most other comparable Western democracies. If countries with compulsory voting are excluded, and comparisons are limited to bi-polar party systems only,* then only New Zealand among the six other comparable nations has experienced an erosion of electoral support for the two main parties that even approaches that in Britain; in all the other states two-party support has remained steady or increased—in the case of West Germany, spectacularly.

Table 3.2    The two-party share of the electorate in elections in or nearest to 1950 and 1974 in Western democracies with bi-polar party systems

| | | | |
|---|---|---|---|
| Austria | Peoples Party and Socialist Party | 80.1 (1949) | 85.9 (1971) |
| Canada | Liberal and Conservative Parties | 59.2 (1949) | 56.7 (1972) |
| Ireland | Fine Gael and Fianna Fail Parties | 54.3 (1951) | 61.5 (1973) |
| New Zealand | National and Labour Parties | 93.0 (1949) | 80.8 (1972) |
| United Kingdom | Conservative and Labour Parties | 77.5 (1950) | 54.7 (Oct 1974) |
| United States | Republican and Democratic Parties | 48.8 (1948) | 54.7 (1972) |
| West Germany | Christian Democratic and Social Democratic Parties | 47.3 (1949) | 82.6 (1972) |

Note:    With the exception of the United States, changes over the twenty years are a result of trends, not cycles.

Sources:    Thomas T.Mackie and Richard Rose, An International Almanac of Electoral History, Macmillan, London, 1974.

The drop in support for the Labour and Conservative parties among the British electorate is partly due to the growing popularity of other parties. The Liberals enjoyed a modest revival of support in 1964, only to slip back in 1966 and 1970 before their major resurgence in February 1974 when they obtained their largest share of both the poll and the electorate for forty-five years (but only a few more parliamentary seats). The fact that this breakthrough in votes was very largely

* Bipolar party systems are defined as those in which the same two parties throughout the postward period have (a) secured the highest and second highest percentage of votes *and* (b) have been the only parties with sufficient parliamentary strength to form a government alone or as the clearly dominant party in a two-party coalition.

maintained in the second election of 1974 suggests that it would be premature to dismiss it as a 'flash' phenomenon. The progress of the Scottish Nationalist Party has been more dramatic: from no seats and less than 1 per cent of the Scottish poll throughout the 1950s (admittedly, reflected by, and in the absence of, many Nationalist candidates) to eleven seats (out of a possible seventy-one) and 30 per cent of the Scottish poll by October 1974.

But the erosion of two-party support owes as much to a decline in turnout at general elections over the last two decades. As Table 3.1 shows, 86.5 per cent of the registered electorate (unadjusted to age of register) cast a vote in 1950; by 1970 the figure had almost monotonically declined to 72.0 per cent. In the extraordinary circumstances of the February 1974 election, fought on a brand new register, it is perhaps not surprising that turnout rose to 78.1 per cent; in the more normal election eight months later, turnout subsided to 72.8 per cent, despite a postwar record number of candidates in the field. Moreover, from the fragmentary evidence available (Hampton, 1970, pp. 313-14; Jones, 1969, pp. 366-7; and Sharpe, 1967, pp. 49, 138) it appears that turnout has also declined a little in local elections since the war.

This fall in national turnout is surprising for a number of reasons. First, there has been a steady increase in the number of candidates presenting themselves for election, from 1,376 in 1951 to 2,252 in October 1974, a 62 per cent increase (see Table 3.1). This might have been expected to result in an increased mobilization of the vote. Secondly, coverage of elections by the mass media, especially television, has become more intensive and at the same time has reached ever-growing proportions of the public (from 4.3 per cent of households in 1950 to 90.8 per cent in 1966). This too might have been expected to raise turnout. Thirdly, while turnout among women (especially the elderly) may still have been slightly depressed in 1950 by the relatively recent establishment of the female franchise (in 1918 and 1928), any residual dampening effect of this kind should surely have disappeared by 1974. And finally, as in the case of the two-party share of the electorate, a persistent and substantial decline in turnout is peculiar to Britain. None of the fifteen comparable democracies has undergone a fall that compares in size with that of Brtain and nine have experienced *increases* in turnout (Mackie and Rose, 1974). As a result turnout in Britain has dropped from fifth to fourteenth in the 'league' of sixteen democracies between 1950 and October 1974 (which excludes those with compulsory voting or restricted franchises).

The growing rejection of the two major parties since 1950 and the successive falls in turnout have been accompanied by a third related trend in British voting behaviour. Since the war, but especially from the late 1950s onwards, shifts in support for the Labour and Conservative parties have become increasingly *volatile,* in general and local elections, byelections and monthly opinion polls. The two party swing at general elections rose from 1.1 per cent in 1950-51 to 4.7 per cent in 1966-70. Between 1970 and February 1974 it was technically 2.1 per cent, but this apparent stability was in fact based on exceptionally high rates of defection from *both* parties: the 8.2 per cent fall in the Conservative share of the poll was the largest suffered by any party since the war; Labour's loss of 5.8 per cent was its worst since 1931. And although the figures are slightly different, the story would be very much the same if we examined the 1970-October 1974 two party swing of 3.4 per cent to Labour. The annual range in the monthly support for the Conservatives combined with that for the Labour Party, as recorded by the Gallup poll, has risen from an average of 9.8 per cent in 1950-54, to

12.5 per cent in 1955–59, to 13.8 per cent in 1960–64, and to 19.8 per cent in 1965–69, although for the period 1970–October 1974 it was slightly down at 16.2 per cent. The number of byelections in which the government's vote fell by 20 per cent or more (compared with the previous general election) has steadily grown from none during the 1950–55 government to 16.5 per cent in the 1959–64 government, 34.2 per cent between 1966 and 1970 and 35.3 per cent under the Conservative

Table 3.3    Indicators of volatility of support between the Conservative and Labour Parties in general elections, by-elections, and opinion polls 1950–1973

| Year | National two-party swing.[1] | % by-elections in which support for govt. party fell by over 20% compared with previous gen. election. | Mean fall in support for govt. party in by-elections. | Range in monthly opinion polls.[4] |
|---|---|---|---|---|
| | % | % | % | % |
| 1950)[2] 1951) | +1.1 | 0.0 (N=14) | 2.0 | 8.0 13.0 |
| 1952 ) 1953 ) 1954 ) 1955 ) | +1.8 | 0.0 (N=43) | 1.9 | 11.0 6.0 9.0 8.0 |
| 1956 ) 1957 ) 1958 ) 1959 ) | +1.1 | 10.0 (N=50) | 8.8 | 8.0 18.0 16.0 12.5 |
| 1960 ) 1961 ) 1962 ) 1963 ) 1964 ) | −2.9 | 16.5 (N=61) | 13.5 | 9.5 12.0 11.5 9.5 12.5 |
| 1965 )[3] 1966 ) | −3.1 | 0.0 (N=13) | 1.8 | 18.0 18.0 |
| 1967 ) 1968 ) 1969 ) 1970 ) | +4.7 | 34.2 (N=38) | 16.8 | 27.0 19.0 17.5 12.0 |
| 1971 ) 1972 ) 1973 ) | −0.8 | 35.3 (N=18) | 13.1 | 20.5 10.5 15.0 |
| 1974(Feb)) 1974(Oct)) | | *[6] | *[6] | 23.0 |

Notes:
1. Swing is defined as the average of the Conservative percentage gain and the Labour percentage loss.
2. Northern Ireland is included in the general election figures, excluded in the others.
3. In the 1950–51 and 1964–66 parliaments Labour was in office but with only a tiny majority. Both periods continued to experience the electoral trends of the previous few years.
4. Range is measured by the difference between the highest and the lowest support for the Conservatives in any one month plus the difference between the highest and lowest support for Labour in any one month. The figures are calculated from David Butler and Jennie Freeman, British Political Facts 1900–1968, for the period until 1968 and from the Gallup Political Index, London, The Gallup Poll, for 1969–1974.
5. Calculations for by-elections between 1970 and February 1974 exclude the Speaker's seat, Southampton Itchen, and those cases (N=12) where there was a non-trivial redistribution of constituency boundaries since the previous general election such that meaningful swing figures could not be calculated.
6. There was only one by-election between February and October 1974.

administration of 1970–February 1974. Local elections reveal a corresponding trend: in the 1950s there were only three years in which one major party won over 500 more wards than the other; in the following decade there were only three years when this did *not* occur—mainly at Labour's expense (Butler and Freeman, 1969, p.243). And by 1971 and 1972 Labour's previously disastrous performance in local elections was immediately and massively reversed as the Conservatives incurred their worst rout (in both years) since 1946. (Since then local government reform has made it impossible to trace trends.) More detailed figures are available in Table 3.3.

These three postwar patterns in British voting behaviour—the fall in the two-party share of the electorate, the decline in turnout and the increasing oscillations in support for each major party—add up to a steady erosion of commitment to the Labour and Conservative parties, the only two parties capable of holding governmental office alone, and therefore to the basis of the British party system. It is this loss of popular appeal by *both* parties rather than the relative appeal of each which stands in need of explanation.

Indeed, there are at least four reasons for regarding it as *more* important than competitive partisan change. *First*, these postwar trends have been *numerically* more substantial. Over the period 1950 to October 1974 the percentage point change in the two-party share of the electorate (22.3 per cent) has exceeded the change in the proportion of the total vote or of the electorate obtained by any single party; and the percentage point change in turnout (13.7 per cent) has equalled it. (The proportion of the electorate supporting the Conservative and Labour parties has ranged by 13.5 and 11.3 per cent, and of the poll by 13.9 and 11.6 per cent respectively. *Second*, these three changes are all more or less peculiar to Britain, running against the trend in other comparable democracies. *Third*, the changes are all more or less linear. And *fourth*, these changes are both inherently important and surprising. They are important because they suggest that, in the country that has been upheld more than any other as the model of a stable and popular two-party system, public allegiance to that system has steadily weakened. Indeed, survey evidence on British schoolchildren suggests that allegiance may well continue to weaken (Dennis *et al.*, 1971). They are surprising not simply because the opposite has occurred elsewhere, but because one might reasonably anticipate turnout to go up as a result of the improved standards of education, the increased exposure to the national mass media and the lengthening duration of universal adult suffrage that have marked the last twenty years. Similarly, the emergence of a new party system in Britain in the 1920s—in response to the extension of the franchise—might have been expected to crystallize by the 1970s, as it appears to have done in other liberal democracies (Lipset and Rokkan, 1969, p. 50) and thereby result in a growing duopoly over the electorate and in a gradual smoothing out of switches of support between the two parties.

## THE MICHIGAN MODEL AND ELECTORAL CHANGE IN BRITAIN

It is the contention of this chapter that the electoral trends described above raise disturbing anomalies for the Michigan 'model' of voting behaviour. Indeed, to put the argument in stronger terms, the model would lead us to expect trends in turnout, the two-party swing and the two-party share of the electorate that are the very reverse of what has, in fact, occurred in Britain since 1950. Applied to the characteristics of the British electorate over the last century, as discovered by a Michigan-based study, the model suggests that turnout should have steadily increased, that the two-party swing should have remained steady or diminished, and, most importantly, that the Labour and Conservative parties should have obtained a steadily increasing proportion of the electorate's support.

An outline of the Michigan model may be derived from *Political Change in Britain* (Butler and Stokes, 1969). Although the study contains no explicit 'model' of voting behaviour, it is nonetheless structured throughout by a recurring set of interdependent analytic frameworks for the description and explanation of voting patterns which collectively could reasonably be described as a 'model'. Most of these frameworks are identical to or elaborations upon those adopted in earlier voting studies by the Survey Research Center at the University of Michigan, and one is tempted to dub them the 'Michigan model Mark III'. As befits a model, it is not a theory of electoral behaviour (i.e. a statement about the empirical relationships predicted to obtain between two or more variables), but a conceptual framework from which inherently interesting theories, some fruitful and others not, may be derived by deduction. It consists of a few simple postulates about voting behaviour which serve as building blocks for the construction of more elaborate hypotheses relevant to a range of subjects connected with voting that is both wider and more specialized than that initially covered in the model. The word 'postulates' is deliberately preferred to the more usual 'axioms', which are *a priori* assumptions, to indicate that the Butler—Stokes model is a mixture of the *a priori* and empirically tested.

The Butler-Stokes model may be reduced to the following statements (page references to *Political Change in Britain* (1969) are added):

### A. Party Identification

(1) The large majority of British electors possess a 'partisan self-image', that is, a deeply entrenched psychological commitment to a party, varying in direction and intensity (p.38).

(2) Partisan self-image is the most *enduring* feature of a voter's political attitudes and behaviour because:

> (*a*) it induces a process of partisan selective perception of the voter's political environment and thus becomes self-reinforcing over time (pp. 35–7, 220–36); and

> (*b*) it tends to divide along fairly immutable social cleavages such as social class or religion (pp. 73–80, 124–44).

(3) Partisan self-image is the strongest predictor of attitudes or behaviour involving the relative evaluation of parties, and particularly

> (*a*) party choice at a single election (p.39, 42);

> (*b*) stability of party choice: the stronger a voter's partisan self-image, the less likely he is to defect from his party allegiance in any single election, and the more consistent will his support be over a series of elections (pp. 39, 41–3);

> (*c*) turnout: the stronger a voter's partisan self-image the more likely he is to turn out to vote (p.39).

### B. Direction of Party Identification

(1) The single variable most strongly associated with the direction of a voter's partisan self-image is parental partisanship (pp. 45–50). Voters are particularly likely

to inherit their parents' partisanship if both parents shared the same, strong allegiance either to the Labour or to the Conservative party, and if they did not experience social mobility, up or down, compared with their parents. Thus the direction of a voter's partisan self-image is most likely to depart from that of his parents:

(a) if the parents were of Liberal, mixed or no party allegiance ('mixed' allegiance refers both to separate support for different parties and to cases where only one parent had a party attachment) (pp.52-3, 250-54);

(b) if both parents identified with the same major party, but the one that obtained the minority of support within their social class (p.51);

(c) if the voter experienced inter-generational social mobility (except in the circumstances cited immediately above) (pp. 98-101).

(2) In each of the cases (a) to (c) parental partisanship is still largely bequeathed to children, especially in their early years as registered electors, but other factors, in particular social class, begins to have an important bearing on the direction of partisan self-image as the voter matures.

## C. Strength of Partisan Self-image

(1) Since partisan self-image is self-reinforcing (A(2a)) its strength increases with the length of time it has been consistently held and excercised in party choice, which in turn is strongly related to, although not the same as, age (p.55). Hence the newly enfranchized and young voters generally, while particularly influenced by the direction of their parents' partisanship, tend to have relatively weak attachments to a party.

## D. Implications for Turnout and Stability of Party Choice

(1) *Stability of party choice.* It follows from A(3b) and C(1) that inconsistent party support is most likely to occur among young voters and the newly enfranchized.

(2) *Permanent* abandonment of previously established partisan allegiances is only likely to occur, however,

(a) when the political tide runs exceptionally strongly in one direction as a result of a cataclysmic national event such as war, economic depression or chronic political instability (pp. 54, 249-54). It is the relatively weak who are most likely to make a once-for-all change; strong partisans are more likely to do no more than temporarily defect;

(b) among voters undergoing *intra*-generational social mobility (pp.98-101).

(3) Since it is those voters with a weak or non-existent party identification who are least likely to vote, and it is new voters who are most likely to have a poorly developed sense of party allegiance, the lowest rates of turnout generally occur among new voters (p.40).

With this theoretical scaffolding in mind, therefore, let us see what follows if it is used to explain recent trends in British voting behaviour.

## THE INABILITY OF THE MODEL
## TO EXPLAIN POLITICAL CHANGE IN BRITAIN

(a) *The decline in the two-party share of the British electorate.* As described above, the model regards the direction of an elector's partisan self-image as the overriding determinant of his party choice at an election, and the strength of that partisanship as an important if somewhat less overwhelming influence on whether he turns out to vote. Since we wish to account for the declining share of the British electorate obtained by the two major parties it follows from the model that we should expect to find a falling proportion of Labour and Conservative identifiers among the most recent electorates, or a weakening of partisanship among Labour and Conservative identifiers, or both. Accordingly, the 1966 wave of Butler and Stokes's panel survey was re-analysed to see whether the distribution of party identification in successive British electorates has changed in the way their model would predict. The results are presented in Table 3.4. Before commenting on the figures a few words of explanation on the construction of the tables are in order. No *direct* evidence on the attitudes or behaviour of any electorate prior to 1963 was collected by Butler and Stokes. They do provide data on the partisanship of different age groups and 'political generations' among the 1966 electorate; but clearly this cannot count towards an accurate portrait of past electorates because (*a*) it excludes members of past electorates who died before 1966, and (*b*) it consists of the current party identification of the respondent, which we know from Butler and Stokes may have changed (but more probably strengthened) over a lifetime, and which therefore cannot tell us about the *past* partisanship of *current* respondents in *past* electorates. Nevertheless, reasonably satisfactory data on the direction and rate of changes in the partisan distribution of electorates in the past can be extracted from the Butler and Stokes survey by analysing the reports of *parental* partisanship by respondents of different age groups. This device admittedly depends on a certain degree of inferential courage and is subject to a number of drawbacks, but it is employed by Butler and Stokes (1969, pp. 247–74). These shortcomings include the absence and inaccuracy of recall among a minority of respondents; the wide range of the historical period of parental partisan behaviour that recall by any ten-year age group of respondents is likely to involve; and the fact that not all electors who are now dead left children to report on their partisanship. In the context of this paper, however, the most important drawback is that Table 3.4 does not prove a *composite* picture of the partisanship of past electorates but merely reveals trends in the partisanship of successive groups of *new* entrants into past electorates. But it proved impossible to construct the partisan distribution of *whole* electorates in the past without raising the number and order of assumptions to an unreasonable level (although a subsequent attempt at such an exercise showed that the substantive results would have been very similar).

It is clear from Table 3.4 that the Conservative and Labour parties have together obtained the allegiance of a steadily *increasing* proportion of new entrants into successive electorates over the last half century, and that to this extent the Butler-Stokes model, which would have predicted a decrease over the last two decades, is contradicted. The figure rises gradually and almost linearly from 54 per cent of the parents of respondents aged 60–69 and 67 per cent of parents of those aged 50–59 to 84 per cent of the parents of respondents aged 20–29, although it is perhaps significant that it then flattens out for *respondents* aged 21–45. There is a corresponding fall in the proportion of entrants into successive electorates without any party allegiance, and a gradual erosion of support for the Liberals which is perhaps slower than one might have expected. If men and women are taken separately it can clearly be seen that the growth in identification with the two parties has been faster

Table 3.4 The party identification of respondents aged 21–32, and 33–45, and of the parents of respondents of different age groups by sex of respondents and parents

**Men**

| Party Identification | Male respondents aged 21-32 % | 33-45 % |
|---|---|---|
| Conservative | 32 | 26 |
| Labour | 56 | 54 |
| Liberal | 9 | 11 |
| Other | – | – |
| None | 2 | 9 |
| N= | (170) | (235) |

**Women**

| Party Identification | Female respondents aged 21-32 % | 33-45 % |
|---|---|---|
| Conservative | 36 | 37 |
| Labour | 49 | 46 |
| Liberal | 10 | 13 |
| Other | – | – |
| None | 6 | 5 |
| N= | (218) | (289) |

**All**

| Party Identification | All respondents aged 21-32 % | 33-45 % |
|---|---|---|
| Conservative | 34 | 32 |
| Labour | 52 | 50 |
| Liberal | 10 | 12 |
| Other | – | – |
| None | 5 | 6 |
| N= | (388) | (524) |

| fathers of respondents aged | 20-29 % | 30-39 % | 40-49 % | 50-59 % | 60-69 % | 70 and over % |
|---|---|---|---|---|---|---|
| Conservative | 30 | 26 | 31 | 38 | 36 | 44 |
| Labour | 62 | 56 | 41 | 32 | 21 | 12 |
| Liberal | 4 | 7 | 14 | 20 | 31 | 34 |
| Other | – | 1 | 2 | – | 1 | – |
| None | 5 | – | 9 | 10 | 11 | 10 |
| N= | (302) | (366) | (440) | (402) | (274) | (221) |

| mothers of respondents aged | 20-29 % | 30-39 % | 40-49 % | 50-59 % | 60-69 % | 70 and over % |
|---|---|---|---|---|---|---|
| Conservative | 30 | 26 | 32 | 40 | 38 | 33 |
| Labour | 46 | 36 | 32 | 23 | 14 | 6 |
| Liberal | 5 | 7 | 9 | 11 | 13 | 22 |
| Other | – | 1 | 2 | – | – | – |
| None | 19 | 31 | 25 | 26 | 38 | 39 |
| N= | (302) | (366) | (440) | (402) | (274) | (221) |

| mothers and fathers of respondents aged | 20-29 % | 30-39 % | 40-49 % | 50-59 % | 60-69 % | 70 and over % |
|---|---|---|---|---|---|---|
| Conservative | 30 | 27 | 32 | 39 | 36 | 39 |
| Labour | 54 | 45 | 38 | 28 | 18 | 9 |
| Liberal | 4 | 7 | 12 | 15 | 22 | 28 |
| Other | 1 | 1 | 2 | – | 1 | – |
| None | 12 | 20 | 17 | 18 | 24 | 23 |
| N= | (302) | (366) | (440) | (402) | (274) | (221) |

Notes: Respondents replying 'Don't know' or giving no answer have been excluded.

Source: Butler and Stokes' 1966 survey.

and sharper among women. This is almost entirely due to the sharper decline of female non-identifiers, who were far more numerous relatively than male non-identifiers among the parents of middle-aged and elderly respondents, but of a similar proportion among the parents of young respondents and among younger respondents themselves. It is not entirely valid to compare respondents' reports of their own partisanship with their recall of their parents': the latter is likely to be less acurrate, and to be biased by the former. Nevertheless, the figures overall confirm not only the trend of general election results over the last fifty years, but also what one might expect from the interwar supplantment of the Liberals by Labour as the main opposition party, together with the establishment of universal adult franchise in the 1920s. One would expect that as the franchise among the working class (especially working-class women) and Labour's rise to prominence became increasingly recognized by the public, and as those who came of age before the First World War diminished as a proportion of the electorate, so an entrenched partisan allegiance to either the Labour or Conservative parties would also grow. (In fact, a whole section of *Political Change in Britain* is devoted to analysing the process whereby this happened.) The question that remains therefore is why this growth of allegiance to the two parties has been accompanied by their growing rejection at the polls in recent years.

One possible explanation, which would remain consistent with the model, is that recent electorates, while identifying with the two major parties in increasing numbers, have been doing so with less intensity. In other words, the overall *strength* of partisanship among the electorate at large may have declined over the last two decades. It proved impossible to discover the distribution of partisan strength in past electorates because Butler and Stokes did not ask respondents to say how strongly their parents supported a party. But respondents were asked to assess both their own and their parents' *interest* in politics and it was therefore possible to compare the degree of interest in politics among successive waves of entrants into electorates in the past. To be very interested in politics is by no means the same as being strongly partisan. Indeed, the possibility that there has developed among recent electorates a growing divergence between political interest and political partisanship is discussed later in this paper. But since the two variables have been shown until now to be closely related (Campbell *et al.*, 1960, pp. 142–5), it seemed reasonable to treat the former as an approximate indicator of *trends* in the distribution of partisan intensity over the last fifty years.

Table 3.5 indicates that a weakening of political interest and thus partisan intensity may have happened to a small degree: the proportion claiming, or reported to be, 'very interested' in politics dropped from about one-quarter of the parents to 16 per cent of those aged 33–45. But the combined figure for those claiming or reported to be either 'very' or 'somewhat' interested in politics has remained remarkably steady. The small extent of the decline in political interest among the public must restrict its importance as an explanation of the growing popular detachment from the two major parties: but it may well indicate the area in which the Michigan model should be improved.

Additional reasons can be derived from the model for expecting the proportion of Labour and Conservative identifiers (and thus voters) to rise among recent electorates. It will be recalled from the earlier description of the model that the *direction* of an elector's party identification depended largely upon that of his parents, and was only likely to differ if:

Table 3.5　Interest in politics of respondents aged 21–32 and 33–45 and of parents of respondents in different age groups by sex of respondents and parents

## Men

| Interests in politics | Male respondents aged | | fathers of respondents aged | | | | | |
|---|---|---|---|---|---|---|---|---|
| | 21-32 | 33-45 | 20-29 | 30-39 | 40-49 | 50-54 | 60-69 | 70 and over |
| | % | % | % | % | % | % | % | % |
| Very interested | 19 | 24 | 25 | 26 | 38 | 41 | 45 | 44 |
| Fairly interested | 47 | 51 | 45 | 38 | 28 | 30 | 28 | 30 |
| Not interested | 34 | 25 | 30 | 36 | 34 | 29 | 26 | 27 |
| N= | (170) | (235) | (302) | (366) | (440) | (402) | (274) | (221) |

## Women

| Interests in politics | Female respondents aged | | mothers of respondents aged | | | | | |
|---|---|---|---|---|---|---|---|---|
| | 21-32 | 33-45 | 20-29 | 30-39 | 40-49 | 50-59 | 60-69 | 70 and over |
| | % | % | % | % | % | % | % | % |
| Very interested | 6 | 8 | 6 | 6 | 15 | 15 | 10 | 9 |
| Fairly interested | 32 | 39 | 35 | 29 | 24 | 24 | 20 | 15 |
| Not interested | 63 | 53 | 59 | 66 | 65 | 61 | 70 | 76 |
| N= | (218) | (289) | (302) | (366) | (440) | (402) | (274) | (221) |

## All

| Interests in politics | All respondents aged | | mothers and fathers of respondents aged | | | | | |
|---|---|---|---|---|---|---|---|---|
| | 21-32 | 33-45 | 20-29 | 30-39 | 40-49 | 50-59 | 60-69 | 70 and over |
| | % | % | % | % | % | % | % | % |
| Very interested | 12 | 16 | 15 | 16 | 24 | 28 | 28 | 26 |
| Fairly interested | 38 | 45 | 39 | 33 | 26 | 27 | 24 | 22 |
| Not interested | 50 | 40 | 46 | 51 | 50 | 46 | 48 | 52 |
| N= | (388) | (524) | (302) | (366) | (440) | (402) | (274) | (221) |

Notes:　Respondents replying 'Don't know' or giving no answer have been excluded.

Sources:Butler and Stokes' survey, 1966. Respondents were asked (i) "How much interest do you generally have in what's going on in politics - a good deal, some or not much?" and (ii) "Do you remember when you were young whether your father/mother was very much interested in politics, somewhat interested, or didn't he/she pay much attention to it?".

(a) the country underwent some widespread social catastrophe;

(b) a new social cleavage with a clear partisan alignment emerged in the country at large;

(c) the elector experienced social mobility, whether *inter-* or *intra*-generationally (except in the circumstances of (e) below);

(d) the parents were of Liberal, mixed or no party allegiance;

(e) the parents both identified with the minority party of their class and the elector remained in the same class as his parents.

Since the Labour and Conservative parties obtained the allegiance of a gradually larger part of successive electorates from 1922 onwards, it follows that the proportion of voters with parents identifying with the two parties must have also increased steadily. But the possibility that the circumstances listed in (a) to (e) may have contributed to a decline or weakening in identification with the two major parties remains to be explored. As regards (a), it is difficult to think of any national event since 1950 that might explain the rise in abstention in and support for minor parties in the way that the two world wars, the interwar depression and the adoption of universal adult franchise all contributed to enduring and major realignments of partisanship in past electorates. It is less difficult, however, to suggest cases of a *series* of events that contributed to a slow but accumulative process whereby increasing numbers of the public lost faith in both major parties. Britain's persistent loss of international power and prestige, and the chronic inability of governments of either party since the early 1960s to solve her economic problems are two examples that come readily to mind. Such an explanation seems realistic but is alien to the Michigan School's emphasis upon single cataclysmic events, the political impact of which is reflected in only one, or perhaps two successive 'realigning' elections.

It is similarly difficult to think of any social cleavages or fundamental changes in the social structure in the last twenty years that could have affected *national* partisan alignments in any way comparable to the substitution of the religious cleavage by the class cleavage in the first three decades of this century. Glacially slow changes in the British social structure have undoubtedly taken place. The emergence of coloured immigrant communities, the growth of white-collar employment (and of white-collar 'trade unionism'), the movement of agricultural workers to the towns and their displacement by commuters and the retired rich, a further spread of secularization and a growing disparity of income between the organized and unorganized working class are all cases in point. (For statistical evidence on these trends see Halsey (1972).) But in all these cases, shifts in party support have been small, often only temporary, and always localized; no shift in the social structure has produced an enduring, nationwide realignment of party support since 1945.

As regards (c) it is possible that both inter- and intra-generational social mobility has increased in the last twenty years: the results of the major occupational mobility study conducted by Hope and Goldthorpe at Nuffield College are still awaited (Hope, 1972; Ridge, 1974). But so far there is no convincing evidence that this has occurred. The most up-to-date analysis shows that the combined proportion of non-manual sons of manual fathers and manual sons of non-manual fathers was 31 per cent in 1949, 28 per cent in 1951, 27 per cent in 1962 and 30 per cent in 1963 (Macdonald and Ridge, 1972, p.146). Such figures should be compared only with caution, but there is no hint of a clear increase in social mobility. Moreover, even if social mobility has increased, this should not have precipitated a fall in support for the two major parties, according to the model, but rather a greater fluidity of support between the parties over time.

We are thus left with possibilities (*d*) and (*e*)—that recent electorates have abandoned the two major parties in growing numbers because, to a greater extent than in the past, their parents have been of Liberal, mixed or no party allegiance, or have identified with the minority in their social class. Table 3.6 shows that this has not been the case. The proportion of electors, both of whose parents agreed in their support of the Labour Party or of the Conservative Party, has steadily risen from 21 per cent of those aged seventy and over to 43 per cent of those aged twenty to twenty-nine. And the proportion of those whose father's party allegiance was class-consonant has gradually risen from 21 per cent of those aged seventy and over to 49 per cent of those aged twenty to twenty-nine. The figures in Table 3.6 therefore help to explain the increasing party identification with the Conservative and Labour Parties among recent

Table 3.6    Age of respondent by (i) whether both parents supported the same major party and (ii) class and partisanship of father

Age of respondent

| | 20-29 | 30-39 | 40-49 | 50-59 | 60-69 | 70 & over |
|---|---|---|---|---|---|---|
| (i) Parental partnership | (N=302) | (N=366) | (N=440) | (N=402) | (N=274) | (N=221) |
| | % | % | % | % | % | % |
| Both parents Conservative | 17 ) | 15 ) | 16 ) | 20 ) | 21 ) | 18 ) |
| | ) 43 | ) 40 | ) 36 | ) 32 | ) 29 | ) 21 |
| Both parents Labour | 26 ) | 25 ) | 20 ) | 12 ) | 8 ) | 3 ) |
| Both parents Liberal or mixed1 | 35 | 33 | 35 | 34 | 42 | 42 |
| No preference, Don't know, No answer | 22 | 27 | 30 | 33 | 30 | 37 |
| (ii) Class and party of father | % | % | % | % | % | % |
| Father was non-manual and Conservative or manual and Labour | 49 | 48 | 38 | 30 | 23 | 22 |
| Father was non-manual and Labour or manual and Conservative | 19 | 16 | 18 | 17 | 23 | 19 |
| Other | 32 | 36 | 44 | 52 | 54 | 60 |

Note: 1. Includes cases of only one parent being reported to have a party identification.

Source: Reanalysis of Butler and Stokes' survey of 1966.

electorates and in this limited sense they vindicate part of the model. But the problem of why a growing minority should then abandon the two parties at elections stubbornly waits for an answer and continues to call the validity of the model into question.

(b) *The fall in turnout.* From the party identification model we should expect Britain's gradual decline in turnout to reflect an overall weakening of partisanship among more recent electorates as well as a shortening in the average duration for which the same party identification has been held. Yet the evidence has pointed to only the slightest weakening in the partisanship of electorates in the recent past. And although it proved impossible to calculate the average duration of consistent party identification in past electorates, circumstantial evidence strongly suggests that it must have been considerably shorter than among the latest electorates.

This is so for two connected reasons. First, since Labour's replacement of the Liberals between 1918 and 1931 as the second major party there has been no shift in the distribution of national support for the parties that can compare in magnitude. The mutation of the two-party system before 1914 into a three-party system in the 1920s and its return to a transformed two-party system by the late 1940s produced a fluidity of party support (and therefore party identification) that has surely not been matched since. Moreover, the rapid rise and fall of parties bridging the old Liberal and Conservative parties, such as the Liberal Unionists, Coalition Liberals and National Liberals, plus the fact that the Liberal decline was chequered by temporary revivals (in 1923 and 1929) and that Liberal losses went predominently to the Conservatives in some elections (1924 and 1931) but to Labour in others (1929), all suggest that shifts in party identification at the time were not once-only affairs. It is therefore reasonable to assume that that period's generation will have had exceptionally inconsistent, short-lived and thus weak party identifications. But this generation will have steadily declined as a proportion of successive electorates after 1945; and since 1945 there has been nothing comparable to produce greater inconsistency and a shorter duration of party identification among the electorate.

The extension of the franchise in 1918 and 1928 provides the second piece of circumstantial evidence. At each election the electorate is replenished by a small proportion of new voters whose partisan inexperience and thus weakness of party identification renders them less likely than the remainder of the electorate to turn out and vote. But the elections of 1918 and 1929, and to a lesser extent those in between, will have added exceptionally large proportions of new voters to the existing electorate. Between 1910 and 1918 the electorate almost trebled, rising from 7.7 million to 21.4 million; it rose a further 7.1 million (32 per cent) between 1924 and 1929 (Butler and Freeman, 1969 p.155). If, as Butler and Stokes argue, the characteristics of each new political generation continue to reveal themselves in subsequent elections, albeit with diminishing impact, the weak party identification of that abnormally large generation should have featured in later electorates but should have gradually disappeared in the electorates of the last twenty years as members of that generation died. It should also be remembered that the 'new' voters of 1918 will have consisted not only of the young, but mainly of middle-aged and elderly women. Thus many will have had too short an electoral lifetime to settle down to a consistent support of one party and thus the development of a strong partisanship. And they will have undergone considerably less 'anticipatory socialization' into partisanship than today's voters because the majority of their parents will not have been entitled to vote and thus will not have possessed a party identification. It thus seems safe to assume that party allegiance was considerably weaker and more short-lived in prewar electorates than in those of the last decade. Whatever the explanation for Britain's falling rate of turnout, therefore, it is hard to find it in a party identification model of voting behaviour.

(c) *The increasing volatility of party support.* In one sense this can be dealt with very briefly. In the party identification model instability of party choice is largely attributed to strength of partisanship and duration of consistent partisanship. But as preceding paragraphs have shown, neither has declined significantly in recent British electorates. To this extent the model fails to explain the growing flux in party support over recent years.

## THE CONCEPT OF PARTY IDENTIFICATION

Any critical discussion of the party identification model should perhaps begin with a fresh examination of the crucial concept of party identification itself. At the time the concept was first formulated in the mid-1950s, it undoubtedly constituted a powerful and original means of understanding important and hitherto unexplained aspects of individual voting behaviour. Previous voting studies had been predicted on an 'economic' model of electoral man whose vote was a 'rational choice'. The most conspicuous feature of the Columbia studies by Berelson and Lazarsfeld, for example, was the emphasis they laid upon voting as a *decision,* on how the voter arrived at a party choice in a single election, on the various stages this process went through, and on the way conflicting social pressures were resolved. The research design adopted in these studies—a panel survey over the duration of the campaign only—reflected this conception of the vote as a decision. The early survey studies of British voters also proceeded on the assumption that voters should act as self-regarding, calculative consumers of party policies and leaders (or, if not self-regarding, at least as conscientious jurors and when they found that most voters diverged from this model, special chapters (as in the Columbia studies) were devoted to the seemingly disturbing implications for representative democracy (Milne and MacKenzie, 1958, Ch. 13; Nordlinger, 1967, Ch. 9; Runciman, 1967, Chs. 2, 3 and 12).

The Michigan studies substituted a socio-psychological model of electoral man whose vote was less self-regarding or calculative, deriving instead from a socialization into an internalization of partisan dispositions. The image of the individual as a 'voter', with its connotations of a conscious act of careful assessment, was relegated in favour of the individual as a 'partisan' or 'party identifier', with its connotation of habitual and unquestioning loyalty, rather than deliberate choice. The voter was regarded more as a religious adherent than a consumer or juror. Like members of a church, voters were 'baptised' into the party of their parents, rarely considered the possibility of 'conversion' but occasionally decided to abstain in the same way the one decides to attend or stay away from church, and they knew as little about the ideology of their party as most worshippers know about the theology of their church. And the rare cases of conversion were more likely to result from social mobility or status passage (e.g. marriage or retirement) than from a genuine change of beliefs. To make party identification the key to an understanding of voting behaviour was therefore both original, in that it differed considerably from previous approaches, and attractive, in that it seemed to encompass the findings not only of the Michigan studies but of previous surveys also.

But considering the theoretical and empirical load that it has to bear, the concept of party identification in a British context has undergone remarkably little systematic treatment or justification. Perhaps the apparent pervasiveness of party identification and the similarity of the concept's relationship with other aspects of voting behaviour among the electorates of a variety of Western democracies, with widely differing electoral and party systems and divergent electoral histories, has led to the belief that no such investigation is necessary. Thus Butler and Stokes (1969, pp. 23–43) persuasively explain the near-universality of party identification in terms of its psychological convenience for the elector in a complex, changing and remote political system, but these arguments are supported by no empirical evidence and thus amount to no more than speculative if imaginative *apercus*.

The closest approach to a more rigorous examination of the concept's applicability in Britain is a concession that the meaning of party identification may differ for the British and American elector. Butler and Stokes (1969, pp. 41-42) show that proportionately more British electors change their party identification to conform with changes of voting preference and conclude that British voters find it more difficult to distinguish between party identification and party choice in a specific election. This disparity between British and American notions of party identification somewhat detracts from the importance attributed by the concept's defenders to the common and widely established existence of the phenomenon across various Western democracies. It also raises a fundamental question about the concept. What are the *meanings* of partisanship for electors and how, if at all, do these meanings vary? What might respondents signify when they agree to classify themselves as Labour or Conservative partisans, or to accept a label as 'very strongly' or 'fairly strongly' partisan?

Rae and Taylor's interesting discussion (1970) of the concept of 'intensity of preference' provides us with a useful point of departure. To discover the subjective meaning of party identification we must ask:

(*a*) with *what* is the respondent comparing his party identification?

(*b*) is the respondent making a positive or negative comparison?

(*c*) in what sense is the respondent claiming party identification?

(*a*) *Party identification compared with what?* If X states that he strongly or intensely prefers alternative A, he could mean any of the following:

   (i)   that he prefers A much more than any of the other *proposed* alternatives;
   (ii)  that he prefers A much more than any other *possible* alternatives, *whether proposed as one or not*;
   (iii) that he prefers A much more than his least preferred alternative;
   (iv)  that he prefers A much more than the alternative most likely to be adopted;
   (v)   that he prefers A much more than the alternative most likely to be adopted *should A be rejected.*

No doubt other meanings could be attributed to X's preference but they need not detain us here. Scattered evidence is now accumulating that suggests that the usual assumptions about party identification confuse meaning (i) with meaning (ii). A respondent's declared partisanship is regarded as an expression of absolute preference (meaning (ii)) rather than of relative choice among familiar and restricted alternatives, that is, vulnerable to change once the alternatives alter (meaning (i)). But intense preference for Labour rather than the Conservatives in no way implies intense preference for Labour *whatever the alternative.* Habitual party support is not the same as a committed party loyalty. Thus in the last decade substantial proportions of Labour and Conservative party identifiers have declared a willingness to vote Liberal (or for a 'new Centre party') if they thought the Liberals had a chance of winning either nationally or locally.* In this context it is also worth reiterating the persistently high proportions of the British electorate who claim to prefer an all-party coalition government to any single party in office. And Goot (1972) has found that only 61 per cent of 'very strong' and 44 per cent of 'fairly strong' Australian party identifiers were satisfied with at least one of the present parties, and about a quarter of both categories wanted a new party. He rightly points out that new parties tend to be formed by the strongest and most active supporters of established parties, the origins of the Labour Party, the Australian DLP and Wallace's American Independent Party being cases in point. What these findings suggest, therefore, is that party identification may not be incompatible with 'availability' to emerging parties or new combinations of parties; and that responses to questions designed to elicit party identification depend on the nature of the current party system and on the likelihood and direction of its changing in the eyes of the respondent.

The rapidity with which the supposedly 'enduring' psychological state of party identification can change, dissolve or emerge in response to alterations in the party system is also supported by recently established evidence from France and the United States (Cameron, 1972; Inglehart and Hochstein, 1972). The marked difference in the level of partisanship between the two countries has been *reversed* between the late 1950s and the present day: the proportion of 'identifiers' in France has risen from 56 per cent in 1958 to 80 per cent in 1969, but has dropped in the United States from 76 per cent in 1958 to 68 per cent in 1970 (Inglehart and Hochstein, 1972, pp. 349, 353). Cohort analysis suggests, moreover, that these trends, although most apparent among young electors, are a generational (not life-cycle) phenomenon and hence can be expected to continue in future years. A variety of research leaves little doubt that French 'realignment' and American 'dealignment' can only be attributed to the rise to political preeminence of Gaullist parties in the Fifth Republic and to the racial and Vietnam crises that split the Democratic Party and led to the intervention of Wallace in the 1968 Presidential election. The proportion of 'strong Democratic' identifiers suddenly fell from 22 per cent in 1964 to 16 per cent in 1968—an unprecedented disturbance of what Campbell *et al.* have described as the 'serene stability' of party

---

* A Gallup Poll in September 1962 reported that 42 per cent of respondents claimed they would vote Liberal if they thought the Liberals had a chance of winning a parliamentary majority. Exactly ten years later a survey by the Opinion Research Centre revealed almost identical figures: 40 per cent claimed they would vote Liberal 'if there was a chance of the Liberal Party getting into power' (including 21 per cent of strong Conservative identifiers and 35 per cent of strong Labour identifiers). The same poll revealed that 40 per cent (including 25 per cent of Labour supporters) agreed that if 'some moderate members of the Conservative Party joined with the Liberals to form a new Centre Party' they would support it, and 35 per cent agreed that if 'well-known moderates like Roy Jenkins, Shirley Williams, George Thompson and Harold Lever joined up with the Liberals to form a new Centre Party' they would vote for it (including 20 per cent of Conservative supporters). See *The Times*, 30 September 1972, p. 14.

identification in the United States (Flanigan, 1972, pp. 42-3). But this 'serene stability' cannot be interpreted as evidence of enduring party *loyalty* among the majority of American electors, for the stability occurred in a period without challenge to the established two-party system, and the test of 'loyalty' is surely the continuation of support for a party when faced with a new substantial challenge.

(b) *Party identification as a negative or positive preference*. The Michigan School's conception of party identification can also be criticized for failing to distinguish between meaning (i) on the one hand and meanings (iii) to (v) above on the other. There is a distinction between positive, overwhelming enthusiasm for one party above all others, and relative, reluctant preference for one party out of hostility to all others, or to the one other that is likely to benefit should the preferred party not be sufficiently supported. To say that Labour is better than the Conservatives is very different from saying that Labour is not as bad as the Conservatives. *Negative* party identification can take two forms: identification with a party for negative reasons (it is not as bad as the rest) and the absence of identification with any party combined with identification *against* a particular party (e.g. the Communist Party in France). Preliminary analysis of the British February 1974 election survey suggests that the incidence of the former is quite substantial, although the latter is negligible. As Table 3.7 shows, 30 per cent of Conservative identifiers and 23 per cent of Labour identifiers felt more negative towards the opposite party than positive towards their own; the

Table 3.7    Negative and Positive Party Identification amongst major
Party Identifiers

| Type of identifier: | Conservative identifiers (895) % | Labour identifiers (1028) % |
|---|---|---|
| 'Polarised' (very strongly for own party and very strongly against other) | 25 | 26 |
| 'Loyal' (very or fairly strongly for own party; not very strongly against other) | 29 | 36 |
| 'Negative' (fairly strongly for own party but very strongly against other) | 26          30 | 20          23 |
| (not very strongly for own party but very strongly against other) | 4 | 3 |
| 'Apathetic' (not very strongly for own party; not very strongly against other) | 17 | 16 |

Source:   Ivor Crewe and Bo Särlvik, British Election Study, February 1974 cross-section survey.

proportion of 'loyalists' (who felt more positive to their own party than negative towards the other) was 29 and 36 per cent respectively. However, the proportion who claimed to be 'very strongly' against the other party but 'not very strongly' (as opposed to 'fairly strongly' or 'very strongly') for their own party was only 4 per cent among Conservatives and 3 per cent among Labour identifiers.

(c) *Party identification in what sense?* The problem of making interpersonal comparisons of preference utilities is well known to economists (and utilitarians) and has never been satisfactorily resolved. It applies to the concept of party identification in that we know nothing about the variety of meanings attached to the partisanship respondents say they possess. We are in no position to understand what the difference between, for instance, 'very' and 'fairly' strong Labour partisanship, or between 'very strong Labour' and 'very strong Conservative' partisanship really amounts to. Users of the concept often believe that because it comes 'naturally' to the great majority of the public (90 per cent) to place themselves in a party camp they can proceed to use party identification both as an explanatory and descriptive variable without further ado. But Runciman (1967, Ch. 8) and Butler and Stokes also 1969, pp. 66–73, 80–91) have shown how similar proportions of the public 'naturally' place themselves in one of the two social classes, yet define their assessment in widely varying ways.

The question of the meanings electors attach to the notion of partisanship is particularly pertinent if we consider the standard way in which information on partisanship is obtained. In Butler and Stokes's study respondents were asked, 'Generally speaking, do you usually think of yourself as Conservative, Liberal, Labour or what?' followed by 'How strongly (chosen party) do you generally feel—very strongly, fairly strongly or not very strongly?'. Two points arise. The first is that the wording may well encourage the tendency discussed earlier to confuse party support with party loyalty by providing the names of the main parties as a cue. The second is that the normal practice is to ask people to volunteer information about themselves which can be consistently scaled and coded according to the researcher's *own* criteria (e.g. inquiries about frequency of church attendance or number of newspapers read). It is surely another matter to ask respondents to assess their own state of mind according to their own subjective scales, for which no fixed standards are provided by the interviewer. Rather different evidence on the electorate's partisanship might have emerged if respondents had been asked whether they regarded themselves as a supporter of *any* political party and if the answers were then coded into categories of intensity without any supplementary question on intensity having been put.

Thus respondents uniformly categorized on the basis of a single response may turn out to be a motley crowd. 'Very strong' Labour/Conservative partisans might well consist of any of the following:

(i) *loyalists:* positive and enthusiastic supporters, who have consistently voted for the party, and could not imagine deserting the party in any circumstances; includes a disproportionate number of activists. This is probably the conventional connotation of the term;

(ii) *negative partisans:* those with an entrenched and intense hostility to the rival party, who nevertheless may well harbour major reservations about their own party. They are clearly vulnerable to defection if the party system changes;

(iii) *temporary partisans:* those with a temporary yet intense commitment to a party as a result of current or recent opposition to the other party arising from some spontaneous (and perhaps frivolous) response to immediate events. The Michigan studies usually imply that the *strength* as well as direction of partisanship is remarkably stable but provide no substantiating evidence;

(iv) *habitual partisans:* consistent but relatively ignorant and indifferent supporters who interpret persistency of party choice as strong partisanship;

(v) *instrumental partisans:* those who strongly support one party because it is identified with (and the other party is identified as against) a policy or group interest that has an overwhelming priority. This is quite compatible with support for the other party on many, even most, other issues of less importance to the respondent.

This list could easily be extended with the exercise of a little imagination: it is simply meant to emphasize that 'strong partisanship' can comprise a wide range of ideological sophistication, political knowledge and interest, consistency in party choice, awareness of other parties and so on.

This dissection of the possible meanings of party identification should not be regarded as trivial nitpicking, for it might explain the inability of the party identification model to account for recent trends in British politics. For example, if the growth in the partisan allegiance to either the Labour or the Conservative Party since 1945 nevertheless masks a change in the meaning of that partisanship to the electorate—from 'absolute' to 'relative', from 'positive' to 'negative', from 'loyal' to 'habitual'—then it is no longer surprising if it is accompanied by a slow decline in turnout and the two-party share of the electorate. If the partisanship reported by respondents expresses not so much an overwhelming enthusiasm for one party but merely a reluctant if consistent preference on the implicit assumption that the party system would remain the same in the future, we can begin to understand why party identification as traditionally measured seems to be losing its usefulness as a tool for the analysis of British voting behaviour. Certain cross-national paradoxes might also be explained in this way. For instance, the level and stability of party identification is as high or higher in the British and American electorates than in any others on which comparable surveys have been done, yet turnout in Britain and the United States is lower than in most Western democracies, and short-term shifts of party support (at the presidential level) in the United States (although not Britain) are substantially greater than in most Western democracies (Rose and Urwin, 1970).

## THE DEVELOPMENT OF PARTY IDENTIFICATION

An elector's partisanship does not simply fall from the sky. How, therefore, is it first developed and then sustained over time? The Michigan School is based on socio-psychological traditions and regards partisanship as a learning process (Butler and Stokes, 1969, Ch. 3; and Converse, 1969). Like any other social role, it is 'learnt' by a process of childhood socialization, youthful experimentation and adult internalization. In their childhood, most electors are nurtured on the party identification of their parents; as young voters they remain largely under parental influence but become increasingly open to the political climate of the times and to the partisan fashion of their social circles; by early middle age they tend to settle for one party, gradually strengthening their partisanship through a process of habit and selective perception until it petrifies and becomes immune to almost any 'disturbance'. This psychological model of partisan development is subject to a number of weaknesses and contradictions however; and in the concluding paragraphs we shall advocate a restoration of sociological and political factors as part of the explanation.

The major weakness has already been alluded to at various points throughout this chapter. The notion of partisanship as a learning process leads to an excessive concentration on changes and processes at the micro-level without reference to those at the macro-level, except in passing. For example, the brunt of Butler and Stokes's answers to the question 'Why did Labour supersede the Liberals between the wars?' rests upon the inter-generational transmission of partisanship among manual workers and Non-Conformists. But the difficulty with citing parental partisanship as a 'cause' of a later generation's politics is that it immediately invites the question 'what causes *parental* partisanship?' and is open to problems of infinite regress. Historians might reasonably claim to provide more satisfying answers by referring to changes at the élite and macro-level: the Taff Vale Court decision in 1901; the Government's need for trade union co-operation during the First World War; the Asquith—Lloyd George split in the Liberal Party in 1916; and the Conservative Government's choice of a conciliatory rather than retaliatory strategy towards organized Labour in the 1930s. The danger of focusing upon changes at the 'grass roots' is that one might be analysing the symptom rather than the cause, a single and intermediate link in a long causal chain.

Ambiguities in the relationship between macro-forces and micro-processes are revealed in a variety of ways. The first concerns Butler and Stokes's treatment of young voters. On the one hand they are characterized as still largely under the influence of their parents. For example, Butler and Stokes show how nearly half the children of Liberal fathers cast their first vote for the Liberals and how this proportion dwindled to about a quarter of the current preference of the same respondents (p.251). On the other hand, new voters are also characterized as unusually amenable to the influence of the issues and events that happen to dominate the national politics of the time. If the political climate of the time is unusually favourable to one or other party, a 'political generation' will emerge which will remain unusually favourable to that party throughout its electoral career. This is the explanation given to the relatively high Labour support among those aged 35–44 in 1964 who therefore must have been new voters in 1945.

There is certainly no logical contradiction here, but these two generalizations about the young voter are used in contradictory ways. For example, the age group that in 1964 gave Labour the biggest percentage lead over the Conservatives (10.6 per cent) was between 35 and 44 and therefore first entitled to vote between 1941 and 1951, a period that includes *both* the pro-Labour war years *and* the massive recovery of the Conservatives from 1947 onwards. The adjacent age group (45–54) was first entitled to vote between 1931 and 1940—the period of massive unemployment and of fascism abroad which supposedly hurt the Conservatives so much—yet the Labour lead drops to 0.3 per cent. Moreover, the parents of those first entitled to vote between, let us say, 1940 and 1946 (Labour's best years) will themselves have probably first voted in the elections of 1910 or 1918, a period that very markedly favoured the

Conservatives. Assuming they, the parents, were also very open to the partisan climate in *their* early adulthood, they should have been disproportionately pro-Conservative. Why, then, was this Conservative partisanship not transmitted to the new voters of 1940–46?

To answer that 'outside' influences tend to override those of the family where the two contradict does not offer a solution; for we should then want to know why other periods that were particularly favourable to a party have not produced a political generation to record the fact. For instance, why was the Liberal landslide of 1906 not revealed in a disproportionate Liberal vote among the elderly? And why do the Conservative landslide of 1924, the massive swing back to Labour between the General Strike in 1926 and Labour's return to office in 1929, and the second Conservative landslide in 1931 fail to reveal themselves in a zigzag trend line for those aged 50–65 in 1964? To argue that political generations will not emerge if a landslide victory for one party is rapidly erased by the subsequent full recovery of the other party is unsatisfactory moreover, because the postwar Labour 'generation' was not precluded by the impressive Conservative recoveries of 1950 and 1951. It could be argued that the new electors of 1945 were exceptionally free from parental influence because the parents of many of them had not been enfranchised long enough to develop a party identification sufficiently strong and enduring to be bequeathed; but in that case the growing rejection of the two major parties by *present-day* new voters, whose parents have always had the vote, becomes more difficult to explain. We are not provided with reasons why new voters are sometimes largely under the influence of parents but at other times largely affected by the national political climate.

The explanation for how British partisanship is sustained also presents some puzzles. Butler and Stokes seem to take their cue from Lord Bryce (1888, p.5): 'When a man has voted, he is committed; he has thereafter an interest in backing the view which he has sought to make prevail.' Thus unswerving loyalty to the same party in successive elections is interpreted as the consequence of long-lasting and strong partisanship: 'the strengthening of partisanship in the ageing voter implies that older electors will be less changeable in their voting' (Butler and Stokes, 1969, p.56). But a few lines down the same page we are given this description of how strong partisanship forms: 'it is duration of party support rather than age itself which strengthens party loyalty'. It is almost tautologous, and certainly uninformative, to argue that strength of partisanship determines constancy of vote and constancy of vote determines strength of partisanship. For example, it becomes difficult to explain how the relatively large proportion of party fluctuaters among new voters whittles down to a much smaller proportion among the middle-aged: we are told *that* the volatile young voter is transformed into a steady partisan by middle age, but not *how*. For it would seem to follow from Butler and Stokes's portrait of the mutually reinforcing interrelationship of party identification and stable party vote that a weak or changing party identification and fluctuating party vote must also be mutually reinforcing. It follows that we should expect the proportion of weak partisans and floating voters in any generation to endure through the lifetime of that generation. The 'acquired habit' of partisanship might well include the habit of switching and indeed it would be interesting to know if instability of party choice can be inherited from parents in the same way that ordinary partisanship can, for if such instability was also found disproportionately among working-class electors, whose fertility exceeds that of the middle classes, we would have a further possible explanation of the growing volatility of party support among recent British electorates.

Butler and Stokes's characterization of older voters (one that finds an exact counterpart in Michigan studies of the United States) also raises more questions than it answers. They are shown to be the most loyal in their party choice but relatively indifferent to party politics with rates of turnout that sink to those of the youngest voters. But why this should be, given that they are disproportionately strong partisans, and given the strong relationship between partisanship and political involvement, including turnout, is never made clear.

All these difficulties in Butler and Stokes's account of how partisanship develops in Britain are no doubt amenable to a variety of common-sense explanations, but explanations that cannot be derived from bare psychological theories of learning and immunization alone. What they require is a supplementation from a more sociological and historical standpoint, which in addition does not ignore factors at the macro- and élite level. Thus, leaving aside Labour's entry into a coalition government, the period 1940–45 may well have witnessed social conditions peculiarly favourable to the formation of a new political generation rather than to the smooth transition of partisanship from parents to children: conscription, military service abroad, the large-scale mobilization of female employment in factories and the evacuation of school children could all have served to strengthen the influence of peer groups at the expense of parents on the partisanship of young voters (Calder, 1969). Similarly, the relative partisan indifference of the elderly can plausibly be attributed to their growing social isolation, and the pattern of more fixed party loyalties developing in middle age may well be connected with the tendency for this stage of life to coincide with a fixed job and residence, and hence colleagues, neighbours and co-members of organizations who are relatively long-lasting. The variety of alternative explanations such as these is endless; the point is not to speculate, however, but to emphasize that partisanship is best understood as something rooted and nurtured in social milieux. It is more than a mere learning process.

## FUTURE LINES OF RESEARCH

The need for a sociological and historical supplementation of the party identification model allows one to suggest the lines of further work on British voting behaviour (and voting generally) that are likely to prove fruitful. One promising line of approach might be a return to the sociological themes of the Columbia voting studies. Berelson et al. (1954, Ch.6) attribute the creation, sustenance and activation of partisanship in the individual voter to the 'primary' face-to-face groups in which he finds himself. One of their major conclusions is that stability and implementation of party preference is strongly related to the stability and social and political homogeneity of an elector's primary group.

Now there is good reason to suppose that gradual changes in the British social structure (changes less dramatic, however, than those envisaged in the party identification model) might have disturbed the traditional stability, sociopolitical homogeneity and *salience* of many voters' primary groups and local cultures since the war. For instance, the literature on the 'new', 'affluent' working class and on the emerging 'spiralist' middle classes (Willmott and Young, 1957; Goldthorpe et al., 1969; Musgrove, 1963; Bell, 1969), suggests that processes of industrial bueaucratization, geographical mobility and 'privatization' have resulted in many more electors than hitherto entering primary groups that are more segmented, politically and socially more heterogeneous, and adopted more frequently out of personal choice rather than economic necessity or physical proximity. At the same time parochial cultures and socially isolated communities are declining as a source of political identity or influence, and the national media, both mass and specialized, predominate as sources of political information and mobilization. In effect, the proportion of voters subject to intensive face-to-face contact with a network of overlapping primary groups of unvarying political persuasion, which instils and activates a deeply entrenched partisanship, is almost certainly diminishing rapidly.

Even if this were not the case, it should be recalled that the Columbia studies also revealed that primary groups were anything but autonomous: they performed their partisan functions only by converting the political messages transmitted by outside agencies such as the media or the party leadership (intercepted perhaps by local opinion leaders). Hence any explanation of postwar trends in the partisanship of British voters would be incomplete without reference to specifically political factors, such as changes in the type of appeals made by the parties and in the relationship of these appeals to the attitudes of their normal supporters.

Four changes of this nature seem worth mentioning briefly, although the lack of hard evidence for confirmation (or contradiction) means that discussion inevitably amounts to no more than 'informed impressions'. They should be regarded rather as an agenda for future research.

(a) *The failure of successive governments to improve the economy.* On the economic issues of growth, inflation and industrial relations, which both parties and public have given most emphasis in recent election campaigns, the two main parties have had remarkably little success. And on other issues that the public consistently declare to be important, such as Ulster, crimes of violence, or pollution, the parties have adopted a broadly bipartisan approach. These are not the conditions to encourage or reinforce strong feelings of identification with major parties.

(b) *The substitution of 'valence' for position issues in postwar British elections.* There has been a gradual shift from group to non-group issues and from explicitly sectional to national appeals in recent British elections. Campaigns have been dominated by issues on which there is a public consensus on goals and dissensus only on the relative ability of the parties to achieve the goals, e.g. inflation, economic growth, foreign policy. Non-divisive issues that do not involve an exclusive appeal to distinct social groups are less likely to activate primary groups and mobilize strong partisanship. Thus in the 1950s the Conservative Party came to accept the welfare state, 'mixed' economy and Commonwealth (as opposed to the Empire), all of which it had bitterly opposed in the 1945–50 parliament. And in the 1960s the Labour Party quietly abandoned explicit class appeals and promoted an image of a party more able than others to harness managerial efficiency and technological advances in the interest of the whole community. Its subsequent adoption of a prices and incomes policy in the late 1960s and its abortive attempt to 'reform' the trade unions demonstrated a willingness to act against the immediate and specific interests of its most habitual supporters. It seems plausible that strong partisanship diminished as both parties converged in policy and renounced traditional group appeals.

(c) *The growing discrepancy between the opinions of party élites and general public.* There is rarely more than a rough fit between the party division and public division of opinion, but a truly radical difference between the two seems to have developed over the last decade. On such fundamental issues as entry into the EEC and governmental control over prices and incomes the two major parties have deprived the electorate of political choice on the matter by managing to agree between themselves, split within themselves and completely reverse their positions without any reference to public opinion. The number of *major* issues on which the Labour and Conservative parties are united among themselves but in serious opposition to each other, with parallel divisions of opinion among their habitual supporters, has steadily diminished. Moreover, both parties largely share a similar position on emotive 'moral' issues, such as coloured immigration, racial discrimination, legislation on sexual behaviour, penal reform and censorship, and in a House of Commons increasingly dominated by the university-educated, have found themselves considerably 'in advance' of public attitudes. King (1969) has suggested that an absence of party involvement in those political conflicts and critical events that directly involve large numbers of people, and political parties' diminishing role in 'aggregating interests' and 'converting demands into general policy alternatives', is an international phenomenon.

(*d*) *Television*. Television has replaced the daily newspaper as the most popular source of political information for the public at large. Unlike the press, however, it is statutorily obliged to maintain impartiality and a 'fair party balance' in its news reports. In addition it is frequently argued that the nature of the medium promotes that aspect of party politics that clearly dissatisfies the majority of electors—rows and other 'yah-boo' aspects of party debate. This seems likely to have a gradual impact on the nature of public attachment to the parties.

## CONCLUSION AND SUMMARY

The argument that has developed in the preceding pages may be summarized as follows. Three political changes have distinguished Britain from comparable Western democracies in the last two decades: (1) a persistent decline in the combined major party share of the electorate; (2) a gradual fall in turnout and (3) an accelerating volatility of support between the Labour and Conservative Parties. These add up to a growing erosion of public commitment to the two major parties in Britain. These types of change not only differ from that on which the Michigan studies have traditionally placed most emphasis—competitive partisan change—but are not as readily explicable in terms of the party identification models associated with the Michigan school. Indeed, if a dynamic party identification model is applied to what is known about the British electorate, it leads to predictions of trends in turnout, shifts of party support and in the major party share of the electorate that are the very reverse of what has in fact taken place since 1950.

In the light of the model's weaknesses some of its key concepts, such as 'party identification' and 'political generations', as well as the psychological model of partisan development as a learning process are subjected to detailed examination. There was insufficient space or data to demonstrate a conclusive explanation of this slow decline in the stability or strength of the major parties' duopoly of public support. But possible reasons are suggested which, while not imcompatible with the main features of a party identification model, place much greater emphasis on sociological and political changes at the macro-level.

## REFERENCES

Beer, S. (1969), *Modern British Politics*, Second Edition, Faber and Faber, London.
Bell, C. (1969), *Middle Class Families*, Routledge & Kegan Paul, London.

60

Berelson, B., P. F. Lazarsfeld and W. McPhee (1954), *Voting*, University of Chicago Press, Chicago.

Bryce, Lord James (1888), *The American Commonwealth*, Macmillan, London.

Burnham, W. D. (1965), 'The Changing Shape of the American Political Universe', *American Political Science Review*, 59, 7–28.

Burnham, W. D. (1974), 'Theory and Voting Research: Some Reflections on Converse's "Change in the American Electorate" ', *American Political Science Review*, 68, 1002–23.

Butler, D., and D. Stokes (1969), *Political Change in Britain*, First Edition, Macmillan, London.

Butler, D., and J. Freeman (1969), *British Political Facts*, Third Edition, Macmillan, London.

Calder, A. (1969), *The People's War*, Jonathan Cape, London.

Cameron, D. M. (1972), 'Stability and Change in Patterns of French Partisanship', *Public Opinion Quarterly*, 16, 19–30.

Campbell, A., P. Converse, W. Miller and D. E. Stokes (1960), *The American Voter*, Wiley, New York.

Campbell, A., P. E. Converse, W. E. Miller, and D. E. Stokes (1966), *Elections and the Political Order*, Wiley, New York.

Converse, P. E. (1969), 'Of Time and Partisan Stability', *Comparative Political Studies*, 2, 139–71.

Converse, P. E. (1972), 'Change in the American Electorate' in A. Campbell and P. E. Converse (eds.), *The Human Meaning of Social Change*, Russell Sage Foundation, New York.

Converse, P. E. (1974), 'Comment on Burnham's "Theory and Voting Research" ', *American Political Science Review*, 68, 1024–7.

Dennis, J. (1970), 'Support for the Institutions of Elections by the Mass Public', *American Political Science Review*, 64, 819–35.

Dennis, J., L. Lindberg and D. McCrone (1971), 'Support for Nation and Government Among English Children', *British Journal of Political Science*, 1, 24–48.

Downs, A. (1957), *An Economic Theory of Democracy*, Harper & Row, New York.

Flanigan, W. H. (1972), *Political Behaviour of the American Electorate*, Second Edition, Allyn & Bacon, Boston.

Gallup Poll (1960–onwards), *Political Index*, The Gallup Poll, London.

Goldthorpe, J., D. Lockwood, J. Platt and F. Bechofer (1969), *The Affluent Worker in the Class Structure*, Cambridge University Press, Cambridge.

Goot, M. (1972), 'Party Identification and Party Stability', *British Journal of Political Science*, 2, 121–5.

Halsey, A. H. (ed.) (1972), *Trends in British Society since 1900*, Macmillan, London.

Hampton, W. (1970), *Democracy and Community*, Oxford University Press, London.

Hope, K. (ed.) (1972), *The Analysis of Social Mobility*, Clarendon Press, Oxford.

Inglehart, R., and A. Hochstein (1972), 'Alignment and Dealignment of the Electorate in France and the United States', *Comparative Political Studies*, 5, 343–72.

Jones, G. W. (1969), *Borough Politics*, Macmillan, London.

King, A. (1969), 'Political Parties in Western Democracies', *Polity*, 2, 112–41.

Lipset, S. M., and S. Rokkan (1969), 'Cleavage Structures, Party Systems and Voter Alignments; An Introduction', in S. M. Lipset and S. Rokkan (eds.), *Party Systems and Voter Alignments*, Free Press, New York.

Lazarsfeld, P. F., B. Berelson and H. Gaudet (1944), *The People's Choice*, Columbia University Press, New York.

Macdonald, K., and J. Ridge (1972), 'Social Mobility' in A. H. Halsey (ed.), *Trends in British Society since 1900*, Macmillan, London.

Mackie, T. T., and R. Rose (1974), *An International Almanac of Electoral History*, Macmillan, London.

Milne, R. S., and H. C. Mackenzie (1958), *Marginal Seat*, Hansard Society, London.

Musgrove, F. (1963), *The Migratory Elite*, Heinemann, London.

National Opinion Poll (1963–onwards), *Bulletin*, National Opinion Polls Ltd, London.

Nordlinger, E. (1967), *The Working Class Tories*, MacGibbon & Kee, London.

Pomper, G. (1967), 'Classification of Presidential Elections', *Journal of Politics*, 29, 535–66.

Rae, D., and M. Taylor (1970), *The Analysis of Political Cleavages*, Yale University Press, New Haven, Connecticut.

Ridge, J. (ed.) (1974), *Mobility in Britain Reconsidered*, Clarendon Press, Oxford.

Rose, R. (1968), 'Voters Show their Scepticism of Politicians', *The Times*, (9 April 1968).

Rose, R., and D. Urwin (1970), 'Persistence and Change in Western Party Systems since 1945', *Political Studies*, 18, 287–319.

Runciman, G. W. (1967), *Relative Deprivation and Social Justice*, Routledge & Kegan Paul, London.

Sharpe, L. J. (ed.) (1967), *Voting in Cities*, Macmillan, London.

Wallas, G. (1910), *Human Nature in Politics*, Constable, London.

Willmott, P., and M. Young (1957), *Family and Kinship in East London*, Routledge & Kegan Paul, London.

# 4

# Party Identification as a Cross-National Concept: Its Meaning in the Netherlands

JACQUES THOMASSEN

## THE CONCEPT OF PARTY IDENTIFICATION

In the United States party identification has proven to be one of the most invaluable concepts in political research. It is defined as 'the sense of personal attachment which the individual feels toward the [party] of his choice' (Campbell *et al*, 1954 pp. 88-9).

In the election studies of the Survey Research Center of the University of Michigan, party identification is measured by the following series of questions: 'Generally speaking do you usually think of yourself as a Republican, a Democrat, an Independent or what?' If the respondent answered 'Republican' or 'Democrat', he was further asked: 'Would you call yourself a strong Republican (Democrat) or a not very strong Republican (Democrat)?' If, on the other hand, he had answered 'Independent', he was further asked: 'Do you think of yourself as closer to the Republican or Democratic party?' A seven-point scale emerges from this series of questions: strong and weak Democrats; independents leaning toward the Democrats, independents not leaning toward a party, independents leaning toward the Republicans; weak and strong Republicans.

This variable has two dimensions, the partisan direction of the identification and its intensity. The following properties have made party identification a key variable in much of the pioneering work in political research.

(*a*) Party identification makes it possible to characterize a great number of people as Republicans or as Democrats.

(*b*) It is an attitude that is stable in the long run.

(*c*) Party identification is strongly related to the vote preference in a particular election but can be distinguished from it. In each election there are people whose vote preference deviates from their party identification. For most people this is no reason to change their identification as well. This makes it possible to distinguish short-term factors (candidates and issues) from long-term factors (Converse, 1966).

(*d*) Strength of party identification is an excellent predictive variable for many forms of political behaviour.

* The following people commented on the first draft of this paper: E. Bijnen, H. Daalder, F. Heunks, G. Irwin, Ph. Stouthard and A. Vissers. Partial support for this research was provided by NSF grant 6536401.

## THE VALUE OF PARTY IDENTIFICATION IN COMPARATIVE RESEARCH

The first attempts to use party identification in comparative political research were highly successful. In a classic article Converse demonstrated that there is a relationship between the length of time during which a country has had a stable political system and the level of partisanship in that country. This phenomenon can be explained as a function of the experience people have with the party system and of inter-generational transmission processes (Converse, 1969). The level of partisanship in a specific country is in turn indicative for the stability of its political system. A system where party identification has developed weakly is in danger of political instability because flash parties can easily garner a great number of votes. On the other hand, when the great majority of people have developed a lasting attachment to a certain political party, the rise of flash parties is much less likely because party identification functions as a barrier against such changes in the party system (Converse and Dupeux, 1966, p. 269). The concept of party identification can only be meaningful in comparative research, however, if party identification has the same meaning and the same properties in different countries. By definition, the concept refers to a psychological attachment to a party, which is relatively stable over time and which is to a certain extent independent of the actual vote. There have been only few attempts to validate the concept of party identification outside the United States.

Most studies escape from this problem by using only the second dimension of party identification, its intensity. A reason for the concentration on this dimension is probably that most of these studies have been done in Western European countries with a multi-party system. This makes the construction of a continuum analogous to the American seven-point scale too complicated. In most countries the intensity of party identification appears to have the same analytical value as in the United States. Thus the correlations between strength of party identification and such variables as political participation, involvement and stability of vote preference are of the same size as they are in the United States, or at least they run in the same direction. However, the meaning of these findings would be greatly reduced if the basic conditions of stability over time and of independence were not met.

The only serious attempts known to us to validate the concept of party identification have been done in the Federal Republic of Germany. Max Kaase found that in December 1967 54 per cent of the adult population identified themselves as convinced or weak adherents of a particular party. In 1969 this percentage was only 29 per cent. (The great difference between the two percentages can at least partly be explained by the fact that the question wording in 1969 was not exactly the same as that in 1967. In 1967 the names of the parties were mentioned in the question, whereas in 1969 they were not. See Chapter 5 in this volume for further details.) Over these two years only 19 per cent identified themselves consistently with the same party. Kaase also found an almost perfect congruence between party identification and vote preference. Apparently party identification in Germany does not meet the two requirements of stability and independence. Schleth and Weede tried to replicate Goldberg's (1966) causal model on American voting behaviour with German data. In the American setting party identification fits into a model where it is causally prior to vote preference. Schleth and Weede (1971) had to reject such a model for the German data.

In view of such findings, it is of interest to test the validity of the concept of party identification on Dutch data. The Netherlands offer a setting that is different from both the American and the German ones. In Germany the democratic process had been interrupted for a period of almost twenty years as a result of the Nazi regime. The theory of Converse predicts that party identification should not reach a high level in such a political system. In this respect The Netherlands is more comparable with the United States. It has known universal adult suffrage for more than fifty years. In this period the basic structure of the party system remained virtually the same. Until the provincial election of 1970 voting was compulsory (more precisely, one had to appear at the polls). Most people in a particular age group have therefore the same voting experience. Universal suffrage has existed long enough for the establishment of a process of inter-generational transmission of party preference. The only interruption of the democratic process occurred during the German occupation from 1940 to 1945.

This interruption was probably too short to have a negative influence on the development of stable partisan attitudes, as becomes evident also from the virtually complete restoration of the prewar system after 1945. In view of these system properties one would expect that the level of party identification would not be lower than in the United States. However, there are a number of differences between the United States and the Netherlands which make a comparison of interest.

The first and most important difference refers to differences in the linkage between the political parties and the structure of the society. In a two-party system like that of the United States the two parties are forced to the middle of the political spectrum to maximise their votes. (Downs, 1957, Ch. 8). As a result political differences between the two parties become minimal or at least less than in a multi-party system. Therefore the political platforms of parties give the voters insufficient clues over time for deciding for which party they should vote.

Shiveley states that in such a situation voters learn to associate themselves with a particular party to avoid the expensive task of gathering enough political information to make their choice on some other basis. 'On the other hand, a voter who is a member of a clear and distinct social or economic group, for which he feels that some party or group of parties is the clear spokesman, may not need a further guide in voting. Since his social and economic position, coupled with the linkage of some party(ies) to that position, provides him with sufficient voting cues, he does not need to identify directly with a party.' (Shiveley, 1972, p. 1222). This hypothesis is consistent with the statement of Campbell and Valen that in a party system with a close relationship between the parties and the social classes, it is difficult to isolate the independent influence that party identification by itself has on the electorate (Campbell and Valen, 1966, p. 268).

If these hypotheses are correct, party identification should score low as an independent motivational force among Dutch voters. The linkages between the political parties on the one hand and religion and social class on the other have traditionally been very strong in The Netherlands. The history of the new parties that are not connected with any religious group or social class has been too short 'to develop a "taught" cadre of supporters' (Jennings, 1972, p. 459).

A second major difference is the electoral system. The United States has a district system. In each election people vote for an individual candidate. Therefore the personal qualities of the candidates play an important role in American elections in addition to political issues and party identification. One of the major heuristic advantages of the concept of party identification is that it offers the opportunity to distinguish short-term influences (candidates and issues) from lasting party attachment.

As election-specific influences seem to be much weaker in The Netherlands than in the United States, Dutch voters should not normally deviate from their possible party identification. The electoral system de-emphasizes the role of individual candidates. A good description of the Dutch electoral system is presented by Daalder and Rusk:

> The electoral law provides for a party-list system of proportional representation, in which votes are aggregated nationally, and seats are divided among numerous contesting parties according to the d'Hondt system of the largest average. Technically there are 18 districts which coincide largely with the boundaries of the 11 provinces. Parties present individual lists across the country for seat allocation purposes. Each voter may mark only one candidate. His vote accrues first to the national party and then to the district list. He can affect the election of a given candidate only if this candidate by himself obtains one-half the district list quotient (which is slightly below 1/150 of the total national vote). But in practice, the overwhelming majority of the electorate tends to vote for the top candidate on the party list. The rank-ordering of individual candidates on these lists, therefore, virtually decides a candidate's chance of election to parliament. This system makes party rather than individual candidates the chief actors in political campaigns. [Daalder and Rusk, 1972, p. 146]

In other words, candidates—as distinct from parties—play a very marginal role in Dutch politics. There is evidence that most people do not even know the names of the candidates. The impact of issues is probably also very modest in most elections. Therefore the sum total of election-specific events has probably much less effect than in the United States. One should therefore expect a very high level of congruence of party identification and vote preference.

### THE DUTCH DATA

We shall test these hypotheses against Dutch data. These data derived from a three-wave panel study that covers three successive elections, the provincial elections in 1970, the parliamentary elections in 1971 and the parliamentary elections in 1972. A nationwide random sample ($N=1,838$) was interviewed in 1970. Because of panel mortality this number was reduced to 1,266 in 1971 and to 972 in 1972. Full panel data are available for 834 respondents. In all three panel waves party identification was measured by this set of questions:

> Many people think of themselves as adherents of a certain party, but there are also people who do not.
> Do you usually think of yourself as an adherent of a certain party? (*If yes:*) Which party do you like best?
> Some people are strongly convinced adherents of their party. Others are not so strongly convinced. Do you belong to the strongly convinced adherents of your party or do you not? (*If not an adherent:*) Is there any party that you are closer to than the others? (*If yes:*) Which?

These questions are as similar as possible to the SRC questions.

## DISTRIBUTION OF PARTY IDENTIFICATION

In Table 4.1 the distribution of strength of party identification as observed in the three panel waves is presented. The aggregate distribution is quite stable over these three years. The percentage of people who spontaneously call themselves adherents of a political party is lower than in the United States (Campbell *et al.*, 1960, p. 124), Britain (Butler and Stokes, 1969, p. 38), Norway (Campbell and Valen, 1966, p. 251), Sweden (Särlvik, 1970, p. 259) and Denmark (Borre and Katz, 1973, p. 72) but higher than the percentage Max Kaase found with a similar question in the Federal Republic of Germany (Kaase, Chapter 5 below). It is hard to draw any direct inferences from the fact that the percentage of spontaneous adherents is lower in the Netherlands than in most of these other countries. There are at least two complications that make a direct comparison somewhat risky.

Table 4.1    Distribution of Strength of Party Identification in Three Successive Elections

|  | 1970 | 1971 | 1972 |
|---|---|---|---|
| Strong adherents | 18.0 | 17.1 | 22.3 |
| Weak adherents | 26.7 | 23.7 | 21.7 |
| Leaners | 32.2 | 31.5 | 33.6 |
| Independents | 23.1 | 27.7 | 22.3 |
|  | 100%(1838) | 100%(1260) | 100% (972) |

The Netherlands is involved in a process of political realignment. The religious parties especially have lost a great number of their adherents. This makes it very likely that the level of partisanship has decreased in the last ten years. A second caveat must be made with respect to the question wording. In the SRC questions the names of the (two) parties are mentioned. In Holland with its long list of parties this is not possible. The lack of this cue can lead to a lower number of spontaneous adherents. That this is so is suggested strongly by the fact that Max Kaase found the level of adherents at 54 per cent in 1967 with a question wording in which the parties were mentioned and only 29 per cent in 1969 when he used a question wording similar to ours (see Chapter 5 below). More important than the overall distribution of party identification, however, is the question whether party identification has the same properties in the Netherlands as it has in the United States.

## THE STABILITY OF PARTY IDENTIFICATION

An essential property of party identification is its long-term stability. On the one hand, the time between our first and last panel wave is too short to prove long-term stability. On the other hand, if we were to find that party identification is not even stable over such a short time, we can be sure that there is no long-term stability either. There is no objective criterion to define how stable party identification should be, especially not in a time of realignment. However, if party identification is a lasting psychological attitude towards a party that is relatively insensitive to short-term factors and does not completely define the vote, it should be more stable than vote preference. Even in a time of realignment one should expect that party identification changes at a slower pace than vote preference.

Table 4.2    Stability of Party Identification and Vote Preference

|  | stable vote preference | stable party identification |
|---|---|---|
| 1970–1971 | 80.3%* | 76.1% |
| 1971–1972 | 77.7% | 74.6% |
| 1970–1972 | 71.1% | 62.6% |

*i.e. 80.3% of the people who voted both times voted for the same party in both elections.

In Table 4.2 the stability of party identification is compared with the stability of vote preference. Party identification is clearly less stable than vote preference. In all three combinations of the panel waves the turnover of party identification is higher than the turnover of vote preference. A possible explanation for this surprising finding could be that party identification only indicates a lasting psychological attachment where this attachment is mentioned spontaneously. This applies to the strong and weak adherents. To test this possibility we have controlled the turnover tables for strength of party identification. The results are presented in Tables 4.3 and 4.4

Table 4.3    Stability of Party Identifcation, Controlled for Strength of Party Identification

|  | Strong | Weak | Leaners |
|---|---|---|---|
| 1970–1971 | 92.2% | 76.3% | 64.3% |
| 1971–1972 | 90.6% | 74.5% | 65.3% |
| 1970–1972 | 80.4% | 63.9% | 47.2% |

Table 4.4    Stability of Vote Preference, Controlled for Strength of Party Identification

|  | Strong | Weak | Leaners | Independents |
|---|---|---|---|---|
| 1970–1971 | 91.8% | 80.2% | 70.8% | 65.1% |
| 1971–1972 | 90.2% | 76.8% | 69.7% | 58.8% |
| 1970–1972 | 82.3% | 74.8% | 56.5% | 44.9% |

Strength of party identification does make a difference: the weaker the identification, the more difference there is between the stability of party identification and the stability of vote preference. There is hardly any difference between the stability of party identification and the stability of vote preference among strong adherents. Among weak adherents and leaners, party identification is less stable than vote preference. These findings make the value of the concept of party identification in the Netherlands very doubtful.

Now that we have found that party identification is less stable than vote preference, we should ask the question whether party identification is something more than an expression of volatile positive feelings toward a certain party at a particular moment, feelings caused by exactly the same circumstances that determine the vote. If this should prove to be the case it is very likely that party identification and vote preference are measuring one and the same phenomenon: the preference for a particular party at a certain moment.

## PARTY IDENTIFICATION AND VOTE PREFERENCE

If party identification and vote preference are measuring the same phenomenon, party identification loses one of its most important functions. In the United States party identification has become such an invaluable analytical concept, precisely because it offers the opportunity to distinguish short-term factors from long-term influences. This made it possible to determine the role of candidates and issues in each election.

A distinction between long-term forces (party identification) and short-term forces can be made only when party identification and vote preference are really different concepts. A perfect congruence between party identification and vote preference means that the two are conceptually the same. It could mean that in a particular election no short-term factors are at work and that therefore everybody is voting according to this party identification. The more deviations there are between party identification and vote preference, the greater the role of short-term influences would be.

Table 4.5    Consistency of Party Identification and Vote Preference, Controlled for Strength of Party Identification

|  | 1970 | 1971 | 1972 |
|---|---|---|---|
| Strong adherents | 98.3%* | 98.5% | 96.1% |
| Weak adherents | 92.3% | 92.9% | 92.2% |
| Leaners | 83.9% | 86.5% | 86.9% |
| Total | 90.9% | 91.7% | 91.2% |

*i.e. of the strong adherents who voted in 1970  98.3% voted for the party they identified with.

Counter-evidence to the hypothesis that there is no conceptual difference between party identification and vote preference is presented in Table 4.5. In all three years about 9 per cent of all voters with a party identification voted for a different party than the one they identified with. This percentage is lower than any comparable figure in the United States.

This is what we expected, mainly because of the differences between the two electoral systems. But although the deviations are small, it appears that, just as in the United States, the relationship between party identification and vote preference varies with strength of party identification (Table 4.5). In 1970 the proportion of strong adherents who voted for the same party as they identified with is 98.3 per cent. Among leaners it is no higher than 84.5 per cent. The traditional explanation for this variation is that people who do not strongly identify with their party are more sensitive to short-term influences and are therefore more likely to vote for a different party. However, this explanation is not the only one possible. Our hypothesis that party identification and vote preference are measuring the same attitude—party preference at a particular moment—can explain the different correlations between party identification and vote preference just as well. If we suppose that party identification and vote preference are two indicators for the same attitude, one should expect a certain level of unreliability of measurement. One should also expect that this unreliability is highest among people whose attitude has been developed less strongly, that means among people with a low level of party preference. If this hypothesis is correct the different figures in table 4.5 are different levels of reliability. There is no way to test this hypothesis directly, but indirect evidence supports our hypothesis very strongly. To test the reliability of questions on voting behaviour we repeated in the third wave the questions on voting behaviour in 1971 that were asked in the second wave (Thomassen, 1973).

In Table 4.6 the relationship between strength of party identification and the consistency of the answers to both questions about the vote preference in 1971 is presented. The strength of the relationship is surprising. The difference between strong adherents and leaners is about 14 percentage points. This is more than the difference between strong adherents and leaners with respect to the congruence of party identification and vote preference. If we now suppose that party identification and vote preference are two different indicators for the same concept, we have found that the reliability of two different indicators measured at the same time is influenced by the same variable that influences the reliability of one indicator over time. Again there is no direct evidence for the hypothesis that party identification and vote preference are measuring the same attitude, but at least this hypothesis can explain the observed deviations from party identification just as well.

Table 4.6    Strength of Party Identification 1971 and the Consistency
of Answers to Questions on Vote Preference 1971

| Answers to question on vote preference 1971 | Strong | Weak | Leaners | Independents | Total |
|---|---|---|---|---|---|
| Consistent | 95.5[*] | 85.7 | 81.0 | 76.9 | 84.7 |
| Not consistent | 4.5 | 14.3 | 19.0 | 23.1 | 15.3 |
| Total | 100% (132) | 100% (161) | 100% (205) | 100% (104) | 100% (602) |

[*]i.e. of those who answered both questions on vote preference 95.5% mentioned the same party.

## PARTY IDENTIFICATION AND VOTE PREFERENCE: CAUSAL SEQUENCE

The theory of party identification is very clear on the causal sequence of party identification and vote preference. Party identification is defined as a lasting psychological attachment towards a party, the relationship between party identification and vote preference being described as the relation between 'the psychological state and its behavioural consequences' (Campbell et al., 1960, p. 122). Goldberg observes that a causal model in which party identification is causally prior to vote preference indeed fits data on American voting behaviour (Goldberg, 1966).

Our findings in the last paragraph suggest that party identification is not conceptually different from vote preference. Another way to formulate this statement is that party identification is simply a reflection of the vote preference. This implies that in a causal model party identification should be found to be posterior to vote preference. If party identification really is a lasting psychological attachment to a party, a change in vote preference should not immediately be followed by a change of party identification. A change of party identification on the other hand—which should not occur very often—would normally not occur unless vote preference changes as well.

No country is more likely than the United States to have such a high degree of independence between party identification and vote preference. Butler and Stokes have shown that party identification changes more often in Britain than the United States. Their conclusion is based upon a comparison of the relation between stability of party identification and the stability of vote preference in Britain and the United States among the same respondents over three time-points (Butler and Stokes, 1969, pp.41-2). In both countries party identification was found to be more stable than vote preference, although there was more stability in the United States (92 per cent) than in Britain (83 per cent). There were a limited number of voters who changed their vote as well as their party identification, although in Britain this percentage was twice as high (13 per cent) as in the United States (6 per cent). In both countries the percentage of people who changed their vote preference but not their party identification was higher than the percentage who changed their party identification but not their vote preference. However, in the United States the difference was much more marked than in Britain. In the United States the ratio was 8:1, in Britain 2:1, which suggests that in Britain party identification is much less independent of vote preference than in the United States.

Table 4.7    Stability of Party Identification and Vote Preference in
Three Dutch Elections

|  |  | Vote preference | | |
|---|---|---|---|---|
|  |  | Stable | Not stable | Total |
| Party | Stable | 61 | 6 | 67 |
| identification | Not stable | 10 | 23 | 33 |
|  | Total | 71 | 29 | 100% |

Table 4.7 presents similar data for The Netherlands. Stable vote preference means that a respondent voted for the same party in 1970, 1971 and 1972. Stable party identification means that a respondent identified with the same party in all three panel waves. There is a dramatic difference between the Dutch data and the British and the American data. Not less than 23 per cent of all the voters in this table changed their party identification as well as their vote preference at least once. (We did not go into the question of whether these changes were symmetric). The most striking finding in this table is the difference between the upper right-hand and the lower left-hand cells. While only 6 per cent of the respondents change their vote preference without changing their party identification, 10 per cent change their party identification

without changing their vote preference. This finding is the exact opposite of what was found in Britain and in the United States.

Table 4.8    (a)–(c) Stability of Party Identification and Vote Preference in Three Elections Controlled for Strength of Party Identification in 1970

Table 4.8 (a)
Strong Adherents

|  |  | Vote preference | | |
|---|---|---|---|---|
|  |  | Stable | Not stable | Total |
| Party | Stable | 80 | 3 | 83 |
| identification | Not stable | 5 | 12 | 17 |
|  | Total | 85 | 15 | 100% |

Table 4.8 (b)
Weak Adherents

|  |  | Vote preference | | |
|---|---|---|---|---|
|  |  | Stable | Not stable | Total |
| Party | Stable | 61 | 5 | 66 |
| identification | Not stable | 12 | 22 | 34 |
|  | Total | 73 | 27 | 100% |

Table 4.8 (c)
Leaners

|  |  | Vote preference | | |
|---|---|---|---|---|
|  |  | Stable | Not stable | Total |
| Party | Stable | 41 | 9 | 50 |
| identification | Not stable | 13 | 37 | 50 |
|  | Total | 54 | 46 | 100% |

Again, one could think that our definition of party identification was too broad. One might argue that only when party identification is mentioned spontaneously, can one be sure that it refers to a lasting psychological attachment. This argument is refuted, however, by the evidence of Tables 4.8 (a)–(c). In these tables the relationship of Table 4.7 is controlled for strength of party identification in 1970. As we already observed, the stability of identification and the stability of vote preference vary with strength of party identification. However, the essential message of Table 4.7 is supported by the three sub-tables. In all cases the percentage of people who change their party identification but not their vote preference is higher than the percentage to which the reversed process applies.

These findings very strongly suggest that party identification is not causally prior to the vote, but simply a reflection of the vote and therefore causally posterior to the vote. We will now test this proposition by using a formal causal modelling technique, the Simon–Blalock method (Blalock, 1964). That this technique is very suitable for panel data was demonstrated by Boudon (Boudon, 1968).

The causal model that we shall test has six variables, party identification and vote preference, each measured at three different times. To explore the causal relations between these variables we will use the product–moment correlation coefficient (Pearson's $r$). This statistic can be used only for continuous variables and in a two-by-two table. Neither party identification nor vote preference meets this requirement. However, both variables can be made dichotomous if we restrict the analysis to one party. We will take the PvdA (Labour Party) as an example.

Party identification then has these two categories:

(a) All respondents who identify with the PvdA;

(b) All respondents who do not identify with the PvdA.

Vote preference has these two categories:

(a) All people who voted for the PvdA;

(b) All people who voted for a different party.

The analysis is restricted to those voting in all three elections and to those for whom complete panel data are available. The correlation matrix for the six variables is presented in Table 4.9.

Table 4.9    Correlation Matrix of Party Identification with and Vote Preference for P.v.d.A. 1970–1971–1972

|   | 1 | 2 | 3 | 4 | 5 |
|---|---|---|---|---|---|
| 2 | .56 | | | | |
| 3 | .49 | .60 | | | |
| 4 | .77 | .65 | .61 | | |
| 5 | .59 | .86 | .67 | .71 | |
| 6 | .52 | .67 | .80 | .66 | .75 |

```
1 = Party identification 1970
2 = Party identification 1971
3 = Party identification 1972
4 = Vote preference 1970
5 = Vote preference 1971
6 = Vote preference 1972
```

Two different models will be tested. Model 1 represents the traditional theory of party identification. Party identification is stable over time and defines the vote preference at each election. (The impact of other variables is excluded from the model.) The stability of vote preference can be explained by the fact that party identification is stable. Vote preference has no stability of its own. The alternative model 2 assumes that vote preference is stable (for whatever reason) and that party identification is no more than a reflection of the vote preference. Party identification therefore has a certain degree of stability because vote preference is stable.

By calculating partial correlations we will test which of the two models fits the data best. The minimal requirements for model 1 are that $r_{45.12}$ and $r_{56.23}$ are equal to zero. In model 2, $r_{12.45}$ and $r_{23.56}$ should be equal to zero. The observed values are $r_{45.12} = 0.30$, $r_{56.23} = 0.30$, $r_{12.45} = 0.08$ and $r_{23.56} = 0.02$.

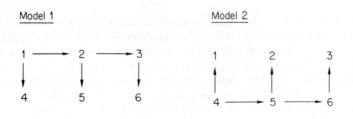

Model 1            Model 2

In model 1 party identification cannot fully explain the stability of vote preference. So the first revision that has to be made in model 1 is a direct link between the vote preference of the successive elections. This has been done in model 3.

Model 3

A complete test of model 2 and model 3 is presented in Table 4.10. It is clear that model 3 does not fit the data at all. Only three of the partial correlations that should not significantly differ from zero, are less than the critical value of 0.10 (with the number of cases in our analysis ($\pm$ 620) partial correlations of $\pm$ 0.10 are significant when $\alpha = 1$ per cent).

Table 4.10    Partial Correlations for testing Models 2 and 3

| | Model 2 | | | Model 3 | |
|---|---|---|---|---|---|
| Partial correlation | Expected value | Observed value | Partial correlation | Expected value | Observed value |
| $r_{42.5}$ | 0 | .11 | $r_{42.1}$ | 0 | .41 |
| $r_{43.56}$ | 0 | .12 | $r_{15.24}$ | 0 | .01 |
| $r_{46.5}$ | 0 | .27 | $r_{43.12}$ | 0 | .29 |
| $r_{13.456}$ | 0 | .02 | $r_{46.1235}$ | 0 | .14 |
| $r_{15.4}$ | 0 | .10 | $r_{13.2}$ | 0 | .23 |
| $r_{16.45}$ | 0 | -.03 | $r_{16.2345}$ | 0 | -.04 |
| $r_{35.6}$ | 0 | .18 | $r_{26.35}$ | 0 | .05 |
| $r_{26.5}$ | 0 | .07 | $r_{35.2}$ | 0 | .38 |
| $r_{12.45}$ | 0 | .08 | | | |
| $r_{23.56}$ | 0 | .02 | | | |

Model 2, on the other hand, fits much better. Not more than 4 of the partial correlations are higher than 0.10. The highest partial is between vote preference in 1970 and vote preference in 1972. This would suggest that people who change their vote at time 2 tend to return to their preference of time 1 at time 3. However, one should be cautious with this interpretation, because in the second category of vote preference all parties but the PvdA are included. But if this interpretation is correct, it fits very well with the 'homing' theory of voting behaviour. The problem is that this 'homing' tendency is normally explained by the fact that people now and then change their vote preference, but are inclined to return to their traditional choice because they have developed lasting feelings of attachment to this party. This explanation cannot be correct in this case, because in the model no causal impact of party identification on vote preference is assumed. Therefore an explanation should be found outside the model.

Model 4

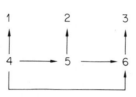

Table 4.11    Partial Correlations for Testing Model 4

| Partial correlation | Expected value | Observed value |
|---|---|---|
| $r_{24.5}$ | 0 | .11 |
| $r_{34.56}$ | 0 | .12 |
| $r_{13.456}$ | 0 | .02 |
| $r_{15.4}$ | 0 | .10 |
| $r_{16.45}$ | 0 | -.03 |
| $r_{35.46}$ | 0 | .11 |
| $r_{26.45}$ | 0 | .05 |
| $r_{12.45}$ | 0 | .08 |
| $r_{23.456}$ | 0 | .01 |

In model 4 the arrow from 4 to 6 has been drawn. Table 4.11 shows that this model fits the data almost perfectly. To account for the few minor deviations from the model in the data we must assume a direct link between party indentification at each successive point in time. This model 5 fits the data completely as is shown by Table 4.12.

Model 5

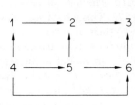

Table 4.12   Partial Correlations for Testing Model 5

| Partial correlation | Expected value | Observed value |
|---|---|---|
| $r_{24.15}$ | 0 | .04 |
| $r_{34.1256}$ | 0 | .08 |
| $r_{13.2456}$ | 0 | .02 |
| $r_{15.4}$ | 0 | .10 |
| $r_{16.45}$ | 0 | −.03 |
| $r_{35.1246}$ | 0 | .08 |
| $r_{26.145}$ | 0 | .04 |

A revision of model 3 such that the final model fits the data is quite complicated. Model 6 does fit the data, but leaves only three partials to predict ($r_{15.24}$ = 0.01; $r_{16.2345}$ = 0.04 and $r_{26.1345}$ = 0.02).

Model 6

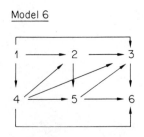

The problem now is that we have no criterion to decide which model is the correct one, model 5 or model 6. The technique of causal modelling does not enable us to prove whether a certain model is correct. Both models do fit the data. However, model 5 is more parsimonious than model 6. We feel that this information, in addition to the evidence that we have presented before, is a sufficient argument to draw the tentative inference that party identification is not causally prior to vote preference.

# THE TWO DIMENSIONS OF PARTY IDENTIFICATION

On the basis of this analysis we might tentatively conclude that the concept of party identification has no real meaning in the Netherlands. However, we have concentrated on one dimension of party identification only: its partisan direction. Using the same data Kent Jennings found that strength of party identification—the second dimension—correlates highly with voting turnout and other forms of electoral participation in The Netherlands. The correlations are even higher than in the United States. The same is true for consistency of voting, decisiveness in the making of electoral choices, and correctness of fit between self-image and party profile (Jennings, 1972, pp.468–9). How can one account for these findings? If party identification is not a psychological attachment, but simply a reflection of the vote preference, one might advance the hypothesis that the intensity of party identification really refers to the motivational strength of the vote preference at a particular moment. That the strength of the motivation to vote for a particular party is correlated with the variables we have just mentioned can easily be explained.

More confusing is the fact that there is a correlation between age and strength of party identification. The classic issue is whether this relationship represents a lifecycle effect or a generation effect. A possible explanation for generation effect could be that the traditional motivational forces of religion and social class have lost much of their impact on political behaviour among younger people. However, we have no evidence to support this hypothesis. The relationship between age and strength of party identification that has been found in several countries is usually explained as a life-cycle effect. Jennings observes that this age effect should not be interpreted as an effect of growing older, but as an effect of experience: 'The more often the voter reaffirms his conviction by supporting the party at the polls, and the more accustomed his perceptual and coding devices become to handling information about the parties in a standard fashion, the more entrenched becomes his attachment to the party' (Jennings, 1972, p.450).

If this conclusion is correct, it is not inconsistent with the results of our analysis *per se*. It would mean that there is a certain psychological attachment to political parties. However, party identification is certainly not a strong attitude, when even among strong identifiers this attitude cannot resist a change in vote preference.

## CONCLUSION

Let us now summarize the essential points in our analysis. The evidence on the question of whether party identification in The Netherlands represents a psychological attachment to a political party or not is inconclusive. However, a number of observations make the use of party identification in relation to voting behaviour in The Netherlands very doubtful:

    (*a*) party identification is less stable than vote preference;
    (*b*) what little evidence exists to the effect that party identification and vote preference can be distinguished can also be explained as unreliability of measurement;
    (*c*) there is strong evidence that party identification is not causally prior to vote preference.

These results leave us with two intriguing questions. Why have lasting psychological attachments to the political parties—as distinct from consistent voting records—developed in the United States but not, or less so, in The Netherlands? And secondly, if Dutch people did not develop strong and lasting attachments to their political parties, how could the party system remain relatively stable for such a long time?

The–speculative–answer to both questions is to be found in the Dutch system of *verzuiling*, or segmentation. Definitions of *verzuiling* have tended to differ and the number of *zuilen* or pillars one chooses to use in analysis depends on the definition chosen. Catholics and Protestants have organized themselves separately at almost every level of society. Lijphart mentions the 'alemene' or 'general' *zuil* as a third piller (Lijphart, 1968, Chapter 2). This really means lumping the remainder together. Within this group social class is an important dividing line. The socialists especially have constructed their own network of organizations, very similar to the way Catholics and Protestants have organized themselves. Therefore the socialist sub-culture is sometimes called a *pseudo-zuil* (Thurlings, 1971, p.15). Each pillar traditionally has its own political party (or parties). The Catholics were politically organized in the KVP, the socialists in the PvdA. The political organization of the Protestant pillar was more complicated. The ARP had its clientele mainly among the orthodox Calvinists, the CHU among the Dutch Reformed. GVP and SGP are two conservative splinter parties with an orthodox Calvinist background. The VVD is the fifth traditional party. It is the antipole of the PvdA on the social class line and is supported mainly by the upper-middle class. So the traditional political parties are deeply rooted in the social structure of Dutch society. For a long time politics provided set alternatives to a great number of Dutchmen. Belonging to a certain pillar, one voted almost automatically for the party that was associated with it. This rigid relationship of the political parties to the different sub-cultures can explain why there was weak psychological attachment to political parties as such and why yet the political system could remain very stable. The identification with the political parties was for most people only indirect. For a Catholic voting for the Catholic party was part of his role behaviour. As far as group identification was important in this process, the identification was probably more with the Catholic sub-culture and much less an identification with the associated political party *per se*. An analogous process applied to Calvinists and socialists. At the same time the system could remain stable as long as the relative strength of the different sub-cultures remained the same and as long as the relationship between religion and social class on the one hand and political behaviour on the other did not change. The rapid changes in the Dutch party system of the last decade can to a great extent be explained by two processes. First, a great number of people lost their religious attachment and therefore indirectly their attachment to the associated political party. Secondly, a number of people no longer allowed their political choice to be determined by their religious attachment.

## REFERENCES

Blalock, H. M. (1964), *Causal Inferences in Non-experimental Research*, University of North Carolina Press, Chapel Hill, N.C.

Borre, Ole, and Daniel Katz (1973), 'Party Identification and its Motivational Base in a Multiparty System: a Study of the Danish General Election of 1971, *Scandinavian Political Studies*, **8**, 69–111.

Boudon, Raymond (1968), 'A New Look at Correlational Analysis', in Hubert M. Blalock, Jr and Ann B. Blalock (eds.), *Methodology in Social Research*, Mc Graw Hill, New York.

Butler, David, and Donald Stokes (1969), *Political Change in Britain*, Macmillan, London.

Campbell, Angus, Gerald Gurin and Warren Miller (1954), *The Voter Decides*, Row, Peterson and Co, Evanston, Illinois.

Campbell, Angus, Philip Converse, Warren Miller and Donald Stokes (1960), *The American Voter*, Wiley, New York.

Campbell, Angus, and Henry Valen (1966), 'Party Identification in Norway and The United States', in Angus Campbell, Philip Converse, Donald Stokes and Warren Miller, *Elections and the Political Order*, Wiley, New York.

Converse, Philip (1966), 'The Concept of a Normal Vote', in Angus Campbell *et al., Elections and the Political Order*, Wiley, New York.

Converse, Philip, and George Dupeux (1966), 'Politicization of the Electorate in France and The United States', in Angus Campbell *et al., Elections and the Political Order*, Wiley, New York.

Converse, Philip (1969), 'Of time and Partisan Stability', *Comparative Political Studies*, 2, 139–71.

Daalder, Hans, and Jerrold G. Rusk (1972), 'Perceptions of Party in the Dutch Parliament', in Samuel C. Patterson and John C. Wahlke (eds.), *Comparative Legislative Behaviour*, Wiley, New York.

Downs, Anthony (1957), *An Economic Theory of Democracy*, Harper and Row, New York.

Goldberg, Arthur S. (1966), 'Discerning a Causal Pattern among Data on Voting Behaviour', *American Political Science Review*, 60, 913–22.

Jennings, M. Kent (1972), 'Partisan Commitment and Electoral Behavior in the Netherlands', *Acta Politica*, 7, 445–70.

Lijphart, Arend (1968), *Verzuiling, pacificatie en kentering in de Nederlandse politiek*, De Bussy, Amsterdam.

Särlvik, Bo (1970), 'An Overview of the Swedish Elections, 1964–1968', *Scandinavian Political Studies*, 5, 241–83.

Schleth, Uwe, and Erich Weede (1971), 'Causal Models on West German Voting Behavior', in Rudolf Wildenmann (ed.), *Sozialwissenschaftliches Jahrbuch für Politik*, 2, 73–97.

Shiveley, W. Phillips (1972), 'Party Identification, Party Choice and Voting Stability: the Weimar Case', *American Political Science Review*, 66, 1203–25.

Thomassen, J. (1973), *De betrouwbaarheid van vragen over kiesgedrag*, mimeo.

Thurlings, J. (1971), *De wankele zuil*, Dekker en van de Vegt, Amsterdam.

# 5

# Party Identification and Voting Behaviour in the West German Election of 1969 *

MAX KAASE

## CONCEPTUAL PROBLEMS IN THE ANALYSIS OF VOTING BEHAVIOUR

The general election of 1969 marks an important political change in the short history of the Federal Republic. It brought an end to twenty years of political dominance by the Christian Democratic Party (CDU) and its Bavarian sister-party, the Christian Social Union (CSU). Many middle- and long-range consequences of this change in political power could have been the legitimate focus of attention and analysis, but it is quite clear that electoral sociologists were particularly fascinated by the new ratio between electoral stability and electoral change that had come to light in the result of the election.

The question of why people voted the way they did this time can be approached from different angles. Those more concerned with the conditions of stability in democratic political systems may be more interested in discovering what leads many people to choose the same party election after election regardless of what goes on in everyday politics and why. Those more interested in the propensities for change in political systems may put their efforts into analyses that enlighten the psephologists about conditions of fluctuations in voting behaviour. Both perspectives are equally legitimate, and common to both is the search for processes of socialization, influence and information as determinants of the individual voting decision.

The stability or volatility of party preferences is, of course, not only relevant for the analysis of *individual* voting behaviour. Individual ballots are aggregated to party shares which reflect the stability or volatility of the party system and overall political system—the case of the Weimar Republic serves as a most suitable though extreme example for the potential system consequences of major shifts in individual party preferences.

The comparisons of aggregate party strength in consecutive elections does not, however, provide an immediate and reliable clue to the ratio of individual voting stability and change (Kaase, 1967). Cohorts move in and out of the electorate at rapid

---

* This is a substantially edited English translation of 'Determinanten des Wahlverhaltens bei der Bundestagswahl 1969', *Politische Vierteljahresschrift*, 11, 1970, pp.46ff. This translation has also been cut in length by eliminating many of the concrete references to the 1969 election. A short paragraph about recent research on party identification in West Germany has been added to bring the reader up to date on the literature.

rates (Butler and Stokes, 1969); different groups are politicized by specific electoral stimuli; and there are, of course, individual changes of voting behaviour. All of these variables have their impact on the outcome of an election, although the full amount of gross movement in the electorate is usually concealed because the effects of the variables have a tendency to cancel each other out.

The concern with elections and electoral behaviour has a considerable tradition in political sociology (Heberle and Rokkan, 1969). A long road has been travelled from the first analyses of André Siegfried to the work of Paul F. Lazarsfeld and his colleagues and the sophisticated approaches of Angus Campbell and his collaborators at the Survey Research Center in Ann Arbor. The initial enthusiasm for the new methodology of survey research has been replaced by a more critical evaluation, and the scepticism about electoral analyses on the basis of aggregate data that culminated in the detection of the ecological fallacy (Alker, 1969) has now made way for new definitions of problems establishing better chances for more complex theories of political behaviour in combining different types of data.

'The style set in the Erie County study of voting, *The People's Choice*, threatens to take the politics out of the study of political behavior' (Key and Munger, 1959, p.281). This style, also characterized as 'static social determinism' (Stokes, 1966, pp.19ff.) and looked upon by many psephologists in a similar manner, has probably been attacked not only because of its limited explanatory power. There is considerable evidence in the literature that the political analysts of democratically organized societies (who usually show a certain amount of personal involvement in their object of analysis) are particularly challenged by the possibility that a large part of the electorate makes political decisions on the basis of a poorly structured and very skinny political belief system (Narr and Naschold, 1971).

An important theoretical consideration that can be brought to bear on the phenomenon of stable party preferences refers to the 'freezing' of social and political institutions like party systems, which may represent the social cleavage structures of the past, but have since long been detached from these cleavage structures (Lipset and Rokkan, 1968). This or a slightly different interpretation of party systems as independent 'systems of channelment' (Sartori, 1968, p.21) are corroborated by the function of parties as generalized means of orientation for the reduction of complex information whenever individual political decisions are required. The symbolic meaning of parties is particularly efficient in reducing information costs if a close relationship between parties and other organized interests like trade unions or churches has been institutionalized. If such a situation exists, a high rate of transmission of generalized preference structures into individual behavioural patterns can be expected. In other words, to the extent that a party system still represents at least symbolically relevant sociopolitical cleavage structures, one can, under conditions of low political involvement and information, assume high levels of stable voting behaviour (Converse, 1962).

When it comes to the analysis of changes in voting behaviour concepts other than those used to explain consistent voting behaviour are apparently needed although even then politics would not necessarily have to come into play. For example, within the framework of reference group theory, one could expect that social and regional mobility would induce changes in voting behaviour as an adjustment to new social contexts. These changes as such would be completely apolitical. Also eliminating the certainly existing but probably very small group of voters that changes party lines accidentally and at random, we arrive at a hard core of those voters for whom political matters have been decisive in changing their party preference.

Only at first sight is the change of party preferences an unambiguous concept, and in fact the operationalization of the floating voter has turned out to be a central and at the same time bothersome problem in the analysis of voting fluctuations. The extensive discussion in the literature does not need to be taken up in this paper (e.g. Daudt, 1961; Key and Cummings, 1966; Kaase, 1967). The important thing to be kept in mind is that the respective analyses are highly dependent on the seemingly technical decision of operalization which in fact reflects specific theoretical concepts.

The discussion of the floating vote among psephologists has been heavily influenced by the work done by Angus Campbell and his associates (Campbell and Kahn, 1952; Campbell *et al.*, 1954; Campbell *et al.*, 1960; Campbell *et al.*, 1966). Their later work on changes in party strength in turn is itself very much based on the concept of critical elections initiably developed by V. O. Key (1955). The core idea here is that voters in so-called 'critical' (or 'realigning') elections establish new and long-term psychological relationships to political parties. The analytically intriguing property of this perspective is that actual voting behaviour at a given election is no longer automatically accepted as a sufficient indicator for a standing long-term party preference. Instead, an intervening analytical concept is added that represents exactly this kind of standing preference, an attachment to a political party that is not weakened by occasional deviations in voting choice at particular elections. This long-term psychological attachment to a certain party has long since made its way into the literature under the label of party identification (Belknap and Campbell, 1952; Campbell *et al.*, 1954; Campbell *et al.*, 1960; Campbell and Valen, 1966; Converse and Dupeux, 1962; Valen and Katz, 1964; Zohlnhöfer, 1965; Butler and Stokes, 1969; Converse, 1969a; Kaase, 1970).

The analytical usefulness of this concept, based on a theory of critical elections, had to be established by a test of whether party identification really reflects a stable attitude dimension from which deviations in voting may occur under specific conditions but which remains basically unchanged by such deviations. At least for the United States, Converse (1964, 1966a, 1969b), in a nationwide three-wave panel study (1956, 1958, 1960), has been able to show that there is indeed a substantial amount of not only aggregate, but also individual stability in party identification over time. Whereas this empirical evidence is by no means overwhelming (Pomper, 1967), it provided at least some safe ground from which to continue working.

The analytical and operational distinction between party identification and the vote is the basis for the separation of the short-term components and long-term components of any particular election. This has far-reaching consequences for the strategies of analysis. Long-term influences may have produced—possibly on the occasion of a critical election—a certain distribution of party identification across the population, and 'the roots of the . . . phenomenon lie so deep in the past that it is doubtful if the data gathered can help to explain them' (Converse, 1966a, p.15). The short-term component, on the other hand lies clearly in the present, acts directly on the voting decision and is basically political in nature. With this conceptualization we have come full circle.

Socio-structural determinants in a given historical and political context have established stable and lasting relationships between individual voters and the political parties. These relationships can be operationalized and measured via the variable party identification of which it itself is no longer in the focus of explanatory interest. The deviation from this 'normal vote' at a given election reflects the political flavour of this election, be it shaped by persons or issues or both (Stokes, 1966). So, finally politics comes back into the analysis of political behaviour.

The relevance of this analytical device for the evaluation of party changes is convincingly documented in the discussion of the importance of the religious factor in the USA presidential elections of 1960 and 1964. It was specifically the calculation of a normal vote for the religious groupings that demonstrated that, contrary to the general interpretation, John F. Kennedy in 1960 actually suffered a net loss because of his Catholic denomination. Even more relevant is the fact that an analysis of change between the 1960 and the 1964 election would have pointed to a religious factor acting also in the campaign of 1964, when in fact only the reduced importance of religion triggered the large return of Protestants with a Democratic party identification to support for the Democratic party (Converse 1966b; 1969b).

Further encouragement along those lines is presented in a causal modelling analysis that evaluates the relative impact of a set of socio-structural and attitudinal variables on the vote (Goldberg, 1966). After testing four different models Goldberg concludes that 'party identification rather than partisan attitudes proves to be the pivotal encapsulator of political socialization' (p.919), a result that is very much in line with what one would expect on the basis of the theoretical reasoning behind the concept of party identification.

## PARTY IDENTIFICATION IN WEST GERMANY

The theoretical rationale behind the concept of party identification has been briefly sketched in the previous section of this article. The cross-national usefulness of the concept depends basically on two related sets of factors. First, the central elements of the concept—stability over time, magnitude and distinguishability from the vote—have to be assessed in comparative perspective. Second, the problem of equivalence of indicator has to be coped with.

There is good reason to anticipate difficulties in trying to use the concept of party identification in Germany. Some of the relevant arguments have been presented very thoroughly by Converse (1969a), and it may at this point suffice to recall his emphasis on the interruption of the democratic process from 1933 to 1945 and the lack of continuity in party labels over an even longer period of time. While both variables would lead one to expect a comparatively lower level of overall party identification, Converse is very careful to point out that time estimates for the establishment of party identifications derived from his model may be unnecessarily inflated when politicized mass organizations are available to mediate between the individual and the party system, an extemely valid assumption for Germany.

The article by Converse also emphasizes a caveat that is typical for comparative research and particularly troublesome in the case of party identification. His analysis is based on the data from the Almond–Verba five nations study and uses a set of questions that, in its manifest meaning, is clearly different from questions about voting intentions or past voting. But does it fully cover the meaning of party identification with all its necessary elements?

For Converse this question is not at stake in his particular analysis, since he is interested only in a general sense of party loyalty and the processes by which it is established. But, as has been pointed out before, this feeling of party loyalty is conceptually and analytically different from party identification in the strict sense, and one can wonder whether it is a wise strategy to use the two concepts interchangeably as Converse does. With respect to this it is interesting to turn to the analysis of political change in Britain in which Butler and Stokes (1969), on the basis of their analyses, make a clear distinction between party identification and 'partisan self-image'.

While one would expect that the interruption of the democratic process in Germany had certain effects on the development of party loyalties—as the Converse analysis does indeed show—it is not surprising that economic growth and the institutionalization of the democratic process in postwar Germany have together encouraged a general acceptance of democratic institutions and behaviour in Germany (Almond and Verba, 1963). Political parties are among those accepted institutions, as the data in Table 5.1 show. These data have been selected from an extraordinary wealth of data on the grounds that, according to the authors who present them, they purport to measure party identification—although the indicators clearly reflect just a general sense of party loyalty (Zohlnhöfer, 1965; Wildenmann, 1968a, 1968b, p.33; Converse, 1969a).

Table 5.1 Different measures of party identification

|  | Zohlnhöfer | Wilden-mann ** | Wilden-mann ** | Converse |
|---|---|---|---|---|
| Party * Loyalty | 1961 % | 1965 % | 1967 % | 1969 % |
| Yes | 72 | 81 | 69 | 68 |
| No | 12 | 15 | 26 | 24 |
| Don't know) N.A. ) | 16 | 4 | 5 | 8 |

\* For full documentation of question wording see the references to the literature. All percentage distributions are based on national samples.

\*\* Identical phrasing of question

The Wildenmann data are particularly problematic because a so-called scalometer, that assesses party sympathy on an eleven-point scale (+5 through 0 to —5), is applied. The party sympathy or 'party identification' percentages in the above table refer to those respondents who evaluate one party better than all the others. The 'non-identifiers' are those respondents who evaluate two or more parties equally well, although one would certainly argue the point that equal sympathy for two or more parties does not necessarily indicate a lack of attachment to parties as democratic institutions.

Undoubtedly the Zohlnhöfer (1965) data are closer to what the party identification concept is about. Nevertheless, he too used a problematic question about the best-liked party which clearly favours the *cognitive* element of party affiliation. He explicitly refers to this difference in cognitive content and justifies it because this specific wording of the questions produces comparable results to the US:

> Wie in Tabelle 1 wiedergegeben, bekennen sich 72,5% der amerikanischen und 76,5% der deutschen Befragten zu einer politischen Partei. Obwohl wir nun diese Werte nicht allzu wörtlich nehmen sollten, so dürfen sie doch als deutliches Anzeichen dafür gewertet werden, daß die hier zu analysierenden Erscheinungen in beiden Systemen von prinzipiell vergleichbarem Gewicht sind. [Zohlnhöfer, 1965, p.133]

The strategy of aiming for an indicator that produces comparable levels of party indentification has obvious pitfalls. Not only does the diverging historical development of the two countries lead one to expect differing *levels* of party identification, but there are also sufficient differences in the makeup of political institutions and the political process in Germany (e.g. a centralized party system) that imply that the *meaning* of party identification as the party preference baseline—the normal vote—is not at all identical in the two systems.

Still, on the other hand, there is the amazing result that a division of parties into right, center and left for the elections to the Reichstag since 1903 showed a surprising similarity to the shares that these groupings won in the elections to the Bundestag since 1949 (Lepsius, 1966). Was it then that the basic political orientations had remained stable with merely the party nomenclature changed?

With all these pros and cons in mind the author, after a one-year research sojourn at the Survey Research Center in Ann Arbor, tried to develop a question that was aimed at capturing the theoretically relevant elements of the party identification concept:

> Generally speaking—do you think of yourself as a CDU/CSU adherent, SPD adherent, FDP adherent, NPD adherent, an adherent of another party, or do you not feel particularly attached to a political party? IF ADHERENT OF A PARTY: Are you a convinced adherent of the . . . or are you not particularly convinced? [The original question in German reads as follows:] Ganz allgemein gesprochen–betrachten Sie sich als CDU/CSU-Anhänger, als SPD-Anhänger, als FDP-Anhänger, als NPD-Anhänger, asl Anhänger einer anderen Partei oder Fühlen Sie sich keiner Partei besonders verbunden? WENN ANHANGER: Sind Sie ein überzeugter Anhänger der . . . oder sind Sie nicht besonders überzeugt?]

In retrospect and after the data became known, one might well tend to agree with Conradt (1972, p.51 n.42) that the word 'Anhänger' is a stronger word than simply 'adherent', and may have deflated the percentage of people willing to accept a clear party label: in December 1967 54 per cent of the German electorate indicated a strong (24 per cent) or weak (30 per cent) identification with a political party.

This was not a completely contra-intuitive result. Nevertheless, the measured level of party identification already violated a first important assumption of the party identification model which requires that a substantial part of the electorate is identified with a political party. The coming election of 1969 then provided an opportunity to test the second equally important assumption of the model, the individual stability of the party identification measure, on a follow-up panel to the 1967 study. This opportunity was unfortunately missed because of an error in questionaire composition: in the 1969 study, a party identification question was used that had been developed in a different context. This question no longer named the parties and asked only whether the respondent considered himself an *'Anhänger'* *(supporter) of a certain party or not (Kaase, 1970, pp.58f.).*

   The *1969 survey with this party identification question showed a dramatic drop in* the rate of identifiers to 29 per cent from the 54 per cent in 1967. The political context of the 1969 election, after more than two years of the 'big' (CDU/CSU–SPD) coalition, initially encouraged a substantive interpretation of this reduction in party identification, particularly because there was reason to assume that the 1967 question already was a 'hard' indicator of party identification. Still, there was sufficient uncertainty and puzzlement to warrant a further test of the impact of question phrasing on the assessment of party identification. In early 1970 the two party identification questions used in the 1967 and 1969 studies were once again put before the West German electorate, although this time in a split-half procedure, i.e. using one type of question with a randomly chosen half sample of the electorate and the other type of question with the other half sample of the electorate. In Table 5.2, results of this test are compared with the 1967 and 1969 results.

Table 5.2    Split-half of level of party identification

| Party Identification | 1967 (2002) | 1969 (992) | Split Half 1967 question (1005) | 1969 question (1003) |
|---|---|---|---|---|
| | % | % | % | % |
| Yes | 54 | 28 | 49 | 27 |
| No | 45 | 71 | 50 | 72 |
| Don't know, N.A. | 1 | 1 | 1 | 1 |

   It can well be argued that both sets of distribution are, considering the sampling error, identical for all practical purposes. Hence the split-half test clearly demonstrated that the changes in overall identification from 1967 to 1969 are a mere artefact of changes in question wording.

   Even if the 'easier' of the two questions is used, the overall extent of party identification assessed by this indicator does not suffice to apply the 'normal vote' model. But what about the relationship between party identification and the vote? As Table 5.3 shows, the expected differences between strong and weak identifiers also did not emerge.

   The observed differences between the two groups of identifiers are very small and, in the case of the SPD-identifiers, they do not even point in the 'right' direction. It seems only fair, however, to raise the question of whether the high correspondence between the two measures is not due to the fact that the 'difficult' 1969 indicator of party identification has been used for this particular analysis. My own analysis, as well as the causal analysis by Schleth and Weede (1971) does, however, corroborate the above data and show that, whichever of the two party identification questions is used, the analytically central postition of party identification in its own right is not borne out. This difference carries particular weight because Schleth and Weede tailored their causal model as much as the data allowed to the model presented by Goldberg (1966).

   The discontinuity of the party identification question in the German 1967–1969 panel does not allow for an exact test of the extent to which changes in party

Table 5.3

Ranking of Parties**                                          Party Identification 1969*
First place

|  | Strong CDU/ CSU | Weak CDU/ CSU | Independents | Weak SPD | Strong SPD | Other parties | Total |
|---|---|---|---|---|---|---|---|
| CDU/CSU | 92 | 90 | 45 | 2 | 6 | 18 | 44 |
| SPD | - | 5 | 39 | 96 | 94 | - | 42 |
| FDP | - | - | 6 | - | - | 64 | 5 |
| NPD | - | - | 1 | - | - | 9 | 1 |
| ADF | - | - | 1 | - | - | 9 | 1 |
| No answer/refused | 8 | 5 | 8 | 2 | - | - | 7 |
| Total | 100% | 100% | 100% | 100% | 100% | 100% | 100% |

\* Both questions were from the September 1969 survey (N = 992)

\** The exact wording of the question was: "Hier sind (nochmals) 5 Karten. Auf diesen Karten stehen die Name von politischen Parteien. Würden Sie bitte diese Karten danach ordnen, wie Ihnen die Parteien gefallen. Ganz oben soll dann die Partei liegen, die Ihnen am besten gefällt und so weiter. Ganz unten liegt dann die Partei, die Ihnen am wenigsten gefällt."

identification co-vary with changes in the vote. That such covariations take place has already been argued by Campbell and Valen (1966, p.268), although their data base is equally unsatisfactory. Their interpretation of the differences between Norway and the United States in this respect is based on the differences in party–class relationships and can be generalized to other European party systems. Fortunately the Butler–Stokes panel data allow a reliable assessment of the relationship between changes in party identification (respondents' partisan self-image) and changes in the vote. They conclude that 'in the main, partisan self-images and electoral preferences travel together in Britain far more than in America' (p.40) and further strengthen the point of class-based voting by stating that 'the links of party to class survived in the minds of many electors whose party preferences shifted during the period of our research and these perceptions must often have contributed to a return to traditional preferences' (p.299).

Although the available data, particularly in the German case, are not satisfactory, comparative analyses of party identification in Western Europe seem to indicate that the elements of party identification that constitute the basis for the sophisticated analyses of changes in voting behaviour in the United States are not sufficiently present in comparable party identification assessment in Western Europe. The respective analyses in European countries have also pointed to the socio-structural roots of party systems and corresponding individual party preferences as the main determinants of the difficulties in generalizing from the specific US party identification model.

The reference to the established cleavage structures and their frozen images in the party systems of Western Europe will probably become more and more meaningless as social change undermines, at an increasing speed, what is still left of the traditional cleavage structures. Therefore it is not at all unreasonable to keep party identification in the standard repertoire of 'priority variables in comparative electoral research' (Converse, 1968). Unfortunately, it could not be put to good use in the analysis of the West German general election of 1969.

## THE POLITICAL CONTEXT OF THE 1969 ELECTION

The general election of 1953 must be regarded as the first step towards the consolidation of the West German party system after the Second World War. The CDU/CSU increased her popular vote from 31.0 per cent to 45.2 per cent, and in the terminology of V. O. Key the 1953 election could be classified as a critical or 'realigning' election. A tremendous wealth of data corroborates the importance of economic factors for the alignment of voters with the CDU/CSU. An additional important factor was undoubtedly the hostile attitude of the Catholic Church towards the Social Democrats, the effects of which can be easily demonstrated in the voting behaviour of social groupings which could be expected to have a 'natural' bias in favour of the SPD (Kaase, 1967; Diekershoff, 1964).

An important aspect of the political system of the Bundesrepublik is the role of the chancellor. Many political 'philosophers' hold the opinion that, even in democracies, a symbolic figure for identification and orientation should be offered to the people. Whether this figure should also wield political power is an open question. In any case, the fathers of the German constitution, with the experiences of the Weimar Republic in mind, decided to create the office of the highest state representative—the Bundespräsident—as an institution without political weight. The lack of significance of this institution for the perception and interpretation of conflict politics may have contributed to a development that has moved the institution and person of the chancellor into the centre of interest. To what extent the dominating personality of Konrad Adenauer has additionally influenced this development cannot be precisely evaluated, but it is already historical truth that he won the election of 1957 with an overwhelming margin for the CDU/CSU.

The election of 1961 also received its flavour—although with opposite signs—from the institution of the chancellor when the controversies about the further chancellorship of Adenauer dominated the discussion rather than the Berlin crisis, which turned out to be of minor importance for the outcome of the election (Kaase, 1967; EMNID, 1962). In 1963, after long internal quarrels, Adenauer was finally replaced by Ludwig Erhard, who—with his fat cigar as a symbol of the economic recovery—once again succeeded in winning the population's sympathies for himself and the CDU/CSU.

Until 1965, the political landscape of the Bundesrepublik can be broadly characterized as follows.

(a) The successful economic policy and attractive personalities of candidates for the chancellorship enabled the CDU/CSU, sooner than any of the other parties, to establish a safe base for a permanent seizure of power by exhausting its socio-structural reservoir of voters;

(b) Exclusion from power in 1949 prevented the SPD from presenting itself as an attractive political alternative to the public. The essential social constituency for the SPD was the urban skilled labour force—groupings that had traditionally favoured the SPD. Decisive for the SPD was the fact, that during the period from 1949 to 1965, it was unsuccessful in even approximately exhausting this potential. Contrary to the CDU/CSU, neither Ollenhauer nor Brandt constituted real alternatives to Adenauer and Erhard for the office of the chancellor. In the area of issue politics the SPD caught up with the development in the Bundesrepublik only with the Godesberger Programm in 1959 which entailed a clear decision in favour of the Freie Marktwirtschaft.

(c) The continuing consolidation of the West German party system was indicated by the steady decrease of the share of the vote that the rest of the parties got at general elections. Interest parties of the 'first hour' representing refugees or farmers disappeared and their voters changed to either of the two large parties. Essentially, the FDP remained as 'third force' in the party system, but with a clear-cut preference for the CDU/CSU. The latter was most successful in the election of 1961, promising to guarantee a CDU/CSU- FDP coalition with Erhard as chancellor. The capitulation of the FDP (Der Umfall) after lengthy coalition talks, resulting in the acceptance of a further chancellorship of Adenauer, produced a public image of a party unable to stick to her campaign promises. The FDP still suffered from this image in 1965.

The 1965 general election once again clearly reinstated the CDU/CSU, with 47.6 per cent of the popular vote, as the uncontested favourite of the electorate. It did much better than expected after the disagreeable personal controversy between Erhard and Adenauer, who had denounced Erhard as being unfit fot the chancellorship. Therefore the interpretation of the election outcome as a personal success for Erhard was generally accepted, which in turn led to a self-definition of Erhard as 'chancellor of the people', separating him from his party and its support, and culminating in his decision to leave the extremely important position of party head to Adenauer.

The outstanding competence in economics ascribed to Erhard by the West German electorate is reflected by a full 75 per cent of the population attributing more competence to Erhard than to Brandt in economic policy; Brandt only got 8 per cent on this issue. But the general competence ascribed to the parties, too, showed the SPD in 1965 as an honorable, but not real alternative to the CDU/CSU (Table 5.4).

Table 5.4    Ascription of issue competence in 1965*

| Issues | CDU/CSU | SPD | Other/ N.A. | |
|---|---|---|---|---|
| Economic policy | | | | |
| Further improvement of economic situation | 61 | 30 | 9 | 100% |
| Stabilization of prices | 47 | 44 | 9 | 100% |
| Foreign policy | | | | |
| Good relationship to the US | 62 | 29 | 9 | 100% |
| European Unification | 60 | 30 | 10 | 100% |
| Reunification of Germany | 40 | 46 | 14 | 100% |
| Domestic policy | | | | |
| Age-protection | 47 | 46 | 7 | 100% |
| Educational policy | 46 | 45 | 9 | 100% |

* Data from 1965 national pre-election study

An evaluation of Ludwig Erhard in historical perspective is still lacking. Decisive for the negative reaction of the population in 1966 was his failure in an area where highest competence had always been ascribed to him: economic policy. The 1966 recession, with public finance almost ruined, removed Erhard from office and helped Herbert Wehner to put the final touches to a development that had been started in Bad Godesberg in 1959: the SPD for the first time entered a postwar federal government and got the chance to demonstrate its capacity to govern.

The establishment of the 'big coalition' was an equation with many unknowns not only for professional politicians and the public, but also for the analysts of politics: what would be the effects on the voter's evaluation of the democratic process, of the parties and the politicians, given that the FDP, with 49 out 496 seats, had become the smallest opposition ever seen in the Bundestag?

The low degree of public internalization of the conflict dimension and the decrease in the ideological distance between SPD and CDU/CSU led many observers to expect that the majority of the voters would settle comfortably with this new form of government. This expectation is indeed corroborated by data from several national surveys:

### The Big Coalition met your expectation

|  | Comple-<br>tely | Partly | Not at all | No answer |  |
|---|---|---|---|---|---|
| March 1969 | 26 | 60 | 8 | 6 | 100% |
| May 1969 | 30 | 58 | 7 | 5 | 100% |
| July 1969 | 29 | 58 | 7 | 6 | 100% |

An open-ended question "What do you think of the Great Coalition in Bonn?" had more negative results:

| 1968 (January) | Approval | 48% | Disapproval | 34% |
|---|---|---|---|---|
| 1969 (September) | Approval | 45% | Disapproval | 21% |

Table 5.5    Evaluation of the three parties 1961, 1965 and 1969

|  | Sympathy for the parties * | | |
|---|---|---|---|
|  | 1961[**]<br>% | 1961/1965[***]<br>% | 1965/1969[****]<br>% |
| **SPD** | | | |
| Positive evaluation (+5 to +3) | 36 | +3 | +23 |
| Negative evaluation (-1 to -5) | 24 | -2 | -18 |
| **CDU/CSU** | | | |
| Positive evaluation | 48 | 0 | +17 |
| Negative evaluation | 13 | +3 | -11 |
| **FDP** | | | |
| Positive evaluation | 17 | -5 | +14 |
| Negative evaluation | 21 | +11 | -16 |

* Each respondent was confronted with an eleven-point scale ranging from +5 to -5 and was asked to rate the parties on that scale.

** Data from the 1961 national pre-election survey of the "Wahlstudie".

*** Data from our 1965 national pre-election survey.

**** Data from our 1969 national pre-election survey.

The coalition did not even contradict long-term expectations: in July 1969 45 per cent of the voting age population wanted a big coalition even after the election, 36 per cent wanted a government formed by only one party and 10 per cent spoke in favour of a small coalition. This demonstrates one of the negative consequences of such a formation of government for a democratic system.

In the light of these data it is not surprising that the evaluation of the parties by the public had not suffered at all. With the exception of its early days, the coalition has stimulated a considerably improved evaluation of all three major parties (CDU/CSU, SPD and FDP), after the successful economic recovery had become apparent as its most visible achievement. This is summarized in Table 5.5.

The greatly improved rating of the SPD was brought about by, above all, a positive change in the mood of CDU/CSU-voters. This can be taken as a justification of Wehner's strategy to bring the SPD into the government. All in all, there is sufficient evidence to drive the point home that the improved party ratings primarily reflected the government's performance in the realm of economic policy.

Clearly, the two coalition parties have profited from this success unequally. Economic policy had always been the domain of the CDU/CSU, but with Professor Karl Schiller the SPD succeeded in bringing a man into office who very quickly gained great esteem for himself and his party. This has also been important for the SPD because of the chance to demonstrate that no socialization, no transformation of private means of production into public property and no slaughter of the 'holy cow' of Freie Marktwirtschaft would follow from her participation in government.

This development is reflected in the changes in sympathy for Schiller and Erhard (Table 5.6).

Table 5.6    Evaluating of Erhard and Schiller 1965, 1967 and 1969

| Sympathy rating | 1965 | 1967 | 1969 |
|---|---|---|---|
| Erhard |  |  |  |
| Positive evaluation (+5 to +3) | 56 | 29 | * |
| Negative evaluation (-1 to -5) | 13 | 25 | * |
|  |  |  |  |
| Schiller |  |  |  |
| Positive evaluation | ** | 40 | 65 |
| Negative evaluation | ** | 4 | 4 |

    * Data for Erhard were not collected in 1969. How forgotten Erhard already was is indicated by the fact that in September 1969 only 41% of the voting-age population remembered him as CDU/CSU candidate for the chancellorship in 1965. 23% named Kiesinger as the 1965 candidate!

  ** Data on Schiller were not collected in 1965.

There are more data to prove that the economic recovery was attributed disproportionately to Schiller. An open-ended question asking who was responsible for the improvement of the economic situation in the first place brought the following results:

| | | | |
|---|---|---|---|
| Big coalition | 15% | Schiller | 33% |
| SPD | 11% | Strauss | 14% |
| CDU/CSU | 11% | Kiesinger | 11% |

| | |
|---|---|
| Brandt | 3% |
| No answer | 21% |

A close-ended question asking who might have the best judgement concerning the problem of revaluation of the German mark, Kiesinger, Strauß or Schiller, yielded the following results:

| | |
|---|---|
| Schiller | 45% |
| Strauss | 21% |
| Kiesinger | 13% |
| No answer | 21% |

How favourable the impact of the big coalition on evaluation of the SPD by the electorate was can also be seen from the changes in issue competence between 1965 and 1969. In accordance with Converse's theoretical approach (1964), five *a priori*-defined belief dimensions were each represented by a series of issues which had to be rank-ordered *within* each given dimension. In the second run each respondent had to choose those five out of the total of twenty-one issues that he deemed most important for him personally. This selection had to be performed independently from the within-dimension rank-ordering. These five most important issues had then again to be rank-ordered.

This is the relative importance of the five dimensions, defined by the percentage of first ranks for each dimension:

| | (%) |
|---|---|
| 'Close to home' | 44 |
| (personal *v.* general welfare) | |
| Political Ideology | 17 |
| (law and order *v.* tolerance) | |
| Nationalism *v.* supranationalism | 12 |
| Representation of group interests | 10 |
| Conservatism *v.* progressivism | 8 |
| Not ascertained | 9 |
| | 100 |

Table 5.7 Evaluation of activism of two main German parties on the six issues ranked most important

| Issues | Percentage of respondents ranking the issue as most important | Parties | |
|---|---|---|---|
| | | SPD | CDU/CSU |
| | % | % | % |
| Increase of income and stable prices | 28 | 57 | 32 |
| Maintenance of law and order | 12 | 43 | 49 |
| Improvement of educational system | 10 | 58 | 39 |
| Representation of the interests of workers | 7 | 74 | 19 |
| Work for European integration even if national rights have to be given up | 7 | 62 | 50 |
| Construction and modernization of hospitals | 6 | 46 | 41 |

In the final stage of this analysis the respondents had to evaluate the political parties on a five-point scale for each of the five issues that were chosen as the most important ones. Table 5.7 shows the result for the six issues that received the highest number of first choices. The percentages for the parties represent those respondents who see the given party as very active in the particular issue area: It is not at all surprising that the 'close-to-home' issues are the most important ones for the public. It is, however, fascinating to see how strongly the balance of political forces has been shifted from 1965 to 1969 in favour of the SPD.

While it is appropriate to speak of very strong pro-SPD forces in the area of issue politics, the contrary is true when it comes to the evaluation of the two candidates for the chancellorship. In 1969, the CDU/CSU once again was in the fortunate position—as in all other general elections—to present with Kurt-Georg Kiesinger an enormously attractive candidate. This can be seen from Table 5.8.

Table 5.8    Sympathy ratings for Kissinger and Brandt 1961, 1965, 1967 and 1969

| Sympathy rating Kiesinger | 1961 | 1965 | 1967 | 1969 |
|---|---|---|---|---|
| Positive evaluation (+5 to +3) | * | * | 77 | 72 |
| Negative evaluation (-1 to -5) | * | * | 1 | 5 |
| Brandt | | | | |
| Positive evaluation | 40 | 35 | 45 | 58 |
| Negative evaluation | 18 | 29 | 12 | 6 |

* Data for Kiesinger were not collected in 1961 and 1965.

This sympathy rating for Kiesinger is particularly interesting if one considers that in September of 1966 an open-ended question, asking for the chancellor the respondent would like best, resulted in a popular vote of 0.6 per cent for Kiesinger, at that time Ministerpräsident of Baden-Württemberg. In December 1967, one year after the establishment of the big coalition, he got—on the same question—a popular vote of 70 per cent. How large, then, is the premium (measured in voter preferences) on the office of the chancellor independent of the person holding that office?

An interesting response pattern can be extracted from Table 5.9. The similarity between the data from 1965 and 1969 in spite of differing CDU candidates indicates that the office *per se* seems to exert a substantial influence. Fortunately the chancellorship of Willy Brandt, who could not bring the population to his side in

Table 5.9    Preference for Chancellor 1965 and 1969

| Preference for chancellor | March 1965 | March 1969 | May 1965 | May 1969 | Sept. 1965 | July 1969 |
|---|---|---|---|---|---|---|
| Erhard | 39 | X | 39 | X | 44 | X |
| Kiesinger | X | 39 | X | 43 | X | 42 |
| Brandt | 14 | 18 | 19 | 19 | 22 | 19 |

1969, will allow an interesting test of the hypothesis. For the election itself, a solid advantage of Kiesinger over Brandt is beyond doubt.

As significant as the establishment of the big coalition for the perceptions and evaluations of the political process in Germany by the population were, there was also a decisive change in the structure of the party system involving the FDP. The FDP as traditional coalition partner of the CDU/CSU had to develop a new self concept reflecting not only the failure of the CDU/CSU–FDP ties, but also the necessity to establish itself as parliamentary opposition against the CDU/CSU as leading government party. This inner conflict culminated in the election of the Bundespräsident in March 1969, when the FDP leadership, without proper legitimization by the party members, decided to vote for the SPD-candidate Gustav Heinemann, thereby almost tearing the FDP apart. Although at the time of the presidential election in Berlin the FDP denied any plans to join the coalition government with the SPD and continued to do so until the general election in September, it was apparent that the uncertainty about the decision of the voters with respect to the FDP added substantial flavour to an election that was already regarded by many as the most important one in postwar Germany.

## IV. STABILITY AND CHANGE IN THE 1969 ELECTION

The absolute number of people eligible to vote, people who voted and valid votes differed only slightly between 1965 and 1969 as can be seen from the following figures:

|  | 1965 | 1969 |
|---|---|---|
| Eligible to vote | 38,510,395 | 38,677,235 |
| Actually voted | 33,416,207 | 33,523,064 |
| Valid votes, second ballot | 32,620,442 | 32,966,024 |

The aggregate percentaged election returns for turnout and the parties in 1969 and 1965 are given in Table 5.10.

Table 5.10   Turnout and party vote (second ballot) in the general elections of 1965 and 1969

| Turnout and party vote (2nd ballot) | General elections | | |
|---|---|---|---|
|  | 1965 % | 1969 % | 1965-1969 |
| Turnout | 86.8 | 86.7 | -0.1 |
| CDU/CSU | 47.6 | 46.1 | -1.5 |
| SPD | 39.3 | 42.7 | +3.4 |
| FDP | 9.5 | 5.8 | -3.7 |
| Other parties | 3.6 | 5.4 | +1.8 |

While at first these figures seem to indicate a considerable stability over time, it is well known that such aggregate stability can conceal substantial movements within the electorate. Statistics show that from 1965 to 1969 roughly 2.5 million voters left the electorate involuntarily (i.e. they died). Another 2.5 million entered the electorate who were eligible to vote at a general election for the first time in their life. This leaves a total of about 33.5 million, or 87 per cent of the 1969 electorate, who were eligible to vote at both the 1965 and 1969 election. Of course, there are further fluctuations between non-voting in 1965 and voting in 1969 and vice versa, and there are also voters who changed party lines in 1969.

Table 5.11    Party choice 1969 (voting intention).

| Party choice 1965 (recall) | SPD | CDU/CSU | FDP | Other parties | Undecided | Nonvoters | Not ascertained | Total |
|---|---|---|---|---|---|---|---|---|
| SPD | 26.5* | 0.8 | 0.3 | - | 3.2 | 0.2 | 0.8 | 31.8 |
| CDU/CSU | 3.3 | 23.3 | 0.5 | 0.4 | 7.2 | 0.2 | 2.2 | 37.9 |
| FDP | 1.0 | 0.6 | 0.9 | 0.1 | 0.9 | - | 0.4 | 3.9 |
| Other parties | - | - | - | - | 0.3 | - | - | 0.3 |
| Nonvoters | 1.3 | 0.6 | 0.4 | - | 1.7 | 2.6 | 0.3 | 6.9 |
| Not eligible to vote | 1.7 | 1.9 | 0.5 | 0.2 | 2.0 | 0.1 | 0.5 | 6.9 |
| Not ascertained | 0.4 | 0.4 | 0.1 | 0.1 | 5.6 | 0.1 | 6.3 | 13.0 |
| Total | 34.2 | 27.6 | 2.7 | 0.8 | 21.0 | 3.2 | 10.5 | 100.0% |

* Percentages are based on the total sample of 992 cases from the September 1969 pre-election study.

In order to assess stability and change in the vote, the researcher has basically two options. If he is lucky, he has panel data for both elections. Usually he does not have such data, so his second best option is—as in this case—a study at time 2 and recall questions for time 1. Table 5.11 contains the matrix of information about voting behaviour in the 1965 election (recall) and the 1969 election (intention).

These data, however, leave much to be desired, since

(a) compared with the final result of the election, the distribution of preferences shows a strong pro-SPD bias in the sample;

(b) the high percentage of undecided voters without information about probable or past party choice eliminate more than one-third of the sample from the fluctuation analysis.

The SPD bias will not disturb comparative analyses between voter groupings too much, and it seems to be a further indication for the pro-SPD forces shaping the election. Moreover, it is known from many analyses that CDU/CSU voters are less politically interested than average so that there is nothing unusual in their under-representation in pre-election surveys. On the other hand, there is an estimation problem that cannot so easily be coped with. First, there is a significant under-representation of FDP strength in the 1965 (recall) vote. Second, there is not sufficient information to evaluate all respondents in terms of stability or change: fully 38.9 per cent of the total sample could not be classified because of lack of information for one or both of the elections.

With such data there is little point in trying to make a detailed analysis of the voter fluctuations in 1969. Consequently we will have to resort to ecological analyses in order to come to grips with the voter movements that reflected the political flavour of this election.

One of the reliable results of electoral research for the last decade in Germany has been the identification of electoral support for the major two parties in special strata of the electorate. The first major cleavage is religious: Catholics vastly prefer the CDU/CSU to other parties. The second cleavage is basically a class cleavage, with the primary sector of the economy heavily favouring the CDU/CSU (ruralism) and the secondary sector of the economy supporting the SPD (industrial working class). The ecological analysis of the 1969 election on the basis of all 248 constituencies clearly demonstrates that these cleavages were also in effect in 1969 (Kaase, 1970, pp.89ff.). As just one example, the two cleavages, when operationalized as percentage of the population who are Catholic or in agriculture, are reflected very clearly in the correlations and in the beta weights of a regression analysis with five independent, orthogonal variables (the additional variables were: percentage of male workers; percentage of female workers; percentage of population over sixty years of age) in Table 5.12.

Table 5.12

| Parties | Total variance explained by regression | Zero-order correlations | | Beta Weights | |
|---------|------------------|------------|------------|------------|------------|
| | | percentage of Catholics | percentage of agricultural population | percentage of Catholics | percentage of agricultural population |
| CDU/CSU | 82% | +0.66 | +0.72 | 45 | 55 |
| SPD | 82% | −0.59 | −0.74 | −35 | −55 |

These same indicators have been successfully used in survey analyses. With individual data more complex theoretical concepts can be tested, and numerous survey analyses have demonstrated that organizational proximity to interest groups representing the two major cleavages is the decisive variable: the closer a person is to his church, the more likely he is to vote CDU/CSU; the closer a person is to his trade union, the more likely he is to vote SPD (Diekershoff, 1964; Kaase, 1967; Blankenburg, 1967; Liepelt and Mitscherlich, 1968).

With the previous emphasis on stability in patterns of voting behaviour, the question that needs to be raised next is the extent to which the political pro-SPD forces governing the 1969 election were able to overcome the socio-structural inertia of the German electorate. The survey data presented above—even under the generous assumption that those respondents who were undecided at the time of the study had a special propensity to change—would not allow for a higher proportion of floating voters than 15 per cent of those eligible to vote at both the 1965 and the 1969 elections. Among those there is one substantial group of floating voters that shows up clearly even in this rudimentary tabulation: previous CDU/CSU voters who had decided in favour of the SPD in 1969. This turn of the tide is also corroborated by the ecological analyses, which show in addition that the CDU/CSU was able to play the game as well as it did only because it could take advantage of the traditional, 'old-middle class' FDP voters who were not willing to go along with an FDP–SPD coalition.

As unsatisfactory as ecological analyses frequently are for more refined demands, it is nevertheless fascinating to observe the extent to which the move of the FDP within the dimensional boundaries of the German party system was already reflected in the bivariate correlations between the FDP vote and socio-structural properties of the constituencies.

Analyses of the socio-structural background of the FDP voters have shown that until 1969 the FDP gained its electoral support from two quite different blocs: the 'old' middle class with well-to-do farmers and small businessmen on the one hand, and the 'new' middle class with prosperous white-collar workers and some skilled blue-collar workers on the other hand (Klingemann and Pappi, 1970). This essential balance is reflected in low correlation coefficients between socio-structural indicators and the 1965 FDP vote. In 1969, particularly when one looks at the regional variations, the FDP gained much clearer social contours keeping her 'new' middle-class voters and losing a substantial amount of her 'old' middle-class voters (Kaase, 1970, p.94).

The FDP move through the German party space is a unique phenomenon that deserves more detailed analysis. At this point it may suffice to stress that the decision of the FDP leadership to venture a coalition with the SPD almost eliminated the FDP from the political landscape. With a forty per cent reduction in voter response, the FDP hardly made it over the hurdle of the 'five per cent clause', and its dowry for the marriage with the SPD was certainly not what both parties had hoped for in order to establish a working coalition.

Nevertheless, the establishment of just that coalition was the decisive political consequence of the 1969 election, and the coalition became possible only because the SPD had been successful in continuing the upward trend that, since 1953, had brought it an average gain of 3.5 per cent of the popular vote in each election. The ecological analysis of the SPD gains in 1969 reveals a clear pattern that also holds in regional analyses: the higher the percentage of the population working in the tertiary sector of the economy, the higher the SPD increase in votes. As the corresponding survey data show, these increases did not make the SPD the majority party among the white-collar workers. They did, however, suffice to eliminate the traditional voter deficit of the SPD in these groups and reflected the essential political thrust in the election most adequately. The basis for this thrust has been characterized in the previous section of the article as trust in the newly proved ability of the SPD to govern, to maintain economic growth and to bring about changes in newly emerging issue areas where the CDU/CSU had failed to establish or corroborate her competence: the 'Ostpolitik' (eastern policy), social policy and educational policy.

## V. FURTHER DEVELOPMENTS IN THE ANALYSIS OF PARTY IDENTIFICATION—A POSTSCRIPT

In the four years since my initial article about the election of 1969 was published, more data have become available on the concept of party identification. In Germany, Günther D. Radtke (1972) has reported a two-wave panel analysis looking at the covariation of voting intention and party identification. Slightly re-percentagizing the original table presented by Radtke (p.77), one gets the results shown in Table 5.13.

Table 5.13

Party Identification

| Voting Intention | Stable (1170) % | Unstable (218) % | Total number of respondents in panel (4082) |
|---|---|---|---|
| Stable | 93 | 44 | |
| | 92 | 8 | % (1184) |
| Unstable | 7 | 56 | |
| | 40 | 60 | % (204) |

These data clearly corroborate previously mentioned analyses that point to the covariation between party identification and voting intention, although Radtke's analysis also suffers from a change in question wording from wave 1 (equivalent to the Kaase 1969 question) to wave 2 (p.70). In addition it must be noted that Radtke, in accordance with the previous analyses, reports that only roughly one-third of his respondents identified with a political party at all.

In the context of the general election of 1972, Manfred Berger discusses the preliminary results of a three-wave national panel study that was conducted in October, November and December of 1972 (Berger, 1973). This analysis is particularly interesting because Berger, in full recognition of the problems with previous party identification operationalizations, decided to move away from the too *literal* translation of the American question and to try a functionally *equivalent* translation. His formulation is:

Many people in the Federal Republic usually adhere to a particular political party for a long period of time although from time to time they may vote for another party, How about you: do you—generally speaking—adhere to a particular party?

IF YES: Which party is this?

How strongly or how weakly do you—all in all—adhere to this party: very strongly, rather strongly, moderately, rather weakly or very weakly?

[The original question in German reads as follows:]

Viele Leute in der Bundesrepublik neigen längere Zeit einer bestimmten politischen Partei zu, obwohl sie auch ab und zu mal eine andere Partei wählen. Wie ist das bei Ihnen: Neigen Sie–ganz allgemein gesprochen–einer bestimmten Partei zu? WENN JA: Welcher?

Wie stark oder schwach neigen Sie–alles in allem zusammengenommen–dieser Partei zu, sehr stark, ziemlich stark, mäßig, ziemlich schwach oder sehr schwach?

[Berger, 1973, pp.218f.]

The important change in this question is, of course, the *explicit* reference to the possibility that a voter may keep a basic preference for a given party and still vote for a different one at an election. Although this operationalization may appear heuristic to some, it nevertheless does not only result in quite comparable levels of party identification in Germany and the United States, but also shows almost identical party identification variations in the two countries over time (both studies were post-election panel studies).

Although the Mannheim 1972 election study is a panel study, it covers much too short a time period to assess the long-term stability of the party identification indicator. Berger's analysis does, however, cover the problem of covariations between party identification and the vote. The results of this analysis are very much in agreement with party identification research in other European political systems in pointing to a significant tendency of those respondents who deviated from their party identification in the vote to later adjust their party identification accordingly.

There is one major exception to this tendency which sheds an interesting light on the impact of institutional factors on voting behaviour. Forty-four per cent of the 'deviant' vote in 1972 goes to the FDP, comes from SPD identifiers and leaves their SPD identification basically (91 per cent) intact. The assessment of deviation is based on the second ballot, which in the German electoral system is decisive for determining the number of seats a party gets in the Bundestag. Clearly this particular SPD 'deviation' merely reflects the strategic choice of many SPD partisans to assure the FDP a sufficient percentage of the vote to overcome the restrictive 'five-percent-clause' that had been put into the German electoral law to prevent a disintegration of the party system as it had occurred in the Weimar Republic.

This information could as well have been gleaned from a combined analysis of the first and second ballot and is a specific reflection of a unique institutional regulation. Therefore, the party identification model does not yield any additional explanatory power. Since this particular group of 'deviant' voters must also be excluded from consideration in the analysis of the party identification–vote relationship, this actually *increases* the percentage of voters who adjust their party identification to a previously deviant vote, a further thrust against the analytical usefulness of the party identification model.

It is not surprising that Berger concludes his analysis on a sceptical note and once again poses the previously raised question of the extent to which it is not really the parties, but other social groups who are the original focus of orientation and attachment for the individual citizen. Likewise, in his excellent analysis of a three-wave panel study of Dutch voters, which also fails to establish the independent role and high stability of party identification, Jacques Thomassen (Chapter 4, above) refers to the primary importance of social reference groups, the well known phenomenon of *verzuiling* in Dutch politics.

On the basis of those analyses it is difficult to share Shively's optimism about 'an interesting development of European voting behaviour, by which it should tend in the future to be based more on party identification than it has been so far' (Shively, 1972, p.1224) One would rather be inclined to support a position shared by Thomassen (Chapter 4, above), Miller (Chapter 2, above) and Jennings (1972) that de-emphasizes the importance of party identification for the analysis of voting behaviour and focuses more on the function of party identification as an element of the individual's political belief system and its capability to reduce information costs as well as to constrain diffuse bits of political perception.

## REFERENCES

Alker, Hayward R. Jr. (1969), 'A Typology of Ecological Fallacies', in Mattei Dogan and Stein Rokkan (eds.), *Quantitative Ecological Analysis in the Social Sciences*, MIT Press, Cambridge, Mass.

Almond, Gabriel and Sidney Verba (1963), *The Civic Culture*, Princeton University Press, Princeton, New Jersey.

Belknap, George, and Angus Campbell (1952), 'Political Party Identification and Attitudes Towards Foreign Policy', *Public Opinion Quarterly*, 15, 601–23.

Berger, Manfred (1973), 'Parteienidentifikation in der Bundesrepublik', *Politische Vierteljahresschrift*, 14, 215ff.

Blankenburg, Erhard (1967), *Kirchliche Bindung und Wahlverhalten*, Walter Verlag, Oeten/ Freiburg L. Breisgau.

Butler, David, and Donald E. Stokes (1969), *Political Change in Britain*, Macmillan, London.

Campbell, Angus, and Robert L. Kahn (1952), *The People Elect a President*, Survey Research Center, University of Michigan, Ann Arbor, Michigan.

Campbell, Angus, Gerald Gurin and Warren E. Miller (1954), *The Voter Decides*, Row, Petersen, Evanston, Illinois.

Campbell, Angus, *et al.* (1960), *The American Voter*, Wiley, New York.

Campbell, Angus, *et al.* (1966), *Elections and the Political Order*, Wiley, New York.

Campbell, Angus, and Henry Valen (1966), 'Party Identification in Norway and the United States', in Angus Campbell *et al.*, (eds.), *Elections and the Political Order*, Wiley, New York.

Conradt, David P. (1972), 'The West German Party System: An Ecological Analysis of Social Structure and Voting Behavior, 1961–1969', *Sage Professional Paper* (28), Sage Publications, Beverly Hills, California.

Converse, Philip E., and Georges Dupeux (1962), 'Politicization of the Electorate in France and the United States', *Public Opinion Quarterly*, 26, 1–23.

Converse, Philip E. (1962), 'Information Flow and the Stability of Partisan Attitudes', *Public Opinion Quarterly*, 26, 578–99.

Converse, Philip E. (1964), 'The Nature of Belief Systems in Mass Publics', in D. E. Apter (ed.), *Ideology and Discontent*, Free Press, New York.

Converse, Philip E. (1966a), 'The Concept of a Normal Vote', in Angus Campbell *et al.* (eds.), *Elections and the Political Order*, Wiley, New York.

Converse, Philip E. (1966b), 'Religion and Politics: The 1960 Election', in Angus Campbell *et al.* (eds.), *Elections and the Political Order*, Wiley, New York.

Converse, Philip E. (1968), 'Some Priority Variables in Comparative Electoral Research', in Otto Stammer (ed.), *Party Systems, Party Organizations and the Politics of the New Masses*, Institut für Politische Wissenschaft an der Freien Universität, Berlin.

Converse, Philip E. (1969a), 'Of Time and Partisan Stability', *Comparative Political Studies*, 2, 139–71.

Converse, Philip E. (1969b), 'Survey Research and the Decoding of Patterns in Ecological Data', in Mattei Dogan and Stein Rokkan (eds.), *Quantitative Ecological Analysis in the Social Sciences*, MIT Press, Cambridge, Mass.

Daudt, Hans (1961), *Floating Voters and the Floating Vote*, Stenfert Kroese, Leiden.

Diekershoff, Karl-Heinz (1964), 'Das wahlverhalten von Mitgliedern organisierter Interessengruppen', unpublished dissertation.

EMNID, (1962), *Der Prozeß der Meinungsbildung*, EMNID-Institut, Bielefeld.

Goldberg, Arthur S. (1966), 'Discerning a Causal Pattern among Data on Voting Behaviour', *American Political Science Review*, 60, 913–22.

Heberle, Rudolf, and Stein Rokkan (1969), 'Zum Problem der Wahlsoziologie', in *Handbuch der Empirischen Sozialforschung*, (II Band), Ferdinand Enke Verlag, Stuttgart.

Jennings, M. Kent (1972), 'Partisan Commitment and Electoral Behavior in The Netherlands', *Acta Politica*, 7, 445–70.

Kaase, Max (1967), *Wechsel von Parteipräferenzen: Eine Analyse am Beispiel der Bundestagswahl 1961*, Anton Hain Verlag, Meisenheim/Glan.

Kaase, Max (1970), 'Determinanten des Wahlverhaltens bei der Bundestagswahl 1969', *Politische Vierteljahresschrift*, 11, 46ff., Koln and Opladen.

Key, V. O. Jr. (1955), 'A Theory of Critical Elections', *Journal of Politics*, 17, 3–18.

Key, V. O. Jr., and Frank Munger (1959), 'Social Determinism and Electoral Decision: the Case of Indiana', in Eugene Burdick and Arthur J. Brodbeck (eds.), *American Voting Behavior*, Free Press, New York.

Key, V. O. Jr., with Milton C. Cummings, Jr. (1966), *The Responsible Electorate*, Harvard University Press, Cambridge, Mass.

Klingemann, Hans D., and Franz Urban Pappi (1970), 'Die Wählerbewegungen bei der Bundestagswahl am 28. September 1969', *Politische Vierteljahresschrift*, 11, 111ff.

Lepsius, M. Rainer (1966), *Extremer Nationalismus*, Kohlhammer Verlag, Stuttgart.

Liepelt, Klaus, and Alexander Mitscherlich (1968), *Thesen zur Wählerfluktuation*, Europäische Verlagsanstalt, Frankfurt/Main.

Lipset, Seymour M., and Stein Rokkan (1968), 'Cleavage Structures, Party Systems, and Voter Alignments', in Seymour M. Lipset and Stein Rokkan (eds.), *Party Systems and Voter Alignments*, Free Press, New York.

Narr, Wolf-Dieter, and Frieder Naschold (1971), *Theorie der Demokratie*, Kohlhammer Verlag, Stuttgart.

Pomper, Gerald (1967), 'Classification of Presidential Elections', *Journal of Politics*, 29, 535–66.

Radtke, Günter D. (1972), 'Gibt es in der Bundesrepublik eine Parteiidentifikation?', in *Verfassung und Verfassungswirklichkeit, Jahrbuch 1972*, Carl Heymanns Verlag KG, Kölns-Berlin-Bonn-München.

Sartori, Giovanni (1968), 'The Sociology of Parties, A Critical Review', in Otto Stammer (ed.), *Party Systems, Party Organizations, and the Politics of the New Masses*, Institut für Politische Wissenschaft an der Freien Universität, Berlin.

Schleth, Uwe, and Erich Weede (1971), 'Causal Models on West-German Voting Behavior', in Rudolf Wildenmann et al. (eds.), *Sozialwissenschaftliches Jahrbuch für Politik*, (Band 2), Olzog Verlag, München.

Shively, W. Phillips (1972), 'Party Identification, Party Choice, and Voting Stability: The Weimar Case', *American Political Science Review*, 66, 1203–25.

Stokes, Donald E. (1966), 'Some Dynamic Elements of Contests for the Presidency', *American Political Science Review*, 60, 19–28.

Valen, Henry, and Daniel Katz (1964), *Political Parties in Norway*, Universitetsforlaget, Oslo.

Wildenmann, Rudolf (1968a), 'Parteien-Identifikation in der Bundesrepublik', in Otto Stammer (ed.), *Party Systems, Party Organizations, and the Politics of the New Masses*, Institut für Politische Wissenschaft an der Freien Universität, Berlin.

Wildenmann, Rudolf (1968b), 'Möglichkeit und Grenzen der Handlungsfähigkeit der Bundesregierung', unpublished manuscript, University of Mannheim.

Zohlnhöfer, Werner (1965), 'Parteienidentifizierung in der Bundesrepublik und den Vereinigten Staaten', in Erwin K. Scheuch and Rudolf Wildenmann (eds.), *Zur soziologie der Wahl*, Westdeutscher Verlag, Köln and Opladen.

# 6

# A Comparative Analysis of Factors
# Correlated with Turnout and Voting Choice

IAN BUDGE and DENNIS FARLIE

## INTRODUCTION

Much of the discussion in preceding chapters has been taken up with the question of whether party identification is an adequate measure of the long-term predispositions underlying voting. Less attention has been paid to the question of what *is* an adequate measure, if party identification is not. Yet given the non-controversial assumption that voting is affected by both predispositions and immediate election cues, some measure of the former is needed. (So is some measure of short-term cues, which are usually identified with reactions to candidates and issues. Whether that equivalence is justified is too large a question for this empirical paper: in any case issue preferences are the only indicators available for the surveys examined below.)

The main purpose of this paper is therefore to examine, on the basis of survey data from nine democracies, the comparative performance of various potential indicators of long-term predispositions towards voting for one party or another. We shall incidentally also be able to assess the degree to which long-term predispositions as such influence voting, as compared with short-term issue-cues. This is the same concern that inspired Converse's construct of the 'normal vote'. Since the standing of party identification as an indicator of long-term predispositions independent of voting is itself under scrutiny, we shall base the measure of predispositions on such solidly antecedent factors as occupation, education, income, religion, region, etc., even though party identification is in many cases more informative than these (indeed often too informative for us to regard as really independent of vote: see below, fifth section).

We must apologize in advance for the necessarily rather dry statement of which factors perform best in a comparative context, and the use of summary statistics which cannot convey the immediate excitement or even the rich cultural life that produced relationships in the first place. The drama of the class struggle is hardly

* This research was supported on grants MR 2129/2 from the British Social Science Research Council. We are grateful to the Political Science Committee and its officers for their financial and other help with the project. In assembling data we drew heavily on the resources of the British SSRC Survey Archive of the University of Essex. Our able research assistant, Roger Barlow, processed all data for the study. The paper is one of a series in which names are alternated to indicate the equal and joint responsibility of the authors for the discussion.

reproduced in the statement that class variables rank first in influence over voting choice in Britain and Norway, while the complex religious and regional conflicts of Canada are equally undervalued by the simple finding that their ranks stand higher in that country. For a statistically sophisticated analysis combined with full appreciation of these cultural complexities see Irvine's assessments of turnout and voting choice in Canada (Chapters 17 and 18 of this volume). Because of the very wide range of data used, we must limit ourselves to a summary recital of the main findings as they relate to the central questions we have raised:

(1) How well does party identification measure long-term predispositions, in comparison with standard social background factors?

(2) How independent is party identification of the dependent variables we examine—particularly of voting choice?

(3) How much connection do long-term predispositions, as measured by social background characteristics, have with voting, compared with short-term cues, measured by issue preferences?

## THE MEASUREMENT TECHNIQUE: LIKELIHOOD RATIO SPACE

### Preliminary considerations

To provide a direct answer to these questions we require a multivariate technique which gives the necessary information about the relative success of different indicators in 'placing' voters in appropriate categories. The technique also has to be adapted to the survey data at our disposal, which are more commonly at the nominal level of measurement (i.e. organized into mutually exclusive and exhaustive categories only) than at the ordinal or interval (i.e. ranked, or associated with numeric scores). Such a technique is to be found in LiRaS (Likelihood Ratio Space) which has been developed by Farlie over the last three years with particular reference to our joint research on voting and party competition.

In the discussion below we shall use the technique to provide estimates (information values) based on the number of respondents 'moved' by each variable towards the correct voting category minus the number 'moved' towards the wrong voting category. These are analogous to the estimates one would get from beta coefficients in regression, but based on purely nominal assumptions about the data. As the name implies, however, the technique also creates a space, which is defined by the number of voting alternatives facing electors (e.g., for a two-party system: voting for Party A, voting for Party B or not voting). If one considers only voters the space is purely party-defined: a straight line with two end-points for a two-party system; a triangle with three end-points for a three-party system, etc.

We are thus dealing with a party-defined space that is very similar to that created by party identification in the two-party case (Figure 1.2 above) but more flexible in that:

(a) it creates a continuous measurement of propensities towards parties;

(b) it measures these propensities for any number of parties, not simply for two.

Being party-defined, this space is closer to the original concept of party identification than either the party-inferred spaces or pure policy spaces created by dimensional analysis or assumed in rational choice models. If it is produced only through the input of long-term indelible characteristics, such as class, religion, region, etc., which may be taken as measuring long-term predispositions, the analogy with party identification is complete. A party-defined likelihood ratio space can also be produced from issue preferences alone, or from a mixed input of background characteristics *and* issue preferences. In these latter cases the space is still party-defined but is not otherwise analogous to party identification, since it is measuring not simply the influence of long-term predispositions but also of immediate election cues. However a comparison between the pure social background space (which is directly analogous to party identification) and the mixed space then tells us how predispositions and cues are interacting to give the final vote.

Here then we have a spatial representation of party systems that differs radically from the policy spaces usually employed, but which is closely analogous to party identification itself. This makes for intriguing theoretical speculation about the interrelationships between different spatial representations, which we shall pursue in Chapter 20.

In this chapter we are not concerned with questions of total spatial representation but with the prior question of what variables should be used to produce the representation. Lack of reflection on this point contributes to a central weakness of most dimensional analyses: if limited or suspect information goes in, only limited or suspect information comes out. Obviously, one way to create a likelihood space of long-term predispositions would be to use the responses to the party identification questions as input, along with social background characteristics. If such questions themselves measure only voting intentions, as several previous papers allege, the ensuing spatial representation of voting propensities might then only reflect voting propensities without itself explaining or predicting them. Answers to the questions posed above, of how independent and antecedent party identification is to voting choice, are therefore required before proceeding to full-scale modelling, and it is these answers that are provided and assessed in this chapter. We give our conclusions on what input should go into an ideal spatial representation in the final section.


### The Logic of the Technique

Given a large number of background characteristics used in combination to predict voting choice, analysts often seek to overcome the disadvantages of cross-tabulation by using multiple regression or discriminant analysis. But regression analysis on these nominal classifications would require as many variables as the total number of internal categories, and all would be dummy variables (scoring 1 if a respondent belonged to that category and 0 if he did not). Being designed to handle interval level data where variables have proper scores, regression is simply not a practical technique for a situation in which every response has to be characterized by scores that are either 1 or 0.

Discriminant analysis—partitioning the groups into sub-groups with as pure as possible sets of, for example, Labour or Conservative voters, is subject to the same disadvantages as regression. Moreover in its most developed form it assumes a multivariate normal distribution to produce the linear discriminant functions on which it splits the groups. This assumption is not met with the categoric nominal data available from surveys.

However, one can build on the distributions of electors over the categoric variables, without stretching nominal measurement assumptions, in order to locate individuals within the party-defined space with which we are concerned. In the most general terms our procedure uses background characteristics to estimate the distribution of individuals within a space of one or more dimensions. Specified background characteristics are used to estimate the likelihood of a given individual's location in categories of a dependent variable which in the simplest case might be the dichotomy Labour-Conservative.

An example of the method of calculation is given in Table 6.1. This is highly simplified since only one background characteristic is used to estimate the likelihood of an individual being Labour or Conservative. Nevertheless, as will become clear below (see Figure 6.1) the procedure proceeds sequentially, characteristic by characteristic, so in a way the calculation illustrated in Table 6.1 constitutes the basic building block of our procedure.

Table 6.1    Estimation of an Individual's Location in a Likelihood Ratio Space of One Dimension, Defined by the Dichotomy Labour-Conservative from Probability Distributions over a Single Background Characteristic

| Background Characteristic | (i) | (ii) |
|---|---|---|
| Self-assigned class: | Labour | Conservative |
| Working | .90 | .48 |
| Middle | .10 | .52 |
| | 1.00 | 1.00 |

The ratio of probabilities of a Labour supporter being working-class as opposed to Conservative being working-class is (.90, .48). These are normalised to add to 1.00 to permit placement of all individuals in a common space (here the straight line below). This normalisation makes the ratios (.65, .35). This results in the placement of the individual under consideration .65 of the way along a straight line to the end defined as complete certainty of being Labour, as shown below:

```
Complete                                               Complete
certainty              working class individual        certainty
of being     1.00            ↓   0.50        0.00       of being
Labour       ├──┼──┼──┼──┼──┼──┼──┼──┼──┤              Conservative
             0.00            0.50           1.00
```

Complete certainty of voting Labour obviously precludes any possibility that an individual is a Conservative, and vice-versa in the case of complete certainty of voting Conservative. Hence the end-points and intermediate points in the line carry two sets of scores - one calculated as distance towards being Labour, and the other as distance towards being Conservative.

In order to produce Table 6.1 one starts with the simple marginal distribution of Labour and Conservative voters over a background characteristic in the example, self-assigned class. From these marginals one obtains the proportions of Labour supporters, out of all Labour supporters, who regard themselves as working-class, and the proportion who regard themselves as middle-class. Most Labour supporters do consider themselves working class—0.90 in Table 6.1. We do the same for Conservatives who divide fairly evenly between working- and middle-class (0.48 working, 0.52 middle, in the example).

These proportions give the best estimate obtainable of the probability distributions of Labour and Conservative over self-assigned class. Looking down Table 6.1 column (i), we can estimate the probability, given that an individual is Labour, of his being working-class (0.90). Looking across Table 6.1 columns (i) and (ii), we can also read off ratios of probabilities from the entries in the two probability distributions. One can ask, what is the ratio of the probability of a Labour voter being working-class and of the probability of a Conservative being working-class? This ratio of probabilities, or likelihood ratio, is (0.90, 0.48), from the comparison of entries for working class in columns (i) and (ii). Given the known probability distributions over self-assigned class, the discovery that an individual regards himself as working-class would obviously increase our propensity to predict that he was Labour. This is because the likelihood ratio reflects the overwhelmingly working-class composition of Labour voters. At the same time there are many working-class Conservatives so there is no complete certainty in the prediction.

Likelihood ratios can be used as spatial coordinates, so the fact that they can be used to indicate whether individuals are more likely to be Labour or Conservative, implies that individuals can be placed in a space. The type of space created by assignments towards two categories (Labour and Conservative) is a line, the ends being defined by complete certainty of being Labour, or the converse, complete certainty of being Conservative. Such a line is illustrated in Table 6.1. Were the likelihoods left as they are, however, the lines on which individuals are placed would be of varying lengths. A working-class respondent in Table 6.1 would be on a line of (0.90 + 0.48) = 1.38, whereas a middle-class respondent would be on a line of (0.10 + 0.52) = 0.62. Obviously one wants to place individuals on the same line. We can do this by adjusting likelihood ratios so that they always add to 1.00. Thus the location of a self-designated member of the working class in Table 6.1 is (0.65, 0.35) in terms of a standardized likelihood ratio. That of a self-designated member of the middle class (0.10, 0.52) becomes (0.16, 0.84). These likelihood ratios then become coordinates which locate each individual nearer or further away from particular party choices. Spatial distributions can be summarized in the form of tables, but these are always based on some spatial distribution like the one shown under Table 6.1. (Note the formal similarity to the party identification line in Figure 1.2.) Where individuals are assigned not to two but to three categories (such as Labour, Conservative and non-voter), tables will be based on a distribution over a triangle (three end-points) rather than a line (two end-points). In such cases the likelihood ratio consists of the ratio of three rather than two probabilities. But the principle is the same.

One can also use the existence of an underlying space to measure the usefulness, or information value, of each background characteristic in predicting whether individuals are more likely to be Labour or Conservative. Each characteristic will move individuals some way along the line or space towards one end-point or another. Some individuals will be moved towards the end to which they actually belong, some towards an end to which they do not really belong. We can thus define the information value of a characteristic in terms of the average movement it produces in the correct direction minus the average movement it produces in the wrong direction. The value will always be positive. (For a detailed description of information values see the note to this chapter).

We are interested in going beyond the calculations in Table 6.1 because our main purpose is to base estimates on a number of background characteristics in combination. In order to do this one must in some way pool the estimates provided by a whole series of calculations like those illustrated in Table 6.1 —as many calculations as the number of background characteristics we wish to use. A method of pooling calculations is provided by the well-known Bayes Theorem. We designate the individual being Labour as 'Hypothesis' $H_1$ and the individual being Conservative as 'Hypothesis' $H_2$. The initial probabilities assigned to these two hypotheses are denoted by $P(H_1)$, the probability an individual is Labour, and $P(H_2)$, the probability an individual is Conservative. The likelihoods obtained from Table 6.1, such as the 0.90 and 0.52, are designated by $P(A/H_1)$ for the likelihood of A for Labour and $P(A/H_2)$ for the likelihood of A for Conservative. For example, $P(\text{Working}/H_1)$ is 0.90. Where we do not wish to specify a particular hypothesis we will use $H_i$ to mean either $H_1$ or $H_2$ depending on the context.

Given this clarification of terms, Bayes' Theorem can be stated formally as:

$$\frac{P(A_1|H_i)P(H_i)}{[P(A_1|H_1)P(H_1)] + [P(A_1|H_2)P(H_2)]} = P(H_i|A_1)$$

$$\frac{P(A_2|H_i)P(H_i)}{[P(A_2|H_1)P(H_1)] + [P(A_1|H_2)P(H_2)]} = P(H_i|A_2)$$

In other words one can get the pooled probability of an individual being Labour (the posterior probability $P(H_1/A)$) by multiplying the appropriate likelihood (0.90 or 0.48 from Table 6.1) by the initial or prior probability assigned to an individual being Labour, and dividing in each case by the sum of the numerators in the two expressions. This division normalizes the results of the two calculations so that they sum to 1.00, as required.

Figure 6.1 shows in detail how Bayes' Theorem is applied to pool the estimates for each individual in turn until a full spatial distribution is generated. It is rather like double-entry bookkeeping. From the right-hand column we bring in the current likelihood ratio of a given individual being Labour. This forms the prior probability for the purpose of a Bayesian calculation of $(P(H_i))$. We then use the first characteristic of the individual under consideration—designating himself as working-class—to draw a likelihood ratio from the probability distribution of all Labour and Conservative electors over self-assigned class, just as in Table 6.1. We substitute these actual figures into Bayes' Theorem, and thus get a new set of current likelihoods, which are transferred to the right-hand column. We then look at the next of the individual's characteristics (in Figure 6.1, being in a manual occupation), get a likelihood ratio from the probability distributions of Labour and Conservative over occupation, and substitute these into Bayes' Theorem along with the new set of current likelihoods. From these calculations we get a new set of current likelihoods for the next calculation. And so on sequentially, until after going through all the available

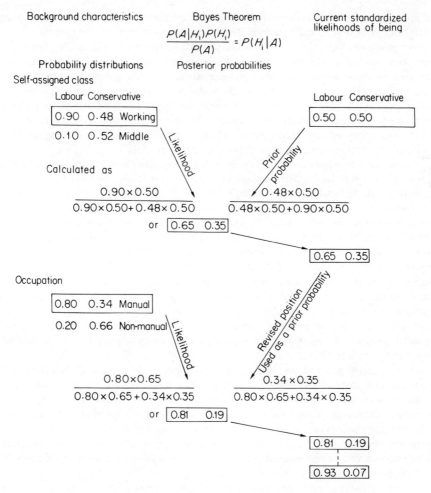

Background characteristics

Bayes Theorem

$$\frac{P(A|H_i)P(H_i)}{P(A)} = P(H_i|A)$$

Current standardized
likelihoods of being

Probability distributions          Posterior probabilities

Self-assigned class

This pattern is repeated until all the variables have been used. The last current position is then plotted on the line below:

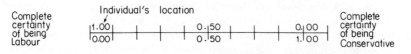

Figure 6.1     Estimation of an individual's location in a Likelihood Ratio Space of one dimension, defined by the dichotomy Labour-Conservative, from probability distributions over a number of background characteristics

background characteristics we emerge with a final placement of the individual on the line, which in the case of Figure 6.1 is 0.89 of the way to complete certainty of being Labour. Although only dichotomized characteristics are used in Figure 6.1, for clarity of presentation, the procedure can accommodate characteristics with any number of categories (within practical constraints).

By going through the same procedure with every individual in the sample, a complete spatial distribution can be built up. Incidentally, assignments are not affected by the order in which variables are introduced: the same placements will be made whatever order is used. The details of the computing procedure which put this series of calculations into effect are given in Appendix B of Budge and Farlie (forthcoming). There is therefore no opaque 'black box' into which the figures go and from which they emerge transformed. They are simply the result of a long series of calculations such as those shown in Table 6.1 and Figure 6.1.

Three further points should be made about the procedure in Figure 6.1. Although Bayes' Theorem is used in the assignment procedure, it is not truly Bayesian since we start with equal probabilities of finding Labour and Conservative (the 0.50 and 0.50 at the top right-hand column in Figure 6.1). This is deliberately naive and in most cases not a true subjective prior, since we know that in certain areas there is a much greater chance of finding Conservative rather than Labour supporters, and vice-versa. On the other hand, treating the occurrence of Labour and Conservative as initially equi-probable allows us to base final assignments exclusively on the data, rather than imposing our preconceptions upon it. Hence, the entries in the right-hand column areas result in standardized likelihoods, adding to 1.00, rather than Bayesian probabilities. However, although equal initial probabilities are used in the example they are not of course necessary for application of the procedure. Whether or not initial 'hunches' are incorporated depends on the analytic purposes for which the representation is employed.

The second point is the procedure's use solely of marginals as probability distributions instead of using joint frequency distributions for all background characteristics in combination. This is because possible combinations over ten or twenty background characteristics would be astronomical in number. The question is whether one chooses to use only a restricted number of variables and make use of their joint distribution, or to 'scan' over large numbers of variables to pick out the most relevant, but with a consequent restriction to marginal distributions. Undoubtedly LiRaS opts for the latter alternative.

The final measurement point about LiRaS is the responsibility on the user to avoid double-counting by first ensuring that all background characteristics used in calculations like those of Figure 6.1 are substantially independent of each other in terms of standard statistics such as chi-square. LiRaS is by intent a robust statistical technique in which small violations of the assumption of independence between variables produce only small and tolerable errors in assignment (an important point, since most social and political variables are weakly correlated with each other). Major violations of the independence assumptions will delay the final assignment rather than produce major errors.

Full spatial distributions resulting from applications of the technique are reported elsewhere (Budge and Farlie, forthcoming). Below we report summary figures on their success in matching propensities (estimated on the basis of optimum combinations of background characteristics and issue preferences) with actual voting choices.

### III THE DATA BASE: NINE VOTING SURVEYS

Most of the surveys used in this analysis come from the Inter-University Consortium for Political Research, University of Michigan. The three that do not were being lodged there at the time of acquisition. Full details of each will therefore be found in ICPR catalogues and codebooks: they also form part of the collection of thirty-three surveys described by us elsewhere (Budge and Farlie, forthcoming, Appendix D). A fair indication of the variables contained in the analysis decks for each survey is given in the following tables and text: numbers of respondents except where otherwise stated are between 1,000 and 2,000, and all consist of some kind of clustered probability sample from a national population. All that is required here therefore is a brief listing and identification of each.

(1) Australia: national election survey of 1969 (Australian National University, Department of Political Science, Study No. 457) obtained through ICPR.

(2) Canada: national election survey of 1965 (ICPR Study No. 7225).

(3) France: national election survey of 1958 (ICPR Study No. 7278).

(4) Germany: national election survey of 1969, carried out by the Zentralarchiv, University of Cologne, under the direction of Dr Franz Pappi, and at the time of acquisition being lodged with the ICPR, from where further details can be obtained.

(5) Great Britain: national election survey of 1963 (ICPR Study No. 7232).

(6) Japan: national election survey of 1967 (University of Michigan, Center for Japanese Studies, Study No. 507, obtained through ICPR).

(7) The Netherlands: national participation survey of 1970, acquired from the Instituut voor Arbeidsvraagstunne, Tilburg University, The Netherlands, obtained through Department of Political Science, University of Amsterdam. (Again, this was being lodged with the ICPR at the time of acquisition and further details can be obtained from their archive.)

(8) Norway: national election survey of 1965, under the direction of Professor Henry Valen, acquired from the Department of Political Science, University of Oslo. This is again now lodged with the ICPR.

(9) United States: national election survey of 1968 (ICPR Study No. 7281).


## FACTORS CORRELATED WITH TURNOUT IN SEVEN DEMOCRACIES

Although our central concerns are with voting choice rather than turnout, it is of some interest to examine the performance of the various indicators in regard to this other aspect of voting behaviour. Normally our spatial representation would treat non-voting as one out of the range of alternatives that can be chosen by electors, along with choices of particular parties. The discussion of party identification has focused on its relationship to voting choice rather than turnout, however. Therefore we treat the two separately in the present discussion. In this section therefore the dependent variable under examination is non-voting v. voting for any party, and movement of respondents is consequently along the kind of straight line shown at the bottom of Table 6.1, defined by complete certainty of voting for some party v. complete certainty of not voting at all. Since Australia has compulsory voting and in Germany reported turnout is very high (94.6 per cent), the relevant surveys are not used in this analysis.

### Predictive Success of the overall representation of turnout

In a crude way we can see how successfully the full sets of variables used in the analysis managed to locate respondents correctly in terms of their actual behaviour. By dichotomizing the line at 0.5, we can roughly predict that all respondents with scores in the range 0.50 to 0.00, towards non-voting, will not vote, while all those with scores in the range 0.50 to 1.00, towards voting, will vote. Cross-tabulating this estimated turnout/non-turnout with actual turnout/non-turnout gives us:

(a) the percentage correctly placed (i.e., respondents predicted to vote who did vote plus respondents predicted not to vote who did not vote, over all respondents);

(b) Goodman and Kruskall's tau_b which tells us how much better the estimate did than the simple guessing rule of allocating individual respondents to voting categories proportionately to the overall marginal distribution;

(c) lambda, which tells us how much better the estimate did than the simple guessing rule of putting all respondents in the largest category (voting).

Table 6.2 shows that, while the behaviour of three-quarters of respondents was correctly predicted, the procedure never does any better than the blind guess that all respondents vote, and little better than reproduction of marginal allocations in the cases of Britain, Canada and Japan.

Table 6.2    Success of LiRaS Assignments in Predicting Turnout

|  | Per cent (%) voting | Non-voting | Per cent (%) correctly placed | Goodman & Kruskall tau_b | Lambda |
|---|---|---|---|---|---|
| Canada | 85.0 | 15.0 | 77.3 | 0.083 | 0.0 |
| France | 66.7 | 33.3 | 72.5 | 0.138 | 0.2 |
| Great Britain | 90.2 | 9.8 | 75.4 | 0.037 | 0.0 |
| Japan | 87.5 | 12.5 | 72.6 | 0.037 | 0.0 |
| The Netherlands | 91.5 | 8.5 | 82.7 | 0.129 | 0.0 |
| Norway | 91.8 | 8.2 | 79.0 | 0.252 | 0.0 |
| United States | 73.8 | 26.2 | 73.3 | 0.550 | 0.0 |

Note:  'Voting' includes all those who stated that they had voted in the recent election or who would vote in a forthcoming one, whilst 'Non-voting' includes all those who stated that they had not voted or would not vote.

As Table 6.3 demonstrates, however, the fault lies neither in the LiRaS technique nor the variables employed. Rather it lies in the well-known tendencies of survey respondents to over-report turnout and of surveys to fail to contact non-voters. Comparisons of reported turnout from the surveys with actual turnout for each country in the nearest election year shows the latter much exceeded in every case except the French. These misreports have the effect not only of blurring distinctions

Table 6.3    Reported Turnout from Seven National Surveys and Actual Turnout in
the Nearest Election Year

|  | Reported Turnout in National Survey % | Actual Turnout in Nearest Election Year % |
|---|---|---|
| Canada | 85 | 75 (1965) |
| France | 69 | 71 (1958) |
| Great Britain | 90 | 77 (1964) |
| Japan | 88 | 74 (1967) |
| The Netherlands | 92 | 79 (1971) |
| Norway | 92 | 84 (1964) |
| United States | 74 | 61 (1968) |

between the voting and non-voting groups, but of 'pulling' even self-reported non-voters over to the voting end-point because there are actual non-voters there who do not report themselves as such but are very similar in characteristics to the self-confessed non-voters.

### Relationship of individual variables to turnout

Against this background of measurement error we can estimate the contribution of standard social background characteristics, and of respondents' own party identification and their father's party identification, to placing respondents 'correctly', i.e. in terms of their reported voting/non-voting. Generalizing across the seven democracies we must do this in very summary fashion and within the following constraints.

(1) We have only a limited number of variables that are 'common' across all seven surveys. These are listed down the side of Table 6.4. We can make comparisons either within the group of common social background variables—how each perform relative to others within the group—or in terms of their performance within all the variables available for each survey. 'In-group' comparisons occur in the first two columns of Table 6.4, and comparisons of relative performance vis-à-vis all other variables, common or not, contained in each survey occur in the third and fourth columns. The entries in the latter give opportunities for comparison between the predictive power of the common social background variables and party identification.

(2) However, these entries consist of rankings only, not absolute information values. This is because the absolute value reflects such extraneous considerations as the number of respondents in each survey. For comparative analysis ranks are therefore more useful than absolute values.

(3) Most variables have fairly obvious coding categories, which are standardized into four or five common categories for inter-country comparisons. Party identification needs special comment, however. Because of the number of categories required in those countries with many parties, it was not possible to include strength of identification in the coding. No-one has ever claimed that simple identification with a party necessarily predicts turnout. It is all the more striking therefore that party identification emerges as the first-ranking and most stable variable from the

Table 6.4    Average Ranks and Standard Deviations of Ranks for Correlates of Turnout
across Countries

| Name | Mean Group Rank | Standard Deviation | Mean Overall Rank | Standard Deviation |
|------|-----------------|--------------------|-------------------|--------------------|
| Age | 4.14 | 1.81 | 10.29 | 15.21 |
| Sex | 5.86 | 3.30 | 20.43 | 4.30 |
| Level of education | 5.57 | 7.31 | 11.57 | 17.28 |
| Region | 4.75 | 4.56 | 11.50 | 6.40 |
| Income | 5.50 | 7.92 | 12.60 | 18.20 |
| Church attendance | 4.75 | 6.69 | 10.00 | 14.63 |
| Religion | 7.83 | 6.99 | 17.33 | 6.07 |
| Occupation | 4.86 | 8.88 | 12.29 | 22.06 |
| Subjective class | 3.00 | 2.33 | 9.17 | 7.40 |
| Union membership | 8.33 | 7.83 | 19.50 | 12.39 |
| Class of family when young | 5.50 | 3.50 | 12.50 | 5.50 |
| Own or rent house | 5.66 | 1.70 | 13.33 | 9.21 |
| Father's occupation when young | 7.50 | 8.31 | 17.75 | 13.29 |
| Urban/rural upbringing | 8.80 | 4.19 | 20.00 | 6.16 |
| Max. possible value | 14 | | 26 | |

| | | | | |
|------|-----------------|--------------------|-------------------|--------------------|
| Party identification | 1.00 | 0.0 | 1.57 | 1.65 |
| Father's party | 2.00 | 0.0 | 13.00 | 23.35 |
| Max. possible value | 2 | | 26 | |

comparisons in Table 6.4. This is because people who say they feel closer to some party are more likely to say they turn out than people who say they feel closer to no party.

The table includes both mean rank of each variable for the within-group and overall comparisons over the seven countries, and also the standard deviation of its ranks over the seven countries. The last statistic gives the extent to which a variable's predictive success in regard to non-voting 'generalizes' across the seven democracies.

Let us now turn to the substantive results. As we have just mentioned, party identification shows the most consistent and strongest relationship with turnout of all variables in the table. Its mean overall rank of 1.57 means that it ranks first or second in every country, as the small standard deviation also attests. The other political variable on the other hand—father's party—which has the additional disadvantage of lying further back in time, has the middling-to-low mean rank of 13.00 and a very large standard deviation, showing it is far from consistent in its effects across the seven countries. The very good performance of party identification is of course consistent with either of the two viewpoints stated previously. One could use its performance on the one hand to assert that it is an antecedent and independent variable which is the best predictor of voting behaviour, among other things; or one could maintain that its good performance is too good, and lends support to the idea that it simply reflects current voting intention. We shall hope to offer more conclusive evidence related to these arguments in the following section, on voting choice.

The socioeconomic variables, however, are indubitably antecedent in character to the voting decision (except possibly for subjective class). This is also reflected in their relatively low overall ranks. No one characteristic emerges as leading: in Japan it is age, as compared with church attendance in The Netherlands, income in Norway, occupation in France and the United States, subjective class in Britain and region in Canada. (This is coded differently from Irvine's categorization in Chapter 17 and the dependent variable is also somewhat different, thus accounting to some extent for our finding that it ranks above the religious indicators.)

Variability across countries is reflected in the middling ranks attained by the leading socioeconomic characteristics in the table. A number bunch around rank 10: (in order) subjective class, church attendance, age. Region and level of education rank on average above occupation, which has a very high standard deviation. Neither class, regional nor religious variables (of the three main groupings of possible influences) consequently emerge as most closely related to turnout.

## FACTORS CORRELATED WITH VOTING CHOICE IN NINE DEMOCRACIES

Voting choice is taken either as reported vote for the election year or current voting intention. Because of the multiplicity of minor parties in some countries the choice is sometimes examined as one between broad political *tendencies* rather than between parties as such. Table 6.5 gives the nature of our dependent variable by country, specifying the groupings between which we divided the vote.

Table 6.5    Nature of Dependent Variable by Country

1. Great Britain    1963 voting intention split three ways:

      (i) Conservative;    (ii) Labour;    (iii) Liberal.

2. Australia    1967 voting intention split two ways: (i) Country party
         and Liberal party;   (ii) Labour party and Democratic Labour party.

3. Canada    1965 reported vote split three ways: (i) Liberal;
         (ii) Conservative:    (iii) New Democratic party, Social Credit
         and Creditise.

4. United States   1968 reported vote split three ways: (i) Democratic
         party; (ii) Republican party; (iii) Wallace.

5. Japan   1967 reported vote split two ways: (i) Liberal-Democratic;
         (ii) Socialist Party and Democratic Socialist party.

Table 6.5 (Cont.)

6. <u>The Netherlands</u>  1970 voting intention split three ways: (i) KVP,

    ARP, CHU, SGP, GPV and alliances, CCP, PCG (the religious parties);

    (ii) VVD, BP (the 'bourgeois' parties); (iii) PvdA, D'66, CPN, PSP,

    PPR, and alliances PAKI, PAKII (the broadly 'Socialist' or 'Left'

    parties).

7. <u>Germany</u>  1969 reported vote split two ways: (i) Christian Democrats;

    (ii) Social Democrats.

8. <u>Norway</u>  1965 reported vote split two ways: (i) Labour and Socialist

    People's party; (ii) Centre party, Christian People's party,

    Liberals, Conservatives.

9. <u>France</u>  1958 reported vote split two ways: (i) UNR, MRP, Conservative

    Indpendents; (ii) Communists, Socialists, Radicals and

    Poujadists.

## Predictive success of the overall representation of voting choice

Proceeding as we did with turnout we can ask, first, how successfully can we predict respondents' actual vote from their score of 0.5 or above on estimated propensity to vote for a particular party? As we noted before, dichotomizing at 0.5 when we have

Table 6.6   Success of LiRaS Assignments in Predicting Voting Choice

| | Per cent: | | | Per cent correctly placed | Goodman & Kruskall tau$_b$ | Lambda |
|---|---|---|---|---|---|---|
| Australia | LCP 57.5 | Labour 42.5 | | 77.6 | 0.16 | 0.47 |
| Canada | Con 30.5 | Lib 44.4 | Other 25.2 | 58.4 | 0.11 | 0.25 |
| France | Gaullists & Allies 64.9 | Others 35.1 | | 77.0 | 0.23 | 0.35 |
| Germany | SPD 49.3 | CDU 50.7 | | 76.6 | 0.28 | 0.53 |
| Great Britain | Con 38.0 | Lab 46.8 | Lib 15.3 | 74.2 | 0.25 | 0.52 |
| Japan | LDP 56.9 | JSP 43.1 | | 70.1 | 0.16 | 0.31 |
| The Netherlands | Rel. 41.9 | Right 14.0 | Left 44.2 | 80.5 | 0.58 | 0.66 |
| Norway | Lab. 51.6 | Bourgeois 48.4 | | 83.4 | 0.45 | 0.66 |
| United States | Dem. 41.2 | Rep. 47.5 | Wallace 11.4 | 72.4 | 0.22 | 0.47 |

Table 6.7    Reported Voting Choice from Nine National Surveys and Actual Vote
in the Nearest Election Year

| | Reported Choices in National Survey (%) | | | Actual Choices in Nearest Election Year (%) | | |
|---|---|---|---|---|---|---|
| Australia | Liberal & Country 57.5 | Labour & DLP (1967) 42.5 | | Liberal & Country 50.o | Labour & DLP (1966) 47.2 | |
| Canada (1965) | Lib 44.7 | Con 30.0 | Other 25.3 | Lib 40.0 | Con 32.0 | Other 28.0 |
| France | Gaullists & Rights 64.9 | Left, Radicals 35.1 | | Gaullist & Right 49.4 | Left, Radicals 50.6 | |
| Germany | CDU-CSU 46.7 | SPD 45.5 | | CDU-CSU 46.1 | SPD 42.7 | |
| Great Britain | Con 38.0 | Lib 15.3 | Lab 46.8 (1963) | Con 43.4 | Lib 11.2 | Lab 44.1 (1964) |
| Japan | LDP 41.2 | JSP-DSP 30.3 | | LDP 47.6 | JSP-DSP 29.1 | |
| The Netherlands | Govt. parties 54.7 | Oppn. parties 45.3 | | Govt. parties 52.1 | Oppn. parties 48.6 | |
| Norway | Labour & SPP 51.6 | Non-Labour 48.4 | | Labour & SPP 49.3 | Non-Labour 48.9 | |
| United States | Dem. 41.2 | Rep. 47.5 | Wallace 11.4 | Dem. 42.7 | Rep. 43.4 | Wallace 13.5 |

continuous scores of propensity is only a very rough indicator of success. Nevertheless, table 6.6 demonstrates that generally a high percentage of votes is correctly placed, and that our predictions improve over the type of guesswork incorporated in either the tau_b or lambda statistics. Predictive success is much lower in the case of Canada: further evidence for Irvine's comments (Chapters 17 and 18 below) on the absence of clear distinctions between Canadian parties. These correct placements are achieved by using all the socioeconomic characteristics and issue preferences available to us, but the party identification responses are not used as input to these representations for reasons discussed below. Table 6.7 shows that, for most countries, the survey estimates of proportions voting for the different parties correspond more closely to the proportions of votes actually cast in the election year than was the case with turnout. The discrepancy in the French figures is unexplained.

Table 6.8 examines the success of representations which use pure socioeconomic characteristics only, and issue preferences only. It will be seen that generally much the same level of predictive success is achieved with the use of socioeconomic characteristics only, as with the use of issue preferences only. Germany and Norway, with an additional 6.7 per cent correctly placed by socioeconomic characteristics, are the countries that reveal the widest gap in favour of socioeconomic variables. France, in the year of De Gaulle's accession to power, has 9 per cent more electors correctly placed by issue preferences.

Table 6.8    Percentages of Electors Correctly Placed (with score of .5 or over towards appropriate party)

|  | Using Issue Preferences alone | Using Socio-Economic Characteristics alone |
|---|---|---|
| Great Britain (1963) | 65.4 | 66.6 |
| Australia (1969) | 75.6 | 72.9 |
| Canada (1965) | 55.5 | 52.3 |
| United States (1968) | 61.3 | 58.3 |
| Japan (1967) | 73.7 | 69.5 |
| The Netherlands (1970) | 71.5 | 75.0 |
| Germany (1969) | 67.9 | 75.0 |
| Norway (1965) | 63.0 | 69.0 |
| France (1958) | 59.9 | 50.4 |

The degree to which issue and background placements duplicate each other's predictive success is of course not surprising given the extent to which issue preferences are shaped by political and social traditions shared with one's associates. Indeed, there might be some debate as to the extent to which issue preferences are produced by voting choices rather than the other way round. Whether or not voters evaluate parties on the basis of independent and autonomous aims (see Chapter 19 below), issue preferences elicited in a rapid survey interview might well be discounted as policy indicators. Given the degree of overlap in correct placements revealed by Table 6.8, one is probably justified in seeking to 'place' voters as much as possible in terms of their socioeconomic characteristics, using only the additional information available from issue indicators (primarily for refining predictions about those electors who are marginal in terms of socioeconomic characteristics alone).

### Relationship of variables to voting choice

Continuing for the moment the comparison between issue preferences and socioeconomic background characteristics, we can make a further estimate of their relative influence by summing the absolute information values for each group of variables within each country and comparing them. This comparison affords some basis for inference (within the admitted limitations of issue preferences as policy indicators) about the effects of immediate election cues on voting compared with long-term predispositions. Analogous estimates using party identification as the measure of predispositions and issue and candidate orientations as measures of short-term cues have been made by researchers at Michigan for the 1968 presidential election (Converse et al., 1969). The measurement of 'short-term forces' against predispositions has also been attempted by Converse through the construct of the 'normal vote'.

Table 6.9 gives comparisons for our nine democracies. We are able to sum the 'information values' (for details on their calculation and meaning, see appendix to this chapter) for each issue to get a grand issue total, and to compare this with the grand total for socioeconomic background characteristics, because each is assumed statistically independent by the LiRaS procedure, and we have in fact checked that only weak correlations exist. Weak correlations slightly distort the comparisons but not to the extent of invalidating the main conclusions. One other point to note is that the absolute information values are very much affected by the dimensions of the figure in which elections are being located and in which movement therefore takes place. If it is a triangle as in Britain and the United States there is much more scope for movement than on a straight line and hence the absolute information value will be much larger than in countries where the representation is a straight line. Of course this does not affect the internal comparison between issues and background characteristics.

Table 6.9    Summed Information Values for Issue—Preferences Compared to Summed Information Values for Background Characteristics, for each of Nine Democracies

|  | Summed Information Value for Issue-Preferences | | Summed Information Value for Background Characteristics | |
|---|---|---|---|---|
|  |  | (No. of issues) |  | (No. of characteristics) |
| Australia | 2.16532 | 14 | 2.01569 | 12 |
| Canada | 5.74089 | 11 | 3.71994 | 12 |
| France | 2.37608 | 10 | 0.68803 | 5 |
| Germany | 1.03961 | 13 | 1.28499 | 11 |
| Great Britain | 7.51219 | 15 | 8.46018 | 14 |
| Japan | 1.64333 | 13 | 1.56584 | 13 |
| The Netherlands | 1.15250 | 12 | 4.08541 | 13 |
| Norway | 3.06402 | 10 | 4.51831 | 12 |
| United States | 15.52947 | 13 | 8.01764 | 15 |

From Table 6.9 it appears that elections influenced more strongly by the latter occurred in Germany, Norway, Britain and (most markedly) in The Netherlands. The last finding provides some support for Thomassen's assertion of the primacy of class and religion there. In Australia and Japan the influence of issues and background characteristics is broadly equal, with a slight imbalance in favour of issues. In Canada, France (1958) and the United States (1968) the balance stands very much in favour of issues. Why issues should loom so large in Canada in 1965 is obscure, but their influence may be due in large part to the absence of strong social cleavages between the parties. France at the advent of De Gaulle, and the United States in the midst of the Vietnam War, had to resolve fundamental political crises, so the influence of issues there is not surprising. But the estimate for the US presidential election of 1968 of a ratio of 2:1 in favour of issue influences as opposed to long-term predispositions contradicts the estimate of 6:4 in favour of predispositions formed by Converse and his associates (Converse *et al.*, 1969, p.1096). Their estimate was of course based on the use of party identification as a measure of predispositions, whereas ours uses background characteristics. Acceptance of one or other estimate will necessarily depend on the value one places on the undoubted antecedence of social background factors to the vote. However, it is worth noting that if the information value for party identification in 1968—3.988—is added to the summed values for the social background characteristics, the balance of influence still favours issues somewhat, though the gap is reduced.

Table 6.10    Average Group and Overall Ranks of Socioeconomic and Political Characteristics for Nine Democracies

1.  Socioeconomic

| Name | Average Group rank | Standard Deviation | Average Overall rank | Standard Deviation |
|---|---|---|---|---|
| Age | 9.25 | 3.60 | 25.25 | 11.68 |
| Sex | 11.40 | 1.80 | 34.25 | 8.24 |
| Education | 6.88 | 3.60 | 18.50 | 8.40 |
| Region | 7.75 | 4.21 | 22.50 | 12.92 |
| Income | 7.12 | 3.18 | 20.90 | 9.79 |
| Church attendance | 5.86 | 3.40 | 17.13 | 10.11 |
| Religion | 5.57 | 3.08 | 15.43 | 8.73 |
| Occupation | 4.60 | 2.04 | 10.88 | 6.64 |
| Subjective class | 4.75 | 2.27 | 14.00 | 12.33 |
| Union membership | 7.25 | 4.10 | 20.95 | 14.01 |
| Class of family when young | 6.25 | 2.95 | 17.25 | 11.12 |
| Urban/rural upbringing | 10.50 | 0.46 | 26.25 | 11.12 |
| Own/rent house | 6.67 | 1.87 | 18.00 | 2.58 |
| Father's occupation when young | 4.67 | 2.17 | 11.50 | 18.78 |

Max. possible value =14                          Max. possible value = 44

2.  Aggregate social and political

| | | | | |
|---|---|---|---|---|
| Size of place metro/urban/rural | 1.88 | 1.69 | 22.25 | 8.88 |

Max. possible value=4                            Max. possible value =44

3.  Political

| | | | | |
|---|---|---|---|---|
| Party identification | 1.00 | 0 | 1.00 | 0 |

Max. possible value=3                            Max. possible value =44

Note:  France is only included in group 3, Germany in 1 and 2.

The fact that party identification is so crucially involved in estimates of long-term versus short-term effects brings us back to the main questions behind our analysis—how predictive is party identification compared with the alternative indicator of long-term trends, social background characteristics? And how independent is party identification from voting choices or intentions themselves? On these points Table 6.10 gives comparative information analogous to that provided by Table 6.4 for turnout. Again, because comparisons across countries are involved, the ranks rather than absolute figures for information values are reported: each entry for each variable consists of its mean rank and the standard deviation of its ranks in the nine countries. Ranks are again given for comparisons within each group (e.g., the fourteen 'socioeconomic' variables) and also for the 'overall' comparison with all other variables included in the analysis. It is the ranks for this last set of comparisons that are relevant for the comparison of socioeconomic variables with party identification, and which will be used in this discussion.

Variables were included in the analysis either because of their inherent interest—e.g., party identification, socioeconomic characteristics and issue preferences have all at some time or another been used to explain voting behaviour—or because of their high predictive power. These last variables include, for example in the United States in 1968, which congressmen respondents voted for, intended vote, senate vote, 1964 vote, feelings towards Wallace and Humphrey, etc. While predictive, such variables are not generally regarded as interesting in a theoretical sense since any antecedent explanatory status is lacking.

With regard to the first question we posed—how predictive is party identification in relation to the socioeconomic variables?—the answer is obvious. Party identification is much more predictive than any individual socioeconomic characteristic. In the overall comparisons with socioeconomic characteristics and issues (not summarized because they differ between countries) it ranks first very consistently. The most predictive of the background characteristics—occupation—is only at rank 11 with a moderate standard deviation of 6.61. It is interesting that all the leading socioeconomic variables are related to class (in rough order: own occupation, father's occupation, subjective class, class of family when young). But not all class characteristics perform as well as religious variables: for example income, education and union membership rank lower than religion and church attendance. Regional variables—region, urban-rural upbringing and size of the place of residence—rank below religious variables. Generally the consistency of effects in terms of standard deviations is roughly proportional to the strength of their influence, apart from the exceptional case of home ownership.

None of these ranks is at all comparable individually with that attained by party identification. This does not settle the first question of relative predictive power, however, because the question is not so much of individual comparison as of using socioeconomic indicators as a group, through the multivariate LiRaS procedure, as an alternative to party identification. The sum of a number of moderately predictive variables may yet be more predictive than one highly informative variable on its own.

Table 6.11 shows, however, that party identification gives more information on its own than the summed background characteristics for all countries except the United States and The Netherlands (in Norway the two values are almost equal). In most countries indeed the information value of party identification much outbalances the summed values.

Table 6.11 Summed Information-Values of Socioeconomic Variables Compared with Information-Value of Party Identification, Within Each of Nine Democracies

|  | Summed Information Values for Socioeconomic Characteristics | Information Values for Party Identification |
|---|---|---|
| Australia | 2.01569 | 5.36177 |
| Canada | 3.71994 | 11.81005 |
| France | 0.68803 | 1.10763 |
| Germany | 1.28499 | |
| Great Britain | 8.46018 | 18.36053 |
| Japan | 1.56584 | 2.01016 |
| The Netherlands | 4.08541 | 2.93066 |
| Norway | 4.51831 | 4.72280 |
| United States | 8.01764 | 3.98761 |

This is an excellent predictive performance which answers the first question conclusively. However, much of the previous argument has not been about the predictive ability of party identification, which is granted, but about its independence from the voting choice itself. Strong predictive success in this context serves only to increase the suspicion that it is not independent, for what better predictor of voting choice could there be than voting choice itself? Put another way, most socioeconomic characteristics are indubitably independent of and antecedent to voting choice. If the party identification questions are so much more predictive, can they be so distinguishable from the voting choice itself?

To answer this question more definitely we return to the most predictive variables—not used in the comparisons in Table 6.10—which were included in our analysis because of this quality rather than any explanatory power they possessed. They were in fact theoretically uninteresting for the very same reasons that gave them their predictive power; i.e., they are difficult to distinguish conceptually from actual voting choice. If party identification actually predicts better than such variables, there must be some doubts about its independence too.

As it turns out, party identification always figures amont the top ten variables in the eight countries in which the relevant questions were asked, and among the top two in six of these countries. Examples of the variables it outranks serve to document the assertion that its very predictive success renders its independence suspect: in Australia, party identification outranks the question 'How would you vote if there was an election tomorrow?'; in Canada, the question 'Which party do you always vote for?'; in France, intended vote; in Britain, direction of the 1959 vote; in Japan, index of voting direction and 1963 vote direction; in The Netherlands direction of vote in the last provincial election; in Norway vote in 1961. Most of the variables outranked refer to past voting behaviour, suggesting that party identification is similarly related to present voting choice.

The exception to all this is the United States. This is particularly interesting because it was in relation to American politics that the concept of party identification was developed and first applied. For the United States presidential election of 1968 party identification ranks tenth of the top ten predictors, having less than half the predictive success of the leading variable, 1968 congressional vote, and coming immediately below 1964 vote. Its very lack of relative predictive success in the American context, compared with the European and Japanese, suggests that the questions there do tap feelings that are independent of and relatively antecedent to the voting choice.

This finding, so far as it goes, does therefore uphold the original Michigan contention that American electors orient themselves to politics through a psychological identification with parties, produced by family socialization in early childhood or by traumatic national crises, which remains thereafter largely invariant through life and which does not in any one election necessarily coincide with Presidential vote. All the original voting studies and investigations of socialization in the United States that rested on these premises are probably right. What our findings equally reveal, however, is that these premises are not appropriate outside the American context, even in Canada (where party identification ranks first of the top ten predictive variables, outranking answers about which party electors always vote for). Paradoxically it is the very predictive success of party identification in these other contexts, relative to the American, that leads one to suspect its empirical independence of voting choice, its conceptual antecedence and its explanatory capacity.

Why should the contrast between the United States and the other countries obtain? It is a tribute to the sophistication and insight of the Michigan investigators that one of them suggested the most likely explanation (Butler and Stokes, 1969). The United States, with separate presidential and congressional elections at the national level, gubernatorial legislative and primary elections at state level (if not others) and innumerable local contests, presents its votes with much more complicated electoral choices than any of the other systems. Given so many frequent choices, with radically different alternatives in each presidential election (compare Goldwater and Johnson in 1964 with Nixon and Humphrey in 1968), the voter needs some stable reference point even if electoral complexities and the shifting nature of the presidential parties often push him away from it. Party identification provides such a reference point. (There may also be other institutional reasons; for example the fact that, in many states, electors must register their party preference in order to participate in primary elections.)

On the other hand, the nature of the parties changes less in the other democracies. It is therefore easier to relate one's class and other interests to the parties and to be reasonably sure the party identified as closer to these in one election will generally remain closer in all elections. Thus on the one hand electors can vote consistently without reference to a psychological identification with party (cf. Thomassen on this very point in Chapter 4 above). On the other hand, when electors transfer their vote they transfer party loyalties as well. Either way the party identification questions will produce answers that are very closely related to current voting intention, contrasting in this with the United States.

These conclusions derive support from the comparative findings on the predictive success of party identification and other indicators of long-term predispositions, which are presented above. But it would be misleading to pretend that they are the only inferences that could be drawn from the findings. Committed proponents of party identification might point to the sustained predictive success of the questions as evidence in their support. To a considerable extent the argument must be resolved—as it has been conducted, even in such a highly statistical discussion as this—on semi-aesthetic grounds of conceptual antecedence and explanatory interest. There is nothing unusual in this: harder sciences than politics resolve many theoretical questions on these grounds. To some extent reactions depend on the degree to which practitioners are willing to trade off easy predictive success for more satisfying theory. There may indeed be no one reaction: different problems and purposes may require a different trade-off. For our own investigations into party competition and voting behaviour, we are prepared to put up with the loss of some predictive power for the sake of the undoubted antecedence and independence of background characteristics. Our reasoning on this point, and the relationship in which the decision leaves us with regard to party identification, are briefly summarized below.

## CONSEQUENCES FOR THE STUDY OF VOTING AND PARTY COMPETITION

Even though the party identification responses seem to reflect genuine and long-standing psychological commitments in the United States, it does not follow that long-term predispositions need necessarily or only be measured through the party identification questions. For it is precisely in the United States that the summed information values of background characteristics substantially outweigh the value obtained by these questions. One can therefore obtain a more accurate estimate of long-term predispositions by using background characteristics in combination. Such an estimate has the advantages (*a*) of being comparable with the estimates obtained on a similar basis in other countries, and (*b*) of being based on factors indubitably antecedent to voting choice, even if in the United States responses to the identification questions seem to be, too.

As a result of this conclusion we shall in our projected representation of voting and party competition base analysis on socioeconomic background characteristics as indicators of long-term predispositions, and on issue preferences as the best available indicators of short-term election cues. Because of the probability that preferences are in most cases adjusted to voting choice, rather than the other way round, we shall further assume that electors' party propensities are primarily shaped by their long-term characteristics, and that only where these leave them in a marginal position between the voting alternatives are they then perforce oriented independently through issue preferences.

None of this implies that our research ignores party identification. One has to recognize an important distinction between the extent to which responses to the traditional questions measure long-term predispositions, which is an operational and measurement problem, and the general conceptual question of how best to relate electors (and politicians) to parties. On the conceptual point we come down firmly on the side of party identification. Like the Michigan researchers we prefer to regard parties as groupings of electors which may be substantially independent of leaders, not as a particular policy programme adopted at one point in time by a united leadership group. In spatial terms we regard a party-defined space—one whose boundaries are set by complete identification with a party—as a more fruitful representation than either a policy space or a party-inferred space. If the LiRaS party-defined space in Table 6.1 or Figure 6.1 is compared with the space based on party identification in Figure 1.2, its form can be seen to be identical in all essential respects, although the impact is different.

In this chaper we have used Likelihood Ratio Space only indirectly, as the context for the average movement of electors from which information values were obtained. This is appropriate for comparisons with the generally non-spatial approaches to voting behaviour considered up to this point. Spatial representations come to the fore with the dimensional analyses and policy-based representations discussed in Parts II and III of this book. In Chapter 20 we contrast the full representation based on Likelihood Ratio Space with these alternatives. In this context it will become even more obvious how closely our basic conceptual approach (as opposed to operationalization) resembles that behind party identification. It is no exaggeration to maintain that in LiRaS, party identification rides again, in a more extended, flexible and powerful explanatory form.

## APPENDIX: INFORMATION VALUES FOR QUESTIONS

The scores used to place the individuals within the party-bounded space are created question by question using a procedure that is exact when the responses to questions are statistically independent within parties. In this case we would need to know only the marginal probability distribution of responses for each question to be able to compile the joint probabilities distribution for any combination of responses to all the questions. The probability of the simultaneous responses $r_1$ to question 1, $r_2$ to question 2, . . . , $r_i$ to question $i$ . . . , up to $r_m$ to question $m$ can be calculated for each possible party as:

$Pr(r_1, r_2 \ldots, r_m) = Pr(r_1) \times P_r(r_2) \times \ldots$ where $Pr(a, b, \ldots)$ denotes the probability of $a$ and $b$ and so on. If we take logarithms of both sides the expression becomes

$\log [Pr(r_1, r_2, \ldots, r_m)] = \Sigma \log [Pr(r_i)]$.

The final scores created by LiRaS treat these probabilities, calculated for each of the respondents by assuming that he belongs to each party in turn, as the likelihoods for the hypothesis that the respondent belongs to the relevant party (regarded as a probability distribution). For these likelihoods, only ratios are meaningful and it is sensible to consider the logarithm of the likelihoods: a constant ratio between likelihoods corresponds to a constant difference between the logarithm of the likelihoods.

The effect of adding one more question to the list would be to add a new response $r_{m+1}$ and the logarithms of the likelihood ratios would have added to them log $[Pr(r_{m+1}$ respondent is in given party)]. The order in which we consider the questions is immaterial, and we can think of each question moving the current position of the elector by adding on these log (probabilities).

A good question will be one for which the overall effect is to move each party nearer its own corner. That is, we need to have the average movement in the right direction (towards the correct corner of the space) to be larger than the average movement in the wrong direction (towards one of the other corners). If we measure movement by the logarithm of the probability we can define net movement in the following way.

Let $P_{ik}$ be the probability of the $i$th response to the question when the respondent is known to be in the $k$th party. The log (probabilities) are the $\log(P_{i1})$, $\log(P_{i2})$ $\log(P_{in})$, where there are $n$ parties. Suppose that the respondent belongs to the $i$th

126

party, then the $\log(P_{ij})$ will be a move in the right direction, the remaining scores will all be moved away from the correct corner, the movement is thus $\log(P_{ij})$ towards the correct corner and

$$\frac{1}{n-1}\sum_{k\neq j}\log(P_{ik})$$

on average towards the wrong corner: the net movement is thus

$$\frac{n\log(P_{ij})-\sum_{k=1}^{n}\log(P_{ik})}{(n-1)}$$

where for convenience $(n-1)^{-1}\log(P_{ij})$ has been added both to the movement in the correct direction and also the movement in the wrong direction. If we now average this net movement over all respondents we get

$$\sum_i \frac{{}^n P_{ij}\log(P_{ij})}{n-1} - \sum_i \sum_{k=1} \frac{P_{ij}\log(P_{ik})}{n-1}$$

A result from information theory shows us that if

$$S(q_1,q_2,...q_n) = \sum_{i=1}^{n} p_i \log q_i, \text{ and } \Sigma q_1 = 1,$$

and $\Sigma q_i = 1$, then $S$ achieves its maximum over variation on $q_i$ when $q_i-2,=p_i$, $-S$ is then the measure of information in the probability distribution. We can see that the net movement we have constructed is essentially positive because of this result. Finally, we can add these movements for each of the parties to give an overall figure. The name information value derives from the association with the measure of information $-S(P_1, P_2, \ldots P_n)$.

It is possible to create partial information values by considering solely pairings of parties and finding the information value for the implied two-party space. When subsets of parties are to be considered separately it is convenient to take as the information value of a question and the quantity $I$, given by

$$I = \sum_{k=1} \sum_{j=1} \sum_{i=1} P_{ik}\left[\log(P_{ik})-\log(P_{ij})\right]$$
$$= \frac{1}{2}\sum_{k=1}^{n} \sum_{j=1}^{n} I_{jk}$$

where $I_{jk}$ is the partial information value
$[P_{ik}\log P_{ik}+(P_{ij}-P_{ik})\log P_{ij}-P_{ij}\log P_{ik}]$.
For any subset of parties we sum $I_{jk}$ over that subset of parties only.

## REFERENCES

Budge, Ian, and Dennis Farlie (forthcoming), *Voting and Party Competition: A Spatial Synthesis and a Critique of Existing Approaches Applied to Surveys from Ten Democracies*, Wiley, London and New York.
Butler, David, and Donald Stokes (1969), *Political Change in Britain*, Macmillan, London.
Converse, Philip E., Warren E. Miller, Jerrold Rusk and Arthur Wolfe (1969), 'Continuity and Change in American Politics: Parties and Issues in the 1968 Election', *American Political Science Review*, 63, 1083-105.

# PART II

Dimensional Analysis

# 7

# Introduction: The Relationship of Dimensional Analysis to Party Identification and Policy-Based Models

The last chapter introduced the idea of a space that has a formal resemblance to the continuum derived from party identification, in being party-defined, but whose input was entirely different. This and the following chapters consider spaces that are generally based on questions like those associated with party identification, but whose formal properties, paradoxically, are very different.

Three broad influences have shaped the development of these 'dimensional analyses' as they are called. Perhaps the most obvious is the fact that new techniques of representing similarity measures spatially have offered political scientists the opportunity for the first time of picturing party relationships directly and simply, on the basis of non-numeric survey responses unsuitable for factor-analyses (Coombs, 1964; Kruskal 1964a, 1964b). A second continuing impetus towards the production of spatial representations has been the development of so-called rational choice theories, based on 'voter rationality' assumptions that electors would advance their policy preferences by voting for the party whose programme most resembled them, and on 'office-seeking' assumptions that party leaders will seek to gain votes by adjusting programmes so as to bring them close to the preferences of most electors (Downs, 1957: for a review of developments since then see Ordeshook, Chapter 15 below). Spatial representations are not essential to this argument, but they present it directly and simply in a one- or two-dimensional space, which shows how under such conditions parties and candidates will 'converge' on the electoral modes.

Downs's hypothetical 'pictures' of distributions of electors over a one-dimensional left–right continuum (measured by degree of government intervention in the economy) have been an inspiration to dimensional analysis but also to some extent a source of confusion. The early excitement of actually deriving from survey data spaces that looked like those of Downs (at least so far as parties were concerned) obscured the fact that for Downs's reasoning to work parties and individuals had to be located in a policy space. As Mauser and Freysinnet observe below (Chapter 11), the locations of electors and parties in terms of their policy preferences have to be measured independently of their voting shifts, otherwise no explanation of voting shifts is being offered. As they further point out, most investigators have nevertheless estimated party distances in terms of feelings of closeness between parties, or even voting intentions, assuming that locations in terms of policy preferences conformed to these.

The assumption may be correct but it is untested, and spaces based on feelings of party closeness cannot therefore form a basis for Downsian explanations of voting and party competition.

They have of course many other uses, and it is here that the third broad influence on their development emerges—party identification. For as we observed in Chapter 1, dimensional analyses have been particularly developed as representations of party proximity in multi-party systems. There the traditional party identification questions failed to yield information on degrees of closeness between parties (since there was more than one voting alternative to the party you identified with)—thus analysts were not able to estimate the prospects for vote transfers and coalitions between parties. Direct questions or thermometers which invited respondents to rank all parties in terms of their relative closeness yielded such information, and were in many ways the obvious substitutes for the traditional questions, with the same types of uses. Rankings even of four or five, not to say ten or twelve parties are difficult to follow when presented in a table, hence the impetus towards spatial representations which give such information at a glance.

The essential reasoning behind most dimensional analyses therefore is that parties whose supporters feel closer to each other, on average, will be represented as closer in the space. Supporters of close parties are more likely to transfer votes between themselves than to more distant parties. Paradoxically, as Frognier points out in the case of the Belgian Liberal Party (Chapter 10), this may turn close parties into strong electoral competitors jockeying for the same voting constituency. One might speculate that in some cases this makes 'distant' parties more likely coalition partners: traditionally in The Netherlands the Catholic Party (KVP) was a preferred coalition partner with the Calvinist parties and one reason for this might have been that they did not overlap into each other's support, so long as religious influences on voting remained strong. On the other hand proximate parties who can be sure of delivering their vote to the other party by strategic withdrawals of candidates or electoral compacts obviously have a strong incentive to bargain and evolve a common policy, with the possibility of a governmental coalition at the end of it. This perhaps accounts for the tendency of analysts to interpret proximity both as predicting vote transfers *and* coalition formation, as in the case of the 'bourgeois parties' in Scandinavia (Converse and Valen, 1971; Rusk and Borre, Chapter 8 below and Damgaard and Rusk, Chapter 9 below). Whether proximity is associated with electoral or governmental competition or cooperation perhaps depends on the nature of the electoral system itself, and the scope it gives for electoral compacts.

Besides giving concise information about parties' relative closeness, analyses usually yield a space of two or three dimensions which can be given substantive interpretations in the light of party positions upon them. No more direct interpretation is possible since formally they are simply those dimensions that define the lowest-dimensional space compatible with information about rankings. Nor need they necessarily dissect the groupings of parties horizontally and vertically but can run from corner to corner obliquely, as pointed out by Mauser and Freysinnet in achieving a more satisfactory left–right interpretation of their French data (Chapter 11 below). In terms of the placements of Socialist and 'bourgeois' parties at opposite ends of a dimension, it can however be inferred to represent a left–right cleavage, like the one investigated in most of the analyses below. Other common inferred cleavages are the two found in different regions of Belgium, and in Switzerland—Clerical/Anti-Clerical and Regional (Chapters 10, 12 below).

Such inferences provide important leads for further research into the politics of the countries concerned. For example, by analysing the perceptions of different types of respondent (most obviously, of different class, regional or religious/ethnic groups, or of politicians and electors) one can see whether they share the same or different features of the political world, and thus refine predictions about vote-transfers or the future shape of party competition (as Damgaard and Rusk do very illuminatingly in Figures 9.5 and 9.6).

Just like party identification, the original concept in terms of which these analyses have been conceived, such spatial representations form a good basis for prediction and speculation about voting behaviour. Like party identification however their explanatory standing may be doubted because perceptions of party closeness are not clearly distinguishable from voting intention itself—indeed, sometimes information about vote transfers is itself used as input to the dimensional analysis. In Frognier's case this is unavoidable as he is careful to point out, because it is the only information available. But in some cases it is used where other information is available: either the purposes of such analyses are severely limited, or not enough reflection has gone into the question of what type of space is desired.

There are also technical constraints on dimensional anaylses based on party placements, and their consequences, which can be summarized as follows.

(1) The averaging process of obtaining mean placements for sets of party supporters, or correlating rank-orders, involves an assumption that the distances between rank-points are equivalent. In the extreme this may lead to misrepresentation, as when one party (such as the Communist) is at a great distance from the others. The difference in this case between Communists' rank 1 and rank 2 is greater both in distance and perhaps in quality than the difference between their other rankings. Also, the fact that there can be only one entry to represent the similarity between a pair of parties means that the mean ranking by *two* sets of supporters must be incorporated in the score. This is satisfactory when both means are close, but in the common situation where communists feel closer to socialists than socialists to communists, it leads to distortion.

(2) These points are specifications of a more general and conceptually more serious consideration. Damgaard and Rusk remark on one usefulness of placements on a 'feeling thermometer' as being that each respondent can bring his own frame of reference to the placement (Chapter 9 below; see also Inglehart and Klingemann's use of a quite contentless left–right distinction in Chapter 13). However, if different sets of respondents view the space they are in quite differently, the idea of any kind of common space comes close to breaking down (cf. Barry, 1970, on a similar argument of Downs's).

(3) Individuals cannot generally be represented in dimensional analyses, since Coombsian techniques that would represent individuals are applicable only with limited numbers of parties and respondents (cf. Mauser and Freysinnet, Chapter 11 below, for an example). Non-metric multi-dimensional scaling on the other hand can deal with large numbers of both but at the cost of averaging and thus representing parties only. We thus lack information on whether for example parties have 'wings' that might break off, or whether one group inside a party might transfer votes to a party proximate to them while the rest go elsewhere.

(4) With such representations the question arises of what precisely is a party? The representations are squarely on the side of party identification in locating the party in groups of electors. But whereas in the spatial interpretation of the party identification

continuum parties are at the end of the line, coincidental with the position of the strong identifiers, parties in dimensional analyses are points in the space defined by their relative distances from the other party points. Parties are the mean of all their supporters, and whether stronger or weaker makes no difference. In the context of party identification, however, parties are located not at the mean of all supporters but at the relatively 'pure' position of the most intense supporters, whether these constitute a numerical majority or not. To an unexploited extent the contrast between the mean or modal position of actual supporters and the pure party position of intense supporters gives rise to interesting predicitions. One could say that, other things being equal, a party where the two coincided was in a more advantageous electoral position than a party where they did not coincide. One cannot pursue this line of reasoning with the parties in dimensional analyses because the mean party position is the only party location.

(5) The discussion of party leads us to reiterate a point already made in Chapter 1 about the contrast between the space inherent in the concept of party identification and the party-inferred space of dimensional analyses. Because the end-points of its space are identified with parties, the former is a party-defined space. In the case of dimensional analyses however space is defined by the inferred qualities of its dimensions: the parties are not at the ends but are points within the space. There is a fundamental difference here, which is what we mentioned at the beginning of this discussion when we said that paradoxically, with similar input, dimensional analyses created a different formal space from that of party identification.

(6) We have stressed throughout this discussion that the dimensions based on party placements have no direct substantive interpretation but are inferred from the location of parties in relation to them (though sometimes candidate and issue locations are introduced to aid interpretation, as in Rusk and Borre's analysis of the Danish electorate (Chapter 8) or Mauser and Freysinnet's discussion of electoral strategies in France (Chapter 11). (To the extent independent interpretation is provided our remarks below apply less.) There are two difficulties with inferring qualities from party locations.

(a) Does the dimension have the same interpretation throughout? It seems clear in Damgaard and Rusk's analysis of parliamentary voting that the underlying dimension is left–right, because it contrasts Communists or socialist People's Party at one end with 'bourgeois' parties at the other. But what is one to make of the 'leftward' placement of the Radical Liberals compared with the Social Democrats in the 1950s? Were we to take the segment of the line encompassing only these two parties, would we not on party placements alone reverse our interpretation of left and right? And does this not mean that on the basis of party locations we must interpret the middle segment of the continuum as involving different qualities from the ends? Perhaps this point will not finally stick with the actual analysis carried out by Damgaard and Rusk, which being based on voting agreements is actually a policy space rather than a party-inferred space, but it does apply forcibly to the common type of dimensional analysis based on party placements by electors.

(b) There are also difficulties with comparisons of such spaces over time. Comparisons of party locations in derived spaces at different points in time have been made (Converse and Valen, 1971). In such comparisons, different locations are qualitatively interpreted as parties moving towards or away from each other. But such interpretations are purely relative. For if one party were to become universally disliked then its descent to lowest ranking would force the other parties closer together, even in the absence of any change in their own relationship. Such changes in the overall pattern of locations would in turn alter the substantive assignment of qualities to the dimensions of the space. These would consequently have different interpretations in each of the time periods, rendering any straight comparison of locations impossible.

To mention these constraints is not to imply that all analyses suffer from them equally, nor to overlook the new approaches that remedy some of the weaknesses of earlier studies. Two of the studies in the following section are of particular interest for the insight they give into probable lines of future development.

(1) Damgaard and Rusk (Chapter 9) present an analysis that uses as input not party placements but policy indicators: these consist of voting agreements between political parties. It is of considerable interest that the study reveals a basic left-right cleavage among parliamentarians which then affects the electorate—by shaping their perceptions of the party system.

This space based on policy indicators is a partial operationalization of Downsian-type policy spaces, although still limited by representing only the politicians' parties and neither the electors' parties nor—most crucially—individual electors. Damgaard and Rusk's representation of Danish electors (Chapter 9 below), following Rusk and Borre relies on electors' party placements, not their issue preferences; and anyway represents electoral parties and not individuals. Strangley, Damgaard and Rusk's handling in their parliamentary study of what must be regarded as the purest policy space yet obtained in dimensional analyses relies on inferences about the nature of the basic dimension based on party placements rather than the issue-stands involved. As pointed out previously, indirect inferences based on party placements are subject to change with the movement of parties, besides being only dubiously antecedent to the voting choices to be explained by them. A pure policy continuum is not only more obviously antecedent but more stable over time and should therefore be utilized to the full. Damgaard and Rusk move towards such utilization in interpreting their space for the 1971-74 period (later in the chapter) in terms of the actual vote divisions involved, rather than placements.

Their paper, therefore, must be seen as a key turning point in the field of dimensional analysis, as it seeks a better operationalization of directly interpretable policy spaces. The transitional nature of their analysis, based on policy spaces among politicians and party placements among electors, slightly undermines some of the substantive conclusions about the greater influence of élite on mass in normal times. Electors' party placements may well be shaped by leaders, since it is natural to view as close two parties that have just been in coalition. But electors' voting reactions to their coalition might well (as rational choice theory suggests) have more to do with whether coalition policy conforms to their own preferences, than with the fact that the party they generally support is now closer to another. In short, dimensional analyses based on party placements may well have an élitist bias (in the sense of politicians' actions predominantly shaping the space) that may be absent where electors are individually located in terms of their autonomous preferences in a policy space. Not for the first time in political science, the type of method used may shape the results. This is a further strong argument for careful reflection on the type of questions used to generate the space, which in turn determines the nature of the spatial representation—a problem about which analysts have been surprisingly unaware to date.

(2) If the future tendency of dimensional analysis will be to create pure policy spaces, how will these relate to party identification? On the face of it they would, if successful, displace it as an analytic concept since they explain voting purely in terms of electors' reactions to party manoevres—in other words, wholly in terms of the short-term election cues provided by parties and not at all in terms of the long-term predispositions that party identification is designed to measure. (On this interpretation, policy spaces, if successful, would also displace other measures of long-term predisposition such as the socioeconomic background characteristics used in Chapter 6.)

As mentioned in Chapter 1, most analysts would agree that voting requires explanation in terms not simply of short-term cues but of long-term predispositions. As many electors will stick to the same broad policy objectives over long periods (e.g. greater welfare expenditure), parties too will find it convenient even in terms of office-seeking to stick to these objectives over many elections. Thus long-term predispositions can be brought back within the policy framework by 'reserving' a particular area of the space to a particular party: electors within this area will always vote for a given party because it will always be nearer to them than any other (Robertson, 1975).

This line of reasoning is implied in Inglehart and Klingemann's interesting attempt (Chapter 13) to develop the notion of a left–right continuum as a surrogate measure of party identification for multi-party systems. Because electors and parties might be expected to remain at particular points in the continuum over long periods of time, psychological or at least fixed predispositions might develop for particular groups of electors to vote for a particular party. Hence the location of an elector on such a continuum would not only give a prediction as to which party he would vote for if its candidates ran, but (given the relatively invariant relative placements of parties on the continuum across the Common Market countries) also a prediction as to which parties he would transfer his vote in the absence of his own party. Since the left–right continuum also plays an important part in theories and investigations of governmental coalition formation (Taylor and Laver 1973) we have here a neat tie-up between voting and coalition theory.

Positions on such a left–right continuum would not of course be entirely fixed by a long-term predispositions—short-term cues might be expected to attract some votes from the supporters of neighbouring parties. Hence placements on the continuum can be examined to see how far they are determined by short-term cues against long-term predispositions, which can be measured by party identification or class or religious indicators.

Use of a left–right continuum on the lines proposed by Inglehart and Klingemann has many attractions. It is simple; it does not predetermine by definition the contributions of predispositions and cues but leaves them to be estimated empirically; and it links the idea of policy space to party identification (but see Robertson, Chapter 19 below, for an argument that these may be conceptually incompatible). There are as always problems, however, of which they themselves directly identify the chief. If forced, by a direct question, respondents will locate themselves and parties on a left–right continuum and they will moreover place themselves closest to the party they usually vote for. As with party identification in Part I, the question is, however, how antecedent or explanatory such placements are for their voting behaviour? When asked directly, large proportions of respondents in various countries will say they do not use left–right placements to decide on their vote (in Britain 20.3 per cent; in Australia 19.1 per cent), or even reveal that they do not understand the terms. Inglehart and Klingemann argue that in multi-party systems electors stand more in need of a simplifying device than in countries with a two-party or two and a half-party system. But to vote one does not need a complete mental map of the party system; one needs only the perception that one party will do better than all the rest. Voting commitments can be regarded as a more likely determinant of left–right placements than left–right placements are of voting commitments.

Inglehart and Klingemann seek to avert this criticism by demonstrating the substantial absence of correlation between left–right placements and social class: this eliminates the possibility of a spurious correlation between placements and voting choices, produced by a common relationship with class. In our opinion the absence of a class influence on the left–right continuum is somewhat surprising and must raise doubts about its validity. For if the working class are not substantially located to the left and the middle class to the right, what meaning does the continuum have? (It is significant that Rusk and Borre actually validate the main horizontal dimension of Danish electors' party space by demonstrating that working-class identification goes to the left; see Figure 8.3.) This raises suspicions that by inviting electors to place themselves between left and right, leaving the interpretation of these terms to electors themselves, each elector may be locating himself in a different substantive space—a similar point to that made earlier about contentless 'feeling thermometers'.

The existence of a single left–right continuum among electors also receives little validation from other studies. It is true that most dimensional analyses do discover a main cleavage interpretable as left–right. But adequate representations also require further dimensions. Moreover, a technique that starts off defining space in terms of the numbers of parties (like LiRaS in Chapter 6) should empirically, if electors' propensities are interpretable on a left–right continuum, find that all electors of whatever party are distributed on a line between the extreme left and extreme right party, since support for any party is then the degree of closeness or distance from the Communists. The fact that such a distribution is not empirically found in Britain, France or The Netherlands, countries that overlap with Inglehart and Klingemann's analysis, casts doubt on many electors' use of this frame of reference.

Nevertheless, whatever the empirical standing of their left–right continuum, there is no doubt that Chapter 13 is extremely valuable conceptually in emphasizing the resemblances between party-defined spaces (such as party identification and LiRaS) and policy spaces with reserved party areas. The fact that one could under certain conditions reduce itself into the other (like LiRaS into a left–right continuum in the last example) points the way to a theoretical synthesis of what might otherwise remain conceptually distinct and confusing alternative approaches. This is a point that we shall pursue in more detail in Part III (Chapter 14 and 20).

## REFERENCES

Barry, B. M. (1970), *Sociologists, Economists and Democracy*, Collier-Macmillan, London.
Coombs, C. (1964), *A Theory of Data*, Wiley, New York.
Converse, P., and H. Valen (1971), 'Dimensions of Cleavage and Perceived Party Distances in Norwegian Voting', *Scandinavian Political Studies*, 6, 107–52.

Downs, A (1957), *An Economic Theory of Democracy,* Harper & Row, New York.

Kruskal, J. B. (1964a), 'Multidimensional Scaling by Optimising Goodness of Fit to a Nonmetric Hypothesis', *Psychometrika,* 29, 1–27.

Kruskal, J. B. (1964b), 'Nonmetric Multidimensional Scaling: A Numerical Method', *Psychometrika,* 29, 115–29.

Robertson, D. (1976), *A Theory of Party Competition,* Wiley, London and New York.

Taylor, M., and M. Laver (1973), 'Government Coalitions in Western Europe', *European Journal of Political Research,* 1, 205–48.

# 8

# The Changing Party Space in Danish Voter Perceptions, 1971-73

JERROLD G. RUSK and OLE BORRE

While all political systems are characterized by elements of both continuity and change, the dominant theme of Danish politics has clearly been that of continuity with the past. Lipset and Rokkan (1967, p.50) speak of the Danish party system as 'frozen' in the 1920s, with but slight modification since that time. Rustow (1956) has also commented on the remarkable stability of the Danish polity, and in a more recent article Damgaard (1974) shows few statistical deviations from this trend in the last fifty years. The four major parties of the 1920s—the Social Democrats, Radical Liberals, Agrarian Liberals and Conservatives—have maintained their 90 to 100 per cent representation in the Parliament up to 1960, to be joined thereafter by a fifth party, the Socialist People's Party, in this continued mandate until the 1970s. Against this impressive backdrop of continuity and stability looms the recent December election of 1973 which suddenly seemed to characterize the Danish electorate as 'unstable', 'protesting', and 'Poujadist-oriented'. What Danish political observers have not been able to witness for half a century has seemingly become manifest overnight—massive sociopolitical change, which has upset the existing coalition framework of 'government' and 'opposition' parties, spurred the rise to power of new parties like the Progressive and Centre Democratic Parties and allowed older minor parties to flex new muscles in Parliament with a strengthened vote from the electorate. If Denmark is ever to become a laboratory setting for studying political change, the time seems clearly at hand.

Many have speculated about this marked change in Danish political patterns. Rejection of the major parties and acceptance of the new and minor parties has most often been seen as a reflection of the electorate's massive distrust of the 'establishment' parties and how they have run the system in the past. Inflation, high taxes and the increased costs of the welfare state—reputed to be one of the most expensive in Europe—have all been cited as reasons for people's feelings of frustration and protest against the government and the established order. Neither the 'socialist' nor the 'bourgeois' blocs in Danish politics have reportedly been able to stem the tide of economic worries experienced by the electorate. In such times of financial anxiety, it is argued that people search for new alternatives—new outlets to express their feelings of distrust and discontent. If there are political vehicles available to capitalize on these frustrations, the necessary 'floating vote' can possibly be realized, even in so stable a society as Denmark's. Two such vehicles emerged for the 1973 election—Mogen Glistrup's Progressive Party, which campaigned, often in a most simplistic manner, to cut government expenses and taxes, and Erhard Jakobsen's Centre Democratic Party, which fought against additional taxes on home-owners. Together these 'flash' parties collected 24 per cent of the vote and were joined in their newly found power by four minor parties—the Christian People's Party, Single-Tax Party, Communist Party and Left Socialist Party—which accrued another 12 per cent of the popular vote. This left the five established parties with a total vote of 64 per cent, a decrease of 29 per cent from their combined vote of 93 per cent in 1971.

Vote changes of this magnitude imply that cleavage lines have seriously changed in Danish politics, even if only temporarily, and that they may well continue to be fluid in the unsettling political atmosphere characteristic of Denmark at present. The purpose of this paper will be to analyse and explain the 1973 Danish vote and the 'change' characteristics of Danish politics witnessed in the 1973 election. With these goals in mind, the paper will be divided into four sections. The first section will deal with the general descriptive parameters of the vote and the electorate's feelings toward the parties in the recent 'change' election as contrasted with the 'stable' election of 1971. The second section will explore, through the use of multi-dimensional scaling techniques, the differing cleavages the electorate perceived in the 1973 and 1971 election settings. The third section will analyse the meaning of these cleavages and determine what caused them and the resulting vote preferences in 1973, with special attention being paid to the motivational basis for the Glistrup Progressive vote. The last section will discuss the implications of the 1973 election for the future of the Danish political system.

The data bases for the analyses in this paper consist of a national cross-section sample of the Danish electorate in 1971 ($N=1,302$) and a randomly selected subset of this sample ($N=533$) which was interviewed again after the 1973 election.* This 1971-73 panel of 533 people will constitute the significant data base for our analysis of individual change characteristics between the two elections.

## THE 1971 AND 1973 ELECTIONS

The 1971 election in Denmark seemed to reflect the normal power struggle between the 'socialist' and 'bourgeois' blocs of parties, with the socialist bloc replacing the bourgeois bloc as the government in this particular election. Political observers at the time seemed to regard the election as simply another element in the continuing series of left-right bloc politics which has been a mainstay of the Danish system since the 1920s. For this reason, the 1971 election seems an appropriately stable reference point by which to judge the volatile affair of December 1973. However, there could

---

* This randomly selected subset of the sample ($N=533$) was interviewed just before *and* just after the September 1971 election, whereas these same people were interviewed only *after* the December 1973 election. They seem to reflect both the characteristics of the master sample in 1971 ($N=1,302$) and such aggregate characteristics as the vote divisions in the 1971 and 1973 elections.

Table 8.1   Popularity of the Danish Parties, 1971–73

| | Mean Thermometer Scores | | Standard Deviation of Thermometer Scores | | Percentage Giving the Party Zero Score | | Percentage Ranking the Party * 1973 | | Percentage in Voting Support | | Official Data Change |
| --- | --- | --- | --- | --- | --- | --- | --- | --- | --- | --- | --- |
| | 1971 | 1973 | 1971 | 1973 | 1971 | 1973 | First | Last | September 1971 | December 1973 | 1971–73 |
| Social Democrats .......... | 19.0 | 19.9 | 23.0 | 25.1 | 20.8 | 16.2 | 37 | 6 | 37.3 | 25.7 | -11.6 |
| Radical Liberals .......... | 18.0 | 19.3 | 18.9 | 18.6 | 14.8 | 15.7 | 25 | 2 | 14.4 | 11.2 | - 3.2 |
| Agrarian Liberals ......... | 11.0 | 18.1 | 24.3 | 24.0 | 21.9 | 14.3 | 29 | 5 | 15.6 | 12.3 | - 3.3 |
| Christian People's Party ... | - 8.1 | 10.8 | 23.6 | 23.3 | 42.4 | 25.7 | 13 | 6 | 2.0 | 4.0 | 2.0 |
| Center Democrats .......... | | 8.7 | | 23.8 | | 27.2 | 12 | 7 | | 7.8 | 7.8 |
| Conservatives ............. | 9.2 | 6.2 | 22.8 | 23.6 | 25.0 | 24.5 | 10 | 12 | 16.7 | 9.1 | - 7.6 |
| Single-Tax (Justice) Party . | - 2.1 | 2.3 | 18.0 | 19.8 | 50.7 | 43.3 | 7 | 6 | 1.7 | 2.9 | 1.2 |
| Socialist People's Party ... | 2.6 | - 5.4 | 25.6 | 27.8 | 22.6 | 23.9 | 11 | 25 | 9.1 | 6.0 | - 3.1 |
| Progressive Party .......... | | - 5.8 | | 32.8 | | 23.3 | 15 | 31 | | 15.9 | 15.9 |
| Left Socialists ........... | -13.1 | -14.1 | 23.4 | 25.1 | 36.4 | 34.3 | 3 | 34 | 1.6 | 1.5 | - 0.1 |
| Communist Party ........... | -22.6 | -18.4 | 25.0 | 28.0 | 25.8 | 24.8 | 5 | 50 | 1.4 | 3.6 | 2.2 |

*These columns add up to more than 100 percent because a respondent could give the same highest or lowest score to several parties.

Note: The data reported here are for the 1971 panel (N = 533). They correspond very closely with the figures for the larger master sample of that year (N = 1302).

have been important undercurrents in the 1971 election which simply did not surface because no vehicle was present to mobilize them adequately. If such undercurrents were present, few recognized them at the time. The only issue of note in the campaign, according to Borre and Katz (1973), was the question of Denmark's entry into the European Community, a matter subsequently resolved in a popular referendum a year later. The exchange in power between the two blocs seemed on the surface to suggest no mass-based discontent or distrust. A mere 2.3 per cent shift in the vote accomplished the change in government, with the Social Democratic Party becoming the new government and using the Socialist People's Party for support from outside. Such minority-based governments with an outside support party (or parties) are a common staple of Danish politics (Damgaard, 1969). The bourgeois parties—the Radical Liberals, Agrarian Liberals and Conservatives—then retired to become the 'loyal opposition'.

The period between September 1971 and December 1973 seemed to focus on two issues that could have been harbingers of the volatility soon to come. In October 1972, the Danish electorate supported entry into the European Community, a proposal heavily backed by the Prime Minister, Jens Otto Krag; these voters would have some fourteen months to reflect on the wisdom of the decision before the next election was called. Shortly after the victorious referendum, Krag resigned his post in favour of another Social Democrat, Anker Jørgensen. The other issue that was becoming increasingly salient during this period was the correlated problem of increasing governmental expenditures and rising taxes. The squeeze on the non-farm population's real disposable income was an inevitable consequence of these trends, and almost simultaneously the Progressive Party appeared, led by the tax lawyer Glistrup, promoting simple remedies for these economic ills. Glistrup promised to abolish the income tax for those earning less than $10,000 a year, to cut seriously the governmental bureaucracy and, indeed, all those who merely 'shuffled paper', and to disband Denmark's army. He strongly criticized the major parties for their inability to solve Denmark's economic problems. Gallup polls record his rapid appeal to the people, registering a 20 to 25 per cent level of support within a few months after his arrival on the political scene. The issue of economic problems continued to command media attention when Erhard Jakobsen, a Social Democrat, walked out on his party in December 1973 because of its proposal to increase taxes on home-owners. By his leaving, Jakobsen caused the government to collapse, necessitating a new general election.

This was the situation in December 1973. Table 8.1 reflects the relative standings of the various political parties in the 1971 and 1973 elections as well as people's perceptions of the parties in these two election years. Most of the table is self-explanatory. The vote losses of the five major parties are evident and, save for the minute loss of the Left Socialists, constitute the only vote losses in the table. Glistrup's 16 per cent and Jakobsen's 8 per cent vote gains are immediately noted. The Christian People's Party, Single-Tax Party and Communist Party all gained sufficient votes in 1973 to pass the seat threshold for Parliament. Their gains are particularly interesting since they represent moves to the left (Communist Party), centre (Single-Tax Party) and right (Christian People's Party), although the dominant move among the electorate was clearly to the right-based parties, with the centre–right Jakobsen Democrats and the rightist Glistrup Progressives registering the biggest increases.

The first eight columns of the table represent the panel respondents' reactions to the parties on a 'feeling thermometer' scale.* Briefly put, the voters were asked to evaluate the parties on a −100 to +100 scale in 1971 and a −50 to +50 scale in 1973, with minus values indicating negative feelings about the parties and plus values indicating positive feelings. Zero was regarded as the neutral point on each scale. Mean and standard deviation values for the parties in 1971 were divided by two in an attempt to obtain a rough comparability with the different scale range used in 1973, although comparisons between the two years must be made with some caution since respondents could use different individual scoring ranges when presented with a 200- and a 100-point scale, respectively. However, this cautionary note need apply only to across-year comparisons of our mean and standard deviation statistics since the different scale ranges used should have but a minimal effect, if any, on the scaling operations to follow.

Table 8.1 makes clear that the most popular parties in 1971 were the five main parties—the parties comprising the 'socialist' and 'bourgeois' blocs. The rest of the parties in the system—the minor parties not represented in Parliament in 1971—all received negative mean values on the 'feeling thermometer'. In 1973 the pattern of mean values changes somewhat for the same respondents. The three parties who received the highest mean scores in 1971—the Social Democrats, Radical Liberals and Agrarian Liberals—continue to hold their rank positions in 1973, but the next two rank locations go to a new party (Centre Democrats) and a minor party (Christian People's Party). After this follow the other two major parties (Conservatives, People's Socialists), and the remaining four parties have negative mean values. The most interesting of these negative values is Glistrup's Progressive Party, which received a large 16 per cent of the vote but was quite disliked by a large percentage of the people, 31 per cent of our respondents giving this party their lowest score on our thermometer scale. Standard deviation figures for both elections are high, indicating a considerable variance among the people with regard to how they rated the parties. The existence of an essentially bipolarized party politics helps to explain the variance for the main parties, the 'socialist' and 'bourgeois' camps, but it is interesting, particularly in 1973, to note that people were quite divided in their sympathies for the new and minor parties as well.

Comparisons, as noted above, should be made with caution. Nevertheless, there appears to be a basic pattern in the across-year comparison of mean values. The major or 'establishment' parties, except possibly for the People's Socialists, did not significantly change in their mean popularity although their vote decreased. What seemed to happen was that these parties were still rated quite high on the thermometer scale by those who defected from them in 1973. The mean scores for the minor parties also did not significantly change between the two election periods.

Some of these comparisons obviously prompt the question of the exact relationship between the vote and our 'feeling thermometer' scores. In an attempt to answer this, we compared people's vote choice with the party they rated highest on the thermometer scale to see if a marked congruence existed. If one also considers ties

---

\* The 'feeling thermometer' scale was originally devised by Aage R. Clausen for social groups and was later revised by Jerrold Rusk and Herbert Weisberg to apply as a device for rating political candidates. It has since been transplanted to Europe to rate political parties. For research conducted with this scale in the United States, see Weisberg and Rusk (1970), Rusk and Weisberg (1972) and Wang, Schonemann and Rusk (forthcoming).

for the first rank, then the correspondence is very high. For the five main parties in the system, 86.2 to 96.2 per cent of the voters for these parties in 1973 also ranked them highest on the thermometer scale. With the exception of the Communists, 81.0 to 100 per cent of the voters of all other parties gave their party the first rank on the thermometer scale. This latter finding is also impressive, given that the voters for the new and minor parties tend to be more volatile in their behaviour. In all, save for the Communists, the range of validity is between 81 and 100 per cent, with the voters of five of the parties in the 90 per cent range. This would seem to say that our thermometer scale taps the vote of the people well, especially given the complexity of doing this in a multi-party state in which the respondent is asked to give scores to eleven different parties. Our thermometer scale can most probably be interpreted as a 'vote preference' variable with the relative scores that a respondent gives the parties on it representing the rank-order of his vote choices from first to last. Obviously some slippage will exist in scoring eleven parties, especially in adjacent rank choices, but the overall order should represent relative vote choices well. This fact has crucial meaning for us, since later we will use the thermometer scale to measure the 'vote preference' construct.

A few additional things should be noted about our thermometer data. First, many people tied two or more parties for their highest score on the thermometer—26 per cent of our respondents in all. This could be interpeted as a natural reaction in an election that created intense cross-pressures and massive vote defections, many voters torn between voting for their old party of long standing and moving to an attractive new party. This tying tendency is particularly noticeable among those who did decide to vote for a new or minor party, which possibly means that a reservoir of support remains for the major parties if the new or minor parties do not satisfy their recently won adherents. These tendencies can also be observed in Table 8.1 in the 'per cent ranking a given party first' on the thermometer scale. The major parties receive a large percentage of first place choices (tied and untied), much larger than their 1973 vote total (with the exception of the Conservatives). This shows considerable room for possible improvement in future elections. On the other hand, the next column, last place choices, shows a decided dislike of four of the parties—the two leftist minor parties (Communists, Left Socialists), a leftist major party (People's Socialists) and the Glistrup party. The figures for the Socialist People's Party comment on the potentially tenuous hold this party has on its 'major party' status. While it has potential for improvement from its first place scores, it is also true that a hard core of 25 per cent dislike it. The Glistrup figure is predictable and reminds one of the George Wallace phenomenon in the United States—a small minority who intensely like the candidate and a much larger group who do not.

An overall summary of the vote and attitudinal data in Table 8.1 would seem to indicate the following. The major parties lost votes in 1973 but at least three of them did not necessarily lose ground permanently with the voters, since they maintained their high mean rankings in 1973 as well as registering a large number of first place choices among the electorate. While the Social Democrats, Radical Liberals and Agrarian Liberals can potentially recoup much of their voting losses in succeeding elections, the future does not appear as bright for the Conservatives and possibly not for the People's Socialists as well. Their loss of votes seems to coincide with psychologically losing any remaining sympathies with their defectors. This judgement may be too harsh, but the losses for these two parties appear across the board on both the attitudinal and vote variables. The picture for the other parties is more complex. Glistrup's Progressive Party and Jakobsen's Centre Democrats have no 1971 base for comparison, but the 1973 attitudinal data indicate at least a bipolarization of opinion on the Glistrup party. The fact that many of the voters for these two parties also rank another party first on the thermometer scale (38 per cent of both the Glistrup and Jakobsen voters) spells possible defections back to these voters' original parties. The minor parties present a mixed picture. All show a larger percentage giving them first place scores on the attitudinal scale than voted for them, but only in the case of the Christian People's Party—a moralist party formed to fight pornography and abortion—does the differential seem marked and hence encouraging for possible future growth for this party.

The basic reading of Table 8.1 is that the stable left-right bloc politics of 1971 seriously changed in certain ways in the December election of 1973. While the table hints that some of the changes may not be permanent, giving the major parties hope for the future, the basis for these present changes, even if the future proves them transitory, must lie in a changing of cleavage lines in the electorate, in a new view of the 'political space' by this electorate. We will now turn to a systematic empirical investigation of these possible, changing, cleavage lines.

## CLEAVAGE STRUCTURES

If cleavage lines have changed in the 1971-73 period, a particularly appropriate way for tapping this is through the use of proximity scaling techniques. As Rusk and Weisberg (1972) have pointed out elsewhere, the Shepard-Kruskal scaling technique, using Pearson correlation data as input information, is the best method for getting at the electorate's perceptions of cleavage lines in politics. Using the 'feeling thermometer' to rate parties allows respondents to freely employ their own frames of reference. Correlations computed between the electorate's ratings of pairs of parties are then interpreted as 'similarity coefficients'—the higher the positive correlation, the more the respondents perceive the parties as similar in some way, and the higher the negative correlation the more they view two parties as dissimilar to one another. These notions of similarity/dissimilarity most usually follow the way the electorate perceives cleavage lines between the parties, and this technique is further enhanced by the fact that correlations act as a standardising device, eliminating idiosyncratic variation unique to any given party while concentrating on the covariation in ratings between parties (see Daalder and Rusk (1972) especially pp.196-8). The Shepard-Kruskal technique then translates these notions of 'similarity' and 'dissimilarity' into a geometric mapping of the parties (Kruskal, 1964).* Simply put, this scaling technique interprets the correlations as monotonic with distances—the closer to +1 the correlation between two parties, the closer together should be their corresponding points in a geometric representation. A 'goodness of fit' measure called 'stress' is calculated to indicate the extent to which the best solution achieved in a given number of dimensions satisfies a monotonic fit with the data. The stress value is at a minimum for the 'correct' solution and increases sharply in value as the number of dimensions being used is cut too far below the correct number.

* The computer program used was developed by E. E. Roskam and J. Lingoes as a particular adaptation of the Shepard-Kruskal scaling logic and is called 'MINISSA-1'. We are grateful to our colleague P. Nannestad Olsen for converting this program to the Control Data 6400 Computer at the University of Aarhus.

144

The scaling solution for the five parties represented in Parliament in 1971 is shown in Figure 8.1. It is a one-dimensional solution since this achieved virtually zero stress. The interpretation of the dimension is straightforward: the electorate perceived the party structure along the left–right cleavage lines which have long characterized Danish politics. This particular manifestation of Danish politics—the bipolarization pattern of 'socialist' and 'bourgeois' parties—has only been in existence since 1966 but the broader left–right model consisting of left, centre and rightist blocs of parties has characterized the system long before this. As Damgaard and Rusk show in the next chapter, this basic left–right model has been the main basis for how parties have voted in Parliament since 1953. Obviously, the electorate has also recognized this cleavage structure and found it a meaningful expression of their political interests and needs.

Figure 8.1    The 1971 party space. The 1971 master sample (N=1302) revealed
the same scaling solution as the panel subset (N=533) used here

In the space, the Socialist People's Party and the Agrarian Liberal-Conservative coalition represent the left–right poles of the dimension. The Social Democratic Party is close to, and can basically be said to cluster with, the Socialist People's Party. This is termed the 'socialist' bloc of parties, and in the last two minority governments formed by the Social Democrats (1966–68, 1971–73) they have relied on the outside support of this other socialist party. (The Socialist People's Party was formed only in 1958 and first received representation in Parliament in 1960.) The three other parties cluster on the right side of the dimension as the 'bourgeois' parties—the Radical Liberals, the Agrarian Liberals and Conservatives—and these parties formed the government in 1968–71.

The basic distance between these left and right clusters is crucial. In 1971 the electorate saw these two blocs of parties as considerably different from one another in terms of policy and programme. There is no 'centre' aspect to this distribution as was the case in earlier days in Danish politics. When this basic scaling analysis was repeated for all parties that contested seats for Parliament in 1971—the five parties in Figure 8.1 who were represented in Parliament and the four minor parties who were not—the basic one-dimensional left–right model again surfaced (not shown). The conclusion that immediately confronts the observer is that the 1971 election continued to reflect a left–right dimension in politics, at least as seen by the electorate. No other dimension of evaluation—no other cleavage lines in essence—seemed to divide the voters.

In the 1973 election, cleavage lines seriously began to change. Whether this is a permanent realignment or not is too difficult to tell at this time of writing, but clearly the electorate no longer viewed politics solely along the left–right dimension presumably so often used in the past. As Figure 8.2 reveals, a second dimension emerges, pitting the two new 'major' parties, Glistrup's Progressive Party and

Jakobsen's Centre Democratic Party, against the five old 'major' parties.* Together these seven parties represented 88 per cent of the vote in the general election. The other dimension in the space, the horizontal axis, shows the element of continuity from the 1971 election, for this is the familiar left–right dimension once again.

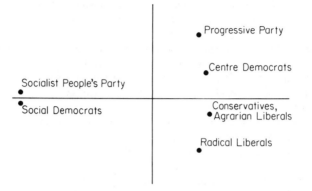

Figure 8.2     The 1973 party space

Figure 8.2 seems to relate two vital points. First, the strong element of continuity is still present in Danish politics. The five old parties are still viewed along the same cleavage lines as before. But this notion of cleavage politics no longer fully describes the Danish electorate. A new dimension has emerged, which contrasts two new and very important parties, which collected 24 per cent of the national vote in the first general election they contested, with the five old 'established' major parties, which collectively lost 29 per cent of their adherents in the last election. The proper interpretation of this dimension may simply be 'new party–old party', but Denmark has had new parties before that have failed to create the impact that the Progressive and Centre Democratic parties did. Several aspects of the current political situation may be correlated with this new dimension and therefore help to explain it. Perhaps frustration or distrust was responsible for the rejection of the five old parties in favour of these two new parties. The past performance of the bourgeois (1968–71) and the socialist (1971–73) bloc governments may have been far from satisfactory in people's minds, opening up channels for new and more attractive alternatives. Particular issues such as rising taxes, increasing inflation, the burgeoning nature of social welfare and reaction to membership of the European Community could be associated with support for Glistrup and Jakobsen.

All we know for sure at this point is that the people perceived the political world in far different terms than before and that this was reflected in their voting behaviour. The next section will attempt to delineate, in more precise terms, the reasons for these changing perceptions—the reasons why Danish politics has entered a new phase of cleavage structures.

* The 'stress' figures for the two- and one-dimensional solutions for these seven parties were not very different, but we decided the second dimension was important because the one-dimensional solution piled all parties up at two points, revealing an unsatisfactory resolution of the distances implicit in the correlation data.

## EXPLANATIONS OF CLEAVAGE STRUCTURES

The fact that people perceived the political world differently in 1973 than before and that this was reflected in their voting behaviour still leaves unanswered questions about the meaning of these different perceptions and what caused them to form. Figure 8.2 has shown us how cleavage lines have changed in Danish politics, but, at best, it has only been able to hint at what these cleavage lines represent and why they were formed. In order to answer such questions more directly, further analysis and tests must be conducted. One such test is to extend the spatial analysis itself by asking how the voters' attitudes on selected aspects of politics fit into the space with their perceptions of the parties. The way in which these attitudes relate to the parties in space can give us a better handle on how to interpret the space—on exactly what the cleavage dimensions represent to Danish voters.

We have selected four attitudinal items to enter into the party space. They are attitudes toward the European Community, political ideology, political distrust and social class identification.* We have also included the respondents' attitudes to all eleven parties in the system, adding the four smaller parties to the more important seven parties originally pictured in Figure 8.2. To achieve this combined space, several additional correlations were needed beyond those required for the scaling solution shown in Figure 8.2. Most importantly, correlations between the respondents' political attitudes and their party perceptions were necessary, but also the interrelations between the attitudinal items themselves, and the correlations between the four parties added to the space, were needed. The result was a correlation matrix which had eighty-four more entries than the one used to produce Figure 8.2. Its translation into a scaling space is shown in Figure 8.3.

There are several things to note about Figure 8.3. First, the locations of the seven main parties in this space are similar to their locations in Figure 8.2, indicating that this enlarged space is only amplifying the basic cleavage lines already depicted in Figure 8.2. This is an important finding because, given the additional statistical relationships that the scaling algorithm must satisfy in order to produce Figure 8.3, the parties' locations could have been different in the two spaces. Second, the locations of the four minor parties which were added to this space tend to follow predictable patterns. The liberal-oriented minor parties—the Left Socialists and Communists—appear on the left, the moderate-to-liberal Single-Tax Party falls just left of centre in the space, and the conservative Christian People's Party is found on the far right. Of special interest is the fact that three of these four parties also appear on the upper half of the vertical dimension with the two new major parties—the Centre Democrats and Progressives—although their loadings on this dimension are much

---

* The European Community item came from the 1971 survey and was worded as follows: 'We should under no circumstances join the European Community.' The respondent was given five response alternatives (Likert format). The political ideology item was represented as a Likert scale based on eight questions, including questions 9, 11, and 12 in Table 8.2. Other questions dealt with the importance of free competition, governmental interference with private property, etc. On each question, five response categories were used. The political distrust item was a Guttman scale composed of questions 1–4 in Table 8.2. The social class identification item was measured by responses to the following questions: 'Do you feel that you belong to any particular social class?' (If belongs) 'Which class is that?' (If does not belong) 'If you were to locate yourself in a particular social class anyway, which one would it be?' This resulted in a five-point scale: 1—belongs to middle class; 2—locates in middle class; 3—does not locate in any class; 4—locates in working class; 5—belongs to working class.

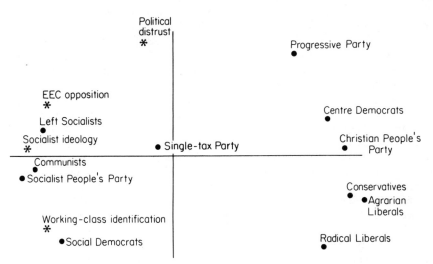

Figure 8.3     The full 1973 party space, including four attitudinal items

lower. Third, and most important, the attitude items are located in the space in such a way as to help us interpret the cleavage lines existing in contemporary Danish politics.

The attitude item that loads highest on the horizontal dimension is 'socialist ideology', and the one loading highest on the vertical dimension is 'political distrust'. The location of these two items suggests an obvious interpretation of these two dimensions. The horizontal axis appears to represent the left–right cleavage to voters as we expected, a cleavage that has dominated Danish politics for over half a century. The division of Danish politics into 'socialist' and 'bourgeois' blocs is well illustrated by the fact that 'socialist ideology' loads high on the left side of this dimension. If we had included the reverse coding of this item in the space, 'conservative ideology' would have appeared on the opposite end of this axis. While 'socialist' and 'conservative' ideologies are obviously less well developed as belief systems among the masses than among the political élites, it is nevertheless true that the masses can and do use definite aspects of these perspectives in viewing the political world and can readily place themselves with their ideological bloc of parties. The fact that the 'working-class identification' item also loads well on this dimension and especially clusters with the main socialist party, the Social Democrats, again validates our interpretation of this dimension. Uncovering such a dimension in our spatial analysis shows the Danish voters' strong ties to their political past.

But the second dimension reflects a reshaping of politics by the electorate to meet current needs and problems. Those discontented or distrustful of the system definitely define cleavage lines along an 'establishment–non-establishment' party axis. All the new and minor parties, save for the Communists, are represented on the upper half of this dimension in contrast to the establishment parties of both the left and the right on the lower end. The leader in this movement to capitalize on discontent and distrust—the Glistrup Progressive Party—is also the party that loads highest on this dimension. The fact that discontent and distrust were the underlying motivating forces for these new cleavage lines is aptly demonstrated by the political distrust scale dominating this dimension. Many people seemed to be unwilling to trust either the bourgeois or socialist blocs of parties, which had formed the previous two governments, to solve the problems with which they were concerned. They were searching for new alternatives, and these alternatives were the parties represented in the upper half of the second dimension.

These new and minor parties were able to benefit from the feelings of discontent and distrust in the electorate, but such feelings do not exist in a vacuum. When discontent is manifest, it is usually tied to specific issues and problems. While it will be a later task to attempt to specify just what these issues and problems were, the attitudinal item on the European Community appears in the space in such a way as to give us some first tangible clues. Reactions to the European Community could be based on a wide variety of motivations, but clearly, since the Community is seen first and foremost as an economic institution, people most probably identified it with their economic problems. Of course, these problems could be different for left-oriented voters than for right-oriented voters. But it seems certain that, since this item was the only other attitudinal variable to load on the upper half of the second dimension, it signals the importance of economic problems in creating discontent and distrust in the electorate. The European Community debate in Denmark in 1972 and the subsequent referendum seemed to have played an important role in generating controversy over economic matters.

Attitude items such as the European Community issue have assisted us greatly in the interpretation of the cleavage dimensions first observed in Figure 8.2. With some necessary reservation, they can also aid us in understanding how these cleavage patterns were formed. The first dimension may well have been the product of social class identifications and various early issues in the country which led to the development of socialist and bourgeois ideologies. The second dimension seems to have been caused by the more immediate factors of political distrust in the older, established parties and concern over more current issues and problems. We base these explanations on the fact that the scaling space geometrically represents the statistical relationships between the attitudinal items and the cleavage dimensions. However, caution in inferring causality must be observed, because correlation does not necessarily imply causation and because not all of these attitudinal items need to have played a causal role in the formation of these cleavages. However, if for the moment we can infer that these were the processes by which these cleavages were formed, and further conclude that these cleavages were directly translated into voting patterns, then the following is a likely scenario of voters' decision-making in the 1973 election. Voters who remained loyal to their party in 1973 basically did so because of their faith in it and the system and because class identification and ideologically related matters (including the 'old' issues that gave rise to these ideologies) were of more importance to them than more current factors, which promoted unrest and discontent among many voters. People who were less trustful of the established parties and more discontented with current problems defected to the new and minor parties on election day. Even their defection, however, was often limited by the presence of the first dimension, as voters who defected did not stray ideologically very far from their party of long standing.

Causal inferences such as these must be regarded as tentative pending a more detailed investigation of these and other attitudinal factors. Spatial analysis plays an important part in establishing such inferences, but as a technique it is limited in the extent to which it can determine causality. As a result we shall look at attitudinal variables from the perspective of percentage distributions and correlation analysis. Table 8.2 lists several attitudinal variables under the five substantive headings of political distrust, the European Community, conventional ideology, new issues and reference groups. (Wordings for these questions are given in the Appendix.) The first three columns of the table list the percentage of our panel respondents who gave 'partly agree' or 'completely agree' answers in 1971 and 1973 to our five-point Likert attitude questions and the percentage change in opinion on these questions between the two elections. The next five columns give the Pearson correlation values between these attitudinal variables and the rankings of the parties (from 1 to 11) as derived from our party thermometer questions. In several cases the correlations have been averaged for groups of parties that tended to show similar correlations and to cluster in our scaling space. Thus the Communist, Left Socialist and Socialist People's Parties have been combined into a left-wing group; the bourgeois coalition of Conservatives, Agrarian Liberals and Radical Liberals have formed yet another group; and the Centre Democratic and Christian People's Parties have constituted a third group. The correlations for the Social Democrats and the Progressive Party were not combined with other parties.* These various correlations closely resemble the earlier correlations between some of these attitudinal variables and the party thermometer questions that helped to form our scaling space in Figure 8.3. By including them in the table, we can analyse these correlations separately instead of relying only on the aggregated solution of the scaling space. Also, since the thermometer question is a good indicator of vote preference, as noted earlier, these correlations will help us to analyse in more detail not only the cleavage space but also the voting decision in 1973 which is closely related to it. These correlations can in fact be said to represent not only sympathies for these parties but the relative vote preferences for them as well. The final four columns focus directly on the vote itself, but on one particular aspect of it—vote changes. These columns give the Pearson values between the attitudinal items and changes in people's vote between 1971 and 1973. The specific 'vote change' categories that are examined are: (1) shifts of socialist bloc voters in 1971 to the Communist, Left Socialist and Single-Tax Parties; (2) shifts of socialist bloc voters in 1971 to the 'new bourgeois' parties, a term we shall use for brevity to refer to the Progressive, Center Democratic and Christian People's Parties; (3) shifts of bourgeois bloc voters in 1971 to the 'new bourgeois' parties; and finally (4) all vote shifts combined (i.e. stable *v.* unstable voters between 1971 and 1973).

## Political distrust

The first four rows of the table contain the political distrust questions that formed the distrust scale shown in Figure 8.3. These questions deal with four different aspects of distrust, and while the distribution of responses varies from question to question, the most salient fact is the large proportion of people who selected the distrust categories in each of these questions. Sixty-seven per cent of the electorate agree that 'politicians give up many of their principles'; 78 per cent believe that 'politicians care very little about what the people think'; and 91 per cent feel that 'politicians are too generous

---

* The Single-Tax Party was not included in this part of the table because of the low correlations found between the rankings of this party and most of the attitudinal items, the most noteworthy exceptions being the high negative correlations with the European Community items.

Table 8.2  Relation of Political Attitudes to Party Sympathies and Vote Switching, 1973

| | % Agreement | | | Correlations with Party Rankings | | | | | Correlations with Vote Shifts | | | |
|---|---|---|---|---|---|---|---|---|---|---|---|---|
| | 1971 | 1973 | Change | Left Wing | Soc. Dem. | Bourg. Bloc | CD & Chr.P. | Prog. Party | To S-T, LS,CP From SB | To PP,CD,Chr.P. From SB | From BB | All Vote Shifts |
| **I. Political Distrust** | | | | | | | | | | | | |
| 1. Pol's Are Too Generous | 80 | 91 | +11 | -.12* | -.15* | .01* | .13* | .20* | .05 | .16* | .23* | .08* |
| 2. Pol's Care Too Little | 72 | 78 | + 6 | .04 | -.01* | -.12* | -.01 | .20 | .05 | .16 | .15* | .10* |
| 3. Pol's Give Up Principles ** | 57 | 67 | +10 | .06 | .08* | -.12 | .00* | .07* | .12* | .02 | .18 | .09* |
| 4. Pol's Make Right Decisions | 60 | 46 | -14 | .04 | -.10 | -.06 | -.08 | .16 | .19 | .09 | .22* | .10 |
| **II. European Community and NATO** | | | | | | | | | | | | |
| 5. We Should Leave NATO ** | 29 | 30 | + 1 | -.34* | -.23* | .31* | .23* | .01 | -.23* | .03 | -.02 | -.10* |
| 6. EC Has Economic Advantages | 45 | 48 | + 3 | -.32* | -.20* | .33* | .22* | .04 | -.24* | .02 | .00 | -.09 |
| 7. EC Is Undemocratic ** | 34 | 45 | +11 | -.28* | -.14* | .32* | .14* | -.01 | -.15* | .11* | -.07 | -.05 |
| 8. EC Threatens Our Independence | 41 | 42 | + 1 | -.29 | -.18 | .27 | .19 | -.01 | -.21 | .13 | .00 | .02 |
| **III. Conventional Ideology** | | | | | | | | | | | | |
| 9. Too Little Investment Control ** | 57 | 63 | + 6 | -.24* | -.28* | .25* | .12* | .08* | -.07 | .15* | -.04 | .06 |
| 10. Impose Wage Freeze | .. | .. | ... | -.20* | -.25* | .20* | .13* | .13 | -.03 | -.07 | .02 | .03 |
| 11. Tax High Incomes More ** | 52 | 71 | +19 | -.20* | -.19* | .18* | .12* | .02* | -.02 | -.02* | .03 | -.03* |
| 12. Strive Toward Equality | 55 | 53 | - 2 | -.24 | -.24 | .18 | .14 | .11 | .01 | .19 | .03 | .08 |
| **IV. New Issues** | | | | | | | | | | | | |
| 13. Morals Are Decaying | .. | .. | ... | -.18* | -.12* | .12 | .22* | .04 | -.10 | .03 | .01 | -.04 |
| 14. Kill Extreme Views in TV | 36 | 42 | + 6 | -.16* | -.06 | .06 | .19* | .11* | -.16 | -.07 | .00 | -.05 |
| 15. Control Welfare Support Better | .. | .. | ... | -.16* | -.07* | .07 | .12* | .13* | -.03 | .09* | .04 | -.06* |
| 16. Too Many Get Social Services ** | .. | .. | ... | -.20* | -.09* | .05* | .14* | .24* | -.05* | .16 | .08 | .08 |
| 17. Tax One-Family Houses More ** | .. | .. | ... | -.20* | -.17* | .11* | .19* | .15* | -.16 | .11* | -.05 | -.01 |
| 18. Employers Should Decide | .. | .. | ... | -.30 | -.12 | .18* | .18 | .14* | -.04 | .16 | .10* | .07* |
| 19. Let A Strong Man Seize Power | 47 | 56 | + 9 | -.01 | -.04 | -.08 | .00 | .25 | -.03 | .08 | .24 | .15 |
| **V. Reference Groups** | | | | | | | | | | | | |
| 20. Working Class Identification | .. | .. | ... | .29* | .33* | -.24* | -.14* | -.14* | .02 | -.19* | -.02 | -.12* |
| 21. Soc./Bourg. Party Id. 1971 | .. | .. | ... | .42* | .60* | -.45* | -.21* | -.30* | -.22* | -.19* | -.21* | -.08* |

*Significant at 5 percent level   **These items were reversed before correlations were computed with the taxpayer's money'. Even 54 per cent disagree with or are ambivalent about the positive-oriented statement that 'political leaders generally make the right decisions'. Such findings obviously show that our earlier emphasis on the importance of political distrust in the 1973 election was not misplaced.

Further indications of the importance of political distrust in 1973 are shown in the correlation data. Feelings of distrust correlate well with both sympathy for the Glistrup Progressive Party and vote shifts to that party and the other 'new bourgeois' parties. There is also some small tendency for distrust to be correlated with left-wing party rankings and vote shifts. Conversely, feelings of trust are most usually associated with sympathy for the socialist and bourgeois blocs of established parties. When feelings of distrust are present, the intensity of these feelings is also related to the vote. Among those giving distrust responses to none or only one of the four questions, only 7 per cent shifted their vote to one of the new or minor parties, whereas this propensity to switch votes between elections rose to 26, 31 and 47 per cent, respectively, for those giving two, three or four distrust responses. These correlation patterns seem to confirm what our scaling space had earlier indicated: distrust of the established parties prompted people to perceive favourably, and in many instances to vote for, either the 'new bourgeois' or left-wing parties. It must be emphasized, however, that such tendencies were much stronger for the Progressive Party than for these other parties.

This tendency for distrust to be related to the vote varied with the particular distrust question being used. While the four distrust questions formed a unidimensional scale, each tapped a somewhat different aspect of distrust. This allowed people to evaluate political distrust from more than one perspective, with important consequences for the prediction of voting behaviour. For example, people who supported the Single-Tax and far-left parties were far more sensitive to the questions of politicians' principles and decision-making than they were to problems of finances or representation. Voters who switched from the socialist bloc to the 'new bourgeois' parties were, however, more concerned about politicians spending too much money and not caring about people's opinions. Only voters who shifted from the bourgeois bloc to the 'new bourgeois' parties cared about equally for all four distrust items; even within this group, the Glistrup supporters were more worried about the first two. Overall, the correlations that stand out for these groups are among the largest in the table, showing that widespread distrust in 1973 was one of the most crucial factors affecting the vote decision.

The widespread distrust in 1973 was not entirely unique to this election year. As the percentage distributions show, considerable distrust also existed in 1971. Since relatively few vote shifts occurred in this earlier election, the distrust existing then, for whatever reason, did not manifest itself in behavioural terms. Perhaps few alternatives existed to excite or mobilize the voters, or the problems confronting them had not reached the level of intensity presumed to have characterized the more recent election. Perhaps the voters were also waiting to see what effect the change in government would have in solving their problems. Whatever the state of the electorate in 1971, there is no doubt that the two-year interim between elections produced a greater intensity and uneasiness among voters, which became evident at the time of the 1973 election. Several things point to this. First, all four indicators of distrust were at higher levels in 1973 than in 1971. Second, campaign figures show that more people paid attention to the 1973 campaign than the previous one, reflecting their greater concern and unrest. Third, vote statistics reveal that more people vacillated in their vote decision in the more recent election, a definite sign of greater uneasiness and anxiety. Despite this greater uneasiness, however, no significant change in feelings of political competence or efficacy occurred between the two elections. Apparently the increased dissatisfaction with political leadership was not accompanied by a growing sense of powerlessness on the part of the voters.

Probably the most significant manifestation of the electorate's increased discontent was the massive vote shifts in the most recent election. Also highlighting this increased dissatisfaction was the fact that the combined responses to our four distrust questions turned out to be a better predictor of vote shifts than the extent to which a voter identified with his party, undoubtedly the only time this has occurred in postwar Danish elections. Increasing political distrust rather than weak identification with the established parties were more important in explaining vote defection in 1973.* When the two variables were interrelated with vote shifts, we received the impression that those who resisted their feelings of distrust, and hence did not switch their votes, relied on strong party ties to counteract these influences. The fact that many of the electorate could not resist these influences says much about the strength of these feelings of distrust. We shall now explore some of the 'issues' and 'problems' that might have helped to create such feelings.

## Issues and problems

The current economic problems of the day seemed to be the most pervasive source of discontent and distrust in the electorate. When asked what they thought were the most important problems the government should take care of, Danish respondents most often mentioned three areas of economic concern. Forty-nine per cent mentioned the related problems of higher taxes and increased public expenditures; 46 per cent noted the unsatisfactory level of income for specific groups; and 36 per cent called attention to the national economic problems associated with inflation and the balance of payments. In contrast, these three problems were mentioned by only 16, 9 and 22 per cent of these respondents, respectively, in 1971, indicating that much of the force of the current issues underlying political distrust occurred after the 1971 election. The fact that economic and financial problems were probably the most important issue component of political distrust was already suggested by our scaling space in Figure 8.3. The European Community debate and referendum in 1972 alerted people to their economic problems and the possible economic advantages and disadvantages of becoming members. Also, one of the four distrust items had an economic aspect to it which suggested the importance of this issue, registering 91 per cent agreement among the electorate that 'politicians are too generous with the taxpayer's money'.

Table 8.2 presents other data confirming the importance of recent economic problems. While most Danes have accepted the concept of the welfare state, an ideological battle fought years ago, their newer economic problems of higher taxes and inflation have prompted them to advocate a greater control over the functions and

---

* For this comparison, 'strength of party identification' was measured in 1971 rather than 1973, since the latter measure would not constitute a 'pure' test of the hypothesis. The 1973 measure would reveal more 'weak' adherents as a result of the increase in political distrust between the two elections.

expense of the welfare system. Items 15 and 16 in the table denoting these attitudes correlate well with sympathy and votes for the 'new bourgeois' parties. These items correlate less well with actual vote shifts, particularly from the bourgeois bloc, because of the particular way these dependent variables were constructed. Both those not moving from the bourgeois bloc and those moving from it to the 'new bourgeois' parties had similar attitudes on these issues, making for weak correlations, but the difference between these two groups was that one group felt more concerned about these issues and hence changed its vote. What is also interesting about these issues is that those favouring the far-left parties took opposite stands on them, presumably because they, being of the lower class, did not wish for a reduction in a welfare system that usually benefited them more than it did the other social classes.

Other economic issues we have discussed are also revealed in Table 8.2 to be important to certain segments of the electorate. The issue of the European Community is shown to be associated with both the far-left and two of the three 'new bourgeois' parties. To the far-left contingent, opposition to the European Community was based on both economic and political grounds. To the 'new bourgeois' parties as well as the bourgeois bloc of established parties, favouring the European Community was the norm because of both its perceived economic advantages and its political potential for forming a European government. While the issue of European Community suggested earlier the importance of economic problems in our scaling space, we can now see that this issue by itself only partly distinguishes between the mainstream and the other parties, and that this tendency to distinguish is more marked, in sympathy and vote-shift terms, on the left than on the right side of the ideological spectrum. Another economic issue—the curtailing of higher taxes on one-family homes—was raised in the 1973 campaign by the Centre Democrats. Traditionally a conventional ideological issue, it seemed instead to reflect in 1973 the newer economic concern of rising taxes and was, as a result, statistically related to sympathies for the 'new bourgeois' parties. A last issue raised in the campaign by the Christian People's Party dealt with a non-economic matter—the problem of moral decay in Denmark. As might be expected, sympathy with, and hence votes for, this party were associated with conservative attitudes on this issue. Two questions were also asked in our survey to tap authoritarian tendencies—whether extreme views should be censored in the media, and if a strong man should seize power in an economic crisis. Both correlated well with our distrust scale and vote shifts to the 'new bourgeois' parties, showing that when distrust exists it can be translated into authoritarian ways of dealing with the situations causing the distrust.

Most of these issues were correlated with feelings of political distrust, suggesting the important causal connection between the two factors. What is also important to know, though, is that different positions on these issues led to different types of distrust. For example, those who were worried about inflation, rising taxes, increased public expenditures and the burgeoning and costly welfare system were most likely to be distrustful of politicians' use of the taxpayer's money (item 1) and of the extent to which politicians listened to the people's opinions (item 2). These were also many of the people who supported the European Community as an attempt to solve some of their and Denmark's economic problems. It is not difficult to understand why these people felt distrustful of politicians. They did not see either the bourgeois or socialist blocs of parties solving their problems when they were in government. Instead, they felt that economic problems were becoming more severe because the politicians did not heed the voters' wishes and did not use their tax money wisely and with restraint. The correlation of the tax waste item alone with the sentiment 'too many get welfare without really needing it' was 0.42. Most of these people can be labelled the 'cynics of the right', to use Miller's term (Miller, 1974). They supported the 'new bourgeois' parties because of the reasons mentioned here and, in the case of the Christian People's Party, also because of the moral decay question. Those supporting the Centre Democrats were most worried about rising taxes, especially on one-family homes, an item that correlated with the tax waste distrust item. Those supporting Glistrup were worried about a wide variety of economic matters, including high taxes, the costly welfare system and the large governmental bureaucracy associated with it. The 'cynics of the right' also tended to be authoritarian, demanding tough measures to deal with these problems. These people actually came from two different sources to support the 'new bourgeois' parties—from both the socialist and bourgeois blocs of parties. Both groups of vote-switchers were similar in being conservative on many of these economic issues, the socialist bloc movers often wanting to curtail taxes and social welfare expenditures almost as much as the bourgeois shifters.

Other people took very different issue stands, which led to a distrust of politicians' principles (item 3) and decisions (item 4). These people wanted, for example, a continuation of the existing welfare system and a separation from the European Community. They did not perceive the European Community as either an economic or political advantage, whereas they felt the existing welfare system to be justified. They also wanted more taxes, not less, on home-owners since they were, by and large, apartment dwellers. The reasons why these issue stands caused distrust of politicians' principles and decisions seems straightforward. Many of these people were socialist voters who saw a socialist government back the initiative to join the European Community, a decision that they considered 'wrong' and against their politicians' 'principles'. They also witnessed Jakobsen, a socialist, leave the party to form a new party to fight against any increase in house taxes. On both the European Community and house tax issues, these people held the minority opinion. The verdict of the most recent election was to place them on the defensive once again, this time attempting to justify a welfare system that was being severely criticized and that seemed destined, at least at that time, to be changed by the politicians according to majority demand. These people even took the minority position on one of the distrust questions—disagreeing that politicians were too generous with the taxpayer's money in an obvious attempt to defend welfare and other governmental expenditures. Because of these various opinions, many of these people shifted their support from the socialist bloc of parties to the Single-Tax and far-left parties. Their discontent with politicians and the system, so obvious in the 1973 election, probably started from at least the time of the European Community debate in 1972 when they lost the referendum. Their particular type of discontent characterizes them appropriately, in Miller's terminology, as the 'cynics of the left' (Miller, 1974). While a unique group, they do have something in common with the bourgeois voters who switched to the 'new bourgeois' parties, because both groups tended to react in the same way to distrust items 3 and 4. While agreeing on two of the same distrust items, these two groups did so for very different reasons. The bourgeois voters switching to the new parties felt that the established bourgeois parties were not sufficiently conservative in their policies, while the socialist voters switching to the Single-Tax and far-left parties thought the established socialist parties were not sufficiently liberal or radical in their policies.

The final scenario of vote change for 1973 appears to follow the expected pattern. Economic issues and problems caused feelings of distrust which were later translated into vote shifts. The direction these vote shifts took depended on which issues and problems were most salient to the voter and what positions he took on them. As long as substantial correlations exist between these issues and political distrust, this explanatory model seems more than adequate. In some cases where the correlations are lower in value, perhaps a simpler explanation is necessary—economic worries being translated into vote shifts without psychological feelings of distrust mediating this process. Both processes were at work, but we assume the first was dominant. We also assume that the bulk of the unrest over these issues occurred in 1972 and 1973, probably starting with the European Community debate in 1972. At least we know that none of the new and minor parties benefited from such feelings until 1973. The four minor parties did not show gains in the public opinion polls until the summer and autumn of 1973, when three of them passed the 2 per cent threshold required for parliamentary representation. Glistrup's party was not formed until January 1973, at which time it received only 5 per cent support in the polls, but by April it had increased its support to 25 per cent before gradually subsiding to the 10–15 per cent level in October. Jakobsen formed his party only two weeks before the election, capitalizing on the current discontent that existed at election time to gain 8 per cent of the votes. While distrust also existed in 1971, as our data show, it dealt in part with issues that did not resurface in the 1973 campaign and, more importantly, with economic issues that did not concern as many people until 1973 or become sufficiently intense until then to affect people's political behaviour.

### Ideology and new cleavages

While new cleavages emerged in 1973 out of current economic problems and the distrust associated with them, the first dimension in our scaling space still reveals the importance of older ideological concerns to many Danish voters. The Danish voters who did not switch to the new and minor parties—those people who would be located in the lower half of our scaling space—still had the ideological beliefs of their parties and the faith in them to solve the current problems demanding attention. In Table 8.2, under the section 'conventional ideology', we can see that the traditional left–right issues of 'controlling private investments', 'freezing wages', 'striving for equality' and 'taxing high incomes more'—issues concerned with the basic role of government in the economy—generally correlated best with sympathies and votes for the established blocs of parties and least with any tendencies for vote-shifting. These particular issues are, of course, merely indicators of the traditional left–right cleavages that are so important to these people. Issues such as these probably were the basis for the formation of the original party identifications of the Danish population, identifications that remained strong for many and correlated well with these traditional issues and the left–right cleavage associated with them. Thus the people who resisted switching to the new and minor parties were motivated by their ideological beliefs, their strong identifications with their parties and their faith in their parties. Even if the newer issues concerned them, their ties to party and their trust in its leadership were sufficient deterrents to any vote-switching proclivities. For those non-switchers who became really distrustful, the strong party attachments they formed from their ideological beliefs were often enough to persuade them to maintain their traditional vote. All in all, those supporting the traditional parties constituted the largest single group in the electorate—the 64 per cent of the voters who defied the current trend to vote for the new and minor parties.

The remaining 36 per cent of the electorate supported the new and minor parties. These people were the vote-switchers who established, at least temporarily, new cleavage lines in the system. They moved in three distinct ways to establish these cleavages—from the socialist and bourgeois parties to the 'new bourgeois' parties and from the socialist parties to the parties of the far left. The first two moves were undertaken by the 'cynics of the right', whereas the last move was initiated by the 'cynics of the left'. What distinguished these people from the established party supporters was their greater political distrust, their greater concern over current economic problems, their weaker party identifications and their lesser interest in traditional issues and ideologies. While having these factors in common, the cynics of the left and the right reacted to these new economic problems in different ways and with different feelings of distrust, causing these various voting movements in 1973. The particular nature of these economic problems and feelings of distrust, however, seemed to overwhelmingly favour, in numerical terms, the voting movements of the 'cynics of the right'.

Danish journalists, noting these voting movements, have generally interpreted the recent election as a major shift towards conservatism. While one would quickly grant that the large proportion of vote-switchers in the 1973 election reacted in a conservative manner to the new economic problems, this does not necessarily mean that these people changed from a liberal to a conservative stance on these issues. Perhaps many of these vote-switchers never changed their orientations on these issues at all, but instead had basically conservative attitudes on them when they first arose and became salient to the public. This seems most likely of those who moved from the bourgeois bloc to the 'new bourgeois' parties. These people were middle-class conservatives who no longer had faith in the established bourgeois parties to handle their economic problems. Most probably they also thought the bourgeois bloc was not sufficiently conservative for them, not even having a spokesman for their interests on the new problems. While these people could have increased the degree of their conservative feelings, their most prominent move in the scaling space was not to the 'right' but 'up' to the 'new bourgeois' parties. The second set of vote-switchers among the 'cynics of the right' presents a more mixed picture. While they moved both to the 'right' and 'up' in the scaling space, some had liberal attitudes on these issues initially and some, conservative. The first group best exemplifies the notion of a move towards conservatism. These people changed their attitudes towards wanting government to spend less, tax less, and grant fewer welfare services.

The size of the second group, however, is surprising. These people already had conservative attitudes on these issues, being lower-middle-class and middle-class identifiers who originally adhered to the conservative wing of the Social Democratic Party (especially on matters of finance) before moving to the Jakobsen and Glistrup parties. The last set of vote-shifters—the 'cynics of the left'—of course contradict the idea of a conservative movement but they constitute only 12 per cent of the electorate at most. Generally speaking, the picture is mixed: many were already conservative on these issues but were simply searching for new voting alternatives because of their lack of faith in the established parties' ability to handle their problems; a lesser number actually changed from liberal to conservative positions on these issues; and a still lesser number defied these trends by supporting the parties of the far left.

A question that remains unanswered is the exact nature of the 'conservatism' expressed by the 'cynics of the right'. Unfortunately, our data can shed precious few clues in the search for an answer. We do know that the traditional issues of the right did not increase in popularity between the 1971 and 1973 elections, suggesting again that the conservatism of the vote-switchers had little to do with older ideological concerns.* What we do not know is whether the conservatism of the vote-switchers is the starting point for the development of a new type of conservative ideology or merely a gut reaction to the important economic problems of the day. Many have perceived this conservatism as simply the product of a basic, yet simple, stimulus-response process. Whatever the situation, we know with certainty that new issues and problems have emerged with a salience and intensity in the last few years to create a profound and widespread sense of distrust in politicians and the political system. This distrust has had important behavioural consequences, manifesting itself in massive vote shifts as people searched for new alternatives to the existing political leadership, especially alternatives on the conservative side of the political spectrum.

## PROSPECTS FOR THE DANISH POLITICAL SYSTEM

Our analysis has shown that a new cleavage dimension has emerged in Danish politics, based on political distrust. The emergence of such a dimension naturally invites speculation as to its durability and consequences for the system. Part of the answer necessarily lies in whether or not the economic problems of the people continue to persist and what the various political parties do in an attempt to solve them, future events that are difficult to predict. At the present moment, what is clear is that a considerable number of voters are expecting and demanding innovation and change in élite politics, although our data cannot tell us when or how such innovations will occur. Leaving future events aside, we can examine what the present electoral situation means for the system. The volatile nature of the 1973 election could signal a permanent change in the existing party system and the cleavage structure on which it is based, or it could merely indicate a more temporary change which later historians will consider to be of little major importance.

Although we do not envisage an exact restoration of the Danish system of two-bloc politics, we believe that the new party space of 1973 is highly unstable and likely to gravitate in the future toward a more or less one-dimensional solution based on left–right politics. In this view, the second dimension of our scaling space is a temporary phenomenon with little chance of survival over the long term. The arguments favouring this position can be stated as follows.

(1) No obvious ethnic, religious, regional, linguistic or other cultural division

---

* The 'private investment' and 'equality/inequality' issues showed little attitudinal change between the two elections, nor did the traditional left–right foreign policy issue involving NATO. (The 'wage freeze' question was not asked in 1971, thereby not allowing a comparison with 1973.) Only the 'taxing high incomes' issue showed much change and this was undoubtedly due to the short-term effect produced by the millionaire Glistrup when he candidly informed the Danish public that he had 'legally' evaded taxes on his income for many years.

underlies the second dimension that could sustain and reinforce it in the future, although the rather small Christian People's Party is attempting to create such a division along moral and religious lines. Even the relation of class to this dimension is probably tenuous. While it is true that certain class elements adhere to this dimension, at least for the moment, it is still definitely the case that the main aspects of the class structure remain anchored to the first dimension and its politics (see Borre and Katz, 1973, pp.89–91). If a new conservative ideology were to develop, a permanent movement of certain class elements to the second dimension might follow, especially among the lower middle class whose incomes are most affected by the current economic problems. What is more likely is that people have reacted in a temporary fashion to these problems and that the volatile voting behaviour of 1973 will restablize in the future along more customary lines. To a large extent, the second dimension exists because of a reaction to uncontrolled taxation and spending. What the 'old' and 'new' bourgeois elements disagree on in these areas is how drastic the measures needed are to solve these problems and who is capable of administering them. The 'new' bourgeois elements are now represented in Parliament, so they can observe if their parties will be able to solve these problems any better or faster than the established parties. One imagines, however, that considerations of 'realpolitik' and coalition formation will come into play between the 'new' and 'old' parties, considerations that will work toward a reestablishment of a one-dimensional party system.

(2) The existence of political distrust in Denmark and its association with the second dimension does not necessarily mean that a permanent change or realignment of the party system has occurred as a result. Indeed, what little research has been done on this topic has failed to demonstrate a connection between distrust and realignment. Instead such research has shown that distrust usually causes temporary rather than permanent changes in voting patterns and cleavage structures, partly because the feelings of distrust themselves cannot be sustained for any length of time. Most of these findings are based on the study of American elections since 1952. For example, Angus Campbell, in analysing the 1952 election, rejected an 'ideological realignment' interpretation in favour of one that stressed more temporary vote changes based on distrust and discontent: 'Accumulated grievances and dissatisfactions over the last years of Democratic government finally led to a vote for a new administration. The voters were not asking for any specific platform of legislation; they just wanted a new bunch of fellows to run things better.' (Campbell 1970). After 1952, the remaining elections of the decade failed to show the prevalence of distrust as a factor in voting behaviour (see Campbell, *et al.*, 1960; Templeton, 1966; Aberbach, 1969; Stokes, 1962). In 1964 feelings of distrust became important again; as Aberbach (1969) shows, the Goldwater vote was strongly related to political distrust. However, unlike the 1950s, distrust continued to remain a strong factor in subsequent elections, although always producing temporary rather then permanent voting changes. In the 1968 election the Michigan researchers state that distrust was associated with sympathy for both George Wallace and Eugene McCarthy (Converse *et al.*, 1969). In the 1972 election distrust was again related to voting, this time being connected with support for McGovern according to the Michigan study (Miller, *et al.*, 1973). In an exhaustive treatment of the 1964–70 period, Miller (1974) discovers both 'cynics of the left' and 'cynics of the right' in the American electorate who oppose the more 'middle-of-the-road' stands of their respective parties.

The development of a new political dimension in a country requires either creating new cleavages to support it or realigning existing ones for the same purpose. The new and minor parties have thus far been unable to form new ethnic, religious, regional or other cultural divisions that could support them. They have not been able, basically, to realign the existing lower class–middle class cleavage either, the cleavage that reflects the left–right politics of the first dimension. What they have succeeded in doing, at least temporarily, is pitting some members of the middle class against one another and, to a much lesser extent, some members of the lower class against each other. They have also been able to produce some conflict between the numerically weak 'cynics of the left' and the much larger 'cynics of the right'. The persistence of economic problems and the performance of the parties in handling them will have much to do in determining whether or not these current reactions will crystallize into a more permanent realignment. At the moment, not knowing the course of future events, a permanent realignment still seems unlikely. The political distrust created by these problems has been shown in other countries to be associated more with a temporary change in voting patterns than with a realignment of the system. Such distrust feelings have also often been shown to exist for only a short period of time. The traditional loyalties to parties and the familiar ideology of left–right class politics will probably reappear as the new parties reveal to the public by their performance that they have no 'quick and easy' solutions to these economic problems. Some of the new parties will weaken and possibly disappear; others will regroup along the left–right dimension. Their most lasting effect will undoubtedly be to motivate the established parties to experiment and try new policies in the hopes of improving economic conditions. Probably they will also, as a necessary byproduct, cause an increased differentiation among the parties to take place along the left–right dimension, which, in its revised form, should continue to shape Danish politics for years to come.

## APPENDIX

The wording of the items in Table 2 is as follows.

1. Politicians are too generous with the taxpayer's money.
2. Politicians generally care too little about what the voters think.
3. People who want to get to the top in politics have to give up most of their principles.
4. In general one may trust our political leaders to make the right decisions for the country.
5. We should leave NATO as soon as possible.
6. Being members of the European Community will mean great economic advantages.
7. The form of government of the European Community is incompatible with Danish democratic traditions.
8. Membership in the European Community will mean abandoning our national independence.
9. The government has too little control over private investment.
10. Wage-earners should be willing to let their wages be frozen if they receive tax relief in return.
11. High incomes should be taxed more strongly than they are today.
12. In politics one ought to strive to give everyone the same economic opportunities no matter what their education or occupation is.

13. There has been some discussion about the moral situation in our society, as, for example, pornography and the 'Jesus film'. Do you think this situation is disturbing or don't you think it is very disturbing?
14. Extreme points of view should be censored from the radio and television.
15. It has been said that some of our social services are being misused. Do you think that we should be more on our guard as to whom we support, or do you think that social services in almost every case go to people who really need them?
16. There are too many who get social services without needing them.
17. The situation of the family home-owners has been under much discussion. Do you think the home-owners have unreasonable tax advantages, or do you think they are treated justly, or do you think that, on the contrary, they are taxed too hard?
18. There has been some talk about the employees having certain decision-making powers at their place of work. Do you think that the employees in private firms should have the right to make decisions on important matters, or should the employer make such decisions himself?
19. It would be sensible to have a strong man seize power in a situation of economic crisis.
20. [See footnote on p.146.]
21. Many people consider themselves adherents of a particular party. There are also many who do not feel that they adhere to any party. Do you usually consider yourself, for example, a Social Democrat, a Radical Liberal, a Conservative, an Agrarian Liberal, a People's Socialist, or something else? Or don't you feel you are an adherent of a party? (If adherent) Some are strongly convinced adherents, whereas others are not so strongly convinced. Do you consider yourself a strong adherent or not such a strong adherent of your party? (If not adherent) Anyway, is there a party which you feel closer to than the others?

Questions 1–12, 14, 16 and 19 have five response categories, ranging from 'completely agree' to 'completely disagree'. Questions 13, 15 and 18 have two categories, and question 17, three categories. For question 21 responses were scored from +3 to −3, positive scores indicating adherence or 'leaning' to the Social Democrats or People's Socialists and negative scores indicating adherence or 'leaning' to the Radical Liberals, Conservatives or Agrarian Liberals. A zero score indicates that the respondent did not feel close to any party. Respondents adhering or 'leaning' to other parties were not included in the construction of this variable.

## REFERENCES

Aberbach, Joel D. (1969), 'Alienation and Political Behaviour', *American Political Science Review*, 63, 86–99.
Borre, Ole, and Daniel Katz, (1973) 'Party Indentification and its Motivational Base in a Multiparty System: A Study of the Danish General Election of 1971', *Scandinavian Political Studies*, 8, 69–111.
Campbell, Angus, Philip E. Converse, Warren E. Miller and Donald E. Stokes (1960), *The American Voter*, Wiley, New York.
Campbell, Angus (1970), 'Voters and Elections: Past and Present', in Edward C. Dreyer and Walter A. Rosenbaum (eds.), *Political Opinion and Behaviour: Essays and Studies*, 2nd edition, Wadsworth, Belmont, California.

Converse, Philip E., Warren E. Miller, Jerrold G. Rusk and Arthur C. Wolfe (1969), 'Continuity and Change in American Politics: Parties and Issues in the 1968 Election', *American Political Science Review*, 63, 1083–1105.

Daalder, Hans, and Jerrold G. Rusk (1972), 'Perceptions of Party in the Dutch Parliament', in Samuel C. Patterson and John C. Wahlke (eds.), *Comparative Legislative Behaviour*, Wiley, New York.

Damgaard, Erik (1969), 'The Parliamentary Basis of Danish Governments: The Patterns of Coalition Formation', *Scandinavian Political Studies*, 4, 30–57.

Damgaard, Erik (1974), 'Stability and Change of the Danish Party System in Half a Century', *Scandinavian Political Studies*, 9.

Kruskal, J. B. (1964), 'Multidimensional Scaling by Optimizing Goodness of Fit to a Nonmetric Hypothesis', *Psychometrika*, 29, 1–27.

Lipset, Seymour M., and Stein Rokkan (1967), 'Cleavage Structures, Party Systems and Voter Alignments', in Seymour M. Lipset and Stein Rokkan (eds.), *Party Systems and Voter Alignments*, Free Press, New York.

Miller, Arthur H., Warren E. Miller, Alden S. Raine and Thad. A. Brown (1973), 'A Majority Party in Disarray: Policy Polarisation in the 1972 Election', University of Michigan, Center for Political Studies (mimeo).

Miller, Arthur H. (1974), 'Political Issues and Trust in Government, 1964–1970', *American Political Science Review*, 68, 951–72.

Rusk, Jerrold G., and Herbert F. Weisberg (1972), 'Perceptions of Presidential Candidates: Implications for Electoral Change', *Midwest Journal of Political Science*, 16, 388–410.

Rustow, Dankwart (1956), 'Scandinavia: Working Multiparty Systems', in Sigmund Neumann (ed.), *Modern Party Systems*, Chicago University Press, Chicago.

Stokes, Donald E. (1962), 'Popular Evaluations of Government: An Empirical Assessment', in Harland Cleveland and Harold D. Lasswell (eds.), *Ethics and Bigness: Scientific, Academic, Religious, Political and Military*, Harper and Brothers, New York.

Templeton, Frederick (1966), 'Alienation and Political Participation', *Public Opinion Quarterly*, 30, 249–61.

Wang, Ming-mei, Peter H. Schonemann and Jerrold G. Rusk (forthcoming), 'A Conjugate Gradient Algorithm for the Multidimensional Analysis of Preference Data', *Multivariate Behavioural Research*.

# 9

# Cleavage Structures and Representational Linkages: A Longitudinal Analysis of Danish Legislative Behaviour

ERIK DAMGAARD and JERROLD G. RUSK*

The general purpose of this chapter is to continue that line of recent empirical research on multi-party systems which uses dimensional models to represent political parties in a policy space (for other relevant research on Denmark see Pedersen, Damgaard and Olsen, 1971, and Damgaard, 1973). More concretely, our objective is twofold. First, we want to analyse the Danish legislative party system by applying a proximity scaling technique to the voting behaviour of legislative party groups on all recorded divisions between 1953 and 1973. This will enable us to describe empirically the cleavage structure in Danish legislative behaviour for a twenty-year period, noting characteristics of both stability and change in such behaviour (for a general description of stability and change in the Danish political system see Damgaard, 1974). Scaling techniques will further be used to plot cleavage lines in specific policy areas deemed to be of major importance to the Danish legislative parties. Few longitudinal studies of this type have been conducted by researchers in multi-party systems, and this seems unfortunate since one of the most crucial aspects of understanding present parliamentary behaviour is its historical evolution and development. Secondly, we shall employ the same scaling technique to tap possible representational linkages between the parliamentary élite and the electorate for the 1971-73 period, the only period in which we have mass survey data bearing on the electorate's perceptions of the party cleavage structure. The proximity scaling technique is particularly appropriate as a test for possible congruences in 'party spaces' between these two sets of political actors, although it cannot directly ascertain the cause-effect sequences that lead to these congruences. Data from our prior longitudinal scaling study of parliamentary voting behaviour since 1953, combined with a necessary amount of inference, will be used to establish tentatively the causal nature of such linkages. A final section will present preliminary data after the December 1973 election to indicate contemporary change in the élite-mass party space configuration.

## THE LEGISLATIVE SYSTEM

The Danish legislative party system has to date been analysed by at least three

---

* Professor Rusk was on a Fulbright leave of absence to the University of Aarhus when this paper was written.

different, although closely related, methods. First, the idea of agreement/ disagreement between pairs of parties in their voting behaviour formed the basis for a study of conflict and consensus in the Folketing (Pedersen, 1967). Second, this way of measuring 'distances' between any two parties was utilized in a very simple way to reveal whether an underlying uni-dimensional model could explain these distances as measured on an interval level scale, which, as it turned out, was not the case, although a fairly strong 'left-right' ordering of parties was clearly visible (Pedersen et al., 1971). Finally, the behaviour of major parties has been analysed within the framework of coalition theory showing that the formation of governmental and other legislative coalitions by and large occurred along a left-right political dimension (Damgaard, 1969, 1973).

What has been missing from such analyses, however, is a rigorous use of proximity scaling techniques to portray the historical development of the legislative party system as well as a similar study of the party system as seen by the electorate when comparable data are available. In this section we shall analyse the legislative system at some length using such techniques, while in a later section the élite-mass linkage problem will be investigated.

To understand the dynamics of the Danish legislative system, our primary focus should be on those parties that (a) comprised the large majority of seats in the 1953-73 period and (b) also constituted the legislative system in the latest governmental period before the December 1973 election, since the parties in Parliament in this latest period represent the end-product of the twenty-year historical period we are studying. This enables our analysis to confine itself mainly to the 'significant' parties in the system and to describe the evolution of the voting patterns of those parties that still controlled Parliament in the 1971-73 governmental period. This latest legislative period was dominated by five parties which controlled all the seats in Parliament. They were the Conservative (C), Agrarian Liberal (AL) and Radical Liberal (RL) Parties—customarily termed the 'bourgeois bloc' today—and the Social Democratic (SD) and Socialist People's (SP) Parties—the contemporarily labelled 'socialist bloc'. The first four parties have been the mainstays of the Danish political system since the 1920s, the Socialist People's Party being formed in 1958. These five parties combined have controlled 94 to 100 per cent of the legislative seats in the 1960-73 period. In the 1953-60 period, the four 'old' parties controlled 91 per cent of the seats, with the Communist Party adding a further 4 to 5 per cent to these totals. We have included the Communist Party (Com) in our data base for this period because it figured in the legislative structure as the far left-wing alternative before the Socialist Party was formed and replaced it in Parliament.

The way these parties voted in Parliament will constitute the data base for our study. We will compute an 'index of distance' for all pairs of parties based on their voting behaviour on the final divisions of all bills and resolutions as well as on 'agenda motions', ('agenda motions' being motions to articulate opinions or demands, especially to the Government, and being equal to a motion of censure in their most extreme form). This set of votes represents the total universe of final votes taken in the Folketing during the 1953-73 period. Since the party groups in Parliament usually behave as voting blocs (see Damgaard, 1973 and Pedersen, 1967), the value of the index for any two parties, A and B, in any given governmental period can be calculated by using the values in Table 9.1 for each vote division, adding up all such values for all vote divisions between party A and B, and then dividing by the number of these

Table 9.1     Voting Values Used for Computation of Distance Index

|  |  | Party A | | |
| --- | --- | :---: | :---: | :---: |
|  |  | Yes | Abstain | No |
|  | Yes | 0 | .5 | 1 |
| Party B | Abstain | .5 | 0 | .5 |
|  | No | 1 | .5 | 0 |

divisions (see Pedersen, 1967, who first devised the 'index of distance'). The resulting index value for a given pair of parties can basically be operationalized as the proportion of times the two parties disagree on their vote. (We say 'basically' because we include abstentions in our model as having data values when combined with 'yes', 'no' or other 'abstention' votes.) The limiting values of the index are 0, indicating complete agreement between two parties' voting patterns, and 1.0, indicating complete disagreement.

These index values can be termed 'dissimilarity coefficients' and can be organized into a party-by-party data matrix, similar to a correlation matrix, and used as input to a proximity scaling computer program that will transform these data, according to certain assumptions, into a geometric space.* The assumptions underlying the Shepard–Kruskal scaling logic used here are basically that (a) notions of dissimilarity can be translated meaningfully into distances in a geometric space and (b) empirically obtained measures of dissimilarities are some monotone distortion of distances in a configuration of 'true' points. The second point, (b), is crucial, for the problem posed for the scaling technique is to recover the true configuration of points from the monotonically distorted input information. In practice, the algorithm merely attempts to get the 'best' possible configuration it can—the configuration that shows the best monotonic fit between the rank-order of the dissimilarity values and the relative distances between the various stimuli in a given dimensional space. Stated in its most simplistic form, pairs of parties with high dissimilarity values should be placed considerably apart in a geometric space while pairs of parties with low dissimilarity values should appear close together in the space, given that the scaling algorithm has to attempt to perform this task for all possible pairs of parties according to the monotonic function stated above. How well it is able to do this—that is, how well the data fit a monotonic function in space—is revealed by a 'goodness of fit' measure called 'stress', which has the limiting value of zero for a perfect scaling solution.

The data we are attempting to scale involve only five stimuli—the five main parties in the Danish political system. With five parties, there are only ten possible dissimilarity coefficients. Having only five parties presents both advantages and disadvantages from the perspective of such scaling techniques. The main advantage is that of 'dimensional parsimony'—if the data have any structure to them at all, we can usually obtain a good scaling solution for five stimuli in one or two dimensions, not needing to resort to higher dimensional solutions with their often sparse explanatory

---

* The particular proximity scaling logic we have used has been developed by Roger Shepard and J. B. Kruskal. See, in particular, Kruskal (1964). The computer program employed was developed by E. E. Roskam and J. Lingoes as a particular adaptation of the Shepard–Kruskal scaling logic and is called 'MINISSA–1'. We are grateful to our colleague P. Nannestad Olsen who converted the program to the Control Data 6400 Computer of Aarhus University.

power and 'noise' factors. The fact that we focus on élite behaviour would seem to go a long way towards assuring 'structure' in the data. The main disadvantage with this set of data is that there are only ten constraints (i.e. ten dissimilarity coefficients) on how the party stimuli move about in a geometric space. One of the advantages of proximity scaling techniques is that, with a large number of stimuli, one can end up with a space that tightly constrains the movement of the stimuli, a space with a 'unique' location for each stimulus that approximates metric-level information. We can make no such pretentions with the data we have—the movement of the party stimuli in space is such that each stimulus can be said to occupy a certain region in the space rather than a single distinct location. Any further movement of a party point within its region could be done manually by the investigator as long as it did not violate the rank-order of the dissimilarity values involved. Normally with such data investigators accept the location of the parties given by the scaling technique and do not bother to move these points further within their regions. The interpretations from such solutions stress first and foremost the order of the stimuli along the dimension and then, within limits, the relative distances they are from one another. This latter comparison is perfectly legitimate as long as the analyst keeps in mind that judging relative distances between parties involves considering the regions they are in as well as the locations the scaling program happens to given them within their respective regions. In our case, we actually attempted to 'improve' the scaling solution by moving parties to particular locations within their regions. Assuming that our index values were interval in nature and reflected 'distances' between the parties, we moved the parties within their regions according to these values while still preserving the basic rank-order solution of the scaling technique. This procedure allows us to discuss, in more definitive fashion, the actual distances between the parties in the space. As a last adjustment, we have also kept the outer limits of the party spaces constant over time for the various governmental periods.*

The data matrices for the various governmental periods were scaled in both two and one dimensions. As we expected, the one-dimensional solutions explained nearly all of the variance in the data and achieved zero or virtually zero stress figures. Figure 9.1 shows the results of these one-dimensional scaling operations. There are several things in the graphs that need to be explored at some length. First is the fact that legislative voting is structured along a single dimension throughout this time period. Second is the observation that the dominant theme in the graphs viewed across time is the continuity or stability of the party structure. Third is the fact that, despite the overriding theme of stability, some meaningful change has occurred in this time period with regard to the relative locations of the parties *vis-à-vis* one another. We will take up each of these points in turn.

The uni-dimensional nature of parliamentary voting is obviously a striking feature of the Danish political system. Given the complexity of modern day politics and the varied problems demanding solution in today's world, some may wonder why only one dimension has been consistently used as a guide to parliamentary voting in each of these legislative periods. There seem to be two possible answers to this question. The most apparent answer is that the one dimension uncovered for each legislative period

* We have also treated stimuli with 'tied' data as having the same location in the scaling space rather than using the 'primary' or 'secondary' approach discussed by Kruskal for resolving ties. Our rationale was that political parties that completely corresponded in their voting behaviour should be given the same location in space.

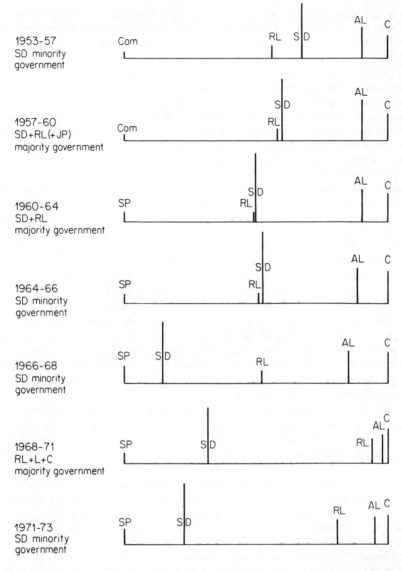

Figure 9.1    Party spaces of the five main Danish parties for all governmental periods, 1953–73: one-dimensional solutions based on all recorded legislative divisions (bars indicate number of seats in the Folketing)

is sufficiently broad yet relevant to act as a meaningful guide to voting on a great many different issues and problems. Another answer is that, although other dimensions may also have been used in any given legislative session as a guide to voting on certain issues or policy areas, they were not sufficiently relevant or generalizable to other areas to be captured by the aggregated nature of our voting index and scaling solutions. Probably both answers play a role in understanding the dynamics of the legislative process, but even so the main point we have made is empirically confirmed repeatedly in the data: that only one dimension is consistently used on a large number of votes within each governmental session. Later we will offer still further proof for this central proposition.

The fact that only one dimension is uncovered for each governmental period leads us to an even more important point: it is substantively the same dimension in each of these periods. What one observes is a left-right ideological dimensioning of party voting. Since, as pointed out by Daalder and Rusk (1972), Shepard-Kruskal scaling is particularly appropriate for tapping political cleavages in a country, one can view legislative voting as the manifest behaviour that is explained by an underlying system of left, centre and right cleavages. While the specific cleavages change in their strength and relative position on the scale over time, the relevant point for the moment is the continuity or stability of this dimension over the twenty-year period. This stability is all the more remarkable because it endures despite variations in the parliamentary basis of governments, i.e. regardless of which parties are in office and whether the government is a minority or majority-based government. Looking across the several graphs, one consistently finds the Communists and later on the Socialist People's Party at the left end of the political spectrum and the Conservatives at the opposite end. Also, the Agrarian Liberals are always closest to the Conservatives and vice-versa. And finally, the Social Democrats and Radical Liberals are always found somewhere in between the Communist/Socialist People's Party and the two parties on the right. This particular ordering of parties—with special reference to the four 'old' parties—reminds one of Lipset and Rokkan's assertion of the 'freezing' of party alternatives in most European countries in the 1920s (Lipset and Rokkan, 1967, p.50). All four of these parties have continued since the 1920s with large majority strength and one would assume with somewhat similar cleavage lines to what is observed for this twenty-year period.

While stability reigns supreme, change is also evident and, as will be shown, important. The most noticeable change in the graphs is not one of party movement but rather one of party replacement. The Communists were effectively displaced from the system in 1960 by a new party, the People's Socialists (at least until the December 1973 election). This is an extremely interesting change since the Socialist People's Party rapidly gained enough strength in the early 1960s to qualify as the fifth 'major party' in the system and the first new addition to this group since the turn of the century. What this seems to show is that there is some 'flux' in what had heretofore seemed an extremely stable system. Unfortunately, without survey data we are at some loss to document the reasons for this change and why it has survived the test of over a decade. What is known, however, is the effect this new party had on the relative movements of other parties in the space. In fact, all of the meaningful movements of parties that take place in this time seem to be traceable to the rise of the Socialist People's Party to the status of a major party.

Before the arrival of the People's Socialists, the Social Democrats were intimately allied with the Radical Liberals, these two parties occupying the centre of the space. From 1953 to 1957 the two parties usually voted together with the exception of votes on defence policy, these latter votes being the main reason why the Radical Liberals are located slightly to the left of the Social Democrats. From 1957 to 1960 the two parties were both members of the majority government coalition, but since they disagreed on a couple of politically insignificant votes the Radicals were once again located slightly to the left of the Social Democrats. The two parties stayed on in office from 1960 to 1964, during which period they agreed completely on all votes taken. Finally, between 1964 and 1966 the Radicals supported the Social Democratic minority government except on three divisions (the Radicals took a more 'leftist' stand on a farm subsidy bill and on a NATO issue, while they deviated from all other parties on a highway project bill). The period 1953-66 was thus one of centre, left and right cleavages, with the Communists and then the Socialists representing the left, the Social Democrats and Radical Liberals representing the unimodal centre of the distribution in which majority coalition building took place, and the Agrarian Liberals and Conservatives representing the right. Such a period was completely stable save for the rise of the Socialist People's Party and the demise of the Communist Party.

The Socialist People's Party made its presence felt starting with 1966, an election in which it received 11 per cent of the vote. It had already displaced the Communists from Parliament and, by its presence, saw the Social Democrat-Radical Liberal coalition get the barest of majorities in 1960. With its strength, this party offered the attraction of a 'socialist government' to the Social Democrats who decided to ally with it in 1966, the Socialist People's Party becoming the outside support party for the Social Democratic minority government, a pattern that was repeated in the 1971-73 period. This left the Radical Liberals with little choice but to move right toward the Conservative and Agrarian Liberal parties. These movements are aptly shown in the 1966-68 figure and the pattern continues from that time on. These moves were important for the system because they changed the older left, centre and right bloc politics to a simpler left (socialist)-right (bourgeois) bloc politics. The modal nature of the parliamentary seat distribution also changed from the centre-based unimodal pattern of the pre-1966 days to the bimodal pattern of the post-1966 period. The power of this bimodal pattern became quickly evident as both blocs of parties were strong enough to form governments in the 1966-73 period.

In sum, then, the left-right dimension seems to be the only salient dimension used on a massive scale as the basis for voting in the Danish Parliament. This dimension has figured prominently in every legislative period, showing a remarkable continuity in Danish élite behaviour. At the same time, the entry of one new party into the system and its subsequent impact on having two parties interchange positions in the space speaks for the fact that important political change can occur within a dimension while still leaving the basic meaning and existence of the dimension intact.

## THE SUBSTANCE OF POLITICAL CONFLICT

The results shown thus far have indicated that a general left-right dimension is used by legislative members to structure their thinking on a large number of roll-call votes. A natural inquiry at this point is whether this left-right model is used in a wide variety of specific policy areas, or whether our earlier aggregated solution is applicable only to certain spheres of legislative policy-making but not to others. In attempting to answer this question, one naturally gets at the heart or substance of political conflict in the legislative arena, for it is in specific issue areas that particular cleavage configurations are most important since they determine the shape and direction of policy in a given domain for years to come.

Five issue areas have been chosen for our scaling analysis: foreign and defence matters, taxation, agriculture, labour and housing. In a separate study (Damgaard,

170

1973), in which agenda motions, however, were not analysed, these areas were shown to have the most political conflict associated with them and can be considered to be among the most important issue areas in Danish politics. In relation to our aggregated data matrices, these five areas constitute 37 per cent of the legislative votes taken from 1953 to 1971, and they also contribute 63 per cent of the sum leading to the aggregated 'distance' values between parties for this period. Figure 9.2 shows the scaling results for these five policy areas for each of the governmental periods in the 1953-71 time span. The most immediate observation from a quick perusal of the thirty-six graphs involved is that our general left–right dimension figures prominently

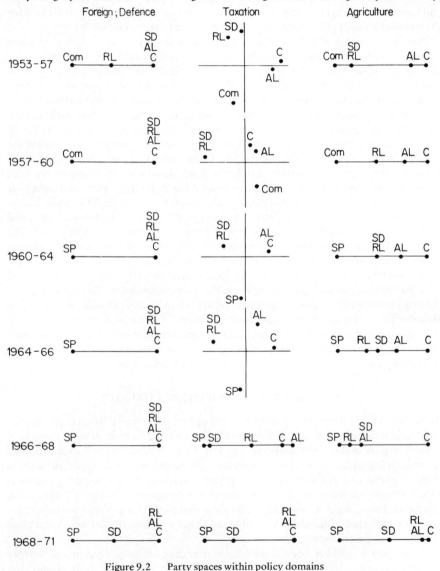

Figure 9.2    Party spaces within policy domains

in all of these specific issue areas. As a general conclusion, we can easily state that our aggregated solutions were quite representative in depicting a large part of the voting behaviour in these various policy areas.

Having noted the overall dominance of the left-right dimension in these policy areas, a more careful look at the graphs reveals some exceptions to this general pattern. In particular, some data matrices in the pre-1966 period clearly required a two-dimensional solution in order for the voting patterns involved to be understood. It is not accidental that such two-dimensional figures occur before the clear bipolarization of Danish politics began in 1966. The earlier legislative periods with their three-bloc configuration dominated by centre-oriented governments produced

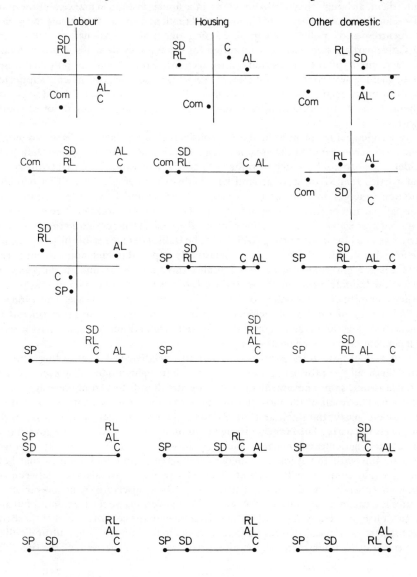

some unique cleavages. While all such two-dimensional figures are still characterized by the basic left–right model as their first dimension, the tendency for parties of the left and the right to vote together on occasion against the centre parties is also noted. This tendency is particularly noticeable in the 1950s and most often occurs on the issue of taxation. In figures showing such tendencies, the Communist Party (and later the Socialist People's Party in some graphs in the early 1960s) occupies one pole of the second dimension, being closer to the Agrarian Liberal and Conservative parties than to the centre parties. In the area of taxation it seems reasonable that the 'unlikely allies' of the left and the right united against governmental proposals for increased taxes. Other 'unpopular legislation' proposed by the Government could similarly unite them, although they probably voted in a similar fashion in many cases for quite different reasons. In general, such behavioural tendencies mean that during the period of 'centre-based' policy-making, 1953–66, our uni-dimensional model of the legislative party system has to be modified for some policy domains in order to take the 'agreement of the oppositions' into account. From 1966 on, however, when policy-making was controlled by either a Social Democratic government (supported on most matters by the Socialist People's Party) or a Radical Liberal–Agrarian Liberal–Conservative coalition, this 'agreement of oppositions' could not of course occur.

A second feature of note in these graphs is the voting patterns displayed within issue areas across time. In the area of foreign affairs and defence, our basic left–right model is seen to hold for all governmental periods. However, the actual figures show that parties tended to move around within this time period. Basically, a two-bloc situation emerges in four of the legislative periods and this has constituted the 'normal' pattern of party voting in this area. This two-bloc situation, however, varies from our aggregated solutions in one respect: the Social Democrats join the other 'old' parties as one bloc in supporting NATO and the Danish defence effort in general. Only the Socialist People's Party is seen as consistently opposed to such policies, but in two instances the governmental periods reveal a three-bloc situation. In the 1953–57 period the 'middle' position of the Radical Liberals is a last reminder of that party's earlier commitment to a policy of neutralism and a limited defence. The 1968–71 period witnessed the Social Democrats' move to the 'middle' position since it no longer had governmental responsibility for defence and hence could chart a more independent course based on its own views.

The area of agricultural issues is another fairly well-behaved set of scaling solutions which basically conforms to our aggregated left–right model. However, as with defence issues, some movement of parties occurs that differs from these aggregated solutions. The result of the most politically relevant move is the relative proximity of the farmers' party, the Agrarian Liberals, to the Social Democrats when the latter was the governing party. The farmers through their unions bargained with the government on certain agricultural matters such as subsidies, which necessarily involved consultation with the Agrarian Liberals, and agreed upon compromises that both parties could support in Parliament. The relative degree of distance between the Agrarian Liberals and the other rightist party, the Conservatives, in several of the figures is explained not only by the 'pull' of the governing Social Democrats but also by the 'push' caused by the rural–urban differences in the constituencies of these two rightist parties, a 'push' that seems apparent only in the domain of agricultural policy.

Several other policy areas also exhibit predictable voting patterns across time. The area of labour relations shows a smooth left-right pattern in four legislative periods and strong elements of such a pattern in the two periods in which a two-dimensional solution is shown. The second dimension in these instances reflects the Communists' (or Socialist Peoples') stand against governmental intervention to settle conflicts in the labour market. The area of taxation, as noted above, has good left-right patterns in the post-1966 period, elements of which are definitely noticeable in the pre-1966 two-dimensional figures as well. The potpourri category, 'other domestic issues', also conforms well to our basic left-right model.

The area of housing is another case in point. Here it is interesting to illustrate the dynamics of legislative bargaining that can cause relative shifts of parties within our left-right dimension. Historically speaking, housing has been a political issue in Denmark since the Second World War, originally because of a housing shortage and later because of rapidly increasing rents for new flats corresponding with substantial tax deductions for home-owners. In 1966 the four old parties finally came together on a compromise package of important housing bills which was designed to settle the issue for the next eight years. Only the Socialist People's Party opposed this package deal and, therefore, the scaling solution for this period shows only two points in the space. In the following period the Social Democrats as the governing party were pledged to pass certain legislation to implement the compromise mentioned, but since it depended for its majority on the outside support of the Socialist People's Party, it was also encouraged to pass new housing bills to benefit flat-dwellers, drawing it as a party somewhat away from its compromise partners as the scaling space shows. Finally, this movement resulted in a complete polarization on the housing question as the scaling space for the next governmental period (1968-71) reveals.

Examples such as the housing issue remind us that bargaining and compromise are an inevitable part of the 'legislative game' and will necessarily be reflected in our voting data. If parties voted only according to their ideologies and party programmes, we would get perfect scaling solutions in virtually all our analyses. The fact that our left-right model is so well supported by the issue domain analysis is all the more remarkable given that considerations of bargaining and compromise exist. Still, the issue analysis also reveals some inconsistencies in the rank-ordering of our parties, calling for some modification in the basic model. To get a better idea of the substantive content of political conflict involved in our basic model as applied to these various issue areas, we have decided to analyse the 1971-72 legislative session (the last session for which complete documentation on the content of bills was available) in greater detail with regard to specific pieces of legislation than we were able to do for the 1953-71 period above with its much larger volume of legislation.

In the 1971-72 legislative session there were sixty-one vote divisions in which disagreement existed among the parties. Eighty-one per cent of these divisions fell into four of our five issue areas. Agriculture was the only area not represented, and the remaining 19 per cent of the divisions dealt either with questions relating to the monarchy or with such diverse items that they had to be labelled a 'residual' area. Detailed investigation of these pieces of legislation can be useful in defining what 'left' and 'right' actually mean in substantive terms for these different policy domains. Figure 9.3 displays the 'aggregate' scaling solutions for each of the policy areas. All areas seem to reflect basic left-right cleavages in voting behaviour.

The foreign affairs-defence area involved twelve vote divisions but only four distinct issues. First, five agenda motions depicted the Danish parties' positions on the

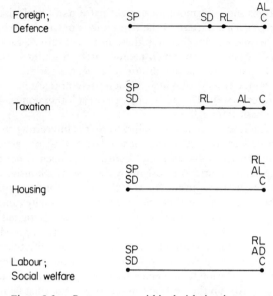

Figure 9.3    Party spaces within legislative issue areas, 1971–72

Vietnam War. The Socialist People's Party revealed itself as strongly anti-American while the Agrarian Liberals and Conservatives took neutral to pro-American stands. The Social Democrats and Radical Liberals placed themselves in between these two blocs but closer to the Socialists. Second, the important European Community issue was involved in five votes, in which the four 'old' parties, as was usual for this issue, were aligned against the anti-European Socialist People's Party. Third, one division was held on a military service bill that improved the situation of conscientious objectors. The Social Democrats and Radicals supported it, the Socialists abstained and the other two parties opposed it because they considered it to be too 'progressive'. Finally, an agenda motion concerning Denmark's relationship with East Germany was passed by the Social Democrats and People's Socialists while the other three parties abstained. Considering the votes on these several issues, an underlying left–right dimension seems adequate to explain each party's position. In terms of what 'left' and 'right' mean in the foreign affairs area, we would be on relatively safe ground if we said that a leftist stance represents anti-NATO, anti-American, anti-European Community and anti-military service attitudes, as well as major cuts in the defence budget. These positions seem to be the province of the Socialist People's Party, while the Agrarian Liberals and Conservatives are seen to be representing the opposite beliefs. In between there are, of course, many shades of opinion which are represented by the Social Democrats and Radical Liberals.

In the area of taxation sixteen bills were voted on in this period, eight of which constituted a unified tax programme of the Social Democratic government. Basically, the Social Democrats proposed the creation of new taxes and increases in existing taxes (other than the income tax), while at the same time sponsoring bills that would guarantee that these tax increases did not work to the disadvantage of low-income groups. All of the bills in this programme were supported by the Socialist People's

Party while the other three parties recommended cutting governmental expenditure rather than raising taxes. In the end, these latter three parties abstained with respect to the measures that would prevent a deterioration of the tax situation for the low-income groups and voted against a new tax on the sale of houses. On the remaining tax bills in the Government's programme, the Agrarian Liberals and Conservatives cast negative votes while the Radicals abstained. Other tax bills in this session dealt with increased taxes for non-salary types of income (e.g. inheritance income, profits on property sales), and two votes were also taken on the Government's proposal to abolish a special plan that granted tax deductions to people who saved money. All of these bills were also opposed by the Agrarian Liberals and Conservatives, and the Radicals opposed the one on property sales as well. Furthermore, the Conservatives deviated from all other parties (cf. Figure 9.3) by opposing a bill granting certain powers to the finance minister that also involved a question of taxing expected stock profits. Finally, a straight government–opposition vote was taken on a temporary duty on imports to reduce the deficit in Denmark's balance of payments.

On the basis of this material, we can define a 'rightist' position on tax policy as involving the following attitudes: preference for reducing governmental expenditures over tax increases and defence of the interests of home-owners, property-owners and generally middle- to high-income groups. In general, this is the position taken by Agrarian Liberals and Conservatives and to a lesser extent by the Radicals. At some risk of oversimplification, we can conclude from this that the fundamental division in the votes taken on tax issues concerns the different interests of low-income groups on the one hand and the middle- to high-income groups on the other. None of the parties deliberately wanted to aggravate the economic condition of low-income people, but they reacted in a quite consistent fashion to the general question of how the burdens and benefits of taxation should be distributed.

The area of labour and social welfare policy revealed many of the same cleavage lines found in the taxation area, as one might expect. Fifteen bills were voted on, all centring on one basic question: should more money be spent on, and more security be provided for, people in low-income groups, including those in economically insecure positions such as old-age pensioners, the disabled, widows and those in situations of unemployment, illness and the like? The Socialist People's Party and the Social Democrats strongly supported such measures while the other three parties said either 'no' to them or 'not at the moment' because of the high costs involved for taxpayers.

Housing policy prior to 1971 has already been briefly mentioned. In the 1971–72 session the eight bills voted on in this area aimed at changing the existing legal and financial state of affairs with respect to the following related sets of contrasting interests: (1) tenants *v.* owners of blocks of flats; (2) government-subsidized housing *v.* private housing; and (3) blocks of flats *v.* one-family houses. The basic left–right cleavage lines again emerged, with the two socialist parties favouring tenants' protection, government-subsidized housing and the construction of blocks of flats, while the other three political parties just as clearly defended the status quo on these matters (i.e., supporting owners of blocks of flats, private housing and one-family house construction). As can be easily seen, the distribution of benefits in this area is also perceived by the two blocs of parties to be structured along economic, class and ideological lines.

These detailed findings from the several policy areas are further evidence that the left–right dimension structures legislative voting and that its substantive content in each policy area most usually coincides with what we would expect 'left' and 'right' to mean in Danish politics. The left–right dimension necessarily has strong economic and class overtones as would be predicted, but it seems to be more than an economic ideology since it generalizes to the area of foreign affairs and defence as well. What seems to be the case is that Danish legislative members—representing the political élite of their country—develop a sophisticated yet general ideological belief system which they apply to several different specific policy areas in a quite consistent fashion. Of course, this statement seems to imply that a certain causal sequence is involved between our aggregated data findings and our findings in these specific policy areas. We are in essence assuming that the dominant pattern for legislators is first to develop a sophisticated ideological belief system and then subsequently to apply it to various specific issue areas. Voting in the specific issue areas would thus act as a reinforcement mechanism for the general belief system. Of course, such ideological systems could have begun in their formative stages through some specific conflict in a given issue area and then been generalized to a broader belief system. All our data tell us for sure is that the general belief system of the Danish legislative members is used in all specific policy areas we have investigated. However, if only one issue area was salient or important to given sets of legislative members in terms of 'left–right' notions, it seems unlikely that they would easily continue this pattern of voting in all of the policy areas. While the data patterns, on the surface, indicate only a continuity in voting over all policy areas, we feel this is strong suggestive evidence for the existence of a more generalized and sophisticated ideological belief system that is the motivating causal force behind such behaviour. The fact that these patterns continue across a twenty-year period further buttresses our notion of the existence and causal nature of such a belief system.

## REPRESENTATIONAL LINKAGES

The existence and duration of a given type of cleavage structure on the élite level necessarily prompts the question of linkages to the mass level of politics. If the élite mainly perceive the political world to be interpretable in only one meaningful way, and if they have persisted in this basic belief for at least twenty years, then an obvious hypothesis would be that this information has been transmitted and embedded in the electorate's 'perceptual map' of the political world. In this situation, the causal sequence would flow from élite to mass, so that the views of the masses 'represent' the beliefs of the élite. To turn the causal sequence around, one could argue that the élite have come to adopt the prior views of the masses on how to view the political world, and by so doing they have become the mere 'representatives' of the masses. This latter hypothesis is a more satisfying one from the perspective of normative democratic theory. The causal process is probably reciprocal, with both mass and élite influencing each other. However, the relative causal flows between these two sets of political actors may be uneven, with one being more influential in shaping and transmitting a belief system than the other. Before we can attempt to answer these questions, however, we must first see if the masses reveal a similar belief structure to that of the élite.

The data base used for this comparison is a national survey of the Danish electorate conducted at the time of the 1971 general election. For the purposes of our study, we have only used the post-election wave of this survey, consisting of 1,302 respondents who were interviewed immediately after the general election in September. In this survey the electorate was asked to rank the parties on a 'thermometer scale'* using whatever frame of reference came to mind. While this data base is not strictly equivalent to our élite data, the common element between the two is the evaluation of the party structure, whether recorded from attitudinal ratings or actual voting behaviour. Correlations could be computed between pairs of parties from the evaluations given by the respondents, resulting in 'similarity coefficients', which, through a simple transformation, could be converted into 'dissimilarity coefficients' to be used as input information to the proximity scaling program in the same manner described earlier for our élite data. The resulting scaling solution for these mass-based party 'dissimilarity coefficients' is given in Figure 9.4.

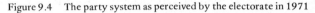

Figure 9.4    The party system as perceived by the electorate in 1971

The one-dimensional solution in Figure 9.4 fits the data with virtually zero stress. More important from a substantive point of view is that it is almost an exact reproduction of the legislative party structure reported in our earlier sections for the élite. Thus, there is a very significant congruence between how the parties behaved and how the electorate perceived these parties in 1971. This result is not surprising, for the reasons mentioned above. The electorate was asked to evaluate a set of parties, most of whom had occupied the political scene since early in the century. The stability of the relationships between these parties has been documented in this paper for a twenty-year period. The one major change in these relationships, which occurred in 1966, provided an even simpler view of the cleavage structure into two opposing party blocs which the voter could readily perceive. The fact that the Danish electorate did so, *en masse*, may imply that the causal sequence between élite and mass is dominated by the élite, as subsequent discussion will show. All in all, the left–right dimension that structures élite political behaviour seems to have a definite parallel in how the voters perceive the political world.

In a methodological sense, however, the graph in Figure 9.4 represents an 'aggregated' scaling solution of how the party system is viewed. At the other extreme one could, in theory at least, describe the party system as it is seen by each individual voter. This would in all likelihood furnish some different scaling spaces, although such a project would be quite impractical and of little theoretical interest. But somewhere in between these two approaches one could possibly define, in a theoretically meaningful way, subgroups of the sample for which the party system might look different. Even with the persuasive evidence of a very stable party structure in 1971, we could possibly expect some variations in the perceptions of parties according to such characteristics as age, occupation, issues salient to the voters, vote choice and party identification. We therefore conducted additional scaling analyses along these lines.

* The 'thermometer scale' is a device by which people rate political objects (in this case, political parties) using their own frames of reference. In the Danish study, it was a 200-point scale which ranged from −100 degrees to +100 degrees, with zero as the neutral point. The thermometer scale was devised by Aage Clausen and revised by Jerrold Rusk and Herbert Weisberg to rate political candidates and has since been transplanted to Europe to scale political parties. For research conducted with this scale in the United States, see Rusk and Weisberg (1972), Weisberg and Rusk (1970) and Wang, Schonemann and Rusk (1975).

Basically, separate scaling analyses using these 'subgroup' variables revealed exactly the same party space as portrayed by our 'aggregate' solution in Figure 9.4. On the age variable, only the older respondents deviated from the 'aggregate' perception, and then only slightly, seeing the Social Democrats as somewhat further away from the 'bourgeois' parties than the Socialist People's Party was from these same parties. The most plausible explanation for this is that older voters were still influenced by their earlier experiences when the Social Democrats on the one hand and the Agrarian Liberals and Conservatives on the other were the main antagonists in Danish politics. As regards occupation, not even a single deviant scaling space was noted, the farmers, professional people, businessmen, white-collar and blue-collar groups all perceiving the same cleavage lines in politics. Issue groups revealed the same pattern, probably for one of two reasons. Either the voters did not feel very intense about the issues in which they expressed interest, or they could not sufficiently relate these issues to the programmes of the parties. Another very plausible explanation is that the issues simply reflected in the voters' minds the basic left–right dimensioning of politics they already knew. The vote and party identification variables revealed the basic left–right structure once again. The only deviation involved the relative placement of the Agrarian Liberal and Conservative parties on the right end of the scale. Socialist People and Social Democratic voters and identifiers placed the Conservative Party furthest to the right while the Radical Liberal and Conservative voters and identifiers located the Agrarian Liberal Party in that position, as did the Agrarian Liberal voters. In general, regardless of which party a person identified with or voted for, he saw his party in relation to others on a strictly left–right scale so familiar to us by now.

As a last investigation into this notion of possible sub-group variation, we looked at the coalition preferences of the voters of each of the parties. When asked which party or parties they thought their party should form a government with, the voters of each party tended to pick possible coalition partners using our basic left–right model as their sole reference point. The data showed that Socialist People voters strongly preferred the Social Democratic Party and that a clear majority of the Social Democratic voters wanted only their own party, with a definite minority favouring the inclusion of the Socialist People's Party. Agrarian Liberal and Conservative voters were strongly in favour of a continued 'bourgeois' coalition, as were the Radical Liberal voters. Two 'possible' deviations occurred in the data: 12 per cent of the Social Democratic voters wanted to include the Radical Liberal Party and a similar percentage of the Radical Liberal voters reciprocated this preference. This way of tapping information on inter-party distances, then, points to the same uni-dimensional structure of the party system that we have seen indicated so often at the parliamentary level.

The fact that both élite and mass show the same structuring of the political world does not mean they view it with the same degree of sophistication and depth of knowledge. As Converse showed in his pioneering analysis (1964), the actual differences in the belief systems of élite and mass are extensive. Élites tend to view specific issues and events within a tightly constrained system of much broader concepts, postures and symbols, which are themselves interrelated. Such a system is complex, long-range in nature and sophisticated, and is sustained by a considerable degree of socioeconomic and political knowledge. A given issue or event is conceptualized as related to a much larger part of the belief system and can rarely drastically change such a system by itself. These truly are 'belief systems' in every sense of the word and give a much-needed sense of 'order' and 'understanding' to the political world. Masses, on the other hand, possess much more rudimentary 'belief systems', and in some ways the term is a misleading one to use for many people. Often only a few issues affecting a person's self-interest are picked up from the maze of political stimuli available and these may constitute his only available basis for evaluating the parties. Issues that the masses cannot relate to one another in any meaningful or consistent fashion are seen by the élite as neatly interwoven into a much broader ideological framework which deals with such concepts as postures toward innovation and change, the welfare state and individual rights and freedoms. What this means in the context of our investigation is that the left–right dimensioning of politics discovered for élites in Denmark probably involves the sophisticated ideological belief system that Converse so carefully defines, while for the masses it can be a combination of various pieces of information such as specific knowledge of the parties' stands on a few issues of particular salience, the remembering of the terms 'left' and 'right' (or, more likely, 'socialist' and 'bourgeois') as they are used by the media, as well as a knowledge of which parties formed governmental coalitions in the past (see Borre, 1973).

With these ideas in mind, it seems much more probable that élites basically form their own belief systems rather than attempting to ascertain what passes for the 'belief systems' of the masses. Issues are formed within such a belief system and communicated to the masses, the amount of information being picked up by the masses probably depending on (a) how long the issue remains an 'issue' over time and (b) how long the élite continue in the general cleavage structure of which this issue forms a necessary part. We know from our analysis that condition (b) is maintained for a considerable period of time, which makes condition (a) all the more critical in determining the amount of 'issue' information picked up by the masses. With many of the economic issues associated with the left–right ideological stance taken by the élite towards the welfare state, we would expect a relatively 'rich' supply of information to be possessed by the Danish voters. Of course, issues can arise from environmental conditions which may have no relation to the 'issue' dialogue being discussed at the élite level. If such issues arise, particularly in 'crisis' situations, élites may be slow to react to them because of the particular way in which they have viewed the political world for so many years. The masses, however, can be receptive to them rather rapidly since they do not have the necessary constraints and perspectives posed on them by a meaningful and well-developed belief system. The tempering nature and long-range perspective of an ideological system are relatively unknown to them. When such issues arise and the élites do not correspondingly respond, new dimensions of political evaluation can emerge, causing both volatility and realignment in the electorate.

From our analysis we know that the period 1953–73 was one marked by a remarkable stability in élite behaviour and, if the 1971 reading of the electorate is any guide to time past, in mass behaviour as well. It seems that élites developed a sophisticated ideological belief system which they applied to a wide variety of specific policy areas. When change in the cleavage structure did occur, as in 1966, it was a decision made at the élite level and subsequently picked up by the masses. The congruence between how the élite and mass view cleavages in the system, while it speaks for this stability, should not be construed as strictly involving the same thought processes. The implications of this statement for 'representation' theory are critical. If élites indeed do have a more sophisticated belief system, it seems unlikely that it was mainly developed from attempts to 'represent' the masses but rather independently or in interaction with other élites. The persistence of common patterns of élite voting in the various policy areas also argues for this point, since one would doubt either that the electorate was interested in all these areas or that they had developed a consistent ideology to embrace all of them. However, specific issues could affect given subsets of the voters and on these particular issues they perhaps could make their voices heard. In such instances, 'representation' would conform more to the democratic norm, and if a given issue or issues were sufficiently 'heated', the parties would obviously be wise to let an 'instructed delegate' mode of behaviour apply in such cases. One would expect few such intense issues to emerge, but when they do occur, they can be expected to mould voters, because of their relative lack of a constraining ideological system, to possible volatile or realigning behaviour if the party élites do not 'represent' their views.

In sum, the Danish political system has been characterized by common cleavage lines for at least the last twenty years on the élite and (most probably) the mass level. These cleavage lines are asserted to be, in part, a product of different ways of thinking and differing degrees of sophistication in the belief systems of the two sets of political actors. The differing nature and complexity of élite and mass belief systems suggest that, while reciprocal influence between the two must certainly occur, the dominant pattern of influence is from élite to mass. However, because of the more fragmented and unconstrained nature of the mass belief system, new issues arising from the environment can have a greater impact in changing the views of the masses than those of the élites, with obvious implications for electoral volatility and realignment. Usually times are 'normal' and the dominant mode is for the electorate to conceptualize, in a more rudimentary way, the cleavage lines and issues structured by the élite. This seems to have been the pattern of stability that has defined Danish politics for twenty years and, as some Danish scholars would assert, for the last half-century. All of this stability was apparently changed suddenly by the 'volatile' election of 1973.

## THE CONTEMPORARY PARTY SYSTEM

The findings reported in the previous sections convincingly demonstrate, we believe, that the uni-dimensional model goes a long way towards describing and explaining the Danish party system over an extended period of time, and that the electorate of 1971 clearly perceived this basic structure of party conflict. Toward the end of 1973, however, things appeared to change dramatically. The 'volatile' election of December 1973 showed a massive change in voting behaviour (see Chapter 8 above). While it would be interesting to explore the micro-level determinants of vote changes in this election, our main purpose here is to probe the nature of such changes as they affect the party system at the macro-level—in short, to analyse this recent change in behaviour within the longitudinal and developmental perspective of this paper. Needless to say, any comments we make must be regarded as tentative at this stage. Before presenting such comments, however, a brief description of the Folketing election, and the events leading up to it, is in order.

In many respects, the unusual nature of the December 1973 election centred on the phenomenal rise of a new party, the Progressive Party. Officially created in January 1973, this party was, within a few months, receiving up to 25 per cent support in the public opinion polls at the expense of the older established parties. Initially this party was a one-man show by a lawyer named Glistrup, forcefully appealing to people who were concerned with such current problems as rapid inflation, increasing tax burdens, 'red tape' bureaucracy and alleged misuse of social welfare money. Generally, this protest party accused all established parties of incompetence in handling governmental affairs—both the ruling left coalition and the previous 'bourgeois' governmental coalition as well. Under these circumstances, none of the established parties had any desire to be confronted by the voters at the polls, but then an unforeseen event occurred which necessitated the calling of an election. In the autumn of 1973, a 'right-wing' member of the Social Democratic parliamentary group left his party as a protest against the 'leftist' policies of the Social Democratic–People's Socialist ruling coalition, particularly on the issue of home-owner taxation. With the loss of this member, the Government could no longer effectively govern because its bare legislative majority disappeared, and consequently new elections were called, with adverse effects for all five parties in the Folketing. The Social Democrats and Conservatives suffered the most, but the Agrarian Liberals, Radical Liberals and People's Socialists also lost several legislative seats. The victorious parties were the Progressive Party, with 16 per cent of the vote, the Centre Democratic Party, with 8 per cent (the party formed by the Social Democratic secession movement mentioned above), the Christian People's Party, the Communist Party and the Justice Party. Thus, instead of the customary five-party Parliament, a new, and completely different, ten-party Parliament came into existence as a result of the 1973 election (see Table 9.2).

Table 9.2    Election Results (Percentages) and Party Composition of the Folketing (No. of Seats), 1971 and 1973

| | 1971 | | 1973 | |
| Party | Per cent of votes | No. of seats | Per cent of votes | No. of seats |
|---|---|---|---|---|
| Social Democrats .............. | 37.3 | 70 | 25.7 | 46 |
| Radical Liberals .............. | 14.4 | 27 | 11.2 | 20 |
| Conservatives .................. | 16.7 | 31 | 9.1 | 16 |
| Agrarian Liberals ............. | 15.6 | 30 | 12.3 | 22 |
| Justice Party ................. | 1.7 | 0 | 2.9 | 5 |
| Communists .................... | 1.4 | 0 | 3.6 | 6 |
| Socialist People's Party ....... | 9.1 | 17 | 6.0 | 11 |
| Christian People's Party ....... | 2.0 | 0 | 4.0 | 7 |
| Left Socialists ............... | 1.6 | 0 | 1.5 | 0 |
| Progressive Party ............. | - | - | 15.9 | 28 |
| Centre Democrats ............. | - | - | 7.8 | 14 |
| Total ..................... | 99.8 | 175 | 100.0 | 175 |

The 1973 election poses two central questions for our study. First is the question of how this election relates to our previous findings about the Danish party system in the 1953-73 period. Second is the question of what the consequences of this election are for the contemporary party system and its future development. Looking back at Figures 9.1 and 9.4, we are reminded of how both the mass and the élite viewed the party structure in the 1953-73 period. Before 1966, a left-centre-right bloc politics was perceived which evolved, in the post-1966 period, into a bipolarized left-right division of the party system. The election results of 1973 seem to indicate a serious change from sole reliance on these left-right patterns. Danish voters appeared to be generally dissatisfied with their economic and social situation under the rule of both the 'left' and the 'right', with the result that this dissatisfaction could no longer be contained within the existing system of left-right politics. The severe impact of recent economic events undoubtedly reinforced and intensified such feelings. Having given both the 'left' and the 'right' their chance in office, a substantial number of dissatisfied voters switched to new party alternatives in 1973. While some of these new alternatives could find a niche in the traditional left-right scale (e.g. the Communists), other parties (such as the Progressive and Centre Democratic parties) did not as easily fit into this customary way of thinking about party system structure. Our 1971 survey results showed that people at that time used such a left-right structure in their political thinking, regardless of whether the five parliamentary parties or all nine parties in the system were included in the scaling solutions. In 1973, using the same 'thermometer' instrument, the new scaling solution shows that the old system has undergone a serious transformation, resulting in the two-dimensional party cleavage structure in Figure 9.5. This graphically illustrates the changing perceptions of the

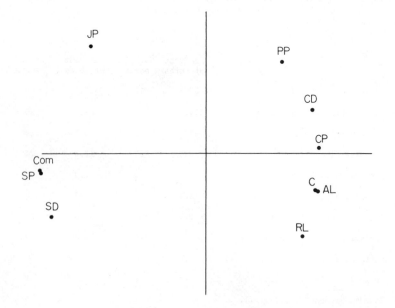

Figure 9.5    The party system as perceived by the electorate in December 1973

electorate that were so evident in their voting behaviour in the December 1973 election.*

The most noticeable aspect of Figure 9.5 is its 'change' element. However, an important element of 'continuity' definitely exists in the Danish system, as the first or horizontal dimension demonstrates. This dimension is the more important of the two dimensions in the scaling solution and remains the same as our previous scaling solutions—a left–right axis which is still used by many Danish voters for evaluating the system. The second or vertical dimension, however, represents a completely new element in Danish politics. Parties perceived on the upper end of this dimension tend to be the new parties (Progressive and Centre Democratic parties) and the minor parties (Justice and Christian People's parties) that have generally been unsuccessful in passing the vote threshold for entry into Parliament until the 1973 election. On the opposite end of this dimension are the established parties of the 'left' and the 'right'. We believe this dimension basically represents a protest against the established parties of Denmark for their inability to handle governmental affairs and solve current domestic problems (see Chapter 8, above). The fact that the Progressive Party—a Poujadist-type of protest party—loads high on this dimension gives further credence to this interpretation. The success of the Progressive Party in the 1973 election—and its opening the way for other new and minor parties to gain votes—is an unprecedented phenomenon in Danish politics, which cannot be fully explained by the data used in our scaling analysis. However, it is relevant to attempt to relate this phenomenon to our earlier discussion of the differing ideological belief systems of élites and masses. While the élites possess a sophisticated and tightly constrained belief system, the masses have a more rudimentary and only weakly structured belief system. The masses, therefore, are more likely to be susceptible to change in periods of anxiety, unrest and distrust, which would favour a party like Glistrup's. Whether this hypothesis is tenable or not, the fact remains that the electorate of 1973—for the first time in recent history—did not merely passively 'receive' or 'accept' the existing structure of legislative party conflict. Instead, it actively 'created' a new party system.

The way in which the electorate responded to the 1973 election leads into our second question of concern: what are the consequences of this election for the contemporary party system and the structure of party conflict in the Folketing? At this stage in writing only half a year has passed since the election, and thus few, if any, definitive conclusions can be drawn on this subject. What can be done is to mention the main events that have occurred thus far in the post election Parliament and give our interpretation of them, including a discussion of what these events imply in terms of the possible shape the party system might take in the future.

The immediate effect of the election on the party system was to end, at least temporarily, the post-1966 pattern of government formation. For sheer arithmetic reasons, the election results precluded majority coalitions being formed by the former coalition partners of either the 'left' or the 'right'. Denmark has been used to minority

* Figure 9.5 displays a 'circular' pattern. Some scaling analysts believe that such a pattern could be basically uni-dimensional in nature. In another study, we found that different explanatory variables correlated with different dimensions of the scaling solution, indicating the independent character of each dimension. Of particular importance was the correlation of such explanatory variables as current economic issues and protest–distrust items with the second dimension. A scaling analysis was also performed in this study using only the seven main parties (in terms of votes received in the 1973 election) as stimuli and the resulting solution was not circular. See Rusk and Borre, Chapter 8 above.

governments in the past, but even this process, so familiar to politicians, became a difficult one given the unusual nature of the election results. The established parties, despite their losses, did not want a government formed that would include the new and minor parties, although some of the new and minor parties were willing to support a government composed of one or more of the established parties. Finally, a minority government was formed, consisting only of the twenty-two-member Agrarian Liberal Party. This party received active support in its bid to be the 'Government' from the Christian People's and Centre Democratic parties, while several other parties decided not to oppose it, including the Social Democratic Party which, shocked by the dramatic split in its ranks and subsequent election losses, did not attempt to stay in office. The Agrarian Liberals became the Government in late December 1973, without a doubt the smallest minority government in Denmark's history, and as such the one most susceptible to shifts in support from other parliamentary parties.

The new Government's major task was to solve, as much as possible, the economic problems of the country. It was, however, this vital yet sensitive area that could so easily unseat a twenty-two-member government. The Agrarian Liberals presented their economic programme to the Folketing in January 1974 and then quickly entered into bargaining sessions with other parties in order to obtain support for as many aspects of this programme as possible. The result was a package-deal compromise which was agreed to by the Christian People's Party, the Centre Democrats and the Social Democrats. Encouraged by this, the Prime Minister, and the leader of the Social Democrats as well, announced publicly that these 'responsible parties' had been able to achieve 'co-operation across the middle'. They stated that, after a period of conflict between the 'left' and the 'right', the electorate wanted this 'co-operation', and the Government and its supporting parties were merely responding to this demand. In the next few months, these parties kept their pledge to support the various bills they had agreed on, although they were strongly opposed on these measures by all other parties. In May, however, this coalition became factionalized when the Government proposed a set of bills to increase sales taxes substantially on various items in order to reduce domestic spending and at the same time improve Denmark's balance-of-payments situation. This started the period of fluid and shifting coalitions and, in essence, demonstrated that the original 'permanent' coalition was far from a stable arrangement. Initially the Social Democrats left the coalition supporting the Government, but the Agrarian Liberals were able to persuade the Radical Liberals and Conservatives to join with the Christian People's and Centre Democratic Parties in backing the sales tax legislation. Even with these added votes, the Government was still unable to obtain a majority, and the situation appeared both confused and hopeless, with the prospect of new elections having to be called to decide the issue. However, at the last moment the Progressive Party—up to this point generally shunned by the élites of both the 'left' and the 'right'—decided to vote for the sales tax bills. Prior to this move, this party had also agreed to support a general plan of the Governments' to cut the budget and reduce income taxes, which would be introduced at the next session of Parliament. The addition of the Progressive vote was sufficient to pass the sales tax increases in May—increases that were vehemently opposed by the Communist, Socialist, Social Democratic and Justice Parties and which caused large-scale, politically motivated strikes for a few days. With the end of these demonstrations, a third issue arose in June, that of housing policy, which caused still new coalition lines to form. This time the Christian People's and Centre Democratic

Parties joined with all the old parties (Social Democrats, Radical Liberals, Conservatives and the governing Agrarian Liberals) to back a compromise package of bills on housing policy for the next four years.

All of these events seem to show that contemporary Danish politics is in a state of non-equilibrium, flux, and change, the outcome of which remains to be seen. Coalitions have been unstable and changing; élites have not been certain of exactly what the electorate wants; new and minor parties, despite their electoral successes, have not been able to enter the Government; and one of the established parties still remains the Government and, within circumscribed bounds, calls the 'shots' for new policy directions.

These are the problems that currently face the élites, the masses and their political system as a result of the 1973 election. It seems clear that the élites have been basically unsuccessful in either understanding the new views of the electorate or changing their own views to correspond with those of the electorate. A formal way of testing this notion is to scale the legislative votes in the January–June session of Parliament and compare the resulting solution with how the electorate viewed the political system in the 1973 voter survey (Figure 9.5). This legislative scaling solution will demonstrate empirically the movement of parties and changes in the relationships among parties after the 1973 election outcome. To obtain such a scaling solution, we used all final vote divisions and divisions on amendments to bills as well—a total of 325 votes, of which 64 concerned legislation associated with the three major compromises mentioned above. Even though this scaling solution might change in the future because of the highly unstable situation that existed at the time of writing, we believe this result is of considerable interest in itself since it represents the Danish legislative system during one of the most turbulent sessions in its history.

Figure 9.6 shows the scaling solution for this legislative session. One immediately notes that the legislative system must now be represented in two dimensions. The main cleavage in the system, according to the élites, remains the left–right dimension (explaining 87 per cent of the variance). Along this dimension the five established parties of the pre-1973 period are located in a familiar order, with the one important exception being the Agrarian Liberals' move toward the Social Democrats and the centre of the space. The Radical Liberals and Conservatives also have a tendency to move somewhat closer to the centre of the space than earlier (1968–73) scaling solutions have shown, but unlike the Agrarian Liberals these parties do not change their 'natural' order on the left–right dimension. One further observes that two of the new parliamentary parties—the Centre Democratic and Christian People's parties— form a cluster near the centre of the space with the governing Agrarian Liberals. Two other new parliamentary parties 'fill out' the dimension by occupying its left and right wings: the Communist Party appears on the far left of this dimension and the Progressive Party is located on the far right. The second dimension of this solution is more difficult to interpret. Presumably various factors are at work here. The most reasonable interpretation is that this axis represents a distinction between 'predominantly compromising' parties (the four old parties plus the Centre Democratic and Christian People's Parties) and 'predominantly opposing' parties (the Communist, Socialist People's, Justice and Progressive Parties). This brings us to an important point which can best be demonstrated by comparing Figures 9.5 and 9.6.

At first glance, there seems to be more dissimilarity than similarity between Figures 9.5 and 9.6. This observation fits well with our idea that a fundamental

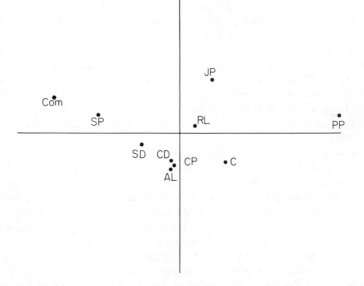

Figure 9.6    The legislative party system of January–June 1974

discontinuity currently exists between how the élites and masses view the cleavage structure of Danish politics. The differences observed can be discussed in both technical and substantive terms. In a technical sense, we could presumably obtain a somewhat better correspondence between the two configurations by a rotation of axes. However, we definitely cannot 'rotate away' the substantial dissimilarity that exists between the two figures. The fundamental difference resides in the existence of a number of parties in the centre region of Figure 9.6, parties that are considered by voters to be from both the 'left' and the 'right'. This is the core cluster of 'predominantly compromising' parties—the Agrarian Liberals, Centre Democrats and Christian People's Party, with the Social Democrats, Radical Liberals and Conservatives at a somewhat greater distance from the Government party. These parties represent the 'co-operation across the middle' that the élites presumed the voters wanted, but from surveying the electorate's voting behaviour in the 1973 election and their perception of the 'party space' in Figure 9.5, one could not easily agree that this was the case. Rather, it seems the voters desired new party alternatives to run the Government, attempting new ideas and solutions for pressing current problems. They probably made this most evident in their voting behaviour by precluding the establishment of the familiar coalitions of either the 'left' or the 'right'.

The differences between Figures 9.5 and 9.6 could be either permanent or transitory. The data available to us cannot easily comment on this point. The élites seem to be moving away from the 1966-73 system of left-right politics, simply because the electoral results compelled them to do so. If they have their way, the resulting compromises 'across the middle' may be indicative of a return to some semblance of the pre-1966 left-centre-right-blocs politics, with the established parties (and two of the new parties) representing the 'centre' and the other new parties representing the 'left' and 'right' fringes. The fact that the second dimension of the mass belief system is founded on contemporary problems and a corresponding protest against the established parties may mean this dimension will disappear if the established parties can reduce or eliminate most of these problems in the near future. If, however, the electorate continues to perceive mismanagement, incompetence, poor decision-making and lack of leadership in governmental affairs, the next election could reinforce the strength of this second dimension and the parties it benefits.

All in all, our contemporary analysis has summarized some quite unique and fascinating developments in the party system, developments with potentially quite different implications for the system from those of the past. Whereas our longitudinal analysis indicated a stable pattern of party conflict between the élite and mass levels, with the élite most probably dominating this reciprocally causal relationship, change entered the relationship between the two sets of political actors in the 1973 election. First the electorate changed its perceptions of the establishment parties in important respects and voted accordingly. Then the legislative élite reacted by trying to build various workable coalitions with the four old parties and two of the new parties as key actors. What has emerged is nothing less than profound—a major changing of a system that has been remarkably stable as a whole and, specifically, in its cleavage lines for at least the past twenty years. As we have noted above, whether these new changes are permanent or transitory will be resolved by future parliamentary actions and succeeding elections. All we can say for sure at this point is that no stable majority pattern has so far emerged from either the electoral verdict or the subsequent parliamentary deliberations, and none is likely to occur in the future until the electorate has once again spoken. Presumably there will be no return to the 1966–73 pattern of politics in the foreseeable future. In one way or another, a politics of compromise among several non-extremist parties seems the only workable solution until new elections are called. Whether these new elections will dictate a revised version of the familiar left–right politics—such as the pre-1966 pattern of left, centre and right blocs of parties—or a continuation of a more volatile two-dimensional cleavage structure is too difficult to judge at this time.

## REFERENCES

Borre, Ole (1973), *Party and Ideology in Denmark,* unpublished manuscript, University of Aarhus, Denmark.

Converse, Philip E. (1964), 'The Nature of Belief Systems in Mass Publics', in David E. Apter (ed.), *Ideology and Discontent,* Free Press, New York.

Daalder, Hans, and Jerrold G. Rusk (1972), 'Perceptions of Party in the Dutch Parliament', in Samuel C. Patterson and John C. Wahlke (eds.), *Comparative Legislative Behaviour,* Wiley, New York.

Damgaard, Erik (1969), 'The Parliamentary Basis of Danish Governments: The Patterns of Coalition Formation', *Scandinavian Political Studies,* 4, 30–57.

Damgaard, Erik (1973), 'Party Coalitions in Danish Law-Making: 1953–1970', *European Journal of Political Research,* 1, 35–66.

Damgaard, Erik (1974), 'Stability and Change of the Danish Party System over Half a Century', *Scandinavian Political Studies,* 9, 103–125.

Kruskal, J. B. (1964), 'Multidimensional Scaling by Optimising Goodness of Fit to a Nonmetric Hypothesis', *Psychometrika,* 29, 1–27.

Lipset, Seymour M., and Stein Rokkan (1967), 'Cleavage Structures, Party Systems and Voter Alignments: An Introduction', in Seymour M. Lipset and Stein Rokkan (eds.), *Party Systems and Voter Alignments,* Free Press, New York.

Pedersen, Mogens N. (1967), 'Consensus and Conflict in the Danish Folketing: the Patterns of Coalition Formation', *Scandinavian Political Studies*, 2, 143–66.

Pedersen, Mogens N., Erik Damgaard and P. Nannestad Olsen (1971), 'Party Distances in the Danish Folketing: 1945–1968', *Scandinavian Political Studies*, 6, 87–106.

Rusk, Jerrold G., and Herbert F. Weisberg (1972), 'Perceptions of Presidential Candidates: Implications for Electoral Change', *Midwest Journal of Political Science*, 16, 388–410.

Wang, Ming-Mei, Peter H. Schonemann and Jerrold G. Rusk (1975), 'A Conjugate Gradient Algorithm for the Multidimensional Analysis of Preference Data', *Multivariate Behavioral Research*, 10, 45–79.

Weisberg, Herbert F., and Jerrold G. Rusk (1970), 'Dimensions of Candidate Evaluation', *American Political Science Review*, 64, 1167–85.

# 10

# Party Preference Spaces and Voting Change in Belgium

ANDRE-PAUL FROGNIER

This research is an attempt to set up the 'psychological', or rather the 'cultural' space of Belgian voters in the three regions of Flanders, Wallonia and Brussels. These regions are becoming more and more autonomous in the Belgian political system, which now has a 'pre-federal character' (*Annales de Droit*, 1972). These 'spaces' will be compared with vote changes between parties, in order to learn whether party 'distances' can be used to explain such behaviour. The method used here has some points in common with that of Rokeach (1960), Roskam (1958), Converse (1966), Converse and Valen (1971) and some others. The particular technique employed is the 'analysis of correspondences'.

## HYPOTHESES

Works of political science dealing with Belgium recurrently study its political system, specifically its party system, with reference to its major cleavages (Lorwin, 1966; Claeys-Van Haegendoren, 1967; Dewachter, 1967; Van den Brande, 1967; Seiler and Raes, 1970; Frognier and Seiler, 1972; Mabille, 1974; Frognier, McHale and Paranzino, 1974). One way or another, there is usually a reference to the standpoint of Lipset and Rokkan (1967). Three cleavages are almost unanimously taken into account:

(a) the 'religious' cleavage, sometimes called 'clerical', which concerns ethical questions and the place of institutions of Christian origin in the state;

(b) the 'socioeconomic' or 'left–right' cleavage, which mainly concerns problems connected with economic power and social class; and

(c) cleavages relating to the form of the State, often called a 'community' cleavage, for it proceeds from the presence of the two (language) communities and has more recently concerned the three regions as well.

These three cleavages do not stimulate constant political opposition. Depending on the situation, they can be expressed in different orders of intensity. For example, in 1960–61 it was clearly the socioeconomic cleavage that was most obvious, whereas shortly thereafter the cleavage connected with the form of the State appeared, and has since been almost continuously visible. Each period, then, sees each of these three cleavages expressed with different intensities. At the same time, it seems that the content itself of these cleavages has varied with time, making a precise definition difficult.

It is natural therefore that our first hypothesis will be that voters also see the parties with reference to this traditional system of cleavages. This means that they consider each party according to its relationship to each cleavage, or only to some of them, depending on such factors as the level of their information. The second hypothesis will be that the party system as seen by the electorate influences its electoral behaviour, particularly vote change from one party to another. The measure of the 'distances' between parties, such as they are revealed by a comprehensive view of their positions on the cleavages, can be associated, according to certain modalities, with the degree of facility with which electors can pass from one party to another.

## PREFERENCE SPACES

In order to test these hypotheses, it was necessary to find data and techniques susceptible to the setting up of cultural spaces with several dimensions, which had a significant character and were ready for interpretation. Only some data on electors' preferences were at hand, and only in the unique form of contingency tables. At the same time research on relations between these data and other material in the same survey was impossible, thus excluding any multivariate space analysis (Converse, 1966). Therefore it was difficult to find an analytical method that could be associated with the structure of the data.* Eventually the analysis of correspondences was used, and it produced interesting results. It was not possible, of course, to seek solutions to the usual problems of such an analysis, which included geometrical distance and the validity of interpretations of factors as cleavages, which in turn raises the problem of the measurement scale.

### Data

The data used here are taken from a survey conducted by the 'Institut de Sociologie' of the University of Brussels in 1968 (Delruelle, *et al.*, 1970). The following three questions were asked:

(*a*) To which party or list did you give your vote [in 1968] ?

(*b*) If the party or list for which you voted had not stood or had not presented a list in your region, for which party would you have voted?

(*c*) For which parties would you not have voted under any circumstances?

About half the respondents could not answer questions (*b*) and (*c*). On the whole, there were more answers to (*c*) than to (*b*).

These questions are very likely to refer to the notion of preference. But there is no question here, as there was in the case of the survey inspiring Converse (1966) or Converse and Valen (1971), of preferences expressed directly towards parties. These are preferences towards votes for parties, i.e. a particular behaviour (real or imaginary). This peculiarity must be underlined because the rank-orders that can be drawn from these two types of preferences might differ from one another. Indeed, voters might not always vote for the party they prefer, but sometimes for another according to certain characteristics of the former, for example, if the former is too

---

* I am most grateful to Professor A. Coxon of the University of Edinburgh for the opportunity to use his programs of multi-dimensional analysis of ordinal data at an early stage of the research.

small to exert any influence, and therefore voting for it is 'losing one's vote'. Voters can do this in reaction to a situation as well; for example, in a crisis one might vote for a party more out of 'fear of adventure' than by real inclination. Voters can also shift votes according to a rational calculation. For example, one might not vote for one's prefered party if it appears to run no risk of losing, but for another party in order to

Table 10.1                                Wallonia [2,3]

(a)  (a) x (b)[1]

|  | No answer | PSC | PSB | PLP | RW | PC | Others |
|---|---|---|---|---|---|---|---|
| No answer |  |  |  |  |  |  |  |
| No opinion | 306 | 15 | 10 | 13 | 18 | 4 | - |
| PSC | 79 | - | 18 | 63 | 14 | 2 | 3 |
| PSB | 93 | 60 | - | 40 | 50 | 29 | 5 |
| PLP | 44 | 55 | 25 | - | 40 | 2 | 1 |
| RW | 16 | 3 | 22 | 16 | - | 3 | 1 |
| PC | 2 | 1 | 9 | 2 | 4 | - | 1 |

(b)  (a) x (c)

|  | No answer | PSC | PSB | PLP | RW | VU | PC | Others |
|---|---|---|---|---|---|---|---|---|
| No answer |  |  |  |  |  |  |  |  |
| No opinion | 231 | 27 | 14 | 32 | 12 | 42 | 107 | 1 |
| PSC | 58 | - | 40 | 12 | 13 | 10 | 115 | 1 |
| PSB | 88 | 73 | - | 118 | 7 | 23 | 75 | 1 |
| PLP | 40 | 22 | 40 | - | 12 | 13 | 110 | 1 |
| RW | 14 | 18 | 8 | 17 | - | 3 | 21 | - |
| PC | 4 | 11 | 1 | 8 | - | 1 | - | - |

1.  For (a), (b) and (c) questions in full, see p.190

2.  In the survey, Wallonia includes the provinces of Hainaut, Liege, Luxembourg, Namur and the administrative district of Nivelles.

3.  PSC = Parti Social Chrétien
    PSB = Parti Social Belge
    PLP = Parti de la Liberté et du Progrès (former Liberal Party)
    RW  = Rassemblement Wallon
    PC  = Parti Communiste
    FDF = Front Démocratique des Francophones
    VU  = Volksunie

Table 10.2                                    Flanders[1]

(a)   (a) x (b)

|  | No answer | PSC | PSB | PLP | VU | PC | Others |
|---|---|---|---|---|---|---|---|
| No answer |  |  |  |  |  |  |  |
| No opinion | 489 | 35 | 20 | 13 | 22 | - | - |
| PSC | 215 | - | 79 | 59 | 146 | 0 | 5 |
| PSB | 100 | 52 | - | 23 | 23 | 13 | 2 |
| PLP | 45 | 42 | 17 | - | 8 | 1 | 2 |
| VU | 38 | 89 | 21 | 15 | - | 3 | - |

(b)   (a) x (c)

|  | No answer | PSC | PSB | PLP | RW | VU | PC | Others |
|---|---|---|---|---|---|---|---|---|
| No answer |  |  |  |  |  |  |  |  |
| No opinion | 372 | 11 | 43 | 46 | 7 | 56 | 184 | 3 |
| PSC | 156 | - | 126 | 93 | 6 | 64 | 234 | 1 |
| PSB | 82 | 42 | - | 59 | 2 | 58 | 38 | - |
| PLP | 31 | 9 | 31 | - | 3 | 51 | 39 | - |
| VU | 33 | 20 | 45 | 85 | 2 | - | 41 | 2 |

1.  Flanders includes the provinces of Antwerp, Western
    Flanders, Eastern Flanders, Limburg and the administrative
    district of Leuven.

'give it a chance'. With this restriction made, for reasons of clarity we will nevertheless talk of 'preferences between parties' and 'distances between parties' in the text that follows. The word 'party' should be understood not as the party itself, but as a vote for the party.

The answers to the questions were accessible only in contingency table cross-tabulations for each region, the answers given to questions (a) and (b) on the one hand, and to (a) and (c) on the other according to the major parties. In a way the tables constitute the very observations of the present study—resulting already from a manipulation of original observations, for it was not possible to obtain the details of the individual answers. Below, we reproduce the data for each region in Tables 10.1, 10.2 and 10.3. The *rows* of the tables are the real vote for the parties (answers to question (a)). The *columns* in each of the three 'a' tables are the parties given as answers to question (b) and in each of the 'b' tables are the parties given as an answer to (c). Each input indicates the number of voters who, after voting for the party corresponding to (a), express their opinion *vis-à-vis* the parties mentioned in answer to (b) or (c).

Table 10.3 Brussels[1]

(a)  (a) x (b)

|  | No answer | PSC | PSB | PLP | RW | VU | PC | Others |
|---|---|---|---|---|---|---|---|---|
| No answer |  |  |  |  |  |  |  |  |
| No opinion | 183 | 9 | 11 | 23 | 10 | 2 | 2 | - |
| PSC | 50 | - | 33 | 54 | 9 | 3 | - | - |
| PSB | 55 | 26 | - | 21 | 31 | - | 3 | 1 |
| PLP | 55 | 41 | 36 | - | 41 | - | 1 | 1 |
| FDF | 21 | 14 | 28 | 36 | - | 1 | 4 | 1 |
| VU | 3 | 7 | 4 | 2 | - | - | 1 | - |
| PC | 5 | - | 4 | 1 | 1 | - | - | - |

(b)  (a) x (c)

|  | No answer | PSC | PSB | PLP | FDF | VU | PC | Others |
|---|---|---|---|---|---|---|---|---|
| No answer |  |  |  |  |  |  |  |  |
| No opinion | 135 | 16 | 8 | 11 | 7 | 55 | 60 | 2 |
| PSC | 31 | - | 15 | 10 | 25 | 43 | 110 | 1 |
| PSB | 29 | 37 | - | 25 | 27 | 34 | 32 | 1 |
| PLP | 17 | 30 | 22 | - | 16 | 83 | 79 | 1 |
| FDF | 14 | 31 | 6 | 11 | - | 56 | 35 | - |
| VU | 3 | 3 | 1 | 4 | 5 | - | 6 | 1 |
| PC | 3 | 4 | - | 4 | 1 | 3 | - | - |

1. Brussels Capital is identical to the district of the same
name, excluding that of Hal-Vilvoorde as well as the so-
called communes with linguistic facilities.

## Method

Tables 10.1 to 10.3 can be considered as reflecting the structure of preference in the electorate, but in a particular way, given their frequential character. We can estimate that these tables contain frequencies of preference judgements. They concern, for 'a' tables, the number of voters of a party-row who rank each party-column second in preference order; for 'b' tables the number of voters for a party-row who rank each party-column last in order of preference. On the other hand, these tables can also be regarded as tables of distances. The higher the frequencies in 'a' tables the nearer the corresponding parties can be estimated; the higher they are in 'b' tables the more distant the corresponding parties can be considered.[*]'[**] We have chosen to apply the same method of analysis to 'a' and 'b' for each region in order to allow comparison. We have used the analysis of correspondences, which allows, in certain cases, a multi-dimensional analysis of such small-sized contingency tables.

As this technique is not frequently used, it seems useful to provide some details (Cordier, 1965; Lebart and Fenelon, 1971; Benzecri *et al.*, 1973). It offers, on the basis of contingency tables, some configurations in a multi-dimensional space. It gives significant results if these tables express a significant association in the sense of $\chi^2$. It actually involves a kind of factorial analysis of probability laws. As in factorial analysis, one builds up a cloud of points in a large dimensional space, each point representing here a row or a column considered as a probability vector. Then one adjusts a sub-space of the least number of possible dimensions by determining successively the major extension directions of the cloud to which one associates a factor, i.e. a straight line on which the points are projected and take a value. The difference from classical factorial analysis lies in the fact that the cloud does not come directly from the data, but is built up from a certain definition of the distance between rows or between columns. The treatment of rows and columns is symetrical and the analysis of correspondences allows representation of both of them in the same space.

It is important to know the meaning of this distance between rows or columns. Usually it is called '$\chi^2$ distance'.[***] Two rows (or columns) are considered more distant as their conditional probabilities of association with their columns (or rows) differ. One could say their 'profile' is distinct. The distance is therefore defined between proportions and not between absolute numbers, which allows consideration to be given to phenomena of structure, or 'form', independent of the weight of each element of the structure. Two parties situated at the head of rows on Tables 10.1 to 10.3, for example, will be close to one another on the configuration if the profile of rows that correspond to them is similar; they will be remote if this profile is different. Conversely, two parties at the head of columns will be close or distant according to the similarity of the profiles of corresponding columns.

---

[*] With an exception as regards the diagonals (see footnote on p.195).

[**] In the works of Rokeach (1960), Converse (1966) and Converse and Valen (1971), the tables to be analysed, based on initial data of the ordinal type, are the result of a mean operation on the orders. Assuming the ranks of the order to be equal intervals, it leads naturally to a manipulation of the measurement scale. However, only the characteristics of the order are again taken into account. In our present case study, no transformation of data has been made.

[***] The '$\chi^2$' distance is established between two rows or two columns, which are considered as probability laws on the central frequencies, according to their difference in relation to an equiprobable law taken as centre. Suppose a contingency table, of which the total component is

$$k = \sum_{i,j} k_{ij}. \quad \text{Then} \quad p_{ij} = \frac{k_{ij}}{k} \text{ is an estimation of probability and}$$

$$p_i = \sum_j \frac{k_{ij}}{k} = \sum_j p_{ij} \; ;$$

$$p_j = \sum_i \frac{k_{ij}}{k} = \sum p_{ij}$$

can be interpreted in terms of marginal laws. Suppose $i$ and $i'$ are two rows of the table, and $j$ and $j'$ two columns. The distance between rows or columns is then measured by the following formulae:

$$d^2 (i,i') = \sum_j \frac{1}{p_{oj}} \left[ \frac{p_{ij}}{p_{io}} - \frac{p_{i'j}}{p_{io'}} \right]^2$$

$$d^2 (j,j') = \sum_i \frac{1}{p_{io}} \left[ \frac{p_{ij}}{p_{oj}} - \frac{p_{ij'}}{p_{oj'}} \right]^2$$

This distance has some particular properties. As we can see, first of all, the quantities between brackets are conditional probabilities, of the $j/i$ in equation (10.1) and of the $i/j$ in equation (10.2). The result then is that the distance between two elements $i(j)$ will be as narrow as their conditional probabilities of being associated to the elements $j(i)$ are identical. If all these probabilities are equal, the distance is non-existent.

For two $i$ we have:

$$V j, P (j\, i) = p (j|i) \Rightarrow d (i,i') = 0$$

Secondly, this distance verifies the principle of distributional equivalance. If two elements $j$ and $j'$ which have the same conditional probabilities of being associated with the elements $i$, are replaced by one single element $j_o$, and if we suppose that

$$p_{ij_o} = p_{ij} + p_{ij'},$$

the distances between elements $i$ remain unchanged.

This distance can be useful as far as it bears on the differences of 'profiles' of rows or columns independently of their level or size. The result is that the analysis of correspondences compares the data shapes, which are actually all balanced. This often leads to a greater stability of results and to a quicker interpretation of them.

## Results

The analysis of correspondences in Tables 10.1 to 10.3 gave statistically significant results, in spite of the narrowness of the contingency tables, for the $\chi^2$ of each table was very high.* Only two factors could be taken into account, which is normal given the size of the tables. At the same time, for each table the configurations of party-rows and party-columns presented themselves in an almost rigorously symmetrical way. We have therefore chosen to take into account only the configurations of party-columns, because they give information concerning a larger number of parties. Finally, we ascertained that the analysis of 'a' and 'b' tables gave almost similar results, subject to some allowable manipulations of factors. Consequently, one will find below a single configuration for each region, with points (●) to represent parties of 'a' tables and points (○) for these of 'b' tables. A dotted line will join each pair of points for each party. The unique configuration for the Brussels region is less obvious and has necessitated an inversion of factors (factor I overlapping factor II and vice-versa.)

## Wallonia

How should we describe the factors? The horizontal factor, in cases of both tables 'a' and 'b' draws out a preponderant part of the variance (respectively 77.3 and 91.8 per

---

\* One should note that for 'b' tables the diagonal inputs have been filled up with frequencies corresponding to 'no-answers' column. The logic is obvious: parties cannot appear as the most distant from themselves.

196

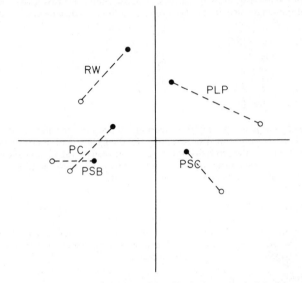

Figure 10.1   Party distances in Wallonia: ● parties in 'a' tables;
○ parties in 'b' tables

cent). It contrasts the Social-Christians (PSC) and the Liberals (PLP) with the Communists (PC) and the Socialists (PSB), the Federalists (RW) being in a more intermediate position. This appears to express a socioeconomic cleavage. This factor seems to differentiate the parties at the level of social class identification. The Socialist and Communist Parties are supported by voters of whom 81.9 and 81.8 per cent claim to belong to the working class, while the figure for Social-Christian voters is 43.5 per cent and for Liberals is only 24.9 per cent (for the Federalist Party it is 42 per cent).

The second factor plays a minor role (variances: 20.4 and 6.9 per cent) but is interesting. It contrasts the Federalists and Communists with the Social-Christians; the Socialists and Liberals are in a more central position, the Liberals being nevertheless nearer to the Federalists. What matters here seems to be the community cleavage. It contrasts parties that were the first to claim more autonomy for the regions with those parties that tend to support the unitary system.*

### Flanders

The horizontal factor, which takes out more variance (57 per cent) than the second, seems to represent the clerical dimension. This dimension contrasts the Social-Christians (PSC), the Federalists (VU) and in a lesser measure the Liberals (PLP)—which are the three parties whose support contains a Catholic majority, respectively 92.7, 72.2 and 65.5 per cent—with the Socialists and the Communists,

---

* In 1968, the Social-Christians departed from normal practice and conducted a rather 'regionalist' campaign on the Walloon scale, while the Liberals offered a very unitary strategy. Soon after the elections, however, the Social-Christians recovered their usual unitary face whereas the Liberals turned to regionalism. In so doing, the two formations went back to their position on the community cleavage as it appears here.

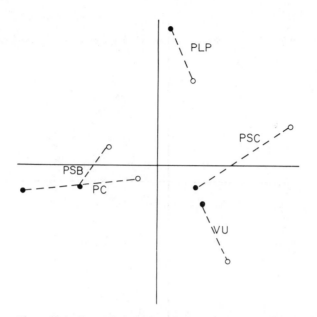

Figure 10.2    Party distances in Flanders: ● parties in 'a' tables;
○ parties in 'b' tables

among whom there is no Catholic majority (34.5 per cent of Socialists (PSB) are Catholic). As for the vertical factor (variance = 39.8 per cent), it appears to express a community cleavage, opposing mainly the Federalists (VU) with the Liberals (PLP). Besides, a rather vigorous anti-Liberal campaign was conducted by the Federalists in 1968 on the theme 'PVV—Pest voor Vlaanderen' (Liberals are a plague for Flanders).

## Brussels

The configuration is reproduced in Figure 10.3. One should note first that it is difficult to assess the impact of the factors here, for factors I and II of the 'a' table correspond to factors II and I of the 'b' table. As for the factors with a unique dimension, we therefore obtain, for the variance drawn from the horizontal factor, 66.9 and 34.8 per cent and for the variance of the vertical factor, 59.5 and 29.6 per cent. We can therefore conclude an approximately equal impact.

If we consider the meaning of the horizontal factor, we notice an opposition between Socialists and Liberals, with the Federalists of the VU and FDF at the centre, and the Social-Christians nearer to the Liberals. It seems to be a case of a socioeconomic cleavage. Class antagonism is sharp between Socialists and Liberals, who are, respectively, of 65 and 14.4 per cent working class. The Social-Christians, the Flemish Federalists and the French-speaking Federalists are in between, with 35.7, 30 and 21.2 per cent: the supporters of these three parties are very mixed. The Communists' position is surprising: one would have expected it on the left side of the Socialists as it is in the other regions. The attraction of the FDF was probably greater to Communists than to Socialists.

As regards the vertical factor, it contrasts the French-speaking with the

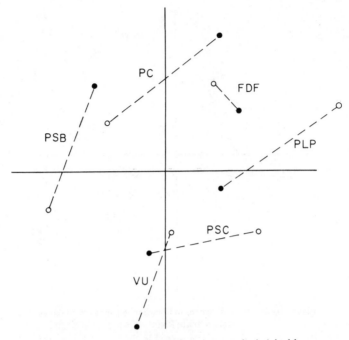

Figure 10.3    Party distances in Brussels: ● parties in 'a' tables;
○ parties in 'b' tables

Flemish-speaking Federalists. Communists, Socialists and Liberals are then on the French-speaking Federalist side and the Social-Christians near the Flemish-speaking Federalists. This is obviously the community cleavage 'as it is', differentiating parties of a more French-speaking composition from those of a more Flemish-speaking composition. One notices that this cleavage is more clearly perceived than the cleavage separating supporters of the Federalist project from the others, the FDF and the VU not being placed beside one other.

## VOTE CHANGE

We have been tempted to inquire, following our hypothesis, whether the distances between parties revealed by Figures 10.1 to 10.3 could disclose something about voting changes. Such a hypothesis lies actually on a physical analogy: one moves more easily between close spots than between distant places. In order to test this hypothesis we have compared the order of distances between parties as they appear on the figures with the order of vote changes revealed by answers to other questions from the same survey (Delruelle *et al.*, 1970). Only a very empirical procedure could be used, given the impossibility of manipulating the original data. In each figure, in order to measure the distances between parties, we have taken the middle of the dotted line joining each pair of points for each party, and have compared these distances with vote changes. However, we included in the comparison only those parties that, in 1968, had made electoral gains or losses amounting to at least 3 per cent compared with the preceeding results of 1965. Therefore we tested only the following cases: in Wallonia, the gains of Federalists (FDF); in Flanders, the gains of the Federalists (VU) and the losses of Social-Christians (PSC); in Brussels, the gains of Federalists (FDF) and Social-Christians (PSC) as well as the losses of Socialists (PSB) and Liberals (PLP).

The comparison of orders is presented in Tables 10.4 to 10.6. For each considered party, the columns of distances indicates the order of classical (Euclidian) distances revealed by the figures, from the nearest party to the furthest. The column of vote change shows the order of parties losing or gaining votes, from the party losing or gaining the most, to the party losing or gaining the least (according to whether the considered party gained or lost in the elections), keeping in mind that the size of the electorate has been balanced.

It is noticeable that the orders are fairly similar except in some isolated cases of inversion. Certainly it would be useful, in further research on new data, to test again these types of relations using more precise measures.

Table 10.4    Order of distances and voting change in Wallonia

| Rank-order | Distances | Voting-change |
|---|---|---|
| | RW (winning party) | |
| 1. | PC | PSB |
| 2. | PSB | PLP |
| 3. | PLP | (PSC[1] |
| | | ( |
| 4. | PSC | ( PC |

1. indicates an equality.

Table 10.5    Order of distances and voting change in Flanders

| Rank-order | Distances | **Voting-change** |
|---|---|---|
| | VU (winning party) | |
| 1. | PSC | PSC |
| 2. | PSB | PSB |
| 3. | PC | PLP |
| 4. | PLP | (no data available for PC ) |
| | PSC (losing party) | |
| 1. | VU | VU |
| 2. | PLP | PLP |
| 3. | PSB | PSB |
| 4. | PC | (no data available for PC ) |

Table 10.6    Order of distances and voting change in Brussels

| Rank Order | Distances | Voting Change |
|---|---|---|
| | P.S.C.  (winning party) | |
| 1. | V.U. | P.L.P. |
| 2. | P.L.P. | P.S.B. |
| 3. | P.S.B. | F.D.F. |
| 4. | F.D.F. | { V.U. |
| 5. | P.C. | (no data available for P.C.) |
| | F.D.F.  (winning party) | |
| 1. | P.C. | P.L.P. |
| 2. | P.L.P. | P.S.B. |
| 3. | P.S.B. | P.S.C. |
| 4. | P.S.C. | (no data avaialble for V.U. and P.C.) |
| 5. | V.U. | |
| | P.L.P.  (losing party) | |
| 1. | F.D.F. | F.D.F. |
| 2. | P.S.C. | P.S.C. |
| 3. | P.C. | P.S.B. |
| 4. | V.U. | V.U. |
| 5. | P.S.B. | (no data available for P.C.) |
| | P.S.B.  (losing party) | |
| 1. | P.C. | F.D.F. |
| 2. | F.D.F. | P.S.C. |
| 3. | P.S.C. | P.L.P. |
| 4. | V.U. | (no data available for V.U. and P.C.) |
| 5. | P.L.P. | |

## CONCLUSION

Bearing in mind all the restraints and limitations of the study with regard to the hypotheses in question, we can nevertheless arrive at some conclusions.

The first hypothesis about the influence of the traditional cleavages of Belgian society in the perception of the electorate has been verified. This verification has been possible concerning at least the presence of two of these cleavages, although the limitation of data did not enable us to observe the existence of a third. The results can be illustrated by Table 10.7.

Table 10.7    Cleavages in the three Regions

|  | Wallonia | Flanders | Brussels |
|---|---|---|---|
| Clerical cleavage |  | X |  |
| Socio-economic cleavage | X |  | X |
| Community cleavage | X | X | X |

We can observe an interesting feature. The new 'linguistic' federalist parties, French-speaking as well as Flemish, are perceived on their own dimension (which is a particular cleavage in terms of the interpretation). At the same time, they are not associated with the left-right cleavage. The nature of this new cleavage certainly deserves to be further investigated. One possible path of research to be followed might be that of R. Inglehart (1973), who discovered that voters for the Belgian federalist parties share, to a high degree, 'post-materialistic' values which do not correspond either to the usual rather materialistic left-right values, or to the traditional nationalistic ones.

The second hypothesis too has been tested with some success, for the order of distances from each party examined corresponded fairly well to the order of vote changes.

The research that has been the object of the present article also stimulated some reflections on what could be called party 'strategy' in the voters' 'cultural' space. We could indeed explain, using the idea of competition, some particular shifts in votes and, among others, the contradictory moves of the Liberals in Wallonia and Brussels. These moves consisted of the quick transformation of an important electoral victory, in 1965, into a defeat in the following elections.* In Flanders, on the other hand, the PLP remained stable during the same period. The configurations seem to allow a clarification of the Liberals' situation in the regions—supposing that the data for 1968 are relevant for 1965 and 1971—as far as the stability of electoral results, mostly in Wallonia and Flanders, allow us to do it. We can indeed consider that the closer two parties are in the configurations, the more likely they are to become competitors if a 'stream' of vote change comes in their direction. In the case of Wallonia and Brussels the Federalists of the RW and FDF are relatively close to the Liberals. All three of them stand in sectors not far from the configurations, and moreover they are situated between two traditional parties: the Socialist Party (PSB) and the Social-Christian Party (PSC). The three winners of 1965 are then in a state of competition.

---

* More precisely, the Liberals, in Wallonia, jumped from 11.77 per cent in 1961 to 25.53 per cent in 1965; in 1968 they reached 26.68 per cent, but in 1971 they fell back to 17.64 per cent. In Brussels they were 17.03 per cent in 1961, 33.46 per cent in 1965 and fell back already in 1968 to 26.27 per cent, a tendency that has since been enhanced in 1971 (16.01 per cent).

In Flanders there is nothing of the kind. The Liberals (PLP) are isolated in their sector and the Federalists (VU) are situated exactly at the opposite extreme of the figure. It is not surprising then that the PLP has experienced in the first two regions, the beginnings of 'bankruptcy' in a conjuncture favouring the RW and FDF while the Flemish PLP has incurred only light electoral losses.

## REFERENCES

Benzecri, J. P. *et al.*, (1973), *L'Analyse des données,* T. II, 'L'Analyse des Correspondances', Dunod, Paris.

Claeys, M.-Van Haegendoren (1967), 'Party and Opposition Formation in Belgium', *Res Publica,* 9, 413–36.

Converse, P. E. (1966), 'The Problem of Party Distances in Models of Voting Change', in M. K. Jennings and L. H. Ziegler (eds.), *The Electoral Process,* Prentice Hall, Englewood Cliffs, New Jersey.

Converse, P. E., and H. Vallen (1971), 'Dimensions of Cleavages and Perceived Party Distances in Norwegian Voting', *Scandinavian Political Studies,* 6, 107–52.

Cordier, B. (1965), *'L'Analyse Factorielle des Correspondances,* thesis, University of Rennes.

Delruelle, N., R. Evalenko and W. Fraeys (1970), *Le Comportement Politique des Electeurs Belges,* Ed. Institut de Sociologie de L'U.L.B, Brussels.

Dewachter, W. (1967), *De Wetgevende Verkiezingen als Proces van Machtsverwerving in het Belgisch Politiek Bestel,* Standaard Wetenschappelijke Uitgeverij, Antwerp.

Frognier, A. P., and D. Seiler (1972), 'Les Clivages Politiques en Wallonie, *C.H. du C.R.I.S.P.,* n° 583, 14, December.

Frognier, A. P., V. McHale and D. Parazino (1974), *Vote, Clivages Socio-Politiques et Développement Regional en Belgique,* Vander, Louvain and Paris.

Ingelhart, R. (1973), 'Industrial, Pre-Industrial and Post-Industrial Political Cleavages in Western Europe and the United States', Annual Meeting of the American Political Science Association, New Orleans.

Ladriere, J., J. Meynaud and F. Perin (1965), *La décision politique en Belgique,* CRISP, Brussels.

Lebart, L. and J. P. Fenelon (1971), *Statistiques et Informatique Appliquées,* Dunod, Paris.

Lipset, S., and S. Rokkan (1967), 'Cleavages Structures, Party Systems, and Voter Alignments', in S. Lipset and S. Rokkan (eds.), *Party Systems and Voter Alignments* Free Press, New York.

Lorwin, V. (1966), 'Belgium: Religion, Class and Language in National Politics', in R. A. Dahl. *Political Oppositions in Western Democracies,* Yale University Press, New Haven, Conn.

Mabille, X. (1974), 'Le Paradoxe de Condorcet dans la Politique Belge', *Revue Nouvelle,* 59, 304–7.

Rokeach, M. (1960), *The Open and Closed Mind,* Basic Books, New York.

Roskam, E. E. (1958), *Metric Analysis of Ordinal Data in Psychology,* Voorschoten, 70–5, Netherland.

Seiler, D. and J. Raes (1970), *Idéologies et Citoyens,* Ed. Vie Ouvriére, Brussels.

Van Den Brande (1967), 'Elements for a Sociological Analysis of the Impact of the Main Conflicts on Belgian Political Life, *Res Publica,* 9, 437–70.

# 11

# Exploring Political Space: A Study of French Voters' Preferences

GARY A. MAUSER AND JACQUELINE FREYSSINET-DOMINJON*

The way in which voters organize their perceptions of the political world influences how they react to political parties and to political leaders. But very little is known about how voters organize their political perceptions. If we can successfully describe the underlying principles that structure voters' perceptions of political parties and leaders, we should then be able to understand as well as predict short-term shifts in political preferences.

This paper presents an approach to describing voters' subjective organization which rests upon the notion of *psychological similarity*. Objects (such as parties or leaders) that are seen to be similar to each other should substitute for each other in a single-choice situation such as an election. Psychological scaling techniques are used here to display voters' perceptions and preferences in a spatial model.

A spatial model is a geometric representation of psychological space of some specified dimensionality—one, two or more dimensions. Political parties, political leaders and voters may be mapped on to points in this space so that the proximity of the points is related to the psychological similarity of the objects. A series of alternative spatial models is developed in this paper and the assumptions of each are examined in the light of the data. The authors hope that such a discussion will give the reader an understanding of the problems involved in fitting spatial models to the data. Discussion centres first on the adequacy of one-dimensional models to account for voters' preferences for political leaders and parties; finally a more complex multi-dimensional model is considered.

Spatial models have been used to analyse electoral behaviour in a variety of democratic countries (Converse, 1966; Mauser, 1972; Pesonen, 1973; Rusk and Borre and Frognier, in this volume). In this paper we examine French voters' preferences for political parties and leaders to determine how the voters conceptualize their political world. How large a role does the right–left continuum play in the preferences of the typical voter? If such a dimension may be said to exist, what are the positions of the

* We would like to take this opportunity to thank all of the people who have worked with us on this study. We are grateful to the students and to our colleagues at the Institut d'Etudes Politiques de Grenoble (IEP) for their generous contributions of ideas, criticisms and plain hard work. Special recognition should also go to the Director of the IEP for his financial help, as well as to Michel Leonard and Michel De Montety for their help with the data analysis.

political parties on this dimension, and, more specifically, which parties are seen to be in the centre—if any? If voters' preferences are not adequately described by a single left–right dimension, what kind of organizing principles do they use? A multi-dimensional structure? A non-spatial structure, or perhaps none at all? Perhaps different groups of voters have different kinds of structures? France under the Fifth Republic offers an uniquely interesting location to study models of short-term preference because of the two-*tour* electoral system. Hypotheses about which candidates or parties are similar may be developed in the first *tour*, and these hypotheses may then be tested in the second *tour*.

In the first section of the paper we briefly present some assumptions that underlie spatial models, and then we introduce the psychological scaling methods. Next we describe the *circonscription* in which the study was conducted as well as the sample and sampling methods. The body of the paper discusses the fitting of spatial models to French voters' preferences for political parties and political leaders.

### THE SPATIAL MODEL

The basic assumptions of the spatial model are presented in this section of the paper.*
We will start with a brief analysis of a one-dimensional model because it is the simplest case and also because one-dimensional models have played a role of historical importance in French politics.

Downs's model (1957) offers a nice point of departure to introduce one-dimensional models. In order to explain political strategy, Downs supposed that voters and political parties are both represented by points along a left–right spectrum depending upon their ideological positions. The political parties manoeuvre along this continuum in an attempt to win elections by advocating the campaign themes that attract enough votes to win. Voters for their part know the positions of the parties and prefer the political party that is the nearest to themselves. This formulation of the model implies that:

(*a*) individual voters determine their position on the dimension without strategic calculation;

(*b*) individual voters can classify political parties in terms of their order of preference for them;

(*c*) the voters' preference orders must be consistent with the parties' ordering along the left–right dimension.

An example may serve to clarify this somewhat. Assume that there are only four political parties and that they are distributed from left to right along the political continuum as illustrated in Figure 11.1. Those voters who prefer the PC (Parti Communiste), because they are located close to this party, choose as second choice necessarily the PS (Parti Socialiste), the RI (Républicains Indépendents) next, and they must put the UDR (Union pour la défense de la République) last. Such a ranking is the only one that respects their ordering along the continuum. A Communist Party voter could not prefer the UDR more than the RI, or the RI more than the PS, and still

---

* The term 'space' in this article refers to a Euclidean space which is defined by the following three conditions (1) $d(x,x) = 0$; the distance between an object and itself is zero; (2) $d(x,y) = d(y,x)$; the distance between $x$ and $y$ is the same as that between $y$ and $x$; (3) $d(x,y) + d(y,z) \geqslant d(x,z)$; the distance between $x$ and $y$ plus the distance between $y$ and $z$ is never less than the distance between $x$ and $z$.

respect the left–right ordering of these parties. Similarly, only one order is admitted for the UDR supporters. However, the supporters of the two 'centre' parties enjoy a somewhat larger variety of possible orders.

Figure 11.1   Hypothesized ordering of four political parties (PC, PS, RI, UDR) along a one-dimensional continuum

Such a model has obvious implications for understanding short-term shifts in preferences. Parties seen by voters as being similar (or close) to each other should show higher rates of shifts between them than parties not seen as being similar or close to each other. This assertion is of course circular unless 'similarity' or 'proximity' is measured independently of 'preference shifts'. Researchers very often measure only one of these concepts, however, and assume that the complementary concept is identical with the one measured (Converse, 1966). In earlier papers one of the authors empirically examined the strength of the relationship in the political arena between psychological similarity and vote switching. A moderately strong correlation was found between perceived similarity and the frequency with which the political leaders substitute for each other (Mauser, 1972; Mauser and Stefflre, 1974). Voters' preferences are analysed in this paper, assuming that similar parties substitute more than less similar parties, so as to determine how voters perceive parties.

Downs's formulation has been the object of vigorous criticism primarily bearing on the over-simplified nature of his model (Stokes, 1966). Specifically, the following four assumptions have been the subject of the strongest criticism: unidimensionality, the continuous nature of the dimension, the common frame of reference, the temporal stability of the model.

*Unidimensionality.* All distinctions that voters can make between the various political parties are limited in Downs's model to those that fall along the single dimension of the model. It is possible to imagine however a society that might have several cleavages that did not all coincide. For example, in Belgium the linguistic cleavages do not coincide with the left–right cleavage (Frognier, Chapter 10 above).

*Continuity of the dimension.* Distinctions made by the voters between the parties are represented in the model by the distance between the parties. If it is possible for parties to differ in such a way that distances could not capture these differences, the model would exclude potentially important information. But it is possible to imagine that a party might be able to improve its 'credibility' with the voters or its perceived ability to govern without changing its position along the left–right axis. The spatial model can not easily take account of such changes. Stokes's (1966) distinction between 'position issues' and 'valence issues' is closely related to this point.

*Common frame of reference.* The assertion that a dimension exists in a polity presumes that there is widespread agreement among the citizens of that polity about the nature of the dimension and a common perception of the positions of the political parties and their leaders. If one group of citizens disagrees with the rest about who goes where on the dimension, it is difficult to talk about a common frame of reference. Moreover, some voters may have no political 'attitudes' in that they may have very unstable or non-existent conceptions of the parties' positions on the political spectrum.

*Temporal stability.* To assert that a spatial model exists it is necessary that its structure not change too rapidly. One could imagine that the 'psychological similarity' of political parties or leaders might change from day to day, or from week to week, in such a way that the idea of 'perceptual' structure would no longer be a very useful analytic concept.

## PSYCHOLOGICAL SCALING METHODS

The assumptions that underlie the spatial model may be tested empirically using psychological scaling techniques. In this paper two such techniques are considered: first, Coombsian 'unfolding' scaling and Young–Torgerson's multi-dimensional scaling (1967). These techniques permit us to describe the nature of the structure that underlies the voters' preferences. Since they are based upon somewhat different approaches to scaling, the use of the two methods provides a check on the results. Because our sample was drawn at only one point in time, we cannot examine the last of these four assumptions, that of the stability of the structure through time.

Coombs's 'unfolding' technique is a method of analysing a set of preference orders to discover the underlying structure. This technique is particularly useful in examining the hypothesis that the underlying structure is uni-dimensional: that is, the one-dimensional structure is capable of *fully* describing voters' preferences. The uni-dimensional hypothesis is quite limiting in that very few preference orders are permitted. This is seen by considering the number of possible ways that four objects can be arranged in order: this is 24 (4!). Now if these four objects are constrained to lie on a single dimension, only 8(2!) orders are possible.*

Consider the example used in Figure 11.1 with the four political parties from left to right (PC, PS, RI, UDR). The eight orders, when no ties are permitted, would be:

(1)   UDR, RI, PS, PC
(2)   RI, UDR, PS, PC
(3)   RI, PS, UDR, PC
(4)   RI, PS, PC, UDR
(5)   PS, RI, PC, UDR
(6)   PS, RI, UDR, PC
(7)   PS, PC, RI, UDR
(8)   PC, PS, RI, UDR

The problem posed for the empirical researcher is just the reverse, however. Instead of knowing the underlying dimension and deriving the possible orders from that, his problem is to *infer* the nature of the underlying dimension from the kinds of orders that are found in the sample. To illustrate the 'unfolding' of the underlying dimension from the orders, we will now work backwards from these same eight orders.

The first question to ask of the data is the number of kinds of orders actually found. A number greater than eight (for four objects) indicates a lack of unidimensionality or erros in the data. Of course in our example there are only eight types of orders. On the other hand, some of the possible orders may not necessarily turn up in the sample.

---

* Eight different orders are possible if the dimension is assumed to be ordinal, that is if no distances are assumed to be known. If distance information is known, only seven possible orders may exist (Coombs, 1964) by the elimination of either the fourth order or the fifth. Whichever order is eliminated depends upon whether the distance between the UDR and the RI is greater or less than the distance between the PS and the PC.

Next, the two end-points of the dimension are identified by examining the parties that are ranked *last*. In principle, only the two extreme parties may be so ranked if the underlying structure is uni-dimensional. In our example, the PC and the UDR are so favoured.

The order of the parties along the dimension may be determined by finding the two orders that are mirror images of each other. There can be only two such orders. In our example, the first and last orders fit this description giving us the ordering of the four parties: UDR–RI–PS–PC. Further analysis can yield the distances between the parties in addition to their orders.

Coombs's 'unfolding' scaling method is used in this paper to examine the hypothesis that one dimension by itself can account for French voters' preferences for political parties and leaders. Unfortunately, the 'unfolding' technique is limited in the number of leaders or parties that can be considered simultaneously. This is due to the rapid rise in the number of permutations with each increase in the number of objects considered. There are 24 possible orders for four parties, 120 for five parties and 720 for six. This is a serious limitation in view of the large number of political parties, movements and coalitions that are active in French electoral politics. In order to be able to consider anywhere the full range of political parties, not to speak of the political leaders, it is necessary to turn to a different method.

The second method used to explore the nature of the underlying preference structure is that of multi-dimensional scaling (MDS). This approach is particularly useful not only because it can accommodate a larger number of objects (12 to 50), but because complex structures such as spheres or typologies may be easily identified. MDS permits the identification of the proper number of dimensions of the underlying structure if the structure is multi-dimensional. Moreover, the assumption of continuity of the underlying dimensions may be examined.

As is characteristic of almost all MDS procedures, the intent is to represent the set of proximity measures geometrically in such a way that the inter-point distances in the scaling model best correspond inversely to the order of the original proximities. The output is a spatial model in which the dimensionality is empirically determined.*

The input to the MDS procedure is an estimate of the 'psychological similarity' of the political parties and political leaders. The similarity index used here is the Spearman correlation coefficient of the parties' and leaders' rankings. This index was selected for three reasons primarily: (*a*) it is an estimate of the overlap in support that a pair of objects receive in an audience, (*b*) it allows a large number of objects to be measured simultaneously, and (*c*) it is simple to calculate for large populations of voters.

## THE FOURTH CIRCONSCRIPTION OF THE ISERE

The founders of the Fifth French Republic modelled their electoral system on that of the Third Republic in that contests for Assembly seats are decided by majority vote, rather than by a proportional vote system as in the Fourth Republic. If none of the candidates receives a majority of the votes cast in the first *tour*, a run-off election (a second *tour*) is held one week later between the candidates who garnered more than 10 per cent of the vote and who wish to stand. A plurality is necessary to win the

---

* The program used in this study was TORSCA 9, written by F. Young and W. Torgerson (1967), adapted for use on the IBM 360/65 at the University of Grenoble.

second *tour*. The *circonscription* is the site of the electoral contests for election to the French National Assembly. The way in which the *circonscriptions* were initially drawn corresponded more to political strategy than to either administrative or technical imperatives. Nevertheless, after fifteen years the artificial character of a *circonscription* begins to diminish owing to the lengthening history of political manoeuvring as well as to the partisan and personal clashes that the voters in each *circonscription* witness in common. Thus the *circonscription* is the natural political unit, better than, say, the *département*, to study the relationship between voters' images of political leaders and political parties and their voting behaviour.

This study was conducted in the fourth *circonscription* of the Department of the Isère by a team of students and faculty members of the Institut d'Etudes Politiques de Grenoble. The fourth *circonscription* was selected from the seven *circonscriptions* in the Isère because it most clearly fits the objectives of the project. The fourth *circonscription* contains a wide diversity of social and economic groupings and is divided, almost equally, between rural and urban regions.

The second *circonscription* of the Isère, which contains the town of Grenoble as well as some of the suburbs, was not selected for study even though it has been the stage of political battles of national importance (Pierre Mendès France and Jean Marcel Jeanneney, and more recently Hubert Dubedout), because it is almost entirely urban.

Moreover, the fourth *circonscription* is interesting because it is a marginal district.* Not only is victory won by the narrowest margins, but it may swing either to the right or to the left. During the Third and Fourth Republics, this *circonscription* traditionally voted for the left, but since 1958 it has swung to the right as often as to the left, frequently following national trends.**

After the success of the right in 1958 when an *'indépendant et paysan'* candidate won election in the fourth *circonscription*, victory went to Gaullist candidates in 1962 and 1968, and to the Socialists in 1967 and 1973. In the latest Assembly election, Jacques Gau (UGSD) managed to beat Alban Fagot (URP) in the second *tour* with only 51.70 per cent of the vote. Francois Mitterrand obtained exactly the same percentage of the vote in the second *tour* of the presidential election on 19 May 1974.

In contrast to the volatility of the vote, the fourth *circonscription* is typified by a remarkable stability as regards political personnel. This is particularly evident with the two largest political groupings—the Gaullists and the Communists. Alban Fagot (Gaullist) has been a candidate for deputy from this *circonscription*, win or lose, since 1951. Jacques Perinetti has been the Communist candidate since 1945. Interestingly enough, Perinetti and Fagot fought together in the French underground during the Second World War in the nearby Vercors mountains as *maquisards*.

The Socialist Party and the Centrists have also tended to present the same

---

* A marginal *circonscription* may be defined as one in which the margin of victory is no more than 3 per cent of the vote in a two-candidate election. Such *circonscriptions* are seen as responsible for most of the fluctuations in the majority in the National Assembly (see G. Le Gall and M, Riglet, 1973).

** The fourth *circonscription* of the Isère is located north west of Grenoble following the curvature of the Rives river in the Lower Isère valley. It is composed of seven *cantons*: Pont en Royans, Rives, Saint Egrève, Saint Marcellin, Tullins, Vinay and Voiron. The suburban part has been characterized as being an 'industralized area which favours the extreme Left', while the Lower Isère valley is rural and tends to support the right (P. Barral, 1962).

candidates throughout this period, but somewhat less consistently. For example the incumbent Socialist deputy who was first elected in 1973 is a *'Parachuté'* and a very recent arrival to the region. In contrast, the candidates of the small fringe groupings (PSU; miscellaneous rightist groupings) almost always put up someone different in each election when they are represented.

Table 11.1    The results of the first *tour* of the 1973 Legislative electionin the Fourth *Circonscription* of the Isere and in Metropolitan France [a]

|  | 4th Circonscription[e] | Metropolitan France |
|---|---|---|
| Parti Communiste | 19.4% | 21.4% |
| UGSD[b] | 23.7 | 20.7 |
| PSU[c] | 4.3 | 3.3 |
| Other Left candidates | — | 1.3 |
| Réformateurs | 14.6 | 12.5 |
| URP[d] | 33.4 | 34.6 |
| Other Majority | -- | 3.3 |
| Other Right candidates | 4.5 | 2.9 |
|  | 100.0% | 100.0% |

(a) Le Monde, Les Forces politiques et les élections de mars 1973 ,supplément aux 'dossiers et documents du Monde' mars 1973.

(b) Union de la gauche socialiste et démocratique

(c) Parti socialiste unifié

(d) Union des républicains de progrès, an electoral coalition of Union pour la defense de la République (UDR), Républicains independants (RI), and the Centre démocrate et progrès (CDP).

(e) Candidates in the Fourth Circonscription were Perinetti (PC), Gau (UGDS), Quezel (PSU), De Galbert (Réformateurs), Fagot (URP-UDR), Graillat (CNIP).

## THE SAMPLE

A sample of 249 respondents was selected to be interviewed for this study from the fourth *circonscription*, using standard quota-sampling techniques, during the first two weeks of February 1974. To qualify for the interview, respondents had to be of French nationality and at least twenty years old. Every effort was made to insure that the distribution of respondents in the sample reflected that of the target population, according to the census figures of 1968, in terms of sex, age, socioeconomic status and *canton* of residence.

Interviews were conducted by students in advanced methodology courses and lasted from thirty to forty-five minutes. The highly structured questionnaire used here focused primarily on the preferences for political parties and political leaders. Political preferences were assessed by two different types of questions: first, respondents were asked to rank-order a set of parties or leaders that was presented to them.* Secondly, respondents were presented selected hypothetical elections, legislative and presidential, past and future, and asked to indicate for whom they would vote in each situation. The hypothetical elections served as a check on the validity of the ranking questions.

## TESTING UNIDIMENSIONALITY

The data analysis is discussed in two phases. First, we examine the hypothesis that the voters' preferences are essentially uni dimensional. Preferences for political parties are examined separately from preferences for political leaders using Coombs's 'unfolding' approach. Next, a multi dimensional model is constructed for both the political parties and leaders together using the Torgerson-Young scaling approach. The implications of these two models for the nature of voters' perceptions are then discussed.

The notion that the primary cleavage in French electoral politics is along the left–right spectrum is as compelling as it is simple. The hypothesis examined in this section of the paper is not only whether this cleavage exists in French politics, but whether this cleavage alone is suffficient to explain voters' preferences satisfactorily. If a uni dimensional structure is not sufficient then it may be necessary to complicate the model by introducing additonal dimensions.

Turning first to an analysis of voters' preferences for political parties, it is useful to focus on the four major French parties: UDR, RI, PS and PC. Table 11.2 shows the percentage of the electorate that shares each of the twenty-four possible orderings of these four political parties. The first impression is that of chaos. The data is nowhere as clean as the one-dimensional model demands. Of the twenty-four possible orders, fully twenty-one are represented in our data, while only eight of these orders are consistent with the one-dimensional structure. Moreover, the end points of the spectrum do not seem clearly defined: every one of the four parties is ranked last by some proportion of the electorate. Thus, the two most elementary assumptions of the one-dimensional model are violated by the data.

On the other hand, the data exhibit some degree of structure despite the wide variety of voters' responses. If we exclude any order representing less than 2 per cent of the sample (all such orders total to approximately 7 per cent), only thirteen orders out of the original twenty-one remain. (Setting the acceptable limit at 4 per cent eliminates all but nine orders). This would indicate a fair agreement among respondents as to the underlying political spectrum. Turning to the question of the end points, we see that the UDR and the PC are rejected by far more voters than the other parties: 41.5 per cent of the sample rank the UDR last and 38.2 per cent rank the PC last, while only 7.9 and 12.4 per cent rank the PS or the RI last respectively. Despite the noisy data a one-dimensional structure emerges with the UDR and the PC as its end points.

* There were two such ranking questions: one in which respondents were to rank-order eight political parties and the other in which they were to rank twenty-five political leaders. Each item to be ranked was presented on a 3x5 card and the respondent was asked to shuffle the cards so that, from top down, the stack reflected the order of his preferences for the parties or leaders. The parties were: CDP, CNIP, PC, PS, PSU, Réformateurs, RI and UDR. The political leaders were: Chaban-Delmas, Debré, Dubedout, Duclos, Fagot, Faure, de Galbert, Gau, Giscard d'Estaing, Graillat, Krivine, Lecanuet, Marchais, Mendès France, Messmer, Mitterand, Mollet, Nicoud, Perinetti, Pompidou, Quézel, Rocard, Servan Schreiber, Tixier Vignancourt, 'Un homme comme DeGaulle'.

**Table 11.2** Comparing the twenty-four possible preference orders for the four parties (UDR, RI, PS, PC) with the one-dimensional models

| | | | | | | Consistency with the model [a] | |
|---|---|---|---|---|---|---|---|
| | | Possible orders | | | | | |
| | 1 | 2 | 3 | 4 | N[b] | % | Model 1 | Model 2 |
| 1. | UDR | RI | PS | PC | 28 | 11.7% | + | + |
| 2. | UDR | RI | PC | PS | 7 | 2.9 | − | − |
| 3. | UDR | PS | RI | PC | 10 | 4.2 | − | + |
| 4. | UDR | PS | PC | RI | 2 | 0.8 | − | + |
| 5. | UDR | PC | RI | PS | 2 | 0.8 | − | − |
| 6. | UDR | PC | PS | RI | 0 | 0.0 | − | − |
| 7. | RI | UDR | PS | PC | 24 | 10.0 | + | + |
| 8. | RI | UDR | PC | PS | 6 | 2.5 | − | − |
| 9. | RI | PS | UDR | PC | 5 | 2.1 | + | − |
| 10. | RI | PS | PC | UDR | 3 | 1.2 | + | − |
| 11. | RI | PC | UDR | PS | 0 | 0.0 | − | − |
| 12. | RI | PC | PS | UDR | 1 | 0.4 | − | − |
| 13. | PS | UDR | RI | PC | 12 | 5.0 | − | + |
| 14. | PS | UDR | PC | RI | 2 | 0.8 | − | + |
| 15. | PS | RI | UDR | PC | 21 | 8.7 | + | − |
| 16. | PS | RI | PC | UDR | 11 | 4.6 | + | − |
| 17. | PS | PC | UDR | RI | 15 | 6.2 | − | + |
| 18. | PS | PC | RI | UDR | 44 | 18.2 | + | − |
| 19. | PC | UDR | RI | PS | 1 | 0.4 | − | − |
| 20. | PC | UDR | PS | RI | 3 | 1.2 | − | − |
| 21. | PC | RI | UDR | PS | 3 | 1.2 | − | − |
| 22. | PC | RI | PS | UDR | 0 | 0.0 | − | − |
| 23. | PC | PS | UDR | RI | 8 | 3.3 | − | + |
| 24. | PC | PS | RI | UDR | 33 | 13.7 | + | − |
| | | | | | 241 | 100.0% | | |

(a) consistent orders are indicated with a "+", inconsistent orders with a "−". Note that ten of the twenty-four orders are inconsistent with both models and two orders are consistent with both.

(b) 8 of the 249 respondents refused to rank the political parties leaving 241 respondents for this analysis.

The first hypothesis (or model) is that the four parties are arranged along the single dimension from left to right in the following manner: PC–PS–RI–UDR. The percentage of voters who have rankings inconsistent with this model serves as a rough index of the validity of this model: 28.9 per cent of the sample are inconsistent with Model 1. Since this is a rather high percentage of voters to exclude from the analysis as being irrational or as having made errors, perhaps another model might prove more suitable. One alternative is one in which the RI are further to the right than the UDR (rather than being to their left as in Model 1). Such a model moreover has the advantage of conforming to what certain observers of French politics think is actually the case. Model 2 would have the four parties from left to right then as: PC–PS–UDR–RI. Unfortunately, this model represents even fewer voters than does Model 1: 58 per cent of the sample have orders that are inconsistent with Model 2. Clearly, Model 1 is the more preferable of the two alternatives.

That neither model does strikingly well in accounting for the data suggests that voters may have only a vague idea of the left–right continuum and may not have a clear picture of the political parties' relative positions. If this is the case, it would be reasonable to expect that knowledge of the parties' positions would vary with voters' interest in politics (Bon and Michelat, 1970). Voters more interested in politics should be more knowledgeable about the political parties, and their political preferences would of course reflect this knowledge. Similarly, voters less interested in politics would be expected to know and care less about the political spectrum and thus their rankings should not reflect such a structure. Table 11.3 compares the inconsistencies

Table 11.3     Interest in politics and success of the one-dimensional models

| Political Interest[a] | Model 1 (PC, PS, RI, UDR) | Model 2 (PC, PS, UDR, RI) |
|---|---|---|
| Interested | 26.9%[b] | 63.9% |
| Not interested | 32.0% | 54.6% |
| Entire sample | 28.9% | 58.1% |

(a) Political interest was based on the respondents' answer to the question "Est-ce que vous vous intéressez à la politique: beaucoup, assez, un peu, pas du tout?".   Responses "beaucoup" and "assez" were classified as indicating interest in politics, while another response, or non-response, consistuted lack of interest.

(b) Entries are the percentage of each category of respondents who have preference orders that are inconsistent with the model in question.

for politically interested voters with disinterested voters. It can be easily seen that for Model 1, the interested voters are a little more likely to be consistent with the model than are the disinterested voters. That is, interested voters have only 26.9 per cent inconsistencies while disinterested voters have 32.0 per cent.

Model 2 on the other hand shows a different pattern: interested voters are less likely to be consistent with the model than are disinterested voters (63.9 per cent to

54.6 per cent). This reversal is somewhat difficult to understand. One possible interpretation is that interested voters, because of their greater knowledge about politics and their greater exposure to the mass media, are more likely to accept the same model of the political spectrum. And, continuing this argument, the disinterested voters, because of their lack of exposure to the mass media, are more heterodox in their views of the political spectrum and so do not reject Model 2 as decisively.

It must be borne in mind however that the small size of our sample ($N=249$) indicates that statistical error may be responsible for variations of this size. Inspection of Table 11.3 does suggest that the differences between interested and disinterested voters are not very large in terms of the extent to which Model 1 is appropriate for both groups of voters, 26.9 per cent to 32.0 per cent inconsistencies. More than two-thirds of the sample, whether interested in politics or not, share the same perception of the political spectrum.

At this point in the paper, we would like to examine the hypothesis that voters have a different view of the political spectrum depending upon their partisan allegiancies. Table 11.4 shows the percentage of inconsistencies with the two models for supporters of each of the four parties. Respondents are classified as supporters of a political party if they rank that party above the other parties in the subset.

Table 11.4    Partisan support and success of the one-dimensional models

| Partisan Support[a] | Model 1 (PC, PS, RI, UDR) | Model 2 (PC, PS, UDR, RI) |
|---|---|---|
| PC | 31.3%[b] | 83.3% |
| PS | 27.6% | 72.2% |
| RI | 19.9% | 38.4% |
| UDR | 42.7% | 18.3% |
| Entire Sample | 28.9% | 58.1% |

(a) Partisan support refers to the party ranked first over the other three parties considered here.

(b) Entries are the percentages of each party's supporters who have preference orders that are inconsistent with the model in question.

Consider first the supporters of the two parties on the right of the political spectrum (the RI and UDR). Model 2 appears to be more consistent for the UDR's supporters, having only 18.3 per cent inconsistencies, while Model 1 is more consistent for those of the RI, with only 19.9 per cent inconsistencies. This result may be due to the reluctance of these voters to accept the image of their preferred party as 'rightist', in preference for the label 'centrist'. The right is far from being in agreement however about the positions of the parties on the right: many of the supporters of these two parties see their own party as being the furthest to the right.

In contrast, no such ambiguity can be discerned on the left. Supporters of both the

PC and the PS agree that Model 1 appropriately captures the ordering of the four major parties. Socialists as well as Communists agree that the PC is further to the left than the PS, and that the UDR is further to the right than the RI.

The ambiguity in the electorate's perception of the positioning of the parties on the right may help explain certain recent political events in France. During the period of campaigning prior to the presidential elections of May 1974, the candidates of both the RI and the UDR claimed to be the candidate of the centre and they both repudiated the right. The results of this study suggest that, while there was some difference of opinion in the electorate, the bulk of the electorate tended to agree with Giscard d'Estaing (RI) rather than with Chaban Delmas (UDR) in placing the UDR to the right of the RI.

It should be noted that, since our survey was conducted in early February, almost two months before the unexpected death of President Pompidou and the subsequent opening of the presidential campgaign, these results could not have been influenced in any way by the events that occurred during the campaign itself—by the actions of the candidates or by the survey findings published in the newspapers. This suggests that, contrary to what some political observers believed at the time, Giscard's campaign was not the primary factor in developing his image and that of his party as that of a centrist candidate, because the RI were already seen by the public as being closer to the centre than the UDR. Nor, by the same token, did the voters see themselves as favouring a shift to the right in choosing Giscard over Chaban Delmas in the first *tour*.

It is interesting to try to estimate the relative proximity of the four parties to each other. This permits several important questions to be answered about the nature of partisan competition. Is the right more unified than the left? Is the major cleavage between the right and the left, between the Communists and the non-Communists or between the Gaullists and the non-Gaullists?

One useful index in this regard is the percentage of a party's supporters who choose each of the other parties in second place. The four parties separate easily into two distinct blocks, the UDR and the RI on the right and the PS and the PC on the left. More than 75 per cent of the supporters on either party on the right rank the other right party second (75.5 per cent for the UDR's supporters and 76.9 per cent of the RI's supporters). On the left, a majority of voters place the other left party in second place. Eighty-five per cent of the PC supporters pick the PS, but only 56 per cent of PS's supporters pick the PC. The left does not seem as tightly knit as the right in view of the massive defection of the Socialists to the right (44.8 per cent). The lack of symmetry appears to favour the Socialists over the Communists, but the Communists may be expected to exact expensive concessions from the Socialists in return.

Coomb's unfolding analysis may also be used to glean information about relative party distances from the rankings. The unfolding analysis confirms that the distance between the UDR and the RI is less than that between the PS and the PC. This stems from the fact that 20 per cent of the supporters of the PS rank the PC last among these four parties while only 8 per cent of the supporters of the RI do likewise with the UDR (Coombs, 1964).

Up to this point, our analysis has been restricted to the four major parties and has not included the Réformateurs or the other centre parties. In order to test the hypothesis that the Réformateurs are on the political spectrum between the left and the right, we will examine selected triads of parties in this section which include the Réformateurs. If all three parties are aligned along the same dimension, the party in the centre cannot be ranked last by voters of any political persuasion. The triad that would be expected to have the greatest chance to be strictly uni dimensional is the triad including the parties the farthest apart along the dimension.

Table 11.5 shows the percentages of respondents who rank the Réformateurs third, or last, in each of the selected triads. The first triad (UDR, Réformateurs, PC) contains the two most distant parties of the political spectrum, but even so manages to elicit 16.5 per cent of respondents who do not follow the hypothesized uni dimensional model. Turning to the other triad (RI, Réformateurs, PS), which contains parties much closer together on the spectrum, the inconsistencies are much more striking: close to one-third of the sample put the Réformaterus last. For neither triad does the variable of political interest play an important role, as the percentages of inconsistencies are nearly identical for interested voters as for disinterested voters. This is further confirmation of the relative lack of importance of political interest for the voters' perception of the political spectrum.

Table 11.5   The Reformateurs and unidimensionality

Political Interest[a]

| Triad | Interested | Not Interested | Entire Sample |
|---|---|---|---|
| UDR, Réf, PC | 17%[b] | 16% | 16% |
| RI, Réf, PS | 33% | 30% | 31% |

(a) see note (a) for Table 11.3

(b) Entries are percentages of each category of respondents who have preference orders inconsistent with a unidimensional model, that is, Réformateurs were ranked third in either of the selected triads.

The evidence in support of the uni-dimensional hypothesis is not overwhelming. Only by excluding close to one-third of the sample, or in the case of the most distant parties 16 per cent, can the electorate be argued as basing their political preferences exclusively on the left-right spectrum.

We now turn to examining voters' preferences for political leaders. Several triads will be examined in turn to test the uni dimensional hypothesis for national as well as local political leaders.

Table 11.6 presents the percentages of inconsistencies found for each of four selected triads. In the preceeding analysis we have seen that the parties that were the farthest apart were the most likely to be uni dimensional. Thus the triads including well-known leaders of these parties should also be the most likely to be uni dimensional. Similarly the parties the most likely to be subject to the influence of additional dimensions—if they exist—would be those that involve leaders of parties closer together on the political spectrum in the centre.

The triad formed by J. Chaban Delmas, F. Mitterrand and G. Marchais is the most clearly uni dimensional. There are only 13 per cent inconsistencies in the respondents' rankings of the leaders as compared with the 9 per cent inconsistencies in the rankings of the parties. Introducing a Réformateur, such as J.J. Servan Schreiber, or removing a

Table 11.6    Unidimensionality and preferences for political leaders

| Selected Triads | Political Leaders | Political Parties (a) |
|---|---|---|
| 1. Chaban, Mitterrand, Marchais | 13%(b) | 9% |
| 2. Chaban, JJ SS, Marchais | 29% | 16% |
| 3. Chaban, Giscard, Mitterrand | 34% | 24% |
| 4. Giscard, JJ SS, Mitterrand | 40% | 31% |

(a) Triads of parties correspond to those of the political leaders:
Chaban - UDR, Giscard - RI, JJ SS - Réformateurs, Mitterrand - PS,
Marchais - PC.

(b) Entries are percentages of respondents who have preference orders
inconsistent with the unidimensional hypothesis, i.e., respondents
who ranked the centre member last in any of the triads considered here.

Communist, such as G. Marchais, increases the percentage of inconsistencies. The triad that is clearly not uni dimensional is that which is comprised exclusively of relatively centrist candidates, for example the fourth triad, which contains Giscard, Servan Schreiber and Mitterrand. Note also that in every case the leaders of political parties are less uni dimensional than the parties themselves. Consider for example the triad containing Chaban, Giscard and Mitterrand. The triad of leaders has 34 per cent inconsistencies while the triad of parties has only 24 per cent. This slippage between the images of the leaders and that of their parties appears to be true for each of the leaders considered here, including the Communist leaders.

How were the three major candidates in the 1974 presidential election viewed by our sample? In the analysis of the parties we found that the UDR is generally seen as being to the right of the RI, with the Gaullist supporters disagreeing with this view. Are the leaders of these three parties seen as occupying the same ideological positions as their parties, or is there some slippage? Table 11.7 compares the successes of two hypothesis: (a) that Chaban is seen as being to Giscard's right, and (b) that Chaban is on Giscard's left. Neither hypothesis can be convincingly supported: neither Giscard nor Chaban is seen as clearly to the right of the other, though the UDR is to the RI's right. One explanation would be that the image of Giscard d'Estaing is more clearly defined than that of his party, the RI, because the supporters of the PS reject him more definitely than they do the RI; and thus Giscard is displaced slightly to the right.

Do the images of the local leaders differ significantly from the images of national leaders of the same party affiliation? Table 11.8 compares the images of local leaders with national leaders, as well as with the images of their political parties. In those triads that do not include the PC, local leaders are more likely to be uni dimensional (as are the parties) than the national leaders. Take for example the first triad of the table, that of the UDR, Réformateurs and PS. There are 24 per cent inconsistencies for

**Table 11.7  Unidimensionality and the 1974 Presidential Election: ambiguity on the Right**

| Hypothesized Left-to-Right ordering of candidates | Political Leaders | | | Parties[a] | | |
|---|---|---|---|---|---|---|
| | Entire Sample | Interested[b] | Not Interested | Entire Sample | Interested | Not Interested |
| 1. Mitterrand, Giscard, Chaban | 34%[c] | 40% | 30% | 24% | 23% | 24% |
| 2. Mitterrand, Chaban, Giscard | 29% | 32% | 27% | 48% | 54% | 37% |

(a) Triads of parties selected to correspond with triads of presidential candidates: Mitterrand – PS, Giscard – RI, Chaban – UDR

(b) See the note (a) for Table 11.3.

(c) Entries are the percentages of respondents who have preference orders inconsistent with the unidimensional hypothesis. Inconsistent orders are those in which the centre candidate (or party) is ranked last.

the parties and 30 per cent for the images of the local leaders, while there are 38 per cent inconsistencies for the images of the national leaders. This suggests that national leaders are not judged so strongly by their partisan affiliations as are the local or regional leaders. This is probably due to the relative lack of information that the average citizen has about local leaders compared to that about the national leaders. The ability of national leaders to command coverage in the newspapers and on television allows them to develop a personal image, widely known in the electorate, which is distinct from that of their party. Thus in times of relative political calm, national leaders are not seen as tied to their political parties as are local leaders.

Table 11.8    Unidimensionality and political leaders: comparing local with national leaders

| Hypothetical Triads | Political Leaders | | Parties |
|---|---|---|---|
| | National | Local | |
| 1. UDR, Ref, PS[a] | 38% | 30% | 24% |
| 2. UDR, PS, PC[b] | 13% | 14% | 9% |

(a) National leaders for the first hypothesized triad are Chaban Delmas, Servan Schreiber, and Mitterrand and the local leaders are Fagot (UDR), De Galbert (Réf), and Gau (PS).

(b) National leaders for the second triad are Chaban Delmas, Mitterrand, and Marchais and the local leaders are Fagot (UDR), Gau (PS), and Perinetti (PC).

(c) Entries are the percentage of respondents who have preference orders that are inconsistent with the undimensional hypothesis.  Inconsistent orders are those in which the hypothesized centre candidate (or party) is ranked last.

In contrast, consider the triad that includes the PC. National leaders and local leaders are equally uni-dimensional, although neither group of leaders is as uni-dimensional as are their parties. The introduction of the PC stresses the existence of the political spectrum that overrides the distinctions between national and local leaders.

In summary, our analysis shows that the political spectrum acts as a powerful determinant of voters' preferences for both political leaders and political parties. Nevertheless, the high percentages of voters who are inconsistent with the uni dimensional hypothesis, in almost all of the groupings selected, indicate that uni-dimensionality is not sufficiently rich enough to explain voters' political preferences adequately. Three possible explanations may be entertained: (a) the respondents have made a large number of errors in their rankings; (b) there is not enough agreement among the voters about the orderings of the parties along the political continuum; and (c) the underlying model is not uni dimensional but rather multi dimensional.

First of all, it is clear that there must be some error in these data. Ranking (as well as rating) several different objects is a difficult task even when the respondents are familiar with the objects under consideration. Moreover, the interviews were obtained under field conditions with relatively inexperienced interviewers, which probably also contributed somewhat to the number of errors in the data. Nevertheless, comparing the results of the ranking task and the hypothetical elections shows a reasonably close correspondence. Further support for the validity of the ranking task has been shown by one of the authors in two earlier papers (Mauser, 1972; Mauser and Stefflre, 1974). There is no compelling reason to reject the results on the basis of widespread respondent errors.*

The existence of sub-groupings of citizens with different views about the political spectrum is a more real possibility. The justification for the assertion that voters share a common view of the political world to a significant extent is that they are all citizens of the same polity and live under the same laws, institutions and leaders. But the supporters of each political party may be imagined to share a basic commmunality of interests and background, so that each party's supporters may view the political spectrum differently. Such an idea is not too implausible at any rate. If we assume that Gaullists differ from the remaining voters in how they view the political spectrum, we could explain many of the problems of the uni dimensional model. We might argue that voters on the right mis-perceive the position of their favoured party owing to the repugnance of the label 'rightist'. They would prefer to imagine that their party is the one in the centre. But, if we make this argument, how can we explain the left's agreement with supporters of the RI? (particularly when we are reminded that the major cleavage in the political system is between the left and the right and not between the Gaullists and the non-Gaullists). Their differences do not seem so great as to oblige us to posit separate models for each party's supporters. Such an approach is somewhat *ad hoc*, and as such cannot really answer the question.

The final alternative to be considered is that the underlying structure is multi dimensional and not uni dimensional. In the next section we discuss the construction and verification of a multi dimensional model of voters' preferences.

## A MULTIDIMENSIONAL MODEL

In this section MDS techniques are used to construct empirical multi dimensional models for political parties and political leaders. First, a model is fashioned for the eight political parties alone, and then a second model is derived for all twenty-five political leaders in addition to the eight parties.

The eight parties may be best analysed together if we make some simplifying assumptions since the number of possible preference orders is too large to be directly handled by Coombs's 'unfolding' technique. Rather than continue to analyse voters' rankings directly, an index of the parties' proximity to each other may be used as the basic datum. The voters' rankings of the parties are correlated for each pair of parties to yield an index (called a preference correlation) of the extent to which each pair of political parties can be said to share the same electorate. Such an index may be interpreted in the following way: a strong positive correlation between two parties indicates that voters who prefer one of these parties prefer the other more strongly than do most voters; and a strong negative correlation indicates that voters who prefer one party reject the other more strongly than do most voters.

---

* It should be noted that, if ties are admitted in the third and fourth ranks, the number of inconsistencies drops considerably: from 29 to 15 per cent for Model 1 and from 58 to 21 per cent for Model 2 (see Table 11.3). Most of the respondents' errors appear to be in their lower-ranked alternatives.

Table 11.9    Inter-party correlations[a]

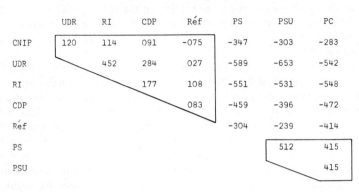

|      | UDR | RI  | CDP | Réf  | PS   | PSU  | PC   |
|------|-----|-----|-----|------|------|------|------|
| CNIP | 120 | 114 | 091 | -075 | -347 | -303 | -283 |
| UDR  |     | 452 | 284 | 027  | -589 | -653 | -542 |
| RI   |     |     | 177 | 108  | -551 | -531 | -548 |
| CDP  |     |     |     | 083  | -459 | -396 | -472 |
| Réf  |     |     |     |      | -304 | -239 | -414 |
| PS   |     |     |     |      |      | 512  | 415  |
| PSU  |     |     |     |      |      |      | 415  |

(a) Entries are Spearman correlation coefficients calculated between
parties from respondents' preference rankings.    The decimal points have
been removed for simplicity.

Table 11.9 gives the correlations between the eight political parties and shows the underlying structure. The major cleavage is clearly seen to be between left and the right. This is evident in the fact that all positive correlations are between members of the same bloc and that almost all negative correlations are between members of different blocs. The right is somewhat elongated in contrast to the tightly knit left. The right is centred around a nucleus of three parties: UDR, RI and CDP, which together make up the URP (the government coalition at the time of the survey). This nucleus has two satellites (CNIP and Réformateurs), which are loosely connected to this bloc. The negative correlation between the CNIP and the Réformateurs (the only example of a negative correlation between members of the same bloc) suggests that, despite their membership in the right, these two parties are quite different from one another. In contrast the left is smaller and more compact. Note however the

Figure 11.2   Two-dimensional configuration of French political
parties. Respondents' preference rankings were intercorrelated for the eight parties and used as input to the
Torsca 9 scaling program ($N$=242). The two-
dimensional solution has a stress of 0.05

ambiguous position of the PSU. The PSU is a little closer to the PS than is the PC, but at the same time it is further away from the UDR than either of the two other parties on the left. This is inconsistent with a simple left–right one-dimensional structure.

Figure 11.2 presents a two-dimensional mapping of voters' preferences for eight political parties.* The same bloc structure is found here as was found in the direct analysis of the correlations. The major cleavage is between the parties of the right and those of the left. There is no ambiguity about which parties are in which bloc, for there is a large gulf between these two groupings. The horizontal dimension of the figure, which spans these two blocs, may be interpreted as the classic left–right political axis. The discontinuity of this dimension suggests that it may not be possible for a political leader to position himself between the two blocs. This hypothesis is put to test in the next section concerning the analysis of political leaders.

Inspection of the figure reveals the internal structure of these two blocs. The right appears to be more dispersed than the left. Part of the explanation for this is that there are more parties on the right than on the left. But such dispersion also reflects the impact of the recent signing of the *programme commun* by the major parties of the left. This suggests that membership in these two blocs is defined by a party's support of, or opposition to, the *programme commun*, so that the right includes all of the political parties, despite their diversity, who are opposed to the *gauche unie* and the *programme commun*.

Interestingly, the parties within each of these two blocs are more clearly differentiated along the vertical dimension than along the horizontal dimension. The left–right dimension serves as only a first rough sort of the parties into two blocs and the second dimension permits a fine-grained comparison within a bloc. On the right, for example, the CNIP is not much further to the right than are the Réformateurs, while these two movements lie on the opposite ends of the vertical axis. Similarly for the left, the vertical dimension is the primary dimension of contrast within a bloc. The introduction of the second dimension explains the negative correlation between the CNIP and the Réformateurs as well as some of the problems that we had in trying to scale the parties with an uni dimensional model earlier.

Note also that the question that bedevilled us earlier, namely which party is the furthest to the right, the UDR or the RI, is difficult to determine in the figure because both parties have about the same position on the left–right axis. It is only along the second axis and not the first that the parties may be differentiated. The relative proximity of the RI to the Réformateurs anticipates the later alliance of these two partie during the presidential elections.

Further efforts to interpret the underlying structure are postponed until later when the political leaders are included in the model.

A multi-dimensional model may be constructed that includes not only the eight political parties but also the political leaders. Such a model permits the comparison of voters' images of leaders with the images of the parties, as well as the examination of the hypothesis of uni-dimensionality, when the full range of parties and leaders is

---

* The two-dimensional configuration presented in Figure 11.2 was selected because the stress (a measure of badness-of-fit) of the one-dimensional configuration was no satisfactory and the three-dimensional configuration did not offer much more additional explanatory power than did the two-dimensional configuration. Splitting the sample into two arbitrary halves and rescaling the stimuli for each sub-sample yielded configurations that were quite similar, so that we believe that the structure shown here is not simply random noise.

considered. This model may be constructed using the same type of proximity index and the same scaling technique as were used in the partisan analysis.

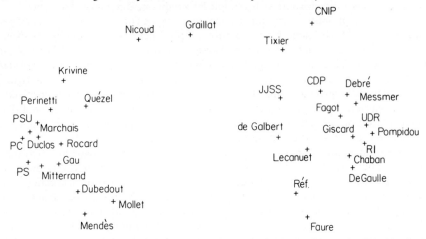

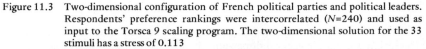

Figure 11.3 Two-dimensional configuration of French political parties and political leaders. Respondents' preference rankings were intercorrelated (*N*=240) and used as input to the Torsca 9 scaling program. The two-dimensional solution for the 33 stimuli has a stress of 0.113

Figure 11.3 presents the two-dimensional mapping of voters' preferences for leaders as well as political parties. Note first that the inclusion of the leaders does not disrupt the original structure. The Parties' positioning relative to each other has not changed, even though the twenty-five political leaders have now been added to the model. Note also that political leaders are found in the model quite close to their own party. Moreover there are, for the most part, no other parties that are closer.

While the associations between political leaders and their political parties are generally respected, there are some striking incongruencies. De Gaulle is placed closer to the RI than to the UDR, for example, and Servan Schreiber is closer to the CDP than to the Réformateurs.

The same two blocs are found again in this model. The centre is strikingly unoccupied, except for Nicoud and Graillat, who are local political leaders, adding further support for the hypothesis that the left–right dimension is discontinuous.

These results yield support for the view that French electoral politics is extremely bipolarized. It appears that it is virtually impossible for any political leader to position himself between the two blocs that dominate French politics, since voters seem to recognize only these two blocs. The unique position of Nicoud and Graillat appears to be due to the marginal roles played in the political system by these two men. Graillat is not very well known by the voters, and Nicoud, as the leader of CID/UNATI, appeals to extremists of both the right and the left.

Turning now to the question of interpreting the underlying structure, the first problem is that of the nature of the vertical axis. On the right the vertical dimension, which extends from the CNIP and Tixier Vignancourt to Edgar Faure and the Réformateurs, might be interpreted as a spectrum ranging from the traditional right (above) to the technocratic centre (below). On the left this dimension shows a somewhat different face: the cleavage between Krivine and the PSU, on the one hand,

and Mitterrand, Mendès France, Mollet and the PS on the other could be seen as the opposition of the supporters of revolution with the supporters of reform. Continuing still further with this analysis, a synthesis might be suggested of these interpretations by arguing that Krivine, the PSU, Tixier Vignancourt and the CNIP share roughly the same view of the political system, while Mitterrand, Mendès France, Mollet and Edgar Faure share another; that is to say, the vertical dimension would be interpreted as reflecting a basic acceptance or rejection of the principles of the existing political system. However, one problem with such an analysis is that it is somewhat forced and artificial because of the extreme heterogeneity of the political parties and leaders involved.

While there are many ways in which this structure might be viewed (as a circle or spheroid, for example), we tend to favour an interpretation in which the explanatory dimensions are seen as spanning the structure obliquely rather than perpendicularly as in the earlier discussion. From this perspective, Krivine and the PSU are at the pole of a dimension running diagonally from Edgar Faure and the Réformateurs, while Mitterrand, Mendès France and the PS are contrasted with the CNIP and Tixier Vignancourt. But both of these dimensions are closely correlated with the left-right axis: the classic left (Mendès France) sits opposite the classic right (the CNIP) and the young, revolutionary left (Krivine) is contrasted with the new right (th Réformateurs). We think that this alternative interpretation of the electorate's view of the political world has the advantage of mirroring better the actual political conflicts that have occurred in contemporary French society.

Such an interpretation emphasizes the importance of the left-right axis in that this cleavage is seen as capable of including many other types of political conflict within its framework. The vertical dimension may then be interpreted as reflecting the historical order in which these conflicts have surfaced in French politics. This implies that, when new conflicts emerge in the body politic, even if they are originally unrelated to the left-right cleavage, they are progressively brought into alignment with the major axis of French political conflict: the left-right axis. The mechanism through which this transformation is effectuated involves the centralized nature of the French political system, which tends to nationalize even local conflicts, as well as the cleavage of the political élites along left-right lines.

The Réformateurs' position is an intriguing one. Their displacement vertically from the other parties on the right explains why there were so many inconsistencies in the one-dimensional models. The Réformateurs are a relatively new movement in French politics, and are seen as in opposition to the classic right as well as in opposition to the left. Some voters therefore see them as properly 'centrist'. Other voters see the new revolutionary left as the fundamental opposite to the Réformateurs while it places both the old right and old left between these two extremes. It appears that while the French voters are clearly in agreement that the left-right opposition is the primary cleavage in their political system, they are not in agreement as to its precise nature.

## CONCLUSION

In this paper we analysed voters' preferences in an effort to uncover the underlying principles that voters used to structure their perceptions of the political world. Spatial models were used to display this underlying structure. Voters were found to be capable of rank-ordering political leaders and political parties in a reasonably coherent and reliable manner. Despite the existence of some error, the rankings exhibited sufficient structure to permit the use of psychological scaling analysis. French voters were found to share similar views of the political system to a large extent despite differences in their social backgrounds, partisan attitudes and levels of political interests. The underlying structure did not appear to be fragile or spurious but rather was strikingly robust and stable. Not only did independent analyses of different sub-groups of voters yield sufficiently similar results, but also the addition of a large number of political leaders to the analysis of political parties did not introduce additional dimensions or disturb the original structure.

A two-dimensional space was required to display adequately the analysis of French voters' preferences. The simple one-dimensional model was not sufficiently powerful to describe the underlying structure. The primary cleavage was found as expected to fall along the classic left–right spectrum. However, political parties and leaders were not distributed along this spectrum at many different positions, but rather were concentrated at only two locations: the right and the left. These two blocs were separated by a void that does not appear to offer a viable niche for centrist or moderate leaders. This does not imply however that voters are unable to make distinctions any finer than a crude classification of political leaders or parties as either 'on the left' or 'on the right'. French voters are able to discriminate rather well, but such distinctions appear to be based more on alternative interpretations of the left–right cleavage rather than on differences in the perceived position of political leaders or political parties along the spectrum.

## REFERENCES

Attali, J. (1972), *Les Modèles Politique*, Press Universitaire Francaise, Paris.

Barral, P. (1962), *Le Departement de l'Isre sous la Ille République*, Colin, Paris.

Bon, F., and G. Michelat (1970), *Attitudes et Comportements Politiques à Boulogne-Billancourt*, Colin, Paris.

Converse, P. (1966), 'The Problem of Party Distances in Models of Voting Change,' in M. Kent Jennings and L. Ziegler (eds.), *The Electoral Process*, Prentice Hall, Englewood Cliffs, New Jersey.

Coombs, C. (1964), *A Theory of Data*, Wiley, New York.

Downs, A. (1957), *An Economic Theory of Democracy*, Harper and Row. New York.

Le Gall, G., and M. Riglet (1973), 'Les Circonscriptions Marginales aux Élections Legislatives de 1967 et 1968', *Révue Francaise de Science Politique*, 21, 86–109.

Mauser, G. (1972), 'A Structural Approach to Predicting Patterns of Electoral Substitution', in R. Shepard, A. Romney and S. Nerlove (eds.), *Multidimensional Scaling: Theory and Applications in the Behavioral Sciences, Vol. II: Applications*, Seminar Press, New York.

Mauser, G., and V. Stefflre (1974), 'Similitude et Substitution dans une Élection', *Révue Francaise du Marketing*, 50 19–38.

Pesonen, P. (1973), 'Dimensions of Political Cleavage in Multi-party Systems', *European Journal of Political Research*, 1, 109–32.

Stokes, D. (1966), 'Spatial Models of Party Competition', in A. Campbell, P. Converse, W. Miller, D. Stokes, *Elections and the Political Order*, Wiley, New York.

Young, F., and W. Torgerson (1967), 'A FORTRAN IV Program for Nonmetric Multidimensional Scaling Analysis, *Behavioral Science*, 12, 498.

## 12

# The Left, The Right, The Establishment and the Swiss Electorate

RONALD INGLEHART and DUSAN SIDJANSKI*

## INTRODUCTION

Since the era of the French Revolution, the concept of a left–right dimension has shown remarkable vitality. Its usefulness has undoubtedly contributed to the concept's longevity in political discourse. Although a nation's dominant political forces and issues may change over time, it is convenient, indeed almost essential, to have a simple shorthand term that provides a general orientation toward a society's political leaders, ideologies and parties.

The left–right dimension is especially helpful to the voter in multi-party systems. In a two-party system electoral choice is relatively simple: the voter is faced with a single pair of alternatives. But in a system with five major parties there are ten pairs of alternatives; in a system with ten parties there are forty-five pairs. In many West European democracies, five to ten or more parties are represented in Parliament. If electoral choice were made by comparing each pair of alternatives, it would be virtually unmanageable. The concept of an underlying left–right dimension simplifies a complex reality and generates a handy set of decision rules: responding to the key issue, the voter decides how far 'left' he or she is and supports the nearest party on the left–right continuum. If that party doesn't present a candidate, or is elminated from a run-off election (as often happens in France), the voter shifts his or her support to the next nearest party. Similarly, when faced with the need to form governing coalitions, political élites have their choices greatly simplified: in theory, they ally with the parties nearest to them on the left–right dimension.

The concept also seems to have explanatory value. Downs (1957), for example, has developed it into a simple but plausible explanation of electoral competition. His model implies that, given a normal distribution of voters on the left–right dimension, the parties will cluster together near the median voter. With a multi-modal distribution, one might expect to find political parties near the mid-point of each cluster of voters.

Although it may be an extremely convenient abstraction, the idea that a left–right

* The authors are indebted to David Handley, Henry Kerr and Hans Klingemann for constructive criticism of this paper. An earlier version of this chapter appeared in *Revue Francais de Science Politique*, 24, 994–1025.

dimension underlies political behaviour has been subjected to considerable scrutiny. Stokes (1966) has raised the question, 'To what extent does Downs's model correspond to reality in a given political system?' He argues that its applicability depends on the extent to which four conditions are present.

(1) *Uni-dimensionality.* Political choice in the given society must be dominated by a single dimension. While Downs's model assumes that the dominant question is the degree of government intervention in the economy, it is quite conceivable that religious or other cleavages might complicate the picture.*

(2) *Ordered dimensions.* It must be possible to rank the parties according to their stand on the dominant dimension.

(3) *A common frame of reference.* In order for political parties to take positions that correspond to the distribution of voters' preferences, both élites and mass must have similar perceptions of the dominant issue dimension.

(4) *A fixed structure.* This is more or less a corollary of point (3): for élites and mass to respond to the same underlying issue, that issue must remain stable over time. The same result might conceivably be attained if both party leaders and voters simultaneously reoriented themselves according to a new dimension, but practically speaking this seems unlikely.

Stokes concluded that American politics did not meet these four assumptions. But analysts of French, German and Italian politics have argued recently that the concept of a left–right dimension does indeed provide a useful basis for analysis of political choice (Deutsch, Lindon and Weill, 1966; Barnes, 1971; Barnes and Pierce, 1971; Klingemann, 1972; Converse and Pierce, 1973). The difference in conclusions may be attributed to a variety of causes.

(1) The latter studies were based on the analysis of multi-party systems. In such systems there is probably a greater need for a simplifying abstraction such as the left–right concept. Both élites and mass consequently have a greater incentive to view politics according to this frame of reference. In a two-party system, one can be either, say, a Republican or a Democrat without needing to seek some underlying ideological dimension that might explain why one prefers a given party.

(2) Stokes's conclusions referred to American politics in the 1950s. At that time and place, political choice seems to have been governed largely by candidate preferences and traditional party loyalties; the electorate showed little tendency to polarize along *any* issue dimension. In contemporary Western Europe, the left–right cleavage may be significantly more important. One can cite a number of reasons why this might be the case. Unlike the United States, France, Germany and Italy have major parties that developed from the Marxist tradition; this may encourage the electorate to polarize along a single Marxist–anti-Marxist axis. Furthermore, the major American parties tend to be organized on a statewide, rather than nationwide basis: the Democratic Party in Georgia may take a quite different stand on issues from that of the Democratic Party of New York. In such conditions, it is difficult for national politics to polarize along a single left-right dimension. In comparison with their American counterparts, the European parties have relatively centralized national organizations. Moreover, the French, German and Italian cultures may have characteristics (apart from their Marxist parties) that are relatively conducive to

---

* Analysing the preference-ordering given to various political parties by French and Finnish voters, Converse (1966) concludes that the underlying party spaces must be multidimensional; and further, that the length of a given dimension varies from voter to voter.

left-right polarization. American society has traditionally placed less stress on one's social class origins, for example: this may minimize tendencies towards polarization along social class lines.

(3) Finally, the 1950s in retrospect appear to have been an era of relatively low political polarization. Contemporary politics in *both* Western Europe and the United States may be more conducive to the emergence of what Stokes called a 'strong ideological focus' than were the bland politics of the Eisenhower era in America (Pomper, 1972; Miller *et al.*, 1976).

In this article we shall explore the extent to which the left-right dimension is a useful concept for the interpretation of Swiss politics, using data from the first representative national survey ever made of Swiss electoral behaviour.* Switzerland provides a particularly interesting site in which to test the applicability of this concept. In several respects she resembles her European neighbours, and consequently we might expect her to show a similar pattern of left-right polarization. Culturally related to Germany, France and Italy, Switzerland has a multi-party political system; moreover, the system incldues both a Socialist Party (which is Switzerland's largest party) and a smaller but well-known Communist Party.

In other respects Switzerland might be expected to show a low level of left-right polarization. For one, her politics in recent years have been characterized by a relatively low level of overt conflict. Governed almost continuously since 1943 by a coalition of the four largest parties, decisions are reached by a process of 'amicable agreement' rather than by majority rule (Steiner, 1973). This decision-making style has obvious advantages in an ethnically heterogeneous society, where linguistic or religious minorities might otherwise risk being perpetually outvoted. But it also implies that the parties rarely present the electorate with a coherent set of opposing programmes. Some major political choices *have* been brought before the people in recent years, but they have been presented in the form of national referenda in which all major parties endorsed a common position. One might argue that much the same is true of the parties in the neighbouring countries—they rarely present drastically different alternatives—but there is undeniably a difference in the *degree* to which this is true. Contemporary Swiss politics have shown an exceptionally low level of conflict. We might expect this to lead to a relatively low degree of political polarization among the electorate.

This tendency might be accentuated by the fact that, until 1971, Switzerland was an anomaly among Western democracies: women could not vote in national elections. Even more than in other countries, women were socialized into a role that tended to exclude politics. For the feminine half of the Swiss electorate, we would expect to find low levels of political interest and consequently low levels of ideological constraint and polarization.

Furthermore, Switzerland has a highly decentralized set of political institutions. With the exception of the German CSU, Swiss parties have a greater degree of local autonomy than those of her neighbours. Despite her small size, cultural and geographic barriers help maintain an extreme political diversity from one canton to

* The survey was designed jointly by Gerhard Schmidtchen of the University of Zurich, Henry Kerr of the University of Geneva and the present authors. Fieldwork was carried out by the Konso-Institut (Basel) in January–June 1972. We wish to express our gratitude to the Swiss National Fund for Scientific Research for awarding a grant which made the fieldwork possible.

another. As in the United States, decentralization may impede the emergence of any clear and commonly accepted left–right orientation at the national level.

For the foregoing reasons, we should expect a left–right dimension to provide a less adequate basis for interpretation of Swiss politics than is the case in Germany, France or Italy. But before we can test this hypothesis, we must clarify an essential point: exactly what does the left–right dimension *mean*?

The research already cited makes it clear that large proportions of the French, German and Italian electorates are able to situate themselves on a left–right scale. But there are two possible interpretations of *why* they place themselves at given locations, and the two interpretations have fundamentally different implications. The traditional interpretation is that the left–right continuum reflects an underlying issue dimension: those who prefer the left are change-oriented in a broad and encompassing sense; those who align themselves with the right support the status quo. The *type* of change one supports is important, of course. The left has historical connotations of egalitarianism, internationalism and social progress; the right connotes support for established authority, nationalism and social continuity. But orientations toward social change constitute the unifying thread of the underlying super-issue or ideology. The traditional interpretation implies that those who favour change-oriented policies see themselves as located on the left side of an ideological continuum; they then vote for given parties *because* of their issue preferences.

An alternative interpretation is possible. It is conceivable that left–right self-placement is not the *cause* of party preference, but a derivative of it. One may prefer a given party because of family tradition or religious or other affiliation. One is also aware of the conventional label attached to one's party: for decades, the mass media have spoken of the Communists as a party of the extreme left, the Socialists as the moderate left and so on. Knowing this, the voter locates himself on the left–right scale at about the same location as the party he prefers. These party preferences can, no doubt, be traced back to some powerful political issue or personality that originally won the voter's allegiance (or that of his parents or grandparents). But they may reflect the impact of actors and ideas that have passed from the scene decades or even generations ago.

Which interpretation is correct? We suspect that both processes are at work; we very much doubt that European electorates are wholly devoid of ideological orientation—but this influence may be a good deal less powerful than is suggested by the fact that most voters can place themselves on a left–right scale. The investigators we have cited attempt to validate the meaningfulness of left–right self-placement by demonstrating that it is a good predictor both of political party preference and of electors' positions on important political issues. The relationship between left–right self-placement and political party preference is somewhat suspect: the former *may* be an influence on the latter—or it may simply be a synonym for given party preferences.

The relationship between issue preference and left–right self-placement is more convincing. If the two *are* strongly related, it is at least plausible to view left–right self-placement as a cause rather than a consequence of party preferences, although we cannot draw any final conclusions without longitudinal data. But if, on the other hand, we were to find virtually *no* relationship between left–right self-placement and one's stand on current issues, it would greatly undermine the traditional interpretation, even in the absence of longitudinal data: the first link in the causal chain would be missing.

Our colleagues have shown that left–right orientation *is* related to current issue preferences in other countries. We believe that this relationship may be comparatively weak in the Swiss setting because, among other things, the dominant political parties are in permanent coalition, ruling by 'amicable agreement'. As a result, new issues are unlikely to become linked with established party loyalties. And in so far as party loyalties provide cues concerning what is 'left' and what is 'right', the left-right dimension would also remain unrelated to current issues.

Thus there are a number of reasons why we would expect contemporary Swiss politics to show a relatively low degree of unidimensionality and relatively little correspondence between left-right self-placement and one's position on current issues. In the following section we shall examine these hypotheses in the light of data from the Swiss electoral survey.

## EMPIRICAL FINDINGS

A first glance at the data seems to confirm the notion that the left-right dimension may be less meaningful in Switzerland than in neighbouring countries. Our colleagues' studies of the French, German and Italian electorates indicate that from 75 to 80 per cent of the public in each of these countries are able to locate themselves on a left-right scale (Deutsch, Lindon and Weill, 1966; Barnes and Pierce, 1971; Klingemann, 1972; Converse and Pierce, 1973). Only 58 per cent of our Swiss sample are able to do so. In part, this contrast reflects the late entry of Swiss women into the electorate. Women were less likely to place themselves on the left-right scale than were men; but even when we control for sex, substantial cross-national differences remain.*

Whether or not an individual can place himself (or herself) on a left-right dimension is closely related to whether or not he or she has a sense of political party identification. And the fact that about 10 per cent more of our respondents have a party identification than can place themselves on a left-right scale might be taken as an indication that party identification precedes left-right self-placement; one cannot explain party preference *entirely* in terms of ideological stance. But clearly, this is not an adequate test of our hypotheses. Some people have party preferences that are not attributable to holding a left-right position; but the question remains whether other people *are* influenced by an underlying super-issue—and if so, to what extent? Another bit of evidence suggests that left-right self-placement may, indeed, reflect exposure to issues and a rational response to them: those who are high on political interest are a great deal more likely to place themselves on the left-right scale than those who rank low on political interest. The same is true of those who report that they 'often' discuss politics with friends and acquaintances, in comparison with those who rarely or never do so.** How well does a left-right dimension 'explain' party preferences among the Swiss electorate? And above all, how accurately does it reflect the major contemporary political issues? The data point to some rather surprising answers. Let us deal with the first question first.

* Women are significantly less likely to place themselves than men in all four countries. But Swiss *males* show a lower rate of left-right self-placement (72 per cent) than the rate for males and females *combined* in any of the other three countries.

** In theory, one might apply causal modelling to sort out this relationship. But it seems very likely that the relationship between left-right self-placement and party identification works in both directions; the same is probably true of the linkages between political interest and party identification and left-right self-placement. Until such time as we have longitudinal data, causal modelling would be of doubtful value.

Our respondents were asked to place themselves and each of the eleven Swiss parties on a scale ranging from 0 to 100; it was specified that 0 represented the extreme left and 100 the extreme right, with 50 being the mid-point.** Table 12.1 shows the mean placement of each party on this scale.

Table 12.1    Left–Right Placement of Parties and Self, Switzerland, 1972*
(Mean rating made by given group)

| Party | Placement of given party by entire sample | Placement of given party by its supporters | Self-placement by given party's supporters |
|---|---|---|---|
| Communist | 15 (925) | 22 ( 23) | 28 ( 21) |
| Socialist | 34 (939) | 36 (249)· | 40 (257) |
| Alliance of Independents | 50 (749) | 51 ( 83) | 52 ( 85) |
| Evang. Protestant | 59 (642) | 65 ( 17) | 61 ( 14) |
| Christian Social | 59 (726) | 69 ( 55) | 64 ( 60) |
| Republican Movement | 63 (607) | 63 ( 17) | 55 ( 21) |
| National Action | 64 (640) | 62 ( 16) | 60 ( 17) |
| Liberal | 63 (767) | 70 ( 59) | 62 ( 64) |
| Christian Democrat | 65 (828) | 73 (150) | 68 (155) |
| Peasants, Artisans, Bourgeois   (UDC) | 66 (818) | 69 ( 74) | 64 ( 81) |
| Radical | 67 (923) | 68 (196) | 62 (207) |

    ∗  The number of respondents making the ranking appears in  parentheses. The average voter placed himself slightly Right of center, at point 55.

A brief discussion of the Swiss parties may be helpful in interpreting this table. Four parties dominate Swiss politics at the federal level: the Socialists, the Radicals, the Christian Democrats and the party of Peasants, Artisans and Bourgeois (in descending order of size). Combined, they normally poll at least 80 per cent of the vote in national elections, and form a virtually permanent governing coalition. Like other socialist parties of Western Europe, the Swiss Socialists adopted a moderate programme in the late 1950s; as Table 12.1 indicates, both the Swiss electorate as a whole and Socialist supporters in particular see the Socialists as a party of the moderate Left—located about one-third of the distance from the mid-point to the extreme Left. Despite their name, the Radicals are the Establishment party *par excellence*. They were, for decades, *the* dominant national party. Together with the

---

\*   The precise wording of the question was: 'People often talk about the political parties of the left, the right or the centre. Here is a scale that goes from left to right. And here are cards with the names of parties. [The cards were presented one by one, in mixed order.] Would you place this card so that the arrow points to exactly where you would place this party on the scale. [Repeated for each party] . . . And where would you place *yourself* on this scale?'

Liberals, they have the closest links with the upper middle class and big business; and the Swiss electorate places the Radicals farther to the right than any other party—but in very close proximity to eight of the ten other parties. Among these other parties, the Christian Democrats are one of two predominately Catholic parties (the other being the Christian Social Party); there is also a small Protestant party. The Peasants, Artisans and Bourgeois are the smallest of the big four, representing a middle-class constituency with a somewhat lower social level than that of the Radicals or Liberals. The Alliance of Independents is the largest party outside the governing coalition; its role is one of mild opposition on economic issues.

The three remaining parties are small but theoretically important. Officially called the Labour Party, the Swiss Communists are more or less comparable to other Western European communist parties and are perceived by the Swiss electorate as situated on the extreme left. The two remaining parties—National Action and the Swiss Republican Movement—might be termed 'reactionary' in the purest sense. They reflect a nativist reaction against cosmopolitan influences that threaten to change traditional Swiss society. Nationalistic, ethnocentric and authoritarian in tone, they are reminiscent of Germany's National Democrat Party, Italy's Neo-Fascists, France's Poujadists or America's Wallace movement. As we shall see, these two parties might be described as genuinely ideological. While they take a coherent stand on a variety of topics, the most important issue underlying their appeal is the problem of foreign workers.

This problem pervades the economically more developed countries of Europe, but nowhere has it reached such an acute stage as in Switzerland. Germany and France have millions of culturally unassimilated and politically powerless foreign workers, and their numbers are growing; but they comprise a rather small minority of the total population. In 1970 foreign workers made up fully 22 per cent of Switzerland's resident labour force—without counting a substantial number of seasonal and daily migrant workers. These foreigners are concentrated at the bottom of the economic scale, performing virtually all of the unskilled and most of the semi-skilled labour in Switzerland. They have caused no unemployment (it is virtually non-existent in Switzerland). But their sheer numbers have given rise to widespread fears that they may engulf Swiss society.

The Swiss Republican Movement and the National Action Party combined have only 11 deputies out of 200 in the national legislature's lower house. But their stand on certain issues evokes widespread support. In 1970 they launched a campaign for a constitutional amendment that would have drastically reduced the number of foreign workers in Switzerland. Although opposed by the leadership of all major parties, the proposal was supported by 46 per cent of the voters in a national referendum. Informed observers would almost certainly locate these two parties on the extreme right. It is astonishing, therefore, to find that the average Swiss voter scarcely distinguishes between these and the other non-Marxist parties on a left/right scale. Indeed, as Table 12.1 indicates, the Republican Movement and National Action are place slightly to the *left* of the three leading bourgeois parties. Could this paradoxical ranking be due to the fact that the two traditionalist parties, being less widely known than the others, are simply misplaced through lack of information? Apparently not. For one thing, they are rather widely known despite their small size. For another, the *supporters* of a given party must have some information about it, even if no one else does. And the supporters of the Republican Movement and National Action *also* place them slightly to the left of the Radicals, the PAB and the Christian Democrats.

This location of course represents the overall mean among all those who are able to locate the given parties. If we examine the distribution of rankings for each party in detail, we find another interesting phenomenon. A substantial portion of the Swiss electorate *does* place each of the two traditionalist parties on the extreme right: more than a third of those who rank them put them in the range 81–100 (See Table 12.2).

Table 12.2    Left–Right Placement of Swiss Parties by Swiss Electorate

| Party | Extreme Left (0-19) | Left (20-39) | Centre (40-60) | Right (61-80) | Extreme Right (81-100) | Total | N* |
|---|---|---|---|---|---|---|---|
| Communists | 69% | 19 | 8 | 2 | 2 | 100 | (925) |
| Socialists | 19 | 39 | 34 | 6 | 2 | 100 | (939) |
| Alliance of Independents | 5 | 16 | 59 | 16 | 4 | 100 | (749) |
| Christian Social | 4 | 11 | 42 | 28 | 15 | 100 | (726) |
| Evang. Protestant | 3 | 7 | 48 | 32 | 9 | 100 | (642) |
| Liberals | 4 | 5 | 41 | 30 | 19 | 100 | (767) |
| Christian Democrats | 2 | 6 | 39 | 30 | 22 | 100 | (828) |
| Peasants, Artisans, Bourgeois (UDC) | 2 | 4 | 36 | 40 | 18 | 100 | (818) |
| Radicals | 3 | 4 | 37 | 31 | 25 | 100 | (923) |
| Republican Movement | 9 | 13 | 24 | 19 | 35 | 100 | (607) |
| National Action | 9 | 13 | 23 | 18 | 38 | 100 | (640) |
| Respondent's placement of self: | 5 | 10 | 53 | 21 | 10 | 100 | (1,111) |

* Numbers in parentheses indicate total number who were able to place the given party on a Left-Right scale. Thus, out of a total sample of 1917, 925 respondents (or 49 percent) were able to place the Communist Party; only 31 per cent could place the Republican Movement; but 58 per cent could place themselves on the scale.

But a surprisingly large portion of the electorate places these two parties on the left or extreme left! Only the Communists and Socialists have larger proportions of placements in the range 0–19. The Republican Movement and National Action are perceived as extremist parties, but it is not entirely clear to the electorate *which* extreme they represent.*

To grasp the peculiarity of this situation fully, one must examine the left–right placement of Swiss parties in comparative perspective. Table 12.3 shows how given

* Almost equal uncertainty exists among the *supporters* of these two parties about where they belong on the Left–Right dimension. Only a few place their party on the Left, but a clear majority place it towards the centre.

parties are located by the Italian, French, German and Swiss electorates.* There is an almost uncanny cross-cultural similarity in where the Communist and Socialist parties are placed in all four countries. Despite important cross-national differences in programmes and leadership, the Communist parties of Italy, France and Germany are

Table 12.3    Left–Right Placement of Selected Parties by Italian, French, German and Swiss Electorates

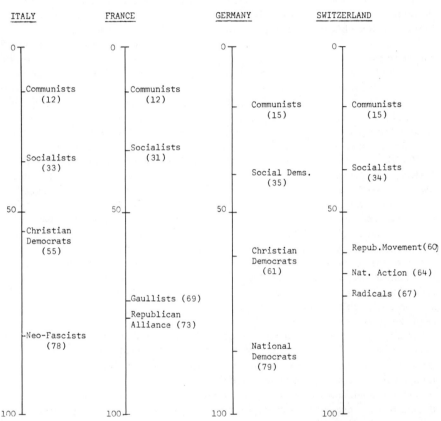

*    The Italian and French data are adapted from Barnes and Pierce, (1971, p.647); the German data are adapted from Klingemann, (1972, p.96). The German sample was asked to place the parties on a scale that had ten locations; in the other three countries a scale was used that ran from 0 to 100. Thus, the lowest score that could be given to parties in the other three countries was 0. We must transform the German data for comparative purposes. The first step is simply to multiply the mean element of distortion: the lowest possible score is now equivalent to 10. To correct for this rightward shift, we have also subtracted 10 per cent from the mean score for each party: thus the mean for the Communist Party is reduced from 17 to 15. Unlike the other three samples, the German sample is not a national one, but is drawn from the *land* of Hesse. It is less comparable to the other three data sets—yet the cross-national similarities are striking. The Italian, French and German surveys were carried out in 1967, 1968 and 1970, respectively. At the time of the Italian survey the two larger socialist parties were merged; Table 12.3 shows the placement given to this combined party which, of course, has since broken up into its two constituent elements.

placed within a few points of where the Swiss Communist Party is located; the same is true of the Socialist parties. The leading non-Marxist parties are relatively heterogeneous, but even among them we find a certain uniformity of placement: they are all situated within the range from 5 (the Italian Christian Democrats) to 69 (the Gaullists). The Swiss Radicals fall near the right end of this range (at 67). The Swiss Christian Democrats and PAB, as we have seen, have virtually the same location as the Radicals. Each of the other three countries has one or more parties that are placed near the extreme right by a consensus of the electorate: in Italy, the neo-Fascists; in France, the Republican Alliance and in Germany, the National Democrats.

In the face of this remarkable cross-national uniformity of party placement it is all the more astonishing to find that there is no consensus among the Swiss electorate about the location of the Republican Movement and National Action: their mean location falls squarely in the middle of the other non-Marxist parties. But this placement results from averaging together two sets of widely diverging perceptions. Examined more closely, the evidence indicates that it occurs *not* because the two traditionalist parties are perceived as similar to the others, but because the prevailing notion of left and right gives no clear orientation concerning their location.

To illustrate this fact, let us refer to Table 12.4 which shows the correlations between self-placement on the left–right scale and preference rankings for eleven Swiss parties.* As this table indicates, left–right self-placement is an excellent predictor of preferences toward the Socialists and Communists and a good predictor of preferences toward most other parties—except that there is virtually no correlation whatever between one's location on the left–right scale and whether one likes or dislikes National Action or the Swiss Republican Movement. Table 12.4 is based on the perceptions of a substantial share of the Swiss electorate, skewed toward the better informed and those most likely to vote. More than 800 respondents ranked each of the two traditionalist parties (in other words, a substantially larger share of the electorate was able to indicate a positive or negative *preference* toward these parties than could place them on the left–right dimension).

In answer to our first question, it seems that the familiar left–right dimension is rather effective in 'explaining' preferences among most parties but virtually meaningless in relation to two 'extreme right' parties; one suspects that Swiss politics must involve at least one additional dimension.

Dimensional analysis of party preference rankings reveals that at least *three* dimensions are needed to provide a satisfactory solution. Interestingly enough, we obtain this same result when we perform dimensional analyses of left–right party

---

* The question about party preferences was worded as follows: 'Here is a deck of cards bearing the names of parties. Could you place the cards on this scale in the following manner: place the party that you like the most in the first box, and the one you like the least in the eleventh box; now would you please place the party which would be your second choice in the second box, and the party that would be your next-to-last choice in the tenth box . . .' The interviewer continued until the respondent had ranked all eleven parties. Not everyone was able to place all of the parties, of course. The two largest parties (the Socialists and Radicals) were ranked by more than 1,000 respondents each, out of a total of 1,917. The Swiss Republican Movement and National Action were ranked by 834 and 838 respondents respectively. Being new and relatively small, the two latter parties were ranked by comparatively few respondents, although they were by no means invisible: the Alliance of Independents was ranked by about the same number of respondents, while three other parties (the Liberals, Christian Social an;Evangelical Protestant Parties) were ranked by a *smaller* number of respondents.

Table 12.4    Correlation Between Self-Placement on Left–Right Scale
And Party Preference

(Positive correlation indicates that those placing selves on Left
give high preference)

| Party | Correlation with Left self-placement |
|---|---|
| Socialists | +.421 |
| Communists | +.417 |
| Alliance of Indpendents | +.150 |
| Republican Movement | .000 |
| National Action | -.040 |
| Liberals | -.108 |
| Christian Social | -.173 |
| Evangelical Protestant | -.187 |
| Radicals | -.197 |
| Christian Democrats | -.252 |
| Peasants, Artisans, Bourgeois | -.275 |

placement: this is surprising, to say the least, because the concept is supposedly uni-dimensional by its very nature. But the Swiss electorate differentiates between the Swiss political parties along three main dimensions, even when we frame the question in terms of left and right.

A clear three-dimensional structure emerges when we analyse party preference-rankings by themselves. But the pattern becomes much more meaningful when we include electors' attitudes toward major political issues and self-placement on the left–right scale in our analysis. Table 12.5 shows the results of a factor analysis of these variables. The first factor that emerges is, unmistakably, the conventional left–right dimension. One reason why we may be sure that this is what the dimension taps is the fact that self-placement on the left–right scale has a very high loading on this factor. But the individual's preference rankings among the various parties provide additional confirmation: support for the Communists or Socialists has strong positive loadings on this factor; support for the Christian Democrats, Radicals, PAB and most other parties has negative loadings. The striking exceptions are National Action and the Swiss Republican Movement. Positive or negative feelings towards these two parties are strongly correlated with the *second* factor. And, surprisingly as it may seem, attitudes towards most of the important questions of contemporary Swiss politics load on this dimension rather than the first factor.

There are some notable exceptions. Attitudes towards income distribution and the housing problem have their strongest loadings on the first (left–right) factor. Those who feel that the present distribution of income in Switzerland is inequitable, and those who favour a public (rather than private) solution to the housing problem, tend to place themselves at the left end of the left–right scale and are likely to favour the Socialists or Communists rather than the Radicals, Christian Democrats or most other

Table 12.5　Party Preferences, Left–Right Self-Placement And Issue Preferences Among Swiss Electorate (Principle Axes Factor Analysis: All loadings above .240 are shown)

| | 1. Left/ Right | 2. Traditional/ Cosmopolitan | 3. Religious/ Secular |
|---|---|---|---|
| Places self on Left | .597 | | |
| Swiss Political system is good | -.397 | | |
| For more vigourous police intervention | | .364 | |
| Allow foreign workers to enter freely | | -.411 | |
| Switzerland should enter Common Market | | -.458 | |
| Switzerland should join United Nations | | -.368 | |
| Conscientious objectors should be obliged to serve | | .295 | |
| Women should play same political role as men | | -.335 | |
| Private enterprise should solve housing problem | -.259 | | |
| Swiss income distribution is fair | -.292 | | |
| Retain ban on Jesuit activities | | .243 | .270 |
| Favourable to Alliance of Independents | | | |
| "　" Peasants, Artisans, Bourgeois | -.399 | | |
| "　" Christian Democrats | -.430 | | -.586 |
| "　" Communist Party | .584 | | |
| "　" Christian Social Party | -.311 | | -.601 |
| "　" Evangelical Protestants | .272 | | |
| "　" Liberal Party | -.304 | | .405 |
| "　" Radical Party | -.345 | | .513 |
| "　" Socialist Party | .509 | | |
| "　" National Action | | .681 | |
| "　" Republican Movement | | .667 | |
| TOTAL VARIANCE CONTRIBUTION: | 10.4% | 9.4% | 6.0% |

non-Marxist parties.* Response to another question is closely linked with the first dimension: we asked whether the respondent felt that the Swiss political system was on the whole very good, good, passable, bad or very bad. Those who placed themselves on the left were relatively likely to give neutral or negative responses.

A left–right dimension does exist, and an individual's stand on socioeconomic issues is linked with this dimension. But electors' positions on the other, more recent, major political issues are virtually unrelated to this classic left–right dimension. This scarcely conforms to the conventional concept of left and right, but it is logical in the context of contemporary Swiss politics. For Switzerland must be something of a limiting case in the degree to which major issues can be raised, debated and decided

* The exact wording of these questions was: 'If you compare what you earn with what other groups earn in this country, would you say that the distribution of income in Switzerland is fair or unfair?' and: 'In your opinion, how should the housing problem be solved—mainly by private enterprise, mainly by the government, or by both combined?'

(through national referenda) without the major political parties taking opposing sides. In each of the past several years, major issues *have* broken the former calm of Swiss politics. In 1970 the Schwarzenbach Initiative led to a national controversy about the role of foreign workers. If this constitutional amendment had passed (as it nearly did) it would have had an immense impace on the Swiss economy and society.\*\* In 1971, after previous unsuccessful attempts, women's suffrage was finally adopted by a national referendum)—doubling the size of the Swiss electorate overnight. In 1972 another referendum was held: this time the sensitive topic of Swiss neutrality was in question. Switzerland had not even joined the UN for fear that it might compromise her neutrality. Finally, in 1972 the electorate voted to end a constitutional ban on the Jesuits which dates back to a Catholic separatist movement and a brief civil war in 1847.† While this amendment will probably have a little practical impact it has great symbolic importance, removing from the Constitution the implication that the Catholic Church was potentially subversive. These were major issues, and they give rise to a major dimension of political cleavage: the second factor, which taps response to these issues, explains nearly as much variance in our factor analysis as does the left-right dimension. But what does the cleavage imply?

Normally one assumes that the Establishment represents conservatism. But in each of the foregoing cases, the élites of all major parties endorsed the 'progressive' stand on the given issue—that is, *against* the Schwarzenbach Initiative and *for* the other three. Despite this endorsement, large portions of the electorate voted against the Establishment in each of these referenda. Only the two small traditionalist parties offered 'a choice, not an echo—except for the Communist Party, which joined them in opposition to the Common Market treaty. The second factor, then, might be viewed as a dimension that pits a relatively cosmopolitan and change-oriented Establishment against a traditionalism that is represented in Parliament only by National Action and the Swiss Republican Movement. Preferences among the major parties are only faintly related to this dimension.

In view of the widespread support that the traditionalist position evokes on certain major issues, the traditionalist parties might appear to draw surprisingly little support. But as we have seen, these parties are opposed by a relatively monolithic consensus among the established élites and the public tends to perceive them as extremist. Moreover, general satisfaction with the Swiss political system is linked with the *first* more than with the second factor. The first factor, we have noted, taps the classic issues of government intervention in the economy but not the more salient recent issues. The bulk of the Swiss electorate seems to judge whether the political system is basically good or bad primarily on the basis of conventional economic issues. And

---

\*\* The public's verdict in 1971 did not lay this issue to rest. Another referendum on the expulsion of foreigners was held in 1974; this time it was rejected by nearly 70 per cent of those voting. Diminished support for the proposal was not simply due to a decline in traditionalist sentiment: the traditionalist movement was split in 1974, with Schwarzenbach himself opposing the referendum as 'too much, too soon'.

† Attitudes toward the Jesuits have a relatively weak loading on the second factor because this item is also drawn into the religious—secular factor. But there was a clear tendency for supporters of the traditionalist parties to resist raising the restrictions on the Jesuits: among those expressing an opinion, 43 per cent of those who supported National Action or the Republican Movement opposed ending the ban, as compared with 21 per cent of our samples as a whole.

Switzerland is, second only to Sweden, the most prosperous country in Europe: an overwhelming majority of our respondents rated the Swiss political system favourably. Finally, much of the Swiss electorate is linked with the various Establishment parties by deep-rooted political traditions. A comparison of the vote in elections and in referenda provides a rough idea of the importance of such political party loyalties. In elections one votes for a given party; in referenda one is more likely to vote according to one's personal opinions. And the traditionalist vote is often eight or nine times as large in referenda as in elections to the federal Parliament. Paradoxically, a conservative electoral behaviour on the part of the Swiss electorate may facilitate the attainment of change by established political élites.

The Swiss elector's religious outlook is an important basis of affiliation with the Establishment parties; and it gives rise to the third principal dimension of Swiss political cleavage. This third factor (labelled 'religious-secular') pits the supporters of the two main Catholic parties against the traditionally secular Radicals and Liberals. The only current issue linked with this dimension concerns the ban on Jesuit activities (which is also linked with the second dimension to a lesser extent). The religious-secular dimension is quantitatively less important than the other two, but it is essential to an adequate description of Swiss politics.

The Catholic parties were once parties of emancipation, struggling against a federal government dominated by the anti-clerical Radicals. With the rise of a militant labour movement, the two sides went into permanent alliance shortly after the first World War, but the heritage of this bygone conflict lives on in the party preferences reflected by our third dimension. Today, whether one identifies with the religious or the secular parties, one is linked to a consensual Establishment that took a united stand on the Jesuit referendum, as on other important matters. The most important practical consequence may be the fact that those who feel affiliated with the Catholic parties (or other established parties) are not available for recruitment to new parties such as National Action or the Republican Movement. The traditionalist parties draw disproportionate support from those who lack religious ties: only 21 per cent of their sympathizers attend church weekly or nearly every week; more than a third of our other respondents do. The religious-secular dimension is important. But it is sufficiently straightforward to seem to require little further discussion.

In addition to factor analysis, we performed multi-dimensional scaling and smallest-space analysis of the items just discussed (Kruskal, 1964a and 1964b; Lingoes, 1964; Guttman, 1968). The various forms of dimensional analysis point to virtually identical conclusions: a three-dimensional solution is optimal, and the three dimensions are readily interpretable as a conventional left-right dimension, a cosmopolitan-traditional dimension and a religious-secular dimension. Figure 12.1 depicts the first two dimensions in a smallest-space analysis. It summarizes the structure of responses in an intuitively meaningul way: the stronger the positive correlation between any two items, the closer together they appear in the two-dimensional space. Thus, support for the Communists and Socialists and self-placement on the left are closely correlated, and these three items cluster together at the left end of the horizontal (or left-right) axis. Support for the Radicals, Christian Democrats and Peasants, Artisans and Bourgeois falls at the opposite end of the horizontal axis (but at different levels on the vertical axis, the PAB being more traditional than the other parties). We suggested earlier that the Radicals are the Establishment party *par excellence*. This seems borne out by the fact that support for them is closely linked with the opinion that the Swiss political system is good: in terms of the left–right axis, the Radicals are clearly a party of the right. But in relation to the vertical axis, the radical electorate is among the least traditionalist. Support for the Republican Movement and National Action falls at one extreme on the vertical axis—virtually at the maximum possible distance from support for free entry of foreign workers. This vertical dimension reflects a coherent structure of attitudes—an ideology, one might say—centring on a concern for maintaining traditional Swiss social patterns. Opposition to the entry of foreign workers goes together with opposition to affiliation with the Common Market, permitting women to participate in politics, permitting conscientious objectors to escape military service or lifting the ban on Jesuit activities.

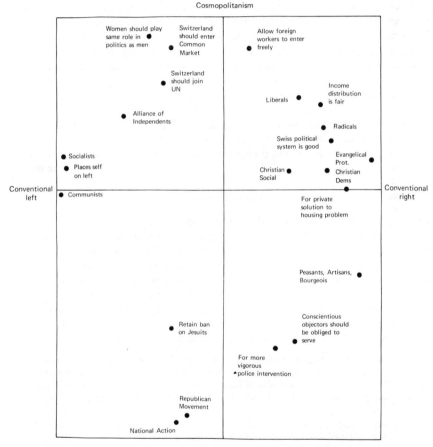

Figure 12.1   Smallest-space analysis: party preferences, left–right self-placement and issue preferences among the Swiss electorate, 1972 (coefficient of alienation=0.124)

This dimension has a flavour reminiscent of authoritarian ethnocentrism—except that the 'authoritarians' do *not* support the authorities. The traditionalist position is in clear opposition to the Establishment's stand on each of these key issues; the traditionalists seem to see the cosmopolitan élite as all too ready to let the Swiss social fabric disintegrate.*

Early in this chapter we noted the astonishing fact that the parties one would normally regard as the extreme right were actually placed to the left of the leading non-Marxist parties on a left–right scale. The traditionalist parties do indeed represent the conservative extreme on several of the most salient current issues, but this fact has little impact on left–right placement. For the Swiss electorate, the terms 'left' and 'right' still refer primarily to a conventional dimension relating mainly to classic economic issues. And as Figure 12.1 shows, the traditionalist parties *are* located to the left of the dominant non-Marxist parties on this conventional left–right dimension.

Inglehart (1971) has presented evidence that the basic values of Western publics are changing in a manner that may gradually tend to shift the axis of political conflict from economic issues to non-economic issues. The items that he used to measure an individual's value priorities were included in our survey. While self-placement on the left–right scale provides a good predictor of preferences among the established parties, value type is a relatively weak predictor. But conversely, an individual's value type is the stronger predictor of preferences toward the traditionalist parties and the issues that load on this second dimension.** Conceivably, such life-style issues may play an increasingly important role in future Swiss politics. If so, attitudes toward these issues might become assimilated into a new and broader left–right dimension—as seems to have happened with the religious–secular dimension, to a certain extent. For the time being, cultural change issues and the left–right dimension are virtually independent in Switzerland.

## CONCLUSION

The left–right continuum has little relationship to the issues that have been most controversial in recent Swiss politics. It 'explains' the political party preferences of this public rather well (apart from support for the two traditionalist parties): the Swiss electorate's preferences are consistent with self-placement on the left–right scale. But these preferences themselves seem to be largely conventional—the result of inherited party loyalties and religious affiliations. Those who lack such loyalties have little sense of where they belong in terms of left and right. In so far as issues *are* involved, the left–right dimension relates mainly to economic issues—which, almost certainly, were the central question a generation ago and might again occupy the centre of the

---

\* The correlations between left–right self-placement and support for the National Action Party and the Swiss Republican Movement, respectively, are −0.040 and 0.000 (as shown in Table 12.4). The respective correlations with value type are 0.107 and 0.134—in other words, the 'post-bourgeois' type is significantly less likely to give a favourable rating to these groups than are the 'acquisitives'.

\*\* The traditionalists not only oppose the Establishment position, but perceive the Establishment parties as ill-equipped to handle these questions. Our respondents were asked which party was most capable of handling various problems, including equal rights for women, Swiss entry into the Common Market and the influx of foreigners. Sympathizers of National Action and the Republican Movement gave relatively low capability ratings to the Establishment parites on these issues. Our sample as a whole gave top ratings to either the Socialists or Radicals in regard to most problems. But in regard to foreign influx, confidence in the Establishment was amazingly low: despite their small number of supporters, National Action and the Republican Movement were the two parties most likely to be judged capable of handling this problem by our sample *as a whole*.

stage in the near future. The left–right dimension is complemented by a weaker but still significant religious–secular dimension; together, these two continua reflect the major cleavages of industrial society. But a third dimension also exists, and many of the most pressing contemporary political issues relate to it, rather than to either of the other two dimensions. Like the United States of the 1950s, Switzerland clearly does not have the 'strong ideological focus' described by Stokes.

We emphasize that these findings apply to the *Swiss* public. For Swiss institutions facilitate the existence of a remarkable degree of independence between parties and issues. And the Swiss public is ideologically less polarized than the French, Italian or German publics; indeed, there seems to be a weaker relationship between issue preferences and the left–right dimension in Switzerland than in most other Western countries (Inglehart and Klingemann, Chapter 13 below). For the Swiss, the long-established left–right dimension is largely unrelated to preferences on non-economic issues—and consequently, to how one voted in crucial recent referenda.

If non-economic issues remain central, the major parties will be faced with a difficult choice. As one alternative they may attempt to maintain consensual government based on the present broad Establishment coalition—in which case the terms left and right would tend to become simply conventional (and increasingly outdated) labels. This strategy might minimize overt political conflict; but it would also tend to minimize the significance of public influence through the electoral process. This tendency is already well advanced, as is suggested by the fact that the Swiss public shows one of the world's lowest rates of participation in national elections, with a turnout generally below even the American rate. In the Swiss case, this problem is mitigated somewhat by the existence of referenda. As another alternative, the leading parties might begin to offer a variety of options along the second of our three dimensions.

On general principles, the latter alternative would seem more compatible with the norms of participatory democracy. Yet there are indications that a loosening up of the Swiss Establishment's political cartel would give greater weight to traditionalist opinion. The existence of a political cartel may tend to dampen the advocacy of social change; but under present conditions its most important consequence may be that it hinders the development of a reactionary movement—which might otherwise have considerable potential for growth.

## REFERENCES

Barnes, Samuel (1971), 'Left, Right and the Italian Voter', *Comparative Political Studies*, **4**, 157–75.

Barnes, Samuel, and Roy Pierce (1971), 'Public Opinion and Political Preferences in France and Italy', *Midwest Journal of Political Science*, **15**, 643–60.

Converse, Philip E. (1966), 'The Problem of Party Distances in Models of Voting Change', in M. Kent Jennings and L. Harmon Ziegler (eds.), *The Electoral Process*, Prentice-Hall, Englewood Cliffs, New Jersey.

Converse, Philip, and Roy Pierce (1973), 'Basic Cleavages in French Politics and the Disorders of May and June, 1968', in Richard Rose (ed.), *Political Behavior in Western Societies*, Wiley, New York.

Deutsch, Emeric, Denis Lindon and Pierre Weill (1966), *Les Familles Politiques d'aujourd'hui en France*, Minuit, Paris.

Downs, Anthony (1957), *An Economic Theory of Democracy*, Harper and Row, New York.

Guttman, Louis (1968), 'A General Nonmetric Technique for Finding the Smallest Coordinate Space for a Configuration of Points', *Psychometrika*, **33**, 469–506.

242

Inglehart, Ronald (1971), 'The Silent Revolution in Europe: Intergenerational Change in Post-Industrial Societies', *American Political Science Review*, **65**, 991–1017.

Klingemann, Hans D. (1972), 'Testing the Left–Right Continuum on a Sample of German Voters', *Comparative Political Studies*, **5**, 93–105.

Kruskal, J. B. (1964a), 'Multidimensional Scaling by Optimizing Goodness of Fit to a Nonmetric Hypothesis', *Psychometrika*, **29**, 1–27.

Kruskal, J. B. (1964b), 'Non-Metric Multidimensional Scaling: A Numerical Method', *Psychometrika*, **29**, 115–129.

Lingoes, James C. (1964), 'An IBM 7090 Program for Guttman↑Lingoes Smallest Space Analysis', *Behavioral Science*, **10**.

Miller, Arthur, Warren E. Miller, Alden S. Raine and Thad A. Brown (1976), 'A Majority Party in Disarray: Policy Voting in the 1972 Election', *American Political Science Review*, **70**.

Pomper, Gerald M. (1972), 'From Confusion to Clarity: Issues and American Voters, 1956–1968', *American Political Science Review*, **66**, 415–28.

Steiner, Jurg (1973), *Amicable Agreement versus Majority Rule: Conflict Resolution in Switzerland*, University of North Carolina Press, Chapel Hill, North Carolina.

Stokes, Donald E. (1966), 'Spatial Models of Party Competition', in Angus Campbell, Philip E. Converse, Warren E. Miller and Donald E. Stokes (eds.), *Elections and the Political Order*, Wiley, New York.

# 13

# Party Identification, Ideological Preference and the Left-Right Dimension among Western Mass Publics

RONALD INGLEHART and HANS D. KLINGEMANN*

## INTRODUCTION

The End of Ideology did not materialize. On the contrary, there are indications that presumably ideological concepts such as left and right are taking on new life and new meaning for Western publics. In the French presidential election of 1974, for example, much of the campaign rhetoric was cast in terms of a left-right dimension that was tacitly assumed to be the main axis of conflict.

The left-right dimension has long been a staple element of European political discourse. But with the rekindling of ideological controversy there has been a re-examination of the role played by an analogous liberal-conservative dimension among the American public. Pomper (1972) and Nie (1974) have documented the extent to which issue voting became increasingly important among the American public during the period 1956-68. In a remarkable analysis of the 1972 presidential election Miller *et al.* (1976) report a continuation of this trend but their findings go a good deal farther. They find that self-placement on a liberal-conservative scale shows robust correlations with the respondent's stand on most of the important issues of 1972, and is a far stronger predictor of vote than any single issue—indeed, a liberal-conservative proximity index actually explains substantially more of the variance in vote than does party identification. This unprecedented finding seems to justify the authors' suggestion that in 1972 an exceptionally large share of the American public responded to politics in an ideological fashion.

A liberal-conservative dimension appears to be an increasingly important factor in American politics. Yet—as we will argue in this article—the left-right dimension seems to provide an even *more* important political cue for West European publics than the liberal-conservative continuum does for Americans. The present study will undertake

* Data for this study have been made available by Jacques-Rene Rabier, special advisor to the Commission of the European Community (surveys covering the nine member nations of the EEC); Dusan Sidjanski and Gerhard Schmidtchen (1972 Swiss National Election Study); and the Inter-University Consortium for Political Research (1972 CPS American National Election Study). We are grateful for this cross-national support. Hans Klingemann wants to express his thanks to the Centre for Political Studies, University of Michigan, which hosted him while writing his part of the article as a Ford Fellow in 1974. The authors' names are in alphabetical order; both authors share equal responsibility for all the wrong-headedness in the paper.

two tasks: (1) a comparative exploration of these analoguous dimensions among different Western publics. We will provide survey-based descriptive material, hoping to offer a useful baseline for other studies; (2) an effort to clarify the role that the left-right dimension plays among mass publics. Let us begin with the latter task.

The classic view of the left-right dimension sees it as a super-issue which summarizes the programmes of opposing groups. Political polarization need not be uni-dimensional, of course. But the left-right dimension is more often than not used by political élites and mass communication to label the most *important* issues of a given era. Downs (1957) hypothesized that electoral choice can be regarded as a process in which the voter decides where the available parties are located on an issue-based left-right continuum and then votes for the one that is nearest to his own location on that dimension. Converse (1964) demonstrated that, in the 1950s, only a small minority of the American public could be regarded as ideologues in this strict sense. Significantly enough, the criterion that he used to distinguish ideologues from the non-ideological public is that the former spontaneously refer to some abstract dimension such as liberal-conservative in evaluating political parties. In a sense, then, those who situate themselves on a liberal-conservative or left-right scale might be considered ideologically oriented by definition. But this operational measure would make sense only if it did imply an evaluation of the respective parties' current political programmes by the individual respondent.

This is not necessarily the case. Short-cuts for the ideological position of parties like left or right are provided by language, and the relationship of such labels to political parties is culturally defined. To be sure, it normally takes a long period of time before mass publics accept certain characteristics of political parties as given. And there is no doubt that it is the political parties' stand on issues in the first place that defines the programmatic image. However, individuals may recognize and use ideological labels in connection with political parties without knowing or considering the implications of such concepts for their own issue positions. If a respondent feels close to a given party and knows that people say it is located on the extreme left, he may place himself accordingly. Thus party loyalties could lead members of the public to adopt ideological labels for themselves that are unrelated to their current issue positions. There may be cases where both ideological label and issue preferences fit perfectly; there may be other cases, however, where the extreme 'leftist' takes a hard line on law and order and favours a nationalistic foreign policy. In short, we suggest that although the left-right terminology does have an ideological meaning to specific Western publics, it also has a major component based on party identification.

Other writers have, of course, recognized the party-relatedness of left and right. Thus Sani argues that 'the acquisition of partisan preference and of left-right identification go hand in hand because of the connections established between specific parties prevailing in the relevant cultural milieu' (Sani, 1974, p.207). Butler and Stokes put more stress on the primacy of party loyalties: 'Voters come to think of themselves as Right or Left very much as a Conservative in Birmingham or Scotland used to think of himself as a "Unionist", because that is what his party was called locally' (Butler and Stokes, 1969, p.260). The difference in emphasis between these two statements may relate to the fact that Sani was studying Italy, while Butler and Stokes used Britain as a point of reference. For we believe that the relative weight of the two components will vary cross-nationally in a systematic fashion. And it should vary among types of individuals as well.

Each of the latter expectations is derived from what might be called a principle of least effort. A taxonomic system like the left–right framework is an efficient way to understand, order and store political information. However, the concepts cannot serve these functions unless their implications are learned. The learning of 'theory', the acquisition of an abstract generalized orientation towards politics, requires motivation, opportunity and effort—and there is much variation with respect to these properties within Western electorates. For those who are not motivated to participate in politics, the relative costs of learning may well be too high. And many of these people might have never been exposed to systematic political education. However, even in the implications of abstract concepts like left and right are learned, the public tends to move to a more sophisticated level of reasoning only when necessary for the understanding and discussion of complex situations. Thus, party identification as the more concrete and close-to-home cue will normally be used for an evaluation of day-to-day political news. Hence one might expect that the party identification component will ordinarily outweigh the ideological meaning component of left–right self-placement.

Converse has proposed a cost–benefit theory of information intake, concluding that 'there is a dramatic inversion between the relative costs and benefits of paying attention to politics somewhere between the upper and lower edges of mass electorates' (Converse, 1974, p.46). The better educated, and those who are involved in politics, are better equipped and more motivated to develop an integrated ideological response to politics. Hence, if only a relatively slight cognitive effort is required for one to be aware of the association between given parties and their left–right labels, we might expect the importance of the party identification component to be more or less equal across all strata of a population—whereas the ideological component of the left–right framework would be present mostly among the educated and those with relatively high political involvement.

Political party identification is not the only form of group loyalty that could provide relatively simple and concrete cues concerning an individual's location on the left–right dimension. Social class and religion could also play this role. From a Marxist viewpoint, the working class should logically form the mainstay of the left in an industrial society. In so far as this is empirically true, any association between party identification and left–right self-placement could prove to be spurious: given individuals might place themselves on the left *and* support given parties simply because they identify both with the working class. From the time of the French Revolution, when revolutionary forces tried to eradiate the Church, the left has often been associated with an anti-clerical stand. Explicit religious questions may constitute a relatively minor theme in contemporary politics, but there can be no doubt that religious affiliation has remarkably strong value implications that are politically relevant (Pappi and Laumann, 1974).

We will examine the impact of both class and religion on left–right self-placement. On the whole, in Western political cultures left–right labels seem to be used in connection with political parties more often than with any other groups; hence we expect that the partisan component will not prove to be spurious but plays an important role.

The role of the left–right dimension should vary across nations as well as among individuals. In keeping with the principle of least effort, it would not be a salient feature of a given political culture unless there is a need for it. Consequently, one might expect this dimension to play a relatively prominent role where there is a multiplicity of salient political alternatives. If there *are* no salient alternatives, obviously it will not play an important role. Nor is it needed much where there are only two alternatives: such a choice already *is* uni-dimensional, with no need for further abstraction. But as the number of pairwise comparisons rises according to the formula $(N^2–N)/2$: three parties entail three comparisons, four parties entail six; with a dozen parties the citizen would have sixty-six pairs of party programmes to compare. The left–right dimension offers an organizing principle that can simplify such complex choices: if the parties are arrayed along a single dimension it becomes relatively easy to decide which is the nearest alternative in a run-off election or when a candidate from one's most preferred party is not available. Thus, as a rule of thumb, we would expect such a dimension to be less important to the publics of the traditionally two-party Anglo-Saxon systems than in most of the continental countries. But multiplicity can exist over time, as well as at a given moment. A left–right dimension can be a source of orientation when parties change or disappear. It can be of help, too, with the politics of foreign countries; in the face of a puzzling parade of strange parties, the familiar left–right terminology may provide orientation.

All this assumes that the politics of a given society can be viewed in terms of some underlying continuum. But certain conflicts have an all-or-nothing nature. Questions of national identity tend to be this way: one either is, or is not, an Irishman, or a Fleming, or a Walloon. It is difficult to see politics as a series of points along a continuum when the political community is at stake.

When politics *can* be assimilated to a left–right dimension, under what conditions will the issue component be relatively important, and under what conditions will left-right self-placement be primarily a reflection of party loyalties? Some fairly obvious answers suggest themselvs. We would expect the latter component to be predominant where party loyalties are relatively strong and widespread—and where the left–right concept has been an element of political culture for a long time. For party labels do not get attached to some point on the left–right continuum automatically. The linkage is likely to reflect a policy position taken by the given party either at some time in the past or in the present. In the latter case, left–right self-placement would show strong linkages with both party identification *and* current policy preferences; only if the given party's left–right label is rooted in long-established tradition would the partisan component be clearly predominant.

Conversely, we would expect the ideological or issue component to be relatively important in cases where political party identification is weak or breaking down. The two probably tend to go together, for strong issue polarization may cause established party loyalties to break down (Inglehart and Hochstein, 1972).

We might summarize our hypotheses about the role of the left–right or liberal–conservative dimension as follows:

(1) The dimension has two main components—one based on issues, another based on political party loyalties.

(2) The partisan component will be about equally important among all strata of a Western society, whereas the issue-based component will play a more important role among the more politically involved and educated. For the population as a whole, the partisan component is likely to provide the dominant cue.

(3) The partisan component is likely to be predominant where party loyalties are strong and the left–right dimension has been salient for a long time; the issue-based

component is likely to be relatively important where issue polarization is high and party identification weak or breaking down.

(4) An 'ideological' continuum such as left–right or liberal–conservative is more likely to play a prominent role in multi-party systems than in systems dominated by two leading parties; and in societies where the leading parties have changed over time more than in those where two or three parties have dominated the system continuously.

(5) Other social characteristics, such as social class and religious affiliation, will also contribute to one's 'ideological' self-placement, but only if there is strong identification with these groups and the political implications of group membership are perceived.

(6) Questions of national identity are less readily assimilated to a left–right continuum than most other types of political conflict.

Let us explore these hypotheses using recent survey data gathered from the publics of a variety of Western nations.

## THE DISTRIBUTION OF WESTERN PUBLICS
## ON A LEFT–RIGHT DIMENSION

In September and October 1973, the European Community sponsored surveys of representative samples of the publics of the Community's nine member-nations. Each of these surveys included the item:

In political matters people talk of 'the Left' and 'the Right'. How would you place your views on this scale?

The respondent was handed a card with the word 'Left' at one side and the word 'Right' at the opposite side, and a scale divided into ten boxes in between. If the respondent hesitated, the interviewer was instructed to note that fact and ask him to try again. No numbers or cues were provided other than the words 'Left' and 'Right' and, since there were an even number of boxes, none of them constituted a halfway house between left and right.

The fact that our scale contains no mid-point is a matter of some importance. Using a scale that does offer a neutral position, one can induce a larger proportion of the population to place themselves on the dimension. For example, Deutsch *et al.* (1966) obtained left–right self-placements from 90 per cent of their French sample, as compared with 78 per cent using our technique. But—as they recognize—placing oneself at the neutral position between left and right can be a concealed form of non-response; a very disproportionate share of those who place themselves at the exact centre have little interest in politics. Consequently, Deutsch *et al.* filter out those nominal 'centrists' who rank low on political interest (about three-quarters of this group), placing them in the same category as those who give no response. Using this technique, they obtain 'true' left–right self-placements for 68 per cent of their sample. There is some tendency for those who place themselves in boxes 5 or 6 or our own scale to show relatively low levels of political interest, but it is considerably weaker than is the case when a mid-point is offered—and this procedure seems theoretically clearer and less arbitrary than the one employed by Deutsch *et al.* For low political interest is by no means limited to those who place themselves at the midpoint of a scale: one is left wondering whether some or all of those who place themselves elsewhere should also be filtered out.

The degree to which European publics are willing to locate their political views on a left–right scale suggests that there is considerable cultural familiarity with these terms. For 83 per cent of our nine-nation sample placed themselves on this scale—with the proportions ranging from a low of 73 per cent in Belgium to a high of 93 per cent in Germany, as indicated in Table 13.1.

Table 13.1  Self-Placement on the Left–Right Scale in Nine Countries

| Country | Mean | Standard Deviation | Percentage of Sample Placing Selves on Scale | Total N |
|---|---|---|---|---|
| Germany | 5.63 | 2.18 | 93 % | (1957) |
| The Netherlands | 5.80 | 2.56 | 93 | (1464) |
| Denmark | 5.41 | 1.93 | 91 | (1199) |
| Italy | 4.69 | 2.29 | 83 | (1909) |
| Great Britain | 5.37 | 2.46 | 82 | (1933) |
| Ireland | 6.30 | 2.54 | 80 | (1199) |
| France | 5.05 | 2.28 | 78 | (2227) |
| Luxembourg | 5.43 | 1.98 | 78 | (330) |
| Belgium | 5.67 | 2.47 | 73 | (1266) |

Moreover, a sense of left–right self-location seems to be more widespread than a sense of party affiliation. Our respondents were also asked:

Generally speaking, do you feel closer to one of the parties on this list or to others? (IF YES): Which one?

In order to minimize non-response due to inability to recall party names—a factor that can be very important in some settings—the respondent was handed a card containing the names of all significant political parties in the given country. In every country, a higher percentage of the population placed themselves on the left–right scale than said they felt relatively close to some party. The gain in classification ranges from a high of 23 per cent in Germany to a low of 7 per cent in Britain, where the same parties have dominated the scene for half a century.

These results confirm previous findings that the terms 'left' and 'right' are readily recognized by European publics. In addition to the findings of Deutsch et al., already cited, Converse and Pierce (1973) found that in 1967 and 1969 up to 80 per cent of the French electorate were willing to place themselves on a left–right scale. Converse and Pierce used still another measure of left–right self-placement—a numbered scale ranging from 0 to 100. This did have a mid-point, but respondents were asked not to place themselves if they were not familiar with the concept. Comparable figures for Italy are 76 per cent in 1968 (Barnes, 1971) and 62 per cent in 1972 (Sani, 1974). In

Table 13.2   Classification Range of Left–Right Self-Placement and Party Identification

| Country | Place Selves on Left-Right Scale | | Do not place Selves on Left-Right Scale | | |
| | Have Party Identification | No Party Identification | Have Party Identification | No Party Identification | |
| Germany (29)[*] | 62% | 31 | 2 | 5 | 100% |
| Ireland (24) | 48% | 32 | 8 | 12 | 100% |
| Luxembourg (20) | 51% | 27 | 7 | 15 | 100% |
| Denmark (19) | 69% | 22 | 3 | 6 | 100% |
| Belgium (16) | 49% | 25 | 9 | 17 | 100% |
| France (15) | 59% | 19 | 4 | 18 | 100% |
| Italy (11) | 70% | 13 | 2 | 15 | 100% |
| The Netherlands (10) | 80% | 13 | 3 | 4 | 100% |
| Great Britain (7) | 67% | 15 | 8 | 10 | 100% |

[*]Figures in parentheses indicate gain in classification through
Left-Right self-placement (column two minus column three).

Germany 80 per cent of a sample from the *land* of Hesse placed themselves on a left–right scale in 1970 (Klingemann and Pappi, 1972, p.42–3). The lowest figure yet reported for continental Europe is one of 58 per cent for the Swiss electorate in 1972 (Inglehart and Sidjanski, Chapter 12 above), but sex differences acccount for much of the cross-national variation: only 45 per cent of the women place themselves on the scale, while 75 per cent of the men do so. The authors themselves attribute this exceptionally large sex difference to the late entry of Swiss women into the electorate—they received the franchise at the national level only in 1971. We must not place too much weight on the latter finding, however. In 1963 a sample of the British electorate was asked:

Do you ever think of yourself as being to the Left, the Centre or the Right in politics, or don't you think of yourself that way?

Only 25 per cent of the sample gave an affirmative reply; on the other hand, when presented with a visual scale, more than three-quarters of the same sample were willing to describe the parties as left-wing or right-wing (Butler and Stokes, 1969, pp.255, 572–3). The British respondents can be induced to place themselves on a left–right scale; however, it does not seem to be the most salient frame of reference in a system where most of the electorate can readily see themselves as either Conservative or Labour.

Aside from the question, to what *extent* does a given public see politics in terms of left–right continuum, it is interesting to note certain features of *how* they place

250

themselves. If a public were symmetrically divided along our left–right continuum, the mean self-placement would be 5.5 (half-way between '1', the code for the box at the extreme left, and '10', the box at the extreme right). In fact, most publics are a little to the right, as Table 13.1 indicates; only Italy, France and Denmark have means below 5.5. The two countries most skewed to the left are the only ones that have sizable Communist parties—whether one views the latter fact as cause or effect. In every country, the modal self-placement is 5 (immediately to the left of centre) except in Britain, where it is 6—and in Ireland, where it is 10! Whyte has argued that 'Irish party politics should be *sui generis:* the context from which they spring is *sui generis* also' (Whyte, 1974, p.648). Our own data indicate that Ireland is indeed a deviant case—not only in this respect, but in several others as well.

The country-by-country distributions of left–right self-placement are shown in greater detail in Figure 13.1. The frequency distributions of all nine nations are similar in one respect—there is a peak around the middle of the continuum, even in Ireland.

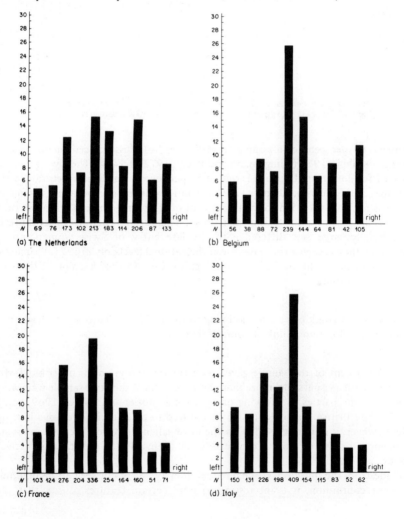

| N | 69 | 76 | 173 | 102 | 213 | 183 | 114 | 206 | 87 | 133 |

(a) The Netherlands

| N | 56 | 38 | 88 | 72 | 239 | 144 | 64 | 81 | 42 | 105 |

(b) Belgium

| N | 103 | 124 | 276 | 204 | 336 | 254 | 164 | 160 | 51 | 71 |

(c) France

| N | 150 | 131 | 226 | 198 | 409 | 154 | 115 | 83 | 52 | 62 |

(d) Italy

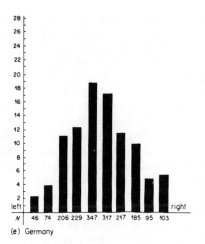

(e) Germany

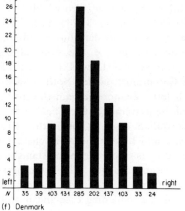

(f) Denmark

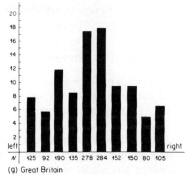

(g) Great Britain

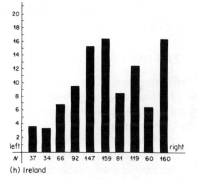

(h) Ireland

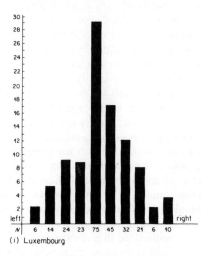

(i) Luxembourg

Figure 13.1   Country-by-country distributions of left–right self-placement

But major differences occur with respect to local modes. The Netherlands and Belgium—with two 'segmented pluralist' countries included here (Lijphart, 1969; Huyse, 1970; Lorwin, 1971)—both have local modes to the left and to the right of centre. Indeed, the distribution obtained for The Netherlands might serve as a textbook example of the type of distribution Downs would associate with a multi-party system (Downs, 1957, pp.114–41). France and Italy, the countries with major Communist parties, both show local modes to the left of centre. Whereas the French left has more to gain toward the centre, the Italian left has an alternative toward the extreme. The left half of the British distribution bears some resemblance to the Italian case, although the British pattern is less pronounced. Germany, Denmark and Luxembourg are characterized by relatively uni-modal distributions. This finding is surprising in the Danish case—a multi-party system undergoing rather drastic recent changes. The hypothesis of a long-established two-bloc coalition government may explain this pattern (Rusk and Borre, Chapter 8 in this volume). Ireland is the remaining case and it alone exhibits two local modes to the right of centre; indeed, the extreme right is more heavily populated than either of the centrist positions. The Irish pattern is indeed peculiar; we will have more to say about this in the following sections.

## THE PARTISAN COMPONENT OF THE LEFT–RIGHT DIMENSION

Our first hypothesis holds that the acquisition of partisan preferences and a left–right frame of reference go together in most political cultures: those who identify with given political parties should locate themselves at a culturally specified point along the left–right continuum.

The present data base does not permit us to examine how the respondent places *all* the important parties of the given system within a one-dimensional left–right space. Where this has been done, the results fit a political culture model quite well (Deutsch *et al.*, 1966, p.45; Barnes, 1971, p.164; Barnes and Pierce, 1971, p.647; Klingemann, 1972, p.96; Sani, 1974, Table 1; Inglehart and Sidjanski, Chapter 12 above, Table 12.3). We can, however, calculate group means for those who identify with given parties and compare the resulting placements with the culturally expected order. A high degree of correspondence would tend to support the present hypothesis.

Table 13.3 shows the mean self-placements of those identifying with the major parties in each country. For two of the parties (Belgium's *Volksunie* and *Front des Francophones/Rassemblement Walloon*) it is difficult to say exactly where they belong. For the other parties, rather clear cultural expectations exist and the results shown in Table 13.3 have a virtually perfect fit with cultural expectations.

The Irish parties have the largest standard deviations found in any party system: among the forty-one other political parties, only one has a standard deviation as high as the lowest figure for Ireland and (apart from Ireland) only in Belgium are the figures predominantly above the 2.0 level. Irish (and to a lesser degree Belgian) party-identifiers are relatively widely scattered on the left–right continuum: and we suspect that this is true because cultural cues concerning the meaning of left and right are less clear in these two countries. For we hypothesized that questions of national identity are less readily assimilated to a left–right continuum than other types of political conflict. And Ireland is a new nation, in that it has been independent only since 1922. The two main Irish parties are rooted in the struggle for independence

Table 13.3 Self-Placement on Left–Right Scale by Respondent's Party Identification

| The Netherlands (80%) | Mean | Standard Deviation | N |
|---|---|---|---|
| Partij van de Arbeid | 4.18 | 2.41 | 394 |
| D'66, PSP, PPP | 4.33 | 1.88 | 145 |
| Demkratieke Socialisten | 6.02 | 1.85 | 44 |
| Katholieke Volkspartij | 7.31 | 1.99 | 193 |
| Volskpartij voor Vrijheid en Demokratie | 7.38 | 1.81 | 205 |
| Anti-Revolutionaere Partij | 7.82 | 1.67 | 84 |
| Christelijke Historische Unie | 7.92 | 1.69 | 56 |

| Great Britain (75%) | | | |
|---|---|---|---|
| Labour | 3.62 | 2.03 | 543 |
| Liberal | 5.60 | 1.75 | 235 |
| Conservative | 7.51 | 1.71 | 485 |

| Italy (72%) | | | |
|---|---|---|---|
| Partito Communista | 1.75 | 1.28 | 207 |
| Partito Socialista | 3.20 | 1.14 | 244 |
| Partio Socialista Democratico | 4.19 | 1.48 | 113 |
| Partio Repubblicano | 4.75 | 1.10 | 64 |
| Democrazia Cristiana | 5.58 | 1.56 | 505 |
| Partito Liberale | 6.62 | 1.52 | 71 |
| Movimento Sociale/Destra Nazionale | 8.65 | 1.36 | 102 |

| Denmark (72%) | | | |
|---|---|---|---|
| Socialistisk Folkeparti | 3.15 | 1.47 | 100 |
| Socialdemokratiet | 4.95 | 1.27 | 296 |
| Radikale | 5.77 | 1.24 | 99 |
| Fremskridtspartiet | 6.09 | 2.25 | 42 |
| Venstre | 6.42 | 1.88 | 124 |
| Konservative | 7.42 | 1.56 | 120 |

| Germany (64%) | | | |
|---|---|---|---|
| Sozialdemokratische Partei | 4.35 | 2.01 | 624 |
| Freie Demokratische Partei | 5.50 | 1.63 | 131 |
| Chrsitlich Demokratische Union/ Christlich Soziale Union | 7.44 | 1.74 | 422 |

| France (63%) | | | |
|---|---|---|---|
| P.S.U. et Extrême Gauche | 2.26 | 1.07 | 62 |
| Parti Communiste | 2.63 | 1.55 | 180 |
| Parti Socialiste | 3.87 | 1.69 | 409 |
| Radicaux de Gauche | 4.51 | 1.60 | 53 |
| Réformateurs | 6.03 | 1.47 | 214 |
| U.R.P. Majorité | 7.19 | 1.59 | 354 |

| Luxembourg (59%) | | | |
|---|---|---|---|
| Sozialistesch Letzeburger Arbechterpartei | 3.72 | 1.56 | 46 |
| Sozialdemokratesch Partei | 5.00 | 2.10 | 11 |
| Demokratesch Partei | 5.72 | 1.36 | 36 |
| Kroestlichsozial Vollekspartei | 7.06 | 1.47 | 71 |

| Belgium (57%) | | | |
|---|---|---|---|
| Socialistes/Socialisten | 3.95 | 2.03 | 180 |
| Front des Francophones,Rassemblement Walloon | 5.32 | 1.92 | 34 |
| Libéraux/Liberalen | 6.25 | 2.29 | 76 |
| Volksunie | 6.42 | 2.35 | 69 |
| Sociaux-Chrétiens/Katholieken | 7.12 | 2.35 | 225 |

| Table 13.3 (cont'd) | Mean | Standard Deviation | N |
|---|---|---|---|
| Ireland (56%) | | | |
| Labour | 5.03 | 2.58 | 84 |
| Fianna Fail | 6.59 | 2.56 | 273 |
| Fine Gale | 6.68 | 2.39 | 146 |

\*Countries are ranked according to the proportion of population identifying with a political party (this percentage appears in parentheses).

from Britain. We suspect that the left-right dimension is less meaningful in Ireland than in most other Western countries.

Belgium, of course, has a much longer recent history as an independent nation than Ireland. Yet the question of national identity is by no means settled—on the contrary, conflicts between Flemish- and French-speaking groups continue to bring down governments and the country is in the process of being remodelled into a bicultural federation. We noted that it is difficult to place certain Belgian parties on a left-right scale. As ethnic nationalist parties, one would be tempted to place Volksunie and Rassemblement Walloon on the extreme right (Weil, 1970, pp.100-8). Yet their supporters do not—and they could both be seen as parties of emancipation (Inglehart, 1973, pp.61-9). The two largest parties, which dominated Belgian politics as recently as 1958, are placed precisely where one would expect them to be, with the Socialists on the moderate left and the Christian Social Party a substantial distance to their right. But the ethnic nationalists fall *between* the two main system parties, straddling the liberals. A somewhat similar phenomenon has been noted in Switzerland, where left-right self-placement corresponds very closely to expectations based on political party preference—except in the case of two parties concerned with the defence of the traditional Swiss social pattern against massive foreign penetration (Inglehart and Sidjanski, Chapter 12 above). Here also, it seems difficult to assimilate questions of national identity to the left-right dimension.

Another feature of Table 13.3 is rather interesting: the fact that standard deviations tend to be higher for the parties of the left; and they all show less variation around the mean than the Social Democratic or Labour Parties of Britain, Ireland, Germany, The Netherlands or Belgium.

In a comparison of data for Italy and France, Barnes and Pierce were impressed by the extent to which 'certain major parties that have common origins or symbols, particularly on the Left, tend to be very similarly located by the electorates of the two countries' (Barnes and Pierce, 1971, p.646). Commenting on the similarity of findings for French, Canadian and North American parties, Laponce concluded that that pattern reflected not merely an ordinal but an interval level of measurement, 'as if the subjects who filled in the questionnaire on different continents at different times were using a similar yardstick to express the relative distance from extreme Left and extreme Right' (Laponce, 1970, p.485; cf. Laponce, 1972, pp.48-52). Whether or not the left-right continuum can be viewed as an interval scale for cross-national purposes, the degree to which parties with common traits are located at similar points is indeed striking. Figure 13.2 shows a cross-national comparison of the locations of the various parties in our nine nations. Practically all of the right-wing parties are placed approximately at scale position 7, while the left-wing parties are located around scale

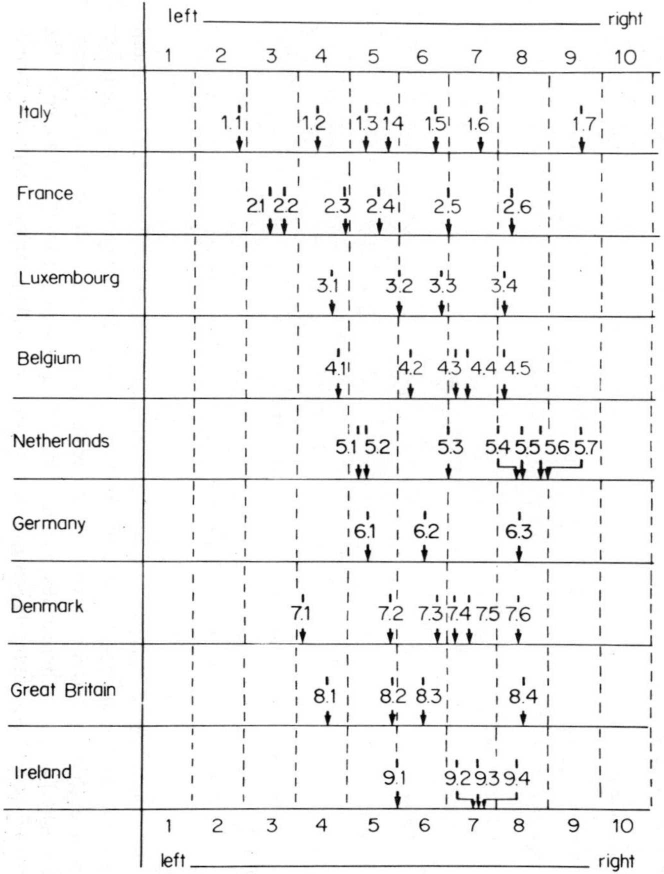

1.1 Partito Comunista
1.2 Partito Socialista
1.3 Partito Socialista Democratico
1.4 Partito Repubblicano
1.5 Democrazia Cristiana
1.6 Partito Liberale
1.7 Movimento Sociale/Destra Nazionale

2.1 PSU et Extrême Gauche
2.2 Parti Communiste
2.3 Parti Socialiste
2.4 Radicaux de Gauche
2.5 Reformateurs
2.6 URP Majorité

3.1 Sozialistesch Letzeburger Archechterpartei
3.2 Sozialdemokratesch Partei
3.3 Demokratesch Partei
3.4 Kroestlichsozial Vollekspartei

4.1 Socialistes/Socialisten
4.2 Front des Francophones, Rassemblement Walloon
4.3 Libéraux/Liberalen
4.4 Volksunie
4.5 Sociaux-Chrétiens/Katholieken

5.1 Partij van de Arbeid
5.2 D'66, PSP, PPR
5.3 Demokratieke Socialisten
5.4 Katholieke Volkspartij
5.5 Volkspartij voor Vrijheid en Demokratie
5.6 Anti-Revolutionere Partij
5.7 Christelijke Historische Unie

6.1 Sozialdemokratische Partei
6.2 Freie Demokratische Partei
6.3 Christlich Demokratische Union/Christlich Soziale Union

7.1 Socialistisk Folkeparti
7.2 Socialdemokratiet
7.3 Radikale
7.4 Fremskridtspartiet
7.5 Venstre
7.6 Konservative

8.1 Labour
8.2 Welsh/Scottish Nationalists
8.3 Liberal
8.4 Conservative

9.1 Fianna Fail
9.2 Fine Gael
9.3 Labour
9.4 National, The Coalition

Figure 13.2  Location of political parties on a left–right dimension. Numbers indicate the specific political parties as given in the key alongside

position 4. We are comparing a considerably larger number of countries than the two discussed by Barnes and Pierce; and for this broader range of cases the parties of the right show even stronger similarity than those of the left.

The mean left–right location of the various parties seems to fit the political culture model quite well: almost without exception, the parties are placed in precisely the order that an informed member of the given culture would expect. There is even a remarkable degree of *cross-national* agreement on where given types of parties are located. Given individuals may make some rather gross misplacements, but with few exceptions the mean scores correspond to the order in which a journalist or politician would rank them.

We will use these mean scores as an indicator of the given party's 'real' location on the left–right dimension. This enables us to create a party identification variable having interval properties: those who identify with the French Communist Party, for example, receive a score of 2.63; those who identify with the Socialists receive a score of 3.87, Gaullist identifiers receive a score of 7.19 and so on. We then calculate correlation coefficients between this party identification variable and left–right self-placement. The results appear in Table 13.4.

Table 13.4    Relation of Left–Right Self-Placement to Party Identification

| Country | Product-Moment Correlation | N | |
|---|---|---|---|
| Italy | .78[*] | 1337 | (70%)[**] |
| France | .73 | 1319 | (59%) |
| Great Britain | .68 | 1299 | (67%) |
| Luxembourg | .68 | 168 | (51%) |
| Denmark | .61 | 827 | (69%) |
| Germany | .59 | 1203 | (62%) |
| The Netherlands | .56 | 1171 | (80%) |
| Belgium | .54 | 610 | (48%) |
| Switzerland | .45 | 850 | (45%) |
| United States | .33 | 1374 | (70%) |
| Ireland | .19 | 574 | (48%) |

[*]All coefficients are significant above the .99 level.

[**]Proportion of total sample reporting both Left-Right self-placement and party-identification is given in parenthesis.

For purposes of comparison, we have incorporated results from American and Swiss national surveys in Table 13.4. Although a different measuring instrument was used in each of the latter countries, the basic principle is similar: the Swiss respondents were asked to place themselves on a left–right scale ranging from 0 to 100, while the Americans placed themselves on a seven-category scale ranging from 'extremely liberal' to 'extremely conservative'. In the latter case, the question was worded as follows:

> We hear a lot of talk these days about liberals and conservatives. I'm going to show you a seven-point scale on which the political views that people might hold are arranged from extremely liberal to extremely conservative [show card] . Where would you place yourself on this scale, or haven't you thought much about this?

Ireland stands out as a deviant case once again in Table 13.4, with a product-moment correlation far below that found in any other country. The United States ranks next above Ireland, but the correlation here is a respectable 0.33. In the other nine nations the figures range from a low of 0.45 for Switzerland to a high of 0.78 for Italy. The latter correlations are remarkably strong for survey data. They are not surprising, of course, for we hypothesized that one's self-location on the left-right dimension is often simply a reflection of where one perceives one's favourite political party to be located. The strength of these relationships is not greatly affected when they are calculated in other ways—for example, with party identification dichotomized according to conventional left-right labels. And the results accord with previous findings: Converse and Pierce (1973, p.12) found correlation coefficients ranging from 0.65 to 0.75 in an analysis of French data; and Barnes (1971, p.165) reports a correlation of 0.65 for Italian data. We will subject our findings to further scrutiny below; thus far the data suggest that partisan preference is, indeed, a major meaning component of the left-right dimension.

## THE IDEOLOGICAL COMPONENT OF THE LEFT-RIGHT DIMENSION

It is more difficult to assess the issue-based component of the left-right dimension than the partisan component. It is easy to draw up a complete list of the political parties in a given society; it is more difficult to list all the important political issues, for they are numerous and often fleeting (reasons why we would expect them to provide a relatively faint cue for mass publics). Moreover, key issues may vary from one society to another, making cross-national comparison difficult. And issues change not only in saliency; they may even change polarity in relation to the left-right dimension. For example, it has been argued that the essence of the left-right dimension lies in disagreements over the scope of government intervention in the economy (Downs, 1957). This notion has not held up very well: a few decades ago, emphasis on centralized controls and planning, in the hands of a strong executive branch, certainly *was* associated with the left; today the left often takes the lead in resisting excessive centralization of power. Similarly, nationalism has traditionally been associated with the right and internationalism with the left. In contemporary American politics, withdrawal from foreign entanglements tends to be supported by liberals at least as much as by conservatives; and on the European scene, opposition to European integration may be becoming linked with the left as much as with the right.

Despite evidence that there has been a change in the issue content of the left-right dimension, we believe that it is possible to identify a persistent and pervasive theme. Lipset *et al.* (1954) have proposed a definition that seems to capture it:

> By Left we shall mean advocating social change in the direction of greater

equality—political, economic, or social; by Right we shall mean supporting a traditional, more or less hierarchical social order, and opposing change toward greater equality. [p.1135]

The salience of *economic* equality may have declined somewhat in recent years, but the left remains characteristically the advocate of change aimed at greater equality, stressing the importance of participation on an equal footing in political and social life. Conversely, the right is characterized by its emphasis on hierarchical order, justifying the hierarchy established in a given society on the grounds that it is an essential defence against the disorders that criminals, dissenters or foreign enemies might bring. Laponce concludes that the left-right concept is cognitively defined by an underlying dimension of authority, either social or metaphysical, stressing the religious, as well as secular, meaning of authority (Laponce, 1972). In a recent enquiry into the political vocabulary of French schoolchildren, Percheron (1973) found that those who responded favourably to the term 'right' also gave relatively positive ratings to 'order' and 'authority', and rejected possible sources of disorder such as strikes and demonstrations; leftists showed an opposite tendency. This opposition between equality and order seems to be a perennial feature of political life, for it reflects a dilemma inherent in politics: the fact that the definitive function of the State is to maintain a monopoly of legitimate power, coupled with the fact that those who control the means of power are *ipso facto* in a position to obtain a very unequal share of whatever is valued in that society.

The 1973 European surveys were not designed to measure attitudes towards the key current issues in each country. Nevertheless, they do provide a set of items that can help us to identify the order versus equality dimension. These items are drawn from a series of questions intended to tap various value domains. Respondents in each of the nine countries were asked to rank the following societal goals (among a set of twelve possibilities):

(1) Seeing that people have more say about how things are done at their jobs and in their communities.
(2) Giving people more say in important government decisions.
(3) Maintaining order in the nation.
(4) The fight against crime.

The first two items focus on support for socioeconomic and political equality, while the third and fourth tend to tap relative emphasis on preserving the hierarchical order of the respective nations. These items contain no explicit reference to a metaphysical aspect of authority; but their face content suggests that they should provide at least a rough indicator of the ideological content of left and right. And the items are cross-nationally uniform—an important advantage for present purposes.

The respondents in the nine European Community nations seem to have had no particular difficulty in answering these items, and the responses show a coherent pattern that is remarkably consistent cross-nationally. In every national sample, high priority for the first two items tends to go together, and to go with *low* priority for the third and fourth items. Furthermore, each of these items has the expected polarity with left–right self-placement in each of the nine countries; the strength of the correlations is modest (ranging from 0.04 to 0.30) but the polarities are in the expected direction without exception.

We have argued that these items should provide an indicator of a key ideological theme involved in the left-right dimension. This argument implies that they should share some variance. Factor analysis is a convenient method to extract the shared variance: we used factor analysis to create a new variable representing the overlapping variance. To allow some country-specific variation in the internal weight of the four items, factor scores were calculated country by country. The percentage of total variance explained by the left-right ideology factor averaged 19 per cent, ranging from a low of 15 per cent in Belgium to a high of 21 per cent in The Netherlands and France. These figures are not high in any absolute sense, and may be taken as simply one more indication of the modest degree of constraint generally prevailing in the belief systems of mass publics. But these items show a relatively clear structure by comparison with other items available in the same surveys—particularly when we bear in mind the fact that they are asked in a forced-choice format which eliminates inflated correlations owing to response set.

Only the second and third of the four items listed above were included in the American and Swiss surveys (which were carried out a year earlier). Experimentation with data from the nine other countries indicated that it was possible to use the rankings of these two items to create an index that correlated very strongly (at the 0.6 or 0.7 level) with the four-item index. For purposes of approximate comparison, we constructed such indices for the American and Swiss respondents.

Our next step was to calculate the correlations between our respective ideological preference indices and left-right self-placement (or liberal-conservative self-placement) for each of the eleven countries. The strength of the relationship is shown in Table 13.5.

Table 13.5   Relation of Left–Right Self-Placement to Left–Right Ideology Index

| Country | Product-Moment Correlation | N |
|---|---|---|
| France | .35[**] | 1744 |
| Luxembourg | .33 | 256 |
| Italy | .32 | 1580 |
| United States | .27 | 745[*] |
| Denmark | .26 | 1092 |
| The Netherlands | .26 | 1356 |
| Britain | .22 | 1591 |
| Germany | .20 | 1819 |
| Switzerland | .12 | 865 |
| Ireland | .12 | 955 |
| Belgium | .10 | 929 |

[*]The ideology items were administered to half of the respondents in the CPS 1972 election survey.

[**]All coefficients are significant above the .99 level.

The left-right dimension *does* seem to have a significant ideological component in each of the European countries, and so does its analogue in the United States. This component is clearly weakest in Belgium and Ireland (a pattern that is by now familiar) but it rises to moderately high levels elsewhere. A comparison of Tables 13.4 and 13.5 shows a striking contrast, however: the partisan component is stronger than the ideological component in all eleven countries. For most countries the correlations with partisanship are at least twice as large as the correlations with the ideological indicator, and in some instances the ratio is considerably higher. But in the United States—and only in the United States—the ideological component is almost as strong as the partisan component. This is not because the American public makes an unusually strong connection between these attitudes and self-placement on an ideological continuum—this correlation is only a trifle above the median figure for Europe. It results from the fact that the liberal-conservative dimension has a reasonably strong ideological component and an unusually weak partisan component among the American public.

Our ideological indices provide a more or less standardized measure that enables us to compare the relative impact of ideology across eleven nations. But it is only a rough measure: it seems highly plausible that nation-specific indices, directly based on the most salient current issues in the given society, might show stronger correlations with the left-right self-placement. The question is, how *much* stronger? Data from surveys that *were* designed to cover the major current issues of the given society give us at least a partial answer. Thus, although our ideology index has a correlation of 0.27 with liberal-conservative self-placement among the American public, Miller *et al.* (1976) report that a set of thirteen key issues in the 1972 presidential campaign had a mean correlation of 0.31 with liberal-conservative self-placement. We must bear in mind the fact that these data were gathered during one of the most ideologically polarized electoral campaigns in recent American history—a fact that probably tends to maximize the strength of issue correlations. In the Swiss setting, on the other hand, where elections usually are *not* polarized, the most salient current issues tend to tap a nativist-cosmopolitan dimension which is virtually unrelated to left-right self-placement (Inglehart and Sidjanski, Chapter 12 above). In the Swiss data, only a few items which relate directly to questions of authority and order (attitudes toward student demonstrations, for example) show substantial correlations with left-right self-placement. Switzerland is a special case, however. In general we expect that the key nation-specific issues probably would produce stronger correlations with the left-right dimension than an ideological index does—but it seems extremely doubtful that the strength of this relationship would compare with that of party preference in the European countries. What evidence is available clearly supports this conclusion (Barnes, 1971; Barnes and Pierce, 1971; Klingemann, 1972; Kaase, 1974).

We have just evaluated left-right self-location as an ideological concept using one particular measure of constraint. Lane has recently criticized this approach, arguing that: 'The mistake underlying reliance on the constraints implied by statistical clustering, scalar ordering or acceptance of an idea clustering by an authoritative elite is based on the fallacious view that if some people see idea-elements properly clustering in a certain way, others should, too' (Lane, 1973, p.103).

This criticism applies if the focus of inquiry is directed toward *private* reasoning processes, leading to individual solutions of the problem of what goes with what and why (Converse, 1964, p.212). We do not doubt that given terms may have rich and complex meanings in the private worlds of given individuals; indeed, Lane himself has demonstrated that they often do (Lane, 1962). But for present purposes we are interested in constraint as an indicator of ideology, not as a sort of IQ test. And for this purpose the *public* meaning component of left and right is most relevant. Lane does not argue that concepts may not also have a public meaning component; on the contrary, there would be no means of interpersonal communication if concepts did not have a shared meaning within a given culture.

Publics learn and understand given cultural models to varying degrees. The evidence indicates that, whereas the partisan preference component of the meaning of the left–right concept seems to be internalized by most people who participate in politics, the ideological meaning component is much less widely shared. We can safely conclude that the former is the dominant meaning component of left and right as far as Western publics as a *whole* are concerned—except, perhaps, in the United States. But another important qualification must be made once we begin to differentiate according to levels of political cognition.

## VARIATION BY LEVELS OF POLITICAL COGNITION

We have argued that an ideological understanding of the left–right dimension demands relatively great cognitive effort, while this dimension's partisan implications may, in given cultures, be almost effortless. Accordingly, we hypothesize that the importance of the former component will vary with the degree to which the individual is motivated and intellectually equipped to deal with political abstractions; whereas the latter component will be about equally important across all strata of the population.

In order to test this hypothesis, we need to measure the respondent's level of what we will call political cognition. The literature suggests that one's likelihood of using relatively abstract and general concepts to orient oneself towards politics varies with the respondent's level of formal education and degree of political involvement (Campbell, *et al.* pp.250–6; Converse, 1964, pp.224–7; Klingemann, 1973, Table 7). Our measure of political involvement is based on response to the question:

When you get together with your friends do you ever discuss political matters? (If 'Yes'): Which of the statements on this card best describes the part you, yourself, take in these discussion? [The alternatives appear in Table 13.6.]

As one would expect, active political discussion is linked with the respondent's level of formal education in a consistent and significant degree. We combined these two variables in the manner indicated in Table 13.6 to produce an index of political cognition. Overall, 20 per cent of our European respondents fall into the 'high' category, 39 per cent rank in the 'medium' level, and 41 per cent are classified as having a 'low' level of political cognition by these criteria. Distributions vary somewhat from country to country: in Germany, Luxembourg, Denmark and The

Table 13.6    Construction of Political Cognition Index

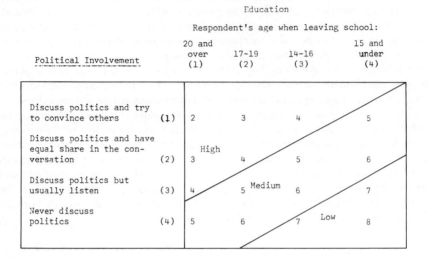

Both variables were scored 1 to 4.

Netherlands only 30 to 37 per cent of the samples fall into the 'low' category; in Belgium and Italy, respectively, 51 and 54 per cent do so.

We are now in a position to test our hypothesis, having calculated the correlations between our respondents' scores on the ideology index and left-right

Table 13.7    Relationship Between Left–Right Self-Placement and Left–Right Ideology Index, by Respondent's Level of Political Cognition
(Product-Moment Correlations)

| Country | High Political Cognition | | | Medium Political Cognition | | | Low Political Cognition | | |
|---|---|---|---|---|---|---|---|---|---|
| | r | N | | r | N | | r | N | |
| France | .50 | 423 | (24%) | .29 | 622 | (36%) | .25 | 699 | (40%) |
| Italy | .46 | 273 | (17%) | .36 | 512 | (32%) | .18 | 795 | (51%) |
| Denmark | .44 | 255 | (23%) | .22 | 448 | (41%) | .20 | 389 | (36%) |
| Luxembourg | .46 | 87 | (34%) | .23* | 112 | (44%) | .19** | 57 | (22%) |
| The Netherlands | .36 | 299 | (22%) | .24 | 577 | (42%) | .23 | 480 | (36%) |
| Great Britain | .27 | 236 | (15%) | .22 | 704 | (44%) | .19 | 651 | (41%) |
| Germany | .27 | 419 | (23%) | .21 | 856 | (47%) | .06** | 544 | (30%) |
| Belgium | .23 | 194 | (21%) | .10** | 323 | (35%) | .03** | 412 | (44%) |
| Ireland | .12** | 176 | (18%) | .08** | 450 | (47%) | .18 | 329 | (35%) |

*= not significant above the .99 level.    **= not significant above the .95 level.

self-placement—the same procedure as was used for Table 13.5 except that this time we stratified by level of political cognition. Table 13.7 shows the results. The first half of our hypothesis is confirmed in every country except (once again) Ireland; and in most instances the differences across levels of political cognition are very handsome indeed. In France, for example, the correlation rises from 0.25 among those 'low' on political cognition to a remarkable 0.50 among those 'high' on this variable. These findings certainly tend to justify Converse's emphasis on the need to stratify along the political cognition dimension when studying ideology (Converse, 1964, 1974). For the relatively politicized and educated 20 per cent of our respondents, the ideological component of the left–right dimension has impressive strength. But it tends to fade out among publics with a low level of political cognition.

It remains to test the second half of our hypothesis. Table 13.8 presents the relevant data. On the whole, the pattern again fits our expectations. There is

Table 13.8    Relationship Between Left–Right Self-Placement and Party Identification by Respondent's Level of Political Cognition

(Product-Moment Correlations)

| Country | High Political Cognition | | | Medium Political Cognition | | | Low Political Cognition | | |
|---|---|---|---|---|---|---|---|---|---|
| | r | N | | r | N | | r | N | |
| Italy | .87 | 239 | (18%) | .78 | 437 | (33%) | .74 | 661 | (49%) |
| France | .80 | 339 | (26%) | .70 | 475 | (36%) | .71 | 505 | (38%) |
| Great Britain | .77 | 185 | (14%) | .68 | 572 | (44%) | .65 | 542 | (42%) |
| Denmark | .75 | 192 | (23%) | .64 | 331 | (40%) | .48 | 304 | (37%) |
| Germany | .68 | 313 | (26%) | .59 | 555 | (46%) | .52 | 335 | (28%) |
| Luxembourg | .66 | 53 | (31%) | .72 | 72 | (43%) | .68 | 43 | (26%) |
| The Netherlands | .62 | 273 | (23%) | .51 | 498 | (43%) | .61 | 400 | (34%) |
| Belgium | .54 | 125 | (20%) | .60 | 213 | (35%) | .52 | 272 | (45%) |
| Ireland | .31 | 106 | (18%) | .23 | 282 | (49%) | .04[**] | 186 | (33%) |

** = not significant above the .95 level.

relatively little change in the strength of correlations between party identification and left–right self-placement as we move away from those having a high level of political cognition to those having a low level. Setting Ireland aside, the mean correlation among those high on political cognition is 0.71; among those low on political cognition it is 0.61; The corresponding figures for the ideology index are 0.37 and 0.17. The partisan meaning component of the left–right dimension is shared by almost all members of European societies; an ideological component supplements this meaning chiefly among those trained and motivated to deal with political matters.

An examination of the means and standard deviations among those who identify with the various parties, stratified by level of political cognition, gives further support to the interpretation that partisan preference is a uniformly shared meaning component. Regardless of level of political cognition, those who identify with a specific party place themselves very similarly on the left–right continuum. Nor do the standard deviations increase dramatically with decreasing level of political cognition: the sense of location is about as sharply focused among the less politicized as among the more politicized.

Since we do not have identical measures of political cognition for our Swiss and American respondents, they are not included in Tables 13.7 and 13.8. We were able to calculate roughly comparable correlations, however, stratifying by the respondent's level of education. The pattern that emerges from the Swiss survey is very similar to what we find for the European countries other than Ireland. But the American results contain one most interesting peculiarity: the correlations with liberal-conservative self-placement increase with education for *both* the ideological component *and* the partisan component. The latter correlation rises from 0.21 among those who have no more than a tenth-grade education to 0.41 among those who have attended college. We believe that this anomaly and the relative weakness of the partisan component among American respondents with lower levels of political cognition spring from the same source: the fact that American political parties have not traditionally been labelled 'liberal' or 'conservative' in the same clear and time-honoured fashion in which most European parties have been labelled 'left' or 'right'. This, in turn, grows out of a number of factors peculiar to the American polity, including the fact that that country has the closest approximation to a pure two-party system among the eleven nations sampled here—hence, there has been relatively little need for an abstract party-space dimension. Ideological polarization is relatively recent among the American mass public (although Stokes [1963] suggests that it may have reached a high level during the period of the Civil War). In 1972 it threatened to break down established party loyalties, but the appropriate ideological labels were not yet part of everyone's intellectual baggage.

## SOCIAL CLASS, RELIGION AND THE LEFT–RIGHT DIMENSION

Our exploration of the left–right dimension would not be complete without at least a brief examination of its relationship to key social background factors. Moreover, we would be left uncertain as to whether the major role that we have attributed to party loyalties were genuine or spurious.

Among the possible sources of a spurious relationship between party preference and left–right placement, social class is probably the first thing that comes to mind. Do people place themselves on the left *and* support a left-wing party because they belong to the working class (or the reverse, if they are middle-class)? The hypothesis is at least plausible. Several indicators of social class are available and we will use three of them in our analysis—family income, respondent's level of education and trade union membership. Table 13.9 shows the relationship between each of these variables and left–right self-placement. The correlations are astonishingly feeble. The assumption that class conflict is the central variable underlying the left–right dimension can be rejected for every country under consideration. The public concept of left and right may have been based on social class conflict once; it is no longer. The *best* of the three social class indicators, trade union membership, shows relationships to the left–right dimension that are far weaker than those associated with our ideological index—to say nothing of the partisan component. Trade union membership explains at *best* three per cent of the variance (in Denmark); in many cases it explains virtually nothing. Indeed, the social class relationships are so weak that one wonders if some other measure might do a better job. Occupational codings were not standardized cross-nationally, so initially we did not use this variable. Searching for *some* reasonably strong indicator, we examined the relationship between left-right self-placement and the respondent's occupation and that of the head of household. These variables did no better than the results shown in Table 13.9. In an analysis of French data, Converse and Pierce report that even the most potent combined index of social status that they were able to construct did not account for as much as 4 per cent of the variance in left-right partisan preference (Converse and Pierce, 1973, p.15). We conclude that the relationship between social class and left-right political location really is astonishingly weak.

Table 13.9   Social Class Indicators and Left–Right Self-Placement
(Product-Moment Correlations)

| Country | Family Income | Respondent's Education | Union Membership |
|---|---|---|---|
| Denmark | -.01 ** | .00 ** | .18 |
| Italy | -.02 ** | -.07 | .16 |
| Great Britain | -.01 ** | .08 | .14 |
| Luxembourg | .02 ** | -.12 ** | .14 * |
| France | -.02 ** | -.12 | .13 |
| Germany | .01 ** | -.09 | .12 |
| Belgium | .08 * | -.03 ** | .08 * |
| The Netherlands | .16 | .02 ** | .05 *** |
| Ireland | -.05 ** | -.01 ** | .04 ** |
| Switzerland | *** | .01 ** | .05 ** |
| United States | .08 * | .08 | .05 ** |

*= not significant above the .99 level.

**= not significant above the .95 level.

***= This variable not available in Swiss data.

Family income was scored 1 (low) to 6 (high).

Education was operationalized as year left school; scores run from 1 (low) to 4 (high).

Trade-union membership is scored 1 (member) and 2 (non-member).

On the other hand, the relationship with religious practice is surprisingly strong. The fact that relatively frequent church attendance tends to go with

266

Table 13.10   Religious Denominations and Left–Right Self-Placement: Summary Statistics

| Country | No Religious Denomination | | | Protestant Denominations | | | Catholic Denomination | | |
|---|---|---|---|---|---|---|---|---|---|
| | x̄ | s | N | x̄ | s | N | x̄ | s | N |
| Italy | 2.56 | 2.03 | 81 | * | * | * | 4.81 | 2.24 | 1495 |
| Ireland | 5.07 | 3.32 | 14 | * | * | * | 6.30 | 2.54 | 906 |
| Luxembourg | 2.96 | 1.14 | 25 | * | * | * | 5.69 | 1.87 | 230 |
| France | 3.37 | 2.03 | 219 | * | * | * | 5.32 | 2.20 | 1459 |
| Belgium | 4.17 | 2.16 | 157 | * | * | * | 5.98 | 2.42 | 760 |
| Germany | 4.53 | 2.25 | 86 | 5.47 | 2.08 | 973 | 5.96 | 2.26 | 746 |
| The Netherlands | 4.66 | 2.43 | 528 | 6.13<br>7.72 | 2.44<br>-.87 | 259**<br>102*** | 6.57 | 2.35 | 432 |
| Great Britain | 4.78 | 2.29 | 397 | 5.60<br>5.61<br>6.11 | 2.38<br>2.54<br>2.34 | 110**<br>749***<br>103**** | 4.99 | 2.40 | 157 |
| Denmark | 4.67 | 2.00 | 167 | 5.53 | 1.89 | 919 | * | * | * |

* too few cases.

The Netherlands: **Hervormd; ***Gereformeerd.

Great Britain: **Free Church/Non-Conformists; ***Church of England; ****Church of Scotland.

Table 13.11  Frequency of Church Attendance and Left–Right Self-Placement

| Country | At least once a week | | | Sometimes during the year | | | Never | | |
|---|---|---|---|---|---|---|---|---|---|
| | $\bar{x}$ | s | N | $\bar{x}$ | s | N | $\bar{x}$ | s | N |
| Ireland | 6.34 | 2.50 | 883 | 6.32 | 2.82 | 44 | 5.04 | 2.97 | 28 |
| Luxembourg | 6.10 | 1.81 | 115 | 5.82 | 1.48 | 80 | 3.64 | 1.82 | 61 |
| Italy | 5.18 | 2.06 | 747 | 4.56 | 2.26 | 592 | 3.48 | 2.55 | 241 |
| Belgium | 6.53 | 2.30 | 366 | 5.75 | 2.40 | 231 | 4.67 | 2.34 | 332 |
| The Netherlands | 7.27 | 2.16 | 446 | 5.96 | 2.30 | 273 | 4.71 | 2.41 | 637 |
| Germany | 6.59 | 2.14 | 395 | 5.64 | 2.05 | 829 | 4.98 | 2.16 | 595 |
| France | 6.25 | 1.98 | 337 | 5.48 | 2.20 | 670 | 4.11 | 2.09 | 737 |
| Great Britain | 5.93 | 2.42 | 246 | 5.68 | 2.45 | 612 | 4.93 | 2.41 | 733 |
| Denmark | 6.06 | 2.00 | 48 | 5.79 | 1.84 | 508 | 4.98 | 1.92 | 536 |

conservative political preference in Europe has been abundantly noted in the literature. Yet one might expect that, given the remarkable extent to which the social class component of left and right seems to have faded out, the still older clerical–anti-clerical component might have faded even more. Our data indicate that this is far from true.

Our respondents were asked two questions concerning religion: (1) what denomination they belonged to, if any; (2) how often they attended church, if at all. The latter variable is the more useful on two counts: it is more uniform, cross-nationally; and it accounts for more variance in left–right self-placement. Tables 13.10 and 13.11 give summary statistics concerning the distribution of our respondents on the left–right dimension according to the two religious variables. The data hold few surprises.

As Table 13.10 indicates, practising Catholics place themselves to the right of non-practising Catholics or Protestants—except that in The Netherlands, the Gereformeerd, or conservative Calvinists, are to the right of any other group; and in Britain Catholics are to the left of Protestants. As Table 13.11 shows, there are no exceptions whatever to the rule that the more frequently a given denomination group attends church, the farther to the right it places itself. The variation according to church attendance is not only remarkably consistent, but rather impressive in size. We conclude that differentiation along the left–right dimension is not linked to particular religious denominations but to religiosity versus secularism.

Table 13.12 shows the correlation coefficients associated with frequency of church attendance. The figures are quite substantial in most cases, apart from Ireland. In the Irish case there is almost no variance left with respect to the

Table 13.12   Relation of Frequency of Church Attendance to Left–Right Self-Placement

| Country | Product-Moment Correlation |
|---|---|
| Luxembourg | .46[*] |
| The Netherlands | .44 |
| France | .37 |
| Belgium | .33 |
| Germany | .26 |
| Italy | .25 |
| Switzerland | .25 |
| Denmark | .21 |
| United States | .17 |
| Great Britain | .16 |
| Ireland | .08 |

*All coefficients are significant above the .99 level

independent variable, for an amazing 91 per cent of the sample claim to go to church at least once a week—making them by far the most devout of our various publics, but leaving little room for religiosity to explain anything.

A comparison of Table 13.4 and Table 13.12 indicates that, although the relationships with church attendance are impressive in many instances, the partisan component is stronger in every country for which we have data—and usually by a substantial margin. A comparison of Table 13.5 and Table 13.12 gives mixed results: in five countries the figures associated with our ideology index are stronger than those associated with religious practice; in five other countries the reverse is true; and in one country (France) the two are about equally strong.

As a rule of thumb, one might say that church attendance outweighs ideology only in those countries that have important Christian Democratic parties. This explanation is gratifyingly simple: the link between religion and politics is more obvious to the public in countries where there are explicitly church-linked political parties. There is only one exception to the rule: Italy, which has a powerful Christian Democratic party but a relatively weak link between church attendance and left-right self-placement. France is a marginal case: the two components are of about equal strength—in a country that formerly had (but no longer has) a major Christian Democratic party.

Multiple regression analyses confirm what is already fairly obvious: that the partisan component of left-right self-placement is not spurious; it seems to be a powerful independent influence. These analyses also reveal another interesting fact: for those with a high level of cognition, the ideology index has more impact on left-right self-placement than does church attendance; this holds true everywhere except in the Benelux countries. Among those with a *low* level of cognition, church attendance accounts for more variance everywhere except in Ireland.

The overall pattern is clear. The evidence supports Laponce's claim that the left-right dimension reflects one's orientation to metaphysical as well as social order.

## CONCLUSIONS

As hypothesized, among European publics one's sense of belonging to the left or right reflects party affiliations more than issue preferences. Left-right self-placement corresponds very closely to political party identification everywhere except in Ireland. Since party identification tends to be established early in life, it is difficult to view it as a *result* of left-right self-placement; it seems more plausible to conclude either that the two are acquired simultaneously, or that left-right orientations are derivative from party identification. Longitudinal data would be required in order to pin down the precise sequence. Religious affiliations are a secondary component of left-right self-placement, especially in countries where certain parties have explicit religious ties.

The classical view of the left-right dimension as primarily a super-issue seems largely untenable for Europe. For one thing, the partisan component seems to be much stronger than the ideological component. Furthermore, the ideological component is markedly stronger among the more politicized strata—which is precisely what we would expect of an issue-based orientation; while the partisan component is about equally strong across all strata—an indication that it reflects conventional culturally given labels, rather than a response to current issues.

This does *not* mean that the left–right dimension lacks ideological content. On the contrary, our data shows some impressive relationships with one's orientation toward order versus equality; these relationships are relatively weak in Ireland, Belgium and Switzerland, three countries preoccupied with questions of national identity. They are strongest in France and Italy, the classic examples of polarized multi-party systems. Nevertheless, the ideological component tends to be greatly overshadowed by the partisan component everywhere except in the United States.

The left–right dimension seems to have a relatively unclear meaning for the Irish public. Both the partisan and the ideological component are weak in Ireland, our persistent deviant case. The poorest and the most heavily rural of our eleven countries, Ireland is still, in a sense, pre-industrial. With a two-and-one-half-party system, Ireland has had little need for an abstract continuum in order to interpret party distances or ideological cleavages. Her politics were rooted in the Irish Question: for decades the main bone of contention between her two dominant parties was whether the independence settlement that partitioned Ireland should have been accepted or not. She remained relatively little influenced by the ideological currents that swept through other Western publics during the Great Depression, The Second World War and the explosive economic development of the postwar decades. With Irish entry into the Common Market, new issues may begin to impinge on her politics at an increasing rate; as of 1973, however, the Irish public did not have any very clear basis for left–right orientation.

Belgium and Switzerland resemble each other in some respects. Both are economically developed countries in which there is a strong traditional meaning attached to left and right, persisting through linkage with party labels. But their contemporary politics tend to be dominated by questions of national identity, which are difficult to assimilate to a left–right dimension: does a populist type of nationalist belong on the extreme right? In the aftermath of the Second World War, such a self-placement is likely to seem unpalatable; yet the extreme left is presumably pre-empted by the Communists and the centre by Establishment. The fact that rather clear traditional labels are *already* attached to various areas of the left–right spectrum tends to hinder positioning oneself on this dimension according to current policy preferences.

In the seven other European countries, both the ideological and the partisan components of the left–right dimension are relatively strong, above all in France and Italy—multi-party systems with strong Communist parties—in which the left–right concept has long been salient. The dimension is somewhat weaker in Germany and Britain, which might be described as two-and-one-half party systems. The Danish and Dutch cases fall at roughly the same level, however: since the latter are multi-party systems, it would seem that the intensity of polarization is more important than the number of parties in determining the salience of the left–right dimension.

In all of the above cases except Ireland, the partisan component accounts for at least four times as much variance in left–right self-placement as does the ideological component. In the United States the two components are of almost equal strength: liberal–conservative self-placement is relatively weakly tied to partisan continuity, but has a rather strong ideological component.

It is tempting to equate the liberal–conservative dimension in the United States with the left–right dimension in Europe—and there certainly is an analogy. But these dimensions have quite different political implications. The American version seems to reflect a rather exceptional situation—the emergence of a *newly* ideological public. For reasons suggested above, the American dimension is relatively unencumbered with partisan attachments in some circumstances. At the time of the 1972 presidential election, liberal–conservative self-placement had a 0.33 correlation with party identification, and a 0.47 correlation with presidential vote. One's position on this dimension was more strongly linked with short-term forces than with partisan tradition—and, indeed, can be used to explain substantial deviations from normal voting patterns. To be specific, liberal–conservative self-placement had a relatively moderate impact on Republican party-identifiers (the great bulk of whom voted for Nixon regardless of ideology): 78 per cent of those Republicans who located themselves on the 'liberal' side of the scale voted for Nixon, as compared with 96 per cent of the 'conservative' Republicans. But among Democratic party-identifiers, one's position on the liberal–conservative dimension had a devastating impact: a bare 16 per cent of the 'liberals' voted for Nixon—as compared with 48 per cent of the 'middle-of-the-road' group and 69 per cent of the 'conservatives'. To a great extent, the shattering of the Democratic Party in 1972 seems to reflect an ideological cleavage among the American public.

If a public is strongly polarized along an axis that cuts across established party loyalties, an ideological dimension may emerge which (like the liberal–conservative dimension in 1972) leads to the fragmentation of existing parties. Given its much stronger partisan component, the left-right dimension in a country like France may play a different but equally important role: it may serve as a surrogate for party identification. For in France, left–right self-placement is to party identification as party identification is to current party preference. Party identification seems to be weaker than in the United States. Important parties have changed their labels repeatedly or disappeared altogether in the last few decades. When this happens, an underlying sense of left-right location seems to provide an important cue in channelling voters from their former party to the nearest equivalent among the new ones. Thus, in the 1974 French presidential election, Valery Giscard d'Estaing inherited the great bulk of a crumbling Gaullist constituency, although he did not bear the Gaullist label and had never been a member of the Gaullist party (under any of its various names). For he *was* generally perceived as the candidate of the right or centre–right (Campbell, 1974); affiliation with this broad political family, together with a favourable personal image, enabled him to win a narrow victory over François Mitterand, who strove to emphasize his image as candidate of the left, rather than his ties with any political party.

Survey data indicate that the French electorate behaved pretty much as would be predicted by a left–right model. Mitterand was supported by 87 per cent of the Socialist electorate, which is not surprising, since he was the leader of the party. But he won an even *larger* share (97 per cent) of the votes of the Communist electorate. This *would* be surprising if one were thinking in terms of party loyalty: one would generally expect a candidate to win more support from his own party than from another, even if the two were allied. But the pattern is perfectly comprehensible in terms of an underlying left–right dimension: on this dimension the Communists are located at the extreme left—and a Socialist candidate is much closer to them than a candidate of the centre–right. Yet a certain portion of the Socialist electorate might, quite conceivably, see themselves as relatively close to a candidate like Giscard.

272

Conversely, the electorate of the right behaved like a mirror image of the left: Giscard was supported by 79 per cent of the centrist Reform Movement's electorate, and (despite a bitter first-round contest with a duly anointed Gaullist) by 90 per cent of the Gaullist electorate (IFOP, 1974, p.62).

The role of abstract dimensions of political competition such as left–right or liberal–conservative varies from one society to another. Representing a relatively high level of generalization, such dimensions are not always part of a mass public's outlook. Yet they provide a valuable tool for the interpretation of politics when group loyalties or party identification break down or become irrelevant. We suggest that they deserve high priority among the variables to be used for the study of long-term political change.

## REFERENCES

Barnes, Samuel H. (1971), 'Left–Right and the Italian Voter', *Comparative Political Studies*, 4, 157–75.

Barnes, Samuel H., and Roy Pierce (1971), 'Public Opinion and Political Preferences in France and Italy', *Midwest Journal of Political Science*, 15, 643–60.

Butler, David, and Donald Stokes (1969), *Political Change in Britain*, Macmillan, London.

Campbell, Angus, Philip E. Converse, Warren E. Miller and Donald E. Stokes (1960), *The American Voter*, Wiley, New York.

Campbell, Bruce A. (1974), 'On the Prospects of Polarization in French Electoral Competition', paper presented at the annual meeting of the Western Political Science Association, Denver, Colorado.

Converse, Philip E. (1964), 'The Nature of Belief Systems in Mass Publics', in David A. Apter (ed.), *Ideology and Discontent*, Free Press, New York.

Converse, Philip E. (1968), 'Some Priority Variables in Comparative Research', in Otto Stammer (ed.), *Party Systems, Party Organizations, and Politics of the New Masses*, Free University, Berlin.

Converse, Philip E., and Roy Pierce (1973), 'Basic Cleavages in French Politics and the Disorders of May and June, 1968', in Richard Rose (ed.), *Political Behaviour in Western Societies*, Wiley, New York.

Converse, Philip E. (1974), 'Public Opinion and Voting Behavior', in F. I. Greenstein and N. W. Polsby (eds.), *The Handbook of Political Science*, (Vol. 6), Addison-Wesley, Reading, Mass.

Deutsch, Emeric, Denis Lindon and Pierre Weill (1966), *Les Familles Politiques*, Les Editions de Minuit, Paris.

Downs, Anthony (1957), *An Economic Theory of Democracy*, Harper and Row, New York.

Huyse, L. (1970), *Passiviteit, Pacificatie on Verzuiling in de Belgische Politiek*, Standaard Wetenschappelijke Uitgeverij, Antwerpen.

IFOP (1974), 'Presidential election survey', reported in *Le Point*, 13 May, 1974.

Inglehart, Ronald, and Avram Hochstein (1972), 'Alignment and Dealignment of the Electorate in France and the United States', *Comparative Political Studies*, 5, 343–72.

Inglehart, Ronald (1973), 'Industrial, Pre-Industrial and Post-Industrial Political Cleavages in Western Europe and the United States', paper presented to the annual meeting of the American Political Science Association, New Orleans, 4–8 September 1973.

Kaase, Max (1974), 'Political Ideology, Dissatisfaction and Protest: A Micro Theory of Unconventional Political Behavior', *German Political Studies*, (forthcoming).

Klingemann, Hans D. (1972), 'Testing the Left–Right Continuum on a Sample of German Voters', *Comparative Political Studies*, 5, 93–106.

Klingemann, Hans D. (1973), 'Dimensions of Political Belief Systems and Levels of Conceptualization as a Variable: Some results for USA and FRG 1968/69', paper presented at the ECPR Workshop on Political Behavior, Dissatisfaction and Protest, University of Mannheim.

Klingemann, Hans D., and Franz Urban Pappi (1972), *Politischer Radikalismus*, Oldenbourg, München-Wien.

Lane, Robert E. (1962), *Political Ideology*, Free Press, New York.

273

Lane, Robert E. (1973), 'Patterns of Political Belief', in Jeanne M. Knutson (ed.), *Handbook of Political Psychology*, Jossey-Bass, San Francisco.

Laponce, Jean A. (1970), 'Note on the Use of the Left–Right Dimension', *Comparative Political Studies*, 3, *481*–502.

Laponce, Jean A. (1972), 'In Search of Stable Elements of the Left–Right Landscape', *Comparative Politics*, 4, 455–76.

Lijphart, Arend (1969), *The Politics of Accommodation*, University of California Press, Berkeley, California.

Lipset, Seymour M., Paul F. Lazarsfeld, Allen H. Barton, and Juan Linz (1954), 'The Psychology of Voting: An Analysis of Political Behavior', in Gardner Lindzey (ed.), *Handbook of Social Psychology* (Vol. 2), Addison-Wesley, Reading, Mass.

Lipset, Seymour M., and Stein Rokkan (1967), 'Cleavage Structures, Party Systems, and Voter Alignments: An Introduction', in Seymour M. Lipset and Stein Rokkan (eds.), *Party Systems and Voter Alignments: Cross National Perspectives*, Free Press, New York.

Lorwin, Val. R. (1971), 'Segmented Pluralism: Ideological Cleavages and Political Cohesion in the Smaller European Democracies', *Comparative Politics*, 3, 141–75.

Miller, Arthur, H., Warren E. Miller, Alden S. Raine and Thad A. Brown (1976), 'A Majority Party in Disarray: Policy Polarization in the 1972 Election', *American Political Science Review*, 70.

Nie, Norman H. (1974), 'Mass Belief Systems Revisited: Political Change and Attitude Structure', *Journal of Politics* (forthcoming).

Pappi, Franz Urban, and Edward O. Laumann (1974), 'Gesellschaftliche Wertorientierungen und Politisches Verhalten', *Zeitschrift für Soziologie*, 3,157–88.

Percheron, Annick (1973), 'Political Vocabulary and Ideological Proximity in French Children', in Jack Dennis (ed.), *Socialization to Politics: A Reader*, Wiley, New York.

Pomper, Gerald M. (1972), 'From Confusion to Clarity: Issues and American Voters, 1956–1968', *American Political Science Review*, 66, 415–28.

Rose, Richard (1974), 'Comparability in Electoral Studies', in Richard Rose (ed.), *Electoral Behavior: A Comparative Handbook*, Free Press, New York.

Sani, Giacomo (1974), 'A Test of the Least-Distance Model of Voting Choice: Italy 1972', *Comparative Political Studies*, 7, 193–208.

Stokes, Donald E. (1963), 'Spatial Models of Party Competition', *American Political Science Review*, 57, 368–77.

Weil, Gordon L. (1970), *The Benlux Nations: The Politics of Small-Country Democracies*, Holt, Rinehart and Winston, New York.

Whyte, John H. (1974), 'Ireland: Politics Without Social Bases', in Richard Rose (ed.), *Electoral Behavior: A Comparative Handbook*, Free Press, New York.

Rational Choice and Party Identification

Political Choice and Party Identification

# 14

# Introduction: Rational Choice, Policy Spaces and Party Identification

The questions that can be posed about the precise meaning of party and of space point to the necessity of clarifying these and other ideas. As we emphasized previously, the great success of dimensional analysis has been in the imaginative handling of survey data to produce empirically derived spaces, and in the use of these to predict voting transfers, party strategies and governmental coalitions. But these developments have been pioneered in the midst of considerable theoretical confusion about what to base such spaces on, and consequently about the information they yield. Analysts seem barely aware, even, that the kind of information they use to produce the space determines what its nature will be and hence its explanatory and predictive potential.

These faults spring from an excess of empirical data and a paucity of theory, exactly the reverse situation from the rational choice formulations we consider in this and the following chapter. As we noted, these formulations have exerted a strong influence on the development of dimensional analysis, particularly in the shape of Downs's uni-dimensional representation of party competition and voting (Downs, 1957).

However, since that time a whole body of formal theory has developed from Downs independently of dimensional analysis—independently indeed of most empirically oriented voting studies. In Chapter 15 Peter Ordeshook, himself a leading builder of mathematical theories based on rational choice assumptions and located in $n$-dimensional policy space, summarizes their present state (see also Riker and Ordeshook, 1973, Chs 11 and 12). His discussion is also in part a plea for the closer integration of these sophisticated models with current empirical work. Their utility in clarifying concepts is demonstrated by the distinction drawn, towards the end of Chapter 15 between the different kinds of spaces within which electors and candidates operate. At a very simple level the spaces necessary to understand the logic of electoral decision are three:

(1) electors' common underlying preference space $(S_1)$, linked to
(2) an action space of issues, governmental programmes, etc. $(S_2)$ by a transformation $T_1$, which from electors' utility functions in $S_1$ permits us to derive their preferences in $S_2$;
(3) a space $(S_3)$ that describes candidates' publicly stated issue-stands, and is linked to $S_2$ (the space of their issue-stands as perceived by electors) by a

second transformation $T_2$ representing electors' interpretations of candidates' campaign strategies.

Ordeshook points out that it is very unclear whether existent multi-dimensional analyses of American elections apply to $S_1$, $S_2$ or $S_3$. The civil liberties dimension that commonly emerges seems indeed to apply not only to actionable issues but also the transformation $T_2$ as well. It is however essential in pursuing this line of reasoning to distinguish very clearly between the various preference spaces and the different transformations.

Thus purely theoretical work based on the rational choice paradigm can form a basis on which to clarify the purposes and concepts of empirical analyses. It is worth noting, however, that the mathematical theorists themselves have not commonly worked on the assumption of separate preference spaces with linking transformations: they have generally simplified (or indeed over-simplified) election processes by postulating the coexistence of candidates and electors within a single $n$-dimensional space of pure policy. The suggestion that several spaces, with linking probability functions, would have to be used to describe electors' decision processes if they actually did cast their vote purely in terms of policy comes from a critique of $n$-dimensional rational choice theories which is expanded by Farlie and Budge in Chapter 20 below. This critique relates to flaws in the basic postulates of rational choice theory. Thus it casts considerable doubt on the practicability of Ordeshook's suggested integration with empirical work through additional assumptions which incorporate findings explicitly into these simplified representations.

The gap that Ordeshook tries to bridge derives from more basic considerations than the relative lack of contact between mathematical utility theorists and survey analysts. It also derives from their different purposes.

(1) Survey analysts have traditionally been concerned with explaining voting behaviour while taking for granted the exact shape and nature of party competition. Rational choice theorists in contrast have been primarily concerned with party competition, particularly the positions taken up by candidates, making only sufficient assumptions about electors' reactions to provide a dynamic for party movement.

(2) Rational choice theory has embodied moral as well as descriptive concerns, while survey analyses have been primarily descriptive. The moral emphasis is found in Downs but has been intensified in the works of his successors. It is posed by the well-known Paradox of Voting (Arrow, 1963).

A succinct illustration of this paradox is as follows. Although each of three electors has a clear preference ordering among the alternatives A, B and C listed in Table 14.1,

Table 14.1    The paradox of Voting: Three Electors' Consistent
Preference Orderings give rise to Cyclical and Unstable Collective
Choices

| Elector | Preference Orderings of Alternative Policies A, B, C |
|---------|-----------------------------------------------------|
| 1 | A → C → B |
| 2 | C → B → A |
| 3 | B → A → C |

Arrows represent preferences among policies:  thus A → B stands for
'A is preferred to B'.

no alternative is dominant in the sense that it obtains a clear majority of choices against all other alternatives. B defeats A (electors 2 and 3, against 1); C defeats B (electors 1 and 2, against 3); and A defeats C (electors 1 and 3, against 2). Thus the social preference ordering—A over C over B over A—is intransitive. If A, B and C represent alternative policies that a party might endorse, leaders cannot find a programme that guarantees them a certain tie, still less a winning majority.

The suggestion that stable majorities cannot exist under reasonable and indeed desirable conditions designed to give equal weight to preferences undermines moral justifications for democracy. But it also raises strategic problems for party decision-makers about what policy stand to adopt to maximize their change of office—indeed, the descriptive problem is the other side of the moral. Hence Ordeshook's assertion at the outset of his discussion that rational choice theory is descriptive, with its general concern being the process by which individual preferences are translated into collective decisions and its particular concern being the establishment of necessary and sufficient conditions under which candidates will have no inducement to move from particular policy positions (i.e., assuming that they wish to gain votes, they cannot gain from altering their programme after taking up optimal positions).

The basic conception of the model is thus of an electoral process involving two groups of participants, the electors and the candidates, in a contest governed by voting rules. The moves in this contest consist of each candidate offering a portfolio of past actions, future intentions and characteristics (such as party, social class or personality) for consideration by electors. On the basis of these portfolios electors establish a preference for a candidate and an inclination to declare that preference in their voting.

The characteristics of candidates and electors differ in several respects, but most noticeably in that the opinions and actions of the candidates are in the public domain—known both to the electors and to the other candidates—while the actions and opinions of the electors are in the private domain and accessible in the main only be sampling techniques, if at all. The mobility afforded to the candidates is restricted to future intentions only. Past actions and background characteristics are known and the only modification possible is the emphasis placed upon them; party affiliation in particular is not an element in the mobile part of the candidate's portfolio. An attempt was made in earlier presentations of the multi-dimensional model to argue that shifts of emphasis on party and other characteristics gave candidates sufficient mobility to include them as continuous dimensions in the model. Recently there has been a tendency to locate candidate positions on pure policy dimensions first, subsequently noting that party bias will have to be taken into account in translating deduced spatial locations into predictions about actual elections (perhaps by viewing party or personality bias as random variables). In marked contrast to candidates, electors are supposed to have unchangeable preferences for policies but complete mobility on party preference. In its simplest form we can then think of electors evaluating every declared policy, deriving a utility for each, and waiting while the candidates waltz in front of them seeking a dominant position from which to win the election on the basis of the electors' aggregated preferences. At the moment of election the electors declare their preferences for candidates as opposed to policies. A variation that turns out to have important consequences is to permit some electors not to declare their preferences—by abstaining.

The location of electors and candidates in some kind of space is implicit in what has been said. The explicit spatial assumptions of the models are as follows.

(1) The most preferred position of individual electors can be expressed as a series of points on each dimension of some multi-dimensional space. Technically these points are regarded as a vector of real-valued coordinates in the multi-dimensional space. We can thus express each elector's position as a vector of co-ordinates, $x = (x_1, x_2, \ldots, x_n)$. Further assumptions are that $n$, the total number of dimensions, is known, and that each elector has a preferred position on each issue. These assumptions will often be augmented by a third: that issue preferences constitute a continuum so that continuous functions of preference can be handled later in the argument.

(2) Candidates and their movements can be mapped into the same space as electors. Thus the policy alternatives they combine into their programme can also be expressed as a vector of points on each dimension, denoted as $\theta = (\theta_1, \theta_2, \ldots, \theta_n)$. This space is deemed neutral, and candidates are equally free to take up any position in the policy space, (which causes the difficulties noted above of regarding party identification as a dimension of the space).

(3) Electors estimate the loss to them of a candidate choosing a policy vector $\theta$ other than their most preferred position $x$ through some calculation based on the distance between $\theta$ and $x$.

Given these spatial assumptions and the general conception of candidate rationality, candidates will seek a position in the space that will persuade electors to vote in sufficient numbers to elect them, using as a criterion the distance of $\theta$ from their particular distribution of preferences $(x_i)$. Supplementing these by more specialized assumptions about (a) electors' utilities, (b) the inclination of electors to vote after evaluating candidates' stands, (c) the distribution of electors' preferences over the policy space and (d) the objectives of candidates (vote-maximization, voting plurality, etc.), we can arrive at results of the following type:
-  ( i) in general, no equilibrium point exists that is undominated by alternative policies;
-  ( ii) an equilibrium point exists to which the candidates will converge, but the position cannot be specified in general;
-  (iii) the candidates converge to the centre of the distribution of electors' preferences, which usually has to be assumed symmetric to get this result;
-  (iv) an equilibrium exists but the candidates may or may not converge.

Ordeshook discusses the possibility that the theory might broaden out by extending this notion of 'equilibrium strategy pairs' to wider concepts such as the 'strong bargaining set'. A very relevant question, however, is whether such a focus overlaps very much with the objects of empirical and particularly survey analyses. Downs made such a general impact partly because the range of phenomena he tried to explain was so wide. Besides strategic party positions and convergence, he sought to cover actual policy content; the ambiguity, consistency and reliability of policy; governmental effectiveness; information economizing; abstention; vote transfers; the shape of the party system; and the rise of new parties. The interest of survey analysts in these last points may be a consequence of their lack of guiding theory. But any synthesis would surely have to accommodate their interests, rather than suggesting that they simply give them up in favour of studies focusing on policy positions. An additional reason for their lack of interest may of course be that, in the real world, party policy stands may be fairly predictable—it is difficult for example to think of the British Conservative Party endorsing nationalization, or Gaullists dissociating themselves from *grandeur,* whatever the electoral consequences. Party manoeuvres may be more a question of selective emphasis on issues that one or other 'owns' rather than on opposed stands on any one issue (Robertson, 1975).

A consequence of this divergence between the *explicanda* of later rational choice theory and of survey analysts is that most of the latter who have concerned themselves with checking rationality assumptions have started from the work of Downs rather than Ordeshook, Davis, Riker, Hinich or their associates (reviewed in Riker and Ordeshook, 1973, Chapters 11 and 12). This is the case with Laver's imaginative reconstruction of the Northern Ireland electoral space of 1973 (Chapter 16 below) and with Robertson's 'oligopolistic' theory of party competition (Robertson, 1975). It is significant that one of the few attempts to use later rational choice models in actual survey analysis (Irvine, Chapters 17 and 18 below) starts from Ordeshook and Riker's explanation of abstention and turnout rather than from their analysis of policy convergence (Riker and Ordeshook, 1973, Chapter 3).

Irvine's investigation is of interest from another point of view than that of the predictive capacity of 'socialization' and other models compared to rational choice. For what he ends up with is a mixed model combining indicators of long-term predispositions (like party identification) with the short-term election cues that alone influence voting under pure rational choice.

Irvine's analysis foreshadows the most important modifications that Ordeshook proposes making to his policy space: that is, restrictions on the free movement of candidates. If candidates or parties are restricted to some areas of the space, it follows that they will always be closer to electors in parts of that area than any other party: hence such electors will always vote for that party. In this way a pure policy space, in which voting is conditioned exclusively by candidate policy stands (i.e. short-term election cues), is modified so as to accommodate long-term predispositions. But in so doing it no longer remains a pure policy space but has become a policy space with party-reserved areas.

To see the ultimate consequences of this kind of modification we can consider a particular example of this type of space, Laver's assumed space for the Northern Ireland Assembly election of 1973 (Figures 16.1 to 16.4). In this space we have the various Unionist factions at the right of the continuum, Alliance and NILP in the middle and Nationalist factions to the left. Parties cannot move out of their particular segments of the continuum: Unionist supporters cannot vote for any Nationalist party or Nationalist supporters for any Unionist party.

Laver considers this a policy continuum whose end-points are defined by the issue-stands of 'protestant Ulster regardless' and its antithesis, 'United Ireland regardless'. An alternative in view of the restrictions on party and elector movement is to view the continuum as bounded by the most extreme Unionist and Nationalist parties. The other factions spread along the continuum in terms of their closeness to the pure party positions. This interpretation renders Laver's space very similar to the space based on party identification (Figure 1.2). In fact, the interpretation views Laver's continuum explicitly as a party-defined space, just like party identification or Likelihood Ratio Space (Chapter 6). More extended arguments for regarding policy spaces with party-reserved areas as substantially equivalent to party-defined spaces are found in Budge and Farlie (forthcoming, Chapter 9).

Viewing Laver's continuum as party-defined permits an alternative interpretation of vote transfers in Northern Ireland in 1973—as influenced by party identification rather than rational choice. (Unionist voters prefer a Unionist faction to all other alternatives, and will consider voting for Alliance, which has some breakaway Unionists, but will never vote Nationalist.)

More generally, however, one can argue that, in so far as restraints are imposed on candidate or party movement within $n$-dimensional policy space, it becomes more of a party-defined space rather than a pure policy space, and increasingly resembles the space based on party identification (Figure 1.2) in its characteristics. It also comes closer to LiRaS, interpreted as a space of propensities towards voting for parties at the end-points—relationships that are explicitly considered in the concluding paper by Farlie and Budge (Chapter 20).

The consequences of restricting candidates' movements are thus far-reaching for the $n$-dimensional rational choice formulations, particularly in terms of the conceptualization of party. This could not under such circumstances be represented simply by the point in policy space the candidate happens to have taken up, since it now also consists of:

(a) the range of policy potentially open to him (and conversely those closed to him), which collectively might represent an enduring ideology as opposed to policies currently and explicitly endorsed;

(b) a body of electors consistently voting for a party. This would involve a view of parties as also existing in terms of electors' partisan loyalties, which is a view embedded in party identification as we noted in Chapter 1.

In Chapter 19, however, Robertson argues persuasively that, even if rational choice formulations incorporate long-term predispositions of electors to vote for particular parties, this cannot be interpreted as party identification in its original sense as defined by Miller in Chapter 2: a deep-rooted psychological loyalty to the party group. For rational choice models must presuppose, if they are to retain rational choice at all, that electors evaluate parties in terms of their autonomous aims, rather than having these aims given to them by parties.

Perhaps for this reason, and certainly because of the other complexities involved, recent work on $n$-dimensional theory has bypassed the idea of imposing explicit restraints on candidates' spatial mobility, in favour of locating their positions on the pure policy dimensions first, subsequently taking party bias into account in translating deduced spatial consequences into predictions about outcomes (perhaps by viewing party bias as a random variable) (Ordeshook, Chapter 15 below). The trouble with this expedient is that long-term predispositions are certainly as important as short-term issue-cues in shaping election outcomes. (If their influence in shaping issue preferences in the first place is considered, they are much more important.) Moreover, precisely because they are long-term and stable, they are more easily analysed and predicted than short-term issues, which fluctuate from election to election. Hence to concentrate analysis primarily on the impact of issues, and to view predispositions simply as unexamined bias, seems to be reversing the order of priorities. The original Michigan emphasis on the nature and development of party identification is more appropriate.

The basic dilemma for rational choice theory in its more recent forms is therefore as follows. It can retain its distinctive and recognizable form only by sticking to the basic postulate of a pure policy space, which precludes dealing seriously with a central concept of empirical voting analysis, the impact of long-term predispositions. On the other hand, the more it incorporates such predispositions into its spatial analysis, the more similar the space becomes to party-defined space, forcing a fundamental reassessment of the associated postulates of the theory. Some repercussions of this are explored in the final chapter of this volume which tries to relate the various spaces employed to represent voting and party competition, and attempts a synthesis. Hopefully this will provide a clear statement of where party identification stands in relation to the various other alternatives discussed in this book.

## REFERENCES

Arrow, Kenneth J. (1963), *Social Choice and Individual Values*, 2nd edition, Wiley, New York.

Budge, Ian and Dennis Farlie (forthcoming), *Voting and Party Competition: A Spatial Synthesis and a Critique of Existing Approaches Applied to Surveys from Ten Democracies*, Wiley, London and New York.

Downs, Anthony (1957), *An Economic Theory of Democracy*, Harper and Row, New York.

Riker, W., and P. C. Ordeshook (1973), *Positive Political Theory*, Prentice Hall, Englewood Cliffs, New Jersey.

Robertson, David (1976), *A Theory of Party Competition*, Wiley, London and New York.

# 15

# The Spatial Theory of Elections: A Review and a Critique

PETER C. ORDESHOOK *

Donald E. Stokes's (1963) critical review of spatial models of elections, especially of Anthony Downs's (1957) model, prefaced a concerted effort to advance spatial theory along the several lines suggested by Stokes and to render Downs's conceptualization more deductive and mathematically rigorous. So voluminous is this research that it is now a major part of the application to political science of the rational choice paradigm. As the literature on spatial theory increases, however, criticisms multiply accordingly. Many of these criticisms—concerning both the adequacy of assumptions and the testability of propositions—are well founded and warrant serious attention. Other criticisms derive from misconceptions about the nature of theories and models in general and spatial models in particular—misconceptions that frequently are shared by the spatial theorist. Whatever their genesis or virtue, however, these criticisms warrant attention lest the contribution of spatial analysis to our understanding of election processes go unrealized and its very real deficiencies go unrecognised.

The purpose of this essay, then is to offer a critical survey of spatial models of election competition. It does not seek, however, to review the definitions, assumptions and theorems of alternative models *per se* (for such a review see Riker and Ordeshook, 1973, Chs. 11 and 12). Rather, it focuses on issues such as the testability of assumptions and contemporary empirical research, the failure of the theory to accommodate particular features of election processes and the general utility of a spatial perspective. We begin with a brief non-mathematical review of the theoretical foundations of spatial analysis and turn, in the following section, to a discussion of stability in election processes and to the issue of an appropriate solution concept for election models. In the third section we directly confront the numerous substantive critiques of the theory and outline a methodology for using spatial analysis to study complex processes. Finally we address ourselves to the basic issue of the reasonableness of a spatial conceptualization of individual preferences.

* The research for this chapter was supported by a National Science Foundation Grant to Carnegie-Mellon University.

## THEORETICAL FOUNDATIONS

Elections in general, and voting behaviour, campaign tactics, candidate motives, election rules etc. in particular, are of interest to the policy scientist because they are part of a mechanism for rendering social decisions (public policy) from individual preferences and choice. Spatial theory's principal focus, then, is elections as a social choice mechanism—rather than voting behaviour, candidate motives or the means by which candidates convert resources such as money into votes. To retain this focus spatial theory abstracts mightily from reality; but in doing so it seeks to provide a structure upon which we can construct an understanding, in a truly scientific sense, of more complex processes of public policy generation. With its roots in the paradigm of rational decision-making, it attempts to provide a flexible theoretical framework (or at least to work within such a framework) that permits theorizing about a variegated class of phenomena in a consistently rigorous manner.

To review spatial theory, its inadequacies and its promise, let us consider its simplest form and trace in detail the assumptions used to derive this form from a more general structure. We begin with these assumptions about citizens:

(1) they employ a common set of criteria for evaluating election candidates;

(2) while their preferences may differ, the admissable range of alternative preferences on a criterion can be represented by a segment of the real line;

(3) citizens' preferences over this range are well defined.

Stated differently, if we interpret each criterion as a public policy issue, then we assume that

(1) citizens evaluate candidates on the basis of their policy stands;

(2) the set of admissable campaign platforms can be represented by an $n$-dimensional ($n$-issue) Euclidean space;

(3) we can represent each citizen by a utility function over that space—a function that defines his most preferred platform (package of policies) and the relative benefit he associates with other platforms.

Taken together, these assumptions are summarized by an assumption about the mathematical form of each citizen's utility function (e.g., utility functions are quadratic as in Davis *et al.* (1970), city-block as in Rae and Taylor (1971) and Wendell and Thorson (1974), or lexicographic as in Taylor (1973)) and by an assumption about the distribution of ideal points in the policy space (e.g., preferences are bimodally or unimodally, symmetrically or non-symmetrically distributed across an issue).

Candidates, in turn, are represented by points in this policy space, i.e. by the positions they 'advocate' on each issue. The presumed objective of candidates in two-party plurality rule systems (the usual setting for spatial theorizing) is plurality maximization—where plurality is a function of our previous assumptions about citizens, each candidate's spatial position and a decision rule for citizens. The simplest such decision rule is that every citizen votes and that he votes for the candidate whose strategy is closest to his own most preferred policy package. Generalizations of this rule include permitting citizens to abstain in accordance with some formulation of alienation or indifference, or permitting citizens to vote probabilistically. Usually, however, all citizens are assumed to share a common perception of each candidate's strategy—thereby eliminating from the analysis any consideration of cognitive dissonance or imperfection in the distribution of information within the electorate.

Finally, spatial theory offers as its definition of a solution to the election (its prediction as to the policies candidates advocate) the notion of equilibrium strategy pairs—a spatial position for each candidate such that, once at such a pair, neither candidate possesses any incentive to move unilaterally. (And here, spatial theory generally introduces another assumption—namely, that both candidates possess unlimited spatial mobility). Since such strategy need not exist, one of spatial theory's central objectives is to establish sufficient (and, on rare occasions, necessary) conditions for a spatial equilibrium. Generally, these conditions are quite restrictive (e.g., if the election concerns more than one issue, if all citizens vote, and if citizen's utility functions are represented by simple Euclidean distance, then an equilibrium exists if and only if preferences are distributed symmetrically), and are the source of many criticisms of the theorems that constitute the theory. These criticisms are exacerbated, moreover, by the fact that spatial theory cannot yet predict the candidate's strategic choices when equilibria fail to exist.

This brief review of spatial theory's perspective and approximate structure should reveal not only its many substantive inadequacies (in the form of its assumptions about, e.g., voter perceptions and candidate motives) but also its limited scope (such as its focus on policy as the sole instrument of campaign strategy). Before we consider these criticisms, however, let us turn to the derivation of the preceeding spatial model from a more general structure. We do this because spatial theory is but a particular formulation of elections as a game in the Von Neuman–Morgenstern sense, and many of its assumptions, as well as its basic structure, attempt simply to add substantive detail to a game-theoretic conceptualization of election competition. To review spatial theory critically, then, we must examine the implicit and explicit processes by which this detail is added.

Beginning within the general rational choice paradigm of game theory, we assume, first, that there exists a set $D$ of *decision-makers* and that each decision-maker $d \in D$ possesses a set $A^d$ of alternative *strategies* and a measure $U^d$ for evaluating each *outcome* $O$ in the set of all possible outcomes (social states). The outcome that prevails is, in turn, a function of the conjunction of strategies chosen by $D$, $a \equiv (a^1, a^2, \ldots)$ and the prevailing state of nature $s \in S$. Thus, we write $U^d(a, s)$ to indicate that since $U^d$ is a function of $O$, and since $O$ is a function of $a$ and $s$, $U$ is a function of $a$ and $s$. As a branch of mathematics, however, game-theory is without substantive meaning. To this point, then, we possess little more than a notation that reveals our intention to address circumstances in which each person's welfare, $U^d$, is a function of the alternatives chosen by other people. Theorizing begins when we specify the substance and mathematical properties of $A, S, P$ and $U$.

Our first step is to partition the set of decision-makers, $D$, into two exhaustive subsets—citizens, $V$, and candidates, $C$—thus:

(A1)   $C$ = [the set of candidates]
       $V$ = [the set of citizens]
       $C \cup V = D$

Our second step is to describe what we feel is distinct about members of each subset in terms of the concepts at hand—$A$, $U$, $O$ and $S$. With respect to citizens, we suppose that

(A2) for all citizens $v \in V$, $A^v \equiv$
$$\begin{bmatrix} a_1^v: \text{vote for candidate 1} \\ a_2^v: \text{vote for candidate 2} \\ \cdot \\ \cdot \\ \cdot \\ a_n^v: \text{vote for candidate } n \\ a_o^v: \text{abstain from voting} \end{bmatrix}$$

Thus, citizens can either vote for a particular candidate or abstain from voting. This assumption, then, precludes consideration of such ballot-related activities as intentionally casting invalid ballots (e.g. casting 'blank' ballots in France to protest against the range of available choices, or casting invalid ballots in The Netherlands to protest against compulsory voting).

Our next sequence of assumptions concerns the indentification of a citizen's actual choice, which we denote by $a^*$, which requires that we specify the set of outcomes that concern citizens. In particular, suppose,

(A3) for all citizens $v \in V$, $O^v =$
$$\begin{bmatrix} O_1: \text{candidate 1 wins} \\ O_2: \text{candidate 2 wins} \\ \cdot \\ \cdot \\ \cdot \\ O_n: \text{candidate } n \text{ wins} \end{bmatrix}$$

This assumption is not trivial. First, it states that the set of relevant outcomes for citizens is a specification of who wins or loses rather than a detailed account of how many votes each candidate receives (ties can be ignored if we assume that coin tosses or some other random mechanism determines the eventual winner). Thus, (A3) does not allow us to consider the possibility that citizens might prefer the candidate of their choice to win by a landslide rather than by a plurality of one vote. Second, (A3) bypasses the question of whether winning is an unambiguous concept. In multi-party proportional representation systems, for example, winning may not be easily defined—especially if a post-election coalition formation process is necessary to choose a government. Winning can include retaining seats previously held, securing a majority of seats or securing enough seats to ensure participation in the government. Even in simple plurality systems augmented by an electoral college, winning for a minor party might include forestalling a determinate outcome and requiring Congress to select the President. Let us suppose, however, that the election entails the simple plurality formula and that a candidate wins if he receives more votes than any opponent.

From the rational choice paradigm, we assume that each citizen possesses a utility or preference function over $O^v$ and that his choice, $a^*$, maximizes the expectation of this utility. That is, $a^*$ maximizes

$$\sum_{i=1}^{n} Pr(O_i)U(O_i),$$

where, presumably, the probability that candidate $i \in C$ wins, $Pr(O_i)$ is a function of each citizen's choice. In particular,

(A4) for all citizens $v \in V$, $i \in C$,

$$Pr(O_i|a_i^v) \geqslant Pr(O_i|a_o^v) \geqslant Pr(O_i|a_j^v), \; j \neq i).$$

By itself, (A4) does little more than rule out negative votes. But if we keep in mind that probabilities are necessarily subjective, then this assumption prohibits people from believing that their votes (or intentions, if they reveal them in, say, public opinion polls) affect the vote of others in an opposite manner. One implication of (A4), however, is particularly important: with it and with the outcomes as defined by (A3), we are assured that, in two-candidate plurality-rule elections, voters vote for their most preferred candidate. That is, the following assumption is necessarily satisfied:

(A5) All citizens vote sincerely.

Assumption 5 is unreasonable, however, in multi-party elections to the extent that citizens engage in *sophisticated* voting—voting for a second or third choice if the most preferred candidate has little chance of winning (see McKelvey and Ordeshook (1972), as well as the debate between Casstevens (1968) and Kramer (1971); for a general discussion of sophisticated voting see Farquharson (1969) and, in a spatial context, Kramer (1972)). Owing to this complication, spatial theory typically focuses on two-candidate contests, while if three or more candidates are admitted, assumption 5 is somewhat arbitrarily imposed (cf. Tullock, 1967, pp.50-6).

Our next step is to assume that the utility a citizen associates with candidate $i$'s victory, $O_i$ is a function of that candidate's 'strategy', denoted by $\theta_i$, and the prevailing state of nature $s$. This, in turn, implies that the citizen's probability of voting for candidate $i$ or of abstaining is a function of $\theta_i$ $i = 1, \ldots, n$ and $s$ thus,

(A6) $U^v(O_i) = f^v(\theta_i, s)$ and $Pr^v(a_i) = g_i^v(\theta_1, \theta_2, \ldots, \theta_n, s)$.

Assumption 6 does little more than introduce some notation and commit us to representing the factors that affect a person's choices in terms of the candidates' choices and states of nature. Substantive limitations arise when we specify the content of $\theta_i$ and $s$, as well as the functional form of $g_i$ or $f$. First, however, we posit an objective for candidates, i.e., we specify the outcomes relevant to candidates and the mathematical form of each candidate's utility function. Assuming that the domain of $\theta_i$ exhausts all of candidate 's campaign-relevant alternatives, spatial analyses typically suppose that the outcome that concerns a candidate is his expected plurality and that his utility is linear in plurality. Since plurality is a function of citizens' choices and since these choices are functions of $\theta_i$ and $s$, plurality is a function of these variables as well. Denoting the function candidate $i$ seeks to maximize by $\varphi^i$, we have,

(A7) (expected plurality maximization) for all candidates $i \in C$;

$$\varphi^i(\theta_1, \theta_2, \ldots, \theta_n, s) = \sum_v g_i^v - \max_{j \neq i} \sum_v g_j^v$$

Note that if only two candidates compete, $i$ reduces to the simple expression for expected plurality, $\Sigma g_i^v - \Sigma g_j^v$. It is evident, of course, that expected plurality maximization is but one possible specification of an objective. Others, which again rely solely on the votes received by each candidate, are easily imagined—including maximizing expected vote, proportion of the expected vote and probability of winning (see Aranson *et al.* 1973, 1974) and Frey and Lau (1968). We shall later reconsider assumption 7 in the context of our criticisms.

Our final step before we interpret $s$ and the $\theta_i$s substantively is to define a solution to the election game, i.e. a prediction about the strategies candidates choose. Our task here differs somewhat from our previous discussion of choice functions for voters. There we assume that citizens' choices are not directly dependent on the choices or preferences of other citizens. Owing to the large number of citizens in most elections, this assumption is reasonable since no citizen by himself is likely to affect significantly the probabilities of alternative outcomes. Thus we do not suppose that citizens are in a game situation with respect to each other. We cannot reasonably impose this assumption about candidates, however, if only because the interdependence of the candidates' choices is our principal focus. Hence, if we impose the additional assumption that

    (A8)  All candidates choose their strategies simultaneously, then, from (A7), we model the election as an $n$-person (-candidate) zero-sum non-co-operative game.

Having thus set elections in a game-theoretic context, our next assumption concerns the strategies candidates eventually adopt. Briefly, we say that $n$-tuple $\theta^* = (\theta_1^*, \theta_2^*, \ldots, \theta_n^*)$ is a pure strategy equilibrium if

$$\varphi_i(\theta^*) \geqslant \varphi_i(\theta_1^*, \ldots, \theta_1, \ldots, \theta_n^*)$$

for all $i$ and $\theta_i \neq \theta_i^*$. That is, $\theta^*$ is an equilibrium if, once there, no candidate, $i$, possesses any incentive to shift unilaterally from $\theta^*_i$. Supposing that $\theta^*$ as a solution to the election game poses some problems if $n > 2$ and if $\theta^*$ is not unique. However, for $n=2$ or for unique $\theta^*$, the usual assumption of spatial theory is

    (A9)  Candidates adopt pure strategy equilibrium $n$-tuples,

which is to say that, if minimax pure strategies exist, candidates converge to or otherwise adopt them.

We do not, of course, know whether $\theta^*$ exists—establishing conditions for existence has been one of the principal occupations of spatial theorists. But, before we consider this issue, we must interpret $s$ and $\theta$ substantively. It is this interpretation and its attendant assumptions that moves us from a quasi-abstract system to a model of election processes.

Remaining within the confines of a simple spatial model, we return to the analysis of citizens and, in particular, to assumption 6. Candidates must, of course, decide a great many things during a campaign including where to campaign, what to say, how to spend money (e.g., television commercials $v$. billboard posters), whether or not to debate an opponent, etc. All of these choices can be subsumed under the heading of tactics. Although we might wish to study tactics, spatial theory addresses itself directly to the *criteria* citizens use to evaluate candidates—their partisan identification, their positions on a particular policy issue or their personality—and thus bypasses the question of how alternative tactics affect their positions on these criteria. The vector $\theta_i = (\theta_i^1, \theta_i^2, \ldots, \theta_i^m)$, then, denotes candidate $i$'s 'position' on each of $m$ criteria. The state of nature $s$, in conjunction with $f^v$, contains the information necessary to define a citizen's evaluation of $o_i$. Generally, $s$ includes the citizen's most preferred 'position' on each criterion as well as that criterion's relative importance (for candidates, $s$ describes preferences and patterns of relative salience across the entire electorate). Altogether, this information is summarized by the assumption that $U^v(\theta_i, s)$ is a particular metric such as the following:

(A10) (example): for all citizens $v \in V$,

$$U^v(\theta_i) = -(\theta_i - x^v)' \Gamma^v (\theta_i - x^v)$$

where $x^v$ is the citizen's vector of most preferred positions and $\Gamma^v$ is an $m \times m$ matrix that weights the criteria. Other more general assumptions are possible, including letting $U^v(O_i) = U^v(\theta_i, x)$ be any quasi-concave, continuously differentiable function of $\theta_i$. The significance of all such assumptions, however, is that we thereby commit ourselves to a spatial representation of election competition.

Our final step is to specify the functional form of $g_i^v$. Basically, after choosing a particular metric representation for $U(\theta_i)$, specification of $g_i^v$ entails assumptions about non-voting, the simplest possibility being:

(A11) for all citizens $v \in V$,

$$Pr^v(a_i) = 1, \text{ if } U^v(\theta_i) > U^v(\theta_j) \text{ for all } j \neq i$$
$$= 0 \text{ otherwise.}$$

With assumption 11, then, a citizen abstains only if two or more candidates are tied for first in his preference order; otherwise he votes with certainty for the candidate he most prefers. Other possible assumptions include letting a citizen's probability of voting decrease as the utility from his most preferred candidate decreases (*alienation*) or as the utility difference between two candidates decreases (*indifference*).

These assumptions ((A1)–(A11)) outline the general theoretical basis for most existing spatial models. It is important to note here, though, that it is only assumption 10 that renders our game-theoretic formulation of election competition spatial. Without (A10), strategies remain uninterpreted variables, which is to say that we can substitute alternative interpretations (e.g., the $\theta_i$s denote resource allocations) without altering the basic structure. For this reason we should not equate spatial models with the game-theoretic analysis of elections, but rather should view spatial models as a special sub-class of such analyses. Consequently, we must ask whether the criticisms of these models concern their spatial interpretation of strategies, their underlying game theoretic structure (e.g. the partitioning of decision-makers) or the applicability of the rational choice paradigm itself. Thus, many criticisms of spatial *theory* are more general than we might otherwise suppose in that they are not criticisms of a spatial interpretation of strategies but of the assumptions we use to model elections in game-theoretic terms.

After having adopted a spatial interpretation of strategies, however, several additional assumptions are imposed in the search for equilibria, which, while they simplify analysis, are of substantive significance also. Hence, for future reference, we list here those that are most frequently imposed:

(A12) all citizens share identical perceptions of each candidate's strategy (e.g. no cognitive dissonance);

(A13) all citizens weight the issues in an identical fashion and thus are concerned with an identical set of issues (i.e., $\Gamma^v = \Gamma^{v0}$).

(A14) $\theta_i$ and $x^v$ are continuous variables;

(A15) $x^v$ is well defined (i.e., all citizens possess a unique most preferred position on every issue unless, from (A13), all citizens have no preference on that issue);

(A16) the domain of $\theta_i$ is identical for all candidates (i.e., one candidate cannot be restricted to 'liberal' positions while his opponent is restricted to 'conservative' policies);

(A17) all citizens are weighted equally;

(A18) $g_i^v$ is of identical functional form for all candidates and citizens.

This last assumption (A18) imposes several restrictions simultaneously (and actually subsumes (A12), (A13) and (A15)), including that all citizens abide by identical decision rules (e.g., they all conform to the abstention from alienation hypotheses) and that the election is not biased in favour of a particular candidate (i.e., ceteris paribus, $g_1^v = g_j^v$).

Using all or some subset of these assumptions, spatial theory turns to its final objective: identifying sufficient conditions for pure strategy equilibria and describing those equilibria. Generally, these sufficient conditions are stated in terms of assumptions about: (1) the functional form of citizen's utilities (quadratic, city block, concave, etc.); (2) the form of non-voting (alienation, indifference, universal turnout); and (3) the electorate's overall distribution of preferences (unimodal, bimodal; symmetric, non-symmetric; and whether one or more issues (criteria) characterize preferences). Pure strategy equilibria, however, are not easily found. This is demonstrated by Plott's (1967) and Sloss's (1973) restrictive *necessary* and sufficient conditions for majority rule (two-candidate, plurality system) equilibria, and the several theorems of game theory that establish sufficient conditions for pure strategy equilibria in continuous, non-co-operative games. Hence, to insure the existence of such equilibria we must necessarily impose restrictive conditions, such as assumptions (A12)–(A18), or require symmetrically distributed or uni-dimensional preferences. That pure strategy equilibrium solutions need not exist to two-person zero-sum games such as those we use to model two-candidate elections is, of course, well known. It is precisely this fact that led Von Neumann and Morgenstern to introduce the concept of a *mixed strategy* and to resolve partially the issue of an appropriate solution by proving that every such game with finite strategies possesses an equilibrium minimax solution in either pure or mixed strategies. Game theory, then, suggests a logical extension for spatial analysis in the event that pure strategy equilibria do not exist—namely, mixed minimax strategies. In conjunction with our assumptions about payoffs, for example, the cycle in which the candidates' strategies are [A, B, C] and $A > B > C > A$ yields the two-candidate constant-sum game in Figure 15.1 (payoffs are to Candidate 1 and represent his probability of winning). Although this game does not possess a pure

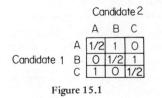

Figure 15.1

strategy equilibrium, it has a mixed strategy equilibrium—(1/3, 1/3, 1/3) for both players. That is, by choosing a strategy randomly, each candidate guarantees himself an *expected* payoff at least 1/2 and no other strategy provides such a guarantee.

Despite the mathematical closure of the problem provided by Von Neumann and Morgenstern, spatial theorists resist this extension. Their argument is twofold. The first objection concerns the inherent lack of specificity of mixed strategies as to the spatial positions candidates eventually adopt. Pure strategy equilibria are appealing (especially if they are unique) because they identify unambiguously the policies candidates should advocate. Mixed strategies, on the other hand, by design seek to disguise a candidate's ultimate choice of policy. For those, then, who desire explicit predictions about the policies engendered by majority rule procedures, the mixed strategy notion seems less than satisfactory.

The second argument against the use of mixed strategies in a simple spatial context concerns the dynamics of campaigns. Specifically, the most reasonable model of the extensive form of the election game is one in which candidates are permitted to adjust their spatial positions sequentially. A pure strategy, then, is not simply an element of $X$, but a 'game plan'—a specification of a spatial response to an opponent's position for each and every period of adjustment. Thus, if we retain our present conceptualization of pure strategies, we necessarily violate the condition for regarding minimax strategies as solutions—the condition being that both candidates announce their pure strategies simultaneously and neither player is permitted to alter his choice thereafter (e.g., payoffs are realized immediately). This violation seems unimportant, though, if the minimax strategy corresponds to a pure strategy equilibrium since neither candidate possesses any incentive to move unilaterally from the equilibrium. But if the minimax strategy is mixed, the abstraction of spatial theory from the true extensive form of the election game seems to preclude its applicability. The essential problem is that the spatial positions that candidates adopt in accordance with a mixed minimax strategy are not in equilibrium. Thus, if no prohibitions to sequential adjustment exist, at least one candidate should change his strategy on the next move. For example, if the candidates abide by the mixed minimax strategy for the game we illustrate in Figure 15.1, Candidate 1 can find himself choosing A and losing the election because his opponent chose B. Clearly, he should shift to another alternative if permitted to do so, and not take solace from the fact that he chose A in accordance with a minimax solution to a myopic model.

Despite these arguments, some recent research suggests that mixed minimax strategies might resolve the spatial theorist's dilemma if his models do not yield equilibria in pure strategies. We examine this research in the next section. For the moment, however, we must conclude that any critical review of spatial theory must address itself to at least these questions:

(1) Does equilibrium (in pure spatial strategies) prevail more generally in real elections?

(2) What are the essential features of election competition that induce equilibria but which spatial theory abstracts away?

(3) Can spatial theory accommodate these features?

(4) To the extent that equilibria do not exist in real elections, can spatial theory be suitably modified to render useful predictions about strategies and outcomes?

We cannot dispute the fact, of course, that many essential features of election competition are not taken into consideration by spatial theory at present. In the context of two-candidate competition, for example, this includes the functioning of political parties, campaign activists, interest groups, opinion leaders and the use of resources such as money, as well as assumptions that are more flexible than (A12)–(A18). Our second task, then, is to consider how (and whether) we can modify spatial theory to accommodate these features or the extent to which we can use the theory to construct more complex models.

Our final task concerns a more basic problem—the reasonableness of a spatial conceptualization of individual preferences. First, is it even a reasonable conceptualization theoretically? Second, if it is reasonable, can we empirically identify criteria and measure preferences on them? While, to the casual observer, it might not appear to be the case, most research in spatial theory is dictated by empirical considerations—including its extension to multi-dimensional issue spaces, alternative assumptions about participation and risky strategies. Spatial theory, then, is intended to be empirically relevant. The answer to this last question will largely determine the extent of that relevance.

We turn first, however, to the issues surrounding the existence of equilibria. Briefly, our conclusion is that, while several features of elections, which are not presently incorporated into the theory, might induce equilibria, spatial theory must abandon its dependence on the solution concept defined by assumption 9 and consider alternative concepts. We also conjecture that, by thus considering alternative solution concepts, spatial theory can make its first significant step towards analysing multi-candidate elections.

## II. PURE STRATEGY EQUILIBRIA AS SOLUTIONS

In asking whether spatial theory is unduly limited because it finds equilibria so difficult to establish we must, of course, ask also whether equilibria are any more pervasive in reality. Unfortunately, we cannot provide a conclusive answer to this latter question. One the one hand, repeated historical references to the absence of meaningful differences between the two major US political parties on policy matters, as well as the belief in the advisability of adopting median positions on issues as expressed by, e.g., Scammon and Wattenberg (1970), suggest the existence of some minimal degree of stability. On the other hand, empirical references to a 'coalition of minorities strategy', coupled with the theoretical result that such strategies are possible only if majority rule equilibria do not exist, suggest the existence of instability (see Oppenheimer, 1973). Rather than debate this issue, let us suppose for the present that stability is more pervasive empirically than in theoretical spatial analysis. We turn, then, to a discussion of some factors that might explain this presumed divergence between theory and reality.

First, however, we can eliminate as a possible source of stability the ambiguity—intended or otherwise—that frequently accompanies the candidates' issue positions. Both Shepsle (1972b) and McKelvey and Richelson (1974) demonstrate that if candidates can adopt risky strategies—strategies that correspond to a probability density on an issue rather than a unique point—equilibria are less, not more, likely to exist. For example, if the election concerns a single issue, and if candidates are limited to unambiguous (riskless) positions, an equilibrium generally exists (if all citizens vote, the equilibrium is the electorate's median preference). But if the candidates' strategies conform, say, to normal density functions, then we require a two-dimensional model—one dimension to represent the candidates' mean positions and the other to represent the variance of their strategies—and the sufficient conditions for equilibria in multi-dimensional as against uni-dimensional situations are more restrictive.

A more reasonable source of stability—or at least a factor that should mitigate against the seriousness of disequilibrium—is the constraints that exist on candidate strategies, i.e. the violations of assumption 16. Clearly, candidates cannot shift their positions about at will during the course of a campaign—adopting 'liberal' positions one month and 'conservative' positions the next—owing to things such as the perceptual inertia of citizens, the candidate's policy preferences and the candidate's unwillingness to alienate activist support. First, citizens may be unable or unwilling to perceive shifts in position during a campaign. They may, for example, wholly disregard campaign pronouncements or at least discount them in the case of an incumbent on the basis of policies implemented or advocated during his incumbency. Equivalently, they might use party labels and the historical performance of parties (e.g., in the United States, the perception that Democrats are the party of war while the Republicans are the party of economic recession or depression) as estimates of the candidate's positions.

Unless there is a shift in party identification, the candidate is thus constrained by the electorate's perceptions of his party's policy predispositions. Finally, we cannot ignore the forces of cognitive balance as outlined by Stokes (1966) and documented in numerous attitudinal studies such as Berelson *et al.*, (1954). By using a candidate's relative position on one issue to constrain the perception of his position on another issue, the citizen thus limits the candidate's ability to change strategies independently on both dimensions. (One implication of cognitive balance, of course, is that assumption 12 is violated.)

Spatial theory's present structure can accomodate these restrictions either by directly limiting the domain of each $\theta_i$ or by reconsidering its assumptions about $g_i^v$. Efforts at directly limiting strategic domains (e.g. requiring one candidate to adopt positions to the 'left' of an opponent or by limiting both opponents to a subset of the entire policy space) include Hinich *et al.* (1972) and Davis and Hinich (1972). The principal problem, though, is that these limitations are *ad hoc* while the universe of conceivable formal limits is nearly infinite. What we require, instead, is a better understanding of citizen perceptions and the relationship between these perceptions and campaign tactics. On this score, the theoretical flexibility of $g_i^v$ is considerably greater than assumption 18 suggests, and it is this flexibility that promises to permit the spatial theorist to incorporate forms of cognitive phenomena, including balance, into his models.

Specifically, some recent work on spatial analysis entirely bypasses assumptions about utility functions and considers instead alternative assumptions about $g_i^v$ (cf. McKelvey, 1973). Many older theorems are now generalized to admit the possibility that citizens are biased in favour of one candidate or the other (i.e., $g_i^v \neq g_j^v$) and to let the functional forms of $g$ vary across the electorate (i.e., $g_i^v \neq g_i^{v'}$). In the first instance this permits incorporating partisan bias into the choice function rather than requiring that party identification be a dimension of the 'issue' space. In the second instance, we can assume that some citizens are more concerned with one issue than another while another set of citizens exhibits the opposite pattern of saliency. Thus, if we might assume that $\theta_i$ possesses an objectively precise value, the distortions occasioned by citizen perception can be reflected in individual variations in $g_i^v$. Admittedly, though, this new focus on choice functions has not sought explicitly to consider alternative hypotheses about, say, cognitive balance, but rather addresses assumptions about participation. We attribute this focus partially to historical momentum and partially to the fact that attitudinal research does not yet reduce greatly the range of possible mathematical formulations of perceptual bias, balance, and so on.

A second source of constraint on strategies is the candidate's personal policy preferences. No doubt, many candidates do not seek simply to win elections—many, in fact, might not be in politics save for ideological or substantive policy commitments. Again, however, such constraints tend to be idiosyncratic and not easily incorporated into a general spatial model other than in an *ad hoc* fashion (but see Wittman (1973)).

An additional source of spatial constraint is the candidate's unwillingness to alienate party leaders and activists, including financial contributors. To the extent that the preferences of these groups differ from those of the electorate, and that their support is considered a prerequisite for a viable campaign, the candidate may be unwilling to shift about publicly on certain issues and prefer instead simply to ignore or down-play them. Several spatial analyses, in fact, seek to model the interplay between party activists and citizens in the sequential electoral process of competition for a party's nomination first and for victory in the general election second (cf. Aranson and Ordeshook, 1972, and Coleman, 1971, 1972). In the next section, however, we examine these efforts more closely and conclude that they are not likely to yield general and non-obvious theorems about competition.

The three general sources of constraint we detail above might explain the spatial immobility of individual candidates and thus the appearance of short-term equilibrium. The structure of spatial theory, moreover, permits us to incorporate them into a model of a specific election process. These three sources, however, cannot fully explain long-term equilibria. Specifically, we cannot disregard a party's ability to shift spatial positions simply by nominating candidates with different histories, personalities and policy predispositions. It is in fact a naive view of spatial theory to assume that it requires perfect positional mobility. If an equilibrium exists, or if an incumbent is constrained to a vulnerable position, the party can 'converge' to the equilibrium or take advantage of the incumbent's vulnerability by simply nominating an appropriate candidate. And while we cannot assert that parties always act to maximize their probability of success or their expected plurality (witness the Democratic Party's nomination of George McGovern in 1972), we cannot also assume that these considerations play *no* role in the selection of candidates. In this respect, we can interpret spatial theory as describing the principal forces of a Darwinian system in which the formal and informal processes of party politics weed out candidates with vulnerable strategies (characteristics) or with positions that cannot respond adequately to the opposition party's nominee. In the long run, then, parties can, theoretically, exhibit the same instabilities we associate with spatially mobile candidates.

Two additional possibilities, however, reduce the likelihood of disequilibrium. First, while the electorate might employ several criteria to evaluate candidates, individual citizens might use only one. That is, farmers might evaluate candidates principally by their public pronouncements on farm subsidies, while trade union members focus on the issue of minimum wage scales. (For an anlysis of such an electorate see Davis and Hinich, 1968.) Since candidates can then address each segment of the electorate independently of other segments, and since each segment is concerned with a single issue, the disequilibrium occasioned by multi-dimensional preferences is avoided.

The second possibility is closely related to the first. Specifically, candidates might act myopically and address themselves to the several issues of a campaign independently. That is, after using public opinion polls to gauge public sentiment on several issues, the candidate might simply adopt the median preference on each issue (for relevant analysis see Kadane, 1972). Wholly disregarding the correlations of preference across issues, the candidate thereby disregards the vulnerability of his strategy. It is reasonable to suppose, moreover, that this is a pervasive decision rule. The public opinion polls upon which candidates rely rarely employ sophisticated multi-dimensional scaling techniques or even analyse the data beyond age, sex, region and partisan identification breakdowns. One could scan Gallup's newspaper columns in vain for any measure of the relationship between preferences on, say, Vietnam and a concern with inflation. To the extent, then, that candidates are the captives of this information, they cannot avoid using myopic decision rules that yield at least short-run pure strategy equilibria.

Despite the variety of factors that mitigate against the seriousness of equilibrium in real elections, spatial theory must nevertheless accommodate instability. It must do this, first, to ascertain the possibilities for placing an analysis of these factors in a less *ad hoc* context. Second, it must attempt to weaken the assumptions of its major theorems while simultaneously retaining some of their predictive capabilities. As we noted earlier, the restrictiveness of these assumptions is a consequence of the search for an elusive creature—a pure strategy equilibrium. Spatial theorists have, then, almost wholly bypassed analysing configurations of weaker assumptions for fear that they yield no prediction about strategy. That is, spatial theory presents us with a dichotomy—equilibrium and a prediction about spatial position *v.* disequilibrium and no prediction whatsoever.

This dichotomy is both unreasonable and unnecessary. Consider the following possibility: sixty million voters with quadratic utility functions and with most preferred positions that are symmetrically distributed in some multi-dimensional space. In two-candidate plurality rule elections, then, the multivariate median preference is an equilibrium and the position spatial theory proscribes for both candidates. But, if we augment this electorate by three citizens whose preferences are not symmetrically distributed with respect to each other, equilibrium disappears. With the addition of three voters to sixty million, then, spatial theory is unable to render predictions about strategies. A reasonable hypothesis, nevertheless, is that, despite this disequilibrium, the candidates should not deviate far from the original multivariate median. To the extent that this hypothesis possesses intuitive appeal, then, spatial theory should formulate it in a mathematically precise and general form.

With this in mind, McKelvey and Ordeshook (1974) re-examine the notion of mixed minimax strategy solutions to spatial games. Limiting their analysis to two-candidate elections in which all citizens vote, in which preferences are represented by weighted Euclidean distance (assumption 10) and in which each candidate seeks to maximize his probability of winning, they derive constraints on the support set of such strategies (i.e. the set over which the density describing the mixed minimax solution is nonzero). Briefly, their argument is that, if this set is small, the hypothesis that candidates abide by mixed minimax strategies—contrary to the example of Figure 15.1—does limit our expectations about the spatial positions candidates eventually adopt. McKelvey and Ordeshook show, in fact, that if the electorate's preference distribution is characterized by a continuous density, candidates that abide by a minimax solution adopt positions near (but not necessarily identical to) the median preference on each salient issue of the campaign.

One partial resolution of the argument that a mixed minimax strategy is an unreasonable solution concept in this context, owing to the sequential (dynamic) aspects of campaigns as against spatial theory's static conceptualization, is the hypothesis that both candidates' sequential choices are made in accordance with the method of fictitious play. That is, if candidates keep record of their opponents' previous positions and adopt strategies that are good against these histories, then in the limit their histories converge to the minimax solution. 'In the long run', then, candidates can be said to act as if they abide by mixed strategy solutions.

This, of course, does not resolve all issues surrounding sequential models of election competition, nor does McKelvey and Ordeshook's analysis necessarily 'solve' spatial theory's dilemma concerning the non-existence of pure strategy equilibria. Some progress has been made, however, that suggests that these issues and this dilemma are not necessarily unresolvable.

## SUBSTANTIVE CRITICISMS

If a theory is subject to repeated empirical application and testing, it is relatively easy to identify its most unsatisfactory and limiting features and to specify how it ought to be modified. Spatial theory's applications to the real world, however, are confined to some 'armchair' empiricism with respect to its theorems and to testing its assumptions about citizens (cf. Riker and Ordeshook 1968; Brody and page, 1973; Rosenthal and Sen, 1973; Aldrich, 1975; and Stratmann, 1974). Moreover, we do not possess the experience and attendant expertise in reconceptualizing variegated empirical phenomena in terms of a single theoretical paradigm. Thus, we are less certain about the scope and extent of the inadequacies as well as the promise of a spatial perspective in particular and of rational models in general. Political science nevertheless possesses considerable substantive knowledge on voting behaviour, candidate motives, party organizations, participation and interest groups. And while this knowledge frequently fails to meet scientifically rigorous standards, we can use it tentatively to evaluate our approach.

As we proceed with this evaluation, we attempt to answer one simple question: is the spatial-rational choice paradigm *theoretically* capable of accommodating feature $X$ of an electoral process? Our conclusion is that while the answer to this question is yes, attempting to accommodate every apparently salient feature of elections into a single analysis renders that analysis incapable of producing general results. To see this, as well as to see how spatial theory should properly be used to model complex processes, we must distinguish between *theories* and *models*. In particular, we must resolve the common confusion between the desirable properties of a deductive theory and an adequate description of reality in terms of such a theory.

Briefly, theory construction consists of formulating general sentences about reality with the realization that these general sentences must be reinterpreted and applied in various combinations to understand complex real-world situations. Thus, science proposes no general 'theory of falling feathers' that seeks to account for every twist and turn of a feather's flight. Instead, if we sought such an account (and if sufficient computer resources are avaiable), we doubtlessly would utilize existing generalizations from physics and aerodynamics in some complex combination. And we would term that combination a model.

The fact that parsimonious propositions about falling feathers cannot be constructed is not interpreted as an inadequacy of Newtonian physics. Similarly, political scientists should not anticipate theories from which we directly deduce general statements about all relevant or interesting aspects of election processes. Instead, we must differentiate between the process of constructing theories and that of model-building, i.e. of applying the theory. Thus, to evaluate a theory empirically, we must isolate those facets of reality that we cannot conceptualize as elements of our theory from those elements that are simply complex combinations of laws we understand theoretically.

To see this let us begin with assumption 1, which partitions the set of decision-makers into two distinct subsets, candidates and citizens. One of the most pervasive critiques of spatial theory is that elections concern citizens who do more than simply vote or abstain. Elections also involve party organizations and their leaderships, opinion élites and activists and interest groups who contribute time, money and advice. (Downs, in his seminal analysis, partitions $D$ into parties and citizens. The criticism levelled at this analysis, however, is that parties—especially American political parties—are rarely well organized, homogeneous teams.) The question then is: can we use the existing propositions of spatial theory in various combinations to model elections characterized by variegated classes of decision-makers? If not, what are the propositions spatial theory must develop?

With respect to political parties, Aranson and Ordeshook (1972) and Coleman (1971, 1972) illustrate the construction of a spatial model that accommodates both the nomination and general election stages of a campaign. In Aranson and Ordeshook's analysis, for example, party activists are concerned not only with how well a candidate satisfies their policy preferences but also with the general election viability of candidates. The significance of this analysis, however, is that the modelling process requires little if any reconceptualization of spatial terms. Admittedly, the analyses are clumsy and the derived propositions are restrictive—but we must anticipate that as we focus more on 'falling feathers'.

For another example, consider activists who, in addition to voting, also contribute resources to the candidates' campaigns. Here it is reasonable to suppose that the participation choices of these citizens conform to the same general set of theoretical propositions that we use to explain the decision to vote (cf. Riker and Ordeshook, 1973, Ch. 3). What is difficult, however, is assessing how candidates weight the preferences of activists relative to those of citizens in general—the difficulty being that spatial theory does not presently admit alternative resource allocations as a strategy. That is, we cannot weight activists because we do not know how to evaluate, say, alternative campaign budgets.

An equivalent problem arises if we attempt to incorporate opinion élites into our analysis; we cannot weight their 'votes' because spatial theory has not yet made formal allowances for their contributions to a candidate's campaign.

The problem clearly centres on the assumptions about $\theta_i$. In particular, having avoided the issue of how candidates seek to manipulate their spatial positions during a campaign, we thus rule out any consideration of campaign tactics. The important point, however, is that a model of campaign tactics can be incorporated into a spatial analysis. Suppose, for example, that candidate $i$ engages in two tactics: publicly advocating position $\theta_i$ and spending $r_{ki}$ dollars in state, region or district $k$ to advertise himself and his position. Now suppose that, within the district, each citizen's perception of his position, $\theta_i^k$, is a function of $r_{ki}$ and $\theta_i$: that is, $\theta_i^k(\theta_i, r_{ki})$. We might, of course, let $\theta_i^k$ be a function of the campaign tactics of other candidates as well. But, for another complication, assume that the candidate's budget constraint is a function of the strategies that each candidate advocates publically: thus

$$\sum_k r_{ki} = R_i(\theta_1, \theta_2, \ldots, \theta_n).$$

Each candidate, then, is confronted with a closed simultaneous system in which he must properly choose $\theta_i$ and allocate his budget optimally. Clearly, now, spatial theory (at least its perspective, if not its existing theorems) can be used to evaluate the consequence, in terms of plurality, of alternative values of $\theta_i^k$. By assuming that contributing money is simply a higher order variant of participation than voting, it can also be used to analyse the function $R_i$. For the candidate to solve the system mathematically, however, he must know the properties of the function $\theta_i^k(\theta_i, r_{ki})$. Unfortunately, rational choice models of the effects of campaign contributions on voting are only beginning to appear (cf. Brams and Davis, 1974; Blydenburgh, 1971; Colantoni et al., 1975; and Kramer, 1966). It is evident, of course, that development of these models must rely not on spatial theory but on the fields of cognitive psychology and, perhaps, marketing. Our point, however, is that these models can be used in various combinations with spatial theory to analyse relatively complex election processes.

In addition to illustrating how we might use spatial theory to model such processes, the previous discussion as well as our discussion in the previous section about the choice function $g_i^v$, suggest how we might weaken several of the restrictive assumptions detailed in the first section about citizens, their preferences and their decision rules for revealing these preferences. We do not know, of course, the extent to which general theorems can be proven as against the more 'engineering-like' enterprise of constructing theoretically based computer simulations. But, if complexity necessitates simulation, then spatial analysis should at least provide for computer models that possess some degree of theoretical justification (see Waltz's (1968) critique of contemporary political simulations that are not well grounded in theory).

With respect to citizens, however, we have not yet considered the criticisms of two additional assumptions—that $\theta_i$ and $x^v$ are continuous (A14) and that $x^v$ is well defined (A15). Clearly, (A14) is a mathematical convenience of immense value because it permits us to use the continuous calculus (see Meek, 1972). But Stokes (1963) and many others question its descriptive validity. In particular, Stokes argues the existence of *valence* issues upon which only two or some finite number of admissable positions exist. Casual empiricism seems to confirm this argument (e.g. the candidate is for or against bussing, honest or dishonest, a member of the Labour, Conservative or Liberal parties). As we argue in the next section, though, we require a better theoretical conceptualization of campaign issues before we can conjecture about their mathematical properties. First, however, we note that, if candidates cannot move on valence issues, then we can absorb their effect into our assumptions about $g_i^v$ in the same way that we absorb partisan bias into this function. But if we wish to model strategic variation on such issues (e.g. as when a party considers nominating alternative candidates), there is no reason to suppose that spatial analysis cannot directly accommodate discrete issue dimensions. The basic concepts of game theory (e.g. equilibrium, pure strategy, decision-maker, payoff function) need not be redefined as we move back and forth between finite and infinite games; and, more importantly, we do not find *qualitatively* different theoretical propositions when comparing these two classes of games. Since spatial theory is but a substantively interpreted game, then, we are not likely to discover qualitatively different theoretical propositions by simply admitting discrete strategy spaces. Thus, given the mathematical convenience of continuity, we anticipate that spatial theory will adhere to a continuous representation of issues and preferences.

A second assumption about citizens that is criticized frequently is that a citizen's preferences on issues are well defined ((A15) and presumably the assumption of well defined utility functions, (A10)). Here, however, we must distinguish between two possibilities. The first is that a citizen does not possess a preference on an issue. But, as we note before, this is easily accomodated by permitting the functional forms of $g_i^y$ to vary across the electorate. The second possibility is that citizens are concerned about the issue but are either uncertain about their preferences or unable to discriminate perfectly between nearly identical alternatives or strategies. Uncertainty can be handled with stochastic utility assumptions. The inability to discriminate, though, is more problematical since it can violate our usual assumptions about preference. Specifically, the transitivity axiom requires, in part, that if a person is indifferent between $x$ and $y$ and between y and z, then he is indifferent between x and z. Suppose, however, that he is indifferent between x and y and between y and z because these alternatives are not sufficiently distinct (e.g. they are close spatially): but if, as is entirely possible, x and z are sufficiently distinct so that x is preferred to z or vice-versa, an intransitive preference is revealed. Fortunately, preference functions with intransitive indifference are being closely scrutinized in the social choice literature in general (Fishburn, 1970) and in spatial analysis in particular (Sloss, 1973). Briefly, Sloss's conclusion is that, while these intransitivities can render equilibria more likely, the general mathematical form of the necessary and sufficient conditions for equilibria are not much different from those derived with the transitivity axiom (e.g. Plott, 1967). The point, however, is that there is no reason to suppose that spatial theory cannot accommodate weaker assumptions about preference.

Another class of extensively criticized assumptions are those pertaining to candidates. We argued earlier that the assumptions of perfect spatial mobility and common domain are easily modified within the context of a specific election. A substantively more important assumption, however, is that candidates seek to maximize their expected plurality (A7). There is, of course, considerable confusion as to what candidates maximize. Many possess idiosyncratic objectives that are unrelated to the votes they and their opponents receive. Others wish simply to provide a forum for a particular ideological view. Unfortunately, even if we restrict ourselves to modelling candidates whose goals can be restated in terms of winning, there are a great many ways to operationalize winning in terms of votes. It would appear, of course, that in plurality systems the simplest assumption is that candidates maximize the probability that they receive more votes than any opponent. In early deterministic spatial models this objective is equivalent to the more mathematically tractable assumption that candidates maximize plurality—hence the historical justification for assumption 7. There are, however, good reasons for supposing that candidates seek instead to maximize votes (if, for example, their information about opponents is imperfect) or proportion of the vote (if a great many candidates compete in say a primary election and if 'winning' requires only that the candidate produce a good showing relative to others). If we further admit uncertainty or risk into our election models, then each of the following objectives can be rationalized:

(1) expected plurality maximization;
(2) expected vote maximization;
(3) expected proportion of the vote maximization;
(4) maximizing the probability that plurality exceeds some prespecified level (zero if the objective is simply winning);
(5) maximizing the probability that vote exceeds some pre-specified level;
(6) maximizing the probability that proportion of the vote exceeds some pre-specified level.

On the basis of this list, it appears that spatial theory focuses on a single special case—plurality maximization—which greatly limits its empirical relevance (for an analysis of vote maximization see Hinich and Ordeshook, 1970). The theory, however, is not so limited. Specifically, it is possible to establish conditions under which these objectives are equivalent either in the sense that they yield identical equilibria or in the stronger sense that they are everywhere interchangeable (cf. Aranson et al., 1973, 1974). For example, if all citizens vote, then maximizing expected plurality, vote and proportion of the vote are equivalent.

This is not to say, of course, that these sufficient conditions are not restrictive or that they are easily satisfied; on the contrary, Aranson et al. conclude that these objectives are not equivalent in general. On the one hand, then, we find that formal models can analyse alternative candidate goals and establish conditions under which these goals yield identical outcomes as well as conditions under which alternative goals might explain variations in strategy and public policy. On the other hand, spatial theory is limited, to the extent that it focuses exclusively on expected plurality maximization. A substantial empirical research effort, however, must precede any intensive theoretical investigation of a plethora of alternative objectives. Little is known about candidates and how they translate votes into objectives in alternative election systems. (An equivalent issue exists in economics, for example, where analysts argue whether firms maximize profits, share of the market, rate of growth in earnings per share and so on.) Contemporary journalistic accounts of campaigns continue to equate (confuse?) the objectives of winning, maximizing plurality and maximizing votes. By requiring mathematically well defined objectives, perhaps the principal contribution of formal election models is the focus it lends to an empirical question.

Before we leave the issue of candidate objectives, however, we must consider another objection to assumptions such as (A7); namely that, regardless of how winning is operationalized in terms of votes, candidates do not maximize but seek instead to form minimal winning coalitions (à la Riker, (1962)). At first glance this seems a reasonable counter-proposal, but it is not inconsistent with (A7), nor is it necessarily pertinent to our analysis. Assumption 7 states, of course, that, given an opponent's strategy, a candidate will adopt strategies of his own that maximize his plurality. But, this is not to say that a candidate can or will proceed from there to build an 'oversized' coalition. In the context of elections, the question is not 'what strategy does a candidate adopt when confronted with a simple maximization problem (against nature or an ignorant opponent)' but, rather, 'what coalitions of citizens do candidates organize if they abide by minimax strategies to the election game?' In general, the answer for symmetric games (the context of Riker's analysis) is that the equilibrium entails the expectation of a tie vote; i.e., the candidates converge and all citizens are indifferent between them, or the coalitions of voters supporting each candidate are of equal size (i.e. are minimal but not winning). Riker's analysis, moreover, is not even pertinent to spatial models of, say, two-candidate competition. The context of that analysis is co-operative $n$-person games as when the electorate acts as a committee without candidates. There we infer the sizes of coalitions by examining the structure of solution concepts such as the core, the V-solution and the bargaining set (cf. Shepsle, 1974). In two-candidate election models, however, the candidates are the active players, thereby rendering the game non-co-operative. And, as McKelvey and Ordeshook (1974) demonstrate, the spatial positions corresponding to the V-solution and the bargaining set do not necessarily possess any equilibrium properties for candidates.

Another criticism of spatial theory, noted earlier, is that it fails to consider the sequential or dynamic aspects of campaigns. Apart from using the notion of fictitious plan to justify mixed-strategy solutions, it reduces the campaign to a 'snapshot' by assuming that candidates choose their strategies simultaneously and that they do not deviate from them thereafter (A8). While this is a valid criticism, it is poorly stated. If our objective is to model the general policy biases of election systems, and if pure strategy equilibria exist, then a non-dynamic model may be wholly appropriate—especially if we take the view that candidates do not move spatially but that parties move by nominating different candidates. If, however, we focus on the candidates' tactics as they progress through a campaign, we require a dynamic model. For example, our research objective might be to study optimal expenditure patterns over time and thereby isolate conditions under which a candidate should spend his resources early rather than late. This objective, of course, addresses the practical question of when a candidate's campaign should peak.

Here again, however, we cannot attribute spatial theory's inadequacies to some flaw in its game-theoretic roots or to the paradigm of rational choice. There already exists an extensive literature on dynamic (differential) and sequential games as well as dynamic control processes that we can apply to model the dynamic properties of elections. Rather, the problem is the paucity of well defined empirical questions and research. It is one thing to state that a model should be dynamic rather than static. It is quite another thing to identify the empirical regularities that a dynamic model should explain. Unquestionably, dynamic models are more mathematically complex and less general than their static counterparts—and without well defined empirical relevance.

Suppose, however, that the question of when candidates' campaigns should peak is sufficiently interesting to warrant a detailed deductive analysis. In particular, let us take the model of resource allocations outlined earlier in this section and augment it dynamically by supposing that $\theta_i^k$ is a function of time thus: the divergence between perceived and actual positions ($\theta_i^k$ versus $\theta_i$) decreases as $r$ increases, but if $r$ goes, say, to zero at time $t$, this divergence increases over time (i.e., the effects of resources spent at time $t$ are subject to 'decay' thereafter). Clearly, before this becomes a mathematically rigorous model, we must specify a great many functional relationships including, for example, decay rates and their laws (e.g. exponential). Unfortunately, we can only begin to speculate on the dynamic relationships between campaign resources and citizens' perceptions and attitudes. Political science is not even secure in its understanding of campaign whistle-stops as they affect the activity of local party organizations. That is, while our research might secure some guidance from cognitive psychology and learning theory, the universe of substantively reasonable functional relationships remains vast.

It seems safe to predict, though, that formal models in general and spatial models in particular will begin to consider certain dynamically stated propositions (see, for example, Frey and Lau, 1971) even if these models assume, in a more or less *ad hoc* fashion, particular functional relationships on the basis of their intuitive plausibility. Our principal requirement, however, is that the critic define explicitly the question he wants answered and the context of his problem.

Closely related to the criticism that spatial theory is static is the objection one might raise to its assumptions about the candidates' information. Implicitly or explicitly, spatial models assume that candidates know the issues, their relative salience and citizens' preferences, decision rules and perceptions. But, since social science is only now beginning to develop the appropriate methodologies for measuring these parameters, it seems unlikely that candidates possess the facts we impute to them. We are confronted, then, with three alternatives. First, if we accept the proposition that spatial theory's assumptions capture the essential properties of elections, we can resurrect the notion of Darwinian processes and argue that the candidates with better information, or who somehow better infer the values of parameters, are more successful while others are weeded out. Second, we might argue that our models model candidate perceptions and thus can explain their actions.

For the sake of additional realism, however, a new class of models should be developed—models in which candidates are constrained by available statistical methods and in which candidates progress through campaigns continually taking measurements (e.g. polls), processing alternative hypotheses about the electorate's preference, etc. That is, we require models of candidates as sequential decision-makers and Bayesian learners. At this point, of course, we can only speculate about the form such models should take, as well as about their tractability. Again, however, while we can lament the fact that they do not yet exist, it seems clear that these more complex models should make considerable use of existing spatial concepts.

The final set of issues we consider in this section concerns the institutional setting of spatial theory. Owing presumably to the simplicity of the majority rule voting procedure, spatial theory (i.e. its theorems if not its perspectives) is virutally irrelevant to the analysis of multi-party proportional representation systems or to systems in which parties are more cohesive and centralized than their American counterparts and in which governments are formed by a post-election process of coalition formation. Even within the American context, spatial theory has little to say at present about the rise, maintenance and decline of minor or third parties. Briefly, then, spatial theory is almost wholly preoccupied with simple two-candidate, plurality rule elections. There are some notable exceptions, including Klevorick and Kramer's (1973) analyses of West Germany's *Genossenschaften,* Rosenthal and Sen's (1973) empirical study of turnout and blank ballots in the French Fifth Republic, Hinich and Ordeshook's (1974) analysis of the Electoral College, Kramer's (1972) and Kadane's (1972) models of sophisticated and sequential issue voting and Rosenthal's (1974) model of French trade union elections. For the most part, though, these exceptions are limited in scope.

Our preceding discussions detail several reasons for spatial theory's special emphasis. These reasons include the difficulty encountered in modelling citizen decision rules in complex environments and the restrictiveness of the pure strategy equilibrium concept. In addition to these, however, there are several theoretical and substantive constraints on the spatial theorist.

The most prominent theoretical constraints concern pre- and post-election coalition processes in multi-party systems. Briefly, if bargaining among parties entails transferable commodities such as money or votes, then we might use the solution concepts of $n$-person game theory (or Riker's theory of minimal winning coalitions) to limit our expectations about outcomes. If, however, the parties bargain over policy, then it is more appropriate to model the situation as an $n$-person (party) game without side payments. The difficulty here, however, is that the most common notions of a solution, the V-set or the bargaining set, need not exist—a difficulty that has received little attention in the context of election processes (cf Wilson, 1971b). Thus, given the spatial positions of parties in a parliament, we may be wholly unable to predict which coalition forms and what policies it adopts. Consequently, we may be unable to anticipate the policies of individual parties if their goals include, say, maximizing the probability that they are included in the government coalition.

While these problems do not arise or are irrelevant if competition is uni-dimensional or if the parties' positions are fixed, we see here how easily we can arrive at the frontiers of knowledge in game theory. The spatial theorists cannot wave these problems away by arguing for a reconceptualization or by making distinctions between models and theories. The fact remains that certain consequential indeterminacies exist at present in the rational choice paradigm.

These indeterminacies will doubtlessly be explored further—either in the context of spatial theory or, more generally, in game theory. Believing that his paradigm is completely general, however, and in lieu of these developments, the spatial theorist must continue to explore the possibility that some forms of determinacy may arise from the exigencies of the real world and that he must search them out and model them. But here we are confronted with a paucity of empirical facts, such as those we outline in the following questions:

First, in parliamentary systems with single-member districts, how do citizens subjectively define competitiveness? Do they focus on predictions about national pluralities or seats won, or are their estimates a function principally of district patterns? A similar question arises in the American context with respect to presidential elections; namely, is the decision about whether or not to vote a function of state or national estimates of plurality? Also, which measures of competitiveness are the best predictors of turnout (the theoretically proscribed measure of competitiveness seems too complex to adopt as a reasonable behavioural model; see McKelvey and Ordeshook, (1972).

Second, to what extent are citizens cognizant of post-election coalition possibilities? It is reasonable, for example, to suppose that citizens vote sincerely and that only parties engage in the complex calculations necessary to ascertain strategic advantage (see Downs, 1957, Ch.9; Aranson, 1972; and Trilling, 1970 for a discussion of alternative possibilities)? Are citizens in proportional representation systems, as against those in single-member district systems, more likely to be concerned with post-election coalition possibilities?

Third, how do citizens define the policy positions of coalition governments? Do they act as if these position are some convex combination of the positions of the parties in the coalition, the position of the relevant minister or a lottery among the positions of the member parties?

Finally, to what extent is it reasonable to suppose that voters' perceptions of a party's candidate in a district are determined by the positions of that party's national leadership as against the candidate's personal policy preferences? How is a party's spatial position affected by pre-election pronouncements of coalition intentions?

No doubt additional questions would arise as the actual process of model-building proceeds. Answers to the preceding set of questions, however, are an essential starting point—with or without a theoretical resolution of the indeterminacy of $n$-person games without side payments. To model complex processes we must adopt simplifying heuristic assumptions about decision-makers (see, for example, Laing and Morrison, 1974). Without some guide to an appropriate set of heuristics, the theorist can do little more than construct a variety of alternative models with no guarantee that these models possess any empiricial validity.

Minimally, though, apart from highlighting some theoretical problems that may be common to all social processes, spatial analysis provides some perspective to empirical analysis. Its principal contribution is its spatial conceptualization of citizen preferences and candidate strategies. And the adequacy of that perspective is the issue to which we now turn.

## THE ADEQUACY OF A SPATIAL CONCEPTUALIZATION

If political science adopted the perspectives of economics in defining the goods and services that governments provide, a spatial perspective would cause little criticism. Classical microeconomic theory begins, in fact, with a spatial conceptualization, except that here, citizens' ideal points are at infinity (i.e., consumers prefer more to less). Preferences of this sort, however, are readily converted to the kind assumed by the spatial theorist (cf. Klevorick and Kramer, 1973; Simpson, 1969; and Bowen, 1943). Suppose, for example, that the world consists of two goods, that both goods are provided by a democratically elected government and that the government's only decision is, on the basis of a fixed budget, to produce a proper mix of these goods. Thus, competition between parties in uni-dimensional (percentage of the budget allocated to producing goods 1) and, if citizens' preferences satisfy the usual convexity assumptions, their preferences are single-peaked along this dimension. For a more complicated possibility suppose that, in addition to the two collectively supplied goods, the market provides two additional but non-identical commodities and that citizens' preferences in the four-commodity space satisfy the usual economic assumptions (e.g. more is better than less). Suppose, further, that citizens are permitted to vote also on the size of the government's budget so that, given a tax structure, they are in effect voting on the amount of their personal incomes they can allocate to purchasing market services. Assuming now that each citizen maximizes his utility in the market (subject to their budget constraints) we can derive, from the several rates of substitution and so on, a two-dimensional utility function, where the first dimension corresponds to a tax rate (the size of the government's budget) while the second dimension corresponds to the issue of how that budget is to be allocated between the government's two services.

Clearly, this is an extraordinarily useful perspective, for it points the way towards the construction of models of collective action that are neither purely economic nor purely political. Rather, these models correspond to the reality of market and political forces intertwined.

For political scientists who follow a more behaviouralist tradition, however, the preceding justification and use of the spatial perspective will seem inadequate. Unlike economics, political science devotes considerably more effort to the definition and measurement of attitudes, preferences and perceptions. Thus, the economist's willingness to deal principally with 'objectively' defined, readily measurable variables is regarded as less than satisfactory—at least for an adequate understanding of people's choices in elections.

An even casual perusal of the literature on voting research seems to confirm the political scientist's bias. But while the discipline delves deeper into the empirical world, it does so almost wholly without its own theoretical perspective. What are the questions this research seeks to answer, other than the all encompassing 'why'? And if there are specific questions, are there too many? The cost of this state of affairs is evident—given a specific question of public policy, no answers are forthcoming. For example, one of the most important questions in the debate over Electoral College reform in the United States is whether abandoning the Electoral College in favour of a direct vote plan increases or decreases the viability of third parties. Political scientists and others testifying before Congress are universally unable to offer any more than 'educated' guesses as answers.

Thus we witness a trade-off, with economics opting for theoretical and deductive rigour within the context of a narrowly but well defined set of issues while political science chooses descriptive accuracy within a broadly but poorly defined context. The objective of spatial theory in particular and the rational choice paradigm in general is to synthesize these two approaches. Hence the question is whether and to what extent a spatial perspective can accommodate the apparent complexity of individual attitudes and preferences that are revealed in voting research without abandoning the goal of parsimonious theory.

Of course, we cannot answer such questions conclusively. What we can do here, however, is review several immediate issues and ascertain the response of spatial theory.

Earlier in this essay, we indicated how spatial theory might accommodate (but not explain) several related problems—including partisan bias, valence issues, variations in patterns of salience across citizens and cognitive balance. Briefly, the theme of that accommodation is the flexibility of the citizen's choice function, $g_i^v$. First, with respect to partisan bias and valence issues, there is no reason to suppose that we require a spatial representation for all criteria citizens employ in their evaluations of candidates. If, for example, citizen $v$ identifies with candidate $i$'s party, so that, *ceteris paribus,* the citizen is more likely to vote for candidate $i$ than $j$, then we can assume simply that $g_i^v(x) > g_j^v(x)$ for all $x$. And, as we note earlier, many of spatial theory's central theorems can be generalized to allow for such variations in choice functions (cf. Hinich *et al.*, 1972, and McKelvey, 1973).

The second accommodation that $g_i^v$ allows concerns variations in issue salience.

Both Stokes (1963) and Converse (1966), in their original critiques of spatial analysis, note that citizens do not all weight the issues in the same way. For the most part, though, early spatial models impose assumptions such as (A13). Again, however, we can weaken these assumptions considerably by focusing on choice functions rather than utility functions that underlie them. It is reasonable to conjecture, moreover, that, as spatial theory considers alternative solution concepts, strong assumptions about patterns of issue salience will be required only to specify, for a particular election, the exact domain of the solution. That is, we can establish existence with weaker assumptions than have heretofore been considered. (Although it might seem as important to isolate the exact location of a solution, location will always depend in general on the particular characteristics of the electorate, i.e. the numerical value of variables. Unfortunately, the questions of existence and location are frequently combined in spatial theory so that in attempting to establish both simultaneously, over-strong assumptions are imposed.)

Finally, we conjecture that cognitive balance can be incorporated into one's models by letting $g_i^v$ depend on the $\theta_i$s in ways that are not permitted currently by a simple multi-dimensional utility representation (e.g. assumption 10). Admittedly, though, this possibility has not been pursued to any great extent, owing largely to the considerable variety of reasonable formal operationalizations of balance. It is evident, then, that a significant opportunity exists here for joint research on the part of the cognitive psychologist and the spatial theorist.

We cannot, however, load everything into the choice function unless we admit outright that a spatial conceptualization of evaluative criteria possesses no relevance to the study of elections. Admittedly, it is only a rather large dose of faith at this point that leads us to reject this possibility. If we look to the literature of political science we find few studies that support the hypothesis that evaluative criteria can be meaningfully conceptualized and measured in a multi-dimensional space (cf. Mauser, 1972; Weisberg and Rusk, 1970; Rabinowitz, 1973; and Cahoon et al., 1973). We can attribute this in part to the relative infancy of spatial theory, the failure of political scientists to conduct sustained research in multi-dimensional scaling techniques and an ill-defined theory of attitudes and the determinants of preference.

Let us turn then to a brief examination of a speculative model of preferences that is less detailed, but similar in spirit, to the model Budge and Farlie (1974) offer, and which raises some serious questions about the adequacy of the multi-dimensional scaling applications that we refer to above. First, we suppose that all citizens possess a common underlying preference space $(S_1)$, that they use this space to evaluate not only candidates and parties but also the goods they purchase in markets and so on (i.e. to evaluate alternative complete social states), and that preferences in this space satisfy the usual economic assumptions about utility (for a similar conceptualization in economics, see Lanchaster, 1966).

Second, we assume another space $(S_2)$, called an *action space*, which describes contemporary political issues, government policies, etc. Third, we assume a transformation, $T_1^v$, which maps from $S_2$ into $S_1$ and thereby permits us to derive citizen vs preferences in $S_2$ from his utility function in $S_1$. The function $T_1^v$, of course, is superscripted with $v$ to indicate that it details for each citizen his beliefs about how a particular policy affects his basic welfare as well as his objective status in the economy (e.g. home ownership, trade union membership and income). Finally, we can extend the model further by imagining a third space, $S_3$, that is identical to $S_2$ except that it records the positions publically advocated by the candidates. For greater generality, however, we should represent these positions by density functions to indicate objective uncertainty in the candidate's public utterances (as in Shepsle, 1972). A second transformation, $T_2^v$, now maps functions from $S_3$ into $S_2$ and represents the citizens' interpretation of a candidate's campaign strategy in terms of his beliefs about the policies a candidate will secure if elected (for example, if the candidate professes a specific policy but the citizen is unsure about the true meaning of the candidate's statements, $T_2^v$ maps from a point in $S_3$ to a density in $S_2$). Of course, the form of the transformation $T_2^v$ is a function of a great many things, including the quality of the citizen's information, the extent to which the citizen trusts each candidate and so on (for additional generality we might also suppose that $T_1^v$ admits uncertainty).

This simple conceptualization seems a reasonable starting point for a model of individual preferences. Admittedly, it is one thing to say 'assume at transformation $T_i^v$' and quite another to ascertain its empirical content. We use this conceptualization, however, to raise a fundamental issue. What *are* the dimensions identified by existing applications of multi-dimensional scaling? The fact is, they do not appear to correspond to either $S_1$ or $S_2$ (or, equivalently, $S_3$). Nearly all of the applications we cited earlier use the same SRC presidential election survey data and among the dimensions observed, all find one that corresponds roughly to attitudes towards civil rights, civil liberties or authoritarianism. On neither intuitive nor technical grounds does this dimension seem to belong in $S_1$. First, we can easily imagine that people's attitudes towards civil rights derive from more basic preferences and beliefs about, say, personal safety and economic security. More to the point, attitudes of a similar sort are a function of personal experience and circumstance— which suggests that the dimension belongs to $S_2$. Technically, moreover, our prejudice is to assume that ideal points in $S_1$ are at infinity and that, much like a budget constraint, $T_2$ establishes interior ideal points in $S_2$.

On the whole, then, the dimension corresponds more closely to our conceptualization of $S_2$. But then we must ask: what are the *actionable* issues of a campaign that determine a candidate's position on this dimension? Unfortunately, we can imagine several, including bussing, fair housing and curbs on campus unrest. Thus, the dimension seems more a composite of several action issues. If a candidate is confronted with preferences on this 'civil rights criterion', he is then likely to wonder how his position is affected by a modified public stance on, say, bussing as against open housing. We cannot provide an adequate answer, however, because the dimension revealed by multi-dimensional scaling is a composite not only of several actionable issues, but of $T_2^v$ as well. Thus, its practical value is minimized.

If we minimize practical value, it is reasonable to ask why one should engage in multi-dimensional scaling in the first place. If the reason is simply prediction, then scaling seems too cumbersome a device to that end. If it is description as well, that description requires a purpose; and, presumably, that purpose is to understand the processes of government and why it chooses one policy rather than another. An essential part of that understanding is a clear account of $S_2$ and $T_2^v$ (and, ideally, $T_1^v$). From this we infer that, while contemporary methodologies are a vast improvement over simple attitudinal questionnaires, much additional research remains.

## CONCLUSION

Review essays, critical or otherwise, seem destined to conclude that 'the past is prologue and the future lies ahead', and this review is no exception. We have, however, sought to outline how spatial theory might be modified to accommodate certain aspects of reality without abandoning its basic perspective. We find, nevertheless, that the theory possesses several major inadequacies as constituted at present. The first is its reliance on the concept of pure strategy equilibria for a definition of a solution to the election game. The second is its failure to consider election systems other than simple majority rule. Its third major inadequacy concerns the development of an adequate conceptualization of attitudes and preference and an appropriate statistical methodology. We agree, moreover, with those critics who argue that spatial analysis provides a poor *model* of election processes; but we disagree strongly with the assertion that it constitutes an inadequate *theory* of those processes.

In this essay we have not, of course, considered the more general issue of the adequacy of the rational choice paradigm itself. Nor have we addressed important and more specific questions such as how citizens ought to be conceptualized so as to render rational 'habitual' behaviour, or at least behaviour that seems to be governed by a set of attitudes learned early in childhood (e.g. partisan identification). Our omissions are due in part to the extensive discussions of the paradigm that exist elsewhere (cf. Buchanan, 1966; Harsanyi 1969; Riker and Ordeshook, 1973). They are due also to the fact that we do not know how to answer such questions adequately. Stated simply, we require a better basic understanding of cognitive processes, of learning and of concepts such as partisan identification. On the one hand we know that the perspectives of rational choice can usefully contribute to research that seeks to develop the requisite understanding (see, for example, Goldberg, 1969). On the other hand we believe that the rational choice paradigm, of which spatial analysis is a part, is sufficiently flexible to accommodate a great variety of alternative models of cognition and learning. And as with any scientific paradigm, we cannot ascertain its limitations until we actually attempt to apply it to diverse empirical phenomena.

# REFERENCES

Aldrich, John (1975), 'Candidate Support Functions in the 1968 Election: An Empirical Application of the Spatial Mode', *Public Choice,* 17.

Aranson, Peter H. (1972), 'Political Participation in Alternative Election Systems', unpublished Ph.D. dissertation, University of Rochester, Rochester, New York.

Aranson, Peter H., and Peter C. Ordeshook (1972), 'Spatial Strategies for Sequential Elections', in R. G. Niemi and H. F. Weisberg (eds.), *Probability Models of Collective Decision-Making,* Merrill, Columbus, Ohio.

Aranson, Peter H., Melvin J. Hinich and Peter C. Ordeshook (1973), 'Campaign Strategies for Alternative Election Systems: Candidate Objectives as an Intervening Variable', in H. R. Alker *et al.* (eds.), *Mathematical Approaches to Politics,* Elsevier, Amsterdam.

Aranson, Peter H., Melvin J. Hinich and Peter C. Ordeshook (1974), 'Election Goals and Strategies: Equivalent and Non-Equivalent Candidate Objectives', *American Political Science Review,* 68, 135–52.

Aumann, R. J., and M. Maschler (1964), 'The Bargaining Set for Cooperative Games', in M. Dresher, *et al.* (eds.), *Advances in Game Theory,* Princeton University Press, Princeton, New Jersey.

Berelson, Bernard, Paul Lazarsfeld and William McPhee (1954), *Voting,* University of Chicago Press, Chicago.

Blydenburgh, John C. (1971), 'A Controlled Experiment to Measure the Effects of Personal Contact Campaigning', *Midwest Journal of Political Science,* 15, 365–81.

Bowen, Howard R. (1943), 'The Interpretation of Voting in the Allocation of Economic Resources', *Quarterly Journal of Economics,* 58, 27–48.

Brams, Steven, and Morton Davis (1974), 'The 3/2's Rule in Presidential Campaigning', *American Political Science Review*, 68, 113–35.

Brody, Richard A., and Benjamin I. Page (1973), 'Indifference, Alienation and Rational Decisions', *Public Choice*, 15, 1–17.

Buchanan, James M. (1966), 'An Individualistic Theory of Political Processes', in David Easton (ed.), *Varieties of Political Theory*, Prentice Hall, Englewood Cliffs, New Jersey.

Budge, Ian, and Dennis Farlie (1974), 'A Model of Party Competition and Voting Behavior Based on a Party-Defined Likelihood Space', unpublished manuscript, University of Essex.

Cahoon, Lawrence, Melvin J. Hinich and Peter C. Ordeshook (1973), 'A Multidimensional Scaling Procedure for Spatial Analysis', unpublished manuscript, Carnegie-Mellon University.

Casstevens, Thomas (1968), 'A Theorem About Voting', *American Political Science Review* 62, 205–7.

Chapman, David E. (1967), 'Models of the Working of a Two-Party Electoral System', *Papers in Non-Market Decision Making*, 3, 19–37.

Chapman, David E. (1968), 'Models of the Working of a Two-Party Electoral System', *Public Choice*, 5, 19–37.

Colantoni, Claude S., Terrence Levesque and Peter C. Ordeshook (1975), 'Campaign Resource Allocations under the Electoral College', *American Political Science Review*, 69.

Colantoni, Claude S., Terrence Levesque and P. C. Ordeshook (1975), 'Rejoinder to Comment', by S. Brams and M. Davis, *American Political Science Review*, 69.

Coleman, James S. (1971), 'Internal Processes Governing Party Positions in Elections', *Public Choice*, 11, 35–60.

Coleman, James S. (1972), 'The Positions of Political Parties in Elections', in R. G. Niemi and H. F. Weisberg (eds.), *Probability Models of Collective Decision-Making*, Merrill, Columbus, Ohio.

Converse, Philip E. (1966), 'The Problem of Party Distances in Models of Voting Change', in M. K. Jennings and L. H. Zeigler (eds.), *The Electoral Process*, Prentice Hall, Englewood Cliffs, New Jersey.

Davis, Otto A., and Melvin J. Hinich (1968), 'On the Power and Importance of the Mean Preference in a Mathematical Model of Democratic Choice', *Public Choice*, 5, 59–72.

Davis, Otto A., and Melvin J. Hinich (1972), 'Spatial Competition under Constrained Choice', in R. Niemi and H. Weisberg (eds.), *Probability Models of Collective Decision Making*, Merrill, Columbus, Ohio.

Davis, Otto A., Melvin J. Hinich and Peter C. Ordeshook (1970), 'An Expository Development of a Mathematical Model of the Electoral Process', *American Political Science Review*, 64, 426–48.

Downs, Anthony (1957), *An Economic Theory of Democracy*, Harper and Row, New York.

Farquharson, Robin (1969), *Theory of Voting*, Yale University Press, New Haven, Conn.

Fishburn, Peter C. (1970), 'Conditions for Simple Majority Decision Functions with Intransitive Individual Indifference', *Journal of Economic Theory* 2, 354–67.

Frey, Bruno, and Lawrence J. Lau (1968), 'Towards a Mathematical Model of Government Behavior', *Zeitschrift fur Nationalokonomie* 28, 355–80.

Frey, Bruno, and Lawrence J. Lau (1971), 'Ideology, Public Approval and Government Behavior', *Public Choices* 10, 21–40.

Garvey, Gerald (1966), 'The Theory of Party Equilibrium', *American Political Science Review* 60, 29–38.

Goldberg, Arthur S. (1969), 'Social Determinism and Rationality as Bases of Party Identification', *American Political Science Review* 63, 5–25.

Harsanyi, John C. (1969), 'Rational Choice Models of Political Behavior vs. Functionalist and Conformist Theories', *World Politics*, 21, 513–38.

Hinich, Melvin J., and Peter C. Ordeshook (1970), 'Plurality Maximization vs. Vote Maximization: A Spatial Analysis with Variable Participation', *American Political Science Review*, 64, 772–91.

Hinich, Melvin J., John O. Ledyard and Peter C. Ordeshook (1972), 'A Theory of Electoral Equilibrium: A Spatial Analysis Based on the Theory of Games', *Journal of Politics*, 35, 154–93.

Hinich, Melvin J., and Peter C. Ordeshook (1974), 'The Electoral College: A Spatial Analysis', *Political Methodology*, forthcoming.

Hoyer, R. W., and Lawrence Mayer (1974), 'Comparing Strategies in a Spatial Model of Electoral Competition', *American Journal of Political Science*.

Kadane, Joseph B. (1972), 'On Division of the Question', *Public Choice*, 13, 47–54.

Klevorick, Alvin K., and Gerald H. Kramer (1973), 'Social Choice on Pollution Management: the Genossenschaften', *Journal of Public Economics,* **2**, 101–46.

Kramer, Gerald H. (1966), 'A Decision-Theoretic Analysis of a Problem in Political Campaigning', in J. L. Bernd (ed.), *Mathematical Applications in Political Science II,* SMU Press, Dallas.

Kramer, Gerald H. (1971), Letter to the editor, *American Political Science Review,* **65** 187–9.

Kramer, Gerald H. (1972), 'Sophisticated Voting over Multidimensional Choice Spaces', *Journal of Mathematical Sociology* **2**, 165–80.

Laing, James D., and Richard J. Morrison (1974), 'Coalitions and Payoffs in Three-Person Supergames under Multiple-Trial Agreements', in A. Rapoport (ed.), *Game Theory as a Theory of Conflict Resolution,* Reidel, Dordrecht-Holland.

Laing, James D., and Richard J. Morrison (1974), 'Sequential Games of Status', *Behavioral Science,* forthcoming.

Lanchaster, Kevin J. (1966), 'A New Approach to Consumer Theory', *Journal of Political Economy,* **74**, 137–57.

Maschler, Michael (1965), 'Playing an *n*-Person Game, an Experiment', Econometric Research Program, Princeton University.

Mauser, Gary A. (1972), 'A Structural Approach to Predicting Patterns of Electoral Substitution', in R. Shephard, A. Romney and S. Nerlove (eds.), *Multi-dimensional Scaling,* Seminar Press, New York.

McKelvey, Richard D., and Peter C. Ordeshook (1972), 'A General Theory of the Calculus of Voting', in J. F. Herndon and J. L. Bernd (eds.), *Mathematical Applications in Political Science VI,* University Press of Virginia, Charlottesville.

McKelvey, Richard D., and Peter C. Ordeshook (1974), 'Symmetric Spatial Games Without Majority Rule Equilibria', mimeo.

McKelvey, Richard D. (1973), 'Some Extensions and Modifications of a Spatial Model of Party Competition', unpublished Ph.D. dissertation, University of Rochester, Rochester, New York.

McKelvey, Richard and Jeff Richelson (1974), 'Cycles of Risk', *Public Choice,* **18**, 41–66.

Meek, Brian L. (1972), 'The Formulation of Models of Party Competition', *British Journal of Political Science* **2**, 116–20.

Morrison, Richard (1972), 'A Statistical Model of Legislative Roll Call Analysis', *Journal of Mathematical Sociology* **2**, 235–48.

Oppenheimer, Joe A. (1973), 'Relating Coalitions of Minorities to the Voters' Paradox or Putting the Fly in the Democratic Pie', unpublished manuscript, University of Texas.

Ordeshook, Peter C. (1971), 'Pareto Optimality in Electoral Competition', *American Political Science Review,* **65**, 1141–5.

Plott, Charles R. (1967), 'A Notion of Equilibrium and its Possibility Under Majority Rule', *American Economic Review* **57**, 787–806.

Rabinowitz, George B. (1973), 'Spatial Models of Electoral Choice', unpublished Ph.D. dissertation, University of Michigan, Ann Arbor, Michigan.

Rae, Douglas, and Michael Taylor (1971), 'Decision Rules and Policy Outcomes', *British Journal of Political Science,* **1**, 71–90.

Riker, William H. (1962), *The Theory of Political Coalitions,* Yale University Press, New Haven, Conn.

Riker, William H. , and Peter C. Ordeshook (1968), 'A Theory of the Calculs of Voting', *American Political Science Review,* **62**, 25–42.

Riker, William H., and William Zavoina (1970), 'Rational Behavior in Politics: Evidence from a Three Person Game', *American Political Science Review,* **64**, 48–60.

Riker, William H., and Peter C. Ordeshook (1973), *An Introduction to Positive Political Theory,* Prentice Hall, Englewood Cliffs, New Jersey.

Rosenthal, Howard (1968), 'Voting and Coalition Models in Election Simulations', in W. D. Coplin, (ed.), *Simulation in the Study of Politics,* Markham, Chicago.

Rosenthal, Howard, and Subrata Sen (1973), 'Electoral Participation in the French Fifth Republic', *American Political Science Review,* **67**, 29–54.

Rosenthal, Howard (1974), 'Game-Theoretic Models of Bloc-Voting under Proportional Representation: Really Sophisticated Voting in French Labor Elections', *Public Choice,* **18**, 1–23.

Rusk, Jerrold G., and Herbert Weisberg (1972), 'Perceptions of Presidential Candidates', *Midwest Journal of Political Science,* **16**, 338–410.

313

Scammon, Richard M., and Ben J. Wattenberg (1970), *The Real Majority*, Coward-McCann, New York.

Shepsle, Kenneth (1972), 'Parties, Voters, and the Risk Environment', in R. Niemi and H. Weisberg (eds.), *Probability Models of Collective Decision-Making*, Merrill, Columbus, Ohio.

Shepsle, Kenneth (1972b), 'The Strategy of Ambiguity: Uncertainty in Electoral Competition', *American Political Science Review*, 66, 535–68.

Shepsle, Kenneth (1974), 'On the Size of Winning Coalitions', *American Political Science Review* 68, 505–18.

Simpson, Paul B. (1969), 'On Defining Areas of Voter Choice', *The Quarterly Journal of Economics* 83, 478–90.

Sloss, Judith (1973), 'Stable Outcomes in Majority Voting Games', *Public Choice* 15, 19–48.

Stokes, Donald E. (1963), 'Spatial Models of Party Competition', *American Political Science Review*, 57, 368–77.

Stokes, Donald E. (1966), 'Some Dynamic Elements of Contests for the Presidency', *American Political Science Review*, 60, 19–28.

Stratmann, William C. (1974), 'The Concept of Voter Rationality', *Public Choice* 16.

Taylor, Michael (1973), 'The Problem of Salience in the Theory of Collectiv Decision-Making', in Alker, Deutsch and Stoezel, (eds.), *Mathematical Approaches to Politics*, Elsevier, Amsterdam.

Trilling, Richard J. (1970), 'Coalition Government, Political Parties, and the Rational Voter', unpublished Ph.D. dissertation, University of Wisconsin, Madison, Wisconsin.

Tullock, Gordon (1967), *Toward a Mathematics of Politics*, University of Michigan Press, Ann Arbor, Michigan.

Von Neumann, John, and Oskar Morgenstern (1947), *The Theory of Games and Economic Behavior*, Princeton University Press, Princeton, New Jersey.

Waltz, Kenneth N. (1968), 'Realities, Assumptions, and Simulations', in W. D. Coplin (ed.), *Simulation in the Study of Politics*, Markham, Chicago.

Weisberg, Herbert F., and Jerrold G. Rusk (1970), 'Dimensions of Candidate Evaluation', *American Political Science Review*, 64, 1167–85.

Wendell, Richard E., and S. J. Thorson (1974), 'Some Generalizations of Social Decisions Under Majority Rule', *Econometrica*, 42, 893–912.

Wilson, Robert (1971a), 'Stable Coalition Proposals in Majority-Rule Voting', *Journal of Economic Theory*, 3, 254–71.

Wilson, Robert (1971b), 'A Game-Theoretic Analysis of Social Choice', in B. Lieberman, (ed.), *Social Choice*, Gordon and Breach, New York.

Wittman, Donald A. (1973), 'Parties as Utility Maximisers', *American Political Science Review* 67, 490–8.

# 16

# Strategic Campaign Behaviour for Electors and Parties; The Northern Ireland Assembly Election of 1973

MICHAEL LAVER*

## INTRODUCTION

The aim of this chapter is to discuss some of the more common propositions about party and voter behaviour generated by the so-called 'rational choice' models of political competition which have sprung in great profusion from Anthony Downs's seminal work (1957). Throughout the discussion, the 1973 Northern Ireland Assembly Election will be used as an interpretive case study. This particular campaign has been chosen for a number of reasons.

Firstly, as an election in extreme conditions, conditions that on the face of it seem hardly conducive to rationality, it will constitute something of a 'destruction' test of the simple Downsian model. There can be little doubt that the previous fifty years of Ulster's electoral history can almost exactly be described in terms of sectarian party identification, with one major party representing each community—the official Unionist Party for the Protestants and the Nationalist Party for the Catholics (see Elliott (1973). The centre party (NILP), while picking up votes of moderates, was heavily under-represented by the electoral system.

Secondly, as a result of the tensions of recent years, and in anticipation of the introduction of the more representative Single Transferable Vote (STV) method of election, the party system had undergone considerable fragmentation since the previous election in 1969, with new parties, and 'new-look' old parties, emerging to take the place of the old sectarian monoliths. Most of these could still be categorized on sectarian lines, although they included a new and aggressive centre party (Alliance).

A third reason for choosing this election is the use of STV itself. This had several effects. The electors were, for the first time since 1925, when STV was abolished and replaced by a first-past-the-post system, asked to decide an *ordering* of the parties rather than a simple first choice. An STV vote is a complex vote since all or part of it can be transferred from one candidate to another, and from one party to another. Voters can hedge their bets by voting for more than one party, while parties can campaign for second and lower preferences from other parts of the political spectrum. This means that an elector may end up casting 75% of his vote, say, for a party A, 20

* This chapter was written with the aid of conversations with Brid Coretti O'Connor and Hans Schadee.

per cent for party B and 5 per cent for party C. However, an STV vote cannot be chatacterized as infinitely or even partially divisable, since the way in which a single elector's vote is divided depends upon the votes of all the other participants, and depends upon it in a way that the elector cannot predict. All he knows is that all his vote goes to his first choice; if this has too many votes, some of it will go to his second choice and if it has too few all of it goes to his second choice, and so on. This does of course allow complex voting strategies, such as not voting for a first choice sure of election so that the vote goes in full value to a second choice, but there is no evidence that such practice in fact occurs. Thus the vote can be realistically seen as a straightforward preference ordering by the voter of *candidates* on the ballot. In fact, as will be shown, this also amounts to an ordering of *parties*, since most voters order candidates of the same party consecutively. Of course it is not possible to obtain access to the complete set of these orderings, and the analysis of them would be a mammoth task anyway, but many inferences can be made about their overall structure from the published result sheets, which give the transfer totals at each stage of the count.

Other features of STV are less helpful as far as simple rational choice models are concerned. Since the elector votes for an *individual* and not a *party*, personality votes assume greater importance, and while such votes can obviously be accommodated by a generalized framework, they are not easily reconcilable with the simple Downsian model, especially when the personality is in a different party from the elector's first choice. This, however, appears to be more of a theoretical than an actual problem. In fact, most prominent candidates' votes did transfer to others of the same party (the interested reader can check the vote transfers of, for example, Faulkner, Bradford, Kilfedder, Paisley, Craig, Fitt, Devlin).

Finally, an STV campaign, since it involves no registration of parties, is organized at constituency level *and* places a high premium on candidates rather than parties, allows new parties to form with relative ease. This means once more than the simple Downsian situation with a fixed number of parties cannot be presumed to obtain. In fact, the ideological breaches into which new parties may step can be quite small—and while the big national parties retain many advantages in terms of access to media and developed organizational structure, a local intensive campaign can reap rich rewards. The success of the West Belfast Loyalist Coalition in this election, in gaining three seats, is a case in point. (The coalition broke up immediately after the election into its constituent elements). New parties *did* emerge in the pre-campaign period, although for the period of the campaign itself the number of parties were more or less fixed.

Fourthly comes the problem of information. Most electors in Northern Ireland will have received a large amount of this in both biased and contradictory form. This, of course, would present no problem if it was randomly distributed, a high level of 'noise' on the information signal, but of course it was not. Most residential areas are now either exclusively Catholic or Protestant, the recent troubles having reversed the trend toward 'mixed' areas. Belfast, for example, has a Catholic and a Protestant morning newspaper (on which see Rose [1971]), and the pattern is repeated in most other areas; political parties representing one community tend not to canvass or speak in the other; for these and many other longer-term reasons, both the formal and informal receipt of political information is largely sectarian. There are, of course, non-sectarian channels of communication as well—the British Press and broadcasting media could possibly be viewed in this light—but what relative weight attaches to these is impossible to determine. Nevertheless, the existence of important sectarian channels cannot but affect the analysis.

The highly selective aspect of information-gathering by the electorate can be accommodated by Downs's notion of party differentials (Downs, 1957, Chapter 8). We are assuming, given the importance of the election and the issues involved, that most electors reckon it to be worth their while to acquire some information about the contestants, and, in a highly politicized society, much more information than is normal will be effectively free. *Free information will largely concern parties representing the electors' own community, however, and electors will probably perceive too little difference between parties of the other community to make it worth their while involving themselves in any expenditure to get information about them.* For either community, it would be rational to gather information about the centre parties, to distinguish them from moderate parties on either side. As far as Alliance was concerned, this was plentiful, with extensive media coverage and their own campaign so carefully balanced that even the controversial name of the Province's second city was randomized between 'Londonderry' and 'Derry'. Additionally, the close correspondence between Alliance policy and Westminster policy made the former's ideological position clearer, since the latter also went to great pains to publicize its views.

It will also be argued that NILP's failure in this election was due at least in some part to the fact that its publicity campaign was far less powerful than that of Alliance, its main opponent for centre votes. Since Alliance has reached a dominant position in the centre, NILP did not state its position clearly enough to enable any differentiation to be made, so that votes went to the party with the greatest apparent chance of success.

From all of this it can be seen that many of the simple Downsian assumptions are not operative, and much of this paper will centre around ways in which the model can be adapted to incorporate these features, while remaining within the rational choice paradigm. Party identification *has* existed in the past, and clearly remains, at least at a residual level; the new parties and issues, however, constitute exactly such a period of shock and realignment in which new identifications emerge. Are these arrived at 'rationally'? Does the need to *order* parties on an STV ballot encourage what looks like rational behaviour? Does the ease of new party entry facilitated by such a system make a difference? Can selective and biased information-gathering be accommodated in a revised model? These are some of the problems that a concentration on Northern Ireland in 1973 raises, and to which some answers will be suggested. We are clearly dealing with an extreme case, but extreme cases often have the fortunate property of drawing attention to phenomena that are commonly present to a lesser degree, but have not yet received the consideration due to them.

Additionally, discussion of the actual behaviour of parties during the campaign will lead to the suggestion of a broader definition of party strategy, one that will encompass more types of action than simple ideological jockeying for position. The *manipulation* of both information flow and differential resource bases needs to be considered, and an attempt will be made to incorporate these into a method of talking about campaign behaviour which will doubtless be viewed by some as falling into an uneasy no-man's-land between 'strategy' and 'tactics'. It may be that such a distinction is not always the most useful one that can be made.

## CONSTRUCTING AN IDEOLOGY SPACE

The ideology space that parties and voters inhabited is going to be constructed from a set of assumptions. It is *not* going to be empirically derived, although a measure of support for its nature can be found in the penultimate section below, *if voter rationality is assumed.* Using the one set of preference data, we can either *assume a particular form of rationality and derive the space* or *assume the space and investigate the nature of voter rationality.* Since, at the level at which it is proposed, the nature of the space in Northern Ireland is almost certainly less controversial than the nature of the rationality involved, the latter course of action has been chosen as the most interesting and useful. If the reader disagrees, he can pretend that the section on voter rationality was written from the former point of view, and he will find empirical substantiation for the space constructed here. He must then ignore the conclusions about rationality.

The sectarian nature of the communication system raised in the previous section highlights a particular problem in constructing this space. This arises from Downs's premise that all electors and parties can be placed on a single ideological dimension, and that political preferences can be ordered from left to right in a manner agreed upon by all electors (Downs, 1957, p.115). The main dimension of political ideology in Northern Ireland is clearly not socioeconomic. It would, of course, present no problem *a priori* to substitute another for this: the problem comes when one wonders what in fact this could be.

Consideration of the issues involved suggests two critical end-points. There are:

(*a*) Protestant Ulster regardless;

(*b*) United Ireland regardless.

(Argument in support of these can be found in Appendix A.) However, the highly segregated nature of political life in Northern Ireland, and the selective receipt and perception of political information, makes the use of two independent spaces an attractive proposition: putting it bluntly, one for Catholics and one for Protestants. Two such spaces would have parties ordered as shown in Figure 16.1(a). It is necessary to repeat that the party *ordering* in these and subsequent spaces is not empirically derived, but is proposed by the author. It is doubted, however, whether any would disagree with it, and those who might are welcome to study the party manifestos, press and broadcasting coverage and policy statements from which this proposition emerged. The ordering of the parties is one of the few non-controversial aspects of Northern Ireland politics.

It can be seen that the centre parties appear in each space, reflecting the paradoxical situation that for each community the centre represents one extreme of opinion. Figure 16.1(a) however does not use all of the information at our disposal, since we also know that there is some ideological relationship between the two spaces: that they are in fact sub-spaces of an overall ideological space, which runs from (a) to (b) through the White Paper. (This was published, prior to the election, by the British Government, and contained a statement of the basic principles under which the forthcoming Constitution Act was to set up the machinery for the Northern Ireland Assembly. It reiterated the Government's intention not to allow the province to leave the United Kingdom except with the consent of a majority of its electorate, while committing them to power-sharing between the two communities, and to a Council of Ireland with certain very limited responsibilities, to be jointly operated by the

Northern Ireland Assembly and the Government of the Republic.) The combined space can be seen in Figure 16.1(b). From this it can be seen that attitude to the White Paper *per se* is being treated as a tactical consideration, considered only inasmuch as it affects long term aims (*a*) or (*b*). The two sub-spaces are being kept discrete. In other words, it is being assumed that occupants of one do not even consider the existence of the other when deciding how to cast their vote. For the moment this remains an assumption, although evidence to support it will be introduced when the analysis of vote transfers is undertaken.

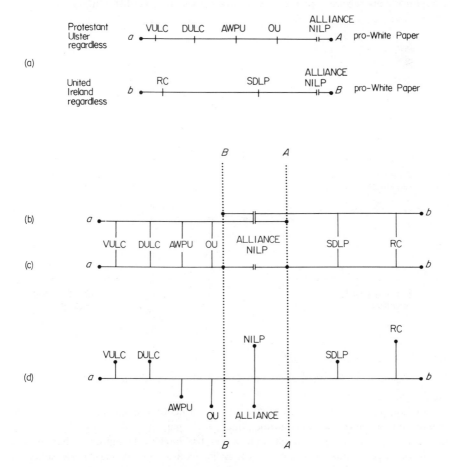

Figure 16.1    Derivation of Northern Ireland party space

If a single space was felt desirable, a similar result could be achieved by making an assumption about the nature of the 'propensity to vote' function of individual electors. Downs stipulates that this should be 'single peaked and slope downwards monotonically on either side of the peak' (Downs, 1957, p.115). If a single dimension is used, as in Figure 16.1(c), the assumption that these 'drop-off' functions look different for electors from different communities will achieve the desired effect.

320

Assume that in Figure 16.2(a) *X, Y, Z* represent the typical drop-off functions of Catholic voters at different points on the scale, each function cutting off at point *B*, beyond which no voter is prepared to consider voting. We can suppose a similar configuration for Protestant electors, staring from the other end, with a different cut-off point, *A* (Figure 16.2(b)). We now have a single dimension, but one with two significant points, *A* and *B*, dividing it into three sections: two with voters from only one community, and one with 'mixed' voters. One of those sections corresponds to the 'centre' and one to each sectarian element. The division makes sense, since party competition in each area centres, as we shall see, on somewhat different issues.

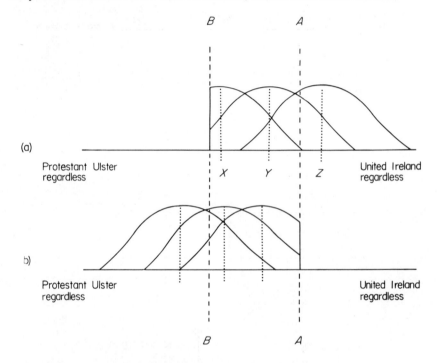

Figure 16.2   Hypothetical 'drop-off' functions for Protestant and Catholic voters

For completeness, Figure 16.1(d) shows the effect of introducing as a second, less salient, dimension the socioeconomic policy of the parties. Fuller discussion of this is found in Appendix A. It was decided, however, for the sake of simplicity, that not too much violence would be done to reality by continuing to regard the space as uni-dimensional, albeit a little 'curled up' at the ends. NILP, probably the least important party in the discussion, will not be well represented by this, but all other parties will.

## PARTY STRATEGY

Party behaviour in the campaign can be usefully split up into the three areas described by the ideology space, representing the fights for the Protestant vote, the Catholic vote and the centre.

Of these, the fight for the Protestant vote was probably the most intense, with four major groupings in the running and Alliance attempting to poach from one end of the spectrum. In general we can see this as constituting two major disputes, one within the various shades of Unionism, and one between the factions of more extreme 'Loyalism'. Laid over this was a high level of uncertainty as to the exact nature of the distribution of the electorate across the spectrum; indeed, at the start of the campaign this was greatly accentuated by considerable doubt about the positioning of many of the politicians themselves.

The dispute between Official and Anti-White Paper Unionists (AWPU) started very much in these conditions, in a situation aggravated by the high degree of autonomy retained by the local constituency organizations, some of which came out in favour of, and some against, the White Paper. Thus in the immediately preceeding local elections, some officially nominated Unionists were for, and some against, it. The party leader, Brian Faulkner, realizing the danger to his position (pro-White Paper) of this confusion, took the risk of crystalizing the situation at the commencement of the Assembly campaign by formulating a pledge to support central party policy; only signatories of this would be allowed to call themselves 'Official Unionist'. This had the predicted effect of completely formalizing the rift into 'Pledged' and 'Unpledged' Unionists (i.e. Official Unionists and AWPU), now two completely distinct groups with clearly identified policies. In initiating the pledge, Faulkner was playing a game closely allied to aspects of rational choice theory. It was his belief that a greater proportion of politicians than of the electorate were opposed to the White Paper; or, in 'rational' terms, he believed that other politicians had misjudged the distribution of the electorate by placing it too far from the centre. The Pledge highlighted the fact that the Official Unionists were the only pro-White Protestant party, and once this was made clear to the electorate, he expected to reap the rewards.

This left three anti-White Paper groups to fight it out. The AWPU attempted to shift as little as possible from their old ground, mainly arguing that they still stood for all of the basis tenets of Unionism, and they fought the campaign as if the Official Unionists, not they, were the deviants. Both sides were probably correct: where once there was one party, which had spanned a wide ideological range, there were now two more rigidly defined parties.

On the other hand, VULC and DULC took advantage of one special feature of STV and buried the hatchet. Forming an electoral coalition, they asked voters to vote first for which ever of the two they preferred, and second for the other members of the pact. VULC abandoned its 'Independent Ulster' policy (already becoming something of a white elephant in view of the barrage of statistics being issued by the British Government on the impractical economics of it) and the two parties more or less converged ideologically, much more emphasis being placed on individual personalities and the common enemy within the Protestant ranks—'sellout'.

Examining the rationality of this in spatial terms, we can see that, taking the combined vote total of the two coalition members, there is nothing to be gained from the coalition in terms of first preference votes. Figure 16.3(a) shows the position at this end of the spectrum. Before coalition, VULC and DULC between them can expect to gain all first preferences between the end of the scale ($M$) and the mid-point between the DULC and the next party ($N$). After coalition, (Figure 16.3(b)), assuming nothing else changes, they can get no more, even if the coalition adopts the same ideological stance as DULC had originally. The only way they can increase this is by closer convergence with AWPU, a strategy that can be adopted more effectively

322

without coalition since if VULC remains stationary, the risk of losing extremists is reduced.

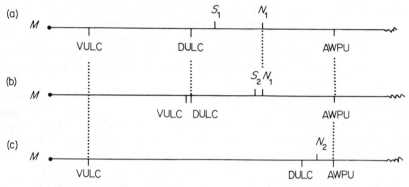

Figure 16.3    Coalition strategies for VULC-DULC

As far as second party preferences are concerned, however, there is some rationality in the move from the situation in Figure 16.3 (a) to that in Figure 16.3(b). Rationally all VULC second preferences should go to DULC in either situation, but before coalition DULC preferences would be split between DULC and AWPU, the break point occurring at $S_1$, the mid-point between the two alternatives. The ideological move of VULC shifts the mid-point towards AWPU, thus increasing VULC'S share of DULC second preferences, and hence the total vote value of the coalition.

This, however, is not the most successful co-operation that could be arranged. This would clearly be to commit themselves to the strategy shown in Figure 16.3(c), a policy of ideological *divergence* with DULC moving up against AWPU and VULC agreeing not to capitalize on this, so that all first preferences from $M$ to $N_2$ would now go to the coalition, and (depending on the position of other parties) a large proportion of the second preferences of the Unpledged Unionists. Conversely, nearly all DULC second preferences would go to the Unionists, but since first preferences have considerably more influence on the result than their preferences, and since the coalition could still use its 'give the other partner your second choice' propaganda, the overall result would almost certainly have been an improvement over the convergence strategy.

The campaign in the centre was a straight fight between Alliance and NILP. Alliance strategy appeared to be to occupy as much of the centre ground as possible. To do this an attempt was made to differentiate its position on separate issues. It thus claimed to be unequivocally in favour of the union with Britain, but also unequivocally in favour of power-sharing and the Council of Ireland. This enabled the party to gain a degree of ideological spread and more or less 'engulf' its opposition in the centre. Inasmuch as there was little difference between the parties, superior funding of Alliance allowed it to win on the other 'non-rational' criteria— 'non-rational', that is, in simple Downsian terms, but highly rational if we recognize that this strategy amounts to a conscious exploitation of the differential resource bases of the two parties. Alliance had more party workers and more money. This fact 'snowballed' to create an advantage in its own right, generating more free publicity depicting Alliance as an 'up-and-coming, dynamic new party'!

One possible and plausible strategy for a centre party in this situation would be to exploit the relative lack of communication between the two halves of its 'clientele' and in fact disseminate different information about itself to the different communities. Obviously this would be possible only within certain limits, since the non-sectarian media would circumscribe the strategy to the extent that it was necessary to be specific about policy. If statements via these media could be kept very general and unclear, then such a tactic could be used. Unfortunately it was not possible to check on this since a good sample of local-level leaflets and other publicity was not available.

Competition on the anti-Partition side of the spectrum was in some ways analogious to that in the pro-Union portion. In one important respect, however, it was different. There was one large party in a dominant position, expected by nearly everyone to gain nearly all of the anti-Partition (pro-United Ireland) vote. SDLP adopted a broadly pro-White Paper stance, concentrating on those aspects of it that seemd favourable to increasing convergence between the Republic of Ireland and the North. Its opposition (coming most realistically from Republican clubs, but also from the remnants of the Nationalists and some Independents) for their part also used the tactic of a pledge. This time the issue was internment. The pledge originated from the Northern Ireland Civil Rights Association (NICRA) and committed politicians and electors to supporting a policy of non-participation in government until internment without trial was removed. SDLP opposed this on the grounds that an end to internment was best achieved by participation. This clarified SDLP's position as very much a centre party, no doubt the intention of the pledge in the first place, since before it SDLP had been unclear on internment, possibly because opposing internment would be characterized by opponents on one side as opposition to the White Paper, while support for it would easily be turned into 'sell out' by opponents from the other side. Thus a fuzzy policy on internment was clearly rational for SDLP as was the forcing of the issue by NICRA via the pledge. The SDLP compromise of opposing internment *via* participation, however, succeeded in postponing any boat-burning until after the election, and more or less nullified the effect of the pledge.

The strategy of Republican Clubs, apart from their support of the pledge, was clearly not dictated solely by vote maximization, and thus in Downsian terms was irrational. In fact, one of the surprising features of the campaign was the lack of challenge to SDLP on its own ground, other anti-Partition parties very much keeping their ideological distances. It is possible that a desire for 'Catholic unity' led to an unwillingness to split this area of the vote, although there can of course be no evidence of this.

The overall picture is one in which ideological manoeuvring of the simple Downsian kind very much played second fiddle. We can detect four basic kinds of alternative strategems which can in a very real sense be called rational, and which there is no reason to suppose could not be found in other elections and other party systems.

Two strategems centre around the precision with which a party's policy position is specified. The first is a pledge, or similar commitment, introduced by a party or actor in the campaign in an attempt to negate any advantage apparently held by opponents as a result of their clouded policy positions. Clearly, when parties do not have perfect information about the policy preferences of their clientele, they want to hedge their bets rather than risk being too specific. Conversely, their opponents may well try and negate this by forcing clarification when this might result in driving the other party out on a limb, for example by a pledge.

The second strategy is the inverse of this. A party (in this case Alliance) may try to 'spread itself out' ideologically by attempting to adopt different policy positions on the same underlying ideological dimension. There is obviously a limit to the extent to which this is possible (and it can be countered with something like a pledge), but to a certain extent Alliance achieved success on these lines. From this example we might speculate that this could involve the playing of complex semantic games (such as the randomization of 'Derry' and 'Londonderry') in order to appear to reconcile the inconsistencies that might arise. This could be strengthened further by attempting to disseminate different positions to different sections of the population, a tendency that could be suspected if national publicity was much vaguer on policy issues than local publicity.

The third possibility involves exploitation of the 'rules of the game'; for example the formation of an electoral coalition. This can be particularly effective if the coalition partners occupy one end of the spectrum, and can thus extract themselves from some of the constraints upon their freedom of ideological manoeuvre.

The fourth possibility is the exploitation of differential resources. Given equal resources, two parties may hold back from total convergence on the grounds that the voters will then choose on 'non-rational' grounds, potentially risky for either. A more wealthy party *should* rationally converge on a poorer one, however, since in effect it can better manipulate those extra features of competition which, while they *may* remain 'non-rational' for voters, are by no means such for parties.

All of these possibilities seem convincingly 'rational' for parties, and in situations where resources and information are not equal and perfect (i.e. always) can assume considerable importance.

## THE VOTERS AS RATIONAL ACTORS

### The theory

Having discussed party competition in strategic terms, we turn now to the electorate. For this section of the analysis, some of the significant features of the situation are rather different from those raised in the previous section. The first of those differences is the role of information. Whereas it is quite possible that parties did not have a very clear idea of the distribution of electors across the various issue spaces involved, the pledges, and the extensive publicity campaigns mounted by most parties, must have gone a long way to ensure that their positions were relatively clear to most electors at least in their ideological catchment area. We can thus suppose that the assumption of perfect information is under less duress as far as voter choice was concerned than it was for party competition, while bearing in mind the assumption that in fact electors from one community will seek and receive little information about parties in the other.

Secondly, the fact that an STV vote is a complex vote does not influence the analysis here if we assume that electors are unable to cast their vote in such a way as to award a certain proportion of it to different parties. Since the 'quota' is difficult to predict (and the surpluses and vote totals transferred are almost impossible to predict), this would appear to be quite reasonable (Lakeman and Lambert,

1974). In any case, if a proportion of the electorate were to start casting such complex or strategic votes, the interaction effect of these would be impossibly difficult for a realistic 'rational' voter to assess. We would therefore appear to be on safe ground assuming that each STV vote case expresses a genuine preference ordering by the voters of the candidates on the ballot paper.

The STV method itself, since it demands of the elector a preference ordering of candidates, and *implicitly* of parties, is unique in that completion of the ballot paper involves a more sophisticated analysis of the political wares on offer than any other electoral system. In a 'pure' election situation the voter does not have to decide which party is closest to his own position, but rather to have in his mind a complete party space, defined at an ordered metric level, involving at least a more rigorous if not more rational evaluation of the party system. This feature of an STV election is immensely significant for a rational choice model, but it is tempered by the fact that there is no way in which an analyst can gain access to these orderings, even if he had a computer power to analyse (to take the Irish example) three-quarters of a million of them. The results of the transfer process at each stage of each count, however, are available, and for these it is possible to make some valuable inferences about the overall structure of preference structures within the electorate.

Since such information is available, we are no faced with a decision as to what in fact we are going to use it to test. One of two constraints can be imposed. Either the rationality of the electorate can be assumed, and the preference orderings can be used to construct the party space; or the nature of the party space can be assumed, and the data can be used to test a rationality proposition. Both alternatives would appear to be useful and interesting, but for the purpose of this paper the latter course was adopted. This was because, firstly the intention was to discuss rational choice rather than Northern Ireland, and, secondly, of the two constraints the latter is easier to defend. The *ordinal* properties of the space proposed, moreover, would seem to be far less controversial than the assumption that the Northern Ireland electorate operated under Downsian rationality.

One important aspect of the theory will not be covered, and that is the problem of abstention. This is for the somewhat unsatisfactory reason that little is known of non-voters in this election beside the fact that they abstained. No survey or similar data are available to help estimate the extent to which this was strategic within the terms of the approach, the result of disfranchisement through faults in the register, mobility or a rational evaluation that the cost of voting did not merit the benfits. For the record, turnout averaged around 70 per cent, but from now on discussion will concentrate, for better or for worse, on *the rationality of voters, not of the electorate*.

The data analysis that follows can thus be seen as an investigation of the *general hypothesis* that '*the voters in the 1973 Northern Ireland assembly election were rational, that is they attempted to maximize their expected utility*' (see Downs, 1957, Chapter 3, on the logic of rational voting). This hypothesis cannot be tested directly, but various propositions can be derived from it, and tested by an analysis of the overall structure of vote transfers.

**Proposition I.** *When votes from a candidate from Party X are being transferred, these should all go to other candidates from the same party, if one is still in the running (i.e. if all other candidates of that party have not already been elected or eliminated).*

326

This proposition is consistent with a version of rational choice that uses parties defined at a single point in space. Thus if all candidates of the same party are perceived by voters to occupy the same ideological position—if the choice between them is made or criteria outside the scope of the theory (personality, image and so on)—a second preference would necessarily go to the same party, since such criteria are dominated by ideology. If vote transfers do *not* conform to Proposition 1, then either the general hypothesis is false, or the assumption that parties are perceived at a single point in space is.

The latter possibility would amount to the need to use a more general form of the model where parties can occupy *sections (or areas)* of the space. In these circumstances, if voters can place the candidates of a party ideology within a section, it is perfectly possible for preferences not to go consecutively to the same party.

Take, for example, the situation in Figure 16.4, showing an area of an ideology space inhabited by parties $A,B,C$. Each occupies the *section* of the space shown and each puts up two candidates at different points within this section. A voter situated at position $X$ would cast a first preference for candidate $b_1$ but his second preference would be for candidate $a_2$. In fact, his *candidate* preference ordering would be $X$ ($b_1$, $a_2$, $b_2$, $a_1$, $c_1$, $c_2$,) while his *party* ordering would be $X(B, A, B, A, C, C)$. Similarly Voter $Y$ would have candidate preference $Y(b_2, c_1, b_1, c_2, a_2, a_1$ ) and *party* preferences $Y(B, C, B, C, A, A)$. There is however no way in which a voter can, having cast a preference for a particular party, rationally case the next preference for a party that was not adjacent to it. Thus voter $Z$, who gives $A$ his first preference, must rationally prefer $B$ to $C$.

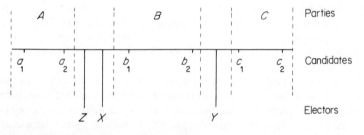

Figure 16.4    Preference structure when parties do not occupy a single point in space

**Proposition 1A:** *When votes from a candidate in Party X are being transferred these should all go to other candidates in the same party, if one is still in the running, or to candidates in ideologically adjacent parties still in the running.*

Given the ideological spaces proposed in Figure 16.1(b) and 16.1(c), the term 'ideologically adjacent' needs some explaining. If all parties are still in the running, then there is no problem: the term means what it says. For example, Alliance/NILP and AWPU are adjacent to Official Unionists; if no AWPU candidate was still in the running, we would take DULC as the adjacent party. However, if no centre candidates are left, the disjoint character of the space means that parties solely in the $aA$ space and those solely on the $bB$ space cannot be thought of as adjacent to each other, since the assumption was made that voters in one did not consider voting for parties in the other. If all other evidence tends to support rationality, but trans-sectarian transfers *do* occur, then this particular formulation of the space would appear suspect.

We shall, however, have to take a 'harder line' when interpreting the data in the light of the addition of adjacent parties to the prediction set, which now includes transfers to one of three parties out of a total of sometimes only five or six. While a test of these propositions sheds some light on the general hypothesis, they could also be explained in other ways, for example that people vote *consistently* but not necessarily *rationally*. While consistency may well be a *necessary* condition for rationality, it is by no means *sufficient*. Consideration of vote transfers from a party when there is no longer a candidate of the same party is a more direct test of rationality, and leads to the next proposition.

**Proposition 2.** *When votes from a candidate in Party X are transferred, and no other candidate of the same party is still in the running, these should all go to candidates of adjacent parties.*

With the qualification that the definition of 'adjacent' is similar to that used in Proposition 1A, the derivation of this from a uni-dimensional Downsian model is reasonably self-evident. In fact, it represents the crucial test, since, to return to Figure 16.4, there is no way within the model for preferences cast for Party $A$ to transfer *en masse* to party $C$ even so long as $B$ is still in the running. If the model is correct, *preferences can only go to B.*

It is not possible to be more specific about to which of two adjacent parties the preferences should go without recourse to a cardinally defined space, and even here the exact distribution of the voting population across it would need to be known. Proposition 2 as it stands, however, is very strong, and needs no qualification. *If the space is uni-dimensional and the voters are rational, it must hold true.*

It was stated earlier that parties can be adjacent only if they occupy the same portions of the space (i.e. $aA$ or $dB$). It is thus possible for votes from party $X$ to be transferred when there is no adjacent party. In this situation, since it is being supposed that voters in one half of the space do not consider parties in the other, and do not care to distinguish between them in the voting process, we would expect no further preferences to be expressed; the votes become non-transferable. This leads to the final proposition.

**Proposition 3.** *If votes from a candidate in Party X are being transferred, and there is no candidate from an adjacent party still in the running, they would become non-transferable.*

This arises directly from the disjoint nature of the space proposed, since if the space is not disjoint there will always be an adjacent party. Its testing can thus be considered a test of the assumption of disjunction.

Between them, the three propositions should now account for all votes transferred, since in all situations there is either a candidate of the same party still in the running or there is not, and if the latter is true there is either an adjacent party or there is not. We can now move on to the actual analysis of transfers.

## The results

The results of the analysis of transfers arising from a count of the 722,000 valid votes are given in Tables 16.1 and 16.2 (the exact method of compilation of these can be found in Appendix B). Since, for the reasons stated in Appendix B, no significance testing was possible, they do not constitute a rigorous testing of the proposition, but nevertheless are a strong indication of their plausibility, since the numbers involved are so large. Table 16.1 relates to Propositions 1 and 1A. The first column shows the average proportion of transfers that went to a candidate of the same party as they originated from, on occasions when this was possible. Of 147 transfer stages analysed

Table 16.1    Destination of Vote Transfers When Candidate Of Same Party Still in Running

| PARTY | Average proportion of votes transferred to same party | Average proportion transferred to adjacent party or same party | Average number of parties in running at time of transfer | No of transfer stages considered N |
|---|---|---|---|---|
| VULC | .60 | .88 | 5.8 | 11 |
| DULC | .62 | .94 | 6.2 | 5 |
| AWPU | .61 | .87 | 7.0 | 5 |
| OU | .81 | .91 | 6.0 | 30 (24)[*] |
| Alliance | .82 | .90 | 6.6 | 18 |
| NILP | .63 | .84 | 6.9 | 7 |
| SDLP | .84 | .94 | 6.6 | 11 (10)[*] |
| Rep. CLUBS | .68 | .82 | 9.0 | 2 |
| ALL PARTIES | .75 | .90 | 6.4 | 89 (82)[*] |

[*]   Total in parenthesis is a total which excludes situations where only adjacent parties are available for transfer, when this is different from N.  This represents the total used in cols. 2 & 3. N is still used in col. 1.

in all (16 were omitted because they related to small parties or Independents, or involved the transfer of more than one candidate) 89 fell into this category. Overall, 75 per cent of transfers in these conditions went to the same party, although there were on average six or seven possible destinations. The three big party machines (Alliance, Official Unionists and SDLP) scored highest on this count, although all parties scored considerably higher than a random selection would have resulted in. Of the three large groups that were successful in the election, but scored lower than average on this test (basically a test of party solidarity), the VULC–DULC electoral pact will have lowered their totals, while the fact that the Unpledged Unionists did not constitute a formal party (more a *grouping* of independents and dissident Unionists) may have affected theirs. Overall however, the results shown in column (1) would seem to provide substantiation for Proposition 1 (although this itself is not a strong test of rationality), while we must bear in mind that by no means all transfers do go to a candidate of the same party.

For the more general model used in proposition 1A, column (2) of Table 16.1 shows that virtually all transfers can now be accounted for. About 90 per cent of all transfers go to candidates of either the same or adjacent parties, while of the remaining 10 per cent, about half are usually nontransferable and half (i.e. 5 per cent of all transfers) do go to other parties. We also note that there is very little variation in this between parties. Of course it is necessary to be more severe in an evaluation of these results, since the theory is predicting that transfers will go to two or three parties out of six or seven on average. Nevertheless, since overall about 90 per cent go to parties specified by proposition 1A and about 5 per cent to the more numerous group of other parties, one would suspect that, were significant testing possible given the high overall vote value of transfers involved, these results would in fact be significant (See Appendix B).

Thus the two propositions concerning inter-party transfers seem to be consistent with the general pattern of vote transfers in the election. In addition it seems that the three parties with big machines do seem to be better able to keep transfers within their party than the others. It will be recalled, however, that Propositions 1 and 1A were *necessary* but by no means *sufficient* conditions for rationality.

Table 16.2 is an analysis of those 45 transfer stages that pertain to Proposition 2. From this it can firstly be seen that the proportion of non-transferable votes that

Table 16.2    Destination of Vote Transfers When No Candidate Of Same Party Still in Running

| PARTY | Average Proportion of vote Non-Transferable | Average Proportion of Transferable vote going to adjacent parties | Average number of parties still in running | N |
|---|---|---|---|---|
| VULC | .13 | .82 | 4.2 | 6 |
| DULC | .16 | .90 | 4.0 | 7 |
| AWPLI | .15 | .86 | 5.3 | 3 |
| OU | .18 | .77 | 5.3 | 4 |
| ALLIANCE | .38 | .90 | 4.3 | 5. |
| NILP | .11 | .56 | 5.2 | 6 |
| SDLP | .18 | .96 | 4.0 | 6 |
| CLUBS | .38 | .84 | 5.6 | 5 |
| NAT | .21 | .86 | 5.7 | 3 |
| REP.LAB. | .16 | .92 | 6.0 | 1 |
| ALL PARTIES | .20 | .86 | 4.7 | 46- |

occur when there is no candidate of the original party left in the running is by no means inconsequential. Broken down by party, there are two quite clear clusters, and while it might be expected that a number of transfers from the parties on the ends of the spectrum might go this way, as extremists (irrationally) refuse to compromise, or (possibly rationally) hope to pull their party towards them ideologically, this is only partially the pattern that emerges. Certainly at one end of the scale (Republican Clubs) this is true, and at the other, the electoral pact will undoubtedly influence the results, lowering VULC's non-transferable totals; but the result for Alliance may seem a surprise. Nearly 40 per cent of those casting a preference for Alliance did not go on to cast subsequent preferences for other parties. In fact, however, the result provides some confirmation of the model of the party space consisting of two superimposed ideological dimensions. In this sense, Alliance and NILP are special sorts of extremist parties, falling at the end of each dimension. Thus, for example, a vote originating with SDLP and transferred to Alliance should go no further. The fact that NILP's non-transferable proportion is not high is almost certainly due to the fact that, since NILP did so badly in the election, its candidates were almost always eliminated before those of Alliance. Thus NILP votes could transfer to Alliance, while Alliance votes could not transfer to NILP.

About 85 per cent of transfers from other parties, however, are in fact valid, and voters casting these were consistent with the simple rationality assumptions. The proportions of these going to adjacent parties are analysed in column (2) of Table 16.2. Overall a figure of 85 per cent went to adjacent parties, the situation consistent with Proposition 2. Since these generally represented one or two parties out of a possible four or five, this was once more considerably higher than would be expected by random choice. This part of the data is once more wholly consistent with the proposition derived from rational choice, and once more it is expected that, had significance testing been possible, the results would have been significant.

Broken down by party, however, there is one striking exception to the general pattern: the case of NILP. It will be remembered however that it was argued earlier that, while a two-dimensional representation is necessary to distinguish NILP from Alliance, its overall relevance was almost certainly quite limited. The relatively low proportion of votes transferred from NILP to adjacent parties (56 per cent) is probably a result of this simplification, and demonstrates the one case where a uni-dimensional representation of the space is inadequate.

Unfortunately, an examination of Proposition 3 was not possible, since relevant transfers (when no other party in the same section of the ideology space was available for transfers) occurred only twice. In the first instance non-transferable votes comprised 99 per cent of the total; in the second, 95 per cent. As far as they go, these results substantiate Proposition 3, but they do not go very far in such limited numbers. Related to this problem, however, is another piece of information from an overall analysis of transfers which is both startling and highly relevant. Out of a total vote value of 722,000 (almost certainly representing at least 3,000,000 preferences), votes to the value of 848 were transferred directly from parties exclusively on one spectrum to parties exclusively on the other. Direct trans-sectarian transfer levels are thus astonishingly low, at 0.1 per cent of the total.

Taking the results of the transfer analysis as a whole, it can be said that it was largely consistent with the propositions derived from the general rational choice hypothesis. They do not constitute a rigorous test of it, since data problems did not allow significance testing (See Appendix B), but the general pattern that emerges quite clearly from the figures is highly suggestive of the validity of a uni-dimensional rational choice model.

## CONCLUSION

This paper has been an attempt to see how a rational choice model could stand up to the analysis of a 'difficult' election, an election in a country where, in old-fashioned political science terms, the main dynamic of political behaviour, sectarianism, might easily be viewed as irrational. If we wish to test the Downsian rationality of all the participants, we are forced to make some rather sweeping assumptions about spatial relationships. To avoid the need for such assumptions we would need to have a time-series of cardinal policy spaces containing the parties (not necessarily defined at a single point) together with frequency distributions of the electorate across them. This is at least theoretically derivable from dimensional analysis of surveys of politicians and voters. In addition, however, it has been demonstrated that there may well be circumstances where the nature of the voter preference functions is crucial to the problem, in which case even more complex data analysis is called for. It is probable that assumptions less sweeping but of the same nature will creep into an interpretation of such data, so that, in terms of expenditure of resources, it is almost certainly more reasonable to jump in at the deep end and make them all in the first place.

This is somewhat of a side issue, however, once it is accepted that the information problems discussed in the section on party behaviour are operative. As far as the parties are concerned it is these problems that would seem to have the most interesting implications for a Downsian model. While nobody would expect the assumption of perfect information ever to be totally valid, the way in which the actors behave should be capable of inclusion in a more generalized framework. It was shown that a major party strategy centred around this information problem, with parties attempting to increase or decrease to their own advantage the degree of precision with which they could be ideologically perceived by the electorate. As far as this 'information engineering' is concerned, the sort of argument proposed by Schelling (1961) would seem appropriate. The pledge as a method of increasing a commitment previously less than obvious to voters; ideological differentiation, or reformulation of the problem as a means of getting off this hook; tacit bargaining between politician and elector around such symbols as the White Paper and internment; the general use of information flow control—all these are more the concern of Schelling (1961) than of Downs. This field would seem a productive one for further development, since there is no reason to suppose it is confined to Northern Ireland.

We have also seen that a relaxation of the assumption of equal resources leads to yet another species of strategy, which could well lead to the consummation of the convergence tendency, or even to wars of attrition. Once more, this is a process the pre-conditions of which are almost universal, and by no means exclusively confined to Northern Ireland.

As far as voter behaviour is concerned, the information problem was less severe. Most voters probably had some idea of where they thought the parties stood (this may have been a wrong idea, but that does not matter). The problem of differential drop-off functions was highlighted and the implications of this could well be further developed, but as far as actual voting behaviour was concerned, this appears to have been at least consistent with a rational choice interpretation, within the assumptions made in constructing the space.

In conclusion it can be said, however, that the kind of allowances that need to be made to interpret the election within a rational choice paradigm do not seem to do too much injustice to reality. This itself is encouraging.

## APPENDIX A: THE IDEOLOGICAL NATURE OF THE PARTY/VOTER SPACE

Having stated that socioeconomic considerations are clearly not the most crucial issues in a Northern Ireland election, the most obvious alternative would be to set

(a) Pro-Protestant Ulster and

(b) Pro-United Ireland

as opposite poles. However, these are not in any real sense the opposite ends of a spectrum; they are almost discrete and mutually exclusive alternatives. Parties cannot be more or less in favour of a United Ireland; they are either for it or against it. It is clear, however, that the space is not degenerate, with parties focused at two points, but that there are extremists and moderates in each camp. Extremes and moderation of what? Considering the parties regarded as moderate (Official Unionists, Alliance, NILP, SDLP) and extreme, (VULC, DULC, Anti-White Paper Unionists, Republican Clubs), we see that the two groups are defined in terms of their attitude towards Westminster policy, as expressed in the White Paper. Taking this as the defining point of an ideological spectrum, we can array the parties along a single dimension. This would be nonsense, however, since it would juxtapose parties such as VULC and Republican Clubs, who clearly have little in common except their attitude to the White Paper. Yet we are not yet in a two-dimensional situation as far as these issues are concerned since opposition to Westminster was felt in terms of the extent to which the White Paper was seen to jeopardize the diametrically opposed aims embodied in (a) and (b) above. The alternatives of supporting British Government policy or defying it if necessary to achieve either a Protestant Ulster or United Ireland do spread the parties along ideological continua. Our two poles have thus in effect been redefined as

(a) Protestant Ulster regardless;

(b) United Ireland regardless.

This means that the space is defined not simply in terms of goals, but in terms of determination to achieve goals in the face of British Government opposition. Thus an element of constitutionalism has been introduced.

While the religious–constitutional issue is clearly the most important in current Northern Ireland politics, that does not mean to say that class issues can be completely ignored. A weak socioeconomic policy dimension can be said to exist. It *is* important in the centre to distinguish Alliance from NILP ideologically, NILP having a more social-democratic flavour than the Alliance party. In general it can be said that a move towards either extreme results in a slightly more radical socioeconomic policy (in the case of Republican Clubs dramatically so), and almost certainly more working-class support (though it is important not to confuse these). The overall picture might well be that of Figure 16.1(d).

## APPENDIX B: THE ANALYSIS OF TRANSFERS

The basic data used in evaluating these rational choice propositions were the transfer totals at each stage of every count in the election. If a candidate's vote total exceeds the electoral quota, the value of his surplus vote is transferred to all other candidates still in the running. To do this all of the ballot papers credited to the candidate are re-examined, and allocated to the next preferred candidate. The totals for each of these candidates are scaled down by a common multiplier to make the total vote value transferred equal to the amount of the surplus. Their transfer totals are thus vote values and not ballot papers. Eliminated candidates have their votes transferred at face value. This means that, while a surplus of value 100 votes transferred from an elected candidate may express the wishes of say, 5,000 voters, the same total from an eliminated candidate may express the wishes of only 100. In other words the *vote values* of the transfers cannot simply be aggregated if we wish to obtain an overall picture of preference structures in the electorate. There is no way of calculating the total number of ballot papers transferred at each stage since these figures are not published, except for the first transfer of each count. It has therefore been necessary to use the *proportions* of the total votes transferred at each stage which go to various destinations. To aggregate the figures for all transfer stages, the *average proportion* has been taken. Obviously such a measure has some unsatisfactory properties, the most serious of which is that, no absolute total being available, no significance testing can be carried out. This is mitigated by the fact that we are using *population* rather than *sample* data and that we know the overall numbers involved to be very large.

An additional problem raised by the use of average proportions is more complex. The method obviously is still not a reflection of all preferences cast in the election, since contributions to the average for small transfer totals will be treated with as much importance as those with large ones. It will be noted, however, that none of the propositions contain any reference to party size, or the total vote gained by a candidate, and that concern is more with proportions of votes going to each destination at each transfer; so that, while 90 votes out of 100 going to Party B from Party A is less *statistically significant* than 900 out of 1,000, the pattern is still the same, and there would seem to be no argument in favour of giving the latter event ten times more weight. Indeed, there is a real sense in which this course of action would distort the picture. Say a success for the theory meant a high proportion of transfers from A to B, and that two transfer results were 10 out of 100 and 900 out of 1,000 from A to B respectively. A weighted average proportion for these two would give an 'A to B' figure of 0.83, itself high, which would conceal the fact that, in one case out of two, the theory had failed completely. The simple average proportion thus places the emphasis on each transfer stage as a separate trial, and since circumstances are not necessarily the same for each stage affecting a particular party (possibly it has different adjacent parties and so on), this would seem realistic. In the Tables 16.1 and 16.2 the number of transfer stages from which an average was computed is given as $N$.

## APPENDIX C: THE PARTIES

### Parties in existence before the 1969 election

*Official Unionists (OU)*. Became Faulkner Unionists January 1974, Unionist Party May 1974;
*Northern Ireland Labour Party (NILP)*;

334

*Nationalist Party.* This had declined to insignificance by 1973;
*Republican Labour Party.* This had declined to insignificance by 1973.

### Parties formed after the 1969 election

*Vanguard Unionist Loyalist Coalition (VULC).* Split off from Official Unionists in 1972;
*Democratic Unionist Loyalist Coalition (DULC).* Formed in 1973 from the Protestant Unionists' 1969 breakaway from Official Unionists;
*Anti-White Paper (or Unpledged) Unionists (AWPU).* Formed May 1973 from dissident Official Unionists. Staged takeover of Official Unionist Party January 1974 (after the election);
*Alliance Party.* Formed 1970 from elements of Official Unionists, NILP and Nationalists;
*Social Democratic and Labour Party (SDLP).* Formed 1970 from elements of NILP, Nationalists and Republican Labour Party;
*Republican Clubs (RC).* Banned 1969, re-legalized May 1973.

### REFERENCES

Downs, Anthony (1957), *An Economic Theory of Democracy,* Harper and Row, New York.
Elliott, Sydney (ed.) (1973), *Northern Ireland Parliamentary Election Results,* Political Reference Publications, Chichester, Sussex.
Lakeman, E., and J. D. Lambert (1974), *How Democracies Vote: A Study of Electoral Systems,* 4th edition, Faber and Faber, London.
Rose, Richard (1971), *Governing Without Consensus,* Faber and Faber, London.
Schelling, T. (1961), *A Strategy of Conflict,* Oxford University Press, New York.

# 17

# Testing Explanations of Voting Turnout in Canada

WILLIAM A. IRVINE*

## THE INSTITUTIONS OF VOTING IN CANADA

By way of introduction to a discussion of voting turnout in Canada, it is always useful to 'put first things first' and examine some of the structural features that may facilitate or constrain each individual's exercise of his franchise. Among the relevant considerations are franchise rules, the ease or difficulty of getting one's name on the electoral rolls and the nature of the ballot and of the choice with which one is confronted upon entering the voting booth. In the few paragraphs that follow, I provide only a summary sketch of Canadian rules regarding each of these features. No attempt is made to survey comprehensively the various qualifications, exceptions and means of redress available, although I can indicate their flavour (for more detail see Ward (1963) and Qualter (1970).

Throughout Canada's history as a state, its franchise rules have followed the usual evolution of such rules in Western democracies. Exclusions on the basis of property were progressively eliminated over the course of the nineteenth century so that, by 1900, almost all men over the age of twenty-one had the right to vote. Exclusions on the basis of sex were eliminated by 1920 and the age limitation for voting in federal elections was lowered to eighteen years in 1970. It is possible to lose citizenship rights by reason of confinement in jails, mental institutions or by virtue of holding certain governmental offices—offices mainly involved in the administration of the election machinery.

There is no permanent electoral list in Canada. Each time an election is called by the government, teams of enumerators call on each household to ascertain the number of qualified voters. Preliminary lists are conspicuously posted, and those excluded have a certain period in which to enter an appeal. Enumerating teams are composed of representatives of the two political parties receiving the highest votes in that constituency at the previous election. If legal prescriptions were invariably good guides to behaviour, one could be confident that the enumerators had put together

* I should like to acknowledge the financial assistance of the Canada Council in support of the writing of this paper, and also the University of Essex for support of computer time involved. My colleagues at Essex provided various forms of comment, encouragement and assistance, for which I was very grateful. Thanks are also due to my research assistant, Mr Phillip Wood.

voting lists that were comprehensive and fair. The only possible exclusions would be those changing residence during the enumeration period. However, as political behaviouralists, we are trained to entertain doubts as to the efficacy of legal prescription. That these doubts are to a certain extent well founded is confirmed by reading the newspaper at the time of any campaign. Some rough perspective on this is given by comparison, in Table 17.1, of turnout as a percentage of those on the voter's list with the percentage of the estimated adult population. Since 1921 the gap has averaged six percentage points. This constitutes an upper limit on *de facto* disenfranchisement in Canada, however, since it is possible to get census data only at ten-, or occasionally five-year intervals, and since the census only permits calculation of the number of people over twenty years of age. There are no secular trends in either series of data. The drop in 1921–26 may reflect initial low turnout among newly enfranchised women, but no election decline accompanied the further extension of the franchise to eighteen- to twenty-year-olds in time for the 1972 election. The drop in 1953 is conventionally attributed to the scheduling of the election in the vacation month of August.

Table 17.1    Turnout At Canadian Federal Elections 1896–1972

| Year | % of voters on list | % of estimated adult population | Year | % of voters on list | % of estimated adult population |
|------|------|------|------|------|------|
| 1896 | 62 | | 1940[c] | 70 | 67 |
| 1900 | 77[a] | | 1945 | 75 | 70 |
| 1909 | 72[a] | | 1949 | 74 | 70 |
| 1908 | 70[b] | | 1953 | 67 | 63 |
| 1911 | 70[a] | | 1957 | 74 | 68 |
| 1917[c] | 77 | | 1958 | 79 | 73 |
| 1921 | 68 | 63 | 1962 | 79 | 73 |
| 1925 | 66 | 60 | 1963 | 79 | 74 |
| 1926 | 68 | 60 | 1965 | 75 | 67 |
| 1930 | 76 | 65 | 1968 | 75 | 71 |
| 1935 | 75 | 70 | 1972 | 77 | |
| | | | 1974 | 73 | |

a.    excluding Prince Edward Island where no voter's lists were established.

b.    excluding Saskatchewan, Alberta and Prince Edward Island.

c.    civilian voters only.

Source:    % of voters on List 1896-1965 from John C. Courtney (ed.), Voting in Canada (1967), Appendix A. 1968 and 1972 figures calculated from relevant reports of the Chief Electoral Officer. The 1974 figure is a preliminary estimate from Canadian Press on the basis of unofficial counts.
% of estimated adult population 1921-1958 from Howard A. Scarrow (1967, p.105).

Finally, theories such as Downs's would lead us to ask such questions as: what kind of effective choice would the voter find if he did go to the polls? Would his vote be assured of contributing to the election outcome? How complicated is the ballot, and how much information would the voter need to make any kind of a reasonable choice? Canadians vote in single-member constituencies in which election goes to the candidate with the highest vote total. At the poll he will find a short ballot, containing only the names of those who hope to represent the constituency in which he lives. Up until 1965 the occupation of each candidate was indicated on the ballot, but not his party affiliation. Since that time, both occupation and party are indicated. The short ballot is usually considered an inducement to vote, since it minimizes the effort required and the complexity of choice (unless one chooses a straight party list). However, the Canadian situation until 1965 required voters to pay close attention to the local campaign—at least to the extent of informing themselves as to the identity of their own party's candidate.

Finally, it continues to be the case that many partisans in Canada have no impact, by their vote, on the outcome of the election. Either their party is so hopelessly behind, or it is so handsomely ahead, that a vote for the party in a 'first-past-the-post' electoral system is irrelevant. Unlike ballot length or format, there is sufficient variance in the competitive positions of Canadian parties for us to undertake some tests of the impact of this feature of the electoral environment.

## DATA AND MEASURES

Using a survey of the Canadian electorate carried out shortly after the 1965 federal election, this chapter will examine the evidence for four theories of voting turnout. This, rather than the more recent 1968 survey, was chosen because it contains more detailed information (albeit based on respondents' reports) on the political interest and commitments of the respondents' parents.

In the course of other work, I have shown that the activity of voting is empirically as well as conceptually separable, in Canada, from other campaign-related activities such as attending meetings or trying to persuade others to vote (Irvine, forthcoming, chapter II). The dependent variable in this paper, voting participation, is an index based on responses to five questions about voting, each response being weighted by the factor score of the question on the first principal factor underlying the five questions.

The independent variables are discussed as they arise in the analysis. In general, however, all are indices derived from standard indicators. These standard indicators were initially run against the dependent variable in a multiple regression containing all the obviously related indicators. They were then combined to form an index with weights assigned according to their regression coefficients. For example, participation was initially regressed on education, occupation and income. These were combined into an index of social integration with heaviest weight given to the variable with the greatest impact on participation. Such a procedure seems justifiable where there is no widely accepted consensus on the appropriate measure of social integration. Indicators are thus chosen on the basis of their face validity, but weights are supplied on the basis of the empirical data at hand. (All indices are fully described in the appendices of Irvine, forthcoming.)

338

## FOUR EXPLANATORY MODELS

In the next few pages I should like to measure the fit of Canadian data to four models: a family persistence model, a social-psychological integration model, an organization-mobilization model and a rational calculus model. Since I do not expect any of these to be fully satisfactory, I shall also offer and test some hypotheses about interrelationships among these models in the following section.

A *family persistence explanation* is a very simple one, and may not even qualify as an explanation in any strict sense of that term. Yet one might expect it to have fairly high predictive power, as persistence models usually do. Essentially, the model says that turnout patterns reproduce themselves through succeeding generations. Some families are interested in politics and have partisan identifications. These they communicate to their children. For other families politics and political parties are exceedingly remote, and this sense of remoteness is also communicated to their children. The model may be diagrammed as in Figure 17.1, where the entries are path coefficients (i.e. standardized regression coefficients) and the arrows depict hypothetical lines of causal force. (On the assumptions required to interpret path relations as causal relations see Blalock, 1971.) All statistically significant paths are included in the figure, but in this and subsequent figures I choose to highlight those paths whose coefficient is greater than or equal to 0.10. It is, after all, not particularly difficult to achieve statistical significance with an $N$ in excess of 2,200. At 0.22 the multiple correlation coefficient is not particularly strong, but the evidence conforms quite well to our expectations. Voting participation is most strongly affected by the respondent's own strength of partisan affiliation. Almost as strong, however, is the direct impact of a politicized home. Indeed, summing the direct and indirect effects, as the simple correlation coefficient does, suggests that coming from a home where father, mother or both had a partisan identity has a slightly greater impact on the respondent's participation than his own strength of identity. One apparently anomalous effect is the negative relationship between the degree of parental interest in politics and the respondent's own strength of identity. This becomes more explicable

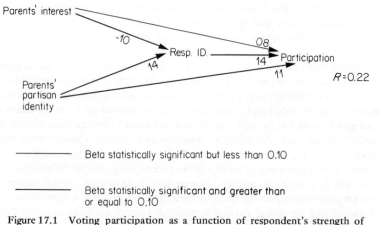

_____ Beta statistically significant but less than 0.10

_____ Beta statistically significant and greater than
or equal to 0.10

Figure 17.1   Voting participation as a function of respondent's strength of
identification, degree of parents' partisan identity and extent of
parents' interest in politics

if we hypothesize that partisanship is, at least in part, a device to minimize the costs of making political judgements (see Goldberg, 1969). Those for whom such costs are lower, at least at the margin, such as the better educated or those with sufficient interest to follow politics as an avocation, will in this view be less likely to develop strong partisan loyalties. The evidence in Figure 17.1 and in other work is consistent with such a concept. (Irvine, forthcoming chapter IV). In general, then, the family legacy is less one of generalized interest than of partisanship—a sense of involvement with the political actors.

The *social-psychological model* informs the work of most analysts of voting participation. Indeed, so pervasive is it that the authors of a recent book refer to it as the 'standard model' (Verba and Nie, 1972, Ch. 8; for a similar and earlier statement, see di Palma, 1970, Ch. 1). The general causal sequence is to see social integration leading to psychological attachment to the political system and thence to participation. The model is essentially mute as to whether social characteristics have any direct effect on participation apart from their mediated effect through psychological orientations.

In earlier analyses, the concept of social integration was treated more or less synonymously with socioeconomic status (SES) and measured by the usual indiciators of SES: education, income and occupation. In testing the model, however, I have sought to include measures of three other dimensions of social integration: subjective social class, age and cultural integration. As noted earlier, the general approach to measurement is to regress participation on various indicators of each concept and then to calibrate an overall index of the concept using the regression results as weight. One advantage of this procedure is its ability to handle non-linear relationships. In measuring the impact of age, for instance, dummy variables were used to represent age groups and the expected curvilinearity emerged—those coming of voting age only since the Second World War are markedly less faithful in coming out to the polls. For Figure 17.2 and the subsequent analysis, the variable AGE is thus not one where scores are assigned chronologically, but one whose highest value is earned by the middle-aged and whose lowest values are those of the very young. There was only one indicator of subjective social class, and the variable in Figure 17.2 labelled 'SOCINT' is measured by income and occupation. With these controlled, education fails to achieve sufficient weight to warrant inclusion. One unexpected feature in the index is that farmers gain high scores, since they are high participants although usually considered to be of low SES. To the extent that the farmer reports a low income, of course, his score will be diminished. As regards the index of spatio-cultural integration (CULTINT in Figure 17.2), ethnicity behaves as expected: English Canadians vote more regularly than French Canadians. Size of place of birth does not achieve sufficient weight to enter into the index, and region enters in as an East-West variable rather than a centre-periphery variable. The highest scores on the cultural integration variable are for English Canadians in the Atlantic provinces; the lowest scores, for the non-English in the West.

In a similar spirit, I have distinguished between two aspects of psychological integration into that political system. One index, labelled RELEVANCE, attempts to measure the extent to which the respondent feels that elections are important and that parties offer meaningful choices. In a sense, this is a measure of the leverage that the political system seems to provide. Somewhat separate from this conceptually, and probably following from it in a causal sense, is the respondent's estimate of his personal ability to influence the political system. This estimate, labelled EFFICACY, does contain the main components of the SRC political efficacy questions ('People like me have no say . . .; Sometimes politics and government seems too complicated . . .') as well as questions measuring general trust in government and the honesty of politicians. There is one slight anomaly in the components of the efficacy index which tends to confirm the criticisms recently levelled at the SRC scale (Mokken, 1971, Chs 7, 8; Balch, 1974; and Asher, 1974): if a person agrees that voting is the only way people can have any say in how the government runs things, is he indicating efficacy or inefficacy? In our data, at any rate, such agreement increases voting participation and so earns a higher score on our index.

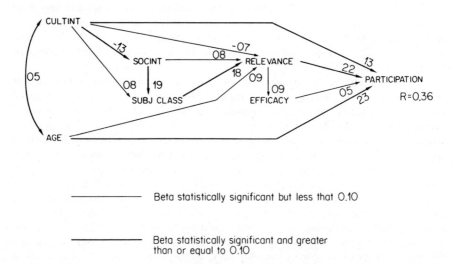

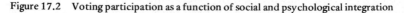

Beta statistically significant but less that 0.10

Beta statistically significant and greater than or equal to 0.10

Figure 17.2    Voting participation as a function of social and psychological integration

This model achieves a much more satisfactory multiple correlation than the family persistence theory just examined. With an $R$ of 0.36, it comes respectably close to the $R$ of 0.39 achieved by Verba and Nie (1972, p.135). They, however, were dealing with a much more restricted concept of social integration which, among other things, excluded age. This is an especially important consideration since the bivariate $r$ between participation and age is 0.25. Canada must be virtually unique among Western democracies in the weakness of the impact of social status, both self-ascribed and ascribed on the basis of more 'objective' indicators, on voting. The total impact of SOCINT, as measured by the bivariate $r$ is a mere 0.03 and the total impact of subjective social class is 0.08. In the causal model posited in Figure 17.2 the impact of these variables, small as it is, derives entirely from the effect of social standing on perceptions of the relevance of electoral choice. The impact of age is almost entirely a direct impact. Except to a very minor extent, it is not the case that the young participate less because they are more cynical about elections and parties. The data tend to confirm the view that the young are probably preoccupied with starting careers and families, so preoccupied indeed that politics is only a matter of peripheral concern. When the intrusiveness of a survey researcher makes politics more central, the young are about as favourable as those of other age groups, but they clearly do not let these orientations govern their political action. The effect of cultural integration is also largely direct; indeed the indirect effects would tend to diminish participation. Largely because of the Quebec and Atlantic residents, those high on CULTINT tend to be low on social status and to have a rather poor estimate of the importance of elections and of the partisan choice being offered. These factors diminish a level of participation that is none the less substantially above average. Of the two psychological variables, the one tapping views of the leverage provided by elections and parties has a much more significant impact than the one measuring a more individualistic orientation of the impact of the self on the system. This is hardly surprising. In the large complex modern state, few voters could realistically expect to have much impact on, or even deep understanding of, the political process. This objective situation tends to override variation in voters' subjective estimates of their importance in determining behaviour.

The *organizational mobilization model* is derived from the re-analysis of the Almond-Verba data carried out by Nie, Powell and Prewitt (1969 and 1969b). They were able to show that in the European countries, and to lesser extent in the United States, membership and activity in organizations was not purely a product of one's socioeconomic status, nor did such membership function only to transmit the effects of socioeconomic status on participation. Rather, they found that membership in secondary associations independently served to activate people into the political process and did so in large part without first modifying the psychological orientations of those affected. (Nie, *et al.*, 1969b). A later survey in the United States confirmed the mobilizing capacity of organizational activity although not simply of organizational membership (Verba and Nie, 1972, pp.184-6). Unfortunately, the 1965 Canadian survey taps only membership and not activity, so Figure 17.3 shows only the relationship between membership in various types of organizations and voting. In presenting this simple relationship, we are not addressing, at this point, the model as formulated by its authors. Unlike the other models considered in this section, the organizational-mobilization argument cannot be properly assessed except in relation to other theories—an assessment we are reserving for the next

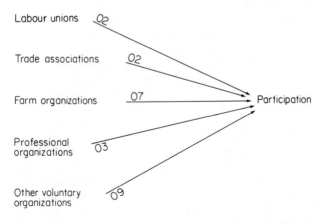

Figure 17.3   Voting participation as a function of memberships in
various organizations

section of this chapter. We may regard Figure 17.3 as simply an introduction to our later discussion. Evident from the diagram is the relatively high impact of farmers' organizations, and of 'other voluntary' organizations, a residual coding category comprising mainly charitable and fraternal organizations.

A good portion of Canadian political history is summarized by the coefficients indicating the strong impact of farmers' organizations and the negligible impact of trade union membership. Farmers in Canada have supported radical parties of both the right and the left and have had to maintain strong organizations to protect themselves against the various middlemen through whom they were obliged to buy and sell. Given the perishability of their product, it could not readily be withheld, so farmer activity has always had a strong political component. By contrast, and as opposed to the European experience, trade unions in Canada have resembled those in the United States in seeking to mobilize their membership only in pursuit of more narrowly defined economic ends. They have, at least until the late 1950s, eschewed the task of political education or mobilization of voting support for particular political parties. Hence, union membership makes no difference in the rate of voting participation. Membership in trade and professional assocations is similarly devoid of any meangingful impact on participation.

In the spirit of the measurement strategy in the rest of this chapter, a general index of organizational membership has been generated from all five of these variables, weighted to reflect the importance of each. The single variable correlates 0.12 with voting regularity. Its interest, however, depends on its interrelationship with other variables from other models. We shall return to this aspect in the next section.

The fourth and final model to be tested, the *rational-calculus explanation* considers the propensity to vote to be a function (for each voter) of:

(1) the probability that his vote could be decisive in the election;

(2) the value to him of producing the outcome even if he could be the decisive voter;

(3) the intrinsic value of voting, less the costs of voting, (Riker and Ordeshook, 1972, Ch. 3).

This model has been subject to quite searching criticism on theoretical and empirical grounds (Budge and Farlie, forthcoming; Barry, 1970, Ch. 2, 5). Item (3) seems to be the decisive one in accounting for the general level of voting turnout in democratic systems and, in its spirit, detracts from the basic calculus underlying this type of theorizing. If item (3) were to be dropped, then one would have to attribute to each voter quite unrealistically high estimates of his own importance. In testing this model, however, I am interested mainly in its ability to account for relative differences in levels of voting rather than for the absolute magnitude of the turnout.

Table 17.2 reports the results of a very crude test of this theory. The probability of decisiveness is captured by broadly categorizing the gap between the top two parties at the 1963 election, that is the election before the survey was conducted. The extrinsic value of the outcome is crudely dichotomized between the case where the outcome was limited to the election of one or the other of the established Canadian parties and the case where one of the possible outcomes was the election of one of the third parties. Since the established parties in Canada are large centrist 'catch-all' parties, while the third parties have more distinctive ideologies and clienteles, we would expect the latter choice to be seen as more valuable than the former, and so to generate a higher level of voting. Finally, we try to capture the intrinsic value of the vote by controlling for the strength of the respondent's partisanship. In operational terms, our rational model would predict that:

(1) for a constant party gap and for constant partisanship, more people ought to vote where a third party has some chance of election than elsewhere;

(2) for constant partisanship and constant class of outcome, more people ought to be regular voters where the contest is closely fought than where one party is very far ahead of its rivals;

(3) for constant class of outcome and party gap, strong partisans ought to vote more regularly than moderate or weak partisans; who, in turn, ought to be more faithful at the polls than those with no partisan affiliation.

Table 17.2    Participation Scores Under Various Conditions of Choice and Personal Stakes In The Outcome

| Extrinsic Value | Intrinsic Value[3] | Probability of Voter Being Decisive[4] | | |
|---|---|---|---|---|
| | | High | Medium | Low |
| Low[1] | None | -.51(81)[5]. | -.83(56) | -.64(53) |
| | Small | .10(81) | .04(70) | -.14(76) |
| | Middling | .11(233) | -.11(221) | .03(253) |
| | Large | .27(129) | .16(135) | .23(139) |
| High[2] | None | .07(50) | -.19(59) | -.33(45) |
| | Small | .04(18) | -.26(61) | -.10(40) |
| | Middling | .11(83) | .19(123) | .12(95) |
| | Large | .23(51) | .06(71) | .04(71) |

1. Contest is between Liberals and Progressive Conservatives.

2. Contest is between either the Liberals or Progressive Conservatives and some third party.

3. Measured by strength of party identification.

4. Measured by the margin separating the top two contestants in the respondent's constituency at the election previous to the one being surveyed (the 1963 constituency margins of victory in this case).

5. Numbers in parentheses are the N over which the mean is calculated.

The results are broadly as we have predicted, although there are numerous departures from strict monotonicity. This ought not to be too distressing given the crudity of our indicators and the very rough way we have had to divide them into categories. It is also possible that there are interactions in the table that detract from perfectly monotone relationships. (For a discussion of this point, see Irvine, forthcoming, Ch. 1.) For example, the impact of the intrinsic value of the contest is greater where the extrinsic value is negligible than where it is large. The participation index was constructed to have a mean of zero and a standard deviation of approximately unity (actually 0.92, given the rounding involved in computing the variable). Thus we see that, where the extrinsic value is low, non-identifiers (intrinsic value = none) differ from strong identifiers (intrinsic value = large) by almost a full standard deviation. Where the extrinsic value is high, the corresponding differences are lower and depend on the strategic value of the vote, ranging from one-sixth to two-fifths of a standard deviation. Similarly, the relationship between the decisiveness of the vote and participation diminishes as the intrinsic value of the contest increases. Both these interactions seem quite reasonable. The first says that, when the act is generally consequential, personal consequences matter less. The second is the converse of this: where an act is seen as personally valuable, it will be engaged in with less regard to the systemic consequences that it might produce. To some extent, therefore, the public outcomes and the private outcomes are substitutes for each other, as predicted in the original formulation (Riker and Ordeshook, 1972). The Canadian data suggest that approximately forty per cent of the population (those unidentified or weakly identified) are quite strongly influenced by the public consequences of their activity, while the remaining sixty per cent are much less affected by this. In this light, it becomes less surprising to find that Western democracies typically have turnouts of 65 to 80 per cent of their population. Although elections rarely swing on a single vote, it is probably not unreasonable to expect 15 to 25 per cent of national electorates to live in areas where outcomes are somewhat unpredictable. If we add to this the proportion strongly partisan in the rest of the country, we would probably get a figure reasonably close to the turnout figure. Performing this addition in Table 17.2 identifies a group that is eighty per cent of the size of the usable sample. This is higher than actual turnout in Canada (by about five percentage points) and approximately five percentage points short of the reported 1965 turnout in this survey.

## INTERRELATING EXPLANATORY MODELS OF TURNOUT

In this section we explore further the interest of each model by seeking to assess whether pairs of models are elaborations of each other, or whether they are complements of each other, or whether one is conditional upon another, or, finally, whether they are redundant. Models may be redundant if they explain essentially the same variance. They will be elaborations if the variables specified in the two models are all part of the same causal sequence with one set of variables transmitting the effects of the other set. In both the case of redundancy and the case of elaboration the two sets of independent variables will themselves be highly intercorrelated. Complementary models, by contrast, specify different sets of independent variables which are uncorrelated with each other. Combining the two sets might thus add substantial explanatory purchase. The logic underlying the preceding types of evaluation of pairs of models is derived from mathematical logic of a general linear model which underlies virtually all data analysis in political science. There is another aspect of this logic—that of analysis of covariance—which is largely ignored, but which underlies the notion of a conditional relationship between models. In this view the occurrence of the relationships posited by one model may depend on the value taken by variables outside the model. Let us consider some examples.

Since there are twelve ways in which models may be paired, and since each combination may be either additive or multiplicative (conditional), we need some theoretical guidance through the thicket of possibilities. The obvious place to start is with a replication of the work of Nie *et al.* (1969a, 1969b), combining organizational mobilization with the standard social-psychological model. The possible mode of combination will be somewhere on the continuum from elaboration to complementarity. In their re-analysis of the Almond-Verba data, Nie and his colleagues found organizational factors to be quite independent of social-psychological ones, particularly in European countries. Activity in groups was not a consequence of high social status, nor was its effect mediated through any capacity of group membership to modify the psychological orientations of those who join. In the United States the independent status of the organizational variable was less, but still quite notable. One would imagine the Canadian situation to be closer to the American, although our *a priori* evidence is somewhat mixed. In the preceeding section, we saw that the major organizational influences were those of farm groups (which do mobilize the lower strata) and of 'other voluntary' groups such as service clubs or the Red Cross. These typically are the preserve of the upper strata of society. Diagrammatically, the elaboration-complementarity (or American-European) continuum is reflected in terms of the width of the causal arrows. Canada will be closer to the American situation if socioeconomic and cultural factors largely determine membership and if this last variable has only a weak direct impact on voting regularity.

The evidence in Figure 17.4 is that in this, as in many other things, Canadian behaviour is a relatively equal mixture of heredity and environment; in this case, a European heredity in an American environment. Adding the organizational variable to

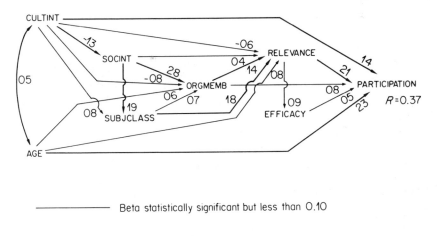

Beta statistically significant but less than 0.10

Beta statistically significant and greater than or equal to 0.10

Figure 17.4    Voting participation as a function of social, organizational and psychological factors

our standard model only raises the multiple correlation from 0.36 to 0.37, but that variable preserves about seventy per cent of its total effect as direct effect. Organizational memberships are, however, highly correlated with socioeconomic

346

status and do have the effect of enhancing interest in the election and the sense that some real choice is being offered. Thus the direct impact of SOCINT on RELEVANCE is cut in half when we allow organizational memberships to intervene: the effect of 0.08 in Figure 17.2 becomes an effect of 0.04 in Figure 17.4. Although the effect is very small, organizational membership is, to some extent, a province of the middle-aged and transmits some of the effect of age. It also transmits some of the ambivalence of the CULTINT variable. We previously saw that, although the direct effect was positive, there were countervailing indirect effects owing to the lower social status and the political scepticism of eastern Canadians. Given these characteristics, it is not too surprising to find eastern Canadians scoring below the mean on organizational memberships, a fact that also serves to diminish their participation below what it would otherwise be.

We may thus take a somewhat Americanized (i.e. strong direct effect of organizational memberships on participation but substantial indirect effects as well) version of the Nie, Powell and Prewitt model as a good approximation of the central process generating participation in Canada, and consider how best to graft our rational and family models to it. Starting with the family model, we recall that the crucial variables were, in fact, partisanship variables: both the respondents' partisanship and their parents' partisanship. We might expect, therefore, that a large part of the impact of our first model would be captured by (and transmitted through) the psychological

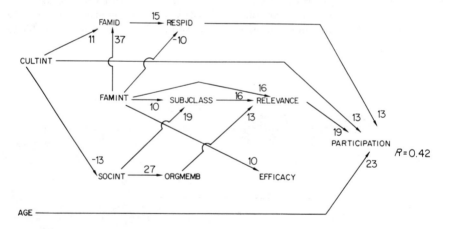

Figure 17.5   Voting participation as a function of family, social, organizational and psychological factors*

* Only betas at least equal to 0.10 are shown. Other statistically significant relationships are as follows:

| | | | |
|---|---|---|---|
| EFFICACY–PARTICIPATION | 0.05 | AGE–ORGMEMB | 0.06 |
| ORGMEMB–PARTICIPATION | 0.06 | RESPID–ORGMEMB | 0.03 |
| FAMID–PARTICIPATION | 0.09 | SUBJCLASS–ORGMEMB | 0.06 |
| RELEVANCE–EFFICACY | 0.07 | FAMINT–ORGMEMB | 0.06 |
| AGE–RELEVANCE | 0.07 | CULTINT–ORGMEMB | −0.09 |
| CULTINT–RELEVANCE | −0.07 | CULTINT–RESPID | −0.08 |
| CULTINT–SUBJCLASS | 0.08 | FAMID–SUBJCLASS | −0.04 |
| SOCINT–FAMID | 0.08 | CULTINT–FAMINT | 0.05 |
| AGE–FAMINT | 0.05 | | |

variables and particularly the one dealing with the relevance of elections and the extent of effective choice. At the same time, constricted partisanship may account for some of the impact of age and culture on participation which remained unmediated and unexplained even in the revised standard model. I have shown elsewhere that identification with federal parties is particularly low among Quebec residents and is due largely to a failure of the family transmission process (Irvine, 1974). In general, then, I do not expect the family model to add much to the explanatory power of our social-psychological-organizational model, but I do expect it to elaborate further the processes involved.

As is evident, our expectations are partially fulfilled. Only some of the anticipated intervening links are indeed present, and these only weakly. The path coefficient from the spatio-cultural variable to respondent identification is 0.08 but that from identification to a sense of the relevance of choice is zero. Necessarily, therefore, the direct paths from these variables to participation are not substantially altered; that from culture is the same (at 0.13) as it was in the simpler version plotted in Figure 17.4, or, indeed, in Figure 17.2, while the link from identification has declined from 0.14 in Figure 17.1 to 0.13 in the more complex theory. Although we have chosen to omit it from the diagram to reduce clutter, even the link from family identification to voting (found to be 0.12 in Figure 17.1) is reduced only to a still statistically significant 0.09 when all variables are considered. With respect to explaining pariticpation, the family persistence and the social-psychological-organizational model are complementary, and the multiple correlation for their combination is now 0.41. For shorthand purposes, we refer in the rest of this paper to this combination as the *comprehensive model*.

The two components of the comprehensive model are also complementary with respect to explaining differences in the perceptions that elections and parties matter, that is in the sense of the relevance of plitical choice. The multiple correlation for the variable we have labelled 'RELEVANCE' increases from 0.27 when family variables are omitted to 0.32 in the comprehensive model. Thus the combined model further specifies the nature of the family inheritance. Being raised in a family where there is considerable political interest raises the respondent's estimate of the meaningfulness of elections and of the degree of choice offered by political parties. It is also associated (possibly because of some causal link) with a heightened sense of personal efficacy. The latter, of course, has only been weakly associated with participation in any of the models considered.

To this point, then, our various models have combined additively and have been interlinked at various points. They captured some of the same variance in turnout, but each made its own contribution as well. It should be clear from the discussion of Table 17.2 that blending in the rationality model will be a significantly more complex business. We have already seen that there is substantial interaction among the various elements that enter into rational choice, and it is to the meaning of this interaction that I should like to turn briefly. In a statistical sense, the term means that the relationship between two variables depends upon the value of some third variable or combination of variables. In our analysis of Table 17.2, for example, we noted that the relationship between decisiveness and voting depended, in part at least, on the extrinsic value of the outcomes with respect to which one was being asked to choose. To be able to determine the outcomes of contest between the Liberal and Progressive Conservative parties was hardly more of a motive to action than if the result of the contest were a foregone conclusion. This particular interaction is theoretically expected in rational models of participation. Half of the basic Riker–Ordeshook participation equation (1972, p.52) is cast in multiplicative form and states that for voting (action $i$) to be preferred to non-voting (action $k$) it is necessary and sufficient that:

$$[P_i(O_j)-P_k(O_j)] U (O_j) + (U_i-U_k)>0.$$

The term in square brackets represents the decisiveness of the vote; $U(O_j)$ the extrinsic value, and $(U_i-U_k)$ the net intrinsic value. As just stated, in this formal theory the contribution of either decisiveness or extrinsic value to participation depends on the value of the other. If $U(O_j)$ is low, as we assume it to be in Liberal $v$. Progressive Conservative contests in Canada, then even high potential decisiveness is unlikely to produce much participation. This indeed is what was found. However, even if $U(O_j)$ is high, outcomes that are foregone conclusions will not generate much participation, or at least not as much as when the potential decisiveness of a ballot cast is greater.

The question that arises, however, is this: if it makes sense to discount extrinsic value when potential decisiveness is low, why does it not make equally good sense to discount the intrinsic value of participation? In other words, why should not the expression in parentheses also be multiplied by the expression in square brackets? This objection is less serious in terms of formal theory, since formal theory does not say how $U_i$ or $U_k$ are to be measured, and it may be that, in arriving at these utilities, the voter has already applied his own discount. If we could trust responses to a survey item reading 'Quite apart from its consequences, how much do you value the opportunity to vote?' we could put the answer into the equation directly and assume that the respondent has already discounted it. Clearly, however, it is beyond our capabilities reliably to measure such things so simply and directly. Hence we are obliged to seek indicators at some steps removed from the utility we hope to measure.

Confronted with the formal theory, the data analyst must reason more circuitously, along the following lines. One source of personal value lies in comformity to powerful group norms. In Canada the norms of British parliamentary democracy are most strongly held by English-speakers in eastern Canada. Therefore, the CULTINT scale used in this paper, which penalizes those who do not live in eastern Canada or who are not English Canadians, can be thought of as a scale of the value derived from conformity to norms. Similar reasoning extends to our other scales. Such indirect measurement obliges us to forego the automatic discounting that each voter supplies for himself. Hence, it is not at all unreasonable for the data analyst to ask: 'Must the value of conformity be everywhere the same?' and 'Might not the voting norm become a less valued object of conformity as the vote becomes a less consequential type of action?' Although this is essentially a question of measurement, it may or may not be sufficiently important to require the recasting of the formal theory. Certainly, I have found sufficient evidence in this and other areas to convince me of the importance of incorporating a rational response to the objective political environment as an important conditioning variable in data analysis.

In the present case we may examine a fairly simple line of evidence, which we present in Table 17.3. If no interactions were present, so that the rate of participation for a French Canadian, or for a farm organization member, or for someone convinced of his own inefficacy were everywhere the same, then it ought to be the case that errors of estimate of the rate of irregular voting will be random with respect to any

Table 17.3   Mean, Actual, and Estimated[1] Participation Scores by Extrinsic Value and
Decisiveness

Value and Decisiveness

| | Actual Participation | Estimated Participation | Difference[3] | N |
|---|---|---|---|---|
| Extrinsic Value[2] | | | | |
| High | .045 | -.010 | .055 | 743 |
| Low | -.009 | .018 | -.027 | 1461 |
| Decisiveness[2] | | | | |
| High | .077 | .023 | .054 | 704 |
| Medium | -.035 | -.009 | -.026 | 750 |
| Low | -.009 | .012 | -.021 | 750 |
| Extrinsic Value=High | | | | |
| Decisiveness=High | .143 | -.002 | .145 | 192 |
| Medium | .029 | -.025 | .054 | 304 |
| Low | -.012 | .002 | -.014 | 247 |
| Extrinsic Value=Low | | | | |
| Decisiveness=High | .052 | .033 | .019 | 512 |
| Medium | -.079 | .001 | -.080 | 446 |
| Low | -.008 | .017 | -.025 | 503 |

1.  Estimated from the Comprehensive Model as follows:

Particip=.001 + .008AGE + .039 EFFICACY + .082 RELEVANCE + .054 ORGMENB
+ .059 RESPID + .041 SUBJCLASS + .060 FAMID + .025 FAMINT - .008 SOCINT +
.011 CULTINT

2.  See Table 17.2 for explanation of these measures

3.  Positive differences indicate more actual participation than would
be expected on the basis of individual characteristics of the residents
in the constituency type.

subset of the data, including subsets defined by the competitiveness of constituency outcomes. On the other hand, if, in certain contexts, a variable produces less participation than it does in other contexts, the residuals will fall into a meaningful pattern of surpluses and deficits. In Table 17.3 we find that competitive and/or highly valued contests have more participants than would be expected on the basis of the characteristics of people resident in those sets of constituencies, while uncompetitive constituencies, or constituencies where the effective choice is one between a Liberal and a Progressive Conservative candidate, have less participation than would be expected given the type of people who live in those areas.

Table 17.3 is thus analogous to Table 17.2, but involving more variables as measures of personal utility. Instead of physically controlling for categories of a single variable of strength of partisan identity, as we did in Table 17.3, we now estimate a level of participation on the basis of the social characteristics and psychological predispositions of the people who are confronted with different types of constituency contests (or, in some cases, non-contests). As before, we consider the extrinsic value of the contest to be higher where a centre party confronts one of the fringe parties than where the two centre parties confront one another. Actual participation is indeed higher in the former set of constituencies than in the latter. What is more remarkable, however, is that we would normally expect the former set of constituencies to be somewhat below the mean in participation, and the latter set to be somewhat above the mean. Just the opposite obtains, suggesting that the predictions of the comprehensive model have been overridden and reversed by the simple nature of the choice being offered the voters. The same sort of thing happens when we control for another very simple variable: the percentage distance separating the top two contestants in the election preceding the one being surveyed. Actual participation does not decline linearly with decisiveness. It is farther below the mean in constituencies of middling competitiveness than it is in very uncompetitive constituencies. However, given the composition of the area, participation *should* be below the mean in the former, but above the mean in the latter. Thus, here again we find competitiveness heightening participation where the contest is close and diminishing it elsewhere, and the pattern of differences is almost monotonic.

The bottom six lines combine both extrinsic value and decisiveness in defining areas in which the choice to participate or not participate must be made. The data show that both elements of the combination are important. Where extrinsic value is high, both actual participation and surplus participation increase monotonically with decisiveness. For this type of contest, only constituencies where the election is a foregone conclusion show participation deficits over what would be expected, given their social characteristics. By contrast, constituencies where the contest is between the Liberal and Progressive Conservative Parties in Canada show participation deficits except where the constituency is in the most marginal third of all constituencies, i.e. one decided by less than seven percentage points.

## CONCLUSIONS

From a comparative point of view, the most interesting features of the Canadian case in explaining participation are the relative weakness of the standard SES variables, the urban-rural variable and the organizational variables. In the latter case, part of the deficiency may be attributable to defects in measurement, but the former are quite unequivocal and are testimony to the power of religion, region and culture to determine not only the direction, but also the incidence of the vote. Only considerations of rationality show any capacity to blunt the impact of spatio-cultural differences. Apart from this feature, other findings confirm our standard notions of what causes political participation.

From a theoretical point of view, the Canadian case is interesting for the encouragement it gives to operationalize and test formal models of participation. Even with the very crudest measures of decisiveness and extrinsic value, some most intriguing findings have emerged, not the least of which is the apparent ability of the objective situation to override certain individual differences.

## REFERENCES

Asher, Herbert (1974), 'The Reliability of the Political Efficacy Items', *Political Methodology*, **1**, 45–72.

Balch, George I. (1974), 'Multiple Indicators in Survey Research: The Concept "Sense of Political Efficacy" ', *Political Methodology*, 1, 1–43.

Barry, Brian (1970), *Sociologists, Economists and Democracy*, Collier-MacMillian, London.

Blalock, H. M. Jr. (ed.) (1971), *Causal Models in the Social Sciences*, Aldine-Atherton, New York.

Budge, Ian, and Dennis Farlie, (forthcoming), *Voting and Party Competition. A Spatial Synthesis and a Critique of Existing Approaches Applied to Surveys from Ten Democracies*, Wiley, New York and London.

Courtney, John C. (ed.) (1967), *Voting in Canada*, Prentice-Hall of Canada, Scarborough, Ontario.

di Palma, Guiseppi (1970), *Apathy and Participation*, Free Press, New York.

Downs, Anthony (1957), *An Economic Theory of Democracy*, Harper and Row, New York.

Goldberg, Arthur S. (1969), 'Social Determinism and Rationality as Bases of Party Identification', *American Political Science Review*, 63, 5–25.

Irvine, William P. (1974), 'Explaining the Religious Basis of Canadian Partisan Identity: Success on the Third Try', *Canadian Journal of Political Science*, 7.

Irvine, William P. (forthcoming), *Strategists, Partisans and Citizens: Political Man in Canada*, (MSS. available from author).

Mokken, R. J. (1971), *A Theory and Procedure of Scale Analysis*, Mouton, The Hague.

Nie, N. H., G. B. Powell Jr. and K. Prewitt (1969a), 'Social Structure and Political Participation: Developmental Relationships I', *American Political Science Review*, 63, 361–78.

Nie, N. H., G. B. Powell Jr. and K. Prewitt (1969b), 'Social Structure and Political Participation: Developmental Relationships II', *American Political Science Review*, 63, 808–32.

Qualter, T. H. (1970), *The Election Process in Canada*, McGraw Hill of Canada, Scarborough, Ontario.

Riker, W. H., and P. C. Ordeshook (1972), *An Introduction to Positive Political Theory*, Prentice Hall, Englewood Cliffs, New Jersey.

Scarrow, Howard A. (1967), 'Patterns of Voter Turnout in Canada', in John C. Courtney, *Voting in Canada*, Prentice Hall of Canada, Scarborough, Ontario.

Verba, S., and N. H. Nie (1972), *Participation in America*, Harper and Row, New York.

Ward, Norman (1963), *The Canadian House of Commons: Representation*, 2nd edition, University of Toronto Press, Toronto.

# 18

# Testing Models of Voting Choice in Canada

WILLIAM P. IRVINE*

The analysis in the present chapter will try to reproduce, as far as is possible given the differences in subject matter, the analysis of the previous one. Again, we shall be examining the separate, and finally the joint, impact of family traditions and social cleavages. We shall also examinine the impact of the nature of the contest on political calculations. However, we must stress that the subject matter *is* different; it is voting choice, and not the decision whether or not to vote. One consequence of the difference is to make important a model we were able to neglect in the preceding chapter. We will here be interested in the impact of issue salience on voting choice and will not examine the impact of organizational memberships.

A second consequence of the difference is the complication introduced into the operationalization of some of the variables, including the dependent variable. Such complications can be avoided by the use of the Budge and Farlie techniques described in Chapter 6 above, but are inevitably present when we attempt to use regression analysis. Briefly, the problem is that of representing voting choices, identifications and parental preferences towards the four Canadian parties as uni-dimensional variables which can be scaled from high to low. There is, in fact, no solution to this problem. It can only be ducked at more or less cost depending upon how 'multi' a multi-party system one is dealing with. In the Canadian case the cost is relatively small since the two traditional antagonists, the Liberal and Progressive Conservative Parties, still managed to attract 72 per cent of the national vote between them in 1965 and 78 per cent of the declared votes cast by the respondents to our 1965 survey (the same data set used in the preceding chapter).

In measuring the dependent variable, LIBVOTER, we choose the largest party in Canada and assign scores of +3 if the respondent remembers voting for the Liberal Party in both the 1963 and 1965 elections; of +1 if he voted Liberal in one election and did not vote in the other; of 0 if he voted once Liberal and once non-Liberal; of −1 for a single non-Liberal vote and of −3 for two non-Liberal votes, even if they were cast for different parties. Respondent identification and parental preferences are coded analogously without differentiating among the non-Liberal choices. With such a

* I should like to acknowledge the financial support of the Canada Council in aid of my general work on voting in Canada, of which this chapter is one aspect.

measurement strategy, we are forced to include among the non-Liberals voters who, in some respects, may resemble the Liberal voters quite closely. It is sometimes held, for instance, that NDP voters are simply 'Liberals in a hurry'. They will want the same sorts of things as Liberals, but will want them more uncompromisingly. To code them with Progressive Conservatives, who may be quite unsympathetic to certain Liberal and NDP stands on English–French relations, is to blur the operative issue dimension and to diminish the correlation between issue concerns and vote. Keeping these sorts of consideration in mind will assist the evaluation of the findings to be presented below.

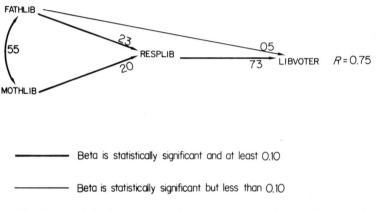

Figure 18.1  Voting behaviour as a function of tradition and respondent identification

The first model tested is also the most powerful and parsimonious one. It sees the vote as mainly a function of party identification, which in turn is largely inherited through the family. As we see in Figure 18.1, there is a very slight, but statistically significant, direct path from father's preference to the vote, but family effects are primarily mediated through the partisanship of our respondents. According to this model, voting choice is quite firmly anchored in the long-run predispositions of the Canadian electorate. The Liberal Party is the majority party in Canada and has been at least since the Depression. As with the Democratic Party in the United States, the Liberal Party in Canada is not unbeatable, but other parties find it extraordinarily difficult to dislodge them from office, or to keep them out of office beyond a single term.

In measuring the various social cleavages that enter into Figure 18.2, the same strategy was adopted, in part, as was used in the preceding chapter. Two variables were entered strictly as dichotomies: Roman Catholic–non-Roman Catholic and French-speaker–non-French-speaker. In other cases, sets of dummy variables were used as predictors of LIBVOTER and a single index was constructed by weighting category memberships according to the impact of that membership on the dependent variable. Thus, the REGION variable is again an East–West one with Quebec and the Atlantic provinces being strongly Liberal and the west very anti-Liberal. AGE is a strictly chronological variable, with the young being more Liberal than older

Canadians. Only the summary variable CLASS is a less obviously meaningful one as one would expect in a country where class cleavages are quite weak. High scores on the class variable go to the self-defined upper and middle classes *and* to the very poorly educated. Both these groups are quite strongly Liberal. Low scores go to low-income earners and to farmers. Apart from the anomalous placing of the poorly educated, this variable constitutes a reasonable scale. The birthplace variable is a strict urban-rural variable.

In a multiple regression of LIBVOTER on these six indices of social cleavage, religion emerges as the clearly dominant cleavage, twice as strong as region, language or class and four and a half times as strong as age. Religion, class and age maintain the same impact in the multivariate case as they do in the bivariate case. Much of the bivariate impact of region and birthplace is captured by other variables, while the bivariate impact of language is reversed under the controls. On the whole, French-speakers are more Liberal than others. When appropriate adjustments are made for religion and region, however, French-speakers become less Liberal than others. This reflects the Social Credit support among a portion of French-speakers who are entirely Roman Catholic and almost entirely resident in Quebec. The impact of size of place of birth is, in a similar manner, almost entirely accounted for by class and age. It is not surprising, of course, to find few city-born farmers, and it is apparently the case that our youngest respondents are disproportionately city-born, clearly reflecting the depopulation of the countryside in Canada. Taken together, these six dimensions of social differences account for only about ten per cent of the variance in voting. The multiple correlation is hardly better than the simple bivariate correlation between voter and religion. Even making allowance for the depression of correlations owing to our inability to differentiate among the anti-Liberal vote, these results are testimony to the lack of social definition in the Canadian party system. (For an argument that even the religious differences are essentially phoney differences, see Irvine, 1974).

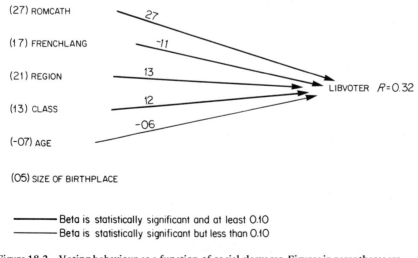

Figure 18.2  Voting behaviour as a function of social cleavages. Figures in parentheses are the bivariate correlations between vote and the various cleavages

In Figure 18.3 we examine the vote as a response to purely current issue stimuli. While such a model may approximate classical conceptions of voter decision-making, it is not one that current students and theorists of voting would take seriously. Even formal rational-calculus models usually incorporate party history as elements of the voter's calculations. Still, as a simple model it is almost as successful as the social cleavages model in accounting for variance in voting behaviour. The concern most closely associated with voting choice is that of corruption in government. Some members of the minority Liberal government elected in 1963 had been shown to have uncomfortably close connections with convicted drug dealers and with reputedly fraudulent bankrupt firms (Gwyn, 1965). Given the concreteness and immediacy of corruption, it is not surprising that it should have had considerable resonance in the mass electorate. The need for a majority government and issues of the proper relationship between French and English Canadians had only half the impact of the corruption issue, while the new Canadian flag or a concern with economic issues tended to be very weakly related to the vote. All of the last four concerns tended to make respondents more likely to be consistent Liberal voters while the corruption issue, of course, diminished Liberal support.

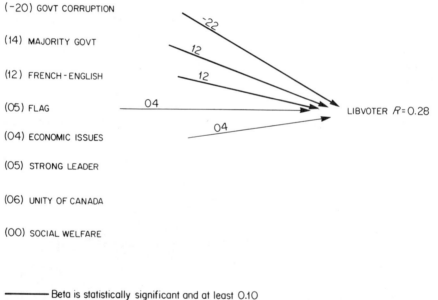

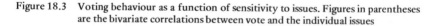

Figure 18.3   Voting behaviour as a function of sensitivity to issues. Figures in parentheses are the bivariate correlations between vote and the individual issues

Three other issues had no significant impact on voting once other issues were taken into account. Social welfare concerns were not linearly related to our vote variable, even in the bivariate case. Two other issues, each moderately related to vote in a bivariate relationship, seemed covered by other, more powerful, issues. In a sense, one could take concern for strong leadership to be a code word for concern for majority government. Expressing concern for Canadian unity was another way of expressing concern for French–English issues. The bivariate correlation between the first pair of issues was 0.33 and that between the last pair was 0.34.

Here again, we have testimony to the weak differentiation among Canadian parties in terms of policy. Corruption, majority government and leadership are classic instances of non-issues. No one supports corruption or weak government and parties simply vie with each other in seeking to associate themselves with purity and strength in their public images. Social and economic concerns were virtually unrelated to our voting dimension, a dimension which, although complicated by the assignment of minor party voters, is essentially a staunch Liberal to staunch Progressive Conservative dimension. Canada's major centrist parties have matched each other so well in these areas that little relevant choice appears to exist. Only French–English issues had the capacity, in 1965, both to stir the electorate and to guide choice, and even here the path coefficient is not impressive.

The theoretical integration of our social, family and issue models is much more straightforward and accepted than was the case for our comprehensive model of participation. In the voting literature this general integration is implicit in the work of the Michigan researchers (Campbell *et al.*, 1960, Ch. 2; Converse, 1966; Stokes, 1966) and entirely explicit in Arthur Goldberg's causal model (1966). For present purposes, the latter is the most useful. Having examined several models, Goldberg finds most

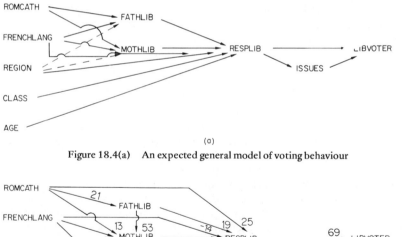

Figure 18.4(a)    An expected general model of voting behaviour

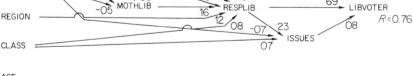

Figure 18.4(b)    An estimated general model of voting behaviour. Some statistically significant paths are omitted. Only paths whose coefficient is at least equal to 0.05 are shown

satisfactory one that sees the father's social characteristics as determining both the respondent's social characteristics and the father's own partisan identification. Both these variables determine, in part, the respondent's partisan identification. The latter variable then determines the respondent's short-term political orientations and influences the vote, both directly and through the respondent's partisan attitudes.

Figure 18.4(a) is an attempt to adapt this model for a data set in which there are no measures of parental social characteristics. Such things as religious affiliation and language use in the home (especially when measured in the broad dichotomies employed in this chapter) change very little between generations. This implies a correlation of nearly 1.0 between father's social characteristics and respondent's social characteristics in these cases and hence justifies the use of the latter as indicators of the former despite the rather curious causality implied in Figure 18.4(a). Since there are no current religious issues in Canadian politics (Irvine, 1974) we may expect the religious effect to be entirely mediated through parental identification. Since there are current language issues, we allow, in Figure 18.4(b), for the possibility of a direct effect of language on respondent identification as well as the indirect effect through the parents.

Our other measures of social characteristics (region, age and class) are much less stable between generations. On the whole, they could not be expected to be highly reliable indicators of parental characteristics, although the situation with respect to region is somewhat less clear since regions are either relatively unattractive to immigrants (in which case, if the son resides there, the father will have done also) or so large as to easily absorb immigrants, so that most of our respondents will have had fathers who were also resident in the region. The Maritimes and Quebec exemplify the first case, and Ontario the latter. Son's region of residence will have a certain component of error as an indicator of father's region of residence but perhaps not so much as to obliterate totally the correlation with parental identification. Hence we show dotted lines in Figure 18.4(a). All of the respondent's social characteristics that are not good indicators of parental social characteristics are expected to influence respondent partisan identification directly.

Although there are a number of additional, very weak but none the less statistically significant, paths that emerge in estimating the model of Figure 18.4(a), and which are not predicted by the model, the major paths, shown in Figure 18.4(b), conform very well to our expectations. In particular, the direct and indirect determination of voting choice is shown quite clearly, as is the major mediating role played by respondent identification. Except for two relatively weak exceptions, social characteristics affect neither the vote nor issue orientations except as they affect respondent identification. An interesting, if relatively weak, exception to this generalization is the case of the variable CLASS. It is now commonplace in analyses of Canadian parties and voting to stress the weakness, or at most the slow emergence, of class cleavages in Canada (Irvine, forthcoming; Alford, 1963, Chapters 4, 9; Schwartz, 1974; Wilson, 1973). The implication of this analysis is that class differences ought not to be deeply rooted in partisan identities. This in turn implies that their emergence ought to be connected with certain issue concerns, which is what is implied in Figure 18.4(b). It must be stressed however that, at least in 1965, the issues were not classic 'class issues'. Rather they were questions of style (probity and stability in government) or of the definition of the country (bicultural as opposed to unicultural English).

The largest discrepancy between Figures 18.4(a) and 18.4(b) is the large direct effect of religion on respondent identification. Surprising, and contrary to the agrument in Irvine (1974), is the direct impact of religion on respondent identity. In part, this is an artefact of measurement. It was shown in the last chapter that strength of parental interest in politics (which is built in to FATHLIB and MOTHLIB as surrogate measures of the strength of their identity) was negatively related to the strength of respondent's identity (which is built in to RESLIB). This no doubt attenuates the correlations between parental and respondent identities in a way that a proper measure of strength of parental identity would not do. Thus, although Figure 18.4(b) implies that religion is an important (indeed, *the most* important) determinant of respondent partisan identity, what is probably happening is that religion is capturing residual differences in strength for which we are not able to account, given our available measures on parental partisan loyalties. (For a fuller discussion, see Irvine, forthcoming, Chapter 6, and particularly n. 15).

A further statistical artefact consists of the various negative paths from language in Figure 18.4(b). These are accurate, given the other controls imposed. What is implied is that *if* French Canadians were as equally divided between Roman Catholics and non-Catholics as other Canadians, and *if* they were distributed across the regions in the same way, then they would be less strong Liberal identifiers than other Canadians. But, of course, it is part of the history of Fench-speaking Canadians to be overwhelming Catholic and to be concentrated in the province of Quebec. While statistical procedures can construct such an artificially de-natured French Canadian, real life has not and one must not over-interpret one's results.

In conclusion, the Canadian case is strongly similar to the American case as captured in Goldberg's causal model. Where there are exceptions, they seem readily attributable to measurement or statistical artefacts, or to the very recent emergence of new cleavages which are not yet embodied in political identities.

At this point, the reader may feel he has been cheated of the promised counterpart to the rationality model of participation offered in the previous chapter. To be sure, it would have been easy to interpret the discussion of Figure 18.3 as an instance of voters sorting themselves out in a space of desirable substantive and stylistic characteristics of a government. Those who preferred majority government and conciliation towards French Canadians, and who were not concerned with the questionable connections of some prominent Liberals, found themselves preferring that party. An opposite set of concerns was associated with support for Liberal opponents.

There is in the voting literature a minor strain of writing that is even more analogous to the discussion in the previous chapter in that it explicitly uses the variable of margin of victory. This is the 'community effects' literature, which interprets large margins of victory not as factors diminishing decisiveness but as indicators of community norms (Miller, 1956; Putnam, 1966; Cox, 1969; Segal and Meyer, 1969; Orbell, 1970; and Butler and Stokes, 1971, pp.71–86). Given this interpretation, the intellectual problem then becomes one of accounting for conformity to community norms, and those who do so turn out to be those who are most centrally placed in communications nets. However, much of this literature is unsatisfactory in that it generalizes about pressures towards conformity without showing that anyone is behaving out of the ordinary. (This objection does not apply to Segal and Meyer, nor to Butler and Stokes.) To find, for example, that the proportion claiming to have voted Republican increases as the Republican Party becomes increasingly dominant in an area *may* indicate processes of conformity. However, given that the generalizations are based on cross-sectional data, the finding may more simply be evidence that the sample is a good one. The problem is essentially one of the direction of the causal arrow: are the people Republican because the area is or is the area Republican because the people are?

Given that this paper too deals with cross-sectional data, we attempt partially to meet this problem by generating an expected mean score on the LIBVOTER variable for each of our sets of constituencies. In the top line in Table 18.1 we find reproduced for the Canadian case what is virtually the first table in all the 'community effects' studies. It confirms that LIBVOTER scores are much larger where Liberals win impressive victories than where they lag equally impressively. Subsequent lines of the table show expected means and residuals from each of the models depicted in Figures 18.1 to 18.3. In each case, the larger the Liberal victory, the larger the surplus of Liberals in the area over what one would have expected given the configuration of parental and respondent loyalties, or given the distribution of social characteristics, or given the pattern of issue concerns. In marginal constituencies, and as the Liberals begin to lose increasingly heavily (although the relationship is not perfectly monotonic), the Liberals become increasingly unable to harvest the voting support which they 'ought' to be getting. (In interpreting poll results in Canada, it is now a commonplace that the Liberals will not do as well in terms of votes or seats as the pre-election polls would indicate; a law that was confounded in 1974, but which obtained in 1965.) The pattern of residuals is flattest for family and identification and steepest for those generated from issue predictions, suggesting that the latter preferences are quite unreliable predictors of actual behaviour.

Such patterns as reported in Table 18.1 admit, I think, of at least two

Table 18.1    Surplus or Deficit in Liberal Support Over Estimate From The Family, Social Cleavage and Issue Models By Area Partisanship

Outcome In 1963

| Margin | Liberal Victory | | | Liberal Loss | | |
|---|---|---|---|---|---|---|
| | Large | Moderate | Small | Small | Moderate | Large |
| Actual Libvoter Score | .672 | .301 | -.313 | -.548 | -.598 | -1.076 |
| Expected From Family Model | .339 | .080 | -.168 | -.322 | -.419 | -.611 |
| Residual - Family | .333 | .221 | -.145 | -.226 | -.179 | -.465 |
| Expected From Social Cleavages | .246 | .076 | -.099 | -.178 | -.387 | -.536 |
| Residual - Social | .427 | .225 | -.214 | -.370 | -.211 | -.640 |
| Expected From Issue Concerns | -.107 | -.115 | -.097 | -.119 | -.210 | -.355 |
| Residual - Issues | .797 | .416 | -.117 | -.429 | -.388 | -.721 |
| N | 646 | 494 | 425 | 392 | 413 | 218 |

interpretations. One is the conventional conformity-to-norms interpretation, but the other says that, where the vote becomes increasingly indecisive, there is no longer any payoff in conforming rationally to the positions indicated by one's social memberships or issue concerns. (For an interpretation of rationality as conformity to one's group memberships, see Goldberg, 1969). Indeed, there may not even be much payoff in emotionally avoiding disturbances in the graves of one's political ancestors. At least one test is possible between these interpretations, provided one is willing to make certain assumptions about the nature of the community consensus. The key assumption is that communities arrive at consensus through processes of communication *through homogeneous groups.*

Suppose, for example, that overall some seventy per cent of Roman Catholics vote Liberal and seventy per cent of non-Catholics vote other than Liberal. It may be that this basic relationship holds true only in those communities that are between 30 and 70 per cent Roman Catholic. Further, it may be that where one or another group is either almost completely dominant in a community, or is a very small and compact minority, processes of social communication intensify the commitment of groups to their own party. Supppose, for example, that in a community 90 per cent Catholic, 90 per cent of the Catholics will vote Liberal and 90 per cent of the non-Catholics will oppose the Liberals. Applying the national relationships to such a community we would expect a 66 per cent Liberal vote ($0.07 \times 0.90 + 0.30 \times 0.10$), but there would actually be an 82 per cent Liberal vote ($0.90 \times 0.90 + 0.10 \times 0.10$). Thus could be generated the surpluses and deficits found in Table 18.1. If this process operates, then we might expect the correlation between a characteristic and a vote to increase as areas become increasingly dominated by one social group and hence by one political group.

On the other hand, suppose simply that the indecisiveness of the vote renders it sufficiently valueless that it ceases to be cast to advance policy interests, the interests of one's social groups or the commitments of one's past. In this case, votes might well be cast more or less randomly by group and so go disproportionately to the traditional winner in the community, who has the general advantages of exposure, organization and so on. This type of process would predict declining correlations between any characteristic and the vote. Note that, without the assumption of communication within homogeneous interests, the community norms model might make the same prediction, holding that conformity to the norms was sufficiently important as to override differences of interests. There would remain, however, the interesting question of why conformity to norms is more important than advancing one's interests. The answer could be that in single-party-dominant areas the vote is ineffective in advancing one's interests in any case. (One other model would also predict declining correlations with declining decisiveness. This would result if the latter were associated with substantial diminution of the variance in either the dependent variable or the independent variables. Inspection suggests that changes in the variances across categories of competitiveness are almost always insubstantial and are often in a direction contrary to the pattern of correlation. That is, the variance sometimes increases as the correlation is decreasing.)

The correlations in Table 18.2 tend to confirm the proposition that, in single-party areas, it is irrational to cast one's vote in conformity with one's interests. Although the differences in the correlations are not particularly striking in magnitude, they generally, except for the issue questions, fall in the predicted pattern: highest in

Table 18.2    Bivariate Pearson Correlations Between Vote And Major Family, Social and
             Issue Predictors By Partisan Context In The 1963 Election

| | Liberal Victory | | | Liberal Loss | | |
| Margin | Large | Moderate | Small | Small | Moderate | Large |
| --- | --- | --- | --- | --- | --- | --- |
| RESPLIB | 71 | 73 | 78 | 77 | 73 | 79 |
| MOTHLIB | 11 | 30 | 34 | 32 | 35 | 25 |
| FATHLIB | 18 | 32 | 39 | 38 | 27 | 19 |
| ROMCATH | 20 | 24 | 27 | 31 | 27 | 19 |
| FRENCHLANG | 13 | 9 | 16 | 17 | 21 | 12 |
| REGION | 8 | 10 | 14 | 18 | 18 | 8 |
| CLASS | 15 | 12 | -3 | 6 | 12 | 8 |
| AGE | -5 | -5 | -6 | -7 | -7 | -12 |
| GOVT CORRUPTION | -15 | -32 | -19 | -16 | -18 | -20 |
| MAJ GOVT | 16 | 16 | 15 | 12 | 8 | 20 |
| FRENCH-ENGLISH | 13 | 18 | -03 | 8 | 7 | 12 |
| FLAG | 3 | 10 | 3 | 13 | 9 | -17 |
| ECONOMIC ISSUES | 8 | 1 | 6 | 11 | -1 | -4 |

the most competitive areas, lowest in the single-party-dominant areas. This is most
strikingly the case with respect to conformity with parental partisanship: the effects
of these variables are cut in half as one proceeds from the competitive to
uncompetitive areas. We should not, perhaps, have expected a substantial decline in
the impact of respondent identity on vote, given that single-party dominance seems to
have some impact on the shape of partisanship as well as vote (Irvine, forthcoming, Ch.
7). Class and age considerations conform to the pattern less well, but these are among
the weakest correlates of voting choice. Rather more troublesome is the more striking
failure of any of the issue salience questions to reproduce the patterns of the long-term
partisanship and of the major social variables. One plausible explanation is that those
who intend to vote contrary to the community norm feel especially compelled to
justify such a vote by reference to some issue of style or substance. In such a case, our
correlations would be distorted by a small number of voter and issue outliers in the
most single-party-dominant constituencies.

At best, therefore, our test between the two interpretations of the 'community
conformity' voting is indeterminate, although it tends to favour the view that the
value of conformity to social or family positions is being substantially discounted.
Since conformity to partisan identity or to family tradition falls under the rubric of a
'private consequence' of the vote, the results in Table 18.2 also argue for the kind of
discounting of private motives to which reference was made in the previous chapter
(see also Irvine, forthcoming, Ch. 1).

To sum up the preceding pages, we have briefly sketched out a party system heavily reliant on general partisan predispositions as a guide to voting choice. These orientations represent, but only weakly, family history and social differences in Canada. The important social differences are religious and cultural, not class or generational. In part, this is the inevitable consequence of a party system dominated by parties that seek out the centre on any continua of economic or social policy preferences. In part, too, it results from the existence in Canada of single-party areas which tend to so devalue the vote as to make conformity to social interests an inappropriate guide to voting choice.

## REFERENCES

Alford, Robert R. (1963), *Party and Society,* Rand McNally, Chicago and London.
Butler, David, and Donald Stokes (1971), *Political Change in Britain,* St Martin's Press, New York.
Campbell, Angus, Philip E. Converse, Warren E. Miller and Donald E. Stokes (1960), *The American Voter,* Wiley, New York.
Campbell, Angus, Philip E. Converse, Warren E. Miller and Donald E. Stokes (1966), *Elections and the Political Order,* Wiley, New York.
Converse, Philip E. (1966), 'The Concept of a Normal Vote' in Campbell *et al.* (1966).
Cox, Kevin R. (1969), 'The Spatial Structuring of Information Flow and Partisan Attitudes', in Dogan and Rokkan (1969).
Dogan, Mattei, and Stein Rokkan (eds.) (1969), *Quantitative Ecological Analyses in the Social Sciences,* Massachusetts Institute of Technology Press, Cambridge, Mass.
Goldberg, Arthur S. (1966), 'Discerning A Causal Pattern Among Data on Voting Behaviour', *American Political Science Review,* 60, 913–22.
Goldberg, Arthur S. (1969), 'Social Determinism and Rationality as Bases of Party Identification', *American Political Science Review,* 63 5–25.
Gwyn, Richard J. (1965), *The Shape of Scandal,* Clark, Irwin, Toronto.
Irvine, William P. (1974), 'Explaining the Religious Basis of Canadian Partisan Identity: Success on the Third Try', *Canadian Journal of Political Science,* 7.
Irvine, William P. (forthcoming), *Strategists, Partisans and Citizens: Political Man in Canada,* (Mss. available from author).
Miller, Warren E. (1956), 'One Party Politics and the Voter', *American Political Science Review,* 50, 707–25.
Orbell, John M. (1970), 'An Information Flow Theory of Community Influence', *Journal of Politics,* 32, 322–38.
Putnam, Robert D. (1966), 'Political Attitudes and the Local Community', *American Political Science Review,* 60, 640–54.
Rose, Richard (ed.) (1974), *Electoral Behavior: A Comparative Handbook,* Free Press, New York.
Schwartz, Mildred (1974), 'Canadian Voting Behaviour' in Rose (1974).
Segal, David R., and Marshall W. Meyer (1969), 'The Social Context of Political Partisanship', in Dogan and Rokkan (1969).
Stokes, Donald (1966), 'Party Loyalty and the Likelihood of Deviating Elections', in Campbell *et al.* (1966).
Wilson, John (1973), 'The Canadian Political Cultures', unpublished paper presented to the 1973 Annual Meeting of the Canadian Political Science Association.

# 19

# Surrogates For Party Identification in the Rational Choice Framework

DAVID ROBERTSON

When two theories exist, each seeming to give a partial explanation of varying aspects of a social phenomenon, there arises a drive in academics to synthesize them. The drive persists notwithstanding the graveyards of academe scattered with the bones of would-be synthesizers. Electoral behaviour is a prime opportunity for this drive. Michigan and its imitators offer one partial analysis of the vote, centred on the idea of the voter's identification with the party. Downs and his disciples offer a rival, intellectually attractive, logical account of the voting act.

Not only are the rivals both hard to dismiss, but it sometimes appears that a work predominantly cast in one mould can solve some problems in its paradigm by borrowing from the other. Hence the drive to synthesize, as for example in Chapman's article (1967). Here a 'quasi'-party identification concept is dragged into an otherwise pure rational choice model to remove undesirable logical consequences.

Downs started the rot perhaps, when he reached somewhat feebly for a psychological motive for voting at all, when forced to the logical conclusion that it was rational only to abstain. The work by Budge and Farlie, particularly in *Voting and Party Competition* (forthcoming), is the most extensive and deliberate of such syntheses. Briefly, their argument is that, as rational choice models explain leadership politics, and party identification explains voter politics, the two together explain all politics. Now this work is very subtle, and I cannot here criticize it. The danger is clear however. There is a *prima facie* case for saying that the underlying assumptions of the two schools are inherently contradictory, and putting them together guarantees not explanation but *reductio ad absurdam.*

As I do not intend here to synthesize choice and identification theory (as I shall hereafter refer to the two traditions), it might be asked what I am doing looking for surrogates in one theory for parts of the other. The sense in which I think we need in choice theory a surrogate for identification concepts is simply that both theories need to account for a recurring set of observed facts about voting. As it happens, identification does offer a sort of account of these observations, and choice theory has usually ignored them. I do not believe, however, that both theories are troubled by this set of facts *in the same way*, or that, in coming to terms with them, they can come *to the same terms.*

The portrait of the voter that has been drawn by virutally every survey ever taken on voting behaviour in any Western democracy has the following main elements:

(1) Most voters only rarely change their vote preference.

(2) Most voters decide for which party they will vote long before the campaign

(3) Most voters vote the same way as most others in the major social, economic, ethnic and religious groups of which they are members.

(4) Most voters are neither active in, interested in, nor knowledgeable about politics.

(5) Most voters do not have well articulated ideologies or political faiths.

All of this is expressed in its impact by a sixth generalization which most survey researchers would have to support.

(6) One can predict anyone's vote as well or better by knowing sociological attributes external to him as by knowing his beliefs or attitudes about the apparent issues of the campaign.

(It is worth mentioning that this portrait is steadily losing its accuracy, when compared with data from British surveys in 1970 and 1974. See Alt *et al.*, 1974.)

These six propositions are sometimes confused with the thesis that voters are motivated by an identification with a political party. They are also held *eo ipso* to invalidate choice theory. Neither belief is accurate, and neither can be derived from the propositions, which are observations only. They do fit together to present a problem for any theory, and they are constantly replicated. I shall refer to them as showing that voters have a *predisposition* to vote at all times for a particular party, and I shall admit that such a predisposition is *apparently* a-rational.

Choice theory must come to terms with this predisposition, and it must do so better than identification theory can. Identification theory is closely tied up with the 'fact' of predisposition, and its claim to be able to explain, indeed to use extensively, the fact of predisposition is its major advantage over choice theory. If this claim can be challenged, and if choice theory can be shown to be better able to account for predispositions, identification theory will be shown to have little remaining value.

I therefore have three aims: first, to show that predispositions are not fatal to choice theory; second to show that they are not well accounted for by identification theory; and finally to insist that what is fatal to choice theory is the incorporation of its rival's account of predispositions.

I do not have space to argue a general criticism of identification theory. Were I to do so my central contention would be that it is neither internally coherent, nor in any real sense a theory at all. It is, rather, a set of *post hoc* explanations linked loosely to a peculiarly selected aspect of the social psychology of group behaviour.

## THE MEASUREMENT OF PARTY IDENTIFICATION

Oddly enough, one of the major difficulties in treating identification is a confusion about what 'party identification' actually means. Even Butler and Stokes (1969), eminent exponents of identification theory, use at least five different expressions. In the context where *The American Voter* would use 'party identification' they refer most frequently to 'partisan self-image', but employ, apparently interchangeably, 'partisanship', 'party allegiance', 'party attachment' and 'party support' as alternatives (Crewe, 1974).

Unfortunately Butler and Stokes do not provide the detailed and careful explication of their theory of identification that is given in, for example, *The American Voter*. It is not just that, as a result, we are often left unsure about what exactly is being used to explain what. There is a more serious problem, in that 'party identification' at least connects identification theory with the established literature on the social psychology of identification, giving it some hard scientific basis. But we are not sure whether Butler and Stokes wish, when using phrases as vague as 'party support', to rely on this backing or, if not, what theoretical system they may have in the back of their minds.

Linked with this ambiguity is a surprising variance in the questions used to 'trap' party identification among the studies using the concept outside America. Even Butler and Stokes do not use exactly the same question as the SRC, because in America it has been usual to offer 'Independent' as a choice along with Republican and Democrat. Indeed, the general idea that most Americans can give themselves a party identification is true only if one forgets the one-fifth of electorate who actually regard themselves primarily as independent, a category never made available explicitly to British respondents.

Difference in questions is most notable in comparative studies. Compare the 'standard' wording (Campbell *et al.* 1960, p. 122) with that used by Thomassen in The Netherlands as reported in Chapter 4 above, and the question used in Norway (Campbell and Valen, 1966):

(*a*) Campbell *et al.*, 1960

Generally speaking, do you think of yourself as a Republican, a Democrat, an Independent, or what?

(*b*) The Netherlands

Many people think of themselves as adherents of a certain party, but there are also people who do not. Do you usually think of yourself as an adherent of a certain party?

(*c*) Norway

Apart from formal membership, would you say that you wholeheartedly support one special party—in other words do you consider yourself a Liberal, a Conservative, or Laborite or what?

These differences do not, admittedly, detract from the ability of the surveys to demonstrate that in each case there exists in the voter an ability to attach himself in some way to a political party, but they are broad enough to make it extremely hard to characterize this attachment in any particular way. In the European cases it is more than likely that the questions invite voters to reply in terms of some quasi-intellectual conformity between their views and those they would attribute to the parties.

'Adherence' is certainly a word that politicians think voters understand. The posters in the French elections of 1974 that read 'Je suis un métallo, j'adhère au Partie Socialiste' bear witness. No one seems to think that respondents could actually handle the idea of party identification. Perhaps we should ask, outright, 'Do you identify with a party?' The impression that one gets of a more intellectual relationship in the Norwegian and Dutch research is strengthened by the way the Dutch question makes it much easier to declare non-identification.

These cues (wholehearted support, adhere to) are missing in the questions as used in Anglo-American studies, just as the interpretation by the researchers of the party-voter link as an intellectual one is missing in the research reports.

One also finds increasingly an odd theme in discussions about party identification.

Thomassen subtitles his paper: 'Party Identification As a Cross-Cultural Concept: *Its meaning in The Netherlands*'. In so doing he is in good company: Butler and Stokes raise the possibility that party identification *means something* slightly different in Britain than in America. Crewe (1974) gives us a thorough discussion on the different possible *meanings* of party identification. He also argues, correctly I think, that previous explanations of party identification are hard pressed by changes in the way people may now be answering the questions survey researchers use to 'trap' party identification.

There is, however, a fundamental confusion in this discussion of the 'meaning' of party identification. Actually the 'meaning' of party identification cannot vary, over time or place. It is a theoretical tool, or it is nothing. Theoretical concepts do not vary corss-nationally, although their applicability, or the coefficient attached to them, may. Consider the Keynsian concept of 'marginal propensity to save'. The meaning of 'MPS' is not different in The Netherlands and the USA, although its value may be. Party identification may not exist outside America, but it cannot have its meaning changed to force its existence. If it is true, as Butler and Stokes suggest, that British voters, unlike American voters, cannot distinguish between a vote decision at time *T* and an enduring party identification, one cannot use the concept of party identification in Britain. Any change in the meaning of 'party identification' is the creation of a new theoretical concept that rivals party identification.

The source of the confusion I suspect is the tendency of sociologists to use the word 'meaning' in all sorts of contexts where it can only be metaphorically akin to the paradigm use in the question, 'what is the meaning of the word . . . ?' Thus Crewe says (1974, p.70) 'What are the *meanings* of partisanship for electors and how, if at all, do these meanings vary?' What Crewe *means* is probably something like 'how do voters think of themselves in relation to parties, what relationships are voters aware of between themselves as elements in a party system, etc.?' For one odd aspect of party identification is that no one has ever asked voters if they had it, or if they had any analogue, like partisanship. The whole body of knowledge about party identification is, as it has to be, inferential.

## PARTY IDENTIFICATION AS AN EXPLANATION OF PREDISPOSITION

If it is accepted that party identification is an inference from predisposition, then we can see the obvious questions that the theory needs to answer. Curtly, one must say, 'Yes, voters often do think of themselves as "A Republican, a Democrat, or what", but why? and with what effect?'

How does one turn that into a theory of elections? The Michigan school have proceeded, roughly, like this. First, they have posited a special sort of social-psychological tie between the voter and the party analogous (or identical?) to the relationship between other social groups and their members. Second, they have characterized a party as one of these basic social groups. Third, they have argued for a cognitive relationship between party and other elements in the political world (mainly 'issues'), which results in a 'normal' vote that is an affirmation of group identity. Finally they have demonstrated a correlation between the possession of party identification and the possession of adequate knowledge and perceptive complexity to vote 'rationally'. This last step is not vital to their theory, but it is vital to the debate between identification theory and choice theory.

The importance of the last point is that if both their interpretation of identification and their beliefs about voters' ignorance are correct, then the only voters who cannot be shown to vote a-rationally (the ones without party identification) are too ignorant and stupid to vote rationally.

My strategy in arguing against identification will be the following one. It is a little disjointed, for the sake of clarity of separate arguments, but I think the argument overall is fairly easy to follow. I wish first to show briefly why identification theory as it is cannot be coalesced with choice theory to make a composite explanation of political life. Once that is out of the way I wish to comment separately on two aspects of identification theory: the idea of a party as a group and the evidence of ignorance. I shall then go on to suggest how I think one ought to use the idea of identification, and try to sketch at the same time a way in which a version of identification theory could be made compatible with choice explanations.

## Identification, issues and votes

Perhaps the strongest methodological difference between choice and identification theory lies in the idea of the normal vote. For identification theory there are two sorts of vote, one that is 'normal' in the sense that it is predictable from the identification of the voter, and one that is not. As used by Converse (1966) the 'normal' vote is tautologous. His argument asserts that people will vote from their identification with a party unless moved by strong, short-term, 'partisan' forces to vote for another party. Unfortunately, as no substantive explanation is ever given for normal vote direction, there is no way of telling in advance that short-term forces are at work. One can only wait until after an election, and then rule that there must have been short-term forces.

The reason for this tautology will be commented on in a later section. I wish here to note only the way in which identification theory has to have two separate sorts of explanation for the vote; party identification explains most votes at any one election, and does so by ignoring any ratiocinative element, while ill-defined 'forces' are then brought in to explain those who cannot be explained by this method.

The theory cannot therefore ever be falsified, and indeed it does not, as such, *explain* a vote at all; it merely predicts. In addition, it effectively separates voting-as-electoral choice (the rarer case of breakdown of normal vote) from voting-according-to-predisposition (the normal case). I would argue that this makes it incompatible with choice theory, whose main advantage is that it has one explanation for every vote cast, and is both a predictive mechanism and an explanatory one. Choice theory *is* falsifiable, and it has no place for special *ad hoc* explanations of awkward data. Choice theory *must be* at least an approximation to a deductive system that specifies exactly what forces will affect what voter in which way ahead of the event, or it is no use at all. Anything like the Normal Vote approach is incompatible with these requirements.

There is a second, related, way in which identification theory is incompatible with choice theory—in its description of the voter's mind. This is the account given of issues by identification theorists. It sometimes seems attractive to use 'party identification', in explaining predispositions, as an information-economising device in choice theory. Thus one might argue that most of the time a voter votes out of a party identification, but at times, when the stakes are high, he will switch from this indirect evaluation to a direct-vote decision based on issues and policies.

The general description of voting given by Campbell *et al.* (1960) seems to allow for this. It places issue attitudes between identification and the vote in some causal sequence. Only people with poor attitude structures will vote directly from identification, and those with strong attitudes will vote for them, even if they are inconsistent with identification. But this concession to attitudes amounts to little, in the end:

> In persons of strong attitude we would expect voting behaviour to follow these attitudes, whatever the individual's sense of party allegiance might be. Of course, the influence of party identification on perceptions of political objects is so great that only rarely will the individual develop a set of attitude forces that conflicts with this allegiance. [p.141]

Earlier they insist, after granting that party identification must itself be influenced by attitudes, 'But this does not alter our judgment that in the period of our studies the influence of party identification on attitudes towards the perceived elements of politics has been far more important than the influence of these attitudes on party identification itself' (p.135).

This is extremely important, from the choice theory position, because it ensures the incompatibility of the two frameworks, and guarantees that one cannot accept party identification as an account of predispositions if one seeks for a rational choice theory. For now it is impossible to say, 'Ah well, most of the vote most of the time comes from an a-rational identification, but when the stakes are high, voters will cast instead a calculated choice-vote based on their estimation of policies and candidates.' If the source of such a calculated vote, the evaluations and attitudes of the voter, are themselves largely determined by an a-rational partisanship, such as leads one automatically to think well of a Democratic candidate *because* he is nominated by the Democratic Party, or evaluate the Republicans as better able to solve economic problems *because* they are Republicans, there is no possibility of synthesis.

### Parties as groups

Even though we cannot now hope to lift elements of identification theory straight into choice theory, it is worth pursuing their method of dealing with the fact of predispositions, for it can tell us much of how we ought to go about dealing with the problem to see why and where identification theory fails. How does this bond of identification with a party work?

Although the Michigan school is avowedly social-psychological in emphasis, it is clear that the concept of 'identification' they use is not the orthodox social psychology version. In social psychology, 'identification', which stems from Freudian analysis, refers to a process, usually among children, of modelling themselves on, and trying to imitate, some particularly admired adult. To identify with someone has a profound effect on one's life, and is an important phase of socialization. Such a concept could indeed be of great use in political research; there doubtless are people who identify with political groups in this way. It is a pity in many ways that little work has gone into a general examination of the impact of party identification, for we might have more faith in its efficacy in the electoral process were it shown to have an effect elsewhere.

In *The American Voter* Campbell *et al.* explain that

We use the concept here to characterize the individual's affective orientation to an important group-object in his environment. Both reference group theory and small-group studies of influence have converged upon the attracting or repelling quality of the group as the generalised dimension most critical in defining the individual-group relationship and it is this dimension that we will call identification . . . the political party serves as the group toward which the individual may develop an identification, positive or negative, of some degree of intensity. [p.121]

To them the study of political parties is a straighforward part of the study of groups; parties, like other social categories, are groups. Let me drive this home: in their section on the effects of group membership Campbell *et al.* discuss Negroes, Catholics, Jews, trade unions and political parties, and expressly set up a theory of group behaviour equally applicable to all of these. The only difference is that parties are seen as directly involved in politics while the other categories are non-political, but with varying proximity to politics. Other groups can be characterized as voting more or less heavily for Democratic candidates, and so can the 'members' of the Democratic and Republican Parties. The political cues of a party have a stronger effect on party identifiers' decisions than do the political expressions of other group leaders, but not a qualitatively different effect.

I am not concerned to deny that political parties may be groups, though they must be somewhat unusual ones. What I need to know, as a choice theorist, is what is entailed by their being groups. If someone whose skin is black identifies with Negroes as a group, we can presume it is by virtue of his expecting other Negroes to share a set of experiences, problems, attitudes and perhaps values. 'Uncle Toms', although indisputably black, are not to be regarded as 'true blacks' (regardless of their own identifications) by black militants because they lack a set of attitudes. Catholics or Jews who identify with their co-religionists do so, one imagines, again in the sense that they expect of another Jew or Catholic a certain set of attitudes and shared experiences, and almost certainly a common moral and philosophical outlook. Indeed, in a secular age we distinguish between those who just happen to be born into a faith from those who are 'really' Catholics or whatever, by this sense of identification, but also by the empirical evidence of the person's practice of the ceremonial and duties of his religion.

What this says is that, in attributing group membership, one expects the person in question (*a*) to have a set of beliefs and properties, and (*b*) to be aware of this set, and to recognize it in other members of the group. Group members identify with something other than a label. This is how one explains the importance of non-political groups in politics. Catholics or blacks can be expected to support a fellow group member in an election, even against their party identifications, for one or more of three reasons. They may vote for him (*a*) out of loyalty and sympathy to a fellow, (*b*) because he can be expected to help them when in office, or (*c*) because they can rely on him to share a world-view and thus rule approximately as they would themselves or according to the source of their beliefs and guidance (Bible, priest, ethic, etc.).

With what, then, does a party identifier identify? Party can no more exist as a label alone than can Jew, Catholic or black. One answer would be that in identifying with a political party one is associating oneself with an ideology. That may be too strong, especially in view of the Michigan school's well-known definition of ideology, and we may do better to talk, as with groups, of a set of properties and beliefs. It is therefore just as necessary to see a party as defined around a belief structure as any other group, and this considerably constrains a party, and limits the role it can have in giving its members attitudes and evaluations.

I do not suggest that there is anything in the writings of the party identification theorists that contradicts this. Rather there is a great vagueness, a great absence of research of specification about the content of party identifications, which allows them to talk often as though the identifier did in fact identify only with the label 'Democratic Party', and then took up whatever attitudes and postures the party suggested. Hence statements like the following:

> Thus the parties appear to have served two important functions in the case of the domestic welfare attitudes. *They* have not only indicated a basic posture for their followers to assume; but *they* have also provided the party follower with cues that facilitate the structure of his opinions. [Campbell *et al.*, 1960, p.202 (italics mine)]

Identification with a party must indeed serve as a key to issues in confusing areas of policy. But it can do so in two crucially different ways. One is a form of 'learning from authority'. Here the voter says something like, 'the party I trust and respect as a warm, friendly figure in a strange universe must be right, so if they oppose farm subsidies, so do I'. Equally he likes the candidate of his party because the candidate has the stamp of approval of this benign entity. The alternative mode is the 'linked cognition' route. 'I identify with party D. By this I mean that I hold to a set of beliefs/properties X, which I find enshrined in party D. I cannot begin to understand the farm subsidy problem, but my party suggests attitude Z, and this must be in keeping with belief/property set X, so it is fitting that I accept Z.' Similarly, if a man is the candidate for party D, he is presumably himself endowed with belief/property set X, something that the voter would find hard to discover for himself.

I argue in other words that a party identification begins to make sense only if it can be given considerable substance. But, as I shall try to show shortly, to give it substance makes it a very different theoretical animal from the one kept in cages at Ann Arbor.

### The facts about ignorance

There is a frequently (though not invariably) replicated research finding that is often held to diminish the plausibility of choice theory. It is the familiar one on ignorance; the voters who are more likely to change either vote or party identification are the ones who are most ignorant. The stronger an elector's party identification, the more information he is likely to have. Independents are also sometimes said to have less information than party identifiers (although the evidence for this, as for most of the invidious comparisons drawn between identifiers and independents, is less than clear).

The more refined version of this differentiates between the totally ignorant and the only abysmally ignorant; those who know absolutely nothing actually *have* to vote from party identification, for they lack any other cue at all, unless, of course, they take their vote from some totally non-political source, as in voting to please a spouse. After this group, however, the tendency to be informed increases monotonically with the tendency to vote according to party identification.

It is obviously a difficult task to explain why people are more likely to vote from identification the more, rather than the less, well informed they are, or to explain why party identification is strongest among the best informed. The idea that these well-informed strong identifiers are simply demonstrating a greater interest in politics, but screen their information so as not to damage their crude faith has been convincingly defeated in Butler and Stokes 1969, (Chapter 10). But how else does one explain the retention, indeed the strengthening, of a contentless psychological tie under the impact of detailed information about politics?

There are other aspects of this phenomenon too: the extent to which a voter's attitudes and beliefs on domestic policies fit into a neat 'scaler' pattern depends on their degree of party identification. Here again independents are thought to be cognitively impoverished. In fact, from the data published, they appear to have 'scalar' structures to much the same extent as strong identifiers (Campbell *et al.* 1960, p.201).

We have to accept the existence of two sorts of voters. One is the 'know-nothing' who has to vote from party identification, and does so safely and regularly. The other is equally loyal to his party identification, but is well informed and politically quite sophisticated. These are not the same people, and cannot be. For the former an extremely vague and nearly contentless identification may indeed be the cause of their voting and any attitudes they may possibly have to political objects.

For the latter, those who are well informed and have relatively complex structures of thought, identification must connote a belief/property set of the sort we have discussed. High information for these can easily yield a regular vote consonant with their party identification. The more information one has, the more one is able to place new issues and events in one's general cognitive apparatus. If party identification actually consists of a complex world view that leads a voter to associate with the party that seems to espouse a similar belief/property set, then most issues or events in the world will ultimately be interpretable in accord with his general belief structure. It is not at all surprising therefore to find education and information positively correlated with the consistency or predictive value of a strong partisan identity. But this does *not* mean two of the things that its observation through surveys has been taken to mean. First, it does not mean that the voter is taking up an issue-stance, or is voting, *because* of his party identification. It means that his party identification and his vote are mutually occasioned ('caused' would be too strong) by the same basic beliefs and characteristics. More important still, it tells us little about the man who does *not* have a strong party identification, or who has not got a regular voting history.

## Information and substantive party identification

I would suggest that the main failing of researchers in the Michigan school has been an unwillingness to think about how a voter or a group of voters should vote. This has restricted them to seeing voting deviancy only in terms of 'average' group votes over time. It follows the insistence on using a contentless notion of identification and has produced, among other things, the tautologous nature of their 'normal vote' concept.

Accustomed to a class structure of voting in Britain, we have long recognized a category of voters who are problematical not because they are ignorant, or lack a firm identification, but because there is something 'strange' about their vote; these are the working-class Conservatives. Now class is much less important a category in America, and no one would suggest that the identification theorists ought to have come up with a similar class-based category. But it is surprising that they have not tried to use such a mode of analysis at all; that is, they have never attempted to work out how any major group *ought* to vote.

Not doing so (perhaps they could not, given the lack of content to either their long- or short-term influences) has led them to work entirely in observational terms, to analyse entirely in terms of macro-sociological and action variable correlations. So while we know the correlation between, for example, political information level and vote changing, we do not have general descriptions of action groups selected because of their oddness or uniqueness. What I suggest we need to help us see the relevance of the correlation between information and identification is the selection of groups who might reasonably be *expected* to change their vote in different elections, or of groups whose party identification is, in some way, 'strange'. For not all vote changers are ignorant, not all strong party identifiers are informed, with well structured attitudes. Deprived of any content for the habit of identification it is, of course, hard to know how to analyse further. But is seems to me unfair and unscholarly to group voters only by macro-characteristics, e.g. 'have voted for more than one party between 1952 and 1960' and to cross-tabulate them against another macro-characteristic, e.g. 'have gained information from more than one medium'. Are there not people who might be thought of as odd if they *did* vote for the same party in both 1956 and 1960? As a crude example, what of men whose livelihood depends on a large technological defence expenditure? The generally right-wing Republican Party, headed by an ex-commander of SHAPE, makes sense in 1956, but the election programme of Kennedy, underlining an (imaginary) missile gap and the need for a space programme, would surely be a better bet in 1960.

They need an analysis of party identification, information levels and vote changing that is sophisticated enough to accept that the tendency to vote regularly for X, or to vary a vote between X and Y must be differently characterized according to the life position of the voter. Some strong identifiers who are well informed may be odd creatures, others less so; some vote changers may be erratic, while some may be people essentially *following*, not deviating from, their true party identification.

This is the core of my argument: if you grant a content to party identification it is an open question, in elections as fluid and non-ideological as those in the United States, just which candidate does come under the identification. One should not therefore distinguish between voting from identification and voting according to short-term partisan forces. Instead, voting from party identification 'correctly' and voting from party identification 'mistakenly' should be distinguished.

By now most of the thrust of how I feel predispositions should be handled must be fairly obvious. I would like to close this section with a final quotation from the identification school to re-assert the extent to which they do seem to see identification as a contentless and a-rational psychological tie, and the way they ignore one whole half of the electoral system. We should be interested not in a theory of voting *as such*, but in the theory of the electoral system, involving both the political party and the voter in a two-way relationship.

Having shown that party identification works disappointingly in Norway mainly because it is tautologically connected to past vote, and because it shows little sign of influencing attitudes, Campbell and Valen (1966) obverse:

It is a paradox that because of these facts the weakly organised American parties may exert a greater independent influence on political attitudes and votes than do the highly organised and more clearly class related parties of Norway. To a voter who has not learned to interpret political events in terms of an ideology of social class, the party is likely to be the most important source of political direction available. In contrast, when a self-conscious segment of the electorate comes to see its party as the instrument for the implementation of its policy aspirations, it may exert at least as much influence on the party as the party does on it. [p.268]

Quite. My argument is mainly that they fail to show how American parties might be any different.

## PREDISPOSITIONS AND RATIONALITY

The heart of the Downsian model is the theory of ideological competition. It is by virtue of linking the behaviour of voters and of parties, presenting the two as aspects of one dynamic system of policy setting and public choice, that the theory has such intellectual force.

In a book like this it is safe to assume a basic familiarity with the Downsian model, and I shall not review it. Let us concentrate simply on the problems raised by the existence of predispositions. Principally the difficulty is this: choice theory relies on each vote being cast as a direct result of the voter comparing his present policy preferences with the actual policy being offered by each party at that time. If, instead, we must accept that voters (a) do not know much about the policy offerings, (b) do not have clear-cut preferences themselves and (c) vote habitually for one party to which they are loyal regardless of its policy, the central mechanism of choice theory is void.

Having said that, one has to enter a caveat; as it happens, despite their predispositions, most voters seem none the less to cast highly 'rational' votes. Bank managers vote Conservative and Republican, trades unionists vote Labour and Democratic. Northern blacks and Southern white vote Democratic, and so on.

Furthermore, when election results do, as they sometimes do, upset such simple predictions, there is at least some ascertainable, and in some sense 'rational', explanation. Rather a lot of blue-collar workers deserted the Democrats in 1972, just as a lot of white-collar executives deserted the Republicans in 1964. The greatest Labour victory in Britain was won, in 1945, partly because many people who ought to have been predisposed to the Conservative party seemed to think that the right-wing politics of the Depression might not be a good way to inaugurate the post-war era; that they returned to their fold in 1950 is only remarkable if one forgets the massive rethinking of Conservative Party politics superintended by R. A. Butler between those two elections.

So much for political science by anecdote. We all need to think carefully about the assumptions we make about these predispositions, and even more, about rational voting. I suggest that it requires only two crucial assumptions to remove any threat that the fact of predispositions might be held to present to choice theory.

First we have to make an assumption about predispositions: why do people have such regular voting habits? How do they develop a firm loyalty to one party? The obvious assumption is that they learn, quite young, to make a connection between the political actions and general ideology of one party and a picture of what is meet, right and fitting in the world, particularly as that world affects them, which they also learn quite young. In other words, they develop a party identification in the sense of a connection between their own belief/property set and a similar belief/property set attributed to a party. The connection between the two belief/property sets is contingent, however, and neither psychologically permanent nor capable of withstanding any great incongruence. If the party does not validate the connection, they will neither vote for it, nor long retain the identification.

It seems fair to say, and it is supported by findings of the Michigan school, that the longer this connection remains intact, the stronger it will become; so if a party seldom or never behaves contrary to the belief/property set one attributes to it, one increasingly discounts the probability that it will ever do so.

We still need a second assumption. As yet all we have argued is that there could be a form of party identification that might be consistent, in explaining predispositions, with the demands of choice theory. The second assumption must do two things. It must demonstrate why a predisposition not to take much notice of politics and policies is likely to be a safe way of casting a 'rational' vote. Of greater importance is its need to show when the identification will not be safe, and to show that for some people all the time, it cannot be safe. For unless some people can be expected not to rely on predispositions, choice theory fails again. If everyone does and can vote from identification, the parties need not compete ideologically, and we lose the complex dynamics of the policy-setting aspect of choice theory. In addition we run across the research finding that many people do change their vote frequently, and that not everyone seems to have a strong party identification.

Where do we get the assumption that works this miracle? It exists already in the form of a thesis, partly normative and partly descriptive, about policy-making. I am referring to the 'incrementalist' thesis associated mainly with the works of Charles Lindblom and D. A. Braybrooke (1963) and, in a more abstract way, the ideas of Karl Popper on the nature and need for 'social engineering' (1960). The general drift of this argument is that policy-making is extremely difficult, because of our ignorance and inability thoroughly to discover the effects and ramifications of any policy change. Lindblom and Braybrooke's version goes further, in pointing out the remarkable difficulty of even making an *a priori* decision, in the abstract, about what might constitute a policy 'maximization' target.

For no very good reason, most choice theory has seemed to assume that policies offered by parties change quite frequently, and by large degrees (despite Downs's stress on the need for reliability and responsibility in policy offerings over time). To suggest otherwise is almost heresy, particularly to identification theorists who suppose elections to demonstrate a set of frequently changing short-term partisan forces. Yet the incrementalist thesis suggests that policy can change only slowly and marginally. Intuitively this fits experience. The raw stuff of politics changes only slowly and erratically. For as long as I have been aware of politics, British party politics has had a few, constant, issues, all tied up with the extent to which different social classes should bear the cost of baling out a badly leaking economy. Much the same is true of most Western democracies. Even where issues have changed faster or more frequently, they have seldom changed in such a way as to invalidate or alter the relevance of the general posture of the major parties ten, or even twenty, years ago.

The easiest way of making the rest of this point is to go to one of the spatial demonstrations that choice theory lends itself to. In Figure 19.1, assume a simple left–right dimension on which voters are distributed according to the belief/property sets that generate their party identifications. We then place two parties, $X$ and $Y$, on the same dimension, showing their positions at any time $t$. All that the incrementalist thesis adds, I suggest, is a range, around the $X$ and $Y$ points bounded, for $X$, by $X'$ and $X''$ and for $Y$ by $Y'$ and $Y''$. Inside these bounds it is quite probable that policy will shift from election to election as parties seek to come up with policies that will both solve commonly agreed problems and win votes. Outside the range however lie most of the voters. It is extremely unlikely that any party will shift its position so as to change the relative congruence between the voter's belief/property set and that of the party with which he previously allied.

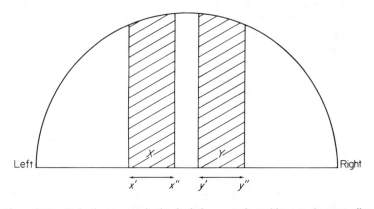

Figure 19.1    Only those voters in the shaded area need consider actual party policy. The area shown larger than is likely for clarity. It is probable that only a small proportion of voters would be inside the ranges $x'-x''$ and $y'-y''$

This demonstration simultaneously identifies those who, because their own position lies inside the range of likely policy change, will need to vote directly from party policy cues, and cannot rely on an identification. They are voters who are 'socially marginal', the middle ground whom parties could chase after, the people, perhaps, whom the Conservative Party strategists in the early sixties used to call 'target voters' (Rose, 1967).

There are many possible candidates for this role; who is likely to be marginal in this sense depends primarily on the cleavage system in the electorate. In a class-based system, as in Britain, one might expect that lower middle class 'white-collar' workers who do not in fact earn very much may at different times find either of the major parties the most rational vote. Similarly, affluent workers, with the salary levels of the middle classes but the expenditure patterns, educational style and requirement for some forms of welfare state provision of the working-class voter, may lie within such a range.

In America, an obvious candidate is the middle-class black who may suffer both from the anti-civil rights attitude of a Republican candidate and the higher tax policies of a Democrat. Farmers in all countries, and the ill-paid but status-conscious liberal professionals like teachers, are other prime candidates. In a way, these are all the people who used to be seen as likely sufferers from 'cognitive dissonance' when that was a fashionable concept; now I suggest, instead, that their tendency neither to have firm identifications nor to vote in a very predictable way follows from their being the only voters who may reasonably be expected to look like Downsian voters.

Other satisfying solutions and explanations follow from this analysis. One obvious variable that will affect the number of such 'marginal voters' is the laxness of party discipline, and indeed the accountability of politicians for the government's actions. The more lax party discipline is, the more variance there is between candidates of the same party. The more such variance there is, the less probable it is that you will be able to vote safely from simply noting the party of your candidates, for your true party identification may well be based on a belief/property set not exhibited by the man who happens to be the Democratic candidate. Which Western democracy has the least party discipline? America. Where is party identification least well correlated with vote? America. European countries are more prone to have programmatic parties, requiring a lower degree of policy change between elections. There vote fluctuation is lower, and actual vote is nearly tautologous with party identification—not, I suspect, because party identification is tautologous, or because it only really arises in classless societies, but because there is less need, or opportunity, to vote from issues.

And, with this interpretation, we can show roughly how to test the model. First, a few pieces of evidence that exist. It is likely that, if class can produce social marginality in Britain, there should be some constituencies where there is an unusual predominance of, for example, affluent workers. In such constituencies, Crewe has shown (1973), that voting has fluctuated more than normally in British elections.

I must refer to another work of mine (Robertson, 1975) where I have demonstrated that the swing to candidates in constituencies where the candidates are relatively extreme for their party is lower than the swing enjoyed in moderate constituencies. This finding I have replicated on American voting figures, using the legislative vote scores produced, for each congressman, by various pressure groups, as indicators of policy extremeness.

Then of course one would expect a change in the life situation of a voter, social mobility being the prime phenomena here, to result in a shift of party identification from that of his parents to that most suitable for his new class. Goldberg (1969) demonstrates just this.


## CONCLUSION

It has been suggested that any difference between my interpretation of predispositions, and identification, and that set by Warren Miller in his contribution here is purely metaphysical. I think this is untrue, because I think that the interpretation I suggest is testable, and points to further research. Before taking this up as my concluding argument, I should review the mass of separate arguments I have so far made.

I have argued, first, that party identification as an account of predispositions cannot be borrowed wholesale, under the guise of its being a voter's information-economising device, by choice theory. Doing so can only produce incoherence, as the basic assumptions of both arguments are mutually incompatible.

Secondly, I reviewed the definition and measurement of identification, and suggested there was very little clarity in its definition, and that the measuring instruments for it vary too much to allow of international comparison. I pointed out also that arguments about 'the meaning of party identification' are confused, and serve only to demonstrate that it is indeed an unsupported inference from the fact that voters have regular predispositions to vote in a certain way.

The idea of a political party as a kind of group, and thus of party identification as analogous to a Catholic's identification with his co-religionists, was examined. I suggested that if the analogy was to hold, party identification had to be given a content based on the voter's perceiving the party as enshrining a set of beliefs and properties.

This point was strengthened by considering the evidence usually quoted about the relationship between information levels and party identification. It was suggested that one could make sense of such macro-sociological variables as consistency of voting and information levels only if one knew exactly what it was that a voter identified with. The possibility of a vote change resulting from *stable* 'true' identification leads into the argument in the final section. Here I suggested a model that divides voters into those who are, and those who are not, able to trust a party identification to guide them well in a political scene where policy changed only infrequently and incrementally. Using these two assumptions, that identification arises from a learned congruence between what a voter believes is right and what a party stands for, and that parties may only make small changes in policy from election to election, I demonstrated the compatibility between a revised notion of identification, as an explanation of predispositions, and a choice theory of the electoral process.

Essentially I have set out a sketch of a way of analysing and explaining voting which is compatible with what we know about voters, is self-consistent and can generate predictions. We do not have enough data yet to test it well, but the way is clear; it involves the analyst predicting first how people with such-and-such a substantive identification ought to vote. This does not seem to me a fault. We should be able to specify precisely how a man with a certain level of information, will perform. If he fails us, we know where to look to refine the theory.

The way to develop such a theory of electoral behaviour is quite easy to see, although very difficult to carry out. The first step is to get a picture of the distribution of political beliefs in the electorate; all we have to date is the distribution of party identification. This, unfortunately, cannot be used, because it measures the intensity with which people hold unspecified identities, and a strong Democrat is not necessarily an extreme Democrat.

Nor, unfortunately, can the existing information on policy attitudes be used. For these are selected on *a priori* grounds of interest or relevance chosen by highly sophisticated political scientists. Only issues that can be shown to be salient, independently, are useful.

The most hopeful avenue, short of a massive survey research project which would be very difficult indeed, is probably a variation of the likelihood space devised by Budge and Farlie, based on characteristics. We need to develop a rational choice description of the electorate which, given the actual policies of parties from time to time, would identify those groups or types of electors who are, as it were, 'at risk' to vote changing. Predisposition voting could then be analysed to see if in fact such voters are or are not efficient in their demands, capacities and uses of information. With such a theoretical and empirical model we would be able to define a group who indeed ought to have unstable voting records. It might, of course, turn out that people were deficient in information and cognitive structures when they most needed to be informed. Then we might well end up with the sort of picture of the electorate that identification theory posits, but at least we would have good grounds for it.

It is actually no part of my thesis that the electorate is rational and well informed, or able to operate as classic democratic citizens. I could not claim such knowledge, and doubt that anyone could. My argument on the whole predisposition-vote problem is much more modest. I am saying essentially that, whatever the electorate may be like, we must analyse voting as electoral choice, because that is why the system exists. Only when we have a framework and appropriate empirical evidence that is devised from the viewpoint of elections as rational public choice mechanisms can we know whether or not the electorate is qualified to operate such a system. Identification theory deals with predispositions on the assumption that they are contra-rational, and therefore finds this to be so. But while it is possible to provide an *a priori* theoretical interpretation of predispositions as being at least consistent with, possibly necessary to, rational choice, it is not possible to confront this with evidence. The evidence we have is created by surveys that, not being designed to test choice theory, are irrelevant to it.

The only way of testing or developing the ideas I have thrown out here is to collect data guided by normative considerations. To differentiate between voters on the observable action variables of consistency of vote, or presence or absence of predispositions, misses the point. We must differentiate voters according to the consistency or inconsistency of their actions and predispositions with the way one would predict a rational voter in the same position to behave. Above all, we must learn what goes on in the voter's mind when he successfully answers the identification questions.

As far as I can see, orthodox identification theory is metaphysical. It explains vote shift tautologously, assumes a causal direction between identification and attitude with no evidence, and explains voters' choice in terms of loyalty to a quite empty label.

My reinterpretation is easily testable, however, and indeed I have cited some existing evidence to support it. Where do we go from here?

## REFERENCES

Alt, J. E., J. M. Crewe and B. Sarlvik (1974), 'Issue Positions, Party Identification and Party Preference', paper presented to APSA annual meeting, Chicago, 1974.

Budge, I., and D. Farlie (Forthcoming), *Voting and Party Competition*, Wiley, London and New York.

Butler, D. E., and D. E. Stokes (1969), *Political Change in Britain*, Macmillan, London.

Cambell, A., P. E. Converse, W. E. Miller and D. E. Stokes (1960), *The American Voter*, Wiley, New York.

Campbell, A., P. E. Converse, W. E. Miller and D. E. Stokes (1966), *Elections and the Political Order*, Wiley, New York.

Campbell, A., and H. Valen (1966), 'Party Identification in Norway and the United States', in Campbell *et al.* (1966).

Chapman, D. (1967), 'Models of the Working of a Two Party Electoral System' in *Papers in Non-Market Decision Making*, 3, pp.19–37.

Converse, P. E. (1966), 'The Concept of a Normal Vote' in Campbell *et al.* (1966).

Crewe, I. M. (1973), 'The Politics of "Affluent" and "Traditional" Workers in Britain: An Aggregate Data Analysis', *British Journal of Political Science*, 3, 29–52.

Crewe, I. M. (1974), 'Do Butler and Stokes Really Explain Political Change in Britain?', *European Journal of Political Research*, 3, 47–92.

Goldberg, A. (1969), 'Social Determinism and Rationality as Bases of Party Identification', *American Political Science Review*, 63, 5–25.

Lindblom, C. E., and D. A. Braybrook (1963), *Strategy of Decision: Policy Analysis as a Social Process*, Free Press, Glencoe, Illinois.

Popper, K. (1960), *The Poverty of Historicism*, 2nd edition, Routledge, London.

Robertson, D. (1976), *A Theory of Party Competition*, Wiley, London.

Rose, R. (1967). *Influencing Voters: A Study of Campaign Rationality*, Faber and Faber, London.

20

# Placing Party Identification within a Typology of Representations of Voting and Party Competition and Proposing a Synthesis

DENNIS FARLIE and IAN BUDGE*

## INTRODUCTION

Robertson's discussion has brought us back to explicit consideration of party identification and its conceptual standing in relation particularly to rational choice models. Putting the matter briefly, both are 'as if' explanations—voting choices can be viewed either 'as if' they were prompted by party identification or 'as if' they were prompted by rational choice calculations. But Robertson argues they cannot be regarded 'as if' they were prompted by both. The long-term predispositions that all recent developments of rational choice model recognize cannot be underlying psychological attachments to parties: within the rational choice framework they must consist in the maintenance of the same relationships between electors and parties over long periods, so that electors in terms of their autonomous personal aims make the same voting choice of party.

It is worthwhile noting that Robertson's argument incidentally rules out any solution to the problem of long-term predispositions in terms of adding a bias term to the outcome of policy-based calculations (cf. Ordeshook, Chapter 15 above). For doing this implies that electors do not or cannot decide how to vote for a party in terms of their rational calculations alone, but are additionally swayed by some a-rational bias (possibly psychological attachment to party). This Robertson's argument would not allow either, since it insists on both moral and empirical grounds that a rational choice framework presupposes the existence of autonomous goals among all (or the vast majority of) electors, which are both necessary and sufficient for the independent evaluation of parties. Abandoning this point of view means adopting a highly élitist interpretation, contrary to normal justifications of representative democracy, in which parties shape electors' preferences (cf. Damgaard and Rusk, Chapter 9 above for an argument rather like this).

As against this, it is true that party identification places great stress on the existence of 'parties' among the electorate that are not the same as leaders' parties.

* This research was supported on grants H.R. 2129/2 from the British Social Science Research Council. This paper is one of a series in which names are alternated to indicate the joint and equal responsibilites of the authors for the discussion.

Nevertheless the Michigan framework as a whole sees party identification as biasing electors towards acceptance of 'their' party's position in terms of issues and candidates, thereby precluding the kind of independent evaluation that Robertson had in mind (cf. Figure 1.1).

If this criticism is accepted, it follows that the only way in which long-term predispositions of electors to vote for particular parties can be represented within a policy space is to limit the spatial mobility of both electors and parties: to say within the British context, for example, that the Labour Party will never repudiate a whole range of policy positions and will therefore in spatial terms always be closer to a particular set of electors, who, therefore, in terms of their long-term independent evaluations of the parties, will always vote Labour (Robertson, 1975, Chapters 2, 3, 6).

Most rational choice models have always assumed electors' preferences to be fixed, and there have been some moves noted by Ordeshook towards limiting candidates' spatial mobility. Implications from this have already been discussed in Chapter 14. Conversion of a pure policy space, whose defining characteristic is free movement, into a policy space with party-reserved areas, makes it very similar to party-defined space. For now the ends of the space need not be interpreted only as policy limits (100 per cent government intervention) but also as 'pure' party positions. And a space limited by pure party positions is defined by party, in much the same way as was the spatial representation of party identification in Figure 1.2 and the LiRaS-based representation (Figure 6.1; Table 6.1). Of course, such representations might still differ in terms of the basis on which the space was constituted—its input. Nevertheless, there is a formal resemblance that is lacking in a pure policy space where the only constraints are limits of policy, and parties are simply points within the space.

The purpose of this chapter is to explore such resemblances and differences further. This explanation will be couched in spatial terms, but will also relate to the discussion of Part I, since party identification, as we have seen, can be interpreted spatially and social background factors such as class and religion (cf. Thomassen, Chapter 4 above; Budge and Farlie, Chapter 6), suggested as alternative indicators of long-term predispositions, can also be viewed as dimensions of a general 'social background space'. Hopefully, therefore, this overview will cover all the approaches suggested in this book and will explicitly state the interrelationships between them. Having discussed the relationship between party identification and Likelihood Ratio Space within this overal typology, we will take up the suggestion made at the end of Chapter 6 that LiRaS (with pure background input) is an improved measure of long-term partisan predispositions. With both background and policy input we shall argue that it retains the measurement strength of other approaches, and is therefore capable of supporting a theory which synthesizes rational choice with the assumptions behind party identification (cf. Chapter 1). With this discussion we move beyond the use of LiRaS as a simple measure of predictive capacity, to the utilization of its potential as a full spatial representation. The method of calculation and the type of distribution produced have already been presented in Chapter 6 (the second section, Table 6.1 and Figure 6.1).

## AN OVERVIEW OF REPRESENTATIONS OF VOTING AND PARTY COMPETITION, INTERPRETED SPATIALLY

We mentioned above that our overview includes the approaches discussed non-spatially in Part I. Such approaches can all be interpreted spatially. Since the advantages of spatial representation have been canvassed extensively in many of the previous chapters, it requires no further justification. But we do emphasize that it is comprehensive and covers, although possibly from an unfamiliar viewpoint, all the common approaches to voting and party competition.

Our discussion centres on the spaces and relationships (or absence of relationships) presented in Figure 20.1. The central spaces here are policy space (P) and background space (B). We have considered policy space explicitly and at length in Parts II and III. Its defining characteristic is free movement. Within pure policy space candidates and leaders are not constrained to any position but can range freely. This implies that policy space can relate only to promises about the future and to future aspirations, since leaders are tied to their past record, party and other characteristics; they cannot alter them at will and in regard to these have the ability to move only within severely constrained limits, if at all.

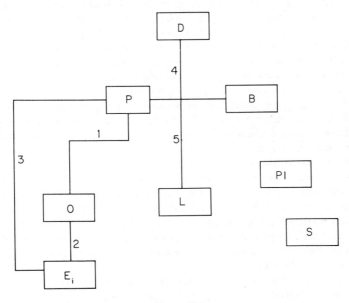

Figure 20.1

Past records, party and other characteristics cannot therefore belong in a policy space whose defining characteristic is perfect mobility. Nor is it satisfactory to represent them as posterior and unexamined bias, since these loom so large in electoral decisions. The solution is to represent them in another space—background space (B)—of equal importance with policy space. This is the space within which fall characteristics like class, religion, region and other factors commonly used by survey analysts.

The contrast between policy and background space is in fact a spatial rendition of the distinction between short-term election cues and long-term predispositions which has underlain much of the discussion of this book. Short-term cues lie in policy space, since they consist of promises about future party performance in office (sometimes deliberately vague promises). Within this space electors too might change their preferences quite freely, in accordance with circumstances and their susceptibility to party persuasion. In background space both parties and electors possess relatively indelible characteristics: since neither can move much, the same relationships between them persist over long periods.

The whole tenor of our previous discussion is that any reasonably predictive and illuminating representation needs to take account of both cues and predispositions—in spatial terms, it needs to be set in the combined space of policy and background (P × B). Equally, the whole combined space cannot be used, since that would be to reproduce the world. It requires to be simplified or condensed in some way, and the various kinds of represenation discussed above can be viewed as alternative strategies for useful simplification. The representations constitute some of the other spaces in Figure 20.1—the links between them and (P × B) are shown by lines.

We start by considering the rational choice models particularly as reviewed in Chapters 14 and 15. In so far as these set their reasoning in pure policy spaces, they represent an attempt at simplification by ignoring background (and hence long-term predispositions) and considering only the policy component of P × B. Our objection to this is that in one way the representation over-simplifies, by ignoring the crucial role of predisposition fostered by such factors as class, religion, etc., in the background space B; while in another way it is too complex, in that the burden of calculation necessary to vote on pure policy grounds is impossibly great.

The spaces within which electors must operate to vote on pure policy are shown on the left-hand side of the figure. The first space is the public policy space (P), within which candidates state their position. This position could be either unambiguous—a point in the space—or ambiguous, in which case it much be represented by a probability distribution over a designated range of policies, which could be designated $\pi_{ij}$ for the $j$th candidate (Shepsle, 1972).

Even for unambiguous policy statements, however, there exists a discontinuity between words and action. Even if a candidate fully intends to carry through the promises, circumstances change and it is by no means certain that he will be able to. This necessitates a separate outcome space 0. With each policy position in P there must therefore be an associated probability distribution $\Pi_2$ over 0, in recognition of the fact that a range of different outcomes may follow from the same policy statement with varying degrees of probability.

So far our discussion has proceeded on lines that are broadly parallel to Ordeshook's suggestions about a space in which candidates publicly state their policies and an 'action space' corresponding to outcomes. These are public spaces, known to everyone and assumed to mean the same for everyone. We differ on a crucial point from Ordeshook in assuming that electors form their preferences and evaluations not in a generally perceived public space but in their individual private spaces—designated as $E_i$ in Figure 20.1—a different space of type E for every elector. Our reason for regarding preference space as essentially private is that each elector's goals are to a considerable extent idiosyncratic and individual and hence more readily expressible in private rather than public space. Typical preferences might be: 'less noise from aircraft near my home'; 'better schools for my children'; 'a good job'. The point about these aspirations is that they are not automatically translatable into public policy stands and could be attained by the individual without being made generally available, or necessarily shared with others, or even revealed to them.

As an example of the relationship between private goals and public policy we could consider a public policy commitment (an element of policy space P) 'to reduce defence spending by 10 per cent'. This generates a probability distribution over the public outcome space consisting of cutbacks of men and materials and commitments such as 'dismiss $X,000$ civilian employees, cancel £$Y,000$ of purchases and close $Z$ establishments'. To the elector the perceived outcome could depend on whether he was one of the $X,000$ civilians, a shareholder in a company with cancelled contracts, a small retailer with trade generated by one of the closing establishments or a taxpayer whose livelihood was unaffected by defence closures.

Voting on pure policy grounds thus requires electors, from the perceived positions of candidates in their private space $E_i$, to choose between them on the basis of a utility function so as to maximize their expected utility. This places the most sophisticated task, evaluating the probable consequences of candidates' promises, with the least sophisticated actor—the elector who has least resources with which to perform an evaluation. The utility function of each elector would provide a single most preferred position in policy space P. The distribution of the most preferred positions of all electors then constitutes the data on which candidates base their choice of position. This distribution we can call $\Pi_3$.

Even as it stands, the burden of calculation imposed on electors renders this formulation implausible as a simplification of the voting process: rather it renders it more complex. The final objection to the representation of voting by pure policy decisions lies in the fact that, if electors could perform such calculations, they would also be capable of acting strategically in regard to candidates: i.e., they could mis-state their utility function in order to create a probability distribution of most preferred positions $\Pi_4$, which would ultimately lead to canditates taking up positions closer to electors' truly preferred positions.

In ruling out strategic misrepresentation as a serious possibility, therefore, we must also rule out the pure policy formulation as a useful representation of voting and party competition. Recognition of these limitations has no doubt been responsible for the attempts chronicled by Ordeshook to represent long-term predispositions within mathematical rational choice models either by a posterior bias or by constraints on movement within the space. This latter expedient, we would argue, transforms a pure policy space into one with party reserved areas and hence into something like a party-defined space.

Moreover, since the difficulties in calculation remain even where electors are deciding between fairly stationary parties, attempts have also been made to introduce information-economizing characteristics, such as party identification, into the spatial formulation. From our perspective we should note that the introduction of such characteristics, which do not permit free movement, converts pure policy space into combined policy-back ground space (P $\times$ B). We would contend that this combined space is where realistic representations of voting and party competition need to be. The failure of attempts to base a representation on pure policy space, and the eventual reversion of such representations towards using (P $\times$ B), uphold this assertion.

Use of the combined space implies, of course, that we need to take account of short-term issue-based cues as well as long-term predispositions based on background characteristics. The fact that party identification was designed purely as a measure of background predispositions necessarily makes the space PI in Figure 20.1 only a partial representation of voting decisions. The impact of issues and candidates which are explicitly stressed in the full Michigan approach (cf. Figure 1.1) cannot be rendered spatially within its framework.

A further weakness of party identification as a spatial representation is that there is no specified link—no probability distribution $\Pi_{PI}$—that summarizes its relationship to the background space B. In so far as B is the actual space within which predispositions form and PI is viewed as a simplified representation of B, our inability to make an equivalence between a particular location inside B and locations inside PI constitutes a serious weakness.

It is possibly unfair, although instructive, to view party identification in terms of a spatial representation that was never originally intended. With dimensional analyses based on party rankings, denoted by the space S (for party similarity space with inferred dimensions), the spatial representation is explicit and intended. The obscurities of the relationship between such spaces and (P × B) are consequently the more serious. They are as follows.

(*a*) Does S represent only B, the background space of fixed predispositions, or does it also reflect cues and thus represent (P × B)? From one point of view the rankings of parties on which it is based are rather like party identification questions, and would in this case reflect only predispositions in B. But it seems likely that estimates of proximity would be much affected by the experience of governmental coalition (cf. Damgaard and Rusk, Chapter 9 above). In this case S is an attempted representation of the combined policy–background space.

(*b*) Whichever of the main spaces it represents, a representation based on party rankings and inferred dimensions still lacks any specific link, and probability distribution $\Pi_S$, which gets one from a location in (P × B) to one in S.

Such difficulties render these spaces theoretically unsatisfactory, whatever their practical merits in providing insights into determinants of voting and the shape of party competition. To say this is not necessarily to rule out dimensional analyses as modes of representation, for it was emphasized previously that the qualities of the space they produce depends very much on the type of input that goes in. Two other types of spaces could potentially be generated by dimensional analyses from different types of input.

First, if only direct policy indicators were used (such as those in Damgaard and Rusk's study in Chapter 9), dimensional analysis would reproduce the policy space P, simplifying it from a space of as many dimensions as there were issues or policies to a limited number of dimensions. Such a space is not represented separately in Figure 20.1 since it is simply one of several alternative forms of the policy space P. As a full representation of voting and party competition therefore it is subject to all the objections of complication and complexity already brought against representations based on short-term policy cues.

There remains the possibility that dimensional analysis might generate the space D, from input consisting not only of policy indicators but also of socioeconomic characteristics. Such a representation would certainly reflect the full combined space (P × B).

However, one source of weakness in the Shepherd–Kruskall non-metric scaling analysis commonly applied to survey and voting data would be the necessity of using averaged input and hence the limitation to placing only parties and other groups and not individuals within D. The alternative, Coombsian, technique would place individuals as well as parties, but is limited to small numbers of individuals (Daalder and Rusk, 1972). As systematic theories of voting and party competition need to deal with individuals as well as parties, this limitation rules out such representation of policy–background space.

Factor analysis could place both individuals and parties within a reduced-dimension representation of (P × B). However, the great objection to factor analysis, and the reason why it has not been employed in any of the papers in Part II, is its requirement of an interval level of measurement. We simply do not have numeric scores for most of the characteristics in B, nor indeed for the issue-stands in P. To impose such scores would be to distort the information we get, and to dichotomize into scores of 1 or 0 would be to lose much information.

A multivariate technique explicitly designed for the nominal, categoric information commonly provided by surveys, and which does simplify (P × B), is provided by the Likelihood Ratio Space already described and partially used in Chapter 6. This does have a known link with policy–background space through the type of probability distributions exemplified in Table 6.1 and Figure 6.1 above. It differs, however, from the kind of representation provided in D in being explicitly party-defined, and always having one dimension less than the number of party or voting alternatives specified (e.g., for two parties the representation is one-dimensional, as shown in Figure 6.1).

Being party-defined implies that the ends of lines in the representation constitute a 100 per cent propensity towards the party, not limits of policy. As pointed out above (Chapter 14), this characteristic makes Likelihood Ratio Space used within this context formally analogous with the space based on party identification, where the ends were also defined by 100 per cent propensity towards the party. If in addition to the formal resemblance a LiRaS representation is based purely on background characteristics, and thus measures only long-term predispositions, its resemblance to party identification is complete. We would maintain that with such input LiRaS represents an improved measure of long-term predispositions, as close to the original aims and measure of party identification as it is possible to get, given the improvements. These are:

(1) the ability to represent up to four party/voting alternatives visually, and to give an exact propensity of each individual to vote for each;

(2) the ability to represent an unlimited further number of parties/voting alternatives non-visually, through exact propensities of individuals to vote for each one;

(3) the ability to give an exact numeric score to voting propensities, rather than representing them in a limited number of 'more' or 'less' categories, and hence to generate a continuous distribution of propensities;

(4) avoidance of the conceptual and measurement difficulties with party identification ventilated in Part I, since the kind of background characteristics (class, religion, region, etc.) used as input are undoubtedly antecedent to voting decisions. Obviously the party identification questions themselves could be used as input to the representation where the question of antecedence was resolved in their favour (as seems to be the case in the United States, see Chapter 6 above).

LiRaS can then be converted from representing predispositions only to representing the full range of electoral influences—(P × B)—by adding available policy indicators as input. Alternatively, one might start by using it to represent only policies (P), and then add background characteristics to make it a representation of the full (P × B) space. Either way, the impact of predispositions and policy cues can be examined separately and together, and their relative influence in a particular election examined as in Chapter 6.

Although as a party-defined space LiRaS resembles party identification most closely, this is not to say that similarities are lacking with the dimensional representations one might find in D. On one interpretation certainly, such spaces are not defined by identifications with parties, but rather by issue-characteristic dimensions such as class (100-0 per cent working class) or religion. In so far as the movement of parties would be almost inevitably constrained to certain areas of this space, however, its end-point could be alternatively defined, for example as 100 per cent socialist or bourgeois. The arguments used above in regard to the substantive equivalence of a party-defined space and a policy space with reserved party areas would certainly apply here. Thus, although they start out from different points, the kind of spatial reasoning applied to each would not differ strikingly.

LiRaS has a further advantage over dimensional analyses of this type, however, in that, by explicitly relating the dimensions of the space to the number of parties, its dimensionality will change only when the party system changes. The number of dimensions of spaces of type D would vary much more than that, over time. Each time new issues emerged and previously obscure cleavages were emphasized, one would expect the modification or even disappearance of old dimensions and the emergence of new ones. Since analyses of voting and competition have to make over-time comparisons, this temporal instability of the space would constitute a severe embarassment. Changes in party systems will also occur, although less frequently (Rose and Urwin, 1969), and to this extent LiRaS offers a better framework for longitudinal analysis.

## LIKELIHOOD RATIO SPACE AS THE BASIS FOR A THEORETICAL SYNTHESIS BETWEEN PARTY IDENTIFICATION AND RATIONAL CHOICE

Our purpose in this section is partly to show that many of the original assumptions associated with party identification can be used to build a descriptive model of voting and party competition based on LiRaS. This is a natural development in view of the similarities between these representations that have been discussed above. Our purpose is also, however, to show how such assumptions can be used in conjunction with others, such as the pursuit of office by leaders under certain conditions, which are generally characteristic of rational choice approaches.

The best place to start the discussion is with the concept of party, which is the real strength of party identification and a weakness of rational choice models—a weakness because it is surely more realistic to regard party as a continuing group with associated ideology and loyalties than purely as a moving point in issue space. The concept of party as such a group is embedded in party identification: parties exist among electors by virtue of their attachments, independently of leaders. What such attachments consist of—whether they are deep-lying psychological attachments or rational long-term evaluations of a party's closeness to one's own position, or both—is, *pace* Miller and Robertson, a theological dispute. The important thing from the point of view of the LiRaS-based model is that electors do have long-term predispositions to vote for particular parties, and that these can be used to locate them through the distribution of social characteristics over party voters. The other influence, short-term issue-cues, can also be used to locate electors by a similar procedure.

The resulting space represents purely electoral propensities to support parties as defined by electors. Propensity is measured as the distance between an elector and the 'pure' or 'ideal' party end-point of 100 per cent support. The formal similarity with party identification is obvious.

Within this overall representation parties themselves could be viewed in two ways—either as the 'ideal' located at the appropriate end-point or as the means of party voters' distribution over the Likelihood Ratio Space. These could approach more or less closely: in so far as the mean party position was further from the 'ideal' party position at the end-point, one could derive predictions about the likely consistency and loyalty of party voters. This exactly corresponds to a use that can be made of the distribution over party identification: in so far as the mode of a party's voters is further from the 'ideal' position of strong identifiers, their consistency and loyalty are likely to be less.

Turning from parties to the individual electors distributed over the Likelihood Ratio Space, one can develop further predictions from the assumptions shared by this representation and by party identification. We predict, for example, that the electors closest to end-points (the equivalent of strong identifiers) will vote more consistently and regularly for the party; that electors in the middle, relatively distant from all end-points, will be less decided and more inconsistent. Electors at end-points who are currently voting for another party will moreover tend disproportionately to return 'home'. If the alternative of not voting is included in the representation as one of the end-points, we can extend such predictions to non-voters. In addition, we can make over-time or inter-system comparisons, in terms of the behaviour we should expect from distributions concentrated mainly at the end-points or mainly in the middle. From these distributions we can also predict which party we would expect to win. If over time the overall distribution of electors remains stable, and is shaped mainly by long-term predispositions, the distribution of votes in elections should also remain stable.

All such predictions are extremely congenial to lines of reasoning pursued by analysts using party identification, and indeed many are borrowed directly from them (for an explicit statement see Crewe, 1974). The full LiRaS representation differs from party identification, as we noted, in including short-term cues as well as predispositions. This provides an opportunity not available with party identification to expand predictions based on electors' space in terms of their differing reactions when influenced by predispositions or by cues. To the extent that they vote mainly in accordance with predispositions, one expects their voting to be fairly predictable and slow to change. Cues, being election-specific, are less predictable and liable to differ sharply between elections. Hence where electors' choices are influenced mainly by cues, their movements will be quicker and final locations may not lie anywhere near their starting point. A conclusion from this reasoning is indeed that, to the extent elections are determined by short-term cues, outcomes may be inherently unpredictable.

So far we have considered the space of electoral propensities, where it is natural to draw as much as possible on survey-based approaches to voting behaviour. When we consider leaders it is equally natural to make use of rational choice assumptions which provide a dynamic for party competition, in particular of the assumption that, where they think they can gain office thereby, they seek to gain votes (for the importance of the qualification see Robertson, 1976).

Note, however, that within the LiRaS representation there is no built-in assumption that leaders' space is necessarily the same as electors'. True, leaders like electors act in terms of the combined policy-background space, (P × B). However, the characteristics and issue preferences within that space that distinguish leaders' parties may or may not be the same as those that distinguish electors' parties. To the extent that they differ we should expect leaders' initiatives not to affect electors' voting choices. Their lack of influence would be accentuated further if electors voted primarily on predispositions rather than election cues. Conversely, if electors were affected mainly by cues and if leaders' space resembled electors' space very closely, leaders' movements in relation to each other should be well reflected within electors' space, particularly in the paths of electors' mean party positions and of party end-points over time. It is here that we should look for evidence of convergence or divergence in the party positions.

In order to act strategically in relation to each other, leaders must have some ideas about which issues to emphasize in order to gain votes. It is unlikely, however, that they have any direct *apperçu* into the distribution of electors within elector space, or of the way in which cues would need to be manipulated in order to move electors from the middle into the appropriate party corner. We do not, after all, assume that electors themselves know anything about the space we locate them in: they react to group pressures, issues, etc., not to spatial proximity or distance. It is much more likely that leaders will react not in terms of electors' space but in terms of their own space, unconsciously projecting it on to electors. Hence the issues they emphasize will be those that would shift electors from the middle towards their own party corner, were they located in leader space. Sometimes this assumption may work, when the two spaces share a close resemblance, but sometimes it may not. Again this consideration emphasizes the importance of the equivalence between leaders' and electors' space. By changing the assumption of the rational choice models that these spaces are the same into a variable condition, we follow the advice given by Stokes in his well-known critique of the Downs's model (Stokes, 1966).

Further derivations can be made from this spatial representation to the possibility of change in the party system, when large numbers of electors and leaders are grouped in the middle of their respective spaces, and hence unattached to existing parties (an extension of Converse's reasoning on the availability of support for 'flash' parties). Enough has been said, however, to indicate the broad lines along which a synthesis between rational choice and party identification can be made on the basis of the LiRaS representation. Detailed work is proceeding on a rigorous statement of assumptions that will logically entail derivations on the lines of the predictions discussed above (Budge and Farlie, forthcoming).

This outline of our attempted synthesis does, however, make the contribution of party identification and its associated assumptions quite clear. While abandoning the original measure based on direct questions, we retain the central distinction between underlying predispositions and short-term election forces and the essential idea of a party of electors independent of (though affected by) the party of leaders. Since this forces us to regard the equivalence between elector and leader space as variable, it substantially modifies the reasoning associated with the rational choice 'office-seeking' hypothesis, which we incorporate in the synthesis with the ideas derived from party identification. Actually these modifications consort with office-seeking very well, and help to make the predicted behaviour more realistic. This good internal fit between assumptions derived from different sources gives us hopes that the synthesis is a reasonable and reasoned theory in its own right. We propose to check this in later reports by comparing its predictions with the surveys from nine democracies already used in the preliminary study described in Chapter 6 above.

## REFERENCES

Budge, Ian, and Dennis Fairlie (forthcoming), *Voting and Party Competition: A Spatial Synthesis and a Critique of Existing Approaches Applied to a Survey of Ten Democracies*, Wiley, London and New York.

Crewe, Ivor (1974), 'Do Butler and Stokes Really Explain Political Change in Britain?', *European Journal of Political Research*, 2, 47–92.

Daalder, Hans, and Jerrold G. Rusk (1972), 'Perceptions of Party in the Dutch Parliament', in Samuel C. Patterson and John C. Wahlke (eds.), *Comparative Legislative Behaviour*, Wiley, New York.

Robertson, David (1976), *A Theory of Party Competition*, Wiley, London and New York.

Rose, Richard, and Derek Urwin (1969), 'Social Cohesion, Political Parties and Strains in Regimes', *Comparative Political Studies*, 2, 7–67.

Shepsle, Kenneth (1972), 'The Strategy of Ambiguity: Uncertainty in Electoral Competition', *American Political Science Review*, 66, 535–68.

Stokes, Donald E. (1966), 'Spatial Models of Party Competition', in Angus Campbell *et al.*, *Elections and the Political Order*, Wiley, New York.